KU-187-918

CROMWELLIAN SCOTLAND
1651-1660

CROMWELLIAN SCOTLAND 1651-1660

F. D. DOW
Department of History, University of Edinburgh

JOHN DONALD PUBLISHERS LTD
EDINBURGH

ISBN 0 85976 049 9

Printed in Great Britain by Bell & Bain Ltd., Glasgow.

Contents

MAPS

Conventions and Abbreviations

Dates: All dates are given in Old Style except where otherwise stated, but the year is deemed to have begun on 1 January.

Money: At all important points sums of money are stated to be in either £s sterling or £s Scots. At other points, where no positive indication is given, the sums are in £s sterling.

The following abbreviations have been used in the text:

Aberdeen Council Register	John Stuart (ed.), *Extracts from the Council Register of the Burgh of Aberdeen 1643-1747* (Scottish Burgh Records Society, 1872).
Add. MS.	Additional Manuscript.
APS	*The Acts of the Parliaments of Scotland*, eds. T. Thomson and C. Innes (12 vols., London, 1814-75).
Baillie, *Letters and Journals*	David Laing (ed.), *The Letters and Journals of Robert Baillie* (3 vols., Edinburgh, 1842).
Baker, *Chronicle*	Sir Richard Baker, *Chronicle of the kings of England from the time of the Romans government unto the death of King James . . . whereunto is added the reign of King Charles I, and the first thirteen years of . . . King Charles II . . . 7th impr.* (London, 1679).
B. L.	British Library, London.
Bodl. Lib.	Bodleian Library, Oxford.
Brodie, *Diary*	David Laing (ed.), *The Diary of Alexander Brodie of Brodie* (Spalding Club, 1863).
Brunton and Haig, *Senators of the College of Justice*	George Brunton and David Haig, *An Historical Account of the Senators of the College of Justice* (Edinburgh and London, 1832).
Burnet, *History*	Gilbert Burnet, *History of my Own Time*, ed. Osmund Airy (2 vols., Oxford, 1897).
Burton, *Diary*	J. T. Rutt (ed.), *Diary of Thomas Burton Esq.* (4 vols., London, 1828).
Cal. Cl. S.P.	O. Ogle, W. H. Bliss, W. D. Macray and F. J. Routledge (eds.), *Calendar of the Clarendon State Papers* (5 vols., Oxford, 1872-1970).
Cary, *Memorials of the Great Civil War*	Henry Cary, *Memorials of the Great Civil War in England from 1646 to 1652* (2 vols., London, 1842).
Casada, 'The Scottish representatives . . .'	James A. Casada, 'The Scottish representatives in Richard Cromwell's parliament', *Scottish Historical Review* li (1972), 124-47.

CJ	*Journals of the House of Commons.*
Consultations	*Consultations of the Ministers of Edinburgh and some other Brethren of the Ministry* (2 vols., Scottish History Society, 1921-30).
CSPD	*Calendar of State Papers, Domestic Series 1651-1660*, ed. M.A.E. Green (11 vols., London, 1877-86).
Davies, *Restoration*	Godfrey Davies, *The Restoration of Charles II 1658-1660* (San Marino, 1955).
DNB	*Dictionary of National Biography.*
Dow, 'Thesis'	F. D. Dow, (The English Army and the Government of Scotland 1651-1660' (York University, D. Phil. thesis, 1976).
Firth and Davies, *Regimental History*	Sir Charles Firth and Godfrey Davies, *The Regimental History of Cromwell's Army* (2 vols., Oxford, 1940).
Firth and Rait, *A & O*	C. H. Firth and R. S. Rait (eds.), *Acts and Ordinances of the Interregnum* (3 vols., London, 1911).
Firth, *LYP*	C. H. Firth, *The Last Years of the Protectorate 1656-1658* (2 vols., New York, 1964).
Firth, *S and C*	C. H. Firth (ed.), *Scotland and the Commonwealth* (Scottish History Society, 1895).
Firth, *S and P*	C. H. Firth (ed.), *Scotland the Protectorate* (Scottish History Society, 1899).
Gardiner, *C and P*	S. R. Gardiner, *History of the Commonwealth and Protectorate* (3 vols., London 1897-1901).
Gardiner (ed.), *Charles II and Scotland*	S. R. Gardiner (ed.), *Letters and Papers illustrating the relations between Charles II and Scotland in 1650* (Scottish History Society, 1894).
Gardiner, *Civil War*	S. R. Gardiner, *History of the Great Civil War 1642-1649* (4 vols., New York, 1965).
Gardiner, *Constitutional Documents*	S. R. Gardiner (ed.), *The Constitutional Documents of the Puritan Revolution 1625-1660* (3rd edn., Oxford, 1906).
Glasgow Burgh Recs.	J. D. Marwick (ed.), *Extracts from the Records of the Burgh of Glasgow 1630-1662* (Scottish Burgh Records Society, 1881).
Gwynne's Memoirs	Sir Walter Scott (ed.), *Military memoirs of the Great Civil War, being the military memoirs of John Gwynne; and an account of the Earl of Glencairn's expedition . . .* (Edinburgh, 1822).
HMC	Historical Manuscripts Commission.
Jaffray, *Diary*	John Barclay (ed.), *Diary of Alexander Jaffray* (Aberdeen, 1856).
Kaplan, *Politics and Religion*	Lawrence Kaplan, *Politics and Religion during the English Revolution: The Scots and the Long Parliament 1643-1645* (New York, 1976).

Lamont, *Diary*	G. R. Kinloch (ed.), *The Diary of Mr. John Lamont of Newton 1649-1671* (Maitland Club, 1830).
Lauderdale Papers	Osmund Airy (ed.), *The Lauderdale Papers* (2 vols., Camden Society, 1884-5).
LRO	J. Y. Akerman (ed.), *Letters from Roundhead Officers written from Scotland and chiefly addressed to Captain Adam Baynes. July MDCL-June MDCLX* (Bannatyne Club, 1856).
McCoy, *Robert Baillie*	F. N. McCoy, *Robert Baillie and the Second Scots Reformation* (Berkeley, California, 1974).
Masson, *Life of Milton*	David Masson, *The Life of John Milton and History of his Time* (7 vols., London, 1859-94).
Minutes of the Synod of Argyll	D. C. Mactavish (ed.), *Minutes of the Synod of Argyll 1652-1661* (Scottish History Society, 1944).
Mitchell and Christie *Records*	A. F. Mitchell and J. Christie (eds.), *The Records of the Commissions of the General Assemblies of the Church of Scotland* (3 vols., Scottish History Society, 1892-1909).
Mukerjee, 'Scottish Members . . .'	H. N. Mukerjee, 'Scottish Members of Richard Cromwell's Parliament', *Notes and Queries* clxvi (1934), 65.
N. S.	New Style.
Nicholas Papers	George F. Warner (ed.), *The Nicholas Papers* (3 vols., Camden Society, 1886-97).
Nicoll, *Diary*	John Nicoll, *A Diary of Public Transactions* (Bannatyne Club, 1836).
NLS MS. Adv.	National Library of Scotland, Advocates' Manuscript.
O.S.	Old Style.
Pinckney	Paul J. Pinckney, 'The Scottish representation in the Cromwellian parliament of 1656', *Scottish Historical Review* xlvi (1967), 95-114.
PRO	Public Record Office, London.
Recs. Conv. RBS	J. D. Marwick (ed.), *Extracts from the Records of the Convention of the Royal Burghs of Scotland 1615-1676* (Edinburgh, 1878).
Reg. P. C. Scot. 1661-1664	*The Register of the Privy Council of Scotland*, ed. P. Hume Brown, 3rd series Vol. I 1661-1664 (Edinburgh, 1908).
Row, *Life of Blair*	Thomas McCrie (ed.), *The Life of Mr. Robert Blair . . . with Supplement . . . by . . . Mr. William Row* (Wodrow Society, 1848).
Scots Peerage	Sir James Balfour Paul (ed.), *The Scots Peerage* (9 vols., Edinburgh, 1904-14).
Scott, *Fasti*	Hew Scott (ed.), *Fasti Ecclesiae Scoticanae* (7 vols., Edinburgh, 1915-28).

SRO	Scottish Record Office.
Steele 3rd pt.	Robert Steele (ed.), *Tudor and Stuart Proclamations* (2 vols., Oxford, 1910) 3rd part (Scotland).
Stevenson, 'The King's Scottish revenues . . .'	David Stevenson, 'The King's Scottish Revenues and the Covenanters, 1625-1651', *The Historical Journal* xvii (1974), 17-41.
Stevenson, *Revolution and Counter-Revolution*	David Stevenson, *Revolution and Counter-Revolution in Scotland, 1644-1651* (London, 1977).
Stevenson, 'Thesis'	David Stevenson, 'The Covenanters and the Government of Scotland 1637-1651' (Glasgow University, Ph.D. thesis, 1970).
Terry, *CU*	C. S. Terry (ed.), *The Cromwellian Union* (Scottish History Society, 1902).
TSP	*A Collection of the State Papers of John Thurloe . . .* ed. T. Birch (7 vols., London, 1742).
Tucker, *Report*	'Report by Thomas Tucker upon the settlement of the revenues of excise, and customs in Scotland A.D. MDCLVI', *Miscellany* (Scottish Burgh Records Society, 1881).
Turner, *Memoirs*	Sir James Turner, *Memoirs of his own Life and Times* (Bannatyne Club, 1829).
Underdown, *Royalist Conspiracy*	David Underdown, *Royalist Conspiracy in England 1649-1660* (New Haven, 1960).
Wariston, *Diary* ii	D. Hay Fleming (ed.), *Diary of Sir Archibald Johnston of Wariston* Vol. II 1650-1654 (Scottish History Society, 1919).
Wariston, *Diary* iii	James D. Ogilvie (ed.), *Diary of Sir Archibald Johnston of Wariston* Vol. III 1655-1660 (Scottish History Society, 1940).
Whitelocke, *Memorials*	Bulstrode Whitelocke, *Memorials of the English Affairs* (4 vols., Oxford, 1853).
Wodrow	Robert Wodrow, *The History of the Sufferings of the Church of Scotland*, ed. R. Burns (4 vols., Glasgow, 1828-30).
Wood, *Extracts Edin. Recs. 1642 to 1655*	Marguerite Wood (ed.), *Extracts from the Records of the Burgh of Edinburgh 1642 to 1655* (Edinburgh, 1938).
Wood, *Extracts Edin. Recs. 1655 to 1665*	Marguerite Wood (ed.), *Extracts from the Records of the Burgh of Edinburgh 1655 to 1665* (Edinburgh, 1940).
Worcester	Worcester College, Oxford.

INTRODUCTION

Scotland's Relations with England, 1637 — 1651[1]

DURING the period from 1637 to 1660, English and Scottish history were more closely interwoven than at any other time between the Union of the Crowns in 1603 and the Treaty of Union of 1707. During the crucial decades of the mid-seventeenth century, the relationship between Scotland and England underwent profound changes. From being the ally of the English Parliament in the early 1640s, Scotland became a conquered province of England in 1651, and although later admitted to a full parliamentary union with England, she remained under military occupation until 1660. The conquest of Scotland by the English army was the culmination of a long period of estrangement between the two countries whose roots lie entangled in the years of political and military alliance of the early 1640s. The road to open war was marked not only by a breakdown in Anglo-Scottish relations but also by a radical realignment of political power within each country and so, when the final breach came, it was as much the product of domestic as of international politics. The battle of Worcester in September 1651 was thus the outcome of a complex series of political manoeuvres in both England and Scotland stretching back to before the Civil War.

From the first, Scottish opposition to the policies of Charles I in church and state was informed by the belief that the union of the crowns was failing to protect Scottish interests. Hopes that the union would strengthen the security of Scotland and would promote the prosperity and influence of Scotsmen had been quickly dashed after the accession of James VI and I to the English throne, for the remoteness of the monarch and his liking for English advisers cut the Scottish nobility off from the mainstream of British political life.[2] Under Charles I, the monarch's neglect of Scottish interests was coupled with another tendency, even more distasteful to Scottish opinion, for Charles, it seemed, had embarked upon a deliberate policy of undermining the traditions and institutions of his northern kingdom and of replacing them with English models. Most important of all, his attempted changes in the liturgy and discipline of the church and the elevation of the bishops' authority in the state smacked of Laudian influence and seemed to threaten the identity and integrity of the Scottish kirk. David Stevenson has argued that '[i]t was *anglicising* policies that were mainly responsible for driving Scotland to rebellion in 1637' and that, in particular, '[t]he plight of the kirk came to be taken as symbolic of Scotland's position under the union of the crowns.'[3] For the subsequent rift between Charles and his Scottish subjects, the union was thus partly to blame, for by providing the king with a power base in England, it had enabled an absentee monarch to introduce foreign influences and institutions into Scotland.

Some change in the nature of the union was therefore essential if Charles's Scottish opponents (the Covenanters) were to secure permanent redress of their grievances. Such, at any rate, was the belief which the Covenanters carried into their dealings with Charles's opponents in England, for from the first they accepted that they must make common cause with the growing number of puritans and others who were fanning the flames of dissent in the south. From the mid-1630s, groups of discontented nobles, ministers and lairds had been building up contacts with the opponents of Charles's policies in England, and by 1637 they had a resident agent in London in the person of Eleazar Borthwick. In the following months, co-operation grew between the Covenanters in Scotland and their sympathisers at the English court,[4] and when, after Charles had denounced the proceedings of the General Assembly of 1638, the Covenanters made preparations for war against the king, they sought to strengthen these links with the opposition in England. By early 1639, they were ready to put forward a view of the future relationship between Scotland and England in which they envisaged more, not less, contact between the two countries. For although the Covenanters believed that the existing form of the union was damaging Scotland, their 'cure for this was not less union, but more'. They sought, in fact, to counter the ill-effects of the personal union of the crowns by closer union at other levels, including the forging of 'permanent links between the parliaments to protect the liberties of the kingdoms from the king'.[5]

In 1639 this policy existed in embryo only, but over the next few years events strengthened its appeal for the Scottish Covenanters. In particular, their growing conviction of the king's untrustworthiness and their fear that, so long as he had a power base in England, the concessions they had wrung from him in 1641 would not be secure, led them to seek a closer alliance with the English Parliamentarians. In 1641 Charles had given his consent to the abolition of bishops and the setting up of full presbyterian church government, as well as to the exclusion of all churchmen from civil office, the abolition of the lords of the articles and the calling of triennial parliaments. He further agreed to appoint officers of state, councillors and judges only with the advice and approbation of Parliament.[6] To ensure that Charles did not reverse these changes, which amounted to a revolution in church and state, the Scots Covenanters were willing to contribute to the English Parliament's victory over the king. The price of their support, and the indispensable foundation for any lasting settlement with the king and for peace between the two kingdoms, was to be co-operation and consultation in civil, and unity and uniformity in religious, matters.

From 1641 to 1643 the Scots actively sought to implement their programme for closer union. At this point, their demands included uniformity in church government, in effect the introduction of the presbyterian system into England; the appointment of parliamentary commissioners to settle disputes between the two kingdoms; the nomination of conservators of the peace to maintain friendly relations and discuss matters of mutual interest; and the establishment of free trade.[7] From the first it was clear that the Scots were much keener on these proposals than the English, who consistently dragged their feet, particularly when the subject of religious uniformity was raised by the Scots commissioners in London. England had no wish to adopt a presbyterian system on the Scottish model, nor did she wish for closer union in civil matters. By 1643, however, the English Parliament's need for military aid forced her to pay lip-service to the Scottish ideals and to send commissioners to Scotland. The Scots, in turn, were invited to send representatives to the Westminster Assembly, where they might seek to convince their English brethren of the merits of presbyterianism. Before the end of the year, not only had five Scots ministers and three elders taken their seats at the Westminster Assembly,[8] but the two kingdoms had signed the Solemn League and Covenant and the Scots had agreed to send an army of 21,000 men to England. In the Solemn League and Covenant, both parties pledged themselves to preserve 'the reformed religion in the church of Scotland' and to reform the church of England 'according to the word of God', a formula which in English, if not in Scottish, eyes might 'leave a door open in England for Independency'. In the civil clauses of the Covenant, the two countries swore to uphold the rights and privileges of the Parliaments and the liberties of both kingdoms, to preserve the king's person and authority, and to work for peace and union between England and Scotland.[9] In February 1644, these plans for civil union were given some substance by the appointment of a committee of both kingdoms to supervise the war effort.[10]

Although these agreements marked in theory the high-water mark of Anglo-Scottish collaboration, the attempt to implement them served merely to emphasise the underlying differences between the Scottish Covenanters and those political and religious groupings which were gaining the ascendancy in England. Over the next year or so, it became clear that the Scots were primarily interested in religious changes, and that they were prepared to negotiate a settlement with the king, if he would agree to establish presbyterianism throughout England, Scotland and Ireland. At the same time, the Scots army in England became increasingly unpopular, while Montrose's successes in Scotland did little to boost the Covenanters' reputation in the south. Thus, win or lose, the Covenanters had little to commend them to the sectaries and the 'war party' in the English Parliament. If they appeared strong, they aroused fears that they would rob the political and religious Independents of victory over the king; if they appeared weak, they seemed a liability as a military ally.[11] But the king's rejection of the Uxbridge peace proposals,[12] his continuing refusal to accede to the Scots' religious demands, and the English Parliament's military needs kept the two sides together up to 1645.

The ambivalent nature of the relationship between the Scots Covenanters, the English Parliament and the king was further highlighted by several developments in the early months of 1646. The revelation that the Scots had been treating separately with the king through the French agent in London, Jean de Montreuil;[13] further evidence of the English Parliament's determination to set up an erastian version of the presbyterian system of church government in England;[14] and Parliament's production in February of a set of peace proposals which sought to weaken the links between the two kingdoms,[15] all indicated the distance that lay between the Covenanters and the Independents. But again Charles's obstinacy on matters of religion compelled the two sides to unite to present terms to the king, this time in the form of the Newcastle Propositions of July 1646.[16] When Charles turned these down, the Covenanters began to reassess their relationship both with him and with the English Parliament. They now agreed to hand the king over to Parliament and to withdraw their army from England. They even gave some signs of recognising that, in the immediate future, they had little hope of having their brand of presbyterianism accepted in England. But because they distrusted the king, they were still anxious to preserve the alliance with the English Parliament and to work for peace and union between the two countries.[17]

At the end of the first civil war, then, the Scots were still committed to the civil and religious policy of the Solemn League and Covenant, but unable in practice to realise their ideals. Yet the last few years had seen much greater co-operation in political and military matters between England and Scotland than ever before, and by their intervention in the south the Scots had succeeded in safeguarding the terms of the 1641 settlement with the king. To some extent, therefore, the Covenanters' policy of closer union had been successful, and in 1647 both sides kept up the facade of wishing to present joint peace proposals to the king.[18] But developments within the two countries worked throughout 1647 to widen the gap between the ruling groups in each nation. In England, the growing political influence of the army made the likelihood of a rigid presbyterian settlement in the south recede even farther, while, more significantly perhaps, it also raised the prospect of greater curbs being put on the king's civil authority. It was this seeming threat to the power of the king in civil matters that aided the rise of a party within Scotland which put the claims of the king before those of the kirk, and which was prepared, by fighting against the English army and the Independents in defence of King Charles, to end the Anglo-Scottish collaboration of the last few years.

This development in Scottish politics culminated in the signing of the Engagement in December 1647. Charles pledged himself to have the Solemn League and Covenant confirmed by Act of Parliament and to introduce the presbyterian system of church government into his three kingdoms for a trial period of three years, a concession which was considerably less than the Scots had asked from him in the Newcastle Propositions. He also promised to work for closer union between England and Scotland in certain civil matters, including the establishment of free trade. In return, the Scots commissioners agreed to defend the king's rights and authority by force of arms — a pledge which was to lead to a Scottish invasion of England a few months later.[19] The signing of this agreement not only caused the English Parliament to abolish the committee of both kingdoms, and so dissolve the main organ of political co-operation between the two countries,[20] but it also unleashed a considerable storm in Scottish domestic politics. By March 1648, it was clear that the prime movers of the Engagement, the Hamiltonian party, had won the support of the Committee of Estates and the Scottish Parliament, but only at the cost of alienating the commission of the kirk and its lay supporters, the party of the Marquis of Argyle. Hamilton's victory in fact signalled the nobility's reassertion of their authority in Scottish politics, and their wish to free themselves from the domination of the presbyterian clergy. It thus marked the rupture of that alliance between laity and clergy which in and after 1638 had made possible the achievements of the Scottish revolution. The rupture was not, however, complete, for Argyle, a few nobles, many lairds and most burgesses sided with the clergy in opposition to Hamilton and most of the nobility, while the Hamiltonians themselves sought to play down the breach by emphasising their commitment to religious as well as political ideals.[21]

Nonetheless, the existence of this cleavage in Scottish political life had important implications for Anglo-Scottish relations, in 1648 and beyond. On the surface it seemed that the triumph of the Engagers marked a breakdown in any form of political or military co-operation between the two countries and thus sealed the estrangement of their ruling parties. This was true insofar as the Engagers' invasion of England marked the dissolution of the alliance between the two Parliaments. Paradoxically, however, the kirk party's hostility towards the Engagers[22] kept alive the ideal of unity between the two countries. For although the kirk party abhorred the religious policy of the English sectaries, they clearly believed that an invasion of England in defence of the king could succeed only at the expense of religion in Scotland. To safeguard presbyterianism at home, therefore, the kirk party was prepared to seek peace with the Independents. Argyle, for one, was prepared to contemplate the presence of the English army just south of the Border, if this would intimidate the Engagers and encourage their opponents in Scotland.[23] In this way the prospect of collaboration between Scots and English was kept dimly alive.

Towards the end of 1648, co-operation between Covenanter and Independent assumed a tangible form, after Hamilton's defeat at Preston had led to the overthrow of the Engagers within Scotland. News of the battle of Preston led to an immediate revolt in the west of Scotland against the power of the Engagers. The attempt to levy men to serve in the army of invasion had already met with some resistance amongst the extreme Covenanters of Galloway and Ayr,[24] and it was principally from these districts and from Clydesdale that several thousand men now marched on Edinburgh to topple the Engager-dominated Committee of Estates. This Whiggamore raid, as it came to be called, put Argyle, backed by the commission of the kirk, in a position of supreme power, but his position was secure only because he had the support of Cromwell and the English army, which by 25 September was camped within six miles of Edinburgh. Cromwell had entered Scotland to ensure the final submission of the Engagers, and although the kirk party had no wish actively to ally with him, they resented his presence less than they disliked the 'malignant' Engagers. Thus, to safeguard the new régime they asked that, when he withdrew the bulk of his army from Scotland, he should leave behind two regiments of horse and two companies of dragoons. Although this force, under the command of Major General Lambert, remained in Scotland for only a month, it enabled Argyle and his supporters to consolidate their hold on the Scottish government.[25] As a precaution against the emergence of a new malignant régime, Argyle later joined in organising a military association of the western shires, namely Argyll, Bute, Renfrew, Dunbarton, Lanark, Ayr, Kirkcudbright and Wigton,[26] and by the Act of Classes of January 1649 all Engagers were debarred from public office.[27]

The precariousness of Argyle's position and the fragility of the kirk party's links with the English Independents were starkly revealed after the execution of Charles I in January 1649. This event forced all Scots to view the competing claims of kirk and king in a new light, for it brought to the fore their allegiance to the concept of monarchy and to the notion of indefeasible hereditary right.[28] At the same time, allegiance to the Covenants dictated that the kirk party's support for the new king, Charles II, could not be unconditional. On 5 February, the Scots Parliament therefore decided that Charles, whom it had just proclaimed King of Great Britain, France and Ireland, could not be admitted to the exercise of his office unless and until he had given satisfaction concerning the security of religion, and the union of the kingdoms, according to the two Covenants.[29] Given the almost unanimous support for the monarchy and the reassertion of covenanting principles, Argyle's position was thus sensibly weakened, not least because of his recent dealings with the English army. He had no alternative, then, but to put out feelers to the king. In February 1649, Argyle and his colleagues sent Sir Joseph Douglas on a mission to Holland to sound out the new king, and in March he was followed by an official body of commissioners appointed by Parliament and the commission of the kirk. By May, however, the negotiations had ground to a halt, with the commissioners insistent upon Charles's acceptance of both Covenants, and Charles, for his part, giving preference to Montrose's schemes for the recovery of his rights and authority.[30] The summer of 1649 thus found the régime of the kirk party politically isolated, resolved on the one hand to resist an invasion by Montrose and on the other to refuse all offers of friendship from the English sectaries.[31]

Although a few extremists in the kirk party still favoured an English alliance, Argyle believed that the only way out of the *impasse* was to reopen negotiations with the king. On 7 August Parliament commissioned George Winram of Libberton to go to the king, but it was not until January 1650 that Charles and his advisers considered the letters Winram had brought from Scotland. By this time the failure of the king's cause in Ireland had made him more amenable to an agreement with the kirk party, and so he asked that commissioners be sent over from the Committee of Estates and the commission of the kirk.[32] In the face of violent protests from the extremists of the kirk party, Argyle and the nobles succeeded in getting commissioners appointed, with instructions to insist upon as strict terms as before. The collapse of his other plans, most notably the lack of any sign from Scotland that Montrose's campaign was making headway there, drove Charles to come to terms, and on 1 May 1650 a draft agreement of the Treaty of Breda was signed.[33] But still Charles had not signed the Covenants, and his failure to do so caused no little tension between those commissioners who supported the policy of Argyle, and those who reflected the views of the extremists of the kirk party.[34] At the same time, the influence of the Hamiltonians at Charles's council table caused some observers to predict that when Charles arrived in Scotland, neither wing of the kirk party would retain the ascendancy. Instead, former Engagers would carry all, and would work to destroy Argyle and his allies.[35] Thus, to the perceptive observer, the negotiations at Breda prefigured the realignment of parties which Charles's presence in Scotland would soon help to produce, with its attendant implications for relations with England.

For the moment, however, the kirk party in Scotland was continuing to pursue a strict policy against former Engagers, not least in its implementation of the Act of Classes. The defeat of Montrose at the end of April reinforced this attitude, and led to the imposition of even more stringent terms upon Charles in the Treaty of Heligoland in June 1650. The commission of the kirk was especially insistent that Charles must signify his personal acceptance of the Covenants, and this he did at Speymouth on 23 June.[36] When Charles reached Scotland, he was subjected to further controls, for the kirk party then demanded that he dismiss all Malignants from his court.[37] The party's horror of Malignancy also influenced the military preparations then in train to meet the threat of an invading English army, a threat which assumed reality when Cromwell crossed the Tweed on 22 July with 16,000 men. Supported by the barons and burgesses, and in opposition to most of the nobility, the kirk urged that the army be purged of Malignants, Engagers and other backsliders. On 21 June, a commission for purging the army was set up, and throughout August the work of purifying the host went on apace.[38] In its ruthlessness, the commission defied much evidence of the king's popularity in the army and in the country as a whole, and it earned the disapproval not only of Malignants, but of Argyle, the nobility, and many moderate ministers as well.[39] The effect on military discipline and morale was disastrous, and undoubtedly contributed to the Scots' defeat at the battle of Dunbar on 3 September 1650.

The effect of Dunbar upon the alignment of political groupings within Scotland was immense. On 4 September, Cromwell gave his estimate of the situation in a letter to Sir Arthur Hesilrige, governor of Newcastle. 'Surely,' he wrote, 'it's probable the Kirk has done their do. I believe their King will set up upon his own score now, wherein he will find many friends.'[40] There was, indeed, in the ensuing months a general move away from support for the covenanting cause, as represented by the kirk, towards support for a national cause, embodied in the king.[41] But Charles's first attempt to 'set up upon his own score' was an ignominious failure. His plans for a royalist rising north of the Tay at the beginning of October ended in disaster, due to his own indecision and the incompetence of his advisers.[42]

Far from benefiting the king, the defeat at Dunbar seemed initially to favour the extreme Covenanters in the west and south-west of Scotland, for it led to the formation of a 'western army' whose power could rival that of the Committee of Estates. In the summer of 1650, the 'western association' had been revived, nominally to protect the shires of Ayr, Renfrew, Lanark and Galloway from the English, but in fact 'to oppose malignant Scots as well as sectarian English'.[43] After Dunbar, the association provided the extremists of the kirk party with the nucleus of a new army, composed only of godly men, which, they hoped, might repeat the glories of the Whiggamore raid and trounce the Malignants of the north and east. The creators of this army, Colonels Archibald Strachan and Gilbert Ker and Sir John Chiesley, had in fact been commissioned by the Committee of Estates to raise levies in the west, but they used their authority to assemble what was virtually an independent force. They had the strong support of a party in the commission of the kirk led by James Guthry and Patrick Gillespie and could count amongst their leading lay supporters Sir Archibald Johnston of Wariston.[44] Until the end of November, although Strachan was willing to negotiate with the English,[45] this army maintained in its military manoeuvres a position of strict neutrality between Cromwell and the Committee of Estates.

Politically, the westerners made their contempt for the king and his cause quite plain. On 22 October they presented a Remonstrance to the Committee of Estates in which 'all intention of fighting for the King until he had given satisfactory evidence of sincere repentance and of honest intention to abandon the company of Malignants was entirely repudiated'.[46] Although the Remonstrants pledged themselves to expel the English from Scotland, they renounced their obligation to restore Charles to his English throne. In so doing they implicitly accepted the triumph of the Independents in England[47] and the dissolution of the union of the crowns. After heated debate, the Committee of Estates issued a declaration denouncing the Western Remonstrance. The commission of the kirk also rejected it, although many extremists on the commission spoke in its favour, and even the moderates admitted it contained many truths. The kirk's decision called forth protests from about sixteen remonstrant ministers and two elders, many of whom then withdrew from the commission, thus leaving it free to pursue a more lenient policy towards Malignants.[48]

Ironically, the need for such a policy in the interests of national unity was brought home to the commission and the Committee of Estates by Lambert's defeat of the western army. Believing that he was soon to be displaced by a nominee of the Committee of Estates, Col. Gilbert Ker had been driven to attack the English at Hamilton in Lanarkshire, but his forces suffered a complete rout.[49] This brought to a sudden end the existence of the western association as a military force, although the Remonstrant party continued to exert a strong political influence in church and state. Lambert's victory and the subsequent loss of the south-west of Scotland to the English made it imperative that as many able-bodied men as possible be enlisted to expel the invader. Hence the ban on Malignants serving in the army had to be lifted, and to this the commission of the kirk consented in the Public Resolutions of 14 December.[50] Thus an important plank in the royalist platform had been won, but at the cost of deepening the split within the church. In their denunciation of the Public Resolutions, the Remonstrants were joined by many others who had not themselves subscribed the Western Remonstrance; together these groups formed the basis of the Protester party of the 1650s whose continuing disputes with the Resolutioners were to dominate church affairs until the Restoration. At the beginning of 1651, presbyteries and synods wherein the Protesters were strong sent in to the commission of the kirk strongly worded protests against the Resolutions and against the employment of increasing numbers of Engagers and Royalists in the army,[51] while in April and May those judicatories which supported the Resolutions issued counter-declarations.[52] It was clear that the Protesters drew most of their support from the south-west, including the synod of Glasgow and Ayr, while the Resolutioners were dominant in the north and east.

Although these disputes revealed that the extremists had little love for the king and were unwilling to fight on his behalf, in fact Charles's cause was becoming steadily stronger throughout the first months of 1651. Not only were his supporters infiltrating the army, but the moderates of the kirk party had increasingly to rely on his support to remain in power. Although they still had control of the Committee of Estates, these moderates suffered a serious setback in March when, with the commission of the kirk's connivance, Parliament admitted Royalists to membership of a new committee for managing the affairs of the army.[53] Although the commission subsequently protested that Parliament was carrying forgiveness for Malignants too far, Parliament went on to display its increasingly royalist sympathies by asking the kirk to agree to the rescinding of the Act of Classes. Reluctantly, at the end of May, the commission of the kirk conceded that persons formerly excluded from office might now be admitted to places of public trust, if they showed repentance for past offences and displayed clear signs of piety and morality.[54] On 2 June the Acts of Classes of 1646 (imposed after the defeat of Montrose) and 1649 were rescinded, and two days later an act was passed condemning the Western Remonstrance.[55]

The passage of these measures marked the final downfall of the kirk party régime. In June 1651, Charles II was stronger than at any other time since his accession, in terms of the internal politics of Scotland. Royalist and Engaging nobles had returned to leading positions in government and in the army,[56] and it seemed that in affairs of state the kirk had really 'done their do'. Argyle, previously the most powerful man in Scotland, had, for some months past, been steadily losing influence, for he was caught between the Remonstrants, whom he had condemned, on the one hand, and the Royalists and Engagers, whose projected march into England he opposed, on the other.[57] The kirk, moreover, was rent by internal divisions, which were made worse by the rescinding of the Act of Classes. The Resolutioners attempted to exclude their opponents from membership of the General Assembly which met at St. Andrews and Dundee in July. In retaliation, on 20 July, over twenty Protester ministers gave in a protestation against the assembly, denying that it was lawfully constituted, and then withdrew.[58] Over the next few years, they continued to maintain that the meetings at St. Andrews and Dundee were illegal in the face of all attempts by the Resolutioners to effect a reconciliation, while their secession from the assembly was soon to be reflected at local level by splits in several presbyteries and synods. On occasion these splits resulted in Protesters and Resolutioners holding separate meetings, each claiming to exercise the rightful authority of the judicatory, but in most instances disagreement was confined to verbal battles at the sitting of each presbytery or synod.

Despite the king's political successes, his military position steadily deteriorated throughout the summer of 1651, and defeat in battle was to follow swiftly on the heels of political triumph. Cromwell's advance into Scotland had progressed slowly but steadily since September 1650. His victory at Dunbar had given him control of the south-east of Scotland and had enabled him to occupy Edinburgh. In October and November, his army had made visits to the west and for a time had occupied Glasgow, but it was only after Lambert's defeat of the western army in December that the English secured a firm hold on the south-west of Scotland.[59] A few weeks later, the surrender of Edinburgh Castle further increased Cromwell's strength and demoralised the Scots — it prompted Sir John Hope of Craighall, for example, to recommend that the southern part of the country be permanently abandoned to the English.[60] From February to June 1651, Cromwell was plagued by illness and for a time the advance of his army was halted, but by the summer it was ready once more to take the offensive. At this time, the Scots army was assembling at Stirling and had withdrawn several regiments from Fife. Cromwell therefore determined to take advantage of Fife's vulnerability, and on 17 July he sent part of his army across the Firth of Forth. After defeating a Scots contingent at Inverkeithing on 20 July, this force was able to overrun Fife in a matter of days and to penetrate as far north as Perth, which surrendered on 2 August.[61]

The English successes drove the Scots to take drastic action. At the end of July, Charles decided that the bulk of his army should march into England in an attempt to draw Cromwell off from his strong position in Scotland, and that only a small part of the Scots forces should remain behind to raise new levies and to attack any detachment of English troops left in the north.[62] Cromwell duly fulfilled the Scots' expectations by following Charles into England, where he caught up with and defeated the Royalists at the battle of Worcester on 3 September. When Charles had crossed the border into England, he had had only about 13,000 men with him: at Worcester Cromwell's army killed around 2000 of them, and captured nearly 10,000 during or just after the battle.[63] Cromwell had left in Scotland a considerable force, perhaps 5-6000 men in the field and another 2000 in garrisons, under the command of Lieutenant General George Monck. This force proceeded to extend its control over Scotland, first by enforcing the submission of the burgh and castle of Stirling on 6 and 14 August.[64] This victory was soon followed by another *coup*, which had important political implications. That part of the Committee of Estates left in Scotland (part had accompanied the army into England) had evacuated Stirling on Monck's approach, but at the end of August Monck learned that they had taken refuge at Alyth in Perthshire. A party of English horse, 7-800 strong, was therefore sent out under the command of Col. Matthew Alured, and on the night of 27/28 August it succeeded in capturing nearly all the members of the Committee of Estates and of the commission of the kirk who were hiding there. Those taken prisoner included the Earl of Leven and the Earl of Crawford-Lindsay; the latter, although nominally subordinate to Leven, had been made commander-in-chief of the king's forces in Scotland by Charles before his departure.[65]

By their victories at Alyth and Worcester, the English had virtually destroyed Scotland's political and military independence. Monck's army was now left free to complete the conquest of Scotland, and English politicians were able to impose upon Scotland a much closer form of union than the Covenanters had ever imagined when they first made contact with their English allies in 1638.

PART ONE

THE CONQUEST OF SCOTLAND AND UNION WITH ENGLAND, 1651 — 1653

1

The Subjugation of Scotland, September 1651 — January 1652

i. The failure of military and political resistance to the English army, September — December 1651

THE capture of the Committee of Estates at Alyth and the defeat of Charles's army at Worcester deprived Scotland, within the space of one week, of her central executive and of the main body of her fighting troops. In effect, she had lost both her government and her army, yet for some months she continued to put up military and political resistance to the English invader. Royalist levies remained active in the north under the Earl of Balcarres, the Marquis of Huntly and several of the lesser nobility and gentry; and a few fortified strongholds, namely the Bass Rock, Dumbarton, Dunnottar and Brodick Castles, held out against the English army. Stalwarts of the old kirk party régime attempted to assume the mantle of political authority. The Earl of Loudoun, backed by Argyle, tried to unite the scattered fragments of the nation's political leadership by summoning first the Committee of Estates and then Parliament to meet in remote parts of the west and the Highlands. But the military and political arms of the Scottish resistance, never strong in themselves, failed to unite, and the superior might of the English army soon prevailed against its weaker opponents. By December 1651, although large areas of the Highlands remained unconquered, and three major fortresses still held out, the English were in control of the far north, the north-east, and the whole of Scotland south of the Tay.

The English army's first priority, after Alured's *coup* at Alyth, was to extend its control up the east coast of Scotland. On 30 August, after repeated summonses, St. Andrews was forced to surrender and its inhabitants fined £500 stg. for their former obstinacy.[1] Two days later Dundee was taken by storm. The English had brought up guns and mortar pieces from Perth and on the night of 30 August these began playing against the town; but bad weather and the need to wait for reinforcements caused Monck to postpone an all-out assault on Dundee.[2] Early in the morning of 1 September, however, the bombardment was resumed. For some hours the garrison retaliated, but around 11 o'clock the English entered the town through breaches in the fortifications on the east and west sides.[3] The Scots sought refuge in the church, but were overtaken by the English, who killed at least 500 soldiers and townsmen, took another 500 prisoner, and seized many ships in the harbour.[4] After the fall of Dundee the English soldiers were given leave to plunder the town for twenty-four hours, but despite Monck's attempts to stop further

Map 1. Scotland

looting, attacks on the persons and property of the inhabitants went on for another fortnight. On 15 September Monck at last took stern action against the looters. Proclamations were issued which forbade plunder and ordered the soldiers to restore all shops, cellars and warehouses to their rightful owners.[5] Courts-martial then imposed swingeing penalties on the soldiers for robbery, drunkenness, swearing and fornication, and thereafter military discipline was stringently enforced.[6]

The capture of Dundee gave the English army command of the northern shores of the Firth of Tay and allowed it to extend its control farther up the east coast of Scotland, as far as Aberdeen. After Dundee Monck himself fell gravely ill, but parties of horse under the command of Col. Overton were despatched to summon the town of Montrose which, it was rumoured, the Scots might try to fortify.[7] After completing that mission, Col. Overton, in the company of Cols. Okey and Morgan and with a mixed force of horse and dragoons, went on to Aberdeen. Before it reached the town the army was met by a deputation from the inhabitants, led by Alexander Jaffray, a former provost. Jaffray, formerly a staunch Presbyterian, had been much influenced by the English divine Dr. John Owen and was now veering towards Independency.[8] He pleaded eloquently for the safety of the town and won from Okey a promise that the army would exact only free quarter. When he entered the town on 7 September, however, Okey reneged on this promise and demanded a fine of £1000 stg. The fine was later taken off, but only after Jaffray and his colleagues had given further pledges of future co-operation and good behaviour.[9]

The submission of Aberdeen marked the culmination of several weeks' successful campaigning by the English along the east coast of Scotland. Operations had continued virtually unhindered since Cromwell's decision in July to ship part of his army into Fife: Perth, Dundee and Aberdeen had all fallen within the space of six weeks, and little resistance had been offered to the English invader. In the south-west, too, the month of September saw further successes for the English army, for here Major Scott quickly mopped up the remaining pockets of resistance. At the end of August, 300 Scottish foot and some horse had quartered in Dumfries, but on the approach of the English army they, and the inhabitants, fled. The English occupied the town and then sent out parties to pursue the fugitives, whose main body had withdrawn to Maxwelton, where they gathered considerable support from the country people. A series of engagements scattered this and other parties, and severe reprisals were visited on those country people who had aided the Royalists. Thereafter the remnant of the Scots forces, although attempting at least one more general rendezvous at Ayr, was kept on the run and by late September serious resistance in the area had been effectively destroyed.[10] Farther north, however, Dumbarton Castle still held out and for some months more challenged English control of the west of Scotland. Not until 29 December did the governor, Sir Charles Erskine, conclude articles of capitulation and a few days later hand over his castle to the English.[11]

From October to December 1651 the army's attention was primarily focused not on the threat from Dumbarton but on the challenge to its control of the north and north-east. In these areas the English army faced two major tasks. First, organised military resistance to the English invader which was still being led by the royalist nobles Balcarres and Huntly had to be crushed. Secondly, the endemic lawlessness of the Highland zone, under cover of which the clans and other unruly elements could continue to resist alien domination, had to be brought under control. It was to these problems that Monck addressed himself after he had secured the submission of the coastal towns between Dundee and Aberdeen.

The royalist levies which were still in arms at the end of September were numerically weak, and their leaders more often than not at odds with each other, but they possessed the advantage of having lines of retreat which stretched into the mountains. They were, therefore, difficult to locate and even more difficult to pursue, if once they could be brought to an engagement. For the English army a campaign into unknown and mountainous terrain possessed inherent disadvantages, but even without these, Monck seriously doubted his capacity to undertake major offensive action. The regiments in Scotland, both of horse and foot, were greatly under strength; many of his soldiers had fallen sick, provisions were running short, and pay was much in arrears.[12] Although he received word in mid-September that the army in Scotland was to be brought up to 12,000 men,[13] no new recruits arrived until October or November. Even then, some of the newcomers were found to be either too old or too young for service, and it was feared that the others would take some time to become accustomed to Scottish conditions.[14] Monck's strategy was, therefore, to wage a war of attrition against the northern Royalists, in the hope that organised resistance would collapse from within. In this respect Monck could count on the fact that time was not on the Royalists' side. Balcarres and Huntly needed a quick victory against the English army to swell their levies; failure to achieve this caused them to lose what little support they already had. This was as true of their civilian supporters as of the number of men actually in arms, for increasingly the English were able to attract and enforce the obedience of the local population. By capitalising on their own strength and on the war-weariness of the country people, the English were able to cut the Royalists off from potential supplies of food, money, men and horses. For the English, nothing succeeded like success: the stronger their control over the Scottish countryside *seemed* to be, the stronger they in fact became.

In late September, the greatest part of the English horse was quartered between Dundee and Aberdeen 'in order to observe the enemies motion'. They received intelligence that Huntly had 600 horse and 1000 foot, most of them inexperienced soldiers, and Balcarres about 250 horse. But these forces were scattered; plans for a general rendezvous failed; and the efforts of the Mackenzies to levy men farther north likewise had little result. Huntly's threat to plunder Aberdeen merely drove the inhabitants farther into the arms of the English.[15] By mid-October, William Clarke, secretary to the English army in Scotland, could report to Parliament only rumours of risings and bustlings among the Highlanders, but no positive military action on either side.[16] In the following weeks, the royalist cause was further weakened by disputes among its leaders over the military command in the north-east. The Earl of Callander, who had links with Argyle and Loudoun and was therefore suspect in the eyes of staunch Royalists, was rumoured to have angered Balcarres by claiming absolute precedence over all other leaders, while Huntly had fallen out with Lord Forbes over the command of such levies as the latter should bring in. Early in November, Monck was told that Huntly had 1500 men and that Balcarres had been seen in Moray and Ross with some parties of horse; one estimate put their combined strength at 2500 or 3000 horse and foot.[17] Even if, as these figures indicate, the total strength of the royalist forces had deteriorated little over the past month, it had not improved dramatically either, and, more ominously, there were signs that the country people were withdrawing their support. Increasingly, the local people were finding it difficult to meet the demands of both the English army and the king's levies, many of whom were posing an additional burden by 'betaking themselves to the High-wayes to play the Tories and Robbers'.[18] In the battle for the support of the local population, the English were at an obvious advantage, not only because they could employ superior force, but because their demands were less capricious than those of the Royalists, and they could hold out the prospect of peace and settled government. The English could, therefore, take heart from reports that the local population were determined to prevent Huntly's troops from crossing the Spey and that they had actually set upon Balcarres' troops when the latter had come to levy contributions.[19] During the next month, the collapse of military resistance was swift. By 6 November, most of the house of Gordon had laid down their arms. By 9 November, Huntly had sent commissioners to treat with the English, and on the 21st articles of capitulation were agreed on by both parties. About the same time, Callander also submitted. By 17 November, Balcarres had come in to the English army, by the 23rd he was disbanding his forces, and on 3 December he too signed articles of capitulation.[20]

With the submission of Balcarres and Huntly, organised military resistance in the shires bordering on the Moray Firth and in the central Highlands was virtually at an end. The way, therefore, was open for the English army to tighten its grip on the far north, to overawe the Highland clans, and to deal with the problem of lawlessness in the Highlands, a problem now exacerbated by those wandering bands of 'Tories and Robbers' who had split off from the main body of the royalist forces and had taken to pillaging the countryside. The English only partly succeeded in achieving these objectives in the winter of 1651-2. Many problems remained, some to be tackled by a campaign into the Highlands in the summer of 1652, others to defy solution for many more years. But by January 1652, the English army could claim to be in effective control of most of Scotland.

By December, John Lambert and Richard Deane had joined Monck as acting commanders-in-chief of the army in Scotland,[21] but the plans then put in motion for reducing the north were essentially those which Monck had evolved two months previously. Their intention was to maintain a strong military presence in the coastal plains of the north and north-east rather than to penetrate into the mountains. This would hem in the 'wilde Highlanders', as *Mercurius Scoticus* called them,[22] cut them off from the support of the population there, and provide a base for future operations into the interior.

By late November, it had been decided to send Col. Fitch's regiment to Inverness and part of Col. Ashfield's with some of Monck's own regiment to Morayshire. Starting off from Aberdeen, the English forces crossed the Spey around 1 December. Having planted a garrison in Inverness, they then in the next few weeks marched through parts of Ross, Sutherland and Caithness.[23] So rapid was their subjugation of this part of the north that within a couple of months they were able to extend their conquest to the Orkneys. Two companies of Col. Cooper's regiment sailed thither on 28 January and were 'civillie entertayned' by the inhabitants.[24]

While the English were notching up these successes, several of the clans were reported to be restive and to have taken up arms, although to what purpose was not made clear. In mid-November, it was alleged that the Macraes and the Maclennans, amongst others, were in arms, while in late December reports came in that 800 clansmen, including Macgriggors, Macduggans, Mackinnons and Macfarlanes, had banded together.[25] But at no time did they attack the English *en masse*, and the problem of enforcing their formal submission to the English Commonwealth was shelved until the following summer.

It was less easy to ignore the activities of the many bands of thieves and murderers who continued to plague the countryside. In the mid-winter months, the English forces which were quartered between Inverness and Aberdeen, as well as those farther south, had to deal with attacks and ambushes from moss-troopers. The term 'moss-trooper' had originally been applied to the lawless elements of the Border country, but it was now generally used by the English to describe the gangs of marauders, many of them ex-soldiers, who roamed throughout Scotland. The most notorious of these 'mossers' in the north were Capt. Augustine and Capt. Gordon, both of whom did much to harass the English army before being forced to give up their resistance around January 1652. Augustine was a German mercenary who had been dismissed from the Scots army before Dunbar. For some time he had harried the English troops in the south of Scotland, and in December 1650 had even dared to reinforce the garrison of Edinburgh Castle shortly before they capitulated to Cromwell. A year later he was still active, this time in the Highlands, where he roamed up and down 'spoiling the country' before escaping to the Orkneys, and from there to Norway, at the beginning of 1652.[26] Capt. Gordon was in command of a party of horse who had fought under the Marquis of Huntly and were now, after their official disbandment, continuing to harry the countryside. On 6 December, Gordon captured four English dragoons and one foot soldier. One of these later escaped and the remainder were released, after being forced to swear on the psalm book to be true to the king and never to take up arms for the English Parliament again.[27]

At the turn of the year many other incidents were reported which showed that, although organised military resistance had been crushed, law and order had yet to be imposed on the countryside. Early in December three English soldiers were murdered near Aberdeen, and another three or four met the same fate near Stirling, while in January some Highlanders killed ten or twelve men at Inverness.[28] The last months of 1651 saw also the return of many stragglers from the Scots army in England. Some had escaped from the battlefield at Worcester, while others had been taken prisoner but had escaped from their gaolers. Being penniless and hungry, they proved a heavy burden on their native country. In November, an Englishman at Leith described them as 'more desperate in their designs and resolutions than all the Lords or Lairds who stayed at home'. The lower elements frequently took to robbery. Thus Robert Bell, with six or seven other men, extorted £10 stg. from a Scotsman in Coupar in Angus under pretence of being a member of the English army. Bell was court-martialled at Dundee on 2 December and sentenced to be hanged as a thief and a spy.[29] In addition to these rootless elements, the country was also the prey of 'an hundred people of severall nations, call'd heere by the name of Egyptians', who rambled up and down the northern Highlands where, like the English gipsies, they cheated and cozened the inhabitants.[30]

To discourage the country people from lending support to the smaller gangs of mossers or robbers, the English army made local communities responsible for delivering up offenders in their midst, under threat of heavy fines. This method of combating disorder, which was to be used extensively by the English during a later phase of royalist unrest, achieved swift results in a number of cases in 1651. After the murder of the soldiers near Aberdeen, Col. Overton told the gentlemen of the district that if they did not find the murderers he would fine the country £50 for each man killed; three of the culprits were promptly handed over and imprisoned at Aberdeen. The country people round Stirling were forced to pay several fines for murders and robberies committed in that area, and this, in turn, encouraged the inhabitants of Coupar to hunt down Robert Bell and two other moss-troopers.[31]

Although the attacks of robbers and mossers were undoubtedly a threat to the English army's control of the countryside, it was clear that they represented a problem of law and order rather than a military or a political danger. The fact remained, however, that if these lawless elements or, indeed, the restiveness of the Highland clans, could be harnessed to the political machinations of a national leader, then the result could be a renewal of co-ordinated and forceful resistance to the English invader. To prevent such a conjunction it was vital that the English, having successfully crushed organised military resistance, should also destroy the one important element of political resistance still remaining in Scotland. This element of political resistance, which at first was represented by the Earl of Loudoun's attempts to resurrect the Committee of Estates and the Scottish Parliament, was, by November 1651, embodied in the Marquis of Argyle's refusal to submit to the English government.

No doubt Argyle and Loudoun did, in the immediate aftermath of Worcester, contemplate some form of *military* resistance to the English, but as a practical matter they did not raise new levies in the west, and they did not succeed in linking up with the existing royalist levies in the north-east. Ironically, Argyle had probably the greatest manpower resources of any man in Scotland, yet he wisely eschewed armed resistance to the English army in favour of more subtle political ploys. For some weeks he threw his weight behind the attempts of Loudoun to maintain the authority of the Committee of Estates, but later he used Loudoun's manoeuvrings as bargaining counters in his single-handed negotiations with the English. When Loudoun's plans had finally collapsed, Argyle continued to trade on his prestige as a clan chieftain and feudal aristocrat, and on the fact that the English could not send an expeditionary force anywhere near the seat of his power in the western Highlands until the summer of 1652, to maintain some semblance of independence in his negotiations with them. Although wary and distrustful of his motives, the English remained confident that in the long run they could force Argyle to submit, but it is a testament to his diplomatic talents that he did not finally do so until October 1652.

After the capture of most of the Committee of Estates at Alyth, Loudoun, in his capacity as Chancellor, summoned all remaining members to meet at Killin in Perthshire on 5 September, but he was opposed by Balcarres who, in addition to his purely military activities, was trying to maintain the pretence of a royalist government in the north-east. Those members, including Argyle, who did gather at Killin by 10 September then ordered Balcarres to attend their next meeting at Dumbarton on the 25th. This order was issued despite the fact that they had also asked Balcarres to rendezvous with his troops at Dunkeld on the 24th; how the two orders were to be reconciled was not made clear. But Balcarres, unwilling to cede precedence to a faction which was led by members of the old kirk party, disdained to obey either command, and so sensibly widened the breach between the military and political arms of the Scottish resistance.[32] Meanwhile, rumours were rife as to the purpose of the meeting at Dumbarton. Wariston heard on the 20th that, although Argyle had until lately been in favour of an armed rising, proposals would now be put forward for a treaty with the English.[33] At the same time, the English were less sure of Argyle's conversion to peaceful diplomacy, for they had received alarming reports that he intended to be present at a general rendezvous on 3 October with 4000 troops.[34] In the event the presence nearby of English troops prevented any meeting from taking place at Dumbarton. The Committee therefore adjourned to Rosneath and then Rothesay, by which time a quorum was no longer present. Argyle was present at Rothesay, but by then Loudoun, and not he, was the sole advocate of further attempts to raise new levies. On 15 October the Committee summoned Parliament to meet at Finlarig on 12 November,[35] and on the same day, Argyle made his first overtures to the English.

In a letter to Monck of 15 October, Argyle suggested that 'some men who have deserved Trust in both Kingdomes' should meet to negotiate a settlement. Thus, far from envisaging an outright submission to the English, Argyle was attempting to assume a mediatory role between the English army and the Scottish nation. He did not mention in his letter who the Scottish representatives at this meeting should be, but he probably had in mind the faction of which he and Loudoun were the head. Monck, however, replied that no such treaty could be concluded without authority from Parliament, and although Parliament heard of the proposal on 31 October, it declined to act upon it.[36] The army in Scotland believed that effectively Argyle was seeking a compliance with them because of the weakness of his position, since reputedly he could get neither country men nor burgesses to join with him, but their trust in the sincerity of his overtures was severely diminished when, about a week after the receipt of his letter, they also learned of the plan to summon Parliament to Finlarig. Their immediate reaction was to suspect Argyle of being the main instigator of the project, whereas in fact it was Loudoun who had been the prime mover.[37] In early November, Argyle sent the Earls of Wemyss and Linlithgow to Monck with a request for a meeting at Perth. Wemyss assured Monck that Argyle had raised no new levies against the English since Charles II had left Scotland, and, indeed, some of the English believed that 'Argylle is unwilling to engage in a new warre, but rather advises every one to capitulate & every man to doe for himselfe.' Monck agreed to appoint two of his officers to treat with Argyle on 19 November but stipulated that any agreement must include Argyle's outright submission to the Commonwealth. He also demanded that Argyle should do his utmost to prevent Parliament from meeting at Finlarig and should certainly not attend in person.[38] In the event, Argyle did not go to Finlarig — only four noblemen, including Loudoun himself, did — but he did not go to Perth either to meet the English officers. The alleged reason in both cases was an illness which made him unfit to travel. Thereafter communication between the Marquis and the English lapsed until late December, when Argyle asked for a meeting with Lambert.[39]

At this time, the English seemed unsure of Argyle's military strength. In mid-November *Mercurius Scoticus* reported that 'It's said those few men Argyle had daily run away, so that few or none are left.' Yet on 25 December Clarke wrote that Argyle still maintained a strong garrison of 300 men at Loch Carron, and on 1 January he reported that several hundred clansmen had answered Argyle's summons to foregather for the choosing of a mere thirty of their number to accompany him to army headquarters, 'soe slavish are those barbarous Creatures to his will'. In January the English alternately believed that Argyle was planning to escape overseas or that he would presently appear in Edinburgh to submit to the Commonwealth.[40] In fact, he refrained from either course and declined to have further contact with the English army until March 1652, by which time the arrival of commissioners from Parliament to settle the civil affairs of Scotland[41] had changed the political context within which negotiations were conducted. Thus, at the beginning of 1652 Argyle was contriving to maintain a defensive posture against the English. Although he had undertaken no offensive military action against them, and although he had abandoned the pretence of an independent government, his resistance was nonetheless a serious obstacle to the army's hopes of subduing the western Highlands. Argyle's opposition, and the fact that three royalist strongholds — the Bass Rock, Dunnottar and Brodick Castles — had yet to be reduced, meant, therefore, that the English conquest of Scotland was still incomplete. But with these exceptions and that of the central Highlands, the English army was the indisputable master of the country. Having effectively destroyed military and political resistance, it could, by the end of the year, proceed to the tasks of restoring the rudiments of civil government and of reconciling the Scottish people to alien rule.

ii. The English army and the Scottish people, September 1651 — January 1652

In the course of its military operations, the English army had had many opportunities to influence its future relations with the Scottish people. In most cases it tried to emphasise that the English were committed to a policy of 'evenhanded justice and good government'[42] and to show that the army was neither capricious nor arbitrary in its demands. Thus in the war against the levies of Balcarres and Huntly, the army had made a bid for the support of the local population not only by the exercise of superior force, but by recognising the country's war-weariness and its desire for settled government. Similarly, in its drive against moss-troopers, the army could contend that the harsh measures adopted against those who sheltered thieves and robbers worked also to the advantage of those who might suffer from the mossers' threats to their goods and property.

The army leaders could further show that they desired to protect the local population by imposing strict military discipline on English soldiers who robbed or killed Scotsmen. Such incidents were not infrequent at this time and were indicative of a general discontent in the army. The campaign in the north was not popular; communications were difficult and the weather was extremely cold. Robert Baynes, an officer in Col. Ashfield's regiment, complained to his brother in London that his regiment was 'much slighted': their pay was either in arrears or insufficient for their needs, the country was too poor to afford them adequate quarters, and since their Colonel was in London, they had nobody to represent their sufferings to the command in Scotland.[43] His complaints find an echo in the records of the courts-martial held at Dundee in December 1651. Many of the cases involving members of the garrison stemmed from the shortage of provisions for the army. Food was stolen from the townspeople, and threats were made to commit atrocities in the town if arrears of pay were not forthcoming. One near-mutiny occurred when the provost-marshal attempted to reprove a soldier who had stolen meat from a Dundee butcher. Insubordination towards officers was not unusual, and complaints — echoed also by Baynes — were voiced against Monck. These disorders were repressed severely, whether they occurred inside or outside the garrison. On 9 December, the court-martial issued a proclamation forbidding soldiers to straggle from their quarters because they abused the population and extorted victuals from them, to the dishonour of the army and the great prejudice of the country.[44]

There was no denying, however, that the army imposed a heavy burden on those districts it occupied. It was the Scottish people who had to provide maintenance for the army, either in the form of free quarters, or of monetary contributions, or both. As garrisons were established throughout the country and the English occupation of Scotland became more entrenched, it became possible to levy a tax or assessment (known as the 'cess') on the district surrounding each garrison. Here the English followed the Scottish practice of using parishes and presbyteries as the unit of collection. Thus in August the area covered by the presbytery of Kirkcaldy began to pay cess to the garrison of Burntisland, and in September the presbytery of St. Andrews paid cess to the English at Perth. The latter paid weekly 21 shillings on every £100 of rent (annual value). By the end of October, Aberdeen was being asked to pay £35 stg. weekly, and in November Edinburgh was charged with the sum of £554. 8s. 10d. stg. per month.[45] In the early months of the conquest, the imposition and collection of these taxes were no doubt organised very much on an *ad hoc* basis, but in most cases, it seems, the English attempted to levy a sum equivalent to two and one-half times the amount the Scots had been asked to pay in the monthly maintenance of 1649-51.[46] This tax, imposed by the Covenanters to maintain their armies, had stood at the rate of £108,000 Scots per month (£9000 stg.), and, in theory, each shire had paid monthly 1/56th of its annual valuation.[47] Clearly, in those areas where the English succeeded in levying the cess, the burden on the local population was great.

Those parts of the army which were not settled in garrisons but were on active field service were more likely to demand free quarters than monetary cess. In October, the forces watching the movements of Balcarres and Huntly were quartered throughout the shires of Angus and the Mearns (*i.e.* Kincardineshire), and in December those sent to settle the far north were distributed throughout Morayshire. Their exactions from the countryside undoubtedly caused much suffering and forced the shires and burghs to petition for relief. The English frequently found it necessary to rearrange their quarters to alleviate the burden, but they turned the situation to their advantage by granting such concessions only after they had extracted formal submissions and promises of good behaviour from the country. Thus Monck authorised the withdrawal of two regiments of horse and five troops of dragoons from Angus and the Mearns after the gentlemen there had promised not to engage further against the Commonwealth and to help bring in those who, like the followers of Balcarres and Huntly, had not already submitted. Similarly, the need to obtain a reduction in their assessment led some gentlemen of Fife to seek a compliance with the English.[48] The burghs were equally assiduous in sending representatives to treat for some relief. Glasgow sent a former provost, John Graham, to Stirling, and Aberdeen sent Alexander Jaffray and Bailie George Cullen, who had succeeded in getting the town's fine of £1000 taken off in September, to Dundee to plead for an abatement.[49]

In December, Lambert and Deane began to organise the assessment on a more regular basis. Free quarter was taken off in most parts of the country, starting with the east, then the west, and finally the north, and was replaced by the monthly assessment.[50] In arriving at an estimate of the yearly rental of each shire on which to base the assessment, the English in many cases worked on figures very close to those in the valuation rolls of 1649, to which they may have had access.[51] It appears that they now wanted to impose sums amounting to one and a half times the monthly maintenance of 1649-51 on Scotland;[52] if applied to the whole country, this would have produced, in theory, £13,500 stg. per month. It is unlikely, however, that such a sum was ever obtained. After Lambert and Deane had made provisional arrangements, tribunals were appointed to hear pleas for further reductions or exemptions, and between December 1651 and January 1652 several changes were made in the original assessments.[53] It was not long, moreover, before commissioners from Parliament altered the nominal rate of the cess to £10,000 per month, thus entailing a further revision of the system.[54] The work of Lambert and Deane, therefore, by reducing the rate of the cess by about 40% — and in some cases more — from the level at which it had stood for the past few months, marked the beginnings of an attempt to rationalise, and make more equitable, the financial burdens on the Scottish people.

By December 1651, the army had also taken steps to remedy the lack of a judicial administration in Scotland. The last meeting of the Court of Session (the highest court in Scotland for civil affairs) had taken place on 28 February 1650,[55] and since then there had been no supreme judicatory functioning either in civil or criminal matters. The English commanders undertook to fill the gap. A committee of officers sat at Leith and despatched cases, some of which had been pending for years before the Scottish courts.[56] In other towns Scotsmen came before courts-martial, but only in matters directly involving the army — as, for example, the killing of English soldiers — and not in civil suits between Scot and Scot, as was the case at Leith. On 29 December the committee at Leith issued a proclamation stating that any person who disobeyed its summonses or orders would be liable to a fine or imprisonment at will.[57] In addition, the officers at Leith and Edinburgh sat also as a regular court-martial and in that capacity regulated the lives of the inhabitants in matters which concerned the army. Proclamations were issued regulating the price of hay, the quality of bread (particularly that sold to the garrison), and the lighting and cleaning of streets (so that soldiers might not be unjustly accused of disorders committed in the dark). Two proclamations concerned the moral welfare of the soldiery. In October, all soldiers in Edinburgh and Leith were forbidden to marry Scotswomen without permission from a superior officer, and in January the employment of maidservants and barmaids (synonymous with loose women) was forbidden in Leith.[58]

By the turn of the year, then, not only had active military resistance to the English been crushed but interim measures had been taken to organise the administration of Scotland on a peacetime basis. The Scottish community had undoubtedly been coerced into submission: it remained to be seen whether it could also be cajoled into reconciliation. The army believed it had already made some progress in this task. The enforcement of strict military discipline, the restoration of law and order, the dispensing of evenhanded justice, the relief in quartering and assessment — these were all seen as benefits for which the Scottish people not only should be, but would be, grateful.[59] On the larger issue of whether the Scots could be persuaded actively to co-operate with their conquerors, the English, both at Westminster and in Scotland, took particular heart from the many divisions within the Scottish community itself. They hoped that these antagonisms would not so much neutralise each other as force the contending parties to compete for English favour, in the hope of scoring off their opponents. During the early months of the conquest, English observers in Scotland were quick to spot any signs of disharmony within the Scottish community which they thought might be turned to their advantage, and to report such developments to their colleagues in London. They held to their belief in eventual reconciliation between conquerors and conquered despite the overwhelming opposition of the presbyterian clergy and their lay supporters to English rule. Indeed the English believed, in the face of much evidence to the contrary, that many Scots desired deliverance from the dominance of the clergy and that in secular affairs the common people wanted to be freed from the power of the nobility and gentry. The assumption that these aspirations would in the long run cause the Scots to turn to the English for support played an important part in shaping Parliament's policy towards Scotland between October and December 1651. Many newsletters expressed these same convictions, but at the same time showed a canny awareness of three more immediate aspects of the Scottish situation. English commentators noted, first of all, the actions of the presbyterian clergy and their lay supporters and paid much attention to the continuing disputes between Protester and Resolutioner; secondly, they observed the small but growing number of sectaries in Scotland; and thirdly, they reported the fact that many gentry who had formerly been supporters of the royalist cause were among the first to seek a compliance with their conquerors.

The behaviour of the clergy was to be the focus of much attention between September 1651 and January 1652. After the English *coup* at Alyth, the commission of the kirk which had been appointed at Dundee (and was therefore known as the Commission of 1651) fled north. Some members convened in Aberdeen around 2 September, and there were other meetings in the far north, but little business could be transacted. Thereafter the commission, which was, of course, composed only of Resolutioners, did not meet again until May 1652.[60] The Protesters and their sympathisers, meanwhile, met in Glasgow towards the end of September. This meeting had been called by Patrick Gillespie and his faction, but the more extreme Protesters such as Wariston and Chiesley refused to attend. Wariston knew that the Earl of Loudoun had asked the Commission of 1651 to join the Committee of Estates at Dumbarton on 25 September, and he suspected that the meeting at Glasgow would be under pressure to unite with those at Dumbarton. In the event, however, the Commission did not meet with the Committee, and the Protesters at Glasgow adjourned their meeting to Edinburgh.[61]

Sixty-six ministers were present at the Edinburgh convention which lasted more than two weeks. Much time was taken up with a confession of national and personal sins, but the substantive work of the meeting was to declare the Public Resolutions unlawful (on 11 October) and to vote that those members of the Commission of 1650 who were free from the taint of defection should exercise the authority of a commission in opposition to that appointed by the 'pretended' Assembly at Dundee.[62] The meeting was in itself much divided. Wariston's party of extremists distrusted the attempts of James Durham to effect a reconciliation with the Resolutioners, while they were equally appalled by the suggestions of Alexander Jaffray that some things in the Covenant were unlawful. Jaffray, supported by three Aberdeenshire ministers, had come south to confer with the

Protesters on no less a point than the lawfulness of the whole presbyterian system of church government. As he was later to express it, Jaffray had come to the conclusion that 'the congregational way comes nearer to the pattern of the word [of God] than our classical form' (*i.e.* Presbyterianism). Jaffray's supporters were not prepared to go as far as this in October 1651, and the Protesters were overwhelmingly against him, [63] but his was not the only dissident voice to be heard at Edinburgh. Some of the assisting elders spoke against monarchy, against the clergy's monopoly of preaching and against infant baptism.[64] Their voices were certainly muted, but they did show that the seed of sectarianism had been sown.

About the same time, there were other reports of the Scots taking an interest in Independency. At the end of October, Clarke noted that the people in and around Edinburgh were anxious to hear some English minister, having been much affected by those that had been there with Cromwell's troops. A few months later, however, it was said that although the people of Sutherland were well disposed towards Independent preachers, these were not popular in the south. Clarke emphasised that the stranglehold of the presbyterian clergy would not be broken unless the English themselves took positive action to provide an alternative. In November he suggested that stipends should be allowed to some able preachers from England to preach in the principal towns of Scotland in order to draw the people off from 'the leaven of their now-Pharisaical and rigid Presbyterian teachers'.[65] His views were echoed by a correspondent in England who wrote that 'the whole cry of Scotch priests' should be prohibited from preaching and that an honest preaching trooper should be put into every parish church instead.[66]

The English army made no attempt to follow such extreme advice nor, indeed, to prevent the presbyterian clergy and lay elders from holding meetings of synods or presbyteries throughout October and November. The English probably hoped that, by allowing Protesters and Resolutioners to vent their spleen on each other in their accustomed assemblies, they would weaken the church as a whole and so deprive the opposition to English rule of much of its strength. Certainly the split within the church was much exacerbated in the next few weeks. The resolutions of the Protesters at Edinburgh were condemned in late October by the four presbyteries of Fife, and in November by the synod of Lothian. The synods of Galloway and Glasgow, on the other hand, supported the Protesters and declared the Assembly at St. Andrews and Dundee to be null and void.[67] The province of Aberdeen voted by a majority to uphold the Assembly of 1651, but a strong Protester element, led by Andrew Cant, Jaffray's father-in-law, registered a formal protest against this vote.[68] In most synods there was in fact some division of opinion, but only in Glasgow and parts of the west were the Protesters strong enough to carry a majority. In the provinces of Aberdeen and Fife, however, they formed a particularly strong minority.

Despite the fact that in the past some Remonstrants and Protesters had had contacts with Cromwell and his army, the Protesters were not, in general, more kindly disposed towards the English than were their Resolutioner colleagues. Both Englishmen and Protesters disliked the person of Charles Stuart, but the fact that the English were Covenant-breakers stood between them, not only because the

Covenant upheld presbyterian church discipline but because it implied the maintenance of the institution of kingship. The signatories to the third article of the Solemn League and Covenant had sworn 'to preserve and defend the King's Majesty's person and authority, in the preservation and defence of the true religion and liberties of the Kingdoms'. Therefore, as the eminent Resolutioner Robert Baillie wrote in 1652, 'to make the third article of our Covenant stand well enough with a freedome to change Monarchie with a Scotish Republick, this to me is a high-enough crime.'[69] Many Protesters, in defence of this interpretation of the Covenant, openly expressed their hostility to the English régime. Andrew Cant in Aberdeen was particularly vehement in spurning offers of protection and friendship from Col. Overton, and indeed proclaimed that whereas all other Parliaments had been called by man, Loudoun's projected Parliament at Finlarig was brought about by God's own hand.[70] The Protester-dominated synod of Argyll likewise recognised the authority of the Finlarig Parliament.[71] On the other hand, Wariston's band of extremists were almost as distrustful of Loudoun and Argyle as they were of the English, and so could be relied on not to bolster that faction's resistance to the Commonwealth.

Whatever their internal differences, all sections of the presbyterian clergy were united in their opposition to those 'Malignants' (many of them former Royalists) who were now putting out feelers to the English. At the end of October, the gentry of Fife, Perthshire, Angus and the Mearns sent representatives to a meeting at St. Andrews to discuss the drawing up of propositions for presentation to the commissioners who were to be sent from England to implement Parliament's long-term policy towards Scotland. The propositions were to deal with the settlement of the civil affairs of Scotland under the authority of the Commonwealth of England. No agreement was reached at St. Andrews and the meeting was adjourned till 6 November at Perth. On that date the delegates agreed that a letter should be sent to every shire and burgh inviting them to elect commissioners to meet at Edinburgh on 21 November. The object of this meeting was to attend the downcoming of the English commissioners and to transact business with them for the good of the kingdom and the cessation of 'these unnatural wars'.[72] Although the meeting scheduled for the 21st was later to be cancelled, many shires went ahead and elected delegates. By 18 November most of the shires in the north, together with Linlithgowshire, Stirlingshire and Fife, had met to choose their representatives, and in all cases, the English asserted, these shires had disowned Loudoun's Parliament at Finlarig. But these elections did not go forward without bitter dispute. The presbyterian ministers were unanimous in their condemnation of the proceedings, and particularly in Fife were supported by the more extreme presbyterian gentry. In Stirlingshire, too, there was a prolonged controversy, for although the shire had convened before the 18th, the commission to the delegates was not drawn up until the 24th.[73]

From the end of November to the end of December, Presbyterians and Malignants refrained from denouncing each other so fiercely, although the controversy between them did not altogether abate. In November, the Malignants were joined in making overtures to the English by 'some few who formerly were accounted pious and gracious men' but were now 'corrupted by sectarian principles'. These sectarians presented a paper consisting of fifteen overtures to the Parliament of England in which they asked for uniformity in government, both of church and state, between Scotland and England and 'many other things prejudicial to the covenant and cause of God'.[74] This small group of men probably had strong links with the Protesters, for at the end of December, when the latter met in Edinburgh specifically for the purpose of giving out a testimony against sinful compliance with the English, these 'sectarian' dissenters met with them. Not surprisingly, the dissenters left after the first session.[75] The meeting then went on (although not without argument) to draft a letter to Cromwell which expressed in the strongest terms its abhorrence of toleration and the loss of the nation's political liberty. The letter was drawn up on 2 January, but a copy of it was not sent to Lambert until later in the month. Lambert refused to grant a pass to the young man who was to convey it to Cromwell, but by the end of January its contents had already been published in the pages of *Mercurius Politicus* in London.[76]

By the end of the year the English reported that 'a very great confluence of the *Gentry*' had arrived in Edinburgh,[77] together with many burgesses and ministers. The English believed that this concourse of people could be divided into two categories: rigid Presbyterians (comprising both parties of the kirk) and former Royalists. The two groups kept separate assemblies, and it was from the Royalists that, in the main, signs of submission and compliance came. Yet at the beginning of January, a newswriter expressed the belief that the Presbyterians were endeavouring tooth and nail to get commissioners to present some overtures to Lambert and Deane, in order not to be outdone by the Malignants. But realising that the Presbyterians, and especially the presbyterian clergy, were still intent on upholding the principles of the Covenant, the English were equally resolved that any application on those terms would not be entertained.[78] On 21 January, a newswriter reported: 'I find the old Royalists generally throughout the Countrie tendring their devoir, but these fiery Kirkists cannot digest a thought of the losse of their infinite power and prerogative.' As an example of this, the writer cited the Protesters' letter to Cromwell of 2 January in which, he said, the subscribers were 'up with that Engine, the Covenant'.[79] Only the Resolutioners, it seemed, harboured suspicions that the Protesters had defected from their covenanting principles.

In setting so much store by the differences between Presbyterians and former Royalists at this point, the English were inclined to ignore the division between Protesters and Resolutioners. The Resolutioners were also present in Edinburgh at the beginning of 1652 and had some conference with the Protesters, but certainly the feuds between them were less important to the English, who were now intent on assessing Scottish opinion before commissioners should arrive from Parliament, than the split between 'Kirkists' (*i.e.* Presbyterians) and Malignants. More surprisingly, English reports, although noting the divisions of opinion at the Protesters' meetings, in December and January, did not allude to the presence of 'sectaries'. Instead they emphasised that debates had arisen over whether the

English government, although not lawful in itself, might yet be lawfully obeyed.[80] Again, such essentially political concerns were, perhaps, understandable at a time when the English were preparing to lay their plans for the future settlement of Scotland before the Scottish people. On 15 January, when commissioners from Parliament finally arrived at Dalkeith, the way was open for the details of these plans to be revealed.

iii. England's politicians and Scotland's future: debates at Whitehall and Westminster, September — December 1651

The policy which the parliamentary commissioners were to implement had been determined after many debates in Parliament and the Council of State. From September to December 1651, while the army was completing the conquest of Scotland and was establishing the rudiments of an administrative system, the English authorities had been considering the nature of the political settlement to be imposed on the country. By December, they had arrived at a scheme for political union, involving the incorporation of Scotland into one commonwealth with England, and at plans for modifying the country's religious and social systems to meet the needs of the English Commonwealth.

Immediately after their army's success at Worcester, the English Parliament gave many signs of regarding Scotland as a conquered province. Their jubilation at Charles Stuart's defeat was expressed in an order of 6 September for a day of public thanksgiving to celebrate the victory, and for an Act to be brought in for the annual commemoration of 3 September, the date of Cromwell's successes at Preston, Dunbar and Worcester.[81] On 9 September, it was resolved that lands of inheritance in Scotland of the yearly value of £1000 stg. should be settled on Major General Lambert, of £500 on Lieutenant General Monck and Commissary General Whalley, of £300 on Col. John Okey, and of £200 on Col. Matthew Alured.[82] On the same day the House prepared to annex Scotland as a conquered province. It was resolved to bring in an Act 'for asserting the Right of this Commonwealth to so much of Scotland as is now under the Power of the Forces of this Commonwealth'. The committee appointed to prepare a draft of the Act was told to report to the House on the 25th, but it was not until the 30th that Lord Commissioner Lisle reported 'an Act asserting the Title of England to Scotland'. This was then read a first time.[83]

At the beginning of October, however, English policy towards Scotland underwent an important change. No more was heard of the Act 'asserting the Title of England to Scotland', for the scheme of annexation was abruptly dropped in favour of a more moderate form of union, that of incorporating Scotland into one commonwealth with England. The reasons for this change in attitude remain unclear, but it is possible that the new policy was the result of Cromwell's personal intervention. Around 22 September John Swinton, who had been with the parliamentary army at Worcester, returned to Scotland and reported that although many in England were in favour of 'declairing this a conquest', yet

Cromwell was 'for making it on[e] nation'.[84] The decision to enact an incorporating union may therefore represent the triumph of his viewpoint in the counsels of the nation.

The new policy of political incorporation was embodied in *A Declaration of the Parliament of the Commonwealth of England, concerning the Settlement of Scotland.* By 13 October, the Council of State had prepared a draft of this document, which Whitelocke then reported to Parliament on the 23rd. On the 23rd and 28th the House debated the preamble and the four clauses of the Declaration and, after making some verbal amendments, agreed to it. On 5 December, the Council, which had been directed to give orders for the printing of the Declaration, was told to keep its contents strictly secret. On the 24th, the House made a minor amendment to the wording of the first clause, and then ordered 2000 copies to be prepared for distribution in Scotland.[85]

The Declaration[86] was fairly short and to the point. It clearly spelled out the guidelines of English policy towards Scotland in political, social and religious matters, and indicated which groups had most, and which least, to fear from the exercise of English rule in the north. Of the four clauses, the first dealt with religion. Without making any specific reference to presbyterian doctrine or discipline, Parliament declared simply that it would be its constant endeavour to promote the preaching of the Gospel in Scotland and to advance the power of true religion and holiness, and in order that God might be served and worshipped 'according to his mind revealed in his Word' all due countenance and encouragement therein would be given to the Scottish people. Thus, in effect, toleration of the kind which obtained in England was to be extended to Scotland.

The second clause enunciated the scheme for political union and promised that it would be made effective 'with such convenient speed as the same can be made practicable' in Scotland.

Next came provisions for repairing the losses which England had suffered since 1648 on account of the wars with Scotland. The property and revenue of the King and Crown of Scotland were declared forfeit, as were the estates, both real and personal, of all those who had taken part in, aided or abetted the Hamiltonian invasion and/or the subsequent activities of Charles Stuart in Scotland and England. Two categories of persons who might otherwise come within the terms of this provision were declared exempt: those who, since 3 September 1650, had laid down their arms and deserted the royal cause, and those who because of special services to the Commonwealth merited 'a more favourable consideration by Parliament'.

The fourth and final clause declared that all persons not comprehended within the former qualifications who should now concur with and promote the ends specified by Parliament would be taken into the latter's protection. In addition, inasmuch as Parliament was convinced that many of the nobility and gentry, 'the chief Actors in these invasions and wars against England', had used their tribal and feudal rights to influence their tenants and vassals to join in their evil designs, such of the latter as should put themselves under the protection of Parliament would be pardoned for all past acts and would be freed from their former dependencies and bondage-services. They were, moreover, to be admitted as tenants, freeholders and heritors to a proportion of the confiscated estates under such 'easie Rents' as might 'enable them, their Heirs and Posterity, to live with a more comfortable subsistence then formerly, and like a free People, delivered (through Gods goodnesse) from their former slaveries, vassalage and oppressions'.

In sum, therefore, the Declaration of Parliament sought to put the blame for the invasions of England in 1648 and 1651, not on the Scottish nation as a whole, but on its social and political leaders. As a corollary, it sought to extend the hand of friendship to those absolved from 'war guilt' through an appeal to their material interests. A similar principle informed the clause on religion. The grant of toleration was aimed at undermining the power of the presbyterian clergy who, the English believed, had provided the moral and spiritual backing for the political activities of the nobility and gentry, by allowing other religious disciplines to compete on equal terms. The offer of political union was designed to extend and reinforce these elements of concession. By attempting in this way to bring into being new social, political and religious forces to redress the balance of the old, Parliament was concerned to give the army in Scotland some basis of support amongst the Scottish people. But, more importantly, the aim of this policy was in the long run to safeguard the revolution in England by exporting some elements of it to Scotland, for as the Covenanters had earlier realised, security lay in union and uniformity between the two countries.

To implement the first stage of its policy, Parliament resolved to send commissioners to Scotland. On 26 September, while the scheme for annexation was still under consideration, the House instructed the Council of State to nominate a number of persons to be sent north 'for the Managing of the Civil Government and settling Affairs there, as may be best for the Advantage of this Commonwealth'. On 30 September, the Council ordered its Committee for Scotch and Irish affairs to consider the matter, and on 23 October, by which time annexation had given way to incorporation, the following were recommended to the House: Chief Justice Oliver St. John, Sir Henry Vane junior, Major Richard Salwey, Col. George Fenwick, Major General John Lambert, Major General Richard Deane and Alderman Robert Tichborne. On the same day, the House confirmed their appointment and added Monck to the list of names. The commission was thus equally divided between civilians and army officers.[87]

The Council had also been directed to draw up Instructions for the Commissioners, and on 23 October it remitted the matter to the Scotch and Irish Committee. On 4 December a draft of nineteen clauses was presented to the House and a week later, after considerable debate, the Instructions were finally passed. On the 18th, those of the Commissioners not already in Scotland — Vane, St. John, Tichborne, Salwey and Fenwick — received their Instructions from the Speaker, and on the 25th they set out on their journey. On 15 January 1652 they arrived in Dalkeith.[88]

The Instructions[89] charged the Commissioners primarily with the execution of that policy enunciated by Parliament in its Declaration of 28 October. The Commissioners were to make Parliament's intentions known to the people of

Scotland and were to endeavour 'to dispose the people there to a complyance with the resolutions' expressed in the Declaration. As a means to this end — but especially, as events showed, to the end of securing compliance in the scheme for political union — the Commissioners were to order the Scottish people to elect deputies, with whom they were to confer concerning the same. The Commissioners were then told to 'prepare and ripen your owne results, upon such your conferences with them for the judgement and resolution of the Parliament'. In no sense did this imply that the Scottish deputies were to have the decisive voice in settling the political future of their country, but merely that the Commissioners were to use them as a sounding-board for Scottish opinion.

The Commissioners were also instructed to promote the power of true religion and holiness in terms of the Declaration. The grant of toleration implied in the latter was made more explicit by the command to provide adequate maintenance 'to such ministers and persons of pious life and conversation, and well affected to the Parliament' as should be most fitted to preach the Gospel and instruct the people. In addition, the Commissioners were to see to the visitation of universities, colleges and schools and were to alter or abolish such statutes of the same as were inconsistent with the welfare of the government of the Commonwealth. In effect, this gave the commissioners wide powers to undermine or overthrow certain institutional aspects of the presbyterian system if these did not accord with the interests of the English Commonwealth.

Similarly, the Commissioners were charged with securing the implementation of the third clause in the Declaration concerning sequestrations, and of the provisos of the fourth clause. Thus they were to lease the confiscated estates to suitable persons, but only at such rates and values as the Council of State should particularly determine.

Other clauses of the Instructions gave the Commissioners wide powers over central and local government. In particular, they were to remove any officials 'dangerous to this Commonwealth' and to administer oaths (in practice, an engagement to be faithful to the Commonwealth) to any person whatsoever. They were to settle the administration of justice on these terms, and were to see 'that the Lawes of England as to matter of government be put in Execution in Scotland'. They could, if necessary, issue proclamations forbidding the exercise of any jurisdiction not derived from the authority of the Parliament of England. They were also to take charge of the raising and disbursing of all sources of public revenue. In addition, they were given sweeping powers to imprison or otherwise restrain any person in Scotland who should be disobedient or dangerous to the authority of Parliament. And to ensure the execution of the whole gamut of parliamentary commands, the Commissioners were empowered to command any officer or soldier of the Commonwealth in Scotland to assist them. They themselves were authorised to be present at Councils of War and to give such advice as they should think fit.

In its Instructions to the Commissioners, Parliament therefore both elaborated and modified the policy it had expressed in the Declaration. It was made quite clear that the touchstone of what would or would not obtain in Scotland was to be the welfare of the Commonwealth of England, as defined by the Westminster Parliament. Nonetheless, the Scottish community was not to be deprived of all semblance of political representation, and in economic, social and religious terms, certain groups of Scots might be allowed to improve their position, but the context within which they could do so was to be controlled by the military and civil arms of the English Commonwealth. If not the policy itself, then certainly the means of its execution, made that abundantly clear.

Two days after the arrival of the Commissioners at Dalkeith, an English officer summed up the attitude of the Scots thus:

> The Scotch people know not what to say to them now that they are comed: some are glad and some are mad now that they see we are in earnest, and that their power is like to change. The Kirk and Cavalier cannot endure one another: each of them endeavours to ingratiate, but the latter is more rationally convinced; the other are yet much unsatisfied. I fear those that seem to have most religion will be most at a loss if they timely prevent it not by a free condescension. I think power will not early and hastily be given to either of them.[90]

Here he put his finger on the one point that was to emerge clearly in the next few weeks, as the Commissioners set about disposing the people of Scotland to a compliance with Parliament's resolutions. Whatever the controversies within the Scottish community, and whatever effect these might have on the attitude of the Scots towards the English, it was the English who held the reins of power in Scotland. Backed by the might of the army, the Commissioners sought conference with the Scots not in order to negotiate, but in order to facilitate the execution of a predetermined policy.

2

The Political Settlement of Scotland and Union with England, January 1652 — April 1653

THE Commissioners from Parliament were resident in Scotland from mid-January until the end of April 1652. During this time they accomplished wide-ranging political and administrative tasks and paved the way for the summoning of Scottish representatives to London later in the year to confer with Parliament on the union with England. The Commissioners had been instructed to dispose the people of Scotland to a compliance with the resolutions expressed in Parliament's Declaration of 28 October, and since Parliament's prime resolve was to put into effect a political union between England and Scotland, the first two months of the Commissioners' stay in Scotland were accordingly taken up with meeting deputies from the shires and burghs and securing their preliminary assent to this union. The manner in which this task was accomplished indicates clearly that what was in theory to be a political merger between the two countries was in fact a take-over bid by the English, and that the success of this plan in its early stages was guaranteed by the presence of the English army in Scotland. Nonetheless, hostility to the proposed union was widespread throughout Scotland, and it is equally clear that the chief impulse behind this opposition was presbyterian feeling and that its most virulent spokesmen were the presbyterian clergy.

The political work of the Commissioners, then, consisted in translating the military conquest of Scotland into an ostensibly voluntary agreement on the part of the Scots to unite their institutions of central government with those of their English masters. By April 1652 this agreement had been secured, but the details of how the proposed union should be put into practice were still undetermined. In order to consult the Scottish community on these details, the English Parliament summoned twenty-one Scottish representatives to London in October 1652. Between October 1652 and April 1653 the Scottish deputies had a series of discussions on this topic with a committee appointed by Parliament, but here again the evidence shows that the Scots were allowed no substantive part in deciding their political fate. Instead, the course of events in London was determined by the exigencies of English domestic politics, and it was Cromwell's dissolution of the Long Parliament, and not the hostility of the Scots, that put an end to the negotiations. In political terms, therefore, the period from January 1652 to April 1653 was one of unremitting and successful efforts by the English to subordinate the Scots to their will.

i. The parliamentary Commissioners and the Tender of Incorporation, January — April 1652

The Commissioners from Parliament arrived at Dalkeith on 15 January 1652.[1] The first week of their stay in Scotland was something of an anticlimax for those who had expected immediate and positive action, for their only recorded decision during this time was the suppression of the newspaper *Mercurius Scoticus*.[2] By 20 January, the Commissioners had received printed copies of Parliament's Declaration of 28 October, but their publication and distribution was delayed until after summonses had been issued to the shires and burghs to send representatives to Dalkeith to hear what Parliament had to offer them concerning the settlement of Scotland.[3] These summonses were despatched on or around 24 January.[4] Each shire was to elect two deputies and each burgh one deputy, although three of the larger burghs — Glasgow, Aberdeen and Edinburgh — were allowed two deputies apiece. The men chosen were to be persons of 'integrity and good affection to the welfare and peace of this Island', and were to be given full powers to conclude agreements with the Commissioners on the spot. These arrangements meant that, although elections were conducted as if for a Parliament, the nobility were specifically excluded from participating in the proceedings as a separate estate, as had been the practice in previous Scottish Parliaments or Conventions.[5] The shires and burghs were divided into groups according to their geographical location, and, depending on their distance from Dalkeith, were told to appear on 9, 12, 16, 23 or 26 February.[6] In these public announcements, and later when the deputies were received at Dalkeith, the Commissioners took great care to suggest that the Scots would be allowed to act freely, but Monck more accurately reflected their intentions when he wrote to Cromwell that deputies would soon arrive 'for to receive such commands from them, as the Parlt. hath ordered the Commissioners to give unto them'.[7]

In the interval between the issuing of the summonses and the arrival of the deputies at Dalkeith, the Commissioners turned their attention to one of the most pressing problems of day-to-day government — the administration of justice. On 31 January, they drew up a declaration which recorded Parliament's desire to see justice done 'to all pepill in Scotland, equalie and impartiallie, without respect of persones', and which stated that the Commissioners would appoint persons to dispense justice on an interim basis until permanent judicatories could be established. Meanwhile, no power, jurisdiction or authority was to be exercised in Scotland which did not derive from the Parliament of England.[8] This meant that all judicatories in Scotland, other than those tribunals staffed by English army officers, were deprived of power: sheriff, commissary, regality and baron courts[9] and, almost certainly, municipal courts, ceased to function. Despite Parliament's promises, no interim appointments were in fact made, and no further action was taken until seven permanent 'Commissioners for the Administration of Justice' were appointed in May.[10] Perhaps the rough justice already being dispensed by the army was deemed sufficient for the time being. The immediate effect of the declaration was therefore essentially negative; it removed all indigenous sources of justice, but it did not replace them with an efficient and comprehensive judicial system deriving its authority from the English Parliament.

The declaration of 31 January was proclaimed at Edinburgh on 4 February, whereupon an English observer remarked, 'The most ingenuous of the Scotts are nott att all offended att itt in appearance but expected some what higher as to the interdicting of their preists & the like of whom they are very wearie.'[11] No doubt any clue about English intentions was welcome at this stage, for still the Scots people had not been told officially what fate Parliament had in store for them. The definitive statement of English policy — the Declaration of 28 October — remained an official secret, although rumours of its contents had been circulating for some time. Its contents were first publicly revealed in Edinburgh on 12 February, when the Declaration was proclaimed from the Mercat Cross. By that date, however, the first batch of deputies had already arrived at Dalkeith.[12] It seems, therefore, that the Commissioners deliberately withheld exact information on Parliament's plans until the deputies could be told of these proposals in person at Dalkeith. This ploy affected not only the deputies summoned for 12 February, but also those from the more remote areas, for, if the Commissioners' timetable were adhered to, they too would have set out on their journey before receiving news of the proclamation. Thus, even if they had some inkling of the general tenor of the Declaration before their departure, it is unlikely that either they or their constituents could have known of its exact contents before the election of the deputies took place.

The English probably employed this tactic in order to isolate the elections and the subsequent activities of the deputies from the response of public opinion to Parliament's proposals. This was eminently sensible from the English point of view, for 'public opinion' was effectively formed by those very groups (the clergy, nobility and gentry) whose political, social, economic and religious interests were likely to be hardest hit by the provisions of the Declaration. This was especially true of the shires: there, above all, the people who had most influence at the elections were also the people against whom the Declaration was aimed. It was, therefore, expedient to keep them in the dark as long as possible, especially since their co-operation was required to give the appearance of voluntary consent to the scheme for political union. This plan was reinforced by the demand that the deputies should arrive with full powers to treat — thus precluding the possibility of the terms being referred back to the constituencies — and by the Commissioners' insistence, once the deputies had been told of the Declaration, that they should return their answer to the offer or 'tender' of incorporation within a matter of a few days.

This demand for a speedy answer to the proffered union was typical of the tight control which the Commissioners attempted to exercise over the proceedings at Dalkeith. For just as they had laid down definite instructions on how and when the deputies should be elected, they also put specific limits on what the deputies were expected to do once they were present at Dalkeith. When they had been received by the Commissioners, the deputies had read to them three documents: the

Commissioners' commission empowering them to act, Parliament's Declaration of 28 October, and an 'Explanation' of this Declaration drawn up by the Commissioners themselves.[13]

The Explanation sought to elaborate and make more explicit those clauses of the original parliamentary declaration which dealt with religion, and with exemptions from confiscation and sequestration. It stated that ministers 'whose consciences oblige them to wait upon God in the administration of the spiritual Ordinances according to the order of the Scottish churches, with any that shall voluntarily joyn in the practice thereof, shall receive protection and encouragement', and that the same protection would also be extended to those 'who, not being satisfied in conscience to use that Form, shall serve and worship God in other Gospel way', provided that they behaved themselves peaceably and inoffensively therein. This confirmed the grant of toleration in Parliament's Declaration. The right to practise as ministers of religion was not to be confined to the presbyterian clergy alone, and the civil power now pledged itself to support anyone who could prove himself to be preaching and worshipping God in a 'Gospel way' — a vague term which implied a serious threat to the monopoly of the Church of Scotland. In addition, in pursuance of the fourth clause of Parliament's Declaration, the Commissioners declared that all merchants owning less than £500 stg. in goods and all others owning less than £200 stg. in lands and goods would be taken into Parliament's protection, provided that they lived peaceably and in obedience to the Parliament of England.[14] This was to some extent an indication that the English were prepared to favour the lower as against the higher ranks of Scottish society, although the figures of £500 and £200 were sufficiently high to encompass most people of the middling sort and to set at rest the minds of many just outside the higher echelons of nobility and greater gentry.

Having heard the contents of these three documents, the deputies were then asked to deliver in writing their answer as to the acceptance of the tender, or offer, of political incorporation between the two countries; their assurance that they would live peaceably under the authority of the Parliament of England; and their recommendations on what was necessary for effecting the union with 'speede and satisfacõn' to the people of Scotland. If the first two propositions were speedily agreed to, then more time might be allowed before the deputies need give in their answer to the third.[15]

By insisting on this procedure, the English hoped to render the results of their consultation with the Scottish community a foregone conclusion. Their aim was to secure the assent of the deputies to Parliament's proposals with a minimum of fuss; and their ultimate success is reflected in the fact that of the 30 shires, 1 stewartry and 58 burghs in Scotland, 28, 1, and 44 respectively accepted the Tender of Incorporation.[16] These figures present simple and unarguable evidence of English domination, but at the same time they mask the strong undercurrent of hostility to the English proposals which was widespread throughout Scotland. This hostility did not materially affect the eventual outcome of the proceedings at Dalkeith, but it did upset the Commissioners' carefully worked-out timetable for securing the assents of the shires and burghs. Whereas they originally hoped to complete the process of consultation by 26 February, or a few days thereafter, they did not in fact receive the last assents (those of Dornoch and Sutherlandshire) until 30 April.[17]

Hostility to the proposed union with England was spearheaded by the presbyterian clergy. Fears that religious toleration would go hand-in-hand with English domination had already aroused violent debate among the clergy and their lay supporters in November and December 1651,[18] and when the exact nature of Parliament's proposals on matters of religion became known in February 1652, the presbyterian clergy launched an all-out attack on this issue. 'The *Ministers*,' reported one newswriter on 17 February, 'take upon them to talk lowdly (and that is all they will be able to doe) against the declarations of the Parliament and the Commissioners.'[19]

Protesters and Resolutioners were equally aghast at the prospect of religious toleration, but despite their common hostility to the English proposals, the two church parties could not agree on a joint course of action. Both sides held meetings in Edinburgh in mid-February at which the topic of their future relations with each other and with the English was discussed. On 23 February the Resolutioners approached the Protesters, who included James Guthry, Patrick Gillespie, Wariston, Chiesley and Alexander Brodie, and proposed that both parties should present a joint testimony against the English. In addition the Resolutioners put forward proposals for healing the breach between the two church parties, but the Protesters rejected these and went on to state that they had already made their attitude to the English sufficiently clear in their letter to Cromwell of 2 January. They also refused to show their colleagues a copy of a paper they had submitted to Col. Fenwick (one of the Commissioners) expressing their opinions on the Declarations of Parliament and of the Commissioners. This led the Resolutioners to suspect that some of the leading Protesters, namely Wariston, Brodie and Gillespie, 'were underhand dealing with the enemy, that they would be pleased to erect Scotland into an independent commonwealth by itself'.[20] Such suspicions were almost certainly unfounded, for although four Protester laymen had had an interview with the parliamentary Commissioners in late January, they had received scant favour from the English, and Wariston, for one, was widely regarded as the main instigator of the kirk's opposition to the union.[21] Nonetheless, the suspicion lingered that 'thes whom they call remonstrators and dissenters' would be the first to come to terms with the English and would use their influence with the conquerors to oppress their opponents in church and state.[22] No amount of mud-slinging between the two parties, however, could disguise the fact that the clergy were overwhelmingly opposed to the union with England, not only because it imposed toleration on Scotland, but because it implied a breach of the third article of the Covenant, which provided for the preservation of kingship. It was this dual interpretation of the Covenant, this acceptance of its provisions in both the civil and religious spheres, that accounted for the ministry's condemnation of the Tender of Incorporation and for their persistence in praying publicly for the king.

Hostility to the notion of treating with the English and of accepting their proposals for a political and religious settlement was also reflected in the constituencies when the voters of the shires and burghs met to elect deputies to serve at Dalkeith. Disputes at these elections not only upset the Commissioners' timetable for acceptance of the Tender. They also accounted for the fact that some of the deputies arrived at Dalkeith with defective commissions and some constituencies sent only one deputy when two were required.[23]

In Fife, the controversy over the choice of deputies was an extension of the dispute between Presbyterians and Malignants which had started in November 1651. On 17 February, an English newswriter reported that the meeting called to choose the deputies for Fife, 'being (for the most part) composed of fiery *Kirkists*', had refused to allow the Commissioners' summons to be read, but that they had, as a committee of war, appointed two of their number to go to Dalkeith 'by vertue of old Powers'. On 1 March, however, a small minority of the shire gentry overturned this decision and elected Sir Alexander Gibson of Durie and William Bruce, the commissary of St. Andrews, to serve with a full commission, as desired by the English.[24] In Edinburgh, on 11 February, John Denholm and James Fairbairn were elected, but Denholm, a member of the extreme presbyterian party, refused to serve; the Commissioners refused to accept merely one deputy from the burgh, and William Thomson was elected in Denholm's place.[25] In Aberdeen, George Cullen and Thomas Mortimer were chosen, but Mortimer, who had already refused to treat with the English in September 1651, made no appearance at Dalkeith.[26] In these instances presbyterian convictions clearly played an important part in shaping the response of the laity to the English proposals. In other cases however the laity, although still receptive to the propaganda and influence of the clergy, were more inclined to moderate their religious convictions to suit their secular interests. Some of the deputies, the English reported, brought two commissions with them to Dalkeith: one signed to please the ministers, expressing the hope that nothing be done prejudicial to the Covenant, the other 'ful and ample to do al things conducible for the setling of the Nation'.[27]

The conduct of these elections showed therefore that the laity felt some tension between the desire to support the stance of the clergy and the desire to close with the English in order to effect a settlement in civil affairs. This tension was implicit also in the replies which the deputies gave in to the Commissioners at Dalkeith, for although the vast majority of constituencies accepted the Tender, some were clearly reluctant to submit to the sectarian foe.

Of the 89 constituencies in Scotland, only three — Glasgow, Morayshire and Kirkcudbrightshire — went as far as lodging a formal dissent from the Tender of Incorporation. Commitment to covenanting ideals in church and state provided the reason in each case. For Glasgow the dissenting deputies were John Spreule and John Graham, both of whom had refused to renounce their support for the Remonstrance of 1650; and Glasgow's reasons for refusal,[28] like those of Kirkcudbrightshire[29] and Morayshire,[30] emphasised the town's dislike of Parliament's religious policy. Kirkcudbrightshire went further and stated explicitly that it held itself, and England, bound by the third article of the Solemn

League and Covenant to 'defend the person of the King In the defence of the Liberties of the Kingdomes wch stand in a distinct relacōn.' The English, however, were determined to override this hostility and to exact from these constituencies a formal acceptance of the Tender. All three refusals were therefore rejected and the constituencies forced to convert them to assents. In the case of Glasgow this was achieved by quartering nine companies of horse and foot on the town.[31]

Sixteen constituencies did not send representatives to Dalkeith at all. Five of these (Sanquhar, Lochmaben, Galloway, Annan and Dingwall) were small burghs which were excused from attendance on account of their poverty, but no official explanation was given for the other absentees. These included the shires of Ayr and Renfrew and the burghs of Ayr, Renfrew, Irvine, Lanark, Dumfries and Kirkcudbright. In the case of Lanark and Dumfries, their absence was almost certainly due to opposition to the Tender.[32]

Seventy constituencies, therefore, registered their acceptance of the Tender of Incorporation.[33] In explaining why so many Scots acquiesced in the demands of the English, the fact that their country was under military occupation undoubtedly plays a large part. The presence of the English army effectively prevented the conquered nation from exercising any real freedom of choice when called upon to give their answer to Parliament's proposals. Glasgow had received abundant proof of English military might when it tried to dissent from the Tender, and other towns, too, feared the English presence: St. Andrews had at first planned to forbid their deputy to sign the Tender, 'but danger being represented, they fainted' and the town's assent was registered instead.[34] Nonetheless, it was, perhaps, the *implications* of English military control, rather than the exercise of brute force by the army, which weighed most heavily with the Scottish laity and led them to assent to the Tender forthwith rather than to put up a pretence of political resistance. The fact that the laity found it expedient to submit to the English does not necessarily imply that they were lukewarm in their support for presbyterianism or that the clergy overestimated the strength of their following among the Scots people; but it does indicate a point at which spiritual and secular interests diverged. For the laity had greater reason to come to terms with the English than their clerical brethren: compliance with the English was necessary if they were to retain their goods and property, and salvage the remnants of their political and social influence in the localities once the union with England had gone through. The presbyterian clergy also stood to lose by the consolidation of English rule — this was why they opposed the grant of toleration to those who 'shall serve and worship God in other Gospel way'. But the most that they could suffer was competition from, not replacement by, alien elements, since their form of worship and church government would be tolerated too. Therefore, unlike the laity, and in particular the nobility and gentry, they could afford the luxury of opposing rather than complying with the English. Indeed, since the clergy's interest was moral rather than material, they had much to gain by appearing to stand out in high-principled opposition to the conqueror. The laity on the other hand were under greater pressure to put their material interests first.

More surprisingly, perhaps, some constituencies not merely assented to the Tender but registered positive enthusiasm for the union. Judging by the verbal forms in which their assents were couched, the most enthusiastic were Wigtonshire, Lanarkshire and Dunbartonshire and the burghs of Wigton and Rutherglen; more moderate, but still marked off from the bulk of the assenters, were Buteshire and the burghs of Burntisland, Rothesay and Dumbarton.[35]

It is not possible to explain this deviation from the normal pattern of acceptance in terms of a distaste for presbyterianism or a longing for toleration. There is no common pattern to be found in the religious views expressed by these constituencies in their assents to the Tender or in the proposals, or 'Desires', concerning the implementation of the union which they subsequently submitted to the English Commissioners. Lanarkshire and Dunbartonshire, for example, are singular in making no mention at all of religion in the Desires which they presented jointly to the English;[36] while Wigtonshire stands out at the other end of the spectrum by virtue of its explicit request that 'ye protestant religion as it is preferred in Scotland in Doctrine Worshipp and Discipline bee in noe sort Innovated or altered'.[37] Nor is it possible to detect particular lay interests which might have impelled the gentry or burgesses of these constituencies to seek especial favour with the English, although it is noteworthy that the deputies from Wigtonshire and Dunbartonshire were all to hold high office in local or national government in the later 1650s.[38]

The most striking characteristic of these 'enthusiastic' constituencies is, in fact, that with the exception of Burntisland they are all located in the west and south-west of Scotland. This was the area which in 1648 and 1650 had produced men willing to seek some accommodation with the English in order to preserve their own position in the internal politics of Scotland. First the Whiggamores in 1648 and then the Remonstrants in 1650 had allowed their hostility towards Malignants to lead them into correspondence with Cromwell and his army. This area was also the home of the Protesters, whose hostility to Charles II and the Resolutioners had in recent months aroused suspicions that they might conclude an agreement with the English. It is tempting, therefore, to view the enthusiasm of some western shires and burghs in their assents to the Tender as the natural extension of these earlier signs of willingness to co-operate with the English.

Nonetheless it is difficult to see how compliance with the English in 1652 could be compatible with the strong support in the area for covenanting ideals in church and state. Paradoxically, it was the very strength of their commitment to those ideals which had led other constituencies in the same area either to *dissent* from the Tender (in the case of Glasgow and Kirkcudbrightshire) or to absent themselves from Dalkeith (in the case of Lanark and Dumfries). Clearly therefore the west and south-west not only differed in the pattern of its response to the Tender from the rest of Scotland but was an area much divided within itself. Feuds and hatreds within the Scottish community — hatred of Protester for Resolutioner, of Covenanter for Malignant, and feuds of a more local character — probably lay behind the particularity of the region in 1652. Whatever the reason, the few instances of enthusiasm which this part of Scotland registered in 1652 were to be latched on to eagerly by successive agents of the English régime in their attempts to build up a party of supporters in Scotland.

After the Deputies had assented to the Tender of Incorporation, they were allowed to present proposals or 'Desires' to the Commissioners in which they made more explicit their thoughts on the union and their expectations of the English government. These Desires recorded not only the complaints which the bulk of the Scottish nation had against their English conquerors, but also specifically local grievances which had their roots in internal history, and for which the Scots now sought a remedy from the English. They showed moreover that some groups in the Scottish community hoped to achieve short-term aims — often at the expense of their neighbours — under the new government, when they had failed to do so under previous Scottish administrations. In this opportunism, this desire to secure specific benefits from the English, and not in any whole-hearted approval of official English policy, lay the possibility of future co-operation between the Scots and their English conquerors.

The Desires, which technically took the form of proposals for effecting the union, implied severe criticisms of English policy and practice to date. The most commonly stated desire was for the maintenance of the Scottish kirk in the face of the proposed grant of toleration. The terms in which the various constituencies expressed this desire varied: some asked merely that the nation be protected in the exercise of the true protestant religion;[39] others that the protestant religion as it had been lately established in doctrine, discipline and government in Scotland be maintained; [40] while a few proposed that a conference be held for establishing uniformity throughout the whole island.[41] These statements may well have embodied sops to the clergy or qualms of conscience towards them, but it would be idle to deny that for many Scots they expressed sincerely held views on a matter of vital concern.

Most of the Desires also contained pleas for the removal of sequestrations, for the passing of an Act of Oblivion, for a reduction in the assessment, for the removal of at least some of the English troops quartered in Scotland, and for the release of the Scottish prisoners still held in England.[42]

The administrative chaos into which Scotland had been plunged since the defeat at Dunbar was reflected in a widespread desire for the restoration of the courts of justice. The lack of judicial machinery had, in fact, been aggravated by the Declaration of 31 January, which forbade the exercise of any jurisdiction not derived from the Parliament of England. The consequent lacuna at the lower levels of the judicial system was reflected in Stirlingshire's plea that baron courts should be allowed to function,[43] while a few constituencies pleaded for the retention of heritable jurisdictions, or at least that former office-holders should keep their places.[44]

The decay in trade and manufacturing resulting from the wars not only of the last year but of the last decade gave rise to demands that commerce should be encouraged and municipal liberties restored. The shortage of ready money, a symptom of wartime taxation and dislocation, was to be remedied by the re-establishment of the Mint.[45] On the question of trade and manufacturing, however, the Scottish constituencies revealed their disparate interests. A group of burghs which included Edinburgh, Aberdeen, Dundee and St. Andrews petitioned that, to promote industry throughout Scotland, able and well-qualified workmen should be induced to come from England and join with the Scots in establishing 'Manufactories of all sorts'.[46] But Stirling expressly moved that only neighbours (*i.e.* inhabitants) or burgesses should be allowed to engage in trade or manufacture within the burgh, for fear of creating unemployment among those who controlled the commercial life of the town.[47] Roxburghshire and Jedburgh asked that the border customs of 'four footit beastis and all uther kynd of merchandize' be discharged, and that disputes over fishing rights in the Tweed be settled according to former agreements.[48] Orkney and Shetland, meanwhile, petitioned for the restoration of their trade with Norway.[49]

Yet another class of complaints concerned the restoration of law and order in the Borders and in the Highlands. The shires of Roxburgh and Selkirk and the burghs of Selkirk and Jedburgh were particularly concerned with the former, while Inverness-shire and a group of shires which included Perth, Stirling, East Lothian, Fife, Peebles, Forfar, Selkirk and Dumfries asked for measures to be taken to secure such shires as bordered upon the Highlands from the incursions of the Highlanders.[50] This last group suggested that they be allowed to appoint armed guards or watches from among their own inhabitants and that these be paid for out of the assessment.

Only Orkney and Shetland, however, included in their Desires any positive sign that they wished to make the union work or facilitate the establishment of English rule in Scotland.[51] In many of their other demands concerning sequestrations, taxation, and the lack of justice, they did not differ significantly from other areas in Scotland. But in their request for authority to punish persons who should refuse to submit to parliamentary authority they were singular. Moreover,

> because theire be sundry persons lately crept into or land, [wrote the petitioners], whose fortunes lyes in ye South laboringe to disturbe ye peace of ye Land and to interrupt ye begun vnion, Therefore wee desire that they may be removed thence as havinge noe interest there, That soe all obstruccōns beingetaken out of ye way wee may carry on the worke intrusted to vs wth greater freedome and alacritye.

Quite what the motive was behind this request is unclear: it may have stemmed from genuine approval of the union, or merely from a desire to make easier the inevitable imposition of alien authority.

The work of gathering in the assents and Desires of the Scottish deputies went on from early February until late April, but by 1 March the Commissioners felt that sufficient constituencies had accepted the Tender for a report to be made to Parliament on proceedings so far. On that date Sir Henry Vane and Col. Fenwick were authorised to go to London, and by 3 March the report, which contained the Commissioners' recommendations for implementing the union, had been drawn up. By then only 17 shires had recorded their assents to the Tender, but since these included the majority of the shires south of the Forth and Clyde as well as Aberdeen, Banff, Nairn, Forfar, Kincardine and Fife, they constituted at least half the population of Scotland.[52] The Commissioners' 'Tender to Parliament' was presented to the House on 16 March along with the names of 20 shires and 35 burghs which had assented to the union to date.[53]

The Tender to Parliament made five main recommendations. First, it was recommended that acts should be passed to give effect to the proposed union and to punish anyone who should try to restore monarchical power in Scotland or to subvert the government as it would be established by the Act of Union. Second, the Act of Union should provide for Scottish representation in the combined Parliament. To settle the details of the new arrangement, 14 deputies from those Scottish shires which had accepted the Tender of Incorporation and 7 from the burghs should come to London to confer with the Parliament of England. This proposal in part reflected the desire expressed by many constituencies that some sort of Scottish Convention should be summoned to consider the exact terms of the union. Next, the Commissioners recommended that Parliament should 'more perticulerly ascertaine ye Persons whose estates shall incurr ye penalty of forfeiture and confiscacõn', and that an Act of Grace should extend pardon to all others, on condition that they accept the Tender of Incorporation. This measure was designed to replace the blanket penalties of the third clause of Parliament's Declaration of 28 October, but the new Act was not to alter the arrangements for abolishing bondage services. The fourth point recommended that the persons who were to be appointed to administer justice in Scotland should be speedily despatched, while the fifth and final clause urged that twelve or more ministers should be sent north to reside in the garrisons and other convenient places in Scotland. All five recommendations were in time adopted by the authorities in London, although it was to be some years before English policy on the major issues achieved final definition.

On 18 March the House debated the Commissioners' Tender and resolved to bring in an 'Act for incorporating Scotland into one Commonwealth with England'. This Act was to declare that Scotland 'upon this Union shall have Power to elect Members to serve in the Parliament of England, in such Proportion and at such Time as this Parliament shall think fit'. The House resolved also to ask the Council of State to prepare a Declaration authorising those shires and burghs which had assented to the Tender to choose representatives, who should in turn elect a smaller committee from their number to repair to England to effect the union. On 25 March the Council reported the draft of the Declaration to the House, whereupon it was passed and ordered to be printed.[54]

The printed document was entitled *The Declaration of the Parliament of England, in order to the Uniting of Scotland into one Commonwealth with England.* After recording the names of those shires and burghs (now numbering 22 and 39 respectively)[55] which had accepted the Tender, and reciting Parliament's resolution to bring in a Bill for Union, the Declaration went on to lay down in meticulous detail the procedure for electing those deputies who were to represent Scotland at the discussions with the English Parliament. The heritors (owners of heritable property) and rentallers (leaseholders) of each shire and the neighbours and burgesses of each burgh which had assented, or should assent, to the Tender of Incorporation before the date of the proposed elections were authorised to choose deputies 'in like Numbers as formerly they were authorised to do by the Commissioners of Parliament residing at Dalkeith in Scotland'. These elections were to take place before the end of July 1652, and the persons elected were to be 'of known Integrity, and such as have declared their Consent to the said Union'. They were, in turn, to go to Edinburgh on or before 20 August 1652, and there elect 21 of their number (14 for the shires, 7 for the burghs) to act as their representatives in England. Before proceeding to this election, the deputies were again to record their assent to the union, this time in the presence of English officials. After the election the chosen 21 were to set out for England and arrive at whichever place Parliament should appoint for the conference by 1 October.

On 30 March, the House ordered a letter to be sent to the Commissioners in Scotland (who by now consisted only of St. John, Salwey, Tichborne and Deane) requiring them to put the Declaration into effect. After they had done this, and had seen to the setting up of courts of justice in Scotland, St. John, Salwey and Tichborne were to return to England, leaving Deane as commander-in-chief of the forces in Scotland.[56] Meanwhile, on 23 March, the House had asked the Council of State to prepare a Bill 'wherein the Names of such Persons in Scotland whose Estates shall be confiscated, shall be ascertained and inserted', and on 13 April the Bill for incorporating Scotland into one Commonwealth with England was introduced, read a first and second time, and referred to a committee.[57]

On 14 April the Commissioners at Dalkeith issued an order for the publication throughout Scotland of the Declaration of 25 March. On 21 April it was proclaimed at the Mercat Cross in Edinburgh; but the Scottish crowd received the news without enthusiasm. '[S]oe sencelesse are this generation of their owne goods,' commented a newswriter, 'that scarce a man of them show'd any signe of rejoycing.' Towards the end of the month, the Commissioners (with the exception of Deane) left Dalkeith; and on 14 May they made their last report to Parliament and then laid down their commissions.[58] With that, the first phase of Parliament's plans for implementing the union with Scotland had been completed.

ii. Negotiations for union, August 1652 — April 1653

Throughout the summer of 1652 the shires and burghs of Scotland met to elect their deputies to serve at Edinburgh in August. Several of the shires started proceedings as early as 4 May, but Fife waited until mid-June, and Glasgow and Edinburgh made their choice in July.[59] In only a very few cases were the persons chosen the same men as had served at Dalkeith in February and March.[60]

Most of the deputies had assembled in Edinburgh by 12 August, whereupon their commissions were subjected to close scrutiny by those 'Commissioners for the Administration of Justice' (or Judges) whose permanent appointment had been announced in May. The shires and burghs met in separate conventions, at which proceedings were by no means cordial. The burghs, in particular, were given to acrimonious dispute amongst themselves, most notably over the qualifications of some of their members, an issue which was finally resolved not by themselves but by the Judges.[61] By 20 August, however, the preliminaries had been completed and 21 deputies — 14 for the shires and 7 for the burghs — were duly elected to attend Parliament's pleasure in London. The men chosen were as follows: for the shires, William Lockhart of Lee (Lanark), George Blair of Garvoch (Dumfries), Sir James Macdowall of Garthland (Wigton), David Falconer of Glenfarquhar (Kincardine), Sir George Stirling of Keir (Stirling), James Crichton (Midlothian), Lord Linton (Peebles), John Sinclair of Tannoch (Caithness), William Drummond (Linlithgow), Sir James Hamilton of Orbiston (Dunbarton), Sir Alexander Gibson of Durie (Fife), John Swinton and John Hume of Renton (Berwick), and James Lord Carnegie (Forfar); and for the burghs, John Jossie and John Milne (Edinburgh), Sir Alexander Wedderburn (Dundee), James Sword (St. Andrews), George Cullen (Aberdeen), Andrew Glen (Linlithgow) and Daniel Wallace (Glasgow).[62]

The proceedings at Edinburgh were to be the subject of searching inquiry when the deputies finally met the committee which Parliament appointed to confer with them at Westminster, and the report which was then drawn up for presentation to Parliament provides much valuable information on who was and who was not present at Edinburgh.[63] Of the 28 shires which had assented to the Tender at Dalkeith, only 19 voted at the election of the deputies at Edinburgh, having first subscribed to the union in the manner laid down by the Declaration of 25 March. A twentieth — Orkney and Shetland — subscribed to the union but arrived too late to vote at the election. Of the remaining eight shires, Inverness, Banff and Perth had sent only one deputy instead of two, and so their votes were discounted. Aberdeenshire's representatives, although duly elected, simply failed to turn up, but the heritors of the shire sent instead a declaration of their consent to the union. Of the 28 assenters at Dalkeith, this left only Bute, Selkirk, Clackmannan and Argyll for whose absence no explanation could be given. In addition, Renfrew and Ayr, who had not sent deputies to Dalkeith, continued to absent themselves, while the stewartry of Kirkcudbright, whose final assent to the Tender did not have the unanimous approval of the shire, likewise stayed away from Edinburgh.[64]

Of the 44 burghs which had assented to the Tender, only 34 subscribed to the union at Edinburgh and voted for the seven deputies. This number included Whithorn, which had been excused from attending at Dalkeith on the grounds of poverty and had then been regarded as part of the shire of Wigton. The representatives of three more burghs — Selkirk, Pittenweem and Dumbarton — had arrived at Edinburgh but had not voted: Dumbarton's man had fallen sick, and the deputy from Pittenweem had gone home for the start of the herring fishing season, on which he depended for his livelihood. Of the eight burghs which had assented at Dalkeith but had sent no representatives to Edinburgh — Crail, Anstruther Easter and Wester, Kilrenny, Rothesay, Lauder, Peebles and Dunfermline — the first five preferred to concentrate their attention on the fishing season, which provided the main source of employment for their inhabitants. Lauder and Peebles stayed away on the grounds of poverty, but the reason for Dunfermline's absence was unknown. The twenty-one deputies later explained in London that the Scottish Parliament had usually excused poverty-stricken burghs (including the fishing towns of Fife) from attendance at their sessions; and this excuse was also advanced for Sanquhar, Lochmaben, Annan, Galloway and Dingwall, whose representatives were present at neither Dalkeith nor Edinburgh. Of the absence from both meetings of Renfrew, Ayr, Irvine, Lanark, Dumfries, Nairn, Thurso and Kirkcudbright no official explanation was given.[65]

The deputies set out from Scotland towards the end of September 1652. They arrived in London on 6 October and had their first meeting with the Committee appointed by Parliament over a week later.[66] Parliament's nominees to serve on this committee included such well-known names as Oliver St. John, Sir Henry Vane junior, Col. George Fenwick, Major Richard Salwey, Oliver Cromwell, Major General Thomas Harrison, Col. Algernon Sidney, Sir Arthur Hesilrige and Lords Commissioner Whitelocke and Lisle.[67] Between 14 October 1652 and 8 April 1653 the Committee met on 35 separate days, but on as many as 13 of these occasions it sat alone and had no debate with the Scottish deputies.[68]

The minute-book of this Committee, which is still extant, recorded in detail the progress of the conferences. The significant factor, however, was not the minutiae of the discussions but their overall tone. 'When they [the deputies] came to London,' commented Row, 'they were much slighted by the Parliament, and thereafter looked upon rather as petitioners than Commissioners.'[69] Indeed, far from there being any suggestion of negotiating with the Scots as equals, the English took pains to impress upon the deputies that their role was a subordinate, purely consultative, one. Thus, as compared with the proceedings at Dalkeith in the spring, the English attitude had hardened: the Scots had never been allowed the substance of equality and now they were denied even the form. There is little or no evidence to suggest that the activities of the Scots in London materially affected English policy on the nature of the union or on the extent of sequestrations. These two matters, which formed the bulk of the discussions between the deputies and the Committee, were decided along lines settled by Parliament, its Committees and the Council. Moreover, the slow progress which the parliamentary Bills embodying these policies had made by April 1653, when the discussions ceased, was the product not of delaying tactics or hard bargaining on the part of the Scots, but of the exigencies of English domestic politics; and it was the dissolution of the Long Parliament that put an end to consideration of both the Bill of Oblivion and the Bill for Union for the time being.

The first meeting of the Committee on 14 October, at which the deputies were not present, was concerned with various procedural matters and with the preparation of an Act for the renewal of the commissions of the judges in Scotland, which were due to expire on 1 November. The deputies were summoned to appear the next day,[70] when the task of scrutinising their commissions and those of their electors began.[71] On 20 October, the deputies were ordered to present a transcript of the proceedings at Edinburgh;[72] this, along with other information given to the Committee by the deputies, was to form the basis of a statement to Parliament, which would have the final say on the validity of these commissions. At this point, then, the deputies' right to treat, to be considered as commissioners from their constituencies in Scotland, had not been recognised. And when the deputies were asked to comment on the provisions of the Bill, now before Parliament, for continuing the judicatories in Scotland, they were informed that their reply would be considered as coming from 'single persons' and not from 'deputies' as such (26 October). The Scots then declined to answer further until their status had been decided.[73] Perhaps in response to this pressure, the Committee's report on the deputies' commissions was then drawn up and communicated to the deputies two days later; on 29 October, Whitelocke presented it to Parliament, whereupon the House accepted it and confirmed the validity of the commissions.[74]

The way was now clear for the Committee to take up the questions of the union and of sequestrations. On 2 November, following an order from Parliament, Lisle and Salwey were ordered to prepare a Bill 'giving the names of persons in Scotland whose estates are to be confiscated, and the rest pardoned'. It was also decided that the Bill for Union, which had lain dormant since its second reading on 13 April 1652, should be transcribed and that conference thereon with the deputies should begin.[75] On 4 November — the first day on which the deputies were really allowed to perform the function for which they had ostensibly been elected — the Committee divulged to them the contents of the Bill for Union. They were not, however, presented with a copy; the Committee consented merely to read it to them as often as they liked, in order that they might take notes. Perhaps because of this unexpected treatment, the deputies again raised the matter of their exact status and asked pointed questions about Parliament's view of their role in these conferences. To this the Committee returned an evasive reply, merely referring the Scots to the orders and Declaration of Parliament which appointed them to be treated with 'as deputies'.[76]

Discussion on the Bill of Union was then resumed, and continued throughout November. The deputies tried to insist that the number of Scottish members in the future British Parliament and the date of their election should be inserted into the Bill itself, but the House of Commons ignored their pleas. The House would agree only that the *proportion* of Scottish members should be stated in the Bill and that the select committee in charge of the Bill for the New Representative should decide what the exact *number* should be.[77] On 17 December, on being told of Parliament's intentions concerning the Bill for Union, the deputies urged that the select committee's proposals on the number of members should be submitted to them before being reported to Parliament, but this request was refused also, on the grounds that such a procedure was not in accord with parliamentary practice. The deputies then urged specifically that 'the assess may not be the rule for proportion, in regard of the inability of the people of Scotland'.[78] In other words, since Scotland was a relatively poor country, and her taxable value low, such a rule would result in proportionately fewer representatives for Scotland in the united Parliament. Instead, the deputies argued on 24 December, Parliament should take three other factors into consideration: the number of representatives in the Parliament of England and in that of Scotland, abstracted from the House of

Lords in each case; the benefits which would accrue to England by virtue of the union 'both by the number and strength of men'; and the assistance which Scotland had already given to England in the 1640s.[79] If the relative taxable values of the two countries were made the basis of representation, Scotland would be entitled to only 20 members, whereas under the Scottish proposals she would get about 60.[80] But, added the deputies, although they did not wish Scotland's poverty to influence Parliament unduly when the matter of representation was under discussion, they begged that it might be given considerable weight when the burden of the assessment itself fell to be decided! The deputies' arguments were rejected by the Committee during a series of debates, and the matter was unilaterally resolved on 2 March 1653 when the House fixed Scotland's representation at 30 members. The deputies then made strenuous attempts to influence the allocation of these seats and to secure a more generous representation for Scotland, but their efforts were foiled by the dissolution of the Long Parliament.[81]

While these debates were going on, the Committee had also done some work on the Bill of Oblivion. On 11 January 1653, the Committee decided definitely that the main scope of the Bill should be for pardon and oblivion, and that the lands to be confiscated should be inserted as an exception.[82] Parliament, meanwhile, had not forgotten the clause in its Declaration of 28 October 1651 which had linked the abolition of bondage tenures and the freeing of the poor people of Scotland to the policy of sequestration. On 26 January 1653, in pursuance of an order from Parliament, the Committee ordered that letters be sent to the authorities in Scotland asking them to certify the nature of the vassalage and bondage tenures of the Scottish people, the nature of all feu duties, and 'what dependence the people there have upon any their superiors',[83] and on 9 February Whitelocke was asked to prepare a clause on these issues for insertion into the Bill. On 3 February, the Bill had been given its second reading in Parliament, and its contents were then communicated to the deputies. Again a written copy was refused, 'this not being parliamentary', but the Bill was read out 'leisurely' to them.[84] For some time after this, the deputies turned their attention to the Bill for Union, but on 11 March they pressed that the exceptions in the Bill of Oblivion be left out and that pardon be extended to all the people of Scotland. The matter was again raised on 16 March, but thereafter the deputies were allowed to make no further comment upon it.[85]

The last meeting of the Committee before the Long Parliament — from which it derived its power — was dissolved, took place on 8 April. A debate was begun on the renewal of the commissions for the judges in Scotland and on proposals from the deputies for maintaining the integrity of Scots law and the Scottish legal system under the proposed union.[86] Further proceedings were prevented by the dissolution of Parliament, but on 3 May the commissions for the Scottish judicatories were renewed until 1 November by an order of the Council of State.[87] Some of the deputies remained in England for another couple of months, during which time the Council of State made tentative efforts to consult them upon the 'present settlement of the civil government and assessment in Scotland';[88] but with the disappearance of the Committee appointed by the Long Parliament to confer with them, a distinct episode in Anglo-Scottish political relations between the years 1651 and 1660 had come to an end.

Substantively, little had been achieved by either the Scots or the English in the months between October 1652 and April 1653. Despite all the debates in Parliament and in the Committee, the Bill for Union had not progressed further than its second reading in the House on 13 April 1652. The House had, indeed, decided that the number of Scottish MPs in the joint Parliament should be thirty, but their distribution was as yet unsettled. The Bill of Oblivion had had its second reading on 3 February 1653, but the names of the excepted persons were still undetermined. In the event, the union was proclaimed on 16 December 1653 when the Council of State proclaimed the Protectorate under the title of 'the Commonwealth of England, Scotland, and Ireland'. In the Instrument of Government, Scotland's representation in the united Parliament was fixed at 30 members, but their distribution was left undecided until an ordinance of June 1654. The union itself was given legislative sanction by an ordinance of 12 April 1654. As for the Bill of Oblivion, the provisions with which it was concerned found final expression in an ordinance of pardon and grace to the people of Scotland, also passed by the Council of State on 12 April 1654.[89]

The Scots diarist John Lamont's comment on the achievements of the Scottish deputies was that 'they returned, [to Scotland] haveing done litell or nothing.'[90] In regard to the Bills of Union and Oblivion this was undeniably true. The Scots had been unremitting in their efforts to alter these Bills in Scotland's favour but they had made little impression on the policy-makers in Whitehall and Westminster. In the conferences between the Committee and the Scottish deputies it was the English who had called the tune and the Scots who had had to dance to it. If therefore the deputies had gone to London expecting to secure a better deal for their country than had been envisaged in the aftermath of Worcester, they must have returned to Scotland sadly disillusioned men.

3

Attempts at Pacification and the Birth of Revolt, March — December 1652

THE procedure which the English Parliament had evolved for implementing its plans for union with Scotland had been exceedingly protracted. The work of submitting the Tender of Incorporation to the Scottish people and of summoning deputies to London had gone on throughout 1652 and discussions had continued into 1653. This business had not, however, been the only concern of the civil and military authorities in Scotland during this time. Much work remained to be done after the early months of the conquest, both in settling the day-to-day administration of Scotland and in subduing the remaining pockets of resistance to the English army. Between March and December 1652 great progress was made in these tasks by the Commissioners at Dalkeith and by the army under Deane's command. On the surface this period witnessed what appeared to be unremitting and successful efforts by the English to subordinate the Scots to their will; yet despite their undoubted achievements in both the civil and military spheres, English policy failed in certain crucial respects. On the one hand the civil policy of the English Parliament created such resentment and such hardship among the Scottish nobility and gentry that these groups prepared once again to lead an armed rising against the English; while militarily the army's failure totally to subdue unrest in the Highlands provided the springboard for future revolt. When in the following year these two elements of resistance united, they produced a rebellion which seriously challenged the army's control over Scotland.

In January 1652 the Commissioners from Parliament had arrived at Dalkeith with instructions not only to submit the Tender of Incorporation to the Scottish people, but also to settle the civil government of Scotland. It was to the tasks of restoring and remodelling the institutions of central and local government and of implementing Parliament's policy on religion and on sequestrations that the Commissioners therefore turned in March and April 1652. In their reorganisation of the machinery of government their guideline was naturally the policy enshrined in Parliament's Declaration of 28 October 1651. Thus the political motive behind many of their measures was to weaken the power of the clergy, the nobility and the gentry — hence the appointment of commissioners to regulate the universities and to sequester estates — while in other aspects of their work they strove to create that system of evenhanded justice and good government which, it was hoped, would reconcile the Scots to the loss of their political independence. In theory, English policy was all of one piece, for the same measures which hit out at the social and political leaders of the nation also favoured the common people; and it was on the common people that the English planned to rely for political support. This design even achieved some measure of success, particularly in the field of justice, where the impartiality and rigour of the English judges encouraged the Scots to bring actions against their social superiors. But in practice, the scheme embodied a fundamental miscalculation. The English grossly overestimated the extent to which the hold of the ministers, the nobles and the greater gentry over the social and political life of the nation could be broken. Instead of bringing new forces into being to counterbalance the old, they merely provoked a backlash amongst the clergy, the nobility and the gentry. This backlash looked for support to two main sources: Charles's court in exile, and the Highlands of Scotland. From the latter help was not slow in coming, for although the army had mounted a campaign in the Highlands in the summer of 1652 and had established a strong English presence in the region, it had not completely suppressed unrest and disorder. This meant that the way was left open for the formation of a new royalist movement which drew its strength militarily and politically from the untamed elements of the Highlands but which spread out from the Highlands to threaten the army's control over the rest of the country during the next two years.

These developments, however, lay in the future. For much of the year 1652 the English in Scotland could congratulate themselves on having reinforced in the civil sphere the gains which their army had made in the early months of the conquest and on having extended the area which lay directly under the army's control.

i. The parliamentary Commissioners and the government of Scotland

During their stay in Scotland, the Commissioners from Parliament made considerable progress in setting up administrative machinery to deal with the day-to-day tasks of government, as well as with the special problems created by the English military victories. In the four months after their arrival at Dalkeith, they restored municipal government; provided for the dispensing of justice at the highest level by seven Commissioners for the Administration of Justice, who thus replaced the old Court of Session; appointed sheriffs and commissaries; established a Court of Admiralty; appointed Commissioners for Visiting and Regulating Universities and Commissioners for confiscated and forfeited lands and estates; and issued orders concerning the laying on of the assessment and the disbursing of the revenue. All officers of government, whether English or Scots, were required to take an oath of fidelity to the Commonwealth, while those who were Scots were in addition required to declare their assent to the Tender of Incorporation.[1]

The granting of permission to the burghs to elect their magistrates and councillors was made a concomitant of their acceptance of the Tender. Only when the burghs had finally registered their assent was a charter[2] issued to them authorising 'the Neighbours and Inhabitants of the towne and Burgh of (blank)

According to their former Rules and Customes from tyme to tyme to Nominate and Chose' their municipal officers. The English intention here was twofold: to revive institutions and methods of local government which had fallen into abeyance in the years of war and invasion, and to ensure that men would now be elected who would be loyal — at least outwardly — to the Commonwealth. Municipal government had suffered badly since Dunbar. The town council of Edinburgh, for example, did not meet between 2 September 1650 and 4 December 1651, and essential government was carried on by a committee of neighbours;[3] but after Worcester there were signs that things were returning to normal. In Aberdeen and Glasgow, municipal elections took place before the end of 1651,[4] but the state of Edinburgh politics, where a faction led by the ex-Remonstrant Sir James Stewart was violently opposed by a group of moderates and Engagers under Archibald Todd, prevented any such solution in the capital. Even in those burghs where councillors and magistrates were elected, the latter were probably not allowed to resume their judicial functions.[5] The elections now authorised by the English in March and April 1652 were certainly designed to hasten a return to normal, but the methods by which they were to be carried out emphasised the overriding objective of securing loyalty to the new régime in the localities. '[W]ee Expect,' declared the Commissioners, 'in such Eleccōns to bee made as aforesaid due Care to bee taken that all such persons Chosen be Men of Integritie and good affeccōn to the peace and wellfare of the Iseland and otherwise fittly quallified for theire trust.' The electors as well as the persons elected were required to subscribe a declaration pledging their 'free acceptance of and Consent vnto the Tender'.[6] As with the officers of the central government, those elected were to swear an oath to be faithful to the Commonwealth of England, while freemen and burgesses, at the time of their admission, were also to swear fidelity to the Commonwealth and obedience to the government of their town.

This requirement of oath-taking provoked protests from some of the burghs. On 14 April 1652 the burghs of Fife presented a supplication asking that the provision be waived. They argued that the Commissioners had promised liberty to tender consciences and pointed out that they had already declared their acceptance of the Tender through their deputies at Dalkeith. The provost and bailies of Dumbarton — a town which had registered enthusiasm for the union — refused to take the oath and were deprived of office, and in other towns many officers refused to serve in circumstances which suggest that their motive was unwillingness to swear the oath of fidelity.[7] In Edinburgh, too, the burgesses had been extremely troubled at the oath which was to be imposed upon their magistrates, but by 9 March the new bailies had been sworn in in the presence of Judge Advocate Whalley. The new provost was Archibald Todd, the leader of the moderates and former supporter of the Engagement. His triumph in the elections of March 1652 after the town had assented to the Tender thus represented a defeat for the extreme Presbyterians, led by Stewart and backed by the ministers of Edinburgh.[8]

One effect of the restoration of municipal government was that judicial processes within the burghs again functioned normally. In the shires, the return to normal was less complete. The baron courts were not replaced, and judicial authority thus devolved solely upon the sheriff courts. In March 1652, new sheriffs-principal were appointed for each county. Here the English finely balanced the needs of coercion and of conciliation; for while the civil office of high sheriff remained unchanged in terms of its power and jurisdiction, it was now occupied jointly by two men — one a Scotsman, and one an English army officer — both of whom had to take the oath of fidelity to the Commonwealth.[9]

A similar concept of an appropriate balance of power was to be seen in the appointment of seven Commissioners for the Administration of Justice. This body consisted of three Scotsmen and four Englishmen, the Scots being John Swinton of Swinton, William Lockhart of Lee, and Sir John Hope of Craighall, and the English Edward Moseley, George Smyth, Andrew Owen and John Marsh. The Scots were paid exactly half the salary of their English counterparts and, initially at least, were excluded from sitting on criminal cases. Acting under separate commissions, the four English judges alone were authorised to execute the powers formerly held by the Justice-General and his Deputes in Scotland.[10] Scotsmen nonetheless predominated in the inferior ranks of the central judicial machine. The Clerks of Session were Scots,[11], and although the Keeper of the Signet was in all probability William Clarke, secretary to the Army, the Keeper of the Great Seal and Director of the Chancellery was none other than ex-Provost Jaffray of Aberdeen, who had now clearly thrown in his lot with the English.[12]

The three Scotsmen who were appointed to the bench in 1652 illustrate, by the diversity of their political pasts, the catholicity of English taste in the choice of their Scottish advisers. These three were the first of their countrymen to be appointed to high executive office by the English, and each was to go on to achieve further prominence in the administration, with Lockhart and Swinton, in particular, becoming trusted servants of the protectoral régime.[13] Of the three, Sir John Hope was the most obviously fitted for judicial office. He was the son of Charles I's Lord Advocate, Sir Thomas Hope of Craighall, and had himself been appointed an ordinary Lord of Session in 1632. He had retained this post in the 1640s, and had also served successive covenanting régimes as a member of the various Committees of Estates. In January 1651, however, he had incurred the displeasure of the king and of the Committee of Estates by his suggestion that the south of Scotland should be abandoned to the English.[14] A few months after Sir John Hope's disgrace, William Lockhart of Lee also received evidence of Charles's disfavour. Lockhart, a man of royalist sympathies and probable ally of Montrose, had seen active service in the 1640s. His service as a member of the army of the Engagement had resulted in his being imprisoned by the English. After his return to Scotland, however, a quarrel with Argyle in 1650 led to his withdrawal from the army. In the summer of 1651, when he attempted to rejoin the Scottish army as a volunteer, his offers of help were, to his chagrin, spurned yet again, this time by Charles.[15] Thus both Lockhart and Hope had, shortly before the English conquest of Scotland, clearly fallen out of favour with the king, and this may have made them all the more willing to co-operate with the English in 1652. John Swinton, on the other hand, approached collaboration with the conquerors by another route. Initially a staunch Presbyterian, he had in 1650 been a firm advocate of the purging of the Scottish host, but after the defeat at Dunbar his extreme covenanting convictions and hostility towards Malignants led him along the path trodden by Archibald Strachan and some members of the western army. Like Strachan, he was suspected of underhand dealings with the English; in 1651 he was excommunicated by the kirk and sentenced to death by Parliament. By all accounts, his religious leanings after 1651 were towards Independency, and later in the decade he was to become a Quaker.[16] Swinton, Hope and Lockhart, then, were men of diverse political backgrounds. The significance of their appointment as judges in 1652 is hard to ascertain. Their willingness to accept office under the new régime probably says more about them as individuals than about the political groupings or local communities of which they were members. Nonetheless, their collaborative instincts must have given the English hope that in time others would join them in co-operating with their new masters and thereby give substance to the English desire to conciliate the Scots by enlisting their countrymen in the service of the state.

The seven Commissioners for the Administration of Justice were publicly installed in the old Session House in Edinburgh on 18 May 1652,[17] amid speculation by the English that the dispensing of impartial justice would do much to reconcile the Scots to the new administration. On 20 April, an English newswriter had optimistically reported that 'peoples mindes are rather intent uppon the setling of their chief Court of Judicature then uppon resetling their Kinge', and had gone on to predict that once the judicial processes were restored, it would do much to silence disputes about 'Governors or Government'. That, in the short term at least, his hopes were realised was suggested by another report of 24 May, which stated: 'The Businesse now most minded by the people of this Country is the obtayning of Justice & a determination of their longe continued suites, & now they begin to meddle with many of their Grandees agt. whom heertofore they durst not complaine.' Suits had been begun against Lord Chancellor Loudoun, the Marquis of Huntly, the Earls of Moray, Morton, Balcarres, Crawford-Lindsay and others, '& noe doubt but Justice will bee administred to all without respect of persons.'[18] This in itself was a contribution to Parliament's declared policy of undermining the power of the nobility and gentry: unhappily for the English government, however, another aspect of that policy — the confiscation of royalist estates — was to have such disastrous consequences that for the sake of peace in Scotland judicial rigour against the upper classes had later to be modified.[19]

In September and October 1652 the four English Commissioners went on circuit throughout Scotland to deal with criminal causes. At this time they certainly sat at Edinburgh, Stirling, Glasgow and Aberdeen, and assizes may also have been held at several other places, including Ayr, Dumfries, Jedburgh and Inverness.[20] The judges' reputation for impartiality and rigour seems to have gone before them, for in Aberdeen many who were summoned to appear were said to be afraid to do so.[21] Judging, however, by the English reports, the sentences actually meted out, although harsh, were imposed sparingly. Many accusations concerned cases of murder, witchcraft, adultery and buggery, some of which were alleged to have taken place 40 years before. But while the last — 'that torrid sin not fit to be named amongst Christians or men' — was punished with hanging and burning, witchcraft was treated more leniently, with many cases being dismissed for lack of evidence. The English were, not unjustifiably, proud of their enlightened attitude to witches. As one writer put it,

> This Judicial sentence of theirs [the English circuit judges] confirms my former assertions that there are verry few if any of those men usually call witches & that the torments they were put to by the witch finders & the Mallice of their neighbours together wth the partiallitye or ignorance of the former Judges in Scotland (and I feare England two), hath taken away the lives not onely of many even persons but Good & pretious Christians too, by condemning them to the severest punishmts of the fire.[22]

Scots writers, too, praised English justice. As the diarist John Nicoll put it, 'And, to speik treuth, the Englisches wer moir indulgent and mercifull to the Scottis, nor wes the Scottis to thair awin cuntriemen and nychtbouris, as wes too evident, and thair justice exceidit the Scottis in mony thinges.'[23]

The enforcement of the civil laws, particularly of those relating to debt, posed some threat to the power and status of the nobility and gentry. The policy of sequestration, however, represented a far greater danger. In December 1651 it had been reported that the 'Royal Party', while not averse to seeking compliance with the English, were nonetheless afraid that their estates would be confiscated, and in February 1652 the authorities in London had been warned that when this policy was implemented 'we must expect what despaire will produce.'[24] By early April 1652, a board of Commissioners, consisting of Richard Saltonstall, Samuel Disbrowe, and Col. Edmund Syler, had been set up at Leith to deal with the matter, but at that time Parliament's policy regarding sequestration still lacked definition. The Commissioners for managing the affairs of Scotland had, in their 'Tender to Parliament' of 16 March, recommended that the sweeping provisions of the Declaration of 28 October be reduced to the naming of specific persons, but this change was still under consideration, and remained so until 1654. Thus it was that in April 1652 rumours were rife as to who would come under the axe.[25]

Even before the official appointment of the board of Commissioners the work of sequestration had begun. The estates of the prisoners who had been captured at Alyth and at Worcester were among the first to feel the blow: the Earl of Leven's estate, for example, had been sequestered some time before 14 May 1652.[26] The Commissioners and their deputies were nothing if not thorough in discharging their duties. Lamont recorded in detail the way in which two of the English sequestrators surveyed the property of the Laird of Lundie in Fife. On 3 April 1652, they came to Lundie and

> tooke vp ane inventorie of every thing in the house, wither in beds, truncks, or chambers. Vpon the 5 Apr. they tooke a note of the oxen, kaye, sheepe, and cornes. Vpon the 15, they called togither the tennants, and took vp a rentall; they wrate vp ther names, the name of the place where they lived, and what they payed yearlie; with the number of ther kene fowles. The 16, they went to Gilstone and tooke ane inventary of the bestiall there.[27]

Little evidence remains of how the commissioners carried on their work throughout Scotland, or how many estates were affected by their actions in 1652 and 1653.[28] It is clear, however, that the results of Parliament's interim policy on sequestrations were sufficiently severe to endanger the hold of the English army over Scotland, for it was the material hardship caused by the confiscation or sequestration of their estates which drove many of the nobility and gentry to join in the royalist rising of 1653-4.[29]

A further aspect of the parliamentary Commissioners' work in the financial sphere was the regulation of the assessment. Here their main task was to set the rate at which the cess should be levied, for the work of valuation and of ironing out the problems attendant upon the transition from free quarter to monthly assessment had already been undertaken by Lambert and Deane. On 18 February 1652 the Commissioners resolved that the sum of £10,000 stg. per month should henceforth be levied on Scotland, out of which abatements not exceeding £2000 per month might be allowed.[30] By the end of February, tables had been drawn up imposing a gross monthly assessment of just under £9500 on Scotland, and allowing for around £1600 in abatements.[31] By the end of the year these figures had been altered to over £9900 gross and £1400 in abatements so that, in theory, the 'cleere assesse' was now just over £8500.[32] In the following year, however, the impossibility of raising this sum from impoverished Scottish landlords and tenants during a period of continuing unrest compelled a reduction in the 'cleere assesse' to £7500.[33]

As well as dealing with judicial and financial matters, the Commissioners from Parliament attended also to the regulation of the spiritual and intellectual life of Scotland. The three Commissioners for Sequestration, along with the four English judges, the commander-in-chief, Richard Deane, and the governor of Edinburgh and Leith, Col. George Fenwick, were appointed Commissioners 'for Visiting and Regulating Universities and other Affairs relating to the Ministry in Scotland'. On 4 June 1652 these Commissioners issued a Declaration in which they announced their intention of altering or abolishing all such statutes of the universities as were inconsistent with the government of the Commonwealth or the proposed union between England and Scotland. They further declared that they would remove all ministers throughout Scotland who should be found scandalous in their lives or conversation, and would replace them with other, more suitable, persons; and that they would hear and determine all causes relating to the maintenance of ministers. Their first sitting was ordained for Monday, 7 June at Edinburgh, and sessions were to be held every Monday fortnight from that date.[34]

The activities of these Commissioners in regard to the plantation of vacant churches and the granting of stipends aroused the fury of clergymen such as the Resolutioner Robert Baillie. Contrary to contemporary opinion, however, the Commissioners did not embark upon a wholesale policy of removing ministers whom they had found scandalous in their lives or conversations, nor did they eject those who opposed the authority of the Commonwealth of England by, for example, praying for the king. And, as a general rule, they did not intrude men into benefices against the wishes of the presbyteries, kirk sessions or congregations.

Where they did interfere, it seems usually to have been to resolve conflicts engendered, or at least exacerbated, by the rift between Protesters and Resolutioners. This was probably the case at Kilbride and Lenzie, two parishes within the synod of Glasgow and Ayr, where Baillie reported high-handed actions by the English, in support of the Protester candidate in Lenzie and an Independent in Kilbride.[35] Although in the following year Robert Lilburne, then acting commander-in-chief of the army in Scotland, continued to urge the Commissioners to favour the Protesters in such cases,[36] no general picture of arbitrary interference by the English in the internal life of the church emerges. Nonetheless, the necessity of seeking approval from the civil power before a minister could be admitted to a vacant stipend was in itself a cause of deep distress to the presbyterian clergy.

The policy of the Commissioners in relation to the universities was, by contrast, more interventionist. By February 1653 the English had succeeded in getting men complaisant to their interest installed as principals in Glasgow, Edinburgh and Aberdeen. In Glasgow, their nominee was Partick Gillespie, a Protester and friend of Wariston, whose antipathy to the Scottish king and concern for personal advancement was now leading him farther along the path of co-operation with the English. The fortunes of the Protesters in their struggle with the Resolutioners in the college, the presbytery and the synod of Glasgow were linked to Gillespie's rise to power, and it was his acceptance of favour from the new régime that helped to draw the Protester camp towards flirtation with the English, and, later, with Independency. In December 1652 the English Commissioners informed Gillespie that he had been chosen Principal of the College of Glasgow; thereafter he received, on 23 January 1653, a formal invitation signed by the Rector — who happened to be George Lockhart, commissary of Glasgow and brother of William Lockhart, one of the Scottish judges — one professor and two regents. Baillie and some of his Resolutioner colleagues protested violently but unavailingly against this intrusion of an English nominee, and on 14 February 1653 Gillespie was formally admitted as Principal.[37]

At Edinburgh, the English chose Robert Leighton, a man of very different leanings from Gillespie. Supporter of the Engagement, even moderate Royalist, Leighton was to become an archbishop after the Restoration, but in 1652 he travelled to London at the behest of the Scottish Church to plead for the liberation of the ministers who had been captured at Alyth and shipped as prisoners to England. There in all probability he staked his claim to the office of Principal at Edinburgh University. The Principalship at this time was vacant, for the choice of the town council for the post, William Colvill, also an Engager, had been opposed by the Edinburgh ministry and vetoed by the English Judge Moseley. In January 1653, probably as a result of an order sent down from London, and certainly as a result of Moseley's promptings, the town council invited Leighton to fill the vacancy. Despite the continuing hostility of the Edinburgh clergy, Leighton assumed the office of Principal in February 1653.[38]

At Aberdeen the Commissioners' choice fell upon John Row, a man clearly dissatisfied with Presbyterianism. Row, like Alexander Jaffray, belonged to a group of men and women in Aberdeen who formally renounced their adherence to the presbyterian system of church government in May 1652 and declared their support for 'the congregational way'. As a result, in July 1652 Row, and three other Aberdeen ministers, John Menzies, William Moir and Thomas Charteris, were suspended by the General Assembly for having 'declared themselves for separation'. Late in 1652 the English Commissioners removed one Dr. Guild from the Principalship of the college in Old Aberdeen and put John Row in his place. Guild was a Resolutioner, and had already been deposed by the Scottish Church in 1650, but he had been restored to his old place by a Committee of the Assembly of 1651. At his earlier deposition, John Row had been invited to replace him, and it was on the grounds that Row had been called to the office by 'the Acts of the Committee and visitation, 1650' that the English Commissioners now justified his appointment.[39]

The fourth Scottish university, St. Andrews, escaped the interference meted out to her sisters. In September 1652 the Commissioners visited the University, summoned all the masters before them, and examined the registers and the statutes. They gave orders that no vacant place in the college should be filled without their approval, but apart from that they did little. They 'were thought to be the more discreet at St. Andrews, because Mr. Blair having acquaintance of Mr. Fenwick when he was at London . . . did confer with him and exhort him to moderation'. Nonetheless, the college authorities had to adopt various expedients to avoid being forced to comply with the English: in 1652, for example, they held the students' laureation in private, without examination, for a public graduation would have meant that the students would be required to subscribe the Tender of Incorporation.[40]

The Church as a whole at this time was much taken up with the internal split between Protesters and Resolutioners. Hostility towards the English was unabated — as late as August 1652 the synod of Dumfries submitted a protestation against the Tender of Incorporation and in Fife those who had subscribed to the Tender were excluded from the communion table[41] — but from May to July 1652 attention was focused on various attempts promoted by Mr. Robert Blair and Mr. James Durham to secure union between the two parties. On 12 May a meeting of synods took place at Edinburgh, but no agreement could be reached between the two parties on the contentious issue of how or when to summon the next General Assembly. In the event, those Resolutioners who had been appointed members of the Commission of 1651 directed letters to be sent to all presbyteries summoning the Assembly for the third Wednesday in July.[42] It was not simply the case that the Protesters' demands for union were exorbitantly high, although they usually made the (to the Resolutioners) unacceptable demand that the Public Resolutions be formally disowned. Many Resolutioners (of whom Baillie was one) also distrusted Blair's overtures, and felt his mediatory efforts were merely creating a third party in the church.[43] The Protesters refused to recognise the authority of the Assembly which sat down at Edinburgh on 21 July and submitted a Protestation against its constitution. The Assembly nonetheless appointed a committee to confer with the Protesters about a possible union, but it proved abortive, as did similar attempts later in the year.[44]

The fact that these meetings of the synods and the Assembly were allowed to take place at all is in itself indicative of the Commissioners' approach to church affairs. English attacks on the Church of Scotland were for the time being directed more against its individual members than its institutions. Some ministers were subjected to harassment by English soldiers when they prayed for the relief of their brethren imprisoned in England, and a particularly strong line was taken with those who prayed publicly for the king.[45] But the persecution was mostly of a petty kind. The army, for example, seemed to take delight in mocking the stool of repentance and ridiculing the preaching of the Presbyterians[46] but sometimes, too, the soldiers became involved in exchanges of a more serious kind, which led them into deep theological argument with the local clergy.[47] Throughout the year 1652 the English thought they saw signs that Independency was taking root, albeit feebly, in some parts of Scotland. In January and again in March separatist groups in the north of Scotland (no doubt including the Aberdeenshire band) sent in testimonies to the English in which they declared their support for the union with England and their abhorrence of presbyterian church government. In November a newswriter averred that 'The Gathered Churches in Scotland go on so successfully that many who derided them, begin to admire them, and love them.'[48] Despite his optimism, however, the number of converts was in all probability very small. Edward Limburgh, a Baptist missionary who came to the Border country in October 1652, certainly thought the prospects for sectarians were dim. He missed the communion and fellowship of his friends in England, he wrote, 'being cast into these parts, where there are no visible saints, but in the midst of a rugged generation, being led by their priest, who bears rule over them, by their power, and the people delight for to have it so'.[49]

Although the impact of the separatists in 1652 was small, it nonetheless indicated the way in which the presence of the English army and the work of the parliamentary Commissioners had struck a blow at established practices in Scotland. By many of their actions in the fields of justice, religion and finance, the Commissioners had already begun to execute that policy of undermining the ruling groups in church and state which Parliament had laid down in its Declaration of 28 October 1651 and in its Instructions to the Commissioners. In the administrative sphere they had helped to resolve the chaos which had existed in central and local government since Dunbar and to provide the framework for settled government in Scotland. At the same time as the Commissioners were going about these tasks, the army in Scotland was preparing for its summer campaign in the hope of setting the seal of military victory on these political and administrative successes.

ii. The English army and the Highland campaign

Between September 1651 and January 1652 the English army had virtually destroyed organised military resistance to the republican régime in Scotland. The army had established a presence in and control over a large part of the country, and even in the unoccupied areas there was no significant military force still in arms against the English government. Yet during and after the spring of 1652 the army's task was not merely one of consolidation. It had still to crush three pockets of resistance which might separately or in concert provide the springboard for a future challenge to the stability of the new régime. Three major but isolated fortresses — the Bass Rock, Brodick Castle and Dunnottar Castle — had still to be captured; the Marquis of Argyle had to be induced to submit to the Parliament of England; and the central and northern Highlands had to be brought within the control of the army and the clan chiefs forced formally to recognise the authority of the English Commonwealth. The surrender of the royalist fortresses and the submission of Argyle were achieved with little difficulty, but the army's success was less complete in the crucial matter of subduing the Highland clans. Their failure here proved costly, for the continuing unrest in the Highlands fed into the plans which were being laid, both in Scotland and in Europe, for a new royalist rising in the north. As links were forged between the court in exile and the Scottish nobility, the endemic lawlessness of the Highlands took on a distinct political tinge, for the leaders of Scottish society now sought to harness the unruliness of their followers in the service of their king and launch a new royalist movement from the north.

If, then, the Highland campaign of 1652 left a legacy of trouble for the English, the prelude to it nonetheless saw successes of a less equivocal nature. Before taking to the field in June of that year, the army strengthened its hold on Scotland by the capture of the Bass Rock and the castles of Brodick and Dunnottar.

Brodick Castle on the Isle of Arran was the first of these fortresses to fall to the English. It surrendered on 6 April 1652 after being invested by a party of English soldiers sent over by ship from Ayr.[50] The Bass Rock followed a few days later, but its surrender was the outcome of protracted negotiations between the army, the owner of the fortress and the governor of the Bass which had been going on since October. For several months the English had held a strong bargaining counter in the person of the owner of the Bass, John Hepburne, laird of Wauchton, whom they had captured on the mainland. But the garrison on the island were reluctant to obey his instructions to surrender since they had in their possession the Registers of the Kirk of Scotland which had been entrusted to them for safe-keeping. On 3 March, however, Wauchton concluded articles of capitulation with Major General Deane and, despite further attempts to secure more favourable terms, the garrison were forced to hand the island over to the English in the following month.[51] The last of the three fortresses, Dunnottar Castle, capitulated on 24 May 1652 after an eight-month siege. Here again several parties were involved in the discussions which led to its surrender. The owner of the fortress, the Earl Marischal, was a prisoner in London and pressure was put on him by the Council of State to instruct his lieutenant in the north, George Ogilvy of Barras, to surrender.[52] Ogilvy however was determined to hold out, not only because the Regalia of Scotland were hidden in the castle, but because he hoped that the

Royalists abroad would send help to the castle by sea.[53] So long as bad weather hindered the English from bringing up their heavy guns from Leith, Ogilvy could maintain his precarious position, but when the weather cleared in May the English moved their ordnance north. On 24 May, yielding to their superior force, Ogilvy surrendered to Col. Morgan.[54] The English did not however gain possession of the Regalia: these emblems of Scottish sovereignty had been smuggled out of the castle sometime during the siege and were buried in a nearby churchyard until after the Restoration.[55]

The reduction of these three fortresses, each of which had occupied a key position on the coast of Scotland, greatly strengthened the army's position by destroying potential footholds for a royalist invasion of the country. There remained the problems of the Marquis of Argyle and of the clan chiefs, without whose submission no régime could consider itself in full control of the country. During the spring of 1652 the army, and the Commissioners from Parliament, were much exercised by the problem of Argyle, for so long as he remained untamed the west coast of Scotland, over which he exerted great influence, continued to present a strategic danger. Even if no invasion from abroad were imminent, Argyle's power within the Highland zone itself still made it imperative that he should be induced to submit. Between October and December 1651 Argyle had been in negotiation with the English authorities, but the result of these exchanges had been inconclusive and had left the English with a deep suspicion of the Marquis's intentions.[56] In the following year the submission of the Tender of Incorporation to the Scottish people introduced a new element into the situation, for now the inhabitants of the lands under Argyle's control were formally required to accept the fact of English domination.

In February 1652, when the summonses went out to the shires and burghs of Scotland to send representatives to Dalkeith, Argyle was reported to be conferring with fellow chieftains at Inveraray. Some observers believed that he was attempting to reconcile the internecine feuds of the Highlanders and to draw both them and the kirk into his plans for a united front against the English. They were convinced too that Argyle was much afraid of being summoned to appear before the parliamentary Commissioners.[57] Nonetheless, by 21 February the Marquis had sent his steward to Dalkeith to act as deputy for Argyllshire. The Commissioners took this as a sign that his submission was imminent and therefore agreed to another meeting between themselves and the Marquis, this time at Dumbarton on 17 March. This meeting merely revealed, however, that Argyle was still trying to secure for himself a semi-independent bargaining position vis-a-vis the English, for he repeated his earlier suggestion that selected representatives from both nations should meet 'for redresing and giving mutuall satisfaction'. The English rejected this proposal outright and were adamant that no negotiations could be entered into outwith the provisions of Parliament's Declaration and the procedure already set down for consulting the Scottish people. They nonetheless succeeded in extracting from the Marquis a promise that he would co-operate with the English if they wished to establish garrisons in his territory and would send properly elected deputies from Argyllshire to Dalkeith. None of this, however, amounted to a personal submission from Argyle.[58] In a further exchange of letters between Inveraray and Dalkeith he still refused to accept that he was to be accorded no special status in the negotiations on the union, while the commissioners merely reiterated what they had told him at Dumbarton.[59]

Argyllshire's deputies, meanwhile, had arrived at Dalkeith and on 26 April they formally accepted the Tender. Along with their assent they delivered two papers representing their Desires. The first expressed, among other things, the shire's hope that the religion of the Covenants would be maintained in Scotland. The second paper related more specifically to the needs of Argyllshire. First came a plea for a severe reduction in the amount of cess demanded from the shire on account of the devastation it had suffered during the late wars; next a plea that the shire might not be burdened with garrisons or quarterings. Then the Commissioners were asked to ensure that justice was administered in Argyllshire by maintaining the heritable jurisdictions of the Marquis and last, but by no means least, the deputies desired that 'the Marquis of Argyle bee looked vpon wth ane favorable eye, That too ready trust must bee not given to every report that may give hard impressions of him'. For as the shire succinctly put it, the Marquis's backing was invaluable in ensuring that the region obeyed the commands of the English Parliament.[60] This point could not fail to be taken by the English: it was after all the reason for their insistence on securing a personal submission from Argyle.

By the early summer of 1652, despite Argyle's prevarications, time was fast running out for the Marquis, for the English were preparing to launch a campaign into the hills. This was the one course of action which could — and did — force Argyle and other Highland chieftains to tender their submission to the English Parliament. The English anticipated Argyle's downfall with glee: 'he is a subtle Fox,' said one newswriter, 'but if he close not quickly, it is not the rockie Earths he hath amongst the Mountains that can secure him this Summer.'[61]

Preparations for the Highland campaign had been going on since March but were not completed until late June. During this period the army was busy with the settling of garrisons at strategic points throughout the country and, as a necessary adjunct to plans for reducing the Highlands to obedience, with the building of a citadel at St. Johnstons (Perth). This was one of five major citadels constructed by the English in Scotland in the 1650s, the others being at Inverlochy, Inverness, Ayr and Leith.[62] At the same time the Council of State ordered the infantry in Scotland to be increased to 15,000 with a corresponding reduction being made in the cavalry regiments to keep the costs of the northern army level.[63] By June 1652 there were eleven regiments of foot in Scotland, but by the end of the summer the cavalry regiments had been reduced to five.[64] In order to cope with the campaign in the hills, Lilburne's forces in the north of Scotland were to be joined by Overton's regiment of foot from Edinburgh, Blackmere's troops of horse and part of Alured's regiment of foot from Ayr, and Reade's regiment of foot from Stirling. The actual strategy of the Highland campaign was that Deane and Lilburne should march into the hills by a double line from Argyle's country and from Inverness.[65]

As a preliminary to Lilburne's advance from Inverness, Deane issued a declaration from Aberdeen on 9 June 1652 addressed to the clan chiefs, gentlemen and inhabitants of the shires of Elgin, Nairn, Inverness, Ross, Cromarty, Sutherland and Caithness. This required the recipients to come in to Lilburne and give him their engagement to live peaceably. They were also enjoined to provide supplies and other assistance for him on his march.[66]

Deane then moved from Aberdeen to St. Johnstons, where he again interviewed Argyle. Here at last, with the English army already on the march, Argyle bowed to the logic of the situation and prepared to submit to the English. The Marquis now consented to receive English forces into his territory, as indeed he had promised he would at the conference at Dumbarton in March, and discussed with Deane the outlines of a formal agreement which was to be signed by the two parties in August.[67] On 3 July Argyle parted from Deane and returned to his own territory to receive the English forces under the command of Col. Overton. By 13 July Overton and his party had arrived at Tarbert in Kintyre, where they were met by Argyle's steward and his entourage. A few days later, Argyle himself entertained the English officers 'with much state' and made 'many pretences of love and affection' to them. But, added one commentator, 'who knows not that it is but constrained. The Marquesse is no stranger in the art of Politicks; but we shal make use of him accordingly.' Despite these doubts, outward appearances remained favourable to the English. At Argyle's instigation, the country people treated them civilly, while the Marquis himself assisted the English 'in person, presence, men, friends, provisions, or anything else'. During July, in anticipation of the terms of the August agreement, the army settled garrisons in Kintyre and progressed to Dunstaffnage, Dunnolly and the environs of Inveraray itself.[68]

The army still feared that when the bulk of their forces returned to the Lowlands, these successes would prove short-lived,[69] but in the meantime they could take comfort from the fact that progress continued to be made in the negotiations with Argyle. Deane was at Inveraray during August, and it was during this visit that the Marquis agreed to put down on paper the results of his discussions with Deane in June and July. On 12 August he signed a formal acceptance of the union of England and Scotland and pledged himself to live quietly 'under the Parliament of the Commonwealth of England and their authority'. But his submission was qualified by a conscience clause: his acceptance was prefaced by the words, 'my duty to Religion, according to my Oath in the Covenant always reserved', and it extended only to the 'Civill part' of Scotland.[70] In other words, Argyle refrained, at least semantically, from acknowledging the introduction of religious toleration into Scotland along with the political aspects of the union. On 19 August, a full agreement between Argyle and Deane was signed. Argyle agreed to live peaceably under the English government and to use his utmost endeavours to see that his children and family did the same; he promised that 'if any walke otherwise' he would inform the English army immediately. This clause, however, was not 'to hinder his Lordshippes good endeavours for the establishing religion according to his conscience', so long as these 'endeavours' did not involve the use of force against the Commonwealth. He further agreed to see that his tenants and clansmen observed the same provisions. As surety for this, it was agreed that Argyle or his son Lorne would give themselves up as hostages if Parliament should so desire. And finally, the English promised that Argyle should enjoy his liberty and estates, free from molestation or sequestration, provided that he and his tenants paid their assessments and other taxes and that he allowed any of his houses, excepting Inveraray and Carrick, to be garrisoned by the English. In practice, only five garrisons were established as a result of these articles — at Dunstaffnage, Dunnolly, Lough, Kincairn and Tarbert — and steps had already been taken to set these up before the agreement was finally concluded.[71]

As the English had feared, however, paper agreements could not guarantee good order in Argyle's country. Late in August, another meeting between the Marquis and Major General Deane provided the occasion for a minor revolt by some of the clans. Deane had invited Argyle to meet him aboard ship and, as a gesture of civility, accorded him a salute of guns at his arrival and departure. This apparently caused the Highlanders to think that Argyle had been taken prisoner; thereupon 'the fires were made and the red Ribbands sent from Clan to Clan', so that a force of 1000 to 1500 Highlanders gathered to threaten the English. The result was that the garrisons of Tarbert, Lough and Kincairn were surprised, and those at Dunstaffnage and Dunnolly were besieged.[72] Only in October, partly through the good offices of the Marquis himself, was peace restored and the prisoners captured by the Highlanders returned to their regiments. The settlement then reached was embodied in a new agreement, dated 27 October 1652, between Argyle and the English authorities, which modified the previous treaty of 19 August. In this new agreement the English acknowledged that Argyle had the right to sign on behalf of the 'Gentlemen and Inhabitants of the shire of Argile', whereas before he had signed only on behalf of 'himself and freinds' — the change perhaps signifying some recognition that the Marquis's writ still ran in the region. The agreement was in the main concerned with the restitution due from the people of Argyll for their attempts on the English garrisons, and with laying down the figure of £100 stg. per month as the burden of assessment for the shire. But the English for their part conceded that only Dunstaffnage and Dunnolly should now be garrisoned within the shire, and that, except in an emergency, no more English soldiers should be marched through the country.[73] In an additional agreement signed on 28 October, the Marquis promised to hand over to the English 16 brass guns and 500 muskets then in his possession, in return for an agreed sum of money.[74]

These agreements marked the end of a chapter in the history of Argyle's relations with the English government. Of Argyle's position after the negotiations of October 1652, his biographer justly writes:

> On the whole, the Marquess succeeded in obtaining better terms for himself than could have been reasonably expected, and he retained at the end of the negotiations his hereditary status of a potentate of almost independent rank.[75]

The Highlanders' attack on the five garrisons in Argyllshire was but one example, albeit the most serious one, of a general uneasiness and muted aggressiveness in the region which the English army encountered at many points throughout their summer campaign. The nature of the terrain posed special difficulties for the English. Not only did the transport of provisions and other supplies become a major logistical exercise, but the mountainous territory — 'where each hill . . . is no lesse [than] an invincible Garrison' — provided ample cover for marauding bands of Highlanders.[76] The harassment which the English suffered ranged in scale from having pot-shots fired at them on the banks of Loch Lochy to the far more serious danger of being confronted by bands of several hundred armed clansmen. On one such occasion, when 600 Highlanders gathered near Blair Atholl, the threat proved false, for the men had come to submit to the English, not to oppose them. But soon afterwards, in mid-August, the army were so concerned at the possible consequences of a report that Macdonald of Glengarry and some confederates had gathered a force of 4000 men to harass the English, and those of the country people who had complied with them, that they permitted some of the Highlanders to retain their arms for self-defence.[77]

In the summer of 1652 some Englishmen were, on the whole, rather pessimistic about the chances of securing lasting peace in the Highlands. English writers emphasised that the army had taken care to treat the country people well and had made orderly provision for securing grass and food for themselves and their horses, but they were clearly aware of being up against a primitive people whose ways were not those of civilised society. The lifestyle of 'these base and beggerly wild beasts' astonished William Clarke, who told the Speaker, in a letter to Parliament, that '[t]he people [in the Highlands] Generally speake Irish goe only wth plads about their middle both men and women, there are scarce any houses of Stone but only Earth & Turfes.'[78] A report from Inveraray in August 1652 was even more strident in its condemnation of native customs:

> . . . the inhabitants are savage, cruell, covetous, and treacherous; the men are proud of their trouses, belted plades and bonnets, as a Spaniard is of his high-crowned hat, long cloak and rapier; indeed they differ in their pace, for this tells his steps in the pace of a grand paw, whilst that runs like a roe, over hill and dale, till time stops him. Their women are pure Indian complexions, unparalleled for deformity; their habitations are like so many inaccessible charnel houses for nasty noysomness . . .[79]

What worried the army commanders most, however, was the dual significance of the lawlessness in the Highlands. As an expression merely of the social and economic instability of the region — as when the Highlanders stole food or money to improve their living standards — it presented a challenge to the army in its role as a police force bent on punishing breaches of the peace. But it had also a more serious aspect, for the endemic violence of the Highlands could also provide the substratum of a *politically* inspired revolt, capable of challenging the army in its capacity as defender of an alien system of government and society. Before they could assume this political role, however, the 'broken men' of the Highlands would have to have their activities linked to, and to some extent controlled by, the ambitions of their social superiors, be they clan chieftains or semi-feudal aristocrats. For the lawlessness of the region could not become a serious threat to the security of the English régime unless and until it was subsumed in a more general revolt led by men with clear political objectives and supported by an organised military force. In the summer of 1652, therefore, the English were aware that, in order to maintain peace and stability, they must try to isolate the sources of political leadership from the groundswell of social and economic unrest: hence the steps they had already taken to secure the formal submission of the Highland chieftains, and their constant anxiety over the manoeuvrings of Argyle. What they did not realise, though, was that political leadership was already being offered, not by Argyle as they most feared, but by other men who had links with the exiled king. At the very time when the English were campaigning in the hills, the conditions necessary for the resurgence of royalist rebellion were already in existence, and in the midst of the period of pacification there was conceived the embryo of a new revolt. As a result of contact being established between the exiled court and some leading figures in the Highlands, the top layer of political leadership was ready to be added to the substratum of endemic violence in the Highland zone.

After his experiences at Worcester, Charles II was disenchanted with Presbyterians in general and with the Scots in particular. From his court in Paris, it was reported that '[h]e complains much against the Scotch for using him servilely, heaping indignities upon him, and making him act directly against his own liking, and giving him no powers till almost the very end of all.'[80] Such distaste, however, did not prevent Charles from retaining an interest in the fate of the Regalia and of his household goods, which had been left in Dunnottar Castle. Nor did it prevent him from trying to keep in touch with the more sympathetic of his royalist supporters, particularly in the Highlands. In March 1652 the king had appointed an agent to go to Scotland, to consult with the lairds of Pluscardine and Glengarry and other Royalists throughout the kingdom, and attempt to rescue the Regalia from Dunnottar.[81] But news came of Dunnottar's surrender when preparations for the mission were still incomplete, and so the project was abandoned. Stronger links between the Royalists at home and abroad were forged in the following June, when two sets of circumstances combined to draw Charles's attention once again towards his northern kingdom. On the one hand, the outbreak of war between England and the United Provinces raised Charles's hopes of persuading the Dutch to assist his plans for a landing on British shores, while at the same time the war itself diverted the English government's attention from the internal security of the realm. On the other hand, a message reached Charles in June from certain chieftains and noblemen in Scotland, in which they represented 'the condicion of Scotlande' and their willingness to raise the standard of revolt once more.[82] Taken together, these events convinced Charles that Scotland would be a useful backdoor through which to regain his rights in Britain as a whole. The embryonic revolt in Scotland was therefore given a European dimension. To the royalist exiles Scotland was but one element, albeit an increasingly important one, in their overall manipulation of the European power struggle through which they hoped to gather enough men and money to restore Charles to his throne. Similarly, because of the link between Charles and the

Dutch, the Cromwellian government regarded the rising as a factor in their conduct of foreign as well as domestic affairs. And in Scotland itself, the hope of help from abroad and in particular the expectation of aid from the Dutch was greatly to influence the strategy of the royalist leaders.

Charles's response to the address from the Scottish nobility was fairly swift. On 25 June he subscribed a circular letter to the noblemen and gentlemen of Scotland thanking them for their 'affection and zeale' for his cause and desiring them to give every assistance to Lieutenant General Middleton, whom he had appointed general of all the forces raised or to be raised in Scotland. Middleton, a former Engager who had fought with the Scots army at Worcester, was currently with the court at St. Germains, and it was to be left to him to decide on the most opportune moment for a landing in Scotland. The feasibility of such an expedition depended first and foremost, however, on the Royalists' ability to obtain arms and money on the Continent. Middleton and his agents therefore began to tout for supplies from the courts of Europe and from well-disposed Scottish expatriates,[83] but they signally failed in the ensuing months to procure anything like the sums needed to mount a full-scale expedition to Scotland. Hence it became increasingly clear to the exiles as the year wore on that, for the time being at least, the Royalists in Scotland would have to stand or fall by their own efforts.

For this reason, it was essential that the king should keep up the morale of his supporters at long range, and impress upon the royalist leaders within Scotland the need for unity. In August, despite his aversion to Presbyterianism, Charles wrote a letter to the Moderator of the General Assembly in which he exhorted the clergy to 'leave no good means unpractized to keep up the spirits of those who are ready to faint'. In the late autumn the court in exile was heartened by the arrival of a messenger from Scotland, one Malcolm Smith, who landed in Holland sometime in October and arrived in Paris in mid-November. He brought word from Macdonald of Glengarry, then acting general of the royalist forces in Scotland, and his associates that Glengarry himself, the clan Fraser, the lairds of Maclean and Macleod, the chief of Clanranald and many others had each pledged themselves to raise 1000 men apiece, and that sundry others had undertaken to raise 2, 3 or 400 men apiece. The Highlanders further begged that commissions and letters of encouragement should be sent from the king to Glengarry and the rest of the association, that arms and ammunition should be shipped from the Continent to Scotland, and that Middleton should speedily join them. By 30 November [N.S.] letters had been drafted to the members of the association and to Glengarry himself, which assured the recipients that help would soon be forthcoming and exhorted them in the meantime to lay aside all factions and mutual jealousies. On 20 December [N.S.] a commission was drawn up empowering Sir James Macdonald of Sleat, the lairds of Glengarry, Lochiel, Keppoch and Foyer and Donald Gorm Macdonald to act as a Council of War during Middleton's absence, with authority to appoint an interim commander-in-chief. Also in December, more letters were drafted for despatch to Sir James Macdonald, the Captain of Clanranald, and other heads of clans.[84] Before sending these letters, and the all-important commission, to Scotland, however, it was decided to submit them to Middleton for his approval. At this point the plans concocted in Paris came unstuck, for Middleton vetoed the design to allow the Highlanders to elect an interim commander and so the Council of War for the moment came to naught.[85]

By the end of 1652, therefore, much ink had been spilled on the Continent, but little tangible result had been seen in Scotland. The exiles' efforts to succour their friends at home had borne little fruit, while in Scotland itself Glengarry's estimate of the number of men who *could* be raised for the royalist cause bore little relation to the number actually in arms at the end of the year. Nevertheless, although they were largely ignorant of the intentions of the leading men of the Highlands, the English could not be altogether happy about the state of the country in the autumn and winter of 1652. In November it was reported that the Scots, particularly the moss-troopers, had revived 'their old Custom of Robbing and murthering the English (whether soldiers or others) upon all opportunity'. In December Captain William Powell, the governor of Braemar, was murdered by a gang of Highlanders who sought revenge for some punishment his lieutenant had inflicted upon them for buying firearms from the English soldiers. Some of the perpetrators of this type of crime were arrested and tried in the criminal courts, but their trials merely reinforced the English opinion that such murders and robberies indicated the present temper of the Scots, 'that many of them would as well bite as shew their teeth'.[86] More seriously, rumours were circulating of plots and designs against the English, some of which were backed by material evidence. Large hoards of arms had been found in Paisley, including some inside the church in which the English soldiers were quartered. Also in December, a search was made in the burgh towns of Fife, and there again the army found many concealed weapons.[87] Although these must in many cases have been the relics of past struggles, the English feared that they might be used in a new uprising. At the same time, the English intelligence network was anxiously watching the Highlanders' movements. In all, therefore, the army was not inclined to relax its vigilance over the country, but although the authorities were uneasy, they did not seriously doubt their ability to keep these symptoms of unrest under control.

It is clear, then, that by the end of 1652 the English were aware that their attempts to impose peace and good order on the Highlands had not been a total success. During the summer campaign in the hills, they had seen how the Highlanders could use the mountainous terrain as cover for the harassment of English troops, and to this awareness of the geographical advantages held by the Highlanders was added a sense of the social differences between English and Gael which, in English eyes, reduced the chances of reconciliation between conquerors and conquered even further. In the last few months of the year, reports of stirrings in the Highlands and of plots in the Lowlands enhanced the English sense of unease, and were a constant reminder to the army of the continuing ill-feeling of the Scots towards their new masters. Yet it is doubtful if the English fully appreciated the nature of the problem with which they were faced. There is little sign that at the end of the year the English were alive to the political implications of the unrest in the Highlands, or that, despite their suspicion of Scottish malevolence, they viewed these disorders as anything other than 'breaches of the peace'. Their belief that they had effectively completed the subjugation, if not the pacification, of Scotland made them slow to realise how easily their control over the Highlands might be dislodged, and their preoccupation with the Marquis of Argyle obscured the reality of the threat from Glengarry and his confederates. In the following year, however, the English began to perceive the true nature of the revolt and to realise that the very pattern of violence and rebellion which they most feared was about to challenge their hold over Scotland.

PART TWO

GLENCAIRN'S RISING AND ITS IMPACT ON ENGLISH POLICY, 1653 — 1655

Introduction

FROM 1653 to 1655 the might of the English army in Scotland and the integrity of the republican régime were threatened by a royalist rebellion, known to history as 'Glencairn's Rising' after the nobleman who led it. This rebellion crucially affected English policy in the middle 1650s but it had its origins in the earlier years of the English conquest. In part it was an extension of that lawlessness which the army had set out to reduce in 1652, had succeeded in controlling to the point where violent incidents became sporadic and small-scale, but had never completely destroyed. The political impetus behind the unrest, which turned the revolt into a specifically 'royalist' rebellion, was provided when links were forged between the Scottish nobility and Charles's court in exile, and this too had happened very soon after Worcester — much sooner in fact than the English ever realised. Hence although the rising reached its height in late 1653-early 1654 and had its greatest impact on English policy in and after these years, it grew out of, and derived significance from, the problems which the English had faced since the earliest stages of the conquest.

It was of the essence of the rebellion that it expressed not only national resistance to a foreign invader, but also the right of the hard core of Scottish Royalists to lead that resistance on behalf of the nation as a whole. As the political record of many of the leaders of Glencairn's rising shows, support for the revolt came in the main from men who had been loyal to Charles I in the 1640s and who had not come to support his son, Charles II, merely as a result of the vagaries of Scottish internal politics between 1649 and 1651. Glencairn himself, for example, had in the early 1640s belonged to Hamilton's party of 'royalist covenanters' and had opposed the sending of a Scottish army to England in 1643; while in 1648 he was a staunch supporter of the Engagement.[1] Balcarres had in the early days of the Scottish revolution been attracted to the covenanting party, but in later years became a prominent supporter of Charles I.[2] In their contribution to Glencairn's rising Seaforth and Huntly were also carrying on a tradition of royal service, both of them having had fathers who fought with Montrose[3]; while Lorne, although too young to have taken part in the events of the 1640s, had become an ardent royalist during his sojourn abroad from 1647 to 1649.[4] In its championship of the king's cause, therefore, Glencairn's rising marked the ascendancy of Royalist over Covenanter as well as the challenge of Scotsman to Englishman. For this reason, the rising has its place in the history of the political, social and religious disputes which had divided Scotland since the late 1630s as well as in the history of Anglo-Scottish hostility since the Hamiltonian invasion of England in 1648. In this respect it is important to stress that the Royalism of Glencairn and his supporters marks a shift away from the covenanting Royalism of the years 1648-51 in favour of a Royalism more akin to that of Montrose. Three aspects of the rising illustrate this point: its geography, its personnel and its ideology.

Geographically and socially, the rising was rooted firmly in the Highlands and in the clan system. It was not merely that the barely suppressed lawlessness of this region provided a foundation on which political ambition could build. It was also the case that the men who contributed most consistently to the leadership of the revolt were primarily nobles and gentry who had interests in the Highland region; and it was their clansmen and tenants who formed the bulk of the organised military levies in 1653 and 1654. The men of the Highlands were never completely united in their support for the exiled king, however: inter-clan rivalries often meant that if one clan or branch of a clan came out for the royalist cause, its enemies would automatically side, albeit temporarily, with the English. 'Royalist' chieftains from time to time wavered or were lukewarm in their support for the revolt, and the rank and file of the levies proved singularly difficult to control, frequently preferring to seek private gain rather than submit to the demands of military discipline. Nonetheless, the revolt began, ended and had its core in the Highlands. This fact not only profoundly affected the military conduct of the campaign, making the rising into a species of guerilla warfare radiating out from the Highland zone and having lines of retreat stretching back into the mountains. It also influenced the ideology of the revolt. For like Montrose and his associates, Glencairn and his supporters were less anxious to impose political restrictions upon the king, and less eager to uphold covenanting principles, than the Committee of Estates had been from 1648 to 1651. In part this reflects the sympathies of the instigators of the revolt: the Highland nobility, whether they were clan chiefs, feudal aristocrats or both, had never assimilated the presbyterian attitude to church-state relations as fully as their counterparts in the Lowlands. They were thus less concerned with ensuring that Charles II should be a fully covenanted king than with the more practical question of how to restore him to his rights and liberties. This shift away from rigid adherence to covenanting principles continued a trend which had been apparent in Scottish politics since the defeat at Dunbar. For many, the lesson of Dunbar had been that the kirk party, with its rigorous insistence on separating covenanting sheep from royalist goats, had proved itself incapable of leading Scottish resistance to the English invader. There had therefore been a shift in support, away from the covenanting cause as represented by the kirk towards a more truly national cause embodied in the king. Thus it was a king's army much more than a kirk army which had been defeated at Worcester. After Worcester it was men like Glencairn and his supporters who were best equipped in ideological and material terms to carry on the legacy of resistance to the foreign invader. For not only were the men of the Highlands fitted by their political and religious attitudes to assume the mantle of Royalism; in strategic terms it was of crucial importance that the Highland region itself was only partly controlled by the English army. Together these factors meant that it was in the Highlands that royalist military activity had the best chance of getting off the ground.

Such, in brief, were the origins of Glencairn's rising. As the rebellion progressed, however, it became increasingly complex in its character, for it was of the essence of the revolt that its aims, its strategy and the kind of support it attracted were constantly changing. Indeed, the movement could succeed in its ultimate objectives only in so far as it *could* transcend its origins. For in order to overthrow the republican régime and restore the king, the rising had to establish itself *in practice* as a movement of truly national proportions. It was not enough that the task of restoring the king should lie with that one section of the Scottish community which had fallen heir to the legacy of resistance after 1651. If Glencairn and his supporters were to fulfil the hopes vested in them they would have to broaden their appeal considerably in social, territorial and ideological terms, for only thus could the army's grip on the country be weakened. In this task they achieved some notable successes. As the movement grew in strength it attracted the active support of nobility, gentry and common people from the Lowlands as well as from the Highlands. As a result, military activity spread from the Highlands into the south of Scotland, even as far as Carlisle, so that the English army was forced to defend itself on several fronts. And in addition, the leaders of the rising adopted a measure of ideological compromise in an attempt to satisfy both the warring elements within their own ranks and the waverers outside their control. Thus in the declarations and other propaganda documents which the leadership issued, care was taken to emphasise the need for national unity, and assurances were given that the Highlanders posed no threat to the social or religious interests of their Lowland brethren. These efforts did not, however, produce a movement which was cohesive either in action or in purpose: those who at one time or another were actively engaged in arms against the English formed not a homogeneous fighting unit, but a series of layers of revolt whose interaction with, and independence of, one another varied greatly throughout the years of the rising.

The motives which, in the end, prompted other sections of the Scottish community to join a movement which had been instigated by the Highlanders were diverse, and illustrated once again the complexity of the rising. On the one hand, there can be no doubt that sympathy for the royalist cause was strong amongst many who in 1653 lay under the physical control of the English army. What was needed to turn them into royalist activists, therefore, was not so much compulsion or propaganda on the part of the Royalists, as simply the opportunity to join the rebels. This could be afforded on a large scale only if and when the army was forced to withdraw into defensive positions; but even before that began to happen, many individuals managed to escape from under the watchful eye of the local garrisons to link up with the rebel troops. On the other hand, the nature of the passive support which the common people in many areas of the country gave at one time or another is more difficult to assess. Such forms of help as sheltering rebels or handing over food, money or horses to them may well have represented a yielding to *force majeure* rather than to ideological conviction, for when royalist troops were actually present in an area, they could effectively press the inhabitants into service whether they liked it or not. Yet again, the movement gained strength, particularly among the Scottish gentry, as the punitive aspects of English policy towards Scotland began to take effect. As sequestration proceeded apace and the courts of justice began rigorously to enforce the laws of debt, material hardship drove many of the gentry to join the rebels in the hope either of making incidental economic gains or of permanently restoring their fortunes by overturning the English government. The burden of the assessment was felt keenly, too, and by the common people as well as the gentry. Thus the economic implications of English social and fiscal policy provided additional reasons for the Scots to resist alien domination.

By the end of 1653 the movement had evolved from a series of violent incidents on the edge of the Highland zone into a full-scale military rising. At the same time the conflict had extended from the field of battle. Increasingly the struggle became one for the support of the population as a whole, and so the Royalists became involved in a challenge not only to the English government's military strength but to the effectiveness of its civil policy as well. As a result of this, the implications of the Royalists' eventual defeat were political and social as well as military. Indeed, what makes Glencairn's rising important in the political history of the Interregnum is that it forced the English government to moderate that policy towards Scotland which had first found expression in Parliament's Declaration of 28 October 1651. In particular, the government was forced to compromise with those very sections of Scottish secular society — the nobility and gentry — against whom its original policy had been aimed. At one level, such compromise took the form of *ad hoc* co-operation enforced by military necessity; during the rising, for example, the army allowed the gentry in several shires to retain their arms and form guards for the defence of their property against raiders. But much more fundamental alterations also took place, the most striking example being the modification of Parliament's sequestration policy by the Act of Pardon and Grace in 1654. Moreover, such compromises, although initially adopted merely as a means of defeating the insurgents, were retained after English victory was secure in a way which profoundly modified the character of the régime: from 1655, the structure of government at the centre and in the localities bore telling witness to the impact of the rising on English policy.

For the student of Cromwellian Scotland, therefore, the importance of Glencairn's rising extends far beyond the military history of the years 1653-55. Its antecedents lay deep in Scottish internal history as well as in the reaction against English policy after Worcester, and so the rising has a place in the context of Scottish politics from 1638 to 1660. In its outcome moreover it represented not simply the defeat of a weak, divided royalist force by the superior might of the English army; for the whole movement exerted a profound impact on the political and social policy of the Commonwealth and Protectorate in Scotland.

4

Lilburne and the Growth of Revolt, January 1653 — April 1654

FROM January 1653 to April 1654 violence and disorder in Scotland increased as Glencairn's rising gathered momentum and challenged the army's grip on the country. During this time the army in Scotland was commanded by Col. Robert Lilburne, for in December 1652 Richard Deane had been recalled by Parliament to serve as a general of the fleet.[1] Since the late 1640s Lilburne's military career had been spent mainly in Scotland and the north of England. In July 1650 he and his regiment had marched with Cromwell to Scotland and had remained there until the time of the Worcester campaign; by November 1651 they had returned to Scotland and in the summer of 1652 had taken part in the campaign into the Highlands.[2] Despite Lilburne's experience of Scottish conditions, however, his appointment to take command of all the forces in Scotland was meant to be only a temporary one, until such time as Cromwell, the Lord General, should send a fully commissioned and more senior commander-in-chief to take his place. But owing to the demands of the Anglo-Dutch war such a replacement could not be provided until May 1654, when Monck again came north, and it therefore fell to Lilburne to cope with the ever-increasing problem of unrest in Scotland. Indeed, soon after Lilburne's assumption of overall command, it became clear to the English that they were in fact dealing with an embryonic royalist rebellion, not merely with the actions of wayward criminals, and that the gatherings of Highlanders, of which they had long been suspicious, were politically inspired. In the course of 1653 'Glencairn's Rising' gathered pace, challenging Lilburne's grasp of military strategy and his understanding of the needs of the Scottish people.

It cannot be said that Lilburne, personally, stood up to the test well. By the spring of 1654 he was desperate to be relieved of his command, describing himself as having been 'a pure drudge almost these 4 yeares in Scotland'.[3] His letters to the authorities in England became querulous in tone, full of complaints about the failure of the Council and the Committee for the Army to listen to his demands for more men and better supplies, and displaying in general an unwillingness to take responsibility or to exercise his own initiative. Lilburne, however, was beset by great problems. He, unlike his successor Monck, had to cope with the rising when it was on the upsurge rather than when its *élan* had been lost after many months of internal squabbling and disillusionment with the promises of help from abroad. His drive against the Royalists also coincided with England's deepest involvement in the Dutch war, so that it was virtually impossible for Whitehall to find enough men and money to satisfy the demands from both theatres of war. Indeed in the very first month of his command Lilburne received an order from Parliament for the disbandment of a part of the army in Scotland. The infantry was to be reduced from 15,000 to 12,500 and lesser reductions were to be made in the horse regiments and the train of artillery.[4] These changes were deemed necessary to release men and money for the Dutch war, but they seriously weakened the army's ability to take offensive action against the Royalists in the coming summer. Throughout 1653 Lilburne constantly stressed that the soldiers' pay was in arrears, that supplies of food and ammunition were running short, and that campaigning in the hills was impossible without substantial reinforcements, but his own lack of authority in government circles further reduced the chances of his pleas being heeded. This contrasted with the attention later shown to Monck, who admittedly succeeded to the Scottish command when the Council had more time and more money at its disposal, but whose standing in Whitehall helped to ensure that his requests for action on both civil and military matters were met with remarkable promptness. Yet despite Lilburne's practical inadequacies, his insights into the root causes of the rebellion and his plans for dealing with the sources of discontent among the Scottish people were sound. During his stay in Scotland, however, his policy towards the civilian population was only moderately successful, partly because the Council of State failed to act on many of his recommendations and partly because military exigencies forced him to compromise in his schemes for winning back the Scottish people to peace and obedience.

i. The course of the rising, January 1653 — April 1654

From the very beginning of 1653 the English had strong intimations that 'a new war was brewing in the Highlands.'[5] On 22 January Col. Matthew Alured, governor of Ayr, informed Lilburne of a report that Glengarry was at the head of a party in the Highlands, and that some of the leading men in Ayrshire were sympathetic to the royalist cause.[6] Two days later, a report was sent from Inverness that, under pretence of reconciling an old feud between the Macdonalds and the Chisholms, Glengarry had summoned the clans of the district to meet him at Strathglass. The object of the meeting had been to pass on news from abroad and to decide on what tactics to employ against the English. Glengarry, however, had been disappointed, for attendance fell well below his expectations. The chiefs of the clans had been reluctant to declare their allegiance openly, since they did not yet know how the royalist cause would prosper, but they had nonetheless allowed some of their clansmen to join Glengarry. The main result of the meeting had been a decision to raise a 'flying army' of 1500 or 2000 men. The writer of this report, probably Col. Fitch, added that, in his opinion, material hardship had driven, and would continue to drive, Glengarry and the clans into armed revolt, for only by robbery and the spoliation of others could these Highlanders subsist.[7] In the same month news came from Brechin that a messenger from the king had landed in Fife, but he had disappeared into the Highlands before the English could catch him.[8]

Lilburne duly passed this intelligence on to Cromwell, adopting as his own the belief that 'necessity' (or straitened circumstances) had impelled Glengarry to take action.[9] During February the English heard more of Glengarry's movements. Among their informants were Sir James Macdonald of Sleat and the Marquis of Argyle, both of whom emphasised that Glengarry was preparing to bring matters to a head between the Royalists and the English army. To Argyle, Lilburne wrote on 18 February that he had been informed that some of Argyle's friends and acquaintances were likely to join Glengarry, but that others 'uppon whom your Lordshippe hath a powerfull influence' would 'willingly' obey Argyle if he directed them otherwise. Lilburne was anxious to use Argyle as a counter-weight to Glengarry, but although Argyle promised to do all he could to preserve peace in the Highlands, Lilburne was not entirely convinced of his sincerity.[10]

By the end of February 1653 English intelligence reports had quite clearly established the existence of royalist conspiracy in Scotland. Yet Lilburne's attitude towards the incipient danger fluctuated considerably in the coming months. It was not only that Lilburne was slow to accept the fact that he had a serious rebellion on his hands; he based his assessment of the danger from the rebels almost entirely on a short-term view of the situation, and seemed incapable of making a long-term appraisal of the developing conflict. In February, he was aware that 'their [the Royalists'] plotts doe ripen, especially amonge the mountaines', and believed that the messenger from abroad was principally responsible for putting 'a great deale of life into these kinde of cattell'. He was also worried lest links be established between the Royalists in Scotland and Northern Ireland, a concern shared by the Council of State, who ordered patrol vessels to ply between the north of Ireland and the Western Isles.[11] But in March Lilburne was cautiously confident that the rebellion would be contained: a body of 2000 Highlanders had lately dispersed to their homes, and the recent defeat of the Dutch fleet off Portland Bill would, he felt, further dishearten the Royalists.[12] In April he was more hopeful still; affairs were in a 'very peaceable posture', and there was 'a great inclination . . . in the commonality to acquiesce and submitt to the present Government'. Lilburne was convinced at this time that any 'forwardnesse' among the Highlanders was defensive rather than aggressive in intent. He admitted that the presbyterian clergy were still blowing their trumpets in the Lowlands, but this was counterbalanced by the 'increase of good people' who, in his estimation, were coming round to the Independent way.[13]

Contrary to Lilburne's expectations, the peace of April was to prove merely the calm before the storm. In the ensuing summer months, the royalist movement changed from an outbreak of Highland violence into a full-scale military revolt. In May, June and July 1653 the rising began to get off the ground. In these months several meetings were held in the Highlands at which various noblemen and clan chiefs declared their support for the royalist cause. At the same time, royalist forces began to assume a greater degree of organisation and exhibited in their attacks on English soldiers and on the country people at least some conception of military strategy. The Royalists also produced a commander-in-chief in the person of the Earl of Glencairn, who in the absence of Middleton assumed nominal control of all the king's forces in Scotland. All of these developments, however, were accompanied by drawbacks. In the first place, although there now emerged a band of royalist leaders whose commitment to the cause was open and explicit, there were many noblemen who still deemed it more politic to hedge their bets. More seriously for the effective prosecution of royalist strategy, the leadership was riven by internal disputes which were made worse rather than better by Glencairn's assumption of overall command. In the course of 1653 Glencairn's authority was challenged by Balcarres; and Lorne quarrelled successively with Kenmore, Glengarry and Glencairn.[14] Such a situation would clearly have had a disastrous effect on royalist progress had it not been for the tactics which the Royalists adopted for the remainder of the year. Instead of planning a concerted attack on the English army, they decided to avoid direct engagements 'but with parties, and that att passes or by infals'[15] until such time as Middleton should arrive, and in the meantime to concentrate on exacting money, horses and other supplies from both friend and foe. Indeed, the belief that help would come from abroad, and the hope that the king himself might come over to assume command, was a crucial factor in determining the leadership's conduct of the rising. Perhaps for this reason, when they had the English army on the defensive, they did not push their advantage even further, but instead allowed the English to ride out the storm until the balance of power tilted in their favour in 1654.

All these factors worked together to make heterogeneity the hallmark of the rising. In all its aspects — in its geography, its personnel, the unity of its command and the efficacy of its tactics — the rising was varied and complex. As a result the exact nature of the Royalists' activities and the strength of their forces were not always clear to observers. This introduced an element of uncertainty into the English army's calculations on how best to counter the rebellion: what was being done where, and by whom, was not always readily apparent — at least not until after it had actually happened. Yet despite these difficulties the army had a remarkably efficient intelligence system working throughout Scotland and succeeded in reaping much information on the Royalists' movements and intentions.

As the army soon learned, one of the first Highland chieftains to take action against the English in the summer of 1653 was the Earl of Seaforth, chief of the Mackenzies. At the end of April Seaforth presided over a royalist council of war at Glenelg. This meeting produced yet another loyal address to Charles, assuring him that many were actively promoting his cause in the Highlands and Islands. Late in May Seaforth's men captured some English soldiers whose ship had put in at the island of Lewis. Lilburne retaliated by imprisoning the Tutor of Seaforth and other leading Mackenzies, and recommended to Cromwell that Seaforth's estates be sequestered. Later in the summer the army sent an expedition to take over the island and garrison it.[16] At the end of May another meeting of royalist chiefs was reported to have taken place at Killin, in Perthshire, followed by a meeting at Rannoch on 3 and 4 June.[17] On 16 June Balcarres wrote to Lilburne from Lochaber, complaining that the articles of capitulation which he had concluded with the English in 1651 had been broken by them, and that therefore he himself had been obliged 'to retire my selfe somewhat further out of the way'. On 18 June Sir Arthur Forbes, who had been included in Balcarres' capitulation, wrote to Lilburne in similar vein.[18] The implication of both letters was that the writers were about to side openly with the Royalists. In addition, around 13 June, letters went out from the Earl of Glencairn in the name of Charles's commissioners to leading royalist supporters summoning them to a meeting at Moy in Lochaber on 1 July.[19] At this time, too, the formal meetings of royalist leaders, which can be tied down to specific dates, were punctuated by an almost continuous series of less formal rendezvous between varying numbers of chieftains and nobles, at which important business might occasionally be transacted. This shifting pattern of meetings and rendezvous came about because the Royalists had constantly to be on the move to avoid detection by the English, and because the men of influence had to engage in a lengthy series of consultations with friends and allies in the Highlands in their attempts to drum up support and concert measures.

Sometime in late June or early July Glencairn was appointed acting commander-in-chief of the royalist forces in Scotland.[20] His election took place in accordance with a procedure laid down by Charles earlier in the year. In December 1652 the king and his advisers had decided that a council of war, composed of leading men in the Highlands, should elect an interim commander, but Middleton had vetoed this plan as it then stood. In March 1653 the court in exile began to see a way out of the difficulty. A letter had arrived from Glencairn[21] in which he expressed his willingness to join with the rebels, and even to lead them in Middleton's absence. Charles determined to accept this offer, but not to appoint Glencairn outright for fear of offending the other royalist leaders. Therefore, a new commission was drawn up naming as the king's commissioners those men who had been chosen in December, plus Balcarres, Seaforth, the laird of Pluscardine and Glencairn himself. These men were, as before, authorised to choose a commander, but now Charles added his personal recommendation that the man for the job was Glencairn. At the same time, Glencairn was issued with an absolute commission which *did* appoint him outright, but he was instructed to produce this only if the commissioners refused to take Charles's hint and elect him voluntarily. In the event, Glencairn did not find it necessary to produce this personal commission at his election, but later in the summer he was to use it to good effect when his authority was challenged by Balcarres.[22]

It is difficult to estimate the exact strength of the Royalists at this point. In July the Royalists abroad believed that 13 'Earls and Barons' had declared for the king, and that those in arms numbered 7000 men; by September Hyde believed this number had risen to 10,000.[23] These figures were almost certainly wild exaggerations. For although the Royalists were split up into small groups, thus making an estimate of their total strength difficult both for contemporaries and for later writers, there was nothing in the reports which the English received in 1653 to suggest that the total could reach these heights. Rarely did any band of men number more than 100, and even when several leaders joined forces, their combined strength was still relatively small. In August, Lorne, Glengarry, Glencairn and one of the chiefs of the Macleans were accompanied by only 1300 men all told.[24] Perhaps the English tended to minimise the strength of their enemy, but certainly the Royalists exaggerated their own numbers, and for good reason. Throughout the summer and autumn, as the English well knew, the Royalists were content 'not so much to doe any thing against the English, as to make some noyse of a partie, to encourage the king's friends abroad to send him supplies of men, armes and money'.[25] Therefore, in order to convince their adherents in Europe that they were worth supporting, the Royalists in Scotland had to stress their successes rather than their failures in the reports which they sent overseas.

The Royalists' policy of avoiding direct engagements with the English and instead concentrating on extorting men, money and other supplies from the countryside began to pay dividends in the latter half of 1653, not least because it put the initiative of individual commanders at a premium and lessened the chances of disagreement between rival officers. In their attempts to raise money, and in particular to force the population to render to them instead of to the English their contributions to the assessment, the Royalists used a nice mixture of the carrot and the stick. Thus Kenmore ordered the inhabitants of Crieff to hand over only three-quarters of their assessment to the Royalists, and to keep the remainder to themselves; but he also threatened harsh reprisals if the parish should default on the stated sum.[26] The Royalists' success in seizing these taxes both from the population and from the tax collectors began to worry the English in the autumn of 1653. In September Lilburne found it necessary to tighten up regulations for the collection of the cess in order to ensure that the local collectors kept the money in the safest place possible, and from then on several orders were issued for the army in the localities to mount guard on the collectors and generally to assist them in the performance of their duties.[27] Even so, in December Lilburne complained to Lambert that only half the assessment could safely be gathered in.[28]

The Royalists were not slow to demand other supplies as well. In July, for example, the laird of Grantully in Perthshire had been ordered to hand over his house to the rebels, and by December, in response to an English proclamation ordering the seizure of all serviceable horses, Glencairn himself had issued a proclamation forbidding the inhabitants of certain shires south of the Forth to sell or deliver up their arms and horses to the enemy. The penalty he pronounced for disobedience was sequestration of goods and gear, and he followed this up in February 1654 by threatening to proceed with fire and sword against anyone who ignored his summons to take up arms for the royalist cause.[29]

The success of these appeals and threats was not as great as the Royalists hoped, principally because of the continuing strength of the English army, but nonetheless the response to them was sufficient to cause Lilburne considerable anxiety. In July and August he noted that many Lowlanders were eluding the watchful eye of the English garrisons and escaping to the hills.[30] By the autumn the Royalists were taking the initiative and swooping into the Lowlands on lightning raids;[31] and by late November they had penetrated as far south as Galloway and

Carlisle.[32] During this period the Royalists also made a significant advance when a party under Lorne and Kenmore penetrated into Argyllshire. Although they were unable to overrun the whole shire, they secured the submission of the men of Kintyre and for a time seemed poised to challenge the army's control over the whole area. Their presence also threatened to upset the recently cemented alliance between the English and the Marquis of Argyle, on whom Lilburne had come increasingly to depend for assistance and information about the Royalists' movements in the west and north-west of Scotland.[33]

In his letters to Whitehall, Lilburne had to strike a balance between emphasising the spread of the insurrection so that his pleas for reinforcements and other supplies would be listened to, and assuring the authorities that the danger could be contained, in order to justify his own handling of the situation. In September he reported that the Highlanders were making little headway in their attempts to strike at the bases of English power in Scotland, although they were having considerable success in murdering stray English soldiers, revenue officers and other officials as they went about their business in the hills.[34] In October, however, after the relative success of Lorne and Kenmore's expedition to Argyllshire, Lilburne had to 'confesse this businesse begins to looke more suspitiously than before', although he was still confident that the Royalists could not achieve much that winter.[35] In the following month Lilburne reported that the insurrection was spreading and that the Scots people as a whole welcomed it; although towards the end of the month his opinion changed again, and he was more inclined to put stress on the impressions of loyalty he had received from some of the Lowland shires.[36]

By December 1653 the main body of the royalist forces, including the troops under the immediate command of Glencairn, Glengarry, Lorne and Kenmore had retreated northwards to the region of Badenoch, to the south of Inverness.[37] This was an anxious month for the army, although the gloom was not entirely unrelieved. Lilburne wrote to Cromwell on the 3rd intimating that although the rising was not general, yet it was very dangerous, and 'people almost universally have a kinde of muttering and expectation of some change.' By Christmas, he had come to the conclusion that the only course open to the army was to pen the Royalists into the hills, although for this he must have more men. Otherwise, he warned Lambert, the enemy would increase in number and the English would have no option but to withdraw into their garrisons and surrender control of the Highlands to the Royalists. The retreat of the enemy northwards had, the English believed, been occasioned by the hope that supplies from the Dutch would be landed there, and so Lilburne naturally pinned his main hopes for a revival of English fortunes on the successful conclusion of the Anglo-Dutch war.[38] But at the same time he was a little cheered by news of two military successes: on 10 and 12 December the Lord Kinoule's regiment was surprised by the English and on 30 December Kinoule and some of his men were captured at Glamis; while also on 12 December Sir Arthur Forbes was defeated in a skirmish at Borthwick Brae.[39] Moreover, in the New Year news reached headquarters of a rift between Lorne and Glencairn, which seriously threatened the unity of the royalist command.[40]

In December a member of Col. Overton's regiment, who had been a prisoner for some weeks in the hands of the Royalists, reported that they had about 8000 men at their call, but Lilburne did not altogether credit this. In January 1654 another English estimate put the number actually in arms at between 4 and 5000.[41] But royalist expectations were much higher. The English intercepted letters from Perthshire which optimistically stated that by March 1654 the royalist levies would have raised 20,000 foot and 5000 horse; that soon the king would land in Scotland with 3000 Dutch horse and 10,000 foot; and that even at the time of writing (January 1654) the royalist army consisted of 9 or 10,000 men.[42]

At the beginning of 1654 Glencairn and his forces continued to ravage the shires of Moray and Nairn and to harass local property-owners. On 18 and 19 January they laid siege to Lethen House, home of Alexander Brodie of Lethen and his sons, and inflicted damage allegedly worth £2109 1s. 8d. stg. '[T]he great swearings, cursings, drinkings, whoorings of that Highland crew' much offended the local people, who greeted Col. Morgan's arrival in the district as 'a great delyverye'.[43] Morgan and Fitch's success in forcing the Royalists to retreat from the open plains was welcomed by Lilburne, but these reverses seemed only to make the rebels more desperate. Shortly after, Lilburne reported that the number of atrocities committed by the king's men was on the increase, and he attributed this to the influence of the young Marquis of Montrose, who had lately acceded to Lorne's command. In the first few months of the year the royalist leadership received other notable additions, including Lord Charles Gordon, the Earl of Mar, Lord Forrester, Lord Dudhope and the Earl of Selkirk.[44]

Despite this, things were quieter at the beginning of February, and Morgan continued to score some successes, as when he routed the forces of Glencairn and Kenmore at Cromar and pursued the latter to Kildrummy. Kildrummy Castle in Aberdeenshire had been garrisoned by the Royalists, but Morgan forced it to surrender and replaced the garrison with his own men.[45] Col. Daniel, meanwhile, was doing well in Perthshire, having captured over one hundred of Atholl's and Forbes's men at Dunkeld.[46] To these reverses for the royalist cause was added yet another dispute in the leadership, this time between Glencairn and Sir Mungo Murray over who should command the Stirlingshire levies.[47]

The one bonus for the Royalists during this month had been the arrival of a messenger from France; this, according to Lilburne, had made them a little more lively than of late. There was no doubt that, despite the positive successes notched up by the English, the Royalists were still planning to unite their scattered forces and hoping for a sudden break-through. As always, their hopes were pinned on help from abroad, and accordingly the news that Middleton had landed at Tarbatness at the end of February quickened the pulses on both sides.[48]

Middleton had at last left Holland for Scotland in accordance with instructions from the king, dated 27 January 1654 [O.S.]. At the beginning of February, there were rumours at court that the king himself was planning on going to Scotland to lead his army, but these, like all the previous stories to that effect, came to naught. When Middleton arrived in Scotland, he had with him Sir George Monro, Lord Napier, Major General Dalziel, Ludovic Drummond and about 80 followers. In addition he brought a quantity of ammunition, described by the English as 'nott many more than ten horse load'. (Later, however, Lilburne put the exact amount at 300 barrels of powder and 5000 arms — much more than the initial estimate.)[49] Such supplies fell far short of the great expectations which the Scots had had of their foreign friends. Middleton, for his part, was sorely disappointed at the state of the cause in Scotland — such, perhaps, was not what he had been led to believe by the glowing propaganda reports that the Highlanders had sent to encourage their allies on the Continent. Indeed, he could not bring himself to write to Nicholas until the end of May, when he explained that he 'did not meet with so cleer a bussiness' as he had expected on arrival, and that therefore he had put off writing until he had more cheerful news.[50]

Nonetheless, in the course of March the English intelligence system reported renewed activity in the north; this led Lilburne to despair lest that 'mouldering away' of the royalist cause which he had noted in February should be halted. On 23 March he told Cromwell that 'there are risinges in all Countries in considerable numbers', and that '[i]tt will bee necessary that provision bee made for the worst that can happen.' On 1 April he was more gloomy still: 'there is still a worse and worse complexion uppon these people . . . within these 14 dayes more are broke out in rebellion then have done all this Winter', and in consequence 'I am doubtfull the flame heere may bee farre beyond what may bee yett imagined by your Highnesse, or indeed by many that are heere.'[51] Royalist strength fluctuated, of course, from one part of the country to another: as the main body of the king's forces moved about the country, one area would fall quiet, only to burst into flame again when the insurgents returned. What really worried Lilburne at the end of March and the beginning of April was that the danger of insurrection seemed likely to overtake the Lowlands. In previous months he had hoped that if the Royalists could be contained on the far side of the Highland line, their power would be dissipated and they would fall to mutual squabbling. Hence when Dumfries and Galloway rose in the last days of March, he was anxious and not a little surprised, as this region was the last he had expected to defect from its loyalty to the Commonwealth. Although the risings in these parts were quickly put down, others broke out again almost immediately: it was this jack-in-the-box quality of the insurrection that made it so difficult to deal with. Moreover, the Royalists were still quite strong in numbers; on an English estimate, early in April the main body of their troops numbered over 5000, and there were many other smaller parties of indeterminate strength.[52]

Meanwhile, in the far north, Morgan was chasing Middleton and by mid-April had advanced to the borders of Sutherland. He had not yet been able to catch up with the royalist forces there and force them to an engagement, but his steady advance had much reduced their morale. News of further quarrels among the commanding officers had also seeped through to Lilburne: Glencairn and Sir George Monro, one of the officers brought over by Middleton, had had a furious duel and a similar fracas between Glengarry and Atholl had been narrowly averted.[53]

Lilburne reported these latter events to the Protector on 20 April 1654: this was almost his last communication from Scotland as acting commander-in-chief. By 22 April George Monck had arrived to take over the command, the cessation of the Dutch war having at last freed him from his duties as General-at-Sea.[54] During the sixteen months since Deane's departure from Scotland, Lilburne had seen the rising grow from a series of uncoordinated disturbances in the Highland zone to a full-scale military revolt which threatened to spread to the Lowlands as well. Clearly, the Royalists had succeeded in driving the English on to the defensive and in threatening the army's ability to maintain control over the country. Yet, despite the progress which the king's cause had made in Scotland, there were major weaknesses in the royalist campaign. These prevented the movement from achieving the strength and coordination necessary to topple English power in Scotland, while at the same time they provided loopholes through which the army could hope to win the allegiance — practical if not emotional — of key figures in the Scottish community. Thus, in addition to the inadequacies of the Royalists' military effort, the intricate pattern of conflicting loyalties and competing interests within Scottish society helped also to undermine the royalist cause.

ii. Patterns of allegiance and support, January 1653 — April 1654

The difficulties which the Royalists encountered in their attempts to build up and sustain their campaign against the English army in Scotland were of two main kinds: first, the difficulty of translating the widespread sympathy for them into active physical support; and second, the difficulty of preventing their supporters, once they had actually taken up arms, from nullifying their advantages by indulging in internecine feuds. These problems were especially important insofar as they affected the higher echelons of command. To a large extent, the history of the rising throughout 1653 and the early part of 1654 can be considered, from the royalist point of view, in terms of the hesitancy of many chieftains, nobles and lairds to declare outright their adherence to the cause and in terms of the disputes within the leadership. As a corollary, the English advantage during this phase of the rising lay in their ability to attract the support of those who saw their personal or material interests threatened by the nature of the royalist campaign, and, in particular, in their ability to secure the co-operation of the Marquis of Argyle.

On the royalist side, examples of the chiefs' and nobles' reluctance to commit themselves to the king's cause can be found at all stages of the rising. At the beginning of 1653, when the royalist campaign was in its infancy, Glengarry had met with the chieftains' unwillingness to declare themselves openly. In May, when Seaforth presided over a meeting at Glenelg, the English learned that the Tutor of Lovat, the Captain of Clanranald, one of the Macleods and some others had refused to attend.[55] But some of the most intriguing examples of this phenomenon come from the response of the Highland nobility to Glencairn's summons of 13 June. John Macdonald (the brother of Glengarry), Macneill of Barra, Maclean of Lochbuy, and Argyle's son, Lorne, all failed to attend the meeting at Lochaber. Macdonald[56] and Macneill[57] each wrote to Glencairn explaining that his letter had arrived too late for them to make the journey in time — perhaps not an unreasonable excuse. But Lorne's reply,[58] although it too mentioned that the time allotted for the journey was too short, included an unconvincing story that Lorne had neither horses nor servants for the journey. Maclean of Lochbuy refrained from giving an explicit excuse on this occasion, but one month later he again refused to come to a meeting with Glencairn on the grounds that his presence was required in his own territory.[59] One may wonder just how sincere the protestations of good faith which the writers included in their letters were, especially since news of English victories in the Anglo-Dutch war was, at this time, having a generally disheartening effect on royalist morale.[60] Since help from the Dutch was considered, in many quarters at home and abroad, to be an essential prerequisite of royalist success, they may have felt it more prudent, when the Dutch suffered reverses, to wait upon events.

Yet many of the nobility and gentry had more immediate and practical reasons for continuing to hedge their bets. The Earl of Atholl, whose lands in Perthshire were vulnerable to attack from both sides, was in a particularly difficult position. Atholl's sympathies undoubtedly lay with the Royalists, and to the best of his ability he tried to lend them active support in the summer of 1653. But the presence of the English army in Perthshire prevented him, or at least his tenants, from yielding to the Highlanders' demands that the assessment should be paid to them and not to the English. Atholl's tenants were only too aware of the reprisals which the English visited on those who did not pay the cess: early in June the refusal of some of the Macnabs to render their assessment to the English had led to a skirmish with the army in which the laird of Macnab was killed.[61] When Atholl's tenants continued to pay taxes to the English, Glengarry was furious and wrote to Atholl informing him that the Highlanders would consider themselves justified in plundering his lands in reprisal. Atholl therefore wrote immediately to Charles to declare his devotion to the royalist cause,[62] but the incident with the Macnabs had clearly impressed on him the need to tread carefully, for his activities on behalf of the king were somewhat muted. In August, Lilburne reported to Cromwell that, in opposition to the wishes of the Perthshire gentry, he had formed a small party of about 20 men and engaged with the Highlanders; but from then until November, when he was again reported to be in arms, he appears to have kept relatively quiet.[63]

Atholl's case is an interesting one not merely because it illumines the Earl's personal dilemma. It also illustrates the tensions and the divergence of interests which could exist between landlord and tenant, and between nobility and gentry. In the three-cornered dispute between the English, the Royalists and Atholl over the payment of the assessment, it seems likely that the short-term material interests of the tenants predominated in the decision to hand over their contributions. This did not mean, of course, that Atholl's interests had been entirely overborne, for in the long run his interests in his property could not be divorced from those of his tenants. Nor did it mean that the tenantry were now safe from all attack, for by choosing to comply with the English, they still ran the risk of being plundered by the Royalists. Nonetheless the actions of the men of Atholl ensured that in the summer months of 1653 the Earl was forced to moderate his royalist ardour and was prevented from taking the body of his tenants over to the royalist cause.

The attitude of the Perthshire gentry to Atholl's activities is also significant. When in August and again in November the Earl took up arms for the royalist cause, they made plain their disapproval of his actions. *Mercurius Politicus* reported in November that 'the considerable Barons of Athole' had refused to assist the Earl, and some of them had fled to the governor of Blair Castle for protection. They had given as their reason for not wishing to join the Royalists the fact that they had 'had too large a share in the former sufferings for the King; and now having engaged to live peaceably, and give submission to the union, they will rather lose their crops than their inheritance.'[64] These gentlemen, or others living nearby, had already in June 1653 presented Lilburne with an engagement not to act against the English government.[65] There is no reason to suppose that this engagement was extorted from them unwillingly or that the sentiments they expressed in November were false: on the contrary, the previous history of the shire suggests that all landholders on the Highland/Lowland line had overwhelming reasons for voluntarily helping the army to maintain peace in the shire. Fear of Highland insurgents and the damage they might do to property was a constant factor in the calculations of the Lowland gentry. Protection from such attacks had been one of the 'Desires' put forward by Perthshire's representatives at Dalkeith in March 1652. In September of that year, eight parishes within the shire had been granted an abatement of their cess to allow them to maintain a guard against Highland robbers, and Lilburne reaffirmed this concession in the summer of 1653.[66] This meant, in effect, that for purely practical reasons the interests of Scots and English in Perthshire coincided, and that the army was able to play on the gentry's fears, which had arisen long before the English conquest, to support its own endeavours during Glencairn's rising.

The attitude of the Perthshire gentry has some parallels with that of Sir James Macdonald of Sleat, who in February 1653 wrote to Col. Thomas Fitch, governor of Inverness, informing him of Glengarry's movements. Sir James's letter[67] held out the promise of future co-operation with the English, but it also indicated that the English would have to pay for such support. Sir James explained to Fitch that he had no intention of joining Glengarry, but that he was worried about the consequences of his loyalty to the English government. He had already been threatened by the Royalists and, he implied, he expected to be recompensed if he suffered for his allegiance to the English. Perhaps Sir James was merely flying a kite on this occasion, to see how the English would react to his enquiries, for the Royalists in exile at this time regarded him as a firm adherent to their cause. In December 1652 he had been named as one of the king's commissioners in Scotland, and in May 1653, months after his first approaches to the English, he may have attended a meeting of royalist chiefs in the northern Highlands.[68] But even if he were hedging his bets in the early months of 1653, Sir James subsequently co-operated with the army, gave them valuable information and assistance, and was suitably rewarded for his pains. Sir James's approaches to the English illustrate the dilemma in which many of the gentry and nobility found themselves in 1653. Quite apart from any ideological commitment to either side, these men had to think of the safety of their property and persons. Thus, as the royalist campaign gathered force, they stood between two fires: if they did not comply with the rebels, their lands and houses might be plundered by the insurgents; if they did go over to the Royalists, their property might be sequestered by the English, or even devastated by the army in the course of its campaigns.

The English faced a parallel dilemma, in that they were torn between cruelty and clemency in the treatment of their enemies. In their dealings with the Scottish people, they had to balance the need to punish recalcitrants with the desire to win friends. Sir James's plea brought this problem into focus for the first time, by stressing that England's allies would expect to receive reparation for any losses they might suffer in their stand against the Royalists. In February 1653 Lilburne made no firm promises to Sir James,[69] but he began to grope towards a solution to the problem. Eventually, the answer was found in the assessment; loyal friends, such as Sir James himself, were granted an abatement of their cess to compensate them for their losses, while others whose allegiance was in the balance were offered a similar concession as an inducement to support the régime. In February, Lilburne put this policy into practice by granting an abatement of a month's cess to the people of Badenoch in the belief that 'nothing will encourage them [to remain loyal] more then their owne particular advantage.'[70]

It was clear, therefore, that the tensions and weaknesses in the royalist cause could provide the English with opportunities for building up support within the Scottish community, but such support would be translated into practical help only if the English offered inducements, and protection, to their allies. The ability to win friends at all levels of society became more important as the guerilla tactics of the Royalists turned the war into one for the support of the local population, but as a practical matter the loyalty of one leading nobleman could count for more than the grudging allegiance of many of the common people. It was greatly to the English advantage therefore that they were able to attract the support of the Marquis of Argyle. Throughout the period of the rising Argyle lent positive aid to the English army, while his eldest son and heir sided openly with the king's men.

The motives which prompted Argyle to co-operate with the English military government, and in particular the extent to which his private sympathies now lay with the English rather than the king, are matters which remain open for debate. Nonetheless it is clear that, having already come to terms with the English, Argyle had good reason to throw in his lot with them. His previous attempts to hold out against the conquerors had been primarily motivated not by sympathy for, or collusion with, the chieftains and noblemen who were then in association with Glengarry but by a desire to manoeuvre himself into a good bargaining position for the sake of his material and political self-preservation. Consequently, although Argyle's interests might in the long term be served by a royalist restoration, in the short term, given the fact of English conquest, he had much to gain by translating his desire for self-preservation into active co-operation with the occupying power. For Argyle himself and the lands over which he ruled were in deep financial and economic difficulties. The devastations of the last decade or so of warfare, and in particular the depredations of the Scottish and Irish Macdonalds, had left Argyllshire and the surrounding territory in a much impoverished state. As a result, the inhabitants professed themselves unable to pay the English assessment. Throughout the Marquis's negotiations with the English, and also in the related activities of the shire deputies at Dalkeith, the question of the cess had bulked large. It had in fact become as much a political as a financial issue: the withholding of payment by Argyle's followers, and the attempts of the English to enforce its collection, became a trial of strength between the two parties. By the agreement of October 1652 the 'Gentlemen and people' of Argyllshire had promised faithfully to render their dues, but in the late summer of 1653, the Marquis was corresponding regularly with Lilburne on the subject of an abatement. Lilburne prevaricated, but in September conceded the point that some of the assessment could be rendered in kind.[71] In trying to beat down the English demands, Argyle may have hoped that his co-operation during the rising would be rewarded by concessions over the assessment. In fact, his most strenuous efforts regarding the cess came in the month or so after he had tried to show his own good faith by publicly denouncing his son's defection to the Royalists. Success in this sphere would, moreover, have political implications for the Marquis: the mere fact that he acted as the representative of the shire's interests was in itself a recognition of his quasi-independent status in the region; while victory in the matter of the assessment would not only strengthen the shire's position vis-a-vis the English, and Argyle's position vis-a-vis the shire, but would also reinforce the Marquis's own standing in relation to the English government. Argyle's own financial position may also have helped to dictate his attitude to the English in 1653. During the 1640s Argyle had contracted enormous debts on behalf of the Scottish nation; these were to be repaid out of public taxation, but the disappearance of an independent Scottish government in 1651 meant that, unless the English government accepted liability, Argyle would have no hope of recovering what was due to him. Having once submitted to the English, therefore, Argyle had every reason for doing all in his power to persuade the conquerors to accept this responsibility for the debts of their victims. In later years, he was to petition the Council of State to that end, and to meet with some success, and it is not unlikely that his collusion with the English in 1653 was the first step in this campaign. Indeed, the letter he wrote to Lilburne in July 1653, in which he informed the commander that his son had left Inveraray to join the Royalists, contained veiled hints about the 'violence of creditours'.[72]

Weighty considerations of material self-interest thus pushed Argyle towards co-operation with the army, but his decision to side openly with the English was probably reached only after much hesitancy and heart-searching. Some observers thought in March and April 1653 that Argyle's loyalties still lay firmly with the king. One English visitor to Scotland reported that 'that great Polititian', the Marquis of Argyle, had sold his cannon to the English in 1652 knowing full well that he could re-arm his castle at any time he liked, for he had 'four and forty piece of brazen canon at his command lying upon the coast of Kintyre, buried within the sea-mark, and recoverable in eight-and-forty hours' time'.[73] In April Sir Robert Moray, Balcarres' brother-in-law, wrote to Charles II assuring him that Argyle still retained some devotion to the king's service but that he thought 'men and things are not yet rype enough to appeare here in armes'; therefore, for his own preservation, Argyle was for the moment lying low.[74]

Possibly in the spring of 1653, Argyle was genuinely in two minds about his relationship with the English government, but Lorne's open defection to the Royalists in July forced him to clarify his own position, at any rate to Lilburne. Lorne's royalist sympathies had been known to the English and to Glencairn for some time, but throughout June and the first half of July he remained in the bosom of his family. His reply to Glencairn's summons to attend the meeting at Lochaber on 1 July was written from Inveraray, the family seat, on 28 June.[75] But sometime during the third week in July matters came to a head between father and son. On 15 July Lilburne had written to Argyle ordering him to keep his shire free from royalist commotions, and to apprehend all suspicious persons within his territory.[76] But before this letter could reach Inveraray, Argyle had already had a stormy interview with Lorne. As Argyle explained in a letter to Lilburne written probably on 20 July, Lorne refused either to confirm or deny that he intended to engage with the Royalists. Actions soon spoke louder than words: on 18 July, immediately after the interview, he took horse and left Inveraray to join Auchinbreck, McNaughton and Sir Arthur Forbes who, with other Royalists, had gathered near Glenorchy. Argyle then sent his son a strongly worded letter, condemning his actions, in which he threatened:

> if there be in you either feare of God, or respect to his law in your obedience to your Parents, or any feare of the curse pronounced in God's word against the setters lightly of either father or mother, or if you desire not their curse to follow you in all your waies, These are requiring you as you will answere for it one day before the Throne of God, and as you desire to be free of all the guiltinesse and prejudice which will follow such waies, and as you desire to enjoy any thing that is mine, or would eschue to deserve my curse, that you will hearken to my counsell to forbeare such courses . . .[77]

The contents of this letter were quite clearly designed for public consumption. Argyle enclosed a copy of it in his letter to Lilburne, and it was undoubtedly aimed at the English as much as, perhaps more than, at Lorne. Argyle was quite desperate to convince the English of his good faith. On the following day, 21 July, he received Lilburne's letter of the 15th. He immediately sent off a reply, again acknowledging his son's defection but assuring Lilburne that 'there is not any at all that concernes this shire that countenances him in his present course and present resolutions', except a few gentlemen of whom the principal was Auchinbreck. For good measure, Argyle also stressed that the gentlemen of the shire were most willing to pay their assessment, if only they could find the money. There also reached army headquarters a copy of a letter sent to Lorne by some prominent members of the clan Campbell in which they too exhorted him to abjure his rebellious ways.[78]

The fact that Argyle's perorations against his son were specifically designed to impress Lilburne must cast some doubt on their sincerity. Yet the same sentiments were expressed in a letter from the Marquis to his kinsman, John Campbell, fiar of Glenorchy, written on 13 August 1653. The first part of this letter concerned a fairly acrimonious dispute between Argyle and Glenorchy over other family matters, but Argyle then went on:

> As for what you say anent my sonne, tho I know nothing of the particular yit I can beleeve your information for I trust nothing to him but that he will run to every exces of ryot with the wyldest that ar his associats, and as I told you before I doe still advyse you not to suffer him nor any of his complices to enter in any of your houses, and I dischairg you of any preiudice by me tho you kill him in keeping him out by force . . . [79]

Such harshness on the part of a father towards his son, especially when the recipient of the letter was none other than Lorne's godfather,[80] appears quite unreal in the context of seventeenth-century Gaelic society. Was this letter too part of an elaborate public relations exercise? Argyle did not send a copy of this letter to Lilburne: but he may have banked on its being intercepted by the English, or on Glenorchy independently informing them of its contents. Whatever the true motive, it seems likely that Argyle's feelings towards Lorne on this occasion were too complex to be contained within the norms of Gaelic society. The outlook of a clan chief was only one factor in Argyle's make-up. It was, to be sure, his position as chief of the Campbells and hereditary overlord of vast tracts of land in the west and north of Scotland that since the 1630s had provided him with his power-base in Scottish politics. But his diverse experiences on the national political scene had left their mark on his character and on the methods which he chose to preserve his interests. By the 1650s, therefore, Argyle's interests had extended beyond those of a mere clan chief, and the methods which he used to uphold these interests were correspondingly complex.

Whatever the sincerity of Argyle's injunction to Glenorchy, the English, for their part, were more likely to be impressed by deeds than by words. In this respect, too, in the late summer and early autumn of 1653, Argyle gave evidence of his loyalty, for during this period he lent tangible aid to the English army and in so doing incurred the wrath of the Royalists. Both the army's success in its expedition to the Western Isles in August/September, and the failure of Lorne and Kenmore's attempt to overrun Argyllshire in September/October owed something to Argyle's intervention. On the other hand, he was not able to induce his followers to help the people of Kintyre in their opposition to his son and to Kenmore when they marched into that part of Argyllshire, so that on balance Lilburne felt justified in retaining some suspicions of the Marquis's sincerity.

In August, the English army embarked upon its one decisive military manoeuvre during this phase of the rising — the reduction of the isles of Lewis and Mull. The assault on Lewis was in part a reprisal for Seaforth's conduct towards the English earlier in the summer, but the larger objective of the expedition was to secure the northern and western isles against invasion. The Council of State still feared that the Dutch would send ships to these coasts with supplies for the Royalists, and so had constantly enjoined the commander-in-chief in Scotland to keep a close watch over the northern waters.[81] The army landed on Lewis around 20 August. Meeting with very little resistance from the inhabitants, they planted a garrison at Loughsternay. From there, on 27 August, Col. Cobbett sailed towards Mull, an island which lay inside the bounds of Argyllshire, but which was under the immediate control of the royalist Maclean of Duart. The Marquis of Argyle, however, used his influence to undermine that of Maclean. Maclean and Glencairn were both on the island towards the end of August, but when the English arrived, they decamped to Tiree. Argyle, meanwhile, induced the heritors of Mull to submit to the English, to promise to pay their cess 'as the rest of the shire of Argile doth', and to withhold payment of their rents to Maclean so long as he should remain in rebellion.[82]

Owing to a storm which wrecked his supply vessels, Cobbett had to return to the Lowlands by land. This involved a hazardous journey through Argyllshire to Dumbarton, during which the English ran the risk of being attacked by the Highlanders under Kenmore and Lorne, who were currently active in the area. Yet again, Argyle came to the assistance of the English. His people acted as guides to the army through the difficult terrain, and Argyle himself played a key part in saving them from a surprise attack by Kenmore. The latter, on hearing of the enemy's march to Dumbarton, had hastened thither from Loch Tay, only to find that 'oure unnaturall cuntriman', the Marquis of Argyle, had stolen a march on them. He in person had conducted the English to Loch Goyle where he had commandeered all the available herring boats to transport them in safety to Dumbarton. Kenmore had to settle for a short skirmish with some of the soldiers in the town. As Lilburne later reported to Cromwell, Cobbett acknowledged 'his saifety was under God in the Lord Argill's favour to him'.[83]

Yet Argyle either could not or would not force his followers in the shire to take up arms against Lorne when the latter penetrated deep into his father's territory. This part of the royalist campaign occupied the months of September and October, and hence overlapped with Cobbett's return from Mull. A key incident in the campaign was Lorne and Kenmore's struggle, stretching over several weeks, to secure the loyalty of the men of Kintyre. The distinctive feature of Kintyre was the presence in the peninsula of a body of Lowland settlers who had in the 1640s been staunch supporters of the presbyterian cause and who enjoyed the special protection of Argyle. Recently, the original settlers had been joined by a group of Remonstrants under the leadership of William Ralston, who had served in the western army of 1650. Their loyalty both to Argyle and to the English government in 1653 was not in doubt. Indeed in August, they had on their own initiative made plans to arm themselves against a possible royalist attack from Colonel McNaughton, a member of Kenmore's party and previously a man of some influence in Kintyre. Lilburne, however, had taken exception to the gentlemen of Kintyre arming themselves without prior authority from him, and remonstrated with Argyle on the subject. This apparent churlishness on Lilburne's part may have made Argyle lukewarm in his later attempts to get the rest of the shire to support the men of Kintyre. At any rate, although on 3 September Lorne complained to Glencairn that his father's power in the shire of

Argyll was hindering him from raising men there, little positive effort seems to have been made by the Marquis or his followers to go to the help of Kintyre. Early in October, Argyle told Lilburne that 'his Country men and Clan doe nott answer his expectation in joyning with him to oppose Kenmore'; and later he attributed the shire's dilatoriness to a desire not to offend Lorne. The English army also refrained from answering Kintyre's pleas for help; the settlers hoped for reinforcements from the garrison at Ayr, but these were not forthcoming. As a result, Kintyre capitulated to Lorne, but the Royalists were not able to press home their advantage to the extent of overrunning other parts of the shire.[84]

Argyle's reluctance to make his co-operation with the English open and explicit, and his undoubted preference for working behind the scenes, may have led the English to believe, as indeed was probably the case, that his willingness to assist them had definite limits; but it did not stop the Royalists from identifying him as their arch-enemy among the Scots. The mere suspicion that Argyle's influence might be at work was enough to create mutual distrust in the royalist camp. In July, the laird of Macfarlane felt it necessary to defend himself against any possible charge that he had been suborned by Argyle, whom he had lately met to discuss purely personal matters; his passivity in the royalist cause, he explained in a letter to Glencairn, was entirely due to other reasons.[85] In October, Glengarry also warned Glencairn that Argyle had restrained Cameron of Lochiel, who in turn was attempting to restrain Seaforth, from attending a royalist rendezvous, and that, moreover, Argyle would do all in his power to prevent Glencairn from raising men in his bounds.[86] The royalist view of Argyle's influence was summed up in the instructions which Glencairn issued to the king's agent, Major Strachan, at the end of 1653, for communication to the king himself. Glencairn asked '[f]irst, and above all,' that Argyle be declared a traitor and that the Highlanders be encouraged to engage against him. To this end, Glencairn suggested, Charles should send letters to several clan chiefs 'assuringe them that his Majesty will deliver them from under those bonds and yoakes which Argyll has purchased over their heads'.[87]

The accession of Argyle to the English cause had, therefore, not only strengthened the army's support in the west and north of Scotland but had helped to sow dissension in the royalist camp. Argyle's relationship with the English government was, however, based on the principle of *quid pro quo*; in return for his help the Marquis clearly hoped for some alleviation of the shire's fiscal burdens and, perhaps, for some support and protection against his enemies in Scotland. Because of his staunch covenanting past, his ambivalent relations with Charles II and his hostility to the house of Hamilton (to which Glencairn was related),[88] Argyle had much to lose in the event of a royalist victory. He therefore had some reason to throw in his lot with the English, who in turn had much to gain by encouraging this latest expression of rivalry with the leaders of the king's cause in Scotland. The case of Argyle was, then, a further example of the way in which the English could hope to turn the existing feuds within the Scottish community to their own advantage in their search for support amongst the Scottish people.

Traditional enmities were also responsible for fomenting disputes within the royalist leadership itself. These disputes, rather than the malevolence of Argyle, were a major factor in halting the further progress of royalist arms in 1653, although Glencairn, for one, was only too ready to lay the blame for the Royalists' failures at the Marquis's door.[89] Ironically, however, Argyle's son, Lorne, whose defection to the king's cause had signified a major victory for the Royalists in July, took a leading part in many of these quarrels.

Baillie aptly summarised the effect of these disputes on the royalist cause when he wrote, 'behold inward division doth hazard all at the very beginning.'[90] Both the Royalists abroad and the Cromwellians at home fully expected the mutual hostility of Highlanders and Lowlanders to be a major cause of dispute. In July, Lilburne was informed that 'the greatest designe the Lowland Lords have, is to make themselves soe strong as is possible of Lowland men [and] of strangers that they may thereby not onely secuer themselves from the barbarous cruelty and treachery of the Highlanders but likewayes they may keepe them in awe.'[91] When Glencairn, a Lowlander, was appointed to the overall command of the royalist forces, some of the Highland chiefs naturally resented this threat to their authority and independence; but ironically the protagonist of the anti-Glencairn faction was another Lowlander, the Earl of Balcarres. The dispute between the two men lasted throughout the summer and winter of 1653, but it crystallised around July/August on the question of the command. Balcarres had already come under some suspicion in orthodox royalist circles at home and abroad because of his connection with Col. John Bampfield. Bampfield was suspected (rightly) of being in Cromwell's pay, although he was ostensibly acting on behalf of the Royalists. In March Nicholas informed Hyde that he believed Bampfield regularly betrayed the Highlanders' plans to Argyle, and hence to the English, and in August Middleton believed Bampfield to be an agent of the Earl of Dysart, whose daughter was on friendly terms with Cromwell.[92] Balcarres' attitude to Glencairn, however, was prompted by personal hostility and not, as his connection with Bampfield might suggest, by pro-Cromwellian leanings. In July and August he and Glencairn had a sharp exchange of letters on the subject of the latter's pre-eminence.[93] Balcarres then went the length of advocating that the Royalists should be ruled by a committee without any supreme officer and tried to win Lorne, Seaforth and Atholl over to his side. This conspiracy was stifled only when Glencairn produced his personal commission from the king.[94] Charles, for his part, tried to pacify Balcarres by explaining that Glencairn's appointment was decided on at a time when the court abroad believed Balcarres to be dead, or at any rate severely wounded. In October 1653 Charles expressly instructed one of his agents to attempt to compose the feud between the two men, but the estrangement continued until Balcarres left Scotland for the Continent in the spring of 1654. Even then, he made many attempts to poison the exiles' minds against Glencairn and Middleton.[95]

Lorne's involvement in this dispute had been slight, but at the same time as Balcarres had been trying to draw him into the plot to oust Glencairn, he himself had been quarrelling with Kenmore and with Glengarry. The quarrel with Glengarry also arose over Lorne's hostility to Glencairn's role as interim commander. Lorne, Balcarres and some others had written to the king expressing their discontent with Glencairn's command, and when Glencairn got wind of this, he promptly despatched Glengarry to arrest Lorne. As a result, when the two men met sometime in September, they drew swords on each other, 'but were prevented from fighting, yet parted great enemies'.[96]

Lorne's dispute with Kenmore arose during their joint expedition to Kintyre in October 1653. The nub of the matter was that when Ralston and his men surrendered the castle of Lochheid, Lorne, mindful perhaps of the interests of those whose lands lay within his family's sphere of influence, gave them better terms than his colleague thought was justified. Kenmore then rode off to lodge a complaint with Glencairn, and the subsequent failure of the two men to co-operate in Argyllshire accounts in some measure for the poor results the royalist campaign achieved in that area.[97] Two months later Lorne was embroiled in another argument, this time with Glencairn.

By December 1653 the main body of the royalist forces under Glencairn had withdrawn to Badenoch. This area lay indirectly under the control of the Marquis of Argyle: the lands belonged to the Marquis of Huntly, Argyle's nephew, but because the latter was his uncle's debtor, Argyle was responsible for taking up the rents. When, therefore, in the last days of December Glencairn ordered the men of Badenoch to be ready to join the royalist cause, Lorne tried to use the region's connection with his father to convince Glencairn that he (Lorne) should have control of any men who were raised in these bounds. Glencairn refused outright. Lorne then stormed out of the royalist camp and tried to betray Glencairn to the English. But the letter which Lorne wrote to Capt. John Hill, the governor of Ruthven Castle, was handed over by its bearer to Kenmore; while Glencairn sent a party headed by Glengarry and Cameron of Lochiel to apprehend Lorne before he could do any more damage. The quarrel was then patched up, but within a fortnight the Campbells had all deserted from the main body of the royalist forces. To make matters worse, rumour had it that Lorne was now thinking in terms of a reconciliation with his father.[98]

These rifts in the royalist leadership were major setbacks, for they prevented united action at a time when the Royalists were seriously threatening the English army's grip on the country. Moreover, the quarrels of December 1653 and January 1654 occurred on the eve of Middleton's long-awaited landing in Scotland, so that although the Royalists then had a leader who might breathe new life into the cause, he found that the officers under his nominal control were incapable of reconciling their feuds and working together. Middleton's presence in fact exacerbated the tensions within the leadership, for his appointment of Sir George Monro, a professional soldier, as his second-in-command angered Glencairn and caused him to withdraw from the main body of the royalist army.[99]

The significant thing about many of these quarrels was that they owed their bitterness not to the issue in dispute at the time but to rivalries which had their roots in previous Scottish history. Thus, in December, Lorne had chosen to emphasise his rights as heir to Argyle in his dispute with Glencairn who, as a cousin of the late Duke of Hamilton, had a hereditary reason for disliking the family of Argyle. This bias in turn may have influenced Glencairn's decisions then and in October to send Glengarry to apprehend Lorne; for it is otherwise hard to account for his extraordinary tactlessness in sending a Macdonald to arrest a Campbell.

The existence of these weaknesses in the royalist command and the army's ability to attract the support not only of men like Argyle or Macdonald of Sleat but of smaller landowners like the Perthshire gentry boded ill for the long-term prospects of the king's cause in Scotland. The fact that loyalties within the political nation were by no means clear-cut and that concern for material interests might pull against ideological conviction allowed the English to secure the help of some important elements in the Scottish community. Despite the Royalists' undoubted success in weakening the army's hold over the country, these factors therefore throw rather a different light on the picture of English frustration and failure conveyed by Lilburne in his letters to the authorities in Whitehall. By April 1654, Lilburne was in fact showing signs of severe strain in his efforts to cope with the royalist problem. Since January, when Monck's appointment as commander-in-chief in Scotland had been decided upon, he had kept an anxious eye on the progress of the Dutch war in the hope that he would soon be relieved of his command.[100] The irresolution and agonised attention to detail which he had brought to bear upon the problems which first confronted him on his elevation to the command in January 1653 had continued to characterise his approach to the military aspects of Glencairn's rising. The sharp and rapid fluctuations in his assessment of the military situation from January 1653 to April 1654 reflected not only the reality of the rising, but also the lack of self-confidence of a man who felt himself overwhelmed by the demands of his job. It was, therefore, with relief and gratitude that he left Scotland to assume the post of governor of York.[101]

5

Lilburne and the Scottish People, January 1653 — April 1654

ALTHOUGH Lilburne's performance as a soldier had shown that he was 'far from being a resourceful commander', his dealings with the Scottish people proved that '[h]is counsels as a statesman were . . . far more worthy of attention than his military schemes.' As Lilburne realised, it was of the essence of the rising that it drew its strength from 'the rooted hostility of the Scottish people'[1] to the English government; that it fed on the grievances provoked by English policy; and that it was supported morally and materially by a large section of the Scottish community. As the conflict thus turned into a war for the allegiance of the Scottish people, Lilburne had perforce to think as a politician as well as a soldier and to devise means of destroying the rising at its source and not merely on the field of battle. The main problem here was that of achieving an effective combination of conciliation and coercion. For Lilburne had not only to ameliorate the grievances of the Scottish people so that 'civilian' support for the guerilla war wasted away, but had also to ensure that those who did aid the rebels were punished for their crimes. The difficulties inherent in reconciling these aims were well-nigh insuperable, so that by the end of his time in Scotland Lilburne was relying more and more on purely punitive measures to defeat the rising. Yet he never quite lost sight of those solutions which he believed would in the longer term ensure peace and stability in Scotland, and he constantly advocated in his letters to London a reform of English policy towards the Scottish nation. In his analysis of the fundamental ills of the body politic, he was cooler and more realistic than in his appraisal of the military situation, and in his desire for conciliation he showed many statesmanlike qualities. Yet he had also his blind-spots, and none more so than in his attitude towards the Scottish clergy. His antipathy towards the Resolutioners and his belief that the Royalists' success owed much to their influence coloured his whole thinking on the nature of the rising and led him to overestimate the support which the English could expect from those whose dislike of the Resolutioners was equal to his own.

Throughout the rising Lilburne believed that two groups of people, between whom he did not always clearly distinguish in his own mind, could be won over to friendship with the English régime: these were the inhabitants of the western shires, and the members of the Protesters' church party. In April 1653 Lilburne reported that '[t]he people in the west, who have bin alwayes accounted most precise (though att this time seemingly att greatest distance with us)' were now tending to a compliance with the government, and he was sure that, if they received suitable encouragement, they would prove to be 'the most confiding people in this Nation'.[2] For the rest of the year and the first few months of 1654 he continued to believe that the western men were not fundamentally hostile to the English occupation. In October 1653 he told Cromwell that the 'Westerne people doe much detest the thoughts of their [the Royalists'] actions or countenancing of them', and even in March 1654 he could still express surprise when he found that the men of Galloway and Dumfries were rising against the English army.[3]

To some extent Lilburne's belief in the good faith of the western men was justified by events. The west and south-west of Scotland certainly gave less trouble to the English army during the royalist rising than many other areas of the country, but the reasons for this were to be found largely in the nature of the rising itself. Since the royalist forces had their bases in the Highlands, and since it was primarily among the Highlanders that the movement found its initial support, its effects took some time to reach the Lowlands. The Lowlanders meanwhile had no independent means of weakening the grip of the army garrisons and field forces, and so they had to wait for the insurgents to advance into their territory before they could oppose the English army. This meant that the army could keep the Lowlands as a whole — not just the west and south-west — under effective control until such time as the Royalists had overrun the Highlands and were advancing south. But from September 1653 onwards, parties of Royalists were active in the south-west of Scotland. In September they were in Dunbartonshire; in October they were making raids into Renfrew and Ayr; by November they were trying to raise men in Galloway (and even Lilburne admitted that the inhabitants were co-operating with the Highlanders); and in December, such was the threat from them in Dumfries and Galloway, Lilburne had to authorise the formation of an armed guard of 24 local men to apprehend 'all Moss Troopers, Tories, or other disturbers of the public peace'.[4]

In the face of such evidence, why did Lilburne cling so long to his belief in the men of the west? It is possible that in forming his opinion of the goodwill of the western men, Lilburne looked back to the response of some constituencies in the south-west of Scotland to the Tender of Incorporation in 1652. Conveniently ignoring other evidence of hostility to the Tender from that region, he may have concentrated instead on the promise of support from the 'enthusiastic' constituencies and have chosen to believe that these areas would translate their passive acceptance of the régime in 1652 into active political support in 1653 and 1654.[5] Yet again, it was open to him to believe that the local people did not sincerely welcome or support the royalist incursions, which for the most part were the work of Highlanders who had extended their operations into the Lowlands, but that they co-operated with the rebels only because of the latter's superior strength and ability to plunder those who resisted them. When the Royalists were in control of a district, it must have been difficult not to yield to *force majeure*. Primarily, however, Lilburne continued to believe that the people in the west were fudamentally well-affected to the Commonwealth, because the basis of his judgement was religious rather than political. He thought that the western men could be won over to support the English régime because he connected their attitude with that of the Protesting party within the church who, he alleged, were also sympathetic to the government. The Protesters of course found their greatest support in the west, having taken over the legacy of their precursors, the Remonstrants. At times, Lilburne seemed almost to equate the two groups — the western men *were* the Protesters — but significantly, as royalist activity increased in the south-west, he put more and more stress on the good faith of the Protesters *per se*. Although his optimism wavered in November, when the Protesting presbytery of Hamilton in Lanarkshire came out in favour of the Royalists, he was still in March 1654 assuring Cromwell that 'the Remonstratours' were very peaceably inclined and much disliked the royalist insurrection.[6]

Lilburne's faith in the Protesters probably stemmed from two distinct sources: from a belief that the Protesters were potential converts to the cause of Independency, and from the knowledge that they were intransigently hostile to the person of Charles Stuart. On the first point, Lilburne could derive hope from the fact that those sectarian groups who had made overtures to the English in the first few months after Worcester had had connections with the Protester party; moreover, the still flourishing band of Aberdeenshire separatists had some former Protesters in their ranks.[7] More significantly, by 1654, there were signs that some Protesters at least were prepared to support a species of Independency in their attempts to break away from the existing institutions of presbyterian church government, which were dominated by the Resolutioner party. The leading figure in this 'conversion' was Patrick Gillespie, the prominent Protester who had been made Principal of Glasgow University in February 1653 and was generally regarded with much favour by the English authorities. In August 1654 Gillespie persuaded the Council in London to pass an ordinance (thereafter known as 'Gillespie's Charter') which laid down that no minister in Scotland could be admitted to a living without first being declared fit by a group of provincial certifiers, composed of ministers and elders, most of whom were to be Protesters or Independents. This meant that in the matter of admission to benefices, the authority of the presbyterian church courts was to be circumvented in favour of a system not unlike the English brand of Independency.[8] Prior to this, Lilburne had been a staunch supporter of Gillespie, representing him in his letters to Cromwell as a true friend of the Commonwealth.[9] It may be, therefore, that contacts between the two men in 1653 and early 1654 led Lilburne to believe that Gillespie's commitment to Presbyterianism was not unshakeable and that Lilburne then assumed that Gillespie's attitude either represented or could be imposed upon other members of the Protesting party.

Yet Lilburne had had clear warning from other quarters that most of the Protesters were fundamentally hostile to the English régime. This had been made clear in their official pronouncements since the initial stages of the conquest, and in March 1653 they had again presented an address to the English deploring toleration and the alleged introduction of heresy into Scotland.[10] Yet this petition had not been the work of the whole party: it had been drawn up in Edinburgh, by men whose influence lay primarily in the east and north-east of Scotland. Wariston was a notable figure among them, and Wariston and his friends were undoubtedly opposed to the faction led by Gillespie. This indicated that a split was developing between the Protesters of the east and west — the latter being led by Gillespie, and being more inclined than their brethren to consider alternative systems of church government as a means of at once defeating their Resolutioner enemies and currying favour with the English. Lilburne's own religious predilections, as well as the pressure on him to find allies amongst the Scottish people, may have led him to ignore Wariston's attitude in favour of Gillespie's and, in his anxiety to capture support for the English government, to overestimate the signs of anti-presbyterian feeling in Scotland.

Lilburne was on slightly firmer ground when he focused his attention on the one issue on which virtually all Protesters were united, and which had a direct bearing on their attitude to the royalist rising. This was their distaste for Charles Stuart, and in particular their belief that his advisers, his supporters and almost certainly he himself were lukewarm in their support for a truly covenanting cause. The Protesters' own adherence to the tenets of the presbyterian doctrine was not, of course, logically consonant with support for the English régime, but in the circumstances of Glencairn's rising, their specific attitude to the person of the king took on a different colour.[11] Since the Protesters and the English shared a common enemy — the king and his royalist supporters — they gave the appearance of being in sympathy with each other. Some time previously, Protester-Resolutioner rivalry had also made the Protesters appear, in their attempts to block any possible approaches by their rivals to the English, to be making such overtures themselves. Now, in the early months of the rising, these two developments became linked, for the Resolutioners prayed openly for the king, and lent their moral support to the rebellion, while the Protesters, on the whole, did not. For Lilburne, the conclusion to be drawn from this was that the Protesters were sympathetic to the government. He constantly stressed in his letters to England that the Protesters disliked the rising, and he held this opinion in the face of some evidence to the contrary, such as the decision of the presbytery of Hamilton in November and the prayers for Charles Stuart which some Protester ministers were said to have put up in August 1653.[12] With even greater consistency, he reported the Resolutioners' support for the king. Indeed, he laid much of the blame for the success of the rising on their efforts to stir up the people;[13] and this profoundly influenced his decision to suppress the General Assembly, ban prayers for the king, and harass the ministry.

Lilburne's antipathy to all but a small section of the Scottish clergy was no new development in English ideas about Scotland. The belief that the church had been largely responsible for promoting the late war against England, and the consequent desire to undermine the power of the ministry in Scotland after the conquest had been important factors in influencing English policy. After 1651 the English continued to regard the pronouncements of the ministry as the barometer of public opinion in Scotland and they tended, therefore, to gauge the success of their efforts to pacify Scotland by the reaction they elicited from the clergy.[14] Yet surprisingly little action had been taken by the English against the clergy as such, if only because the toleration which they extended to other 'sects' included the Church of Scotland as well. There had indeed been many cases of harassment, but the main target of English wrath was the clergy's political influence, not their spiritual functions.

The clergy's, and particularly the Resolutioners', support for the king took on an added political significance during the summer of 1653, when the royalist rising was gathering momentum. Lilburne therefore viewed with apprehension the approaching meeting of the Resolutioners in full General Assembly at Edinburgh in July 1653, and resolved on a plan to dissolve it. On 12 July he asked Cromwell if 'in regard of the fiklenesse of the times' he should 'prevent that meeting or nott',[15] but by the time the Assembly had sat down on 20 July, he had received no reply to his plea for direction. For once, however, he went ahead on his own initiative. Once the Assembly had formally convened, a party of soldiers led by Lt. Col. Cotterell entered the Assembly hall and demanded to know by what authority the delegates sat. Did they have the permission of Parliament, or of the commander-in-chief, or of the English Judges in Scotland? The Moderator replied that as 'ane Spirituall court of Jesus Christ', their 'authoritie was from God, and established by the Lawes of the land yet standing unrepealed'. This exchange made little impression on the soldiers, who then dissolved the meeting and led the ministers 'all through the whole streets a myle out of the towne'. Thereupon Cotterell forced them to hand in their commissions, forbade them to re-assemble in groups of more than three, and ordered them to be quit of the town by eight o'clock the next morning.[16]

Ironically, this attack on the Resolutioners was condemned by the Protesters as much as by the victims themselves. On 21 July, before he was in possession of the full facts of the case, Lilburne reported to Cromwell that the Protesters 'seeme very joyfull at the dissolution of the assembly'; he also stated that the people generally believed that the Protesters had connived at the plan to disperse the Resolutioners by force, but he assured Cromwell that this had not in fact been the case. The idea of Protester complicity was nonetheless seized upon by some leading Resolutioners: Baillie, for one, implied that this was so.[17]

The truth of the matter was that the Protesters were not only free of such involvement, but that they too protested, in writing, at the way in which the Resolutioners had been treated. Moreover, the Protesters themselves had not gone unharmed by the actions of the English soldiers. At the same time as the Resolutioners had convened in Edinburgh, the Protesters had also foregathered in order to present a paper to their brethren which, in effect, denied the Resolutioners' right to constitute themselves as a General Assembly.[18] Some of their representatives were present at the Resolutioner meeting when Cotterell and his men burst in. Cotterell detained these men, demanded to see the papers which they were about to lay before the Assembly, and asked for the names of all those who were present at the Protesters' own meeting. The Protesters had perforce to comply with these requests. Thereafter, on 21 July the English issued a proclamation ordering 'all Lords, Gentlemen, Ministers or any others who are nott inhabitants in Edinburgh' and who had no public or legal business to transact there, to leave the city before 8 a.m. on the 22nd. This meant that the Protesters had to dissolve their own meeting, so that in effect they suffered the same fate as the Resolutioners.[19]

On 21 July the Protesters drew up a paper to present to the English in which they condemned the actions of the soldiery so far.[20] Not only did they protest at the treatment they themselves had received, but they also condemned the dissolution of the Resolutioners' meeting. The subscribers made it clear that they repudiated any idea that the meeting of the Resolutioners was a lawful General Assembly; instead they stated that their complaint was against the grounds on which this meeting had been dissolved, and the manner in which it had been done. The incident, they claimed, involved the wider issue of the right of the church to hold meetings and to have jurisdiction other than by the authority of the English Parliament or the commander-in-chief. They themselves wished to bear witness for the Lord's sovereign authority over his own house, which precluded any interference by the civil power.

Lilburne, then, had succeeded in preventing the clergy from formulating plans to aid the Highland rebels only at the cost of drawing the two warring church parties closer together. This temporary alliance between Resolutioner and Protester was further cemented as a result of the next stage in Lilburne's campaign against the church. On 2 August, the Commissioners for Visiting and Regulating Universities (who had authority over the affairs of the ministry) issued a proclamation which forbade preaching or praying for the king. One result of this edict was to provoke a pamphlet war between the clergy and the English, in which each side sought to justify its position, with the clergy declaring not only that they ought not to be troubled for praying for Charles, but that 'in conscience' they had a positive duty to do so. The clergy suited actions to words, and continued their now illegal practice. Most significantly, in the aftermath of the events of July, the Protesters who till then had 'been either silent, or but cold in their petitions for' the king, joined in the practice of putting up prayers for him.[21]

The army, for its part, embarked on a campaign of harassment against those who defied the ban. Its treatment of wrongdoers, however, was usually confined to admonitions and threats of future punishment rather than immediate punitive action. On 12 September, for example, four ministers from Fife were arrested by the army for praying for the king. They were kept in custody in Edinburgh for a week, but thereafter released on promise of good behaviour.[22] Similarly in November, Mr. William Row of Ceres in Fife was tricked by some English soldiers into an admission of support for the rebels. Row was arrested and sent to Cupar and Burntisland for interrogation, but he had merely to sign an engagement to do nothing prejudicial to the safety of the Commonwealth, under pain of a fine of £100 stg.[23] Nonetheless, it appears that the English had little success in stamping out the practice, for, in January 1654, Lilburne again saw fit to issue a proclamation banning prayers for the king. This time offenders were threatened with deprivation of their livings and 'farder punischement in their bodyes'.[24]

The third aspect of Lilburne's dealings with the ministry was his interference with church meetings at the local level. On 6 August, he asked Cromwell for advice on whether or not he should 'discharge' the church's provincial assemblies, adding that in his own opinion 'the people are not well able to beare any more against their ministers' and that it would be a mistake to 'distemper their minds too much'.[25]

Although this cautious policy was in fact the one subsequently adopted, and no wholesale disruption of presbyteries or synods took place during the next few months, the army did make occasional checks upon clerical meetings, which in some cases led to the temporary dissolution of the church assemblies. On 11 August, Lilburne reported that he had given orders for the dispersal of a meeting of 60 Resolutioner ministers at Biggar in Lanarkshire, and around the same time the presbytery of Aberdeen was forcibly dissolved. Late in September, the synod of Fife meeting at St. Andrews was interrupted by a party of soldiers, but on this occasion the English allowed proceedings to continue while they remained as observers.[26]

In his relations with the clergy, Lilburne was on the horns of a dilemma, for his belief that the ministry was primarily responsible for whipping up royalist support and hence deserved severe punishment clashed with his desire to conciliate the people over whom the clergy held sway. His difficulties were further increased by his determination to distinguish between Resolutioners and Protesters on this point. His frequent complaints about the role of the ministry during the rising were usually qualified by an expression of faith in the goodwill of the Protesters, although this faith was based on slim evidence. Conversely, it is doubtful whether his charges against the Resolutioners were fully justified. The clergy's role in the rising probably did not extend to active participation, but instead stopped short at moral suasion, which nonetheless may have had a considerable impact on the people. Baillie at any rate positively asserted that 'in all this Northland ryseing . . . there is no minister in Scotland who has had the leist hand or any medling',[27] although Baillie's desire to exculpate the clergy no doubt coloured his opinion of their part in the rebellion.

In the context of his policy towards the Scottish community as a whole, Lilburne undoubtedly regarded the clergy as a special case. Yet in some respects the restrictions imposed upon the ministry were comparable with, and derived from the same motives as, Lilburne's policy towards secular society. The disruption of church meetings, and the banishment of ministers and elders from the capital in July 1653, reflected a general fear that large gatherings of Scotsmen would inevitably lead to the hatching of plots and conspiracies against the English. Historians of royalist conspiracy in England are aware of the effect which the government's fear of political intrigue had on the social life of that nation. The same was true in Scotland: in July 1653 the gentlemen of Angus and Mearns were forbidden to meet for the purpose of hawking and hunting in the Highlands, and for several years the annual race-meeting at Cupar in Fife was banned.[28]

More serious, however, was the effect of such restrictions on the operation of political processes and institutions in Scotland. On or before 8 July 1653, the commissioners from the royal burghs of Scotland had their general convention at Cupar forcibly dissolved by the army. The reason subsequently advanced for the army's conduct was that the burghs had not given the commander-in-chief prior notice of their meeting. In September, after representatives from Edinburgh had petitioned for permission to reconvene, Lilburne authorised a new meeting to be held on 25 October, and this did in fact take place.[29] Lilburne, perhaps, was all the more anxious to conciliate the burghs on this score in order to soften the impact of another prohibition which had recently been imposed on local government. On 17 September, acting not on his own initiative but in accordance with orders from the Council of State, Lilburne notified the provosts and bailies of the Scottish burghs that the municipal elections due at Michaelmas were to be suspended.[30] This ban affected civil officers in the shires as well as in the burghs, with the result that all civilian local government officials were continued in office until further notice. The motive for this ban was probably twofold. The authorities must certainly have feared the possibility of unrest at the time of the elections; but more important, perhaps, was the desire to continue in office men whose loyalty to the Commonwealth had been tried and proven. The volatility of public opinion and the increasing unrest in the country made it imperative that the civil as well as the military powers in the localities should be dependable arms of the state. In the event, the normal electoral procedure was not restored until 1655.

These measures were no doubt useful for preserving political calm, but they only scratched the surface of the problem. Lilburne's real difficulty lay in containing the threat from the Highland clans, who were the major source of support for the rising. For some months, Lilburne had been considering the most effective way of dealing with them, and by June he had reached a decision. He determined to make the chiefs responsible for the good behaviour of their tenants and clansmen, not by using new methods deriving from English authority, but by enforcing old Scottish Acts of Parliament for the preservation of peace in the Highlands. That way, he explained to Cromwell, 'their mouthes can bee lesse open'd against us, by reason these lawes of the Nation are but putt in execution, and that there is nothing of force uppon them but what is necessary, and which they cannott except against.'[31] Accordingly, on 27 July the Commissioners for the Administration of Justice issued a proclamation which ordered the nobility, gentry and clan chiefs north of the Tay to give security for the good behaviour of their tenants and followers before 1 October 1653. The principal authority for this measure was cited as the laws against sorners, broken Highlanders and borderers of the 11th Parliament of James VI (1587). Very few of the leading men of the Highlands were omitted in this order, although the name of Macdonald of Glengarry was a conspicuous exception.[32] Whether or not the army made strenuous efforts to enforce this proclamation remains unclear, but the further progress of the rising testifies to its lack of practical effect.

The idea behind this approach to the problems of agitation and disturbance was clearly that the community should be made responsible for the conduct of its members. The same line of thought was evident also in Lilburne's policy of securing engagements from the Lowland gentry, and even more so in his attempts to control the movements of ordinary people who might be tempted to join the Royalists in the hills.

From the summer of 1653 onwards the gentry of various shires and districts throughout Scotland began to tender engagements of loyalty to the English government. In June the gentlemen of several parishes in Perthshire, and in August the gentlemen of Renfrewshire and of Ayrshire, gave an engagement to remain loyal to the Commonwealth;[33] in the last two cases the subscribers spoke on behalf of the whole shire. These testimonies were probably tendered voluntarily to the English, but by the autumn Lilburne was thinking of making the practice compulsory. By October drafts of bonds to be subscribed by the gentlemen of Scotland had been drawn up at army headquarters, and in November Lilburne took the initiative and demanded that the heritors of certain shires south of the Tay should enter into engagements for their peaceable living. The testimony of the gentlemen of Stirlingshire, which was probably typical, showed that the engagement covered not only the subscribers but also the tenants and inhabitants under their control.[34]

As the rising gathered momentum, Lilburne saw a way of translating the gentry's natural desire to protect their property from the depredations of the rebels into a more active peace-keeping role. By the summer of 1653, he had allowed the gentry and inhabitants of the shires of Inverness, Ross, Cromarty, Banff, Aberdeen, Kincardine, Forfar, Perth and Stirling to organise armed guards against the insurgents; in the autumn he extended this privilege to Argyllshire, and in December to Dumfries and Galloway.[35] He also issued numerous licences to noblemen and gentlemen of quality allowing them to retain their arms for use against possible 'invaders'. Both these measures were in fact an admission that the army's might alone was not sufficient to preserve law and order in Scotland.[36]

The English régime, like any government in the early modern period, was much exercised by the threat which vagabonds, beggars and masterless men posed to the peace of the countryside. In Scotland in 1653, the problem became acute when it was realised that much of this mobility among the lower orders masked the escape of dissident elements from the Lowlands to swell the royalist forces in the hills. Restrictions had therefore to be put on the movement of people from place to place. On 4 July the Commissioners for the Administration of Justice issued a proclamation which put the responsibility for the care of 'Vagabonds, masterfull Beggars [and] strong and idle persons' on to the parishes in which they had been born or had had their last residence. These people, it was asserted, were liable to commit 'many Insolencies, Mischiefs and Robberies' as they wandered about the country, and hence it was vital for the peace of the nation that they be put to work.[37] As with the proclamation of 27 July concerning the Highland clans, this measure rested on the authority of several Scottish Acts of Parliament passed in James VI's reign. By September, however, the problem of 'vagrancy' was seen in more overtly political terms, and the army began to play a greater role in the attempt to solve it. On 27 September 1653 a proclamation issued by the commander-in-chief expressly mentioned as its *raison d'être* the ineffectiveness of the order of 4 July, but instead of merely reiterating the need to enforce the Acts of James VI, it began by citing an army order of Cromwell's dated 5 November 1650 which imposed penalties for damage inflicted on the English army. The proclamation then went on to require all magistrates and officers, both civil and military, to keep a watch on any suspicious persons travelling through or residing within their bounds, and take them into custody if necessary. Any such arrests should then be reported to the Judge Advocate of the army. The proclamation finally gave warning that any person found aiding, abetting or giving intelligence to the rebels would be deemed an enemy of the Commonwealth.[38]

This measure was reinforced late in October, when Lilburne ordered his garrison commanders to ensure that the officials in the burghs and parishes under their control kept lists of all persons known to have left their homes to join the enemy.[39] Measures were also taken to ensure that strangers who came into the towns to stir up disaffection there were apprehended. Under pressure from the English authorities, Edinburgh's town council passed several orders forbidding the reception of strangers except under stringent conditions.[40] The culmination of these measures was reached in April 1654, when a proclamation from the commander-in-chief forbade any person whatsoever to travel more than 5 miles from his home without a pass from the army; a fee of one shilling stg. had to be paid for every pass so issued.[41]

The effectiveness of these orders was in inverse proportion to their number. The last in the series frankly admitted in its preamble that 'nothing to this time hath been effectually done', but that on the contrary rebels and spies were roaming the countryside, gathering intelligence, committing robbery and murder, and enticing the country people to join them. This state of affairs had continued despite the frequent exaction of heavy fines from parishes which were known to have harboured the enemy.[42] Faced with overwhelming anti-English feeling and the impossibility of directly controlling every centre of habitation in Scotland, the English army had signally failed to contain the royalist threat.

As well as the loss of manpower to the enemy, the number of horses which were carried off by, or given to, the rebels greatly worried the army, for on this depended the type of campaign which the Royalists could mount. When Lilburne had been drafting the bonds of loyalty which he wished the gentlemen of Scotland to subscribe, he had included a provision that they should surrender their good horses to the army to prevent them falling into royalist hands.[43] On 14 December he went further and issued a general proclamation which ordered all owners of horses worth £5 stg. or more to bring them in to the nearest English garrison. There they could sell them outright to the army, or else have them kept in custody for the time being. Lilburne's instructions to his officers on how they should execute this order revealed a mixture of fair-mindedness and low cunning. Proper provision was made for assessing each horse's value and for making sure the owner had a receipt for its sale or surrender; but the officers were also to use the opportunity to make neighbour inform upon neighbour and so ferret out possible evasions of the order.[44] This measure was naturally extremely unpopular with the country people, but Nicoll put it on record that the English eventually restored the horses to their owners, unlike the Royalists who seized on 'all the maist considerable horsses, saidles [and] brydles' but made no reparation for them.[45] Furthermore, the English frequently gave dispensations to noblemen and gentlemen to keep a few horses above the value stated in the proclamation, on condition that they were not used against the Commonwealth.[46]

The procedure adopted for the seizure of horses illustrates another facet of Lilburne's thinking on how to win the support of the Scottish community. He believed that good behaviour and fair dealing on the part of the army would commend the military régime to the people. This idea had been an integral part of English policy since the early days of the conquest; it had prompted Monck's disciplinary actions after the sack of Dundee in 1651, and the maintenance of such discipline had been a prime concern of Deane, and was now carried on by Lilburne. In the summer of 1653 a series of orders forbade the soldiery to take advantage of the country people under their control. In May, soldiers were forbidden to shoot rabbits or pigeons; in June they were ordered to cease extorting money from the local population under false pretences; and in July a stop was put to the raiding of gardens and orchards, especially those which belonged to landowners on whose ground the soldiers were quartered.[47] Commissions of inquiry were set up to examine allegations of wrongdoing by the army: thus in May a committee of officers was appointed to inquire into the conduct of some regiments which had lately been quartered in the shires of Banff and Aberdeen.[48] Steps were also taken to see that the system of quartering, although burdensome, was arranged equitably: in July and September, for example, Lilburne ordered the redistribution of troops quartered in Edinburgh, lest one part of the city bear a heavier load than any other.[49] And if this was a burden on the population, how much more anxious was Lilburne to prevent the army having to fall on free quarter, where the people would receive no recompense at all for feeding and housing the army. In the summer of 1653, when the Treasury was running dry, and pay for the army in Scotland was much in arrears, Lilburne pleaded with the authorities in London to send up some money to keep the army from free quarter; such a move, he opined, would be most 'unseasonable' at this juncture.[50]

Lilburne's anxiety over the financial burden which the upkeep of the army imposed upon Scotland was part and parcel of his belief that the fundamental reason for the growth in royalist support was material hardship among many sections of the Scottish community. This belief, in turn, underpinned his more far-reaching proposals for destroying the rising at its roots. In particular, it led him to advocate some measure of compromise with the nobility and gentry, who formed the backbone of the political revolt.

As a first step towards alleviating hardship, Lilburne concerned himself with the assessment, the chief form of taxation on the Scottish people. His task was a difficult one, for there were many competing considerations. On the one hand, the impoverished state of the country and the army's desire to win the goodwill of the people demanded that the tax burden be kept low; but the cost of maintaining the army and of building fortifications, to which purposes the yield of the assessment was in the main assigned, dictated that the rate be kept high. During the period of the rising, it became imperative to achieve some sort of balance. In the summer of 1653 Lilburne ordered a revaluation of all the shires and burghs in Scotland in the hope of answering complaints about the inequitable distribution of the assessment. In May the collectors were told to authorise the gentlemen of each shire to select one or two of their number for a conference in Edinburgh on 12 July. There they were to consult with a committee of army officers on the proportion of the assessment which each shire, and each burgh within a shire, should bear. The results were produced on 22 July, although not without bitter argument from some of the representatives. The shires of Dumfries, Wigton, Orkney and Shetland, Inverness and Aberdeen refused to consent to the tables of taxation which were finally drawn up, but their protests were rejected by the English.[51] After the conference was over, Lilburne ordered the 'heritors etc. in the several counties' to nominate committees for rectifying and revaluing the rents in each shire. These committees for valuation were composed of lairds or gentry,[52] who were thus given the opportunity to participate in the government of the localities in a matter of crucial importance to all landowners. Even before the summer of 1653, it is probable that the English had allowed the local gentry some say in the valuations for and apportioning of the assessment, if only because the army was heavily dependent on their expertise and local knowledge to make the system work. Clearly, therefore, the imposition of the assessment was one matter in which the army found it both necessary and desirable to incorporate the gentry into the task of governing Scotland, however antipathetic to their influence the official pronouncements of Parliament might be.

The ostensible purpose of the conference at Edinburgh had been merely to correct the relative valuation of each shire within the fixed overall tax burden, but it seems that in practice the conference also agreed on an absolute reduction in the amount of tax demanded from the Scottish people. On 18 February 1652, the assessment had been nominally set at £10,000 per month, with the provision that abatements from this total should not exceed £2000; these sums had been confirmed by Parliament on 26 October 1652 and by the Council of State on 3 May 1653.[53] Now, however, the commissioners at Edinburgh agreed on £8500 as the nominal monthly total *and* made provision for further abatements, which brought down the amount the army could expect to gather to just over £7500 per month. All this was done without actually conceding that the sum of £10,000 was outdated in theory as well as in practice, for to wipe this higher figure completely from the record-books would have required an order from Parliament.[54] Lilburne doubtless hoped that the reduction in the assessment would help to secure the goodwill of the Scots. But primarily it reflected not the dispensation of grace and favour to the Scottish people but the practical necessities of the army's position. It had always been difficult to raise the full yield of the tax from a country as impoverished and economically backward as Scotland; but now the disruption caused by the royalist rising made the previous levels totally unrealistic. Nor did this revaluation mark the nadir of Scotland's fiscal potential, for as the devastation caused by the rebellion mounted, yields were to fall very much lower.

Given these difficulties, Lilburne was understandably aggrieved when on 12 November 1653 Parliament demanded that the full £10,000 should henceforth be levied on Scotland. He immediately represented the unwisdom, and indeed the impossibility, of so doing in a letter to William Rowe, secretary to the Committee for the Army. This must have evoked no response, for on 6 December Lilburne sent a fuller statement of the yield of the cess, the abatements, and the use to which the money was put to the Committee itself. He pleaded that 'during the continuance of these distempers heere' the total should not be raised above £8500, nor the abatements reduced.[55] No formal concession was made by the authorities on this point, despite Lilburne's further complaints. In practice, however, the yield dropped drastically, so that by late January 1654 Lilburne had to report that only £6000 per month could actually be gathered in.[56]

Lilburne's concern over the assessment was heightened by the fact that the flexibility of the old system of abatements had made it a useful weapon for rewarding loyalty to the Commonwealth. Early on in the rising, Lilburne had realised that those who were to suffer for their loyalty to the English would require some form of compensation. He had also realised that inducements would have to be offered to the waverers, and beginning with the men of Badenoch in February 1653, he had hit on a reduction in their assessment as the most likely method of winning their favour. Blanket concessions to the Scots were not enough; the one drawback to a lenient policy towards all was that it failed to distinguish the innocent from the guilty, and did nothing to help those whose persons and property had been under particular attack from the Royalists. As a remedy which could be applied with discrimination, a tax abatement fitted the bill, for it was a relatively simple matter to waive the cess on devastated lands, if the owners had shown by their good behaviour that they merited special consideration. Lilburne thus began the practice, which was to be continued by Monck, of abating the cess on despoiled lands. The Earl of Linlithgow and the lairds of Lethen, Meginch and Grantully were four of those who were favoured in this way; each was to have his case considered by Monck also, and was to be in receipt of further marks of English favour in the years 1653 and 1654.[57] Prominent supporters of the régime, such as the Marquis of Argyle, Sir James Macdonald of Sleat, and the laird of Glenorchy, were likewise accorded abatements as a reward for their services throughout the rising.[58]

As a second string to his bow, Lilburne was also willing to explore the possibilities which old Scots law offered for granting reparation to those who suffered at the hands of the rebels. In July, he told the Council of State that the Scots themselves, many of whom were being robbed and plundered by the Royalists during their summer campaign, were now demanding redress under these laws, and in August he mentioned to Cromwell that steps to enforce the relevant statutes might favourably influence public opinion.[59] These proposals were taken no further, but Lilburne did pursue the idea of granting compensation to the sufferers out of forfeited royalist estates. In February 1654 he suggested that the estates of some of the leading rebels, especially those of Atholl, Glencairn and Kenmore, should be specifically assigned to this purpose, for in no other way could the state find sufficient funds to recompense the loyalists.[60] This meant that the English government's sequestration policy would be affected in some degree, and so Lilburne further recommended that the whole question of an Act of Oblivion, and the exceptions which would have to be made to it, should be clarified there and then. The Council of State were in fact considering the matter of sequestrations when Lilburne wrote, not simply in response to the current rebellion but as an issue which had been outstanding since the early days of the conquest; for no final decision had ever been taken on how the relevant clauses of

Parliament's declaration of 28 October 1651 should be implemented. Thus the exact amount of 'pardon and grace' which the Scots could expect from their conquerors was still unknown. Lilburne advocated a speedy decision and recommended that those who had remained loyal to the Commmonwealth during Glencairn's rising should be exempted from sequestration. The sooner all this was done, he explained, the sooner the enemy would be defeated.[61]

Lilburne's plan for restoring loyalists to their forfeited estates was marked off from his other schemes for reparation by the fact that the former was essentially a *preventive* measure. To grant compensation after an injury had been sustained was important; but even more vital was the need to provide a positive inducement to people to stay loyal in the first place. Lilburne was quite sure that the root cause of the growth in support for the rising among the nobility and gentry of Scotland was their material hardship, and that the main reasons for this were twofold: the harsh enforcement of the laws of debt, and the forfeiture of their estates. His most far-reaching proposals for dealing with the revolt therefore centred on these two points. He wished in effect to turn a situation in which the nobility and gentry had nothing to lose by attacking the Commonwealth into one in which they had everything to gain by remaining loyal. Lilburne was not alone in identifying material loss as the motive force behind the growth in royalist support. Scottish commentators drew attention to the straits to which the leaders of Scottish society were reduced.[62] The wars of the 1640s had been economically ruinous, with many of the leading families having contracted debts, both public and private, which could never be repaid. On top of this came the fear, and in many cases the reality, of sequestration, and the certainty of a heavy tax burden imposed by the English. Impoverishment seemed inevitable under the English régime: a reversal of fortune could come only with the restoration of the young king. Although the picture painted by Scottish contemporaries might be a little overdrawn, English commentators of the time substantially bore out their stories. As early as January 1653, the reporter of the first major rendezvous at Strathglass had expressed fears that 'necessity' would drive many to swell the royalist ranks. Lilburne accepted this analysis of the situation, and from then on constantly emphasised the point in his letters to London.

At the time of the setting up of the new judicial system in Scotland, the authorities had been confident that the impartiality and vigour of the new judges would be generally welcomed by the common people. But what they had not foreseen was that the practical effect on the nobility and gentry would be to impel them towards political revolt. This was especially true of the enforcement of the laws of debt, which hit the Lowland gentry particularly hard. In July 1653, an English intelligencer noted: 'for all the faire flourishes the Lowland Lords make before the Highlanders they would gladly be att home if they knew how to live secuerly from his and their debters.'[63] Lilburne accordingly began to make special representations to the Judges asking that they be lenient towards certain noblemen whose loyalty he was anxious to retain. At various times throughout 1653, pleas were advanced on behalf of the laird of Mersington, Lord Frendraught, the Earls of Lothian and Mar, and the Marquis of Huntly, among others.[64]

In November, Lilburne began to press for a more sweeping solution to this problem, and in a letter to the Council of State meticulously explained the effect which enforcement of the laws of debt was having on the rising. He asked that the Judges be authorised to suspend judicial proceedings in certain cases, arguing that it was 'better that some particular men's debts were awhile longer delayed unsatisfied, rather than by their too earnest pressing the peace of the whole Nation should bee disturb'd'. In December he reiterated to Cromwell his belief that the 'strickt proceedings' of the courts were driving men 'to desperate courses'.[65] By this time Lilburne and his officers had drawn up a formal statement of the remedies which in their opinion should forthwith be applied to the troubled state of Scotland.[66] Their proposals on the laws of debt were that sentences should be moderated; execution of the Judges' decreets should be postponed; and creditors should be forced to take land as payment for debts or for the interest on debts. This last proposal was designed to overcome the shortage of ready money in Scotland which in itself was causing great hardship to debtors who were being pressed for payment in cash. Lilburne's desires were not met, however, and in the New Year he was still agitating for some solution.[67] In the longer term, however, his advice was accepted: an ordinance for relief of debtors was passed by the Council on 16 May 1654,[68] but by this time Monck was in command and in a position to reap the benefit.

The proposals put forward by Lilburne and his officers in December 1653 also contained some advice about sequestrations, which Lilburne considered to be as vicious as the laws of debt in their effect on the rising. Lilburne recommended that all sequestrations and forfeitures should be cancelled, except for those on '5 or 6 grand offendors' who should be penalised 'for examples sake'. Moreover, an Act of Oblivion should be passed with a free pardon for all those currently in arms if they should agree to live peaceably under the Commonwealth. But — and here the coercive streak in Lilburne's policy showed itself — rewards should be promised to anyone who captured any of the rebels dead or alive, 'especially the Heads and Cheif of them that will not otherways submitt'. Here again, the eventual decision of the Council of State betrayed something of Lilburne's influence. The Ordinance of Pardon and Grace of 12 April 1654[69] was much less harsh than many had anticipated, although the number of the Scottish nobility made liable to forfeiture and/or fines was greater than Lilburne had suggested.

As well as the clauses on judicial proceedings and on forfeitures, the proposals contained three other recommendations: that Scotsmen might be allowed to levy regiments for service overseas and so rid the country of troublesome elements; that the army in Scotland be reinforced by both horse and foot; and that men of war should patrol the coasts to prevent Middleton's landing from the Continent. Thus Lilburne showed himself concerned about both the military and the civil aspects of the rising, with defeating the enemy on the battlefield and in the hearts and minds of the people. In general terms, the former corresponded to a harsh policy, and the latter to a lenient one. The trouble was that the two aspects of the rising were not as easily divorced in practice as they were in theory. In part this was because the rebellion took the form of guerilla warfare, rather than a series of pitched battles and set engagements, so that conventional assumptions about military conduct did not always apply. But the real core of the problem was that the rising derived its strength from the bedrock of hostility which the Scots felt towards their conquerors, and that it depended for its growth on the passive support of the local population. Once the attitude of the people had become a military problem, Lilburne was forced towards coercive measures, such as the numerous edicts he passed on lending succour to the Royalists and on moving about from place to place. But because the army could not control the activities and movements of the people completely, sufficient leeway remained for them to give covert support to the rebels. Lilburne was thus caught in his own cross-fire: his attempts to combine conciliation and coercion were not, during his time as commander-in-chief, destined to succeed.

Paradoxically, however, by the time of Lilburne's departure in April 1654, there were signs that the rising was on the wane, but these were due not so much to Lilburne's efforts as to the internal contradictions of the royalist cause itself. The difficulties of welding the royalist levies into an organised military force; the squabblings among the leadership; and the failure of help from abroad — these were the vital factors which prevented the king's men from inflicting major defeats on the English army. Indeed, in the first few months of 1654 the army could itself claim some military successes and hope that before long it would have the royalist forces on the run. As a result, when Monck took over the command he had to deal with a movement which had lost its *élan*. This loss of spirit in the royalist cause was not so obvious at the time, however; Monck, for one, was surprised at the strength of the insurrection when he arrived in Scotland, and considered his future task no easy matter. Nor in accounting for the eventual defeat of the Royalists should one ignore the very positive achievements of Monck himself in the coming months. Had it not been for his brisk, confident approach to the military problems and his ability to get his requests listened to in Whitehall, the rising might have regained its spirit and strength. In the event, however, a combination of the two factors — the decline in the royalist cause and the upsurge in the army's capacity to deal with it — proved fatal to the hopes of the king in Scotland.

6

Monck and the Suppression of Revolt, April 1654 — September 1655

FROM his arrival at Dalkeith on 22 April 1654 until the setting up of a Scottish Council in September 1655, Monck was the supreme head of the civil and military government in Scotland. Between his period of command in 1654 and 1655 and that of Lilburne in the previous sixteen months, there were many elements of continuity. The immediate objectives of the two men were the same: the reduction of the royalist rising, and the reassertion of English rule in both its civil and its military aspects throughout Scotland. Within this context Monck, like Lilburne, had three main areas of concern: the reinforcement and supply of the English army to the point where it was capable of mounting an effective campaign in the hills; the enactment and enforcement of measures to prevent the civilian population from abetting the royalist forces; and the final settlement of the problems of the union and of the policy of oblivion. Lilburne had been aware of the interrelationship of these three aspects of English policy, and of their joint impact on the progress of the rising. He had made specific recommendations on each point, but his advice had produced little tangible result during his time in Scotland.

Monck, by contrast, received directions and help in each of these fields within weeks of assuming the command in Scotland. During the early summer, he received substantial reinforcements of both horse and foot. Sums of money were also sent up to re-stock the depleted treasury, which at his arrival in Scotland contained a mere £500.[1] In the civil sphere he secured an ordinance for the relief of debtors, in which the judges were ordered to mitigate their proceedings under the laws governing debt; and he was given wide authority to deal with members of the community who allowed those under their charge to join with the rebels. In addition, Monck presided over the proclamation of the Protectorate in Scotland, and it fell to him to announce the Ordinance of Union between the two countries and to implement the so-called Act of Pardon and Grace, which finally determined who amongst the Scottish nobility and gentry should be liable to fines and forfeiture.

Monck's reputation in England and his authority in government circles go a long way towards explaining why his demands were attended to in Whitehall, whilst Lilburne's complaints had been ignored.[2] Nonetheless, although Lilburne had received little satisfaction in answer to his pleas, nearly all the expedients which were eventually adopted to assist Monck had been suggested by Lilburne

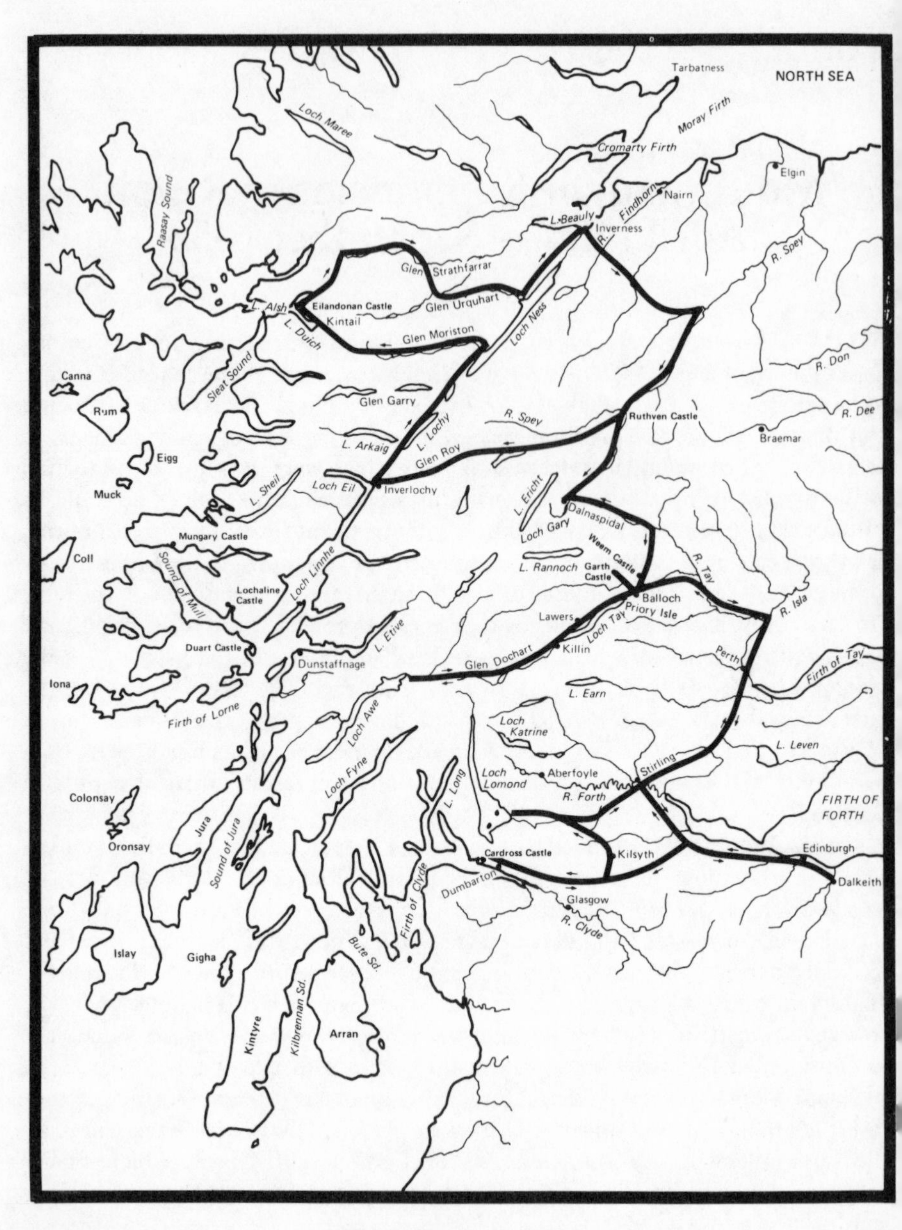

Map 2. Monck's Campaign

and had begun to be discussed in Whitehall before he left Scotland. From the very beginning of the year there had in fact been signs that the authorities were looking afresh at the Scottish problem. This new energy was due largely to two factors: first, the overthrow of the loquacious and inefficient Barebones' Parliament and its replacement by the executive competence of Protector and Council; and secondly, the virtual petering out of the Anglo-Dutch war, which promised the release of supplies for use in Scotland. Ironically, one of the first signs of the new order was the appointment of Monck himself as commander-in-chief in Scotland. Lilburne had taken over from Deane only as acting commander, and the question of a fully accredited successor to him had been kept open throughout the year 1653. The names of John Lambert and Edward Whalley, among others, had been occasionally canvassed, but the new government in January 1654 settled on Monck.[3] Hence, in their subsequent deliberations they knew full well that, unless the Dutch war suddenly flared up again and so prevented Monck from going to Scotland, it would be he who would put their decisions into practice. The knowledge that they would soon have a man in whom they reposed great trust and confidence to execute their decisions no doubt spurred them on to positive action. But in formulating the policy which Monck would implement, it was to Lilburne's analysis of the Scottish problem that they consciously or unconsciously subscribed. Most notably, Monck's formal Instructions,[4] and the resolves of the Council of State of 5 April 1654 which embodied the Council's ideas on how best to assist the new commander,[5] bear the imprint of Lilburne's advice.

The Council's deliberations on the military and civil assistance to be given to Monck, and the measures which resulted from these debates, form the essential background to Monck's military campaign in the summer of 1654. For by the time Monck took to the hills, not only did he have a better-supplied and stronger army at his command, but the political context within which the army would conduct the campaign, and within which the ultimate fate of the rebels would be decided, had been clearly defined.

i. The military and the civil background to the summer campaign, April — June 1654

Of all the Council's concerns, its need to strengthen the army in Scotland was the one most fraught with difficulty. This was due primarily to the government's lack of money, and to competing claims for men and supplies from other quarters of the Commonwealth. Broadly speaking, Lilburne had wanted more ships on patrol around the coasts of Scotland to prevent royalist forces landing from abroad; more men, both infantry and cavalry; more money to pay the soldiers' arrears of pay; more food and clothes; and a tighter control over his officers, many of whom were absent from their regiments for long periods of time.[6] Before he left Scotland, Lilburne had received promises of more men, money and ships, but all of these commodities were slow in arriving in the north. In February he had been told that two additional regiments of horse, those of Whalley and Lambert, would be sent north, but they arrived too late to be of much service to him.[7] On 29 March the Council ordered £50,000 to be provided for the forces in Scotland. Of this a mere £13,000 had been received by 22 April, and by mid-July over £23,000 was still needed to make up the arrears of pay.[8] On 5 April the Council agreed that ten ships should be appointed altogether for the coast of Scotland, but three months later the Scottish coasts still did not have their full complement of patrol vessels.[9]

When Monck took up residence at Dalkeith in late April, he immediately began to send a series of strongly worded despatches to London, in which he demanded that the orders already passed by the Council should be fully implemented and that, in addition, another regiment of horse and a regiment and a half of foot should be sent north.[10] In June the Council ordered £30,000 to be sent to Scotland in fulfilment of its earlier resolution, but the money did not arrive until September.[11] Monck had better luck, however, with his requests for more men. By the time the army embarked on its summer campaign, it had been reinforced by Col. Pride's regiment of foot and seven companies of Sir William Constable's, as well as Col. Hacker's regiment of horse. This greatly improved the army's cavalry strength in the north, for Whalley's and Lambert's regiments of horse, promised in Lilburne's time, were by then on active service in Scotland.[12]

The arrival of 1000 foot from Ireland further improved the army's prospects of hunting down and penning in the rebels in the hills, for these forces were destined to garrison the important strategic area around Lochaber. Plans for shipping them to Scotland were drawn up in April and May. On 24 April, the Protector appointed Col. Matthew Alured commander of the forces to be brought from Ireland, at which time it was thought best that they should be disposed on the islands of Mull and Skye. On 8 May, however, Monck gave notice to Alured that they were to march to Inverlochy. This move had been accomplished by 14 June. But in the course of the month Alured had been removed from his command on suspicion of disloyalty to the régime and had been replaced by Col. William Brayne.[13]

By June 1654, then, Monck had some reason to be pleased with the improvement in his military potential, but he was in fact far from satisfied with the treatment he had received. Such concessions as he had wrung from the authorities in London had been granted grudgingly, and were by no means as efficacious in practice as they seemed on paper. Certainly after the summer of 1654 Monck was concerned not so much with increasing the size of his army, as with merely ensuring that the forces he already had were not directed elsewhere, once the worst of the royalist danger had been averted. But on the point of money his demands were insatiable — never at any time were sufficient funds released to meet the arrears of pay and the many other contingencies to which the army's presence in Scotland gave rise.

Nonetheless, given the undoubted improvement in the state of the army, the prospects for defeating the rebels in the summer of 1654 were by no means gloomy, and Monck could take some comfort from the fact that progress had also been made towards dealing with the rising at its roots, among the local population. The Council had at last paid attention to two points first mooted by Lilburne: that measures should be adopted to deal with parents and guardians who allowed their charges to join the rebels,[14] and that something should be done to relieve those oppressed by the laws of debt.

On 28 March Lilburne had hinted to Cromwell that many noblemen and gentlemen, although cautious enough to stay at home themselves, were nonetheless willing to allow their sons and servants to join the enemy. He wished these connivers to be fined and to be forced to contribute for the service of the Commonwealth as many men, and as many horses, as had gone missing from under their jurisdiction. A little over a week later, the Council went some way towards answering Lilburne's demands when it came to draw up the Instructions for his successor. By Article 13 Monck was authorised to lay fines on anyone who could be proved to have encouraged his friends or relations to join the rebels with horses, money, victuals or arms; should the individual culprit not be found, then the parish wherein the rebel had last lived was to bear the penalty. Two other articles supplemented and complemented these powers. By Article 5 Monck was authorised to imprison anyone found 'disobedient to' the present government, and by Article 11 he had power to make every shire responsible for robberies or murders committed within its bounds.[15]

Monck, however, apparently did not feel that these powers exactly fitted the case. On 22 April, the very night of his arrival at Dalkeith, he specifically asked Cromwell for authority to imprison the fathers of all who were engaged in arms against the Commonwealth. On 3 May the Council formally added to his Instructions the power to imprison any father or master who had consented to his son or servant joining the rebellion. But on 4 May — before he could have heard of this decision — Monck had already issued a proclamation which covered this and certain other matters.[16] The proclamation ordained that all parents, brethren and tutors who had assisted or connived at their sons', brothers', or pupils' defection should within twenty days cause their charges to surrender; if this were accomplished the parents or guardians would be freely pardoned, but if not, then they would be imprisoned until the rebels in question were captured. This decree also covered the case where a parish or presbytery helped one of its inhabitants to go over to the Royalists: fines were to be imposed on such communities. These provisions clearly showed the coercive streak in English policy, but other clauses in the same proclamation showed the more conciliatory side of English rule. One clause decreed that pardon would be extended to all rebels who should submit within 20 days, provided only that they had not committed murder in cold blood and that they were not 'excepted persons' within the meaning of the Act of Pardon and Grace. Another clause laid down that rewards would be given to any person who apprehended one or more of the rebels, with particularly generous rewards being promised to the captors or slayers of Middleton, Atholl, Seaforth, Kenmore, and Major General Dalziel. The proclamation ended with the promise of reparation out of the rebels' estates, or out of the pockets of those communities which sheltered the rebels, for those whose property or person was injured by the royalist forces. The proclamation of 4 May was thus comprehensive in scope. It put a double-edged weapon into the hands of the English, for by combining the threat of punishment with the promise of reward it allowed the army to show the face of conciliation or of coercion, whichever best fitted the case. Surprisingly, however, Monck did not seem to make extensive use of his powers to imprison parents and kinsmen of royalist dissidents;[17] nor did he fine many parishes for abetting the rebels.[18] In practice, it seems, the English were often content to rely on words rather than deeds to frighten the Scots into submission.

The conciliatory aspect of English policy was further displayed in the Council's decisions on the laws of debt, which put another weapon at Monck's disposal before the summer of 1654. The need to mitigate judicial proceedings against debtors had been one of Lilburne's most frequently voiced recommendations to Whitehall. The first sign that the Council was willing to listen to this advice came on 5 April 1654, when it resolved that the Commissioners for the Administration of Justice in Scotland should be authorised to moderate their decrees against debtors.[19] If debtors were not able to procure money to pay off their creditors, then the Judges were to impose a moratorium or else compel the creditors to accept land in lieu of ready cash. This resolution met Lilburne's demands in full, but it still required an ordinance to put the resolve into formal effect. Such an ordinance was read and committed to the committee for Scotch business on 14 April but it did not come before the full council again until 10 May. Meanwhile, on 29 April, Monck had written to Lambert urging the passing of just such a decree and emphasising the good effect this would have on the royalist revolt. On 16 May the ordinance was finally passed, with the provision that it should remain in force until 12 May 1655.[20]

Whitehall's efforts so far had succeeded in strengthening the army's hand against the Royalists in two ways: the military's own effectiveness had been increased by supplies of men and money, and the powers at its disposal for dealing with the civilian population had been made more wide-ranging and flexible. But the troubled state of Scotland owed something, too, to the uncertainty which existed at the highest level of Anglo-Scottish relations. The political settlement between the two countries, which had first been set out in Parliament's Declaration of 28 October 1651, had never been fully implemented. Not only did the union still lack legislative sanction, but the extent of fines and forfeitures, by which the nobility and gentry would be required to expiate their 'war-guilt' for the events of 1648-51, was still unknown. Although English officials had been sequestering the estates of known offenders since the early days of the conquest, the final roll-call of the guilty remained in the balance. By 1654 the need to suppress Glencairn's rising, and in particular the realisation that material hardship was a major cause of the revolt, had introduced a new element into the situation. It was now clear that when the Council of State finally decided whose estates should be sequestered or fined, the severity or leniency of its decisions would profoundly affect the course of the rising. Lilburne, for one, had spelled this out fully when he wrote to the authorities in Whitehall.

Before Monck arrived in Scotland in April 1654, the Council had completed its task of dealing with the necessary 'Acts'[21] of Union and of Oblivion. The Bill of Union which had been introduced into the House of Commons on 13 April 1652 had of course died along with the Parliament which gave it birth in April 1653. On 4 October 1653, Barebones' Parliament considered a new Bill of Union; by the time that that assembly had gone the way of its predecessor, the Bill had had its second reading and had been considered in committee, but had not yet become law. But on 16 December 1653 the union was given formal recognition when the Council of State proclaimed the new Protectorate under the title of 'the Commonwealth of England, Scotland and Ireland'. The Instrument of Government went further and laid down that Scotland's representation in the forthcoming protectoral Parliament, summoned for 3 September 1654, should be thirty members. But still a formal Ordinance of Union was required, and to this the Council of State turned in January 1654. The basis of the ordinance was the Bill which had been considered by Barebones' Parliament, and in its new guise it was given a first and second reading by Council on 20 January. Further consideration was given to it on 23 January and 2 February, and on 12 April 1654 it was finally passed with the approval of the Protector. On 22 April copies were ordered to be sent to Scotland for publication there.[22]

In addition to declaring the fact of the union, the ordinance formally discharged the people of Scotland from their allegiance to the descendants of the late king. The office of kingship and the right of the Scottish Parliament to assemble were also taken away. Instead Scotland's right to send thirty members to Westminster was acknowledged, and various other 'privileges', consequent upon the union, were announced. These included free trade between the two countries, and the promise that taxes would be levied 'proportionably' upon the whole people of the united Commonwealth. The ordinance then harked back to the social policy of the Long Parliament in 1651 and declared that henceforth vassalage and feudal incidents were abolished in Scotland. Tenants were to hold their land by rent only, without any other duty save heriots; they were also discharged from the duty of appearing in their lords' superior courts of justiciary, regality, or barony.[23] Instead the judicial powers of the local magnates were transformed into courts baron, modelled on the English manor courts.

The setting up of courts baron in Scotland was accomplished in a separate ordinance which also received the final approval of Protector and Council on 12 April 1654. The text had first come before Council on 26 January, and in the course of February it had been amended and provisionally approved. The ordinance provided that courts baron should meet once in three weeks in every 'place or circuit of land which realie is, or hath commonly been called, knowen or reputed to be a Mannor'. Their jurisdiction was to extend to cases of contract, debt, and trespass where the sum involved did not exceed 40 shillings stg., and where the question of freehold or title to land was not in dispute. They had also the power to make by-laws for the 'publick weall, Rule & government' of the inhabitants of the manor.[24]

The ordinance for erecting courts baron was therefore complementary to those provisions of the Ordinance of Union which fulfilled the Long Parliament's desire to undermine the feudal powers of the nobility and gentry over the lower classes. The real attack on the country's political and social leaders, however, was reserved for the 'Act' of Pardon and Grace to the people of Scotland, which was the third of the ordinances affecting Scotland to be passed by the Council on 12 April 1654. This ordinance was, in effect, the Act of Oblivion which had, like the Act of Union, been under consideration since 1652 and for whose passage Lilburne had constantly agitated. The nobility and gentry were crucially affected not by the element of 'pardon and grace' in the Act, but by the exceptions to that pardon; for within the category of 'excepted persons' came the names of many of the leading families of Scotland. The conciliatory aspect of the Act was embodied in the provision that, allowing only for the stated exceptions, all fines and forfeitures imposed since 1651 were to be taken off, and a general pardon was to be extended to the people of Scotland for their previous wrongdoings. But by the exceptions, all those engaged in the current revolt were excluded from the benefit of the Act; whilst the estates of 24 persons were confiscated outright, and fines were imposed on 73 more. The fines ranged from £15,000 on the heirs of the Earl of Buccleuch to five or six hundred pounds on such lesser lairds as Anstruther and Rothiemay.[25]

Although the Act was not occasioned solely by the exigencies of Glencairn's rising, all the protagonists in that revolt were affected in one way or another by it. Many of the royalist leaders came within the named exceptions, either because their participation with Glencairn or Middleton was known, or because their previous record demanded it. The others, such as Macdonald of Glengarry, who were not named, were caught by the blanket clause which excluded all those engaged in the current revolt from mercy. This sweeping provision was, however, contradicted by the proclamation which Monck issued on 4 May in accordance with Article 6 of his Instructions. In that edict Monck promised pardon to certain categories of rebels, provided that they had not been named as excepted persons in the Act of Pardon and Grace.[26] This meant that the proclamation promised mercy, whereas the ordinance threatened punishment, to those unnamed persons who were in arms in support of the king; and *both* edicts were announced to the Scottish people in the early days of May.[27] Perhaps this ambivalence was intentional. On the one hand, by pointing up the very exactness of that clause in the ordinance which singled out by name nearly one hundred of the leading men of Scotland, the confusion over the *unnamed* persons served to emphasise the distinction between the royalist leadership and their more lowly followers which Parliament had stressed so much in 1651. At the same time, however, the confusion also kept the sword of Damocles hanging over the heads of *all* who had been, or would be, tempted to defect from their loyalty to the English régime. Nonetheless both edicts made it quite clear that, for the time being at any rate, the strictest penalties and the least chance of mercy were reserved for those persons actually named in the Council's ordinance. Later on, the fines on the 73 named persons were to be substantially reduced,[28] but in the weeks before Monck's summer campaign, every indication was given that the royalist leadership would be harshly treated.

The Act of Pardon and Grace was sent north along with another ordinance 'for settling the estates of several excepted persons in Scotland to the uses herein expressed'.[29] Both were passed by Protector and Council on 12 April 1654 after consideration and amendment during the months of February and March.[30] The second of these ordinances vested the forfeited estates in the hands of trustees who were named as Sir John Hope of Craighall, William Lockhart, Richard Saltonstall, Edward Syler, Lt. Col. Timothy Wilkes, David Barclay and John Harper (the first two and last two being Scotsmen). The trustees were responsible for satisfying the creditors of the sequestrated persons out of the confiscated estates; for reserving a certain yearly revenue for the maintenance of the wives and children of the forfeitees; and for discharging the donatives granted by Parliament to certain army officers and other deserving persons out of these lands.

The four ordinances passed on 12 April were duly proclaimed in Edinburgh. The Ordinance of Union was proclaimed on 4 May, along with the first formal intimation of the establishment of the Protectorate in Scotland. This was made the occasion of Monck's solemn reception into Edinburgh by the provost and magistrates of the city; he was treated to a sumptuous banquet, at which he was waited on by the bailies of the city; and he was also entertained by a fireworks display. On the day after the banquet, on 5 May, the other ordinances were duly proclaimed and thereafter were published in other towns in Scotland.[31]

Monck did not give much indication in his letters to England of how the local populace reacted to this latest expression of English policy. But Wariston, in his diary, recorded the fact of 'every body's dissatisfaction with these proclamations', and their particular resentment of the general clauses in the Act of Pardon and Grace, which threatened ruin to so many people. Other diarists, such as Nicoll and Lamont, also took pains to record in full the names of the excepted persons in the Act, and on the whole it was this ordinance rather than any of the others which received the closest attention.[32] Thus, although the whole corpus of executive legislation contained many elements which were conciliatory and even beneficial to the Scots people, the temper of the times dictated that it was the coercive aspects of English policy which were remarked on by the Scots.

ii. The crushing of revolt and the wasting away of the royalist cause, May 1654 — September 1655

These developments in civil policy were announced to the Scottish people whilst Monck was forming plans for his military campaign. Some felt that the harsher aspects of that policy were a fitting counterpart to the vigour with which Monck would conduct the army's march against the Royalists. Wariston, after lamenting the punitive nature of the Act of Pardon and Grace, commented: 'I thought I aprehended Cromwel's designe in sending doun Monk, that as he had tryed Scotland be faire means with Dean and Lilburne, now he would trye it with rigor and ruyne by Monk.'[33]

'Rigor and ruyne' was an apt description of the tactics and the attitude which Monck adopted in his forthcoming campaign. At the end of it, many areas of Scotland had suffered at the hands of an army bent on destroying the enemy's chance of living off the countryside, and on punishing those who had succoured the rebels. Monck himself displayed great resolution in pursuing the rebels and in concerting his own march with that of Col. Morgan, whose peregrinations in the north of Scotland were as important as Monck's in wearing down the royalist forces. Monck's actual march into the hills began on 9 June 1654, but the success of that venture owed much to his clearsighted and vigorous preparations for the campaign in the preceding few weeks.

When Monck arrived in Scotland, he appeared to be surprised by the extent of the royalist threat. He told Cromwell that 'the designe of this insurreccion is more universall then I expected', and that danger was present not only in the hills, but right down to the borders of England. A few days later, on 25 April, he said he was more and more convinced that 'the people of [this] Country are generallie engag'd in this rising'. Yet he also reported that, apart from a few disturbances in Dumfries and Galloway, the Lowlands were quiet and most of the royalist forces were drawn northwards.[34] Middleton was presumed to be in Sutherland — where Morgan kept watch from a camp at Dingwall — while other royalist commanders were roaming around the central Highlands in search of fresh troops.[35] The reason for his early emphasis on the gloomy aspects of the situation must surely have been the desire to reinforce his demands for more men, money and supplies; only by stressing the potential danger to the stability of the régime could he hope to have his complaints answered. Even when, in May, he adopted a more confident approach and assured Cromwell that the Lowlands were peaceful, he kept up his pleas for reinforcements.

The distinction between Highlands and Lowlands was a crucial element in Monck's strategy. The main object of his preliminary manoeuvres was to seal off the Lowlands from incursions by the Highlanders, thereby depriving the rebels of the superior supplies of horses and men which could be got south of the Tay. His measures to make parents and kinsmen responsible for the whereabouts of their dependants complemented this design by attempting to cut off the drift of volunteers from south to north. Extra care in pacifying the Lowlands was important, too, in ensuring that once Monck had marched into the hills, there was no insurrection in his rear. His first task, therefore, was to stop up the passes on the Highland line. Thereafter he could hope to pen the main body of the royalist forces into a progressively smaller area and so inflict on them a decisive defeat. At the beginning of May, he had hopes that the Royalists could be forced to retreat *en masse* into Caithness and Sutherland, but in the event Middleton's manoeuvres, and those of his officers, kept the struggle going on a much wider front during the summer months.[36]

When he looked beyond his immediate objectives to the actual campaign in the hills, Monck knew he could count on the support of several very able colonels and the strategic advantage of a few well-placed garrisons. Morgan, destined to play the most important role, was already in the field in the far north; Daniel commanded the garrison at St. Johnstons, the modern gateway to the Highlands; Hill was at Ruthven Castle in Badenoch and Fitch at Inverness; while Brayne was in command of the troops from Ireland in the newly established garrison at Inverlochy. Brayne's position was strong in the western Highlands, but his grip on that region could only be improved if the Marquis of Argyle lent his support also.

Monck was careful, therefore, to exchange friendly greetings with Argyle and to express the hope that his co-operation would be forthcoming in the summer campaign.[37] In March Lilburne had declared that Argyllshire's freedom from unrest owed much to the Marquis's influence, and that Argyle himself was 'very peaceably inclin'd.' But the Marquis was not as convinced as Lilburne that all was well in his own country; he wanted English troops to march in and protect it and was nervous about appearing there himself. In May, however, he did make efforts to prevent Glencairn — who had hived off from the main body of the Royalists after his quarrel with Monro and Middleton — from entering the shire, and he was duly thanked for his pains by Monck. At a meeting between the two men at Kilsyth, Monck got an assurance from Argyle that he would co-operate with Brayne's garrison at Inverlochy. Argyle further suggested that if a second garrison were established at the head of Loch Tay, his followers would be so much heartened by the English presence that they would join in clearing the enemy from the area between Dumbarton and Inverness.[38] In June Monck allowed Argyle to raise and arm a force of 100 men for the defence of his shire, by which time the prospect of a conjunction between the forces of Brayne and the Marquis was visibly frightening the enemy.[39]

The conference between Monck and Argyle in May took place while Monck was in process of sealing up the Highland frontier. He left Dalkeith on 10 May and marched to Stirling, where he remained until the 14th. By 16 May he was at Cardross; from there he marched back eastwards to Kilsyth, where he remained until the 25th. All this while, Monck was unable to draw his forces closer together because of insufficient provisions, and was prevented from marching further into the hills by a shortage of grass for his horses.[40] From Kilsyth he moved to Buchanan Castle near the banks of Loch Lomond and gave orders that all the boats on the loch should be destroyed lest they be used for transport by the enemy. He also took care to establish four additional troops of horse near Glasgow to catch the enemy if, by chance, they came into the Lowlands. From Buchanan, he moved back to Stirling for a short stop, and from there to St. Johnstons where he had arrived by 2 June.[41] From there he intended to march into the hills.

During this preliminary phase of the campaign, royalist activity was muted, but it had not stopped altogether. There were reports of minor skirmishes between the rebels and English troops in areas as far apart as Ayrshire and Perth; and royalist recruiting agents were active in several places. This made the English realise that if the Royalists were ever able to draw their forces together, Monck and his colonels would have to face an army of considerable strength. There were also reports, however, that some of the rebels, afraid of the consequences of Monck's campaign, were beginning to submit.[42]

Monck left Perth (St. Johnstons) on 9 June[43] with two regiments of horse and three and a half of foot. He marched to the foot of Loch Tay where he secured the surrender of a castle situated on an island in the loch, held for the rebels by Capt. Donald Robertson. The negotiations for surrender took place between 12 and 14 June, after which Monck established a garrison of forty men on the island. At the same time he put parties of soldiers into houses at Balloch and Weems, to keep the country round about in subjection. Little difficulty was experienced in securing the surrender of an enemy garrison at Garth Castle; on the approach of a party of soldiers, the rebels fled from the stronghold and it was duly occupied by the English.[44]

At this point (14 June), Monck received intelligence that a general rendezvous of the royalist forces had been appointed to take place near Loch Ness, and so he set out in that direction. His first major stopping place on the way was Ruthven in Badenoch, where he hoped to meet up with Col. Morgan.[45] Morgan meanwhile had been moving gradually south from his camp at Dornoch in pursuit of Middleton, who had given Morgan's forces the slip and had thus been able to break out of Sutherland and Caithness. Morgan had passed through Inverness on 14 June, and on the 15th had encountered at the head of Loch Ness a party of 600 horse and foot under the command of Drummond, Irvine, Mercer and the Earl of Selkirk. The engagement resulted in a rout for the Royalists. Two days later, Morgan captured a small enemy garrison on an island in Loch Tarff, after which he received word to join Monck at Ruthven (20 June).[46]

Despite Monck's plans, however, the projected meeting with Morgan at Ruthven did not take place, because by the time Morgan received the instructions Monck had already moved on after hearing further news of Middleton's whereabouts. Middleton was reputed to be marching into the territory of Macdonald of Glengarry, and one estimate put his strength as high as 3500 horse and foot. A premature report on 19 June stated that Middleton had failed to penetrate into Lochaber (a district which cannot easily be distinguished from Glengarry's bounds) and, being afraid of the combined strength of the Marquis of Argyle and Col. Brayne, had retreated instead towards Sutherland and Caithness. What seems actually to have happened around this date was that Middleton divided his forces, sending the foot to Kintail, whence they were to take ship for Skye, and the horse to Lochaber. Middleton himself went towards Kintail, so that although he did not make it to Sutherland, he was certainly travelling farther north. By the end of the month, Monck was prepared to give some credence to the story of a mass retreat to the far north, for on 1 July he ordered Morgan to march into Caithness. There he was to destroy the corn, cattle and houses of the inhabitants to prevent them from sheltering the rebels or sending supplies to succour them farther south. This order was not executed, owing to a reported change in Middleton's position.[47]

Monck left Ruthven on 20 June and was in or around Kintail from the 26th to the 29th. During this time his army performed prodigious feats of marching and counter-marching. 'To give you account of our daily marches since [19 June] . . . is too tedious, and to give it exactly for our way is almost incredulous,' wrote one member of the expedition on the 29th. 'Since Tuesday was se'nnight we have not rested one day, nor scarce any part of a day in our way for 8 days past.'[48] From Ruthven Monck had marched to Cluny, from there to Glenroy, and so onwards to Inverlochy. As he passed through the bounds of the Clan Cameron, he gave orders for their houses to be burnt, in reprisal for their having taken up arms against the English 'invaders'. At the head of Loch Lochy on 23 June he met with Argyle and

Brayne and heard that the Camerons had lately killed more than 60 of the soldiers shipped from Ireland. By this time, Monck was sure that Middleton was in Kintail. On the 24th he came to Glenmoriston, having on the way met up with Col. Morgan whom he despatched to the head of Loch Ness, in case the enemy should be driven that way. From Glenmoriston Monck marched into the region of Kintail, where he learned that Middleton's horse had gone to Glenelg, slightly further west. Monck then harried the lands around Loch Alsh, which belonged to the Clan Mackenzie. By the 29th it had been decided to make for Inverness, where the army could stock up on provisions.[49]

In the course of their march from Ruthven in Badenoch, Monck's army had received many reports of Middleton's whereabouts, but they had never managed to catch up with him. The Royalists were able to 'find out so many back doors' that they could always keep one step ahead of their pursuers. Nonetheless, Monck's progress through the central and north-west Highlands had not been in vain; as a result of the army's pillaging and burning the lands of the Camerons, the Macdonalds and the Mackenzies, vast areas of the country were no longer able to support the rebel troops. The devastation which the Royalists themselves had wrought in this and previous campaigns also added to the havoc. Thus the English believed that despite their short-term failure, in the long run the royalist cause was hopeless. As one writer put it, 'at his [*i.e.* Middleton's] return into the parts where we have been, he will find little to live upon; and so must either disperse, starve or come into the Lowlands where we shall deal with him.'[50]

Immediately, however, Monck continued on his way to Inverness, meeting with Morgan on 1 July in Glenstrathfarar, about 25 miles to the west of that town. It was there that Morgan received his orders to march to Caithness. Two days later Monck was at Dunain, just south of Inverness, and there news reached him which changed his view of the situation. Middleton was reported to be moving not towards the far north, but into the heart of the Highlands. He had been sighted near Blair Castle in Atholl in company with 4000 horse and foot and was making for Dunkeld. Other royalist leaders had been left in Skye and Lochaber to raise fresh levies there. Later information showed that these attempts must have yielded little, at least in Skye, for Sir James Macdonald and the Captain of Clanranald stood firm for the English. The threat from Middleton and the forces under his command was, however, sufficient to compel Monck to march for Atholl and to order Morgan to make for Braemar. Ideally, either Monck or Morgan would succeed in overtaking Middleton, but failing that, Monck hoped to ensure that the royalist forces would be worn out by the chase and that the countryside through which the English passed would be made unfit to harbour the rebels.[51]

By 7 July, Monck was back at Ruthven and Middleton was reported to be at Dunkeld and making for Loch Lomond. This meant that the Royalists had a considerable head start in the march south. By the 10th, Monck had reached Weems Castle in Atholl, where he paused to take in provisions. While Monck was at Weems, he sent out a party of 200 horse and over 200 foot under Col. Okey to investigate reports of enemy movements nearby. A party of Okey's men stumbled on some of the Earl of Atholl's forces, but although the English pursued the rebels, they were unable to draw their own forces together quickly enough to deal with the whole of Atholl's contingent, which numbered about 800. Not only did Atholl escape, but he was also able to send warning to Middleton that the English were approaching. This showed, incidentally, that Monck had closed the gap considerably between himself and Middleton, who must have tarried in the area to the south of Atholl for several days. Now, however, he was reported to be gone to the west of Loch Earn. Monck gave chase on the 12th, making for the head of Loch Tay, which would put him slightly to the north of the enemy's supposed target.[52]

From Weems, Monck marched to Lawers on the north side of Loch Tay, to find that on the previous day Middleton had been at Finlarig at the head of the loch.[53] This meant that in the race westwards Middleton had been about a day's march ahead of Monck and had reached the territory of Campbell of Glenorchy. On the 14th Monck marched farther west through Glen Dochart to Glen Lochy, and in the course of the evening the army got its first real sight of Middleton. The English scouts found the Royalists in Glen Strae to the north of Loch Awe, but the two armies were separated by a 'very high hill' and a distance of about five miles. Thus, although Monck sent parties after them, the Royalists escaped, leaving behind them some baggage horses and provisions. It was difficult to discern in which direction they then turned, because the main effect of the surprisal at Glen Strae had been to disperse their forces and send them packing in disarray. One contingent, however, was known to be heading north-east towards Loch Rannoch, and later information suggested (correctly) that the main body of Middleton's now depleted army was striking out for Badenoch.[54] This meant in effect that the Royalists, in trying to escape from Monck, were marching into the arms of Morgan, who was waiting at Ruthven.

The knowledge that Morgan was in a good position to close in on Middleton from the north, and the realisation, too, that his own troops were nearing exhaustion, caused Monck to slacken the pace of his pursuit after the incident at Glen Strae. On the 15th, he marched almost due east to Strath Fillan, where he had another meeting with the Marquis of Argyle. Argyle once again declared his readiness to 'engage in bloud' with the English and to raise a party of armed men on their behalf. Monck had already on 23 June given Argyle permission to do so, but now he took the opportunity of securing the Protector's final approval of this move. The letter to Cromwell outlining this and a further scheme for engaging the Highlanders in the state's service was written from the army's camp at Glen Dochart, whither Monck had moved by 17 July.[55] That the commander-in-chief had time for such letter-writing was in itself, perhaps, an indication that he had slackened the pace for his own troops, and was relying on Morgan to apply the *coup de grâce* to Middleton.

The period of time spent in camp at Glen Dochart allowed other members of Monck's expedition to take stock of the situation and commit their thoughts to paper — William Clarke wrote to the postmaster at Newcastle, and Cornet John Baynes penned a letter to his cousin in London.[56] The tone of these letters was overwhelmingly optimistic, and showed that the army firmly believed that Middleton's days as the commander of an effective military force were numbered.

The cumulative effect of the five weeks of harrying and pillaging which Monck's army had wrought on the royalist levies and their supporters was decisive. Even the royalist counter-attacks on those clans who were loyal to the government worked ultimately to their disadvantage. Their depredations on the lands of Argyle's followers, for example, served only to strengthen the Marquis's determination to co-operate with the English, and to render yet another area unfit to shelter the rebel troops. Clarke believed that Middleton and his forces no longer deserved 'the name of an enemie', for they had been broken up and dispersed so many times. Monck reckoned that by forcing the rebels to keep on the march he had reduced Middleton's contingent from 3000 to 1200 in number. This method was all the more effective because it reinforced a tendency which had always been inherent in the royalist levies. Even in the days of Lilburne, when the Royalists and not the English had held the initiative, the king's lieutenants had had great difficulty in combining Highland recruits into an organised, disciplined force. Many of the rank and file had stayed with the army only so long as it suited their personal or material interests. Recruits from the Lowlands had, perhaps, been more amenable to military discipline, but the frequent disputes among the leadership had prevented their being welded together into a unified army. Thus the king's army had had fissiparous tendencies at the best of times, and Monck's tactics exploited these to the full.

It is worth emphasising these factors, if only because the size of the defeat which Morgan inflicted on Middleton on 19 July cannot in itself account for the subsequent collapse of the royalist cause. Its effect on the Royalists was disastrous only because it came as the last straw, after months of internal difficulties and weeks of external pressure.

By 19 July Monck had moved camp to Kinnell in Breadalbane, at the head of Loch Tay. There he intended to remain for some time, at least until he had heard how Morgan was faring in his drive against Middleton. But Monck had not completely abdicated from the hunt himself. His stay at Kinnell was designed to block any possible move by the enemy to return to Argyle's country, which had already suffered from their depredations,[57] and it also gave him a base from which he could send out parties to harass the Royalists' rear. On the 19th one such party was sighted by the royalist scouts, with the result that the rebels quickened their march from Rannoch to Badenoch. This, as Monck had planned, pushed them closer to Morgan, for having 'an eye of fear backwards upon the generall, and being soe intent upon the waies of avoiding him',[58] the Royalists had neglected to find out Morgan's position. At some stage during this march, Middleton's foot had separated from his horse, so that they lay about 4-5 miles apart. Morgan had meanwhile progressed southwards from Ruthven to Dalnaspidal at the northern tip of Loch Garry, and in the evening of 19 July his 'forlorn hope' sighted the enemy's horse. Although the strategy of pushing Middleton into Morgan's arms had been carefully planned, the actual encounter seems to have taken the English by surprise. Middleton had with him about 800 horse, whose main line of retreat lay back through a narrow pass from which they had just debouched. The difficulties of escaping along such a route allowed the English horse to catch up with them, put them to the rout, and pursue them for about six miles, despite the fact that they had dispersed in three different directions. Many of the royalist horsemen managed to escape by dismounting and taking to their heels, but the English got the rich prize of over 300 horses, several portmanteaux containing valuable papers, and about 25 prisoners. The royalist foot, numbering 1200, were untouched by this encounter, but were soon pursued by Morgan in the direction of Lochaber.[59] Middleton, who was reported to be badly wounded, escaped on foot, and a week later was back in Sutherland.[60]

The clash between the two forces at Dalnaspidal hardly ranks as a great set-piece engagement, yet its effect on the royalist cause was as serious as any formal battle. The key to the long-term significance of Morgan's victory lies in the fact that it disastrously weakened the enemy's cavalry strength. By capturing 300 horses and dispersing the rest, Morgan had ensured that 'not above 250 of them'[61] could remain together at any one time. By comparison with the horsemen, the royalist foot were of little worth in military terms, not only because they were less disciplined and less well-equipped than the horse, but because the foot alone could not form an army capable of entering the Lowlands and challenging the English in conditions which were suited to formal engagements rather than guerilla warfare. Thus, by dispersing the enemy's horse at Dalnaspidal and in the preceding few weeks of the summer campaign, Monck's army had gone a long way towards destroying the Royalists' potential as an effective political and military threat to the English régime.

Monck and Morgan, however, had by no means destroyed the Royalists' ability to harass the local population and the English troops in the Highlands; nor could they be sure that Middleton would be unable to recoup his former strength. Other royalist leaders still commanded sizeable parties of horse and foot in other parts of the Highlands, and if the ubiquitousness of the English troops made it unlikely that they could come together to form an army, nonetheless they could still inflict considerable damage on the persons and property of the Highlanders. As Monck realised, raids and skirmishes, even if they were confined to the Highlands, could still seriously threaten the peace and stability of Scotland.

Monck's estimate of the difficulties still ahead of him is amply attested by the stringency of the measures which he adopted after Morgan's success at Dalnaspidal. There was to be no let-up in the army's pursuit of those Royalists who were still in arms, and the policy of devastating the countryside was to be continued. As the Royalists also burned and looted many of the areas through which they passed, the month of August saw an increase in chaos and poverty among the Highland clans.

The immediate effect of Dalnaspidal was to cause the forces under Middleton's command to break up and disperse. Many of the foot ran off to their homes; those who remained in a body were pursued by Morgan; and those horsemen who, without their mounts, tried to escape from the region were set upon and robbed by the local inhabitants. Some idea of the demoralisation which then set in amongst the royalist levies was given by Sir James Turner, an ardent king's man, who had landed in Scotland from the Continent in June 1654. After Middleton's defeat

Turner lurked around Loch Earn, where he noticed numerous horsemen passing by on their way home, 'having taken a liberty to themselves to disband'; these men declared themselves willing to rejoin the king's service, but only if they could be found new horses and equipment, which was at present in a sorry state. In August, Turner collected a party of followers and had a successful encounter with the English on the way to Fife, but the party broke up when Turner discovered that they were more interested in plundering than in fighting for the king.[62]

Monck, on hearing news of Morgan's victory, was anxious to round up the stragglers. On 20 July he had set out from Kinnell for Glen Lyon, and from there he despatched a party under Major Bridge to pursue the escapees around Loch Rannoch. Bridge fell upon a party of horse and foot under the Earl of Atholl and succeeded in capturing some prisoners and a fair amount of baggage. Bridge then rejoined Monck, who on 21 July was encamped near Weems.[63] By 23 July Monck had reached St. Johnstons, and by the 28th he had retired to Stirling. This was only a temporary respite, however, for Monck intended to march back into the hills within a few days so that he could continue the work of harassing the rebels and burning the countryside.[64]

The month of August saw the effective prosecution of these tactics. Monck and that part of the army immediately under his command concentrated on those areas which the rebels had been known to shelter in during the previous winter. Perthshire, particularly the area round Aberfoyle, and that region of Dunbartonshire around Loch Lomond suffered heavily. In contrast to the feats of long-distance marching which the army had performed in June and July, Monck's progress was now slow, not, however, out of consideration for his troops but because there was so much grass and corn in these areas that it took some time to destroy it all effectively. From time to time, parties of Royalists were sighted, but on only a few occasions did the English actually bring them to an engagement. The Royalists were certainly demoralised, but they could still put up a spirited, if fruitless, rearguard action. They, too, burned and pillaged the lands through which they passed and perpetrated great cruelties on any English soldier unwise enough to stray from the main body of his regiment.[65]

While Monck's activities in the southern Highlands threatened such royalist leaders as Glencairn, Atholl, Forrester and Montrose, Middleton had travelled farther north into Caithness, well out of reach of the English commander. But Morgan was on hand to follow up his victory at Dalnaspidal. Estimates of Middleton's strength at the beginning of August put his capability at 200 horse and 600 foot, but other reports suggested that dissension in his army would seriously reduce its effectiveness. Morgan was ordered to follow Middleton into Caithness and, whether or not he caught up with the royalist general, to burn the lands and houses of the populace. As a complement to Morgan's presence in Caithness, two frigates, the *Assistance* and the *Sparrow*, were detailed to ply the coasts between the Pentland Firth and Inverness. Their task was to prevent supplies being landed from abroad and to guard against the recurrence of an incident in which one of Middleton's men-of-war had set upon some English merchant vessels. The frigates were, in fact, instrumental in forcing the surrender of the royalist Sir James Sinclair's house on the coast near Thurso. As for Middleton, he again eluded his pursuers, this time by fleeing westwards to Seaforth's fastness of Eilandonan, whither he was followed by a detachment of Morgan's men. Meanwhile, the royalist population of Caithness surrendered to the English and were spared from further devastation on condition that they made restitution to those who had suffered at Middleton's hands.[66]

As a result of the measures which Monck adopted during this month, many of the royalist forces, both officers and men, were induced to submit to the English. One factor which greatly influenced the rank and file was the English practice of sending prisoners taken during actual engagements to the Barbadoes. To avoid this fate many small parties began to submit voluntarily, offering to give bonds for their future good behaviour.[67] August also saw the surrender of several of the leading royalist commanders and the conclusion of formal treaties of capitulation with them. The first to sign was the Earl of Atholl on 24 August. He was closely followed by Glencairn on the 29th, and in the course of the next few weeks by Lord Forrester, Viscount Kenmore and the Marquis of Montrose. Each of these treaties naturally included the subordinate officers and the private soldiers who had submitted along with their commanders.[68] Thus, by the end of September, even if Middleton himself had escaped the English clutches, a sizeable portion of the royalist leadership, not to mention the rank and file, had been siphoned off and rendered harmless.

The terms of these treaties were, on the whole, remarkably lenient. On condition that the signatories laid down their arms and gave security for their peaceable living, they were allowed to retain their estates, both real and personal. The only exception to this was that any donative made by Parliament or the Council from these estates must still be honoured. The securities demanded were, however, set at very high figures (£5000 stg. in Glencairn's case), and some of the signatories had difficulty in raising the necessary bonds. But this was more than offset by the fact that they were absolved by the terms of their capitulations from any penalties they might have incurred under the Ordinance of Pardon and Grace of April 1654.[69] On balance, therefore, they stood to gain substantially by submitting to Monck, and indeed in some cases ended up in a better position than many of their more law-abiding countrymen who had taken no part in the rising but had still to pay heavy fines under the April ordinance.

In addition, the defeated royalist leaders were given permission to levy regiments for service overseas. From the English point of view, this was no mere incidental, but an important element in their plans for preventing a recurrence of royalist-inspired violence. English observers had long believed that Scotland's troubled state stemmed partly from poverty and overpopulation: men were forced to turn to robbery and violence to improve their living standards. Thus if the population could be reduced by several thousands, greater peace and harmony would ensue. Lilburne had first put forward the idea of diverting men from the royalist cause by allowing them to enlist for service overseas in his letters south in 1653; Monck had lent his support to the plan when he arrived in Scotland; and it finally found expression in the treaties of 1654 and 1655. The practical effect of this proposal was, however, small. None of the royalist noblemen seems to have seized on the opportunity, perhaps because Charles II had already declared himself against any such idea.[70]

In other ways, too, Monck showed himself capable of thinking ahead and planning against fresh outbreaks of trouble. For, although the victories of the summer had in fact struck the death-blow to the royalist cause in Scotland, much remained to be done, not only to capture Middleton, but to restore order and tranquillity to the Highlands. As early as 5 August, Monck had asked Cromwell to continue the garrison at Lochaber for at least another year, for it 'will bee of that concernment to us for the reducing of the Highlands, that I doe not know how wee shall bee able to compasse our worke without itt'.[71]

The retention of this force at Lochaber was part of a general policy of settling garrisons at strategic points throughout the Highlands. Many of these were established in castles or country houses, some of which had been captured from the rebels, while others were commandeered from loyal supporters of the government. One of the latter was Argyle's seat at Inveraray, but this received its complement of English soldiers only after an unfortunate incident, which threatened to rupture diplomatic relations between Monck and the Marquis.

The garrison at Inveraray was to consist of five companies of foot and four troops of horse. On Argyle's advice, Monck sent a supply ship, containing 600 bags of biscuit and 10 tons of cheese as well as a fair quantity of ammunition, to Inveraray ahead of the land forces so that when the latter came to Argyllshire they would not be dependent for food on the impoverished countryside. But as the supplies were being landed on the shore in front of the Marquis's house, a party of royalist horse, led by Argyle's son, Lorne, swooped down upon them, captured the guard and the vessel, and made off with some of the provisions. What was left was immediately seized on by the country people.[72]

Monck was enraged, but could not stop the forces intended for Inveraray from reaching their destination. He strongly suspected Argyle, or 'Archgyle' as one English source nicknamed him,[73] of double-dealing, but he could not prove his suspicions. He insisted, however, that the country people make reparation for the loss they had inflicted and was no doubt strengthened in this decision by the knowledge that Argyle's tenants had on previous occasions shown their partiality for Lorne and, by implication, for the royalist cause. Argyle, of course, made haste to assure Monck that he was entirely innocent of any part in the affair. He stood to lose much by incurring Monck's disfavour, not least because he needed an English presence to bolster his power in Argyllshire and ward off possible attacks from those Royalists who, like Lorne, were still at large. He was thus particularly sensitive to suggestions that Monck might cancel his orders for a garrison at Inveraray, and was fulsome in his expressions of innocence and regret. His fears about the withdrawal of the garrison were not realised; but Monck did take this opportunity to inform the Marquis that the men he had raised for the public service would no longer be paid for by the state and must be disbanded.[74]

The upkeep of all these garrisons in terms of manpower alone was considerable. At the beginning of October, Monck stressed in a letter to Cromwell that the total number of the forces in Scotland should on no account be reduced, for the task of pacifying the Highlands must not be put in jeopardy. There were still three or four clans which had not yet been reduced to obedience and, besides, the impoverishment of the Highlands meant that many of the natives must soon revert to robbery and violence.[75]

This constant harping on the theme of poverty and violence shows that Monck, like Lilburne, was alive to the socio-economic origins of the unrest in Scotland. He was aware, too, that in some ways the army had itself contributed to the problem, for its campaign of devastation in the Highlands had destroyed the livelihood of many people. It was for this reason that he was anxious to establish garrisons and to maintain the strength of his forces, for past experience indicated that the greater the hardship, the more likely the Highlanders were to provoke disorder. The extent of the damage which the English army had inflicted on the lands north of the Tay can be judged from the figures which Monck gave Cromwell on the yield of the assessment. In August he stated that not more than £6000 per month could be expected from the cess 'by reason of the late burnings and destruccion', and in a later letter he indicated that the actual cost of the summer campaign in terms of lost taxation was about £1000 per month. By November, his estimate of the yield had risen to £7300, and by the spring/summer of 1655 it had reached £8000,[76] but still Monck was convinced that it represented a severe burden on the Scottish people. Moreover, he believed strongly that any attempt to squeeze more out of the Scots would only fan the flames of unrest once more.[77] This point was especially important in the autumn of 1654, for at that time Monck was under particular pressure from Whitehall to raise the full £10,000 per month from Scotland. This, he flatly declared, was impossible.[78] In a sense this weakened Monck's case in the other battle he was waging with Whitehall in these months: the struggle for money to pay his army. The assessment had always been designated for the upkeep of the army of occupation and hence, as its yield lessened, the greater became the demands on the wider resources of the central treasury. Monck, however, did not hesitate to demand that money be sent up from England. In September he was particularly mollified by the arrival of £30,000 and by the anticipation of £25,000 more, although by the time the bulk of the latter arrived in November, expenditure had once again gone up steeply.[79]

Undeterred by these administrative difficulties, Monck turned in the autumn of 1654 to the vigorous prosecution of the next stage in the mopping-up operation. For although the capitulations of September had marked the end of the most important phase in the war against the Royalists, this was no reason for the army to relax its vigilance. As well as the fear of disorder inspired by hunger, there was also the knowledge that Charles II had sent messages to Middleton urging him to keep the campaign going throughout the winter.[80] Thus the enemy were still Royalists, and not merely robbers.

One can sense in Monck's letters at this time a certain impatience, almost exasperation, with Middleton and his crew, a feeling that, since further resistance must in the long run be futile, it was stubborn and even impertinent of the rebels not to submit forthwith. This impatience was translated into a hardening of

Monck's attitude towards recurrent offenders (*i.e.* those rebels who took up arms again after initially agreeing to submit). In October, he asked for and got an addition to the Articles of War which ensured that anyone captured for a second time in arms should die without mercy. The same provision was to apply to anyone found guilty of burning the property of those loyal to the government.[81] Monck's annoyance with men who failed to realise they had lost, as well as his determination to put an end to the remaining pockets of resistance, was further expressed in January 1655. By then, several of the second rank of royalist leaders — namely Kinoule, Dudhope, Sir Mungo Murray and Lt. Col. Mercer — had been captured, and Monck proposed that they 'or any more pillageing rascalls who staide oute after many oppertunities of coming in' should be executed for terrorism *pour encourager les autres*.[82] This proposal was not accepted by the central government, and so other measures had to suffice.

By far the easiest and most effective way of defeating Middleton in the winter months of 1654/5 was to allow the royalist cause to destroy itself. This could be achieved most effectively if the Scottish community were induced to withdraw support from those rebels who were still in arms; for without supplies of men, money, food and horses from the local population, the royalist forces could not sustain themselves. By the end of 1654, the rebel army had been dispersed and its remnants confined to a relatively small area of Scotland, so that Middleton and his men no longer had the strength to force large numbers of Scots to contribute to their maintenance. Even in those areas where the Royalists still had troops, their chances of success were small, for by the simple expedient of destroying their food supplies the English army had also destroyed the inhabitants' wish to succour the Royalists. As Monck had anticipated, the Scots now fell out amongst themselves and the rebels were deprived of their winter shelter. In essence, therefore, Monck's overall strategy involved a delicate balance of risks, for the policy of devastation could equally well lead to further disorder. Monck could, however, rely on the presence of the garrisons in the Highlands to tip the odds in the army's favour.

The success of the policy was shown in one particular incident around Lochaber in late October. Middleton was on a recruiting drive in the district, but met with little success. His men therefore turned to the seizure of provisions where before they had been unable to gather men. They attempted to carry off some cows belonging to the country people, but met with stout resistance. In the skirmish which followed, both the Royalists and the men of Lochaber suffered casualties, but the latter succeeded in regaining possession of their beasts. Col. Brayne, commander of the nearby garrison of Inverlochy, attempted to follow up this advantage by despatching 700 men to pursue Middleton, but the latter escaped and made off in the direction of Kintail. Monck specifically attributed the incident to the Highlanders' desire to conserve their food supplies in order to ward off starvation and predicted that such disputes would grow more frequent and would lead to the disintegration of the royalist cause.[83]

Middleton was reported to have about 300 men, mostly foot, with him at this time, a number which he found it impossible to augment. Despite his threats to 'kill, burn, hang and destroy all before him' — threats which in any case he could not carry out unless he recruited more men — most of the clans stubbornly refused to join him. Even those chieftains who, like Seaforth, Glengarry, Macleod of Dunvegan and Cameron of Lochiel, were personally loyal to him could not promote a similar enthusiasm among their followers. A general rendezvous planned for 22 or 25 November was an undoubted flop, if indeed it took place at all.[84] The English for their part scored a major success by capturing Kinoule and company on 20 November, and Argyle lent further support to their cause by driving Lorne out of Argyllshire.

Towards the end of October Argyle took up arms against his son, and with the assistance of Capt. Nicholls and the garrison at Inveraray, forced him to quit his territory in Argyllshire. Lorne, in company with the Chancellor, Loudoun, was then reputedly seeking to rejoin Middleton, his royalist ardour apparently undiminished by his recent reverses.[85] Argyle's forthright action against his son had doubtless been prompted by a desire to atone for the unfortunate incident in September, when Lorne's men had attacked the English supply vessels at Inveraray and when the Marquis's own good faith had been cast in doubt. Certainly his reprisal against Lorne was encouraged by Monck, and on 16 November Argyle got his reward when Monck acknowledged his fidelity and support in a letter of commendation to the Protector. Such favour was especially valuable to Argyle at this time, for he was being harried by his creditors and was anxious to obtain the full benefit of the ordinance for relief of debtors.[86] The relationship between Monck and Argyle seems, indeed, to have been firmly established on a *quid pro quo* basis, for in December the general was again dropping hints, and even threats, to the Marquis that a *rapprochement* with his son leading to the latter's formal capitulation would be welcome. Argyle did his best, but the bad blood between father and son made agreement difficult.[87] The negotiations for Lorne's surrender dragged on well into the New Year and, despite Argyle's efforts, it was really the capitulations of other royalist leaders in the spring of 1655 that induced him finally to submit.

December 1654 was a very bad month for Middleton, and for the other royalist leaders. The efforts of Glengarry to appoint a rendezvous in his bounds and to join with the men of Cameron of Lochiel came to nothing, for Cameron's men failed to turn up. Lord Reay had a potential force of 200 men at his command in Strathnaver, but he could not rely on them coming together at one time. Middleton himself was roaming the north-west, but his followers numbered less than 100 — one report put his personal following as low as 20. But the greatest misery the Royalists had to endure was the weather: fierce snowstorms raged, the worst the Highlands had seen for 20 years.[88] Ironically, but not unnaturally, as the plight of his Scots supporters worsened, the king, from the safety of his court at Cologne, redoubled his efforts to keep up their morale and to sustain their campaign throughout the winter. There was even a fresh burst of rumour that he himself would soon land in Scotland, and court officials continued to press for the supply of money, arms and ammunition from friendly merchants and private persons overseas.[89]

But even as Charles was composing a fresh set of messages to his loyal friends in Scotland, a new wave of surrender had begun. In December, both Lt. Col. Irvine and the Earl of Seaforth had offered to treat. On 10 January 1655 articles of agreement were concluded with Seaforth and several of the name of Mackenzie.[90] The terms were much the same as those which had been granted to Glencairn and others the previous autumn, but with one important difference. Seaforth and his clan were expressly allowed 'to carry theire armes for theire owne defence against broaken men and theeves within theire owne bounds'. This provision, which had not appeared in the treaties of 1654 (there all the signatories had been disarmed indefinitely and without exception), was to crop up again in the agreements signed in May 1655 with other clan chiefs. It was, in fact, a privilege reserved especially for those with influence in the Highlands (into which category none of the signatories of 1654 came), and it was designed specifically to deal with the problems of unrest and disorder in that region. As such, it represented an admission by Monck that peace and tranquillity in the Highlands could not be maintained by the English army alone; instead the men of the Highlands themselves had to be enrolled as constables to watch over the malefactors in their midst. But if Monck was thereby acknowledging that the feuds and jealousies of the Highlanders, not to mention the effects of poverty and disruption, were potentially greater than his forces alone could cope with, he was also attempting to turn this state of affairs to his own advantage. For his aim was to play the internal squabbles of the clansmen off against each other, and so produce a kind of stalemate from which the English army, as peacekeepers, would benefit. These ideas, which were first hinted at in the terms of Seaforth's capitulation, were to be given much fuller expression in the course of 1655, not only in the terms which Monck granted to the royalist clansmen in their treaties of surrender, but also in the way in which the general and his officers handled relationships between the royalist leaders before their coming in. Thus, for example, a whole series of inducements were held out to certain chieftains and officers in the spring, urging them to help the English capture their more recalcitrant colleagues, and so obtain better terms for themselves. In April, when Monck was again negotiating through Argyle for Lorne's surrender, he asked the Marquis to remind his son that by arranging for Col. McNaughton's capture, he could improve his own lot; likewise McNaughton could obtain better terms for himself if he apprehended Cameron of Lochiel. The final link in the chain would come, as Monck explained a week later to Col. Thomas Cooper, governor of Ayr, if Cameron of Lochiel would undertake to apprehend Macdonald of Glengarry; if he did so, Monck would reduce the amount of security demanded from him, or else would force Glengarry to give back a piece of land which he had previously filched from Lochiel.[91]

Monck's policy of playing the rebels off against each other, and of then allowing them to share in the enforcement of law and order within their own bounds, did not, however, represent any especial cunning or subtlety on his part. It was merely a clear-sighted recognition of the practical realities of the situation. For as Monck explained in a letter to Col. Cooper on 29 March, he was content that those who lived in the hills should keep their arms, not only to protect themselves against thieving neighbours, but also because no matter what the army did, the Highlanders would always find a way of retaining their weapons — they would probably hand in a few and conceal the rest, but even if they were disarmed completely, they would somehow or other find a way of obtaining more.[92]

At the time of Seaforth's submission, it must have seemed to Monck that the surrender of the other Royalists would be accomplished swiftly and that there might be no need for double-dealing in the spring, for the discouragements of December had induced even Middleton to open negotiations with the English. On 15 December he wrote to Monck asking that a pass be granted for three negotiators to travel from his hideout to the general's headquarters, and that a cessation of arms be declared in the meantime. Monck acceded to the first request but not to the second. Nonetheless, negotiations were opened in the course of January, and by 8 February terms had been agreed on. These included the harsh provision that, unlike the others who had submitted to that date, Middleton, Dalziel, Drummond, Lord Napier and Sir Robert Moray were to forfeit their entire estates, saving only the fifth part which would go towards the maintenance of their wives and children. At the very last moment, however, the negotiators declared to Monck that they could not stomach such severe penalties, and on 10 February they broke off the treaty and returned to the hills.[93]

By this time Middleton had taken refuge in the isle of Skye, where Macleod of Dunvegan was a staunch supporter of the royalist cause. There he got word of Charles's efforts to send over supplies from the Continent. Charles counselled patience to his supporters, but as Middleton remarked to Lord Reay, 'that is an herbe not to be founde in manie of our gardens.'[94] The only crumb of comfort which could be afforded the Royalists was that disaffection in his own army was causing Monck no little anxiety. In December 1654 and January 1655 the details of the so-called 'Overton plot',[95] in which Major General Robert Overton was alleged to have fomented a conspiracy to seize Monck and march the army into England to overthrow the Protector, were gradually unravelled. The truth of the matter was probably rather different: Overton was certainly guilty of the same kind of seditious activity as the 'three colonels', Okey, Alured and Saunders, with whose views on religion and politics his own very much corresponded; but his complicity in a design for mutiny and even revolution is rather more open to doubt. During the time which it took Monck and his trusted subordinates to root out those officers who shared Overton's sympathies, and to trace their connections with seditious elements in England, the problems of dealing with the Royalists had to take second place. These were certainly not neglected — it was, for example, during this time that the abortive negotiations with Middleton took place — but Monck's energies were necessarily divided. It was, perhaps, fortunate that the diversion took place during the winter months, when military action against the Royalists was in any case at a standstill.

The impact of the 'Overton plot' and its offshoots on the Royalists' fortunes was, in effect, minimal. Monck had, however, been very concerned lest the unrest in England should lead to a diminution of the forces at his command, for such a move would endanger not only the final push against the Royalists but also the cohesion of the army itself. In December, he had received orders for the withdrawal of Major General Lambert's regiment of horse and Sir William Constable's companies of foot, but he begged Cromwell not to issue any further orders of this kind, for only if the present establishment were continued would he be able 'to keepe both Scotts (and English of our owne army) in quiett'.[96]

In March, after the repercussions of the 'Overton plot' had died away, and the leading offenders had been court-martialled, Monck could concentrate once more on hunting down Middleton. A new sense of urgency was injected into the task by the news of Penruddock's rising in England: this royalist fracas in Dorset and Wiltshire was quickly suppressed, but the authorities in England and Scotland were on their guard lest disaffection should spread. On 20 March Monck reported that rumours of the trouble in England had caused the Scots 'to prick upp theire eares, and have thoughts of riseing againe'. A party of about 24 Tories had formed in Galloway, and Middleton, along with Lorne, McNaughton, Macleod of Dunvegan and others, was reported to be planning a rendezvous not far from the head of Loch Ness. But Monck was confident that the presence of the English garrisons, together with the extra security measures he had introduced, such as the arrest of all strangers without a special pass and the strict examination of everyone entering or leaving the country, would quickly quell any unrest.[97] News of Penruddock's defeat more than anything else dampened Scottish spirits and allowed Monck's plans for bringing the last of the Royalists to book to come to fruition.

In late March and early April, Monck's ideas on how to play the rebel leaders off against each other were put into practice. On 27 March he stated his belief that Lorne, McNaughton and the Earl of Selkirk were 'upon comeing in', and that Lord Reay and Macleod of Dunvegan were no longer willing actively to aid Middleton.[98] There then began the complicated series of threats and promises by which he hoped to ensnare, in turn, Lorne, McNaughton, Cameron of Lochiel and Macdonald of Glengarry. In this proposed sequence of events, the Marquis of Argyle held a key position, for it was through him that Monck was negotiating with Lorne. At the same time Monck was using another prominent member of the Campbell clan, Sir James Campbell of Lawers, to put pressure on Macleod. Probably while the negotiations for Middleton's submission were going on, Lawers arrived on the isle of Skye to offer very advantageous terms to Macleod if he would desert the cause. Macleod at first refused and Lawers left the island; but when negotiations were reopened in March, Macleod's people refused to rise on his behalf and so he was forced to yield.[99] It was some little time before negotiations with Monck on the actual treaty finally took place; but on 12 May a pass was granted to Macleod to come to treat, and the articles of agreement were signed on the 29th.[100]

When Middleton learned of Macleod's defection, he wrote to Lord Reay warning him to lose no time in seeking means for his own preservation. Clearly Middleton believed that all was lost, and that it was now a case of *sauve qui peut*. Reay accordingly put out feelers to Monck through the agency of a certain Mr. Alexander Macdonald. On 5 May Monck sent word back to him that he must agree on terms within five weeks, but Reay took less than a fortnight to make up his mind — on 18 May an agreement was signed between Monck and Reay's representative, Hugh Mackay.[101]

On 17 May treaties were also signed with Lorne, McNaughton and Cameron of Lochiel; and on 19 May articles were concluded with the Earl of Selkirk.[102] John Graham, laird of Duffra, signed somewhat later — 17 July — but the negotiations for his surrender had long been under way, certainly since May.[103] Likewise in May Macdonald of Glengarry agreed to treat; although the articles for his surrender had been substantially agreed on by the first week in June, the formal signing did not take place until later in the month.[104]

It is impossible to say exactly how much influence Monck's promptings and promises of reward had on the Royalists' decision to submit. In one sense, their capitulation was the logical outcome of that downward trend in royalist fortunes which had been going on unchecked since the defeat at Dalnaspidal. Long after their cause was lost, some of the leaders maintained a touching loyalty to and faith in their commander; indeed, it was only Middleton's express permission that induced Reay, and also Lorne, to begin final negotiations with Monck.[105] But in the discussions which then ensued, many of the Royalists were only too happy to bargain with Monck in order to secure lenient terms, and also to enlist the army's aid in their attempts to settle old scores with domestic rivals. The request most frequently made — and the one most often granted — was for some abatement in the amount of cess due from the delinquents' estates. But there were also demands of a more varied kind. Glengarry, for example, wanted Monck to grant him indemnity for all wrongs committed since 1644; this, in effect, would have extended the period of indemnity granted in the Act of Pardon and Grace by four years and so would have covered the time when he was active in Montrose's service. Monck did not formally accede to this request in the terms of Glengarry's surrender, but in August he did warn Lt. Col. Blount, the deputy governor of Inverness, not to allow Glengarry to be prosecuted for crimes committed 'in the former wars' — a phrase which could be taken to include the years 1644-5 — if Glengarry conducted himself well after the current rising.[106] Cameron of Lochiel succeeded in getting some concessions actually written into the terms of his agreement: thus he was freed from the arrears of rent he owed William McIntosh of Torcastle for some lands in Lochaber, on condition that he allowed a panel of arbitrators comprising Monck, Brayne and Argyle to decide upon the amount he should pay in the future.[107]

Monck, for his part, saw to it that the resources of the defeated chieftains were harnessed to the army's efforts to maintain law and order in the Highlands. As had been the case in Seaforth's treaty, the signatories of the spring and summer, along with their tenants and clansmen, were allowed to keep their arms for purposes of defence, on condition that they gave bonds for their future good behaviour. This provision did not, however, apply to Macleod of Dunvegan — presumably Monck felt that he could best ensure peace on the isle of Skye by relying solely on Sir James Macdonald of Sleat. But Macleod was made responsible for the good behaviour of his uncles, Norman and Rory Macleod, both of whom were ardent

Royalists, and for the laird of Raasay. As compensation for the trouble involved, Dunvegan was to enjoy the life-rents of his uncles' estates, and the profits from Raasay's.[108] The capitulations of Lorne and his colleagues brought to a satisfactory conclusion Monck's efforts to destroy the last shreds of royalist morale and to force the final remnants of their battered army to submit. But to the last, Middleton eluded his enemies. Sometime in April he took ship for the Continent, where he began almost immediately to plot afresh for the resurgence of the king's cause in Scotland.[109] Others of his associates were not induced to submit until later in the summer — Sir Robert Moray, for example, agreed to come in only in July.[110] But the surrender of Glengarry in May had really marked the end of that complex series of events which historians have labelled 'Glencairn's Rising'.

On 8 May Monck assured the authorities in Whitehall that there was little for the army to do that summer 'unlesse it bee the reduseing of some stubborne Clanns in the Hills to obedience'.[111] By this he meant not so much that the clans in question still presented a politically inspired military danger, but that their natural unruliness and disobedience to the normal law enforcement agencies was a potential threat to the completeness of his grip upon Scotland. With this admission the wheel had come full circle, for Monck was implying that the endemic violence of the Scottish Highlands, which in 1652-3 had provided the springboard for military revolt, had outlasted the suppression of that revolt. Its containment in the future was to be one of his major concerns, if only to prevent a recurrence of that spirit of rebellion which Glencairn, Middleton and others had so successfully fomented.

For that reason, at the same time as Monck was triumphantly reporting the final submission of the royalist leaders in the spring and summer of 1655, he was impressing upon the central government the absolute necessity of maintaining the garrisons in the hills and of keeping the forces in Scotland well supplied, well paid and up to strength.[112] These requests he reiterated in the face of a reduction in the army establishment ordered by the Protector and Council in July: this provided that the army in Scotland should consist of 13 regiments and 1 company of foot (reduced in October to 11 regiments), 7 regiments of horse and 4 companies of dragoons. As part of the policy of retrenchment, each company of foot was to be reduced from 100 to 80 men. In August, in order to save a further £3500 per month in the cost of the army in Scotland, the Council ordered more cuts to be made.[113] Monck was concerned not so much with the reduction in the size of his forces, but with the implications which the details of the new establishment had for his policy of garrisoning strategic points throughout the country. The more settled state of the country meant that the withdrawal of a certain proportion of the foot could be effected without undue harm. The horse had, perhaps, a more vital role to play in maintaining peace, especially in the Highlands, but even here Monck was concerned not so much with mere numbers as with settled conditions of pay and service. He recommended, for example, that even if every three regiments of foot were to be reduced into two, and every two regiments of horse into one, some of the regiments which remained should be put on permanent service in Scotland so that the officers and their families could settle in the country and absenteeism could be reduced.[114]

Monck was, of course, constantly worried about the soldiers' arrears of pay. The money designated out of the English assessment for payment of the army in Scotland was, he declared, inadequate, especially since the two major sources of maintenance from the Scottish revenue — namely the assessment and the newly introduced excise duties — were not likely to yield anything like the sums expected. But his main criticism of the new establishment was that it allowed only £800 per month for contingency charges of all kinds, including the building of fortifications. The work in progress on the new fortifications alone, principally the citadels at Ayr, St. Johnstons and Inverness, along with other repair work at Leith, came to over £1000 per month; and in addition to that, the smaller garrisons, some of which were established in country houses, had to be provided with such necessaries as beds, bed-clothes and food. Other claims on the contingency monies included the cost of keeping prisoners in custody. In all, Monck reckoned, he needed a minimum of £1000 per month for the new building programme, plus £800 for other contingency charges.[115]

These points Monck pressed home in a series of letters to the Protector, to Lambert and to the Council throughout August and September 1655. He stressed the importance of keeping up the garrisons and building the fortifications many times, but never more forcibly than in a letter to President Lawrence on 7 September:

> Wee have already quitted as many guarrisons as possibly wee may with safety; the rest that are now kept must necessarily bee repaired and provided for; otherwise wee shall leave some part of the Country without any forces, and by that meanes loose people willbee apt to get together againe, seing those Country men are still forward to waite for an opportunity to doe the same, and want not advice or incurragement from Charles Stewart to doe it.[116]

Monck thus highlighted the two areas in which he and the army were to be most active in the coming years: the suppression of domestic disorder, and the interception of correspondence from Royalists abroad. Past experience had taught him that if these two elements should come together — the political motive and the social unrest — the result could be armed rebellion. The facility with which Monck could accomplish his task depended in part on the kind of relationship which had been formed between the army and the Scottish community in 1654 and 1655. For Monck, like Lilburne, had had to deal with the civil as well as the military aspects of Glencairn's rising. His efforts in this respect not only affected the aid and allegiance which the Scottish people gave the Royalists in the last stages of the rising. They influenced also the work of postwar reconstruction which took place after 1655, when the authority which Monck had exercised over civil affairs was largely taken over by the newly formed Council for Scotland.

7

Monck and the Scottish People, April 1654 — September 1655

IN his dealings with the Scottish people, Monck gave further expression to Lilburne's belief that the rising had its roots in the local communities, and that it could be defeated only if the support which the local people gave to the royalist forces was effectively cut off. For this reason the military and the civil aspects of Monck's policy were always closely intertwined. In the preliminaries to his military campaign in the summer of 1654, for example, he had not only taken steps to strengthen the army in Scotland, but had also adopted various measures to deal with the Royalists' civilian support. At many points in the campaign, his military objectives had been inseparable from his policy towards the local people — thus his devastation of parts of the Highlands and the consequent destruction of the inhabitants' livelihood had been integral to his strategy for forcing the royalist levies to submit.

But in addition to the factors which came into play during Monck's drive against Middleton, the commander-in-chief adopted many other expedients in his treatment of the civilian population in 1654-55. The nature of this treatment was conditioned not merely by the need to accelerate the process of royalist defeat, but also by the desire to ensure that after the revolt was over, Scotland remained a governable country. Monck's policy, like Lilburne's, was inevitably a mixture of conciliation and coercion. Like Lilburne, Monck aimed at making the community responsible for the conduct of its members, in part by allowing trusted elements to participate in suppressing disorder; while in the long term he showed the same calculating concern as Lilburne had done for the material lot of the Scottish people, particularly the politically articulate classes.

Monck continued the policy of allowing local communities to maintain armed guards for their defence against robbers and royalist invaders. Indeed, in the permits which he issued to groups of parishes, to the gentry in a particular shire, and to certain specified individuals, he did not always make a clear distinction between 'the enemy' in a political or military sense, and the everyday social menace of thieves, loose men and vagabonds. This showed how closely the two categories were connected in Monck's mind, and how strongly he felt that in future the maintenance of everyday law and order would be a key element in ensuring the stability of the régime. Monck's order-books, from which much evidence about his dealings with the Scots comes, contain detailed references to the guards which were mounted by certain parishes in the shires of Perth and Stirling,[1] to the watches mounted by the High Sheriff of Roxburgh and 'the gentlemen' of Caithness,[2] and to a whole host of lairds who were allowed to arm their tenants for their own defence. The gentry to whom this privilege was granted included such stalwart supporters of the régime as the fiar of Glenorchy, and men who had been threatened by the royalist forces in their heyday, such as Sir Thomas Stuart of Grantully.[3] In November 1654, as the winter storms began to make the remnants of Middleton's army more desperate in their search for food and shelter, Monck found it necessary to let the men of Strathspey, Badenoch and Lochaber[4] take up arms for their own defence, but here the unsettled state of the region and its ambivalent political loyalties led him to demand that English officers be in charge of the guards. The year 1654 also saw commissions being granted to individuals who were neither greater gentry nor lesser lairds but who, to judge by their surnames, were in many cases ordinary Scotsmen, to hunt the enemy, and to apprehend moss-troopers, thieves or idle persons.[5] For every prisoner these men succeeded in handing over to the English garrisons, they usually received a fee of £1 stg. This employment could be quite lucrative: in May 1655 it was disclosed that Capt. William Roy Menzies had, over an unspecified period of time, brought in 40 prisoners, and, not surprisingly, he then applied to have his warrant renewed.[6] But the system, useful as it was in supplementing the peace-keeping functions of the army, was sometimes liable to abuse. Some of the parishes in Perthshire, for example, commissioned Lt. Col. Daniel (or Donald) Macgregor to command their watch, but it came to Monck's ears that he was claiming maintenance from the country for 30 men, instead of the 24 who had initially been authorised.[7] And Mr. John Dempster, who in July had been authorised to raise 12 honest and faithful Scotsmen 'and others' to hunt down moss-troopers, had his warrant taken away from him in the following month because he had stolen horses from the country people.[8]

Such measures as these complemented Monck's decision to allow the royalist lairds and chieftains who were comprised in the treaties of capitulation of 1655 to retain their arms for defence against marauding neighbours. Both were an admission by Monck that the traditional methods of bringing offenders to book had their place alongside the might of the English army and, in peace-time, the power of the English Judges. In his efforts to bring the Highlands into obedience, Monck was thus prepared to use a variety of agencies, both civil and military, English and Scottish. In June 1655, a series of orders which he issued to his key men in the Highlands, Col. Fitch at Inverness and Col. Brayne at Inverlochy, illustrated the complexity of his task.

In a letter to Fitch of 21 June,[9] Monck expressed concern at the number of thieves and vagabonds who roamed around Inverness and district; he stated that he was particularly worried about the unwillingness of the country people to proceed against these malefactors through the normal processes of criminal justice. For, wrote Monck, the law so seldom inflicted capital punishment on the wrongdoers that they were able to seek revenge upon their prosecutors and so beget new troubles. He therefore ordered Fitch to step in. With the assistance of the local people, he was to apprehend the felons and, on his own authority, give orders for their transportation to the plantations. If this was an admission that the army could operate more effectively than the civil judicatories, a second order to Fitch, of the same date,[10] implied the opposite — or at least, it recognised that the army's police powers could not be all-pervasive. In this instance, Monck's principal concern was cattle-rustling. Fitch was to allow any clan chief, but particularly the Earl of Seaforth, to appoint a gathering of his clan for the purpose of pursuing cattle thieves across clan boundaries, for, said Monck, this was the most reliable means of catching the thieves and recovering the stolen property.

In his instructions to Brayne on 6 June, on the other hand, Monck recognised that certain regions, and certain problems, could be handled only by the firm exercise of military authority.[11] Brayne was given jurisdiction over a wide area around the garrison at Inverlochy, comprising Lochaber, Appin, Glencoe, Rannoch, Glengarry, Knoydart and adjacent districts. He was empowered to arrest any persons suspected of committing or abetting murder, felony or robbery and to try them by court-martial; he was in addition charged with the general responsibility of keeping the public peace within these bounds. The justification for such sweeping powers being granted to an army officer, when civilian authorities such as the Commissioners for Administration of Justice already existed, was given thus: the district was so remote from any judicature, either civil or criminal, and

> the inhabitants soe barbarous that publicque Justice could not bee executed there wch hath been the cause that the people thereof have infested a great part of this Nation wth their frequent murders and robberies wch they comitt openly by force of armes, justifying the same as lawfull (they never having as yet been subject to the lawes of Scotland otherwise then as they were compell'd by armes).

Whereas the powers granted to Fitch later in the month to override civil justice in the interests of law and order were an *ad hoc* expedient, Brayne's new authority was an attempt to find a long-term solution to the problem of the western Highlands. He apparently exercised his authority,[12] with some measure of success, until his departure for Jamaica in 1656, and thereafter judicial power in the region was transferred to his successor, Lt. Col. Cotterell.[13]

Justice administered by a military governor had the advantage of being ever-present; one of the faults of the ordinary circuit judges, Monck had found, was that they seldom visited the troublesome areas, even in such 'border' shires as Perth, and so malefactors had high hopes of impunity. His concern with the problem in Perthshire in fact led him to ask the Judges to grant special powers to someone (perhaps Col. Daniel) to execute 'exemplary justice' in the shire, for he was afraid that when winter came on, troubles in that area would increase.[14]

Under the stress of immediate difficulties, then, Monck was ready to emphasise the army's authority as a peace-keeping force. But when he had first arrived in Scotland, in April 1654, his long-term plans for maintaining justice and order had envisaged a more intricate arrangement. In a letter to Lambert of 29 April 1654, Monck recommended that the Council authorise the appointment of justices of the peace and constables in Scotland, for 'it would much conduce to the setling the Country, especially the Highlands, where the next to the cheife of the Clan might bee appointed a Justice of Peace, which would probably keepe them in awe or divide them'.[15] Monck was not only suggesting that an agency of civil administration be set up to help maintain peace; he was combining this suggestion with the idea that the power structure *within* a clan should be manipulated in favour of the English government. This, then, was a more subtle version of his later attempts to play one clan off against another. In the event, justices of the peace on the English model were not established until December 1655, when Broghill rather than Monck was in charge of civil affairs. Even then, however, the new system maintained the policy of combining military with civil authority by putting the leading army officers of every district on to the commission of the peace.[16]

These measures to maintain order and promote justice, during and after Glencairn's rising, had involved the army with various groups among the Scottish laity, notably the gentry and the clan chiefs. But Monck, like Lilburne, was also concerned with the clergy, and in particular with the moral support they lent to the royalist cause. His attempts to bring the clergy to heel led him to prohibit their assemblies, and to reinforce the ban on prayers for the king. As one might expect, after the spring of 1655, when the rising had been finally crushed, the prohibition on the meeting of church assemblies was greatly relaxed. But in the summer of 1655 Monck continued to use this weapon to promote different ends; where before the ban on meetings had expressed the army's fear of the Royalists, it was now employed to promote the government's religious policy, by singling out the Protesters for special favour. At this time the government's hopes for a long-term religious settlement in Scotland rested on the promotion of 'Gillespie's Charter', the ordinance touching admission to stipends which had been passed by the Protector and Council on 8 August 1654. The provincial certifyers named in that ordinance were almost all Protesters or sectarians. To make the system work, therefore, it was necessary to boost Gillespie's influence within the Protesting party, promote the interests of the Protesters as a whole against those of the Resolutioners, and encourage co-operation between Protesters and ex-Protesters of various shades of opinion. Although no wholehearted effort was made to put the Charter into operation until November 1655,[17] the months after the passage of the ordinance saw various attempts by Monck to promote these ends.

In 1654 the dual motive of Monck's policy — to silence the royalist clergy and to bolster Gillespie's faction — was apparent in his decisions to cancel or disperse meetings of the ministry at Edinburgh. On one occasion the Resolutioners were involved, and on another two, the Protesters.[18] The dispersal of a gathering of Protesters at Wariston's house on 23 August revealed the complexity of Monck's concerns. His order to Lt. Col. Gough to disperse the meeting gave the current unsettled state of the country as the reason, but some commentators suspected that it was a move to thwart Wariston's faction among the Protesters in favour of Gillespie's group. News had just broken of the passage of 'Gillespie's Charter' and it was known that Wariston's faction opposed the grant. Wariston, however, believed that the ban might have been occasioned by the tone of their debates on debarring the sinful from communion.[19]

Whatever the main reason on this occasion, renewed fears of royalist conspiracy in England and Scotland certainly led to a blanket prohibition on meetings in the capital in March 1655. This affected not only the ministry, but also gentry and burgesses from several shires, who had planned to convene in Edinburgh at the beginning of April. In addition, local army officers were warned not to permit any meetings of the clergy in the districts under their command.[20] As a result, the synod of Fife, meeting at Kirkcaldy on 3 April, was forcibly dissolved by Major Daveson and some other English officers. Also in March, the proclamation against preaching or praying for Charles Stuart was renewed.[21]

The fears of a serious royalist resurgence proved, however, to be short-lived; and soon after the dissolution at Kirkcaldy, Monck was relaxing the ban on church meetings elsewhere. Significantly, the first judicatories to receive permission to convene were the synod and the presbyteries of Dumfries, and the synod of Galloway,[22] each of which contained a strong representation of Protesters. Moreover, Monck had first been moved to consider the case of the synod of Dumfries by a letter of recommendation from Mr. Robert Traill, the leading Protester minister in Edinburgh. Thereafter, in the course of April, May, June and July, licence was given to the presbyteries and/or synods of Berwickshire, Lothian, Perthshire, Aberdeenshire, Fife, Caithness, Angus and the Mearns to meet to discuss ecclesiastical matters, the assemblies usually being asked to give an undertaking not to meddle in civil affairs.[23] On two occasions permission to convene was granted only after the interests of the person or party most favoured by the English government had been taken into account. When the synod of Aberdeen applied for permission to meet on 1 July 1655, Monck decreed that it could do so only if Mr. Andrew Cant (a diehard Protester) and Mr. John Menzies (an Independent) thought fit.[24] Elsewhere, at Chirnside, Monck was equally tender of the interests of the parish minister, Mr. Francis Craw, who had been put into the charge by the Commissioners for Visiting Universities in Scotland in September 1653. Craw had been supported by the Protester party, but probably had Independent leanings. The general forbade the presbytery of Chirnside to meet within the parish for fear they might disturb Mr. Craw in the exercise of his duty, but he did permit the assembly to meet elsewhere in the shire.[25]

The spring and summer of 1655, therefore, saw a relaxation of the ban on church meetings at the local level. At no time, however, was there any likelihood of the General Assembly being restored. When Lilburne had first begun the policy of prohibiting meetings of the church courts, the danger to public peace from gatherings of men who supported the Stuart cause had been his prime concern. But the overall religious policy of the English régime had been interwoven with this concern — hence Lilburne's more lenient stance towards, and more optimistic appraisal of, the actions and attitudes of the Protesters as against their Resolutioner brethren. Similarly, with Monck, the rise and fall of the royalist danger was mirrored in his orders to prohibit or permit church assemblies, but intermingled with this concern were the long-term requirements of a religious settlement in Scotland.

Some sections of the laity fared rather better than the church in their attempts to preserve their institutions. The royal burghs of Scotland were allowed to hold both particular and general conventions throughout 1654 and 1655. General conventions were held in July 1654 and 1655, and the latter meeting, while still in session, received Monck's permission to reconvene exactly one year later.[26] Particular conventions were held in August 1654 (to discuss the implications of Scottish burgh representation in the forthcoming Parliament); in November 1654; and in February 1655 (when the proposed date had to be brought forward a week on Monck's orders).[27] Monck on occasion declared himself in favour of protecting the burghs' interests; in a letter to Cromwell of 3 October 1654, in which he pleaded the case of continuing their abatements from the cess, he described the burghs as 'generally the most faithfull to us of any people in this Nacion'.[28]

One of the immediate reasons for the burghs' submissiveness was, perhaps, the existence of municipal corporations which had been moulded to the English will. In 1653, municipal elections had been suspended, so that when the time came round for the Michaelmas elections in 1654, those magistrates and councillors who had been elected in 1652 were still in office. On 11 August 1654, however, the Council of State in London passed an ordinance which, if implemented, would have riveted the government's control on the Scottish burghs even more forcibly. This ordinance gave power to the Commissioners for the Administration of Justice in Scotland to appoint magistrates and council for the year ensuing, thereby suspending the burghs' right of freely electing their officers.[29] The English Judges began to send word of this new order to the burghs early in September, but shortly thereafter the order was countermanded. Instead, after representations had been made to the Protector by William Thomson, the town clerk of Edinburgh and the burgh's official agent in London, it was decided that the old magistrates and council should remain in office for another year. This less provocative solution to the problem aroused some discontent, even amongst the current office-holders — some of the bailies of Edinburgh, for example, maintained that if they served any longer their private fortunes would be ruined — but all protests were in vain.[30] Intent upon preventing potentially subversive gatherings which might, in this case, result in the election of local officials not well-disposed to the English government, the Council refused to rescind its ban on municipal elections.

The success of the army's attempts to dampen down the expression of anti-government sentiment and to control the institutions through which it could be channelled was put to a further test in August 1654, when the first elections for Scottish MPs to sit at Westminster took place. The occasion was the summoning of the first Parliament of the Protectorate, due to convene on 3 September. Over a year previously, four Scottish members had taken their seats in Barebones' Parliament, but they had, of course, been nominated, not elected. The four chosen had been William Lockhart of Lee, Sir James Hope of Hopetoun, John Swinton of Swinton and Alexander Jaffray; a fifth, Alexander Brodie of Brodie, had also received a summons, but had refused to attend.[31] Now, however, in accordance with the Instrument of Government and the Ordinance of Union of April 1654, Scotland was entitled to send 30 members to the Parliament of Great Britain —

twenty from the shires and ten from the burghs. The division of Scotland into the requisite number of electoral districts had been achieved by another ordinance which was passed on 27 June 1654.[32] Each constituency was allotted one member, with the exception of Edinburgh, which got two. On 29 June, the Council despatched to Monck the writs for the elections, together with the forms of indenture between the sheriffs and the electors, and copies of the Instrument of Government, which were to be read when the writs were proclaimed.[33]

In a sense, the elections of August 1654 ought to have symbolised for both English and Scots the culmination of the long-drawn-out process of debate on Scotland's political future which had begun in 1651. Yet they aroused little interest on either side, and have left few traces in contemporary records. For they came at a crucial time in the history of Monck's drive against Middleton, when the final stages of the summer campaign were being put into operation and the fate of the Royalists seemed to the Scots to hang in the balance. Monck and the more important of his field officers were absorbed in the details of the military operation, hence it fell to those officers left in charge of the garrisons to superintend the elections. The relegation of such an important matter to the attention of subordinate officers did not, however, prevent the army from being in full control of the situation. Apart from the ever-present display of armed might in the localities, the system of appointing army officers as sheriffs-conjunct in every shire now proved its usefulness. For the sheriffs, in their capacity as returning officers, had the duty not only of supervising the casting and counting of votes, but of scrutinising the qualifications of the electors. This task was of some importance, for the Instrument of Government had debarred various classes of Malignants from voting in these and subsequent elections.[34] As a result, proven supporters of the royalist cause in Scotland were disfranchised.

Undoubtedly the vigilance of the occupation forces accounts in large measure for the successful outcome, in English terms, of the 1654 elections. On the other hand, it is hard to avoid the conclusion that the response of the Scots to this opportunity for political activity was one of overwhelming apathy — but whether through lack of interest in the union, or through fear of army scrutiny, it is impossible to judge. In some places, however, the failure of the Scots to participate in the electoral process was the product of necessity: the disfranchisement of Malignants led five shires to report that 'not one fit to be a parliament man was to be found within their liberty', while in Aberdeenshire the gentry informed the returning officer that not one of them was even qualified to vote.[35] Partly because of this problem, of the twenty-nine constituencies in Scotland, only twenty-one (including Edinburgh) returned members at the August elections, thereby making Scotland's total representation at Westminster twenty-two.[36] Later on, however, some of the vacancies may have been filled up at a second round of elections. In October Monck wrote to William, Lord Cochrane of Dundonald suggesting that, since no member had been returned for the constituency of Ayrshire and Renfrewshire, an election should be held, even at this late date; this, he represented, could be done without hazard, 'divers members who were chosen by the shires after the time appointed by the ordinance having been accepted of notwithstanding the Qualifications of the persons electing'.[37] This was perhaps a discreet indication that in order to put a respectable face on the Scottish elections, the authorities were willing to waive the franchise restrictions imposed by the Instrument.

Despite this apparent concession, the biographical details of the 22 known members indicate a signal victory for the English interest in Scotland. Out of the 22, 13 were Scots and 9 were English. Only one of these nine, Benjamin Bressie of Dolphinton, the member for the shire of East Lothian, held neither a military nor a civil office in Scotland. Bressie had at one time been a captain in the English army, but had now settled down and apparently acquired lands in Dolphinton in Lanarkshire. Sometime before 1654, he had turned from soldier to trader and now owned several vessels, some of which had been contracted out to the English army for use during Glencairn's rising. This had involved Bressie in some difficulties: in the summer of 1653 one of his ships had been seized by Seaforth, and in the month of his election to Parliament another was captured by Middleton.[38] His selection for East Lothian may have been the army's way of rewarding him for his services and indemnifying him for his losses.

Aside from Bressie, the other English members were either executive officials or army officers. The five soldiers were Lt. Col. William Mitchell (member for Inverness-shire); the governor of Carlisle, Major Jeremiah Tolhurst (Dumfries and adjacent burghs); Col. John Okey (Linlithgow and adjacent burghs); the governor of Stirling, Col. Thomas Reade (the shires of Linlithgow, Clackmannan and Stirling); and George Downing (Edinburgh), Scoutmaster General of the Forces in Scotland. The three civilians were John Thompson (Selkirk and Peeblesshire); Samuel Disbrowe (Edinburgh); and George Smyth (Midlothian). All three were commissioners for claims on forfeited estates; in addition Smyth was a Judge, Disbrowe was one of the Commissioners for the revenue at Leith and for the Visitation of Universities, and Thompson was the Auditor-General of the revenues of Scotland.[39]

Of the 13 Scots, little is known of two of them: John Wilkie of Broomhouse[40] (Glasgow and adjacent burghs) and James Stuart of Maynes (Orkney and Shetland). The remaining eleven were Col. David Barclay of Urie (the shires of Forfar and Kincardine); Col. James Hay (Fife and Kinross); George, second Earl of Linlithgow (Perthshire); Sir James Hamilton of Orbiston (the shires of Argyll, Bute and Dunbarton); William Lockhart of Lee (Lanarkshire); John Swinton of Swinton (Berwickshire); James, Earl of Hartfell (Dumfriesshire); Sir James Macdowall of Garthland (Wigtonshire); Sir Alexander Wedderburn (Forfar and adjacent burghs); James Sword (the burghs of Fife); and William Thomson (Haddington and adjacent burghs). These eleven fall most obviously into one or more of the following groups: those who had served as deputies either at Dalkeith or London in 1652/3; those who held and/or were about to hold some administrative post under the English régime; and those who had some pressing economic reason for wanting to exert influence on English counsels.

Of the eleven members, six had been elected as commissioners to the Parliament of England in August 1652 (although one of them, Sir James Hamilton, may not have fulfilled the office).[41] Four of the six had previously been deputies at Dalkeith, as had one of the other MPs, William Thomson.[42] And in addition, two had served in Barebones' Parliament.[43] This meant that just over half of the Scots elected in 1654 had previously been passed by the English as 'safe', as men who were fit in the circumstances of the time to represent their country in consultations with their conquerors. But it also meant that, from the Scottish point of view, a sizeable proportion of the members had gained some experience of English parliamentary practice and might be better placed than others of their countrymen to exploit the system to Scotland's advantage. Since, however, the business of the first protectoral Parliament rarely comprehended Scottish affairs, this experience had little chance to blossom, but the expectation that it could be put to good use may have influenced the electors' choice at the August poll.

If the Scots stood to gain from having as their MPs men who had some familiarity with English politics at Whitehall and Westminster, they might also benefit from representation by men who held posts in the Scottish administration. Of the eleven members with whom we are concerned, five held some office of trust under the English régime. Swinton and Lockhart were the most important; both were Judges, Swinton was a commissioner for claims on forfeited estates and Lockhart was a trustee for the estates of excepted persons. Lockhart was, in addition, married to Cromwell's niece.[44] Sir James Macdowall was also commissioner for claims on forfeited estates, and Col. David Barclay was a trustee for the estates of excepted persons.[45] The fifth, Sir Alexander Wedderburn, a lowlier being, was a mere collector of the assessment.[46] Swinton, Lockhart and Macdowall were to go on to achieve even more glittering honours in the central administration of Scotland, while the first two, along with four others out of the eleven (including Barclay), were to be appointed JPs in 1656 (one of them, Sir James Hamilton, was also a sheriff).[47] In all, therefore, eight of the Scottish MPs had, or were to have, some involvement in the government of Scotland under the English régime.

The existence of these present (and future) officeholders in the list of MPs betokens strong English influence in the elections themselves, as well, perhaps, as a predisposition on the part of the persons concerned 'to do or say anything they found tolerable to their own large mind',[48] in order to promote their own advancement. But this did not, *ipso facto*, preclude them from representing Scottish interests.[49] Was it coincidence that at a time when so many of the nobility and gentry of Scotland were affected by the Ordinance of Pardon and Grace, whether as excepted persons or as the creditors of such, five MPs (two Scots and three English) were commissioners for claims on forfeited estates, while two others were trustees for these estates? Moreover, on 19 August 1654 the Council appointed a committee, composed of the Judges in Scotland and the Commissioners for Sequestrations, to hear petitions for the mitigation of fines imposed by the Act of Pardon and Grace: four of the men involved were among the new MPs.[50] The 'pluralism' among the English officials — some of the Judges, for example, served almost *ex officio* on several other commissions — perhaps inflates the importance of these figures, but still it seems that many MPs, both English and

Scots, were in an excellent position to aid their constituents.

That some of the Scots MPs had good reason to seek election in the hope of advancing their personal or family fortunes, and that the English may have regarded this as a legitimate concern, is suggested by the third category into which these members fall: those who had a particularly compelling economic motive for wishing to be returned. There are four cases here — the Earls of Linlithgow and Hartfell, and Cols. Hay and Barclay — with Sir James Hamilton as a possible fifth. Hartfell is, at first sight, an unlikely choice for an MP in 1654. He had been imprisoned by the English in September 1651, and in the Ordinance of Pardon and Grace had been fined £2000. He was, therefore, a 'Malignant', but in English eyes his good behaviour in recent years apparently offset his earlier misdemeanours. Moreover, he was a man of considerable influence in Dumfriesshire and therefore a useful political asset. In 1656, Broghill, whose wife was a kinsman of Hartfell's, successfully engaged his electoral influence on behalf of two English candidates for the constituencies of shire and burgh; and in the same year he was made a JP for Dumfriesshire.[51] In 1654, Hartfell must have been anxious to secure a mitigation of his fine, as well as relief from his creditors, and so may have sought to co-operate more closely with the English. His compliance eventually paid dividends, for in November 1655 his fine was wholly remitted.[52] Col. James Hay, the member for Fife and Kinross, was another whose family had been hit by the Act of Pardon and Grace: his brother, the laird of Naughton, had been fined £1000. His connections with the English had already been established; in September 1651, he had been one of the first in Fife to make formal submission to the conquerors, and at the time of his election, Lamont described him as 'a gentleman intimat with the English, and for them'.[53] David Barclay also had personal as well as professional reasons for wishing to stand well with the English. His fortunes were tied up with those of the Earl Marischal, whose estates had been forfeited and who was himself a prisoner in London. Barclay wished to strengthen his title to the barony of Urie which he had bought from the Earl in 1648, but which the English government claimed was still part of the forfeited estates. His office as trustee for the estates of excepted persons put him in a privileged position on this matter, but he was also independently engaged in petitioning the Council for satisfaction of a debt of £1500 owed to him by the Earl Marischal. Ironically, his claims on the Keith family made him all the more anxious to promote the Countess Marischal's own petitions to the Council on behalf of her husband and children, so that Barclay's personal and political allegiances were by no means clear-cut.[54] Closer contact with the English authorities, however, could do him nothing but good.

George, Earl of Linlithgow, was one of the luckier men of his class in Scotland, for he had incurred no penalty under the Act of Pardon and Grace. But he had suffered for his loyalty to the English during Glencairn's rising. His lands in Perthshire had been burnt by the enemy, and earlier in the year Lilburne had made repeated requests to Whitehall that he be compensated for his losses. Monck also recommended him to the Protector. On 19 September, he wrote to Cromwell giving express testimony that the new MP had, since 1651, behaved very peaceably and that he had suffered much for his refusal to obey the rebels' commands.[55] The hope that he might secure some reparation for these losses may have induced Linlithgow to stand for election in August. Likewise, Sir James Hamilton of Orbiston, who had been captured by Kenmore in November 1653 as a punishment for aiding the English, may have sought compensation for the damage done to him by the Royalists.[56]

The performance of Linlithgow and Hamilton during Glencairn's rising also showed that only men of proven loyalty could secure election in 1654. No matter how much a Scotsman might want to enter Parliament, his acceptance by the English depended on his usefulness to them. This was true not only of the administrative officials, but of the men who, like Linlithgow, Hartfell or Hamilton, had political and social influence. That six of the Parliament men of 1654 were to become JPs in 1656, for example, is probably a reflection not of their faithful service to the Protector at Westminster, but of their established standing in the local communities; and it was precisely this standing, coupled with evidence of loyalty since 1651, which commended them to the authorities in Scotland in 1654. The reasons why the 22 men identified above put themselves forward as candidates, were elected by the voters, and were acknowledged by the army to be suitable representatives for Scotland were no doubt varied. Overall, however, their election certainly signified an overwhelming victory for the occupation forces, for nearly all of them had some tie with the English interest. Nonetheless it is worth emphasising that, precisely because of this fact, many of the members were capable of working, within the context of the conquest and the union, for Scottish interests. Taken together, these factors meant that the election results of 1654 reflected the two-sided policy which Monck was currently pursuing towards the Scottish people. The elements of co-operation and coercion were both present. The first was manifest not only in the army's readiness to permit Scotsmen prominent in the central administration to serve as MPs, but also in its willingness to tolerate the election of men of influence in the localities, men whose basic social and economic interests did not differ greatly from those of the rebel leaders in the hills, but whose political support was vital if the English were to continue to govern the country effectively. The element of repression, on the other hand, was made clear by the army's intervention at all stages of the electoral process and by its attempts not merely to exclude unrepentant Malignants from securing election but positively to encourage the choice of men who had some reason to bind themselves to the English interest.

Thus in his dealings with the parliamentary electorate, as in his dealings with the church and the burghs, Monck had shown great firmness in eliminating the expression of opinion which might further the cause of the rebels in the hills. But such measures did not reach to the roots of the problem of government. Monck was aware that the key to the pacification of Scotland lay, in the long term, in alleviating the worst forms of material hardship. His concern with the relationship between poverty and revolt had been an important element in his conduct of the military campaign in the summer of 1654. At that time he had come up against the hard fact that to pursue a policy of rigour against the Royalists to its logical conclusion would prove self-defeating. He had aimed to contain the danger that the destruction of the summer would result in more unrest and violence by maintaining garrisons at strategic points in the hills, but the success of this policy was jeopardised by the fiscal demands of the central government. To the request that Scotland be forced to yield the full £10,000 of its assessment, Monck had returned a firm 'no', on the grounds that it was not only unwise, but impossible to boot.

The question of the assessment was crucial to Monck's plans in many respects. Not only was the total burden a matter of interest for his general policy of pacification, but the system of granting abatements was a key weapon in his attempts to single out those especially deserving of English favour. For it provided the most flexible and effective way of granting reparation to those who had suffered materially for their loyalty to the English. In many cases, of course, a reduction in the amount of cess was merely a formal acknowledgement of the fact that the country could and would produce no more; but it is also clear from the orders Monck issued that the people who were picked out by name to receive this favour were usually those who had either performed some positive service for the English or else had incurred loss through their refusal to join the rebels.

As one would expect, the names of known supporters of the régime crop up in the lists. Sir James Macdonald of Sleat, John Campbell, fiar of Glenorchy, Sir Thomas Stuart of Grantully, the Earl of Sutherland and Sir James Campbell, laird of Lawers, all figure prominently.[57] Several of the lesser nobility and gentry whose estates had been devastated by the enemy also appear: the lairds of Foulis, Lethen and Luss, Viscount Arbuthnott, and Baron Comrie are of this class.[58] Yet abatements were also granted to the Earl of Atholl and to Macdonald of Glengarry,[59] both of whom had been leaders among the rebels. Probably this reflected practical necessity (Glengarry's remission was specifically for 'burnt' and Atholl's for 'wasted' lands), but it was also consonant with Monck's general policy of combining conciliation with coercion. Atholl's tenants had, perhaps, been particularly unfortunate, for as Atholl himself had learned earlier in the rising, Perthshire, lying as it did between two fires, was an extremely vulnerable area. Others who received abatements for lands in this shire included the laird of Edinample, Mr. David Drummond, the Earl of Perth, and Sir Thomas Drummond.[60] The last two had certainly, and the others had probably, suffered at the hands of the enemy, but compensation was also granted where the damage had been caused by the English. Such may have been the case for Glengarry (his lands had been particularly viciously attacked by the army); and it was avowedly so for the Countess of Moray,[61] who received an abatement for losses inflicted by English troops.

Sometimes, however, an abatement of cess was not considered the most suitable form of reparation. On occasion, cash payments were made to unlucky victims. Ronald Macdonald was given £100 for damage done by the enemy; the fiar of Glenorchy got £200; and smaller sums were allotted to two victims of the army's enthusiasm: Robert Menzies got £15 compensation for corn spoiled by English troops in the parish of Dull, and Sir Mungo Stirling got £18 for his house at

Craigbarnett, which had been damaged by the garrison there.[62]

Slightly different was the case of Dougal Macpherson of Badenoch, whose loyalty had been of great value to the army in that area. In March 1655 he was awarded £50 to build himself a house near the English garrison at Ruthven Castle. It was not safe for him to live elsewhere, Monck recorded, since the Highlanders regarded him as their sworn enemy because he had adhered to the English interest. The English were certainly not slow to compensate Macpherson for the losses he had incurred on their behalf: he was allotted some money out of the fines levied on excepted persons, and he was promised a grant of the lands from Viscount Dudhope's estate.[63]

The plan to compensate Macpherson from Dudhope's estate was part of Monck's schemes for making those rebels who had caused the damage help to pay for it. At one time he contemplated recompensing the laird of Glenorchy from out of the estates of the Macnabs, and letting Macleod of Assynt claim satisfaction for his losses from Seaforth's Mackenzies. But such plans rarely came to fruition. Not only would they have provoked further ill-feeling among the Highlanders, but Monck discovered that the responsibility for damage inflicted by one clan on another was rarely clear-cut. Macleod's claim on the Mackenzies was cancelled because it was found that he had raised armed men to oppose the English; while Glenorchy's failure to gain anything from the Macnabs was not unrelated to Monck's suspicion that many of his tenants had joined the rebels.[64]

Tangible material rewards, such as a reduction in taxation or a specific grant of money, were sufficient to satisfy many of the deserving cases which came before Monck and his officers. But undoubtedly one of the most serious long-term problems which the nobility and gentry faced was how to meet the claims of their creditors and pay off their debts. The poverty which had resulted from the Judges' enforcement of the Scottish laws of debt had, in Lilburne's opinion, driven many of the upper classes to join the rebels, and he had pressed continually for some easing of their burden. The ordinance of May 1654, which Monck too had advocated, had partly remedied the problem, but still Monck found it expedient to plead the cause of some loyalists who were being oppressed by their creditors. In May 1654, on the very day when the ordinance for relief of debtors was passed by the Council in London, he had asked for legal proceedings to be stayed against Sir Peter Hay of Meginch, on account of his sufferings at the hands of the enemy.[65] Later in the year he several times recommended that leniency be shown to the Earl of Home, and on receiving little co-operation from the Judges was moved in March 1655 to write to the Protector himself, complaining that the ordinance was not being fairly applied. If the Judges were more forward in allowing gentlemen to satisfy their creditors in land, he observed tartly, it would keep the country much more peaceable than it was.[66] Two months later, he made a similar point in a series of letters to the bench of Judges collectively and to Judges Goodyear and Swinton individually: the pressure of creditors on some of the excepted persons, who were at that time trying to pay off their fines would, he said, inevitably result in their ruin and would drive them to take up arms again unless they were permitted to settle their debts in corn, cattle or lands. This plea, made on 22 May,[67] was lent urgency by the fact that ten days earlier, the ordinance for relief of debtors had expired and was apparently not to be renewed. Unfortunate though this was, the problems posed by the poverty and indebtedness of the Scottish nobility could not have been solved by any one ordinance; and in ensuing years the Councils in Scotland and at Whitehall were to spend much time hearing petitions from both debtors and creditors. Nonetheless Monck's concern about the ordinance had at least shown that he was aware of the role which English policy on this subject could play in ensuring future peace.

In addition to promoting directly the financial affairs of the government's supporters, Monck could serve their interests and his own in other ways. By appointing men of proven loyalty to office in the localities, he could reward faithful service and consolidate the régime at one blow. Thus in 1654 he recommended Sir James Macdonald of Sleat to be sheriff and commissary of the Western Isles, and Sir Andrew Bruce of Earlshall to be sheriff-conjunct of Fife,[68] both of them having given ample testimony of their loyalty to the Commonwealth. And when the lists were drawn up for the first batch of JPs at the end of 1655, they contained the names of many who had remained loyal during Glencairn's rising and whose influence in the localities was useful to the régime.[69]

The political and social influence of the gentry was incorporated into another scheme which bore more directly on the problem of alleviating material hardship. In July 1653, Lilburne had summoned gentlemen-commissioners from every shire to consult with the army at Edinburgh on a more equitable distribution of the assessment. This had resulted in new valuation tables being drawn up and in the appointment of local committees for valuation, staffed largely by gentry and lairds. But few shires remained satisfied with the new valuations for long, and individual gentlemen within each shire constantly complained that they were overrated compared with their neighbours. The rateable value of estates did, of course, fluctuate from one year to another, not least of all in a time of unrest, and so there was a strong case for ordering periodic revaluations. This was especially so where a specific abatement to one landowner meant that his neighbours had to reapportion the total burden amongst themselves. In 1655, therefore, Monck ordered the revaluation of several shires and, as before, this work was to be undertaken by committees of gentlemen: the shires involved included Roxburgh, Midlothian, Sutherland, Inverness, Clackmannan, Ayr, Berwick, Kirkcudbright and Perth.[70] In fact, revaluation was to become almost a continuous process throughout the 1650s, and it provided one of the channels through which the gentry learned to co-operate, albeit from an unequal standpoint, with the army in the running of the country. An institution which performed a similar function was the general shire committee.[71] This met to discuss all manner of business, including negotiations with the army on quartering, the provision of horses, and the payment of coal and candle money to the garrisons.

All devices such as these were useful to Monck in his attempts to remove the fundamental causes of unrest, but in their influence upon the opinion of the politically articulate classes they were insignificant compared with the greatest single bone of contention: the policy of fines and sequestration embodied in the

Ordinance of Pardon and Grace. This ordinance, as we have seen, was lenient in its terms compared with the swingeing penalties forecast in Parliament's Declaration of October 1651, but still it had provoked a howl of outrage. Although it affected directly the fortunes of only 97 families (the estates of 24 persons had been declared forfeit and another 73 had been fined), its repercussions extended to many more creditors, clients, dependants and tenants. Before the ordinance was passed, Lilburne had reported that the threat as well as the reality of sequestration had driven many nobles and gentry to join the rebels; by the summer of 1654 the exact extent of Parliament's vengeance was known, but this did little to improve the situation, at any rate for the excepted persons. Even when an individual escaped sequestration, the fine was often so crippling that full payment was out of the question. Clearly one of the most effective ways in which the English government could pacify Scottish opinion was by mitigating the severity of the penalties imposed in the ordinance.

The speed and facility with which the machinery for so doing was set up suggests that either the Council were shocked into unusually rapid action by the strength of the Scottish protest, or, more probably, that they had already contemplated the wisdom of climbing down. Few could have believed that the heavier fines, such as the £15,000 stg. levied on the heiress of Buccleuch,[72] had a realistic chance of being paid in full. Certainly the Scottish nobility were not slow to demand redress. In May and June, several petitioned the Council at Whitehall individually; and a joint petition from all the nobility and gentry who had been fined was presented also.[73] On 7 July the Council ordered that if the persons concerned paid in one-third of their fines, a committee composed of the Judges in Scotland and the Commissioners for Sequestrations would be authorised to hear what they had to plead for mitigation of the remainder. An ordinance setting up the new commission was prepared, and finally approved by the Protector on 19 August. It took effect two days later.[74]

The fined persons were not, in fact, required to pay one-third before the committee heard their case; but the choice of this fraction was not without significance. For in the preliminary order of 7 July, the Council anticipated what was in the end to prove the overall result of the commission's investigations: that this amount did represent a fair imposition on the majority of the excepted persons. Indeed, the actual terms[75] of the ordinance of 19 August implied that the mitigation of the remaining two-thirds was a foregone conclusion. The preamble virtually admitted that the fines had been out of proportion to the offences committed, and to the offenders' ability to pay; and the speed with which the commissioners were to act and the authority they were given to put their decisions into effect also suggested that the final issue was not in much doubt. In the event, when the commission's decisions were debated by the Council in April 1655, not one was overturned to the detriment of the victim: the only alterations made by the Council *lowered* the fines of the persons concerned.

The committee was empowered to consider pleas for mitigation under six heads: (1) the value of the petitioner's estate, (2) whether he had actively participated in the war with England from 1648 to 1651, (3) whether he was a papist, (4) whether he had assisted the war effort against England either in Parliament or in the Committee of Estates, (5) whether his deceased parents or predecessors had been guilty of these offences and (6) whether his estates had been exempted from fine by any articles of capitulation. Petitioners were given two months to lodge their case with the committee. Copies of the petitions which have survived amongst private collections of family papers[76] indicate that each conformed to a fairly regular pattern imposed by the ordinance. In support of their contentions that they had, variously, not invaded England in 1648 or 1651, had not supported the Engagement, and were not papists, the petitioners produced certificates sworn under oath from their parish ministers, the gentry of the district and other local worthies.

It is notable that the six conditions which were apparently to determine the petitioners' fate contained no mention of their behaviour during Glencairn's rising. Apart from a reference to the fact that many of the nobility and gentry felt that their present deportment towards the government had not been sufficiently taken into account in computing their fines, the ordinance was silent on this point. This clearly reflected the fact that the Ordinance of Pardon and Grace was primarily a response not to the current rebellion but to events between the Hamiltonian Engagement and the battle of Worcester. Nonetheless, its effects were to be felt during the present troubles, and its enforcement or otherwise was a potential weapon in the work of defeating Middleton and his crew. In this respect, the merit of the new ordinance was not that it would penalise the government's opponents, but that it could be used to reward its supporters. On this specific issue, it was less important that the enemies of the régime should be singled out than that its friends should receive some favour, for in the context of civil policy it was conciliation, defined in this case as the mitigation of material hardship, that was the crucial factor. Monck lent support to this view when he wrote to the Protector in October 1654 to put in a good word for the fined persons.[77] He knew many of them personally, he said, and he assured Cromwell that there were not more peaceable men in Scotland than they; moreover, they were ready to give assurances of their continuing support for and submission to the English government. On this and other occasions, he specifically recommended the Earl of Perth and his son, the Earls of Ethie and Tullibardine, the lairds of Balhousie and Craigmillar and Sir John Scott of Scotstarvet.[78]

By March 1655 the commission had submitted its decisions to the Council at Whitehall for ratification or alteration. On 6 April 1655 an order was agreed upon which embodied the results of the Council's debates.[79] The original Ordinance of Pardon and Grace had imposed fines on 73 people. In the new order four were totally absolved because they had been exempted by the terms of their treaties of surrender; six were discharged completely subject only to the approval of Parliament; fifteen had their fines reduced to *less* than one-third of the original sum; forty were fined *exactly* one-third; and eight were fined a proportion higher than one-third but in no case exceeding one-half. For only eight out of 73, therefore, was the promise of the order of 7 July not fulfilled.

It is difficult to say what prompted the committee to recommend special favour for some of the fined persons and not for others, but some examples do stand out. The Earl of Tullibardine, whom Monck had recommended because of the part he had played in getting the Earl of Atholl to surrender, had his fine reduced from £1500 to £250; Sir John Scott of Scotstarvet, whom Monck had also recommended, was absolutely discharged; and the Earl of Hartfell, an MP and a leading supporter of the régime in Dumfriesshire, enjoyed a reduction from £2000 to £500. Recent testimony of good service to the Commonwealth was therefore likely to stand one in good stead.

Nor did the Council's concessions end there. The order of 6 April stipulated that the reduced fines should be paid in two instalments, the first by 21 May 1655, and the other by 2 July. But the fined persons immediately protested that they could not possibly raise the money by then, 'the sums being so great, and the time so short'. The Council therefore altered the dates to 25 June and 29 September following. In all this, there remained one catch: the Council's rulings were the subject of an order, not an ordinance, and they could be overturned by the next session of Parliament, but on this point the petitioners' fears of parliamentary vengeance were never realised.[80]

Overall, these transactions had resulted in a major concession to an important section of the Scottish community. That in many cases the amounts finally imposed represented a fair and realistic assessment of the nobility and gentry's wealth is suggested by the fact that several managed to pay their fines on or near the stipulated dates.[81] Some, however, continued to petition for a further remission, and the whole matter dragged on for a considerable length of time.[82] Nothing, moreover, had yet been done to improve the lot of those who had merited outright confiscation of their estates. Eight out of the 24 who were liable to forfeiture were reprieved by the terms of their capitulations with Monck — for some of the men who followed Glencairn, therefore, crime assuredly did pay — but for the others a solution was not produced until 1656.[83]

The Council's decision to reduce the fines on the excepted persons took place at almost the same time as Monck was rounding up the last of Middleton's supporters and concluding articles of agreement with them. In a sense this epitomised the manner in which conciliation and coercion had combined, not without difficulty, to restore order to Scotland by the summer of 1655. Not since 1652 had the army been so completely in control of the country, but its military victory had been won through co-operating with, as well as coercing, certain elements among the Scottish people. Implicit in many of the measures which Lilburne and Monck adopted for quelling the rebellion was an acknowledgement of the continuing power of the nobility and gentry to unsettle the régime, and an admission that the policy, so proudly proclaimed in 1651, of undermining these groups in favour of the common people was not feasible in practice. A recognition that the political and economic interests of the gentry and nobility had to be considered if the government of Scotland was to run smoothly was the lesson learned by Lilburne and Monck from 1653 to 1655. When passed on to the authorities in London, this lesson resulted in a reappraisal of English policy towards Scotland in many of its aspects. The same trend is to be observed in the history of the Protectorate in England, but a study of Glencairn's rising and the army's response to it disposes of the idea that the Scottish developments were merely mirrors of, and were caused by, equivalent tendencies in England. The expedients employed to counteract the Royalists' influence in the local communities, and the evolution of such expedients into long-term measures to promote the stability of the régime in the north, were direct products of the army's experiences in Scotland. Always, of course, there was some interchange with English influences, and the fascination of the story lies in the curious intermingling of the two. This was to be amply demonstrated in the year after the rising was finally crushed, when something of a new era in the history of English policy towards Scotland began.

In September 1655, the setting up of a Council in Scotland to take charge of its civil government marked a lessening of the military nature of the conquest. The decision to establish the Council was a product of English politics as well as Scottish, but it was the logical culmination in many ways of the lessons which the army had learned in the previous two years. Moreover, just as Monck's Instructions had borne testimony to the wisdom of Lilburne's policies and their adoption by the authorities in London, the Council's Instructions reflected the milder and more conciliatory of Monck's proposals for settling Scotland. Under the presidency of Lord Broghill, the execution of these Instructions proceeded apace, in a manner which, more than at any other time in the 1650s, attempted to blend together Scottish and English influences, both civil and military, with a measure of sophistication and hard-headed realism.

PART THREE

THE ARMY, THE COUNCIL AND THE GOVERNMENT OF SCOTLAND, 1655 — 1658

Introduction

THE period from the setting up of the Scottish Council in September 1655 until the death of Oliver Cromwell in September 1658 saw significant changes in the nature and scope of the English government in Scotland. Most of these changes, whether in the insitutions of government or in the type of men who staffed them, took place during the first year of the Council's life, when Roger Boyle, Baron Broghill and son of the Earl of Cork, was its President. After Broghill's departure from Scotland in August 1656, few major decisions affecting policy were made, but the remaining members of the Council were able to consolidate the political and administrative achievements of the previous year, so that by the time of Oliver's demise, the régime in Scotland was on a sound and stable footing. Lending unity to the whole period, however, was the continuing importance of the army in the running of the country, for on the army's ability to maintain peace and order at home and to gather news of Charles Stuart's intentions abroad depended much of the administration's success.

Broghill's period of office as President witnessed a shift in the balance between civil and military power in the government of the country. During this time the Council established institutions of government staffed mainly by civilians, paid heed to Scottish law and practice, and encouraged Scottish participation in political and administrative affairs at both local and national level, so that in many ways the year 1655-6 seemed to mark a victory for the forces of conciliation and co-operation over those of coercion and repression. The setting up of the Council over which Broghill presided was in itself a sign of the relaxation of overt military rule which had been a feature of the early years of the conquest and which had been continued, even strengthened, in the recent years of royalist uprising. Henceforth, the highest authority in Scotland for the determination of civil matters was to be a civilian body, and, as Monck himself recognised, it was no longer considered fit that any military officer should meddle with civil affairs without its authority. As a corollary, Monck himself was overshadowed in policy-making circles by Broghill: whereas before the commander-in-chief had held the reins of civil *and* military power in his hands, he now for this twelvemonth took something of a back seat in Scottish affairs.

After the setting up of the Council, Broghill promoted the reorganisation of other civil institutions, which indicated, on the surface at least, that the affairs of Scotsmen were no longer so much in the hands, or at the mercy, of Englishmen, be they civil servants or army officers. A new Court of Exchequer was erected; the judicial system was remodelled to allow the reintroduction of the 'outer house' of the old Court of Session; the excise was settled on a basis which kept army involvement in its collection to a minimum; and, most importantly, at the local level, a system of justices of the peace on the English model was established.

This last meant that responsibility for maintaining law and order, for the punishment of crime, and for the day-to-day administration of the localities now lay in part with the gentry and smaller clan chiefs.

In all these institutions, Scotsmen could be seen to be participating in the government of their country. At the highest level, the English régime relied on a small group of tried and tested Scottish 'Cromwellians' to fill executive posts: the two Scottish councillors, Swinton and Lockhart, were no strangers to office under the Republic, and appointments to the bench and to the commission for customs, excise and sequestration embraced men whose loyalty had already been proven in other spheres. The commission of the peace cast its net wider, numerically and politically, for it brought into the business of government many whose immediate loyalties lay firmly within their local communities and whose ability to rule stemmed from their experience of, and influence over, local conditions.

These attempts to conciliate and co-operate with the Scottish community, and to give English rule a more civilian character, did not mark a completely new turn in English policy. The attitudes they embodied had always been implicit in the policy of the conquerors, and where the practical expression of this now differed from that which had obtained immediately after Worcester, the change could often be traced to the exigencies of Glencairn's rising. Thus Parliament's initial desire to hit hard at the Scottish nobility and gentry had been modified in 1653 and 1654 to take account of the economic hardship of the Scottish upper classes and to harness their political and social influence to the English cause. This trend was now continued by the Council, with the local gentry being brought ever more into the service of the government, whether as justices, commissioners of assessment, or on *ad hoc* shire committees. Ironically, therefore, royalist rebellion, which in the short term had caused a reassertion of military rule in all its harshness, had contributed also to the development of greater concessions in the civil sphere.

But neither in 1655 nor at any other time during the English conquest of Scotland was conciliation the only element in English policy. Rather was the essential quality of English rule to be found in a mixture of conciliation *and* coercion, of co-operation *and* conquest; and this dual characteristic, albeit with a shift in emphasis between its two parts, was as important a feature of the period after September 1655 as it had been in the years since Worcester. For, despite the trend towards 'civilian' government, the military and/or coercive aspects of English power were still to the fore: decision-making by the Council could not mask the fact that the army was ultimately responsible for the implementation of civil policy, and the setting up of 'civilian' institutions at local or national level did not preclude these agencies from being staffed in part by English army officers. The joining together of Scotsmen and Englishmen (the latter often being members of the army) on the same governmental commission had become standard practice in the administrative settlement of Scotland. This had been true of the judicial system in the shires, where in 1652 English officers and loyal Scotsmen had been appointed sheriffs-conjunct, and of the commission for the administration of justice on which originally four English judges had sat with three Scots to hear civil causes. On other commissions since, such as those appointed to deal with the estates of excepted persons or to hear pleas for the mitigation of fines, the two nations had likewise been represented. Only on tasks hitherto considered particularly sensitive, such as the work of sequestration or, in the initial stages of the conquest, the judgment of criminal causes, were Englishmen alone employed. The motive behind the employment of Scotsmen was not merely to conciliate the subject nation, but also to tap the expertise of men with knowledge of Scottish law and custom. The use of Scotsmen on administrative, particularly quasi-judicial, bodies thus reflected the conquerors' need and desire to integrate their new ideas with established practice, and to seek the advice of those with experience of Scottish precedent. This form of token representation in government was continued in and after 1655, with Scots members serving, although usually being kept in the minority, on the Council, the commission for administration of justice, the commission for customs and excise, and other bodies.

In all these cases, it was, of course, the English majority, rather than the Scots minority which set the prevailing tone of the administration, and this was no less so after 1655 than before. Even on the commission of the peace, where the local lairds predominated in numbers, it was the army officers on the commission who exerted most influence. For each shire the régime nominated not only the local landowners but also the chief army officers of each district to serve as justices, along with a few Scots, like Lockhart and Swinton, whose service to the Republic was of such longstanding as to identify them with the English, rather than their native, interest. The local lairds were assuredly in the numerical majority; but curbs on their freedom of action were imposed by the presence of these 'alien' influences on the commission. In this way the English ensured that, as with the other institutions of central and local government, their interest on the commission remained paramount.

The importance of the army in the localities, and the vital part it played in ensuring that decisions made at the centre (whether in Edinburgh or London) were implemented and law and order preserved, cannot be overstressed. The civilian organs of government, strengthened now by the institution of a Council, could function only so long as the army performed its peace-keeping role; while for the oversight of day-to-day administration throughout Scotland Monck and his officers were likewise ultimately responsible. The *sine qua non* for the effective exercise of civil policy, moreover, was a settled country free from royalist agitation; to this end Monck and his subordinates operated a far-reaching intelligence network to control the movements of enemy agents and clamped down on all signs of disorder and unrest which, if left unchecked, might erupt into rebellion. The demands of internal security and the preservation of law and order sustained the army's underlying importance in the government of Scotland; however much the new Council might give the appearance of civilian government, it relied for support on the omnipresent armed forces. For this reason Monck, although temporarily eclipsed by Broghill during the latter's year as President, continued to be, as a member of the Council and commander-in-chief of the army, the very lynch-pin of the whole governmental structure in Scotland.

8

Monck, Broghill and the Council, September 1655 — August 1656

i. The setting up of the Council

THE decision to establish a Council in Edinburgh was first mooted when the Council of State appointed a committee on 28 February 1655 to consider the settlement of a civil government in Scotland. This committee, composed of eight members of the Council at Whitehall, reported back at the end of March,[1] and between then and the end of July the full Council debated the membership of, and the instructions to be given to, its offshoot in the north. At the beginning of April, rumours circulated in Westminster that the matter was almost entirely settled, and that eight men, including four Scots — the Earl of Tweeddale, William Lockhart, Sir James Macdowall of Garthland and Alexander Jaffray — had been named as councillors.[2] These reports proved to be premature, for it was not until a month later, on 4 May, that the Protector personally approved the appointment of nine members of Council. These were Monck, Broghill, Samuel Disbrowe, Cols. Charles Howard, Adrian Scroope and Thomas Cooper, Nathaniel Whetham, and the two Scots, John Swinton and William Lockhart. Later on, Sir Edward Rhodes was also added to the Council and was present in Edinburgh with the other members when they took up their duties in September.[3] The choice of Broghill to be President was, on the face of it, a surprising one: aged only 34, he had until six years previously been a staunch Royalist and his political experience had been largely confined to Irish affairs. Yet his conduct in Ireland in the 1650s had greatly impressed Cromwell, in whose counsels he was to become increasingly important as the decade progressed, and so, whatever his other disadvantages, he came north in 1655 with the full trust and confidence of the Protector.[4]

The appointment of the councillors gave rise early in June to speculation that they would set out within the next week or so on their journey to Scotland, but it was not until 12 September that they were all present in Edinburgh.[5] One of the reasons for the delay in their departure from London was the length of time the Council of State took to provide them with a set of formal Instructions. Although Instructions had been substantially agreed on by 30 March, they did not receive final approval until 24 July, but once this had been done, it was ordered that they bear the date 24 June.[6]

The Instructions contained various general clauses enabling the Council to exercise supreme authority in Scotland. The councillors were charged with preserving the union between the two countries, promoting the preaching of the Gospel, and maintaining the peace of the country by imprisoning, taking security from, or deporting any who opposed the government. They were granted power to reform schools and universities, remove 'dangerous, disaffected, or scandalous' office-holders, see to it that no papist was admitted to a position of trust, and encourage trade, commerce and manufactures. This last provision apart, these clauses differed little from some which had appeared in Monck's Instructions over a year previously;[7] they were enabling clauses of a general kind which said little about the specific policies to be adopted by the Council. Some indication of the particular concerns with which the new body was charged was, however, given in the remaining clauses.

In clause five, which enjoined the Council to see peace preserved and justice well administered, Broghill and his colleagues were asked to 'promote the union by having the proceedings in courts of judicature conducted agreeably to the laws of England, as far as the rules of the courts will permit'. This aspiration, that eventually the laws and judicial systems of the two countries should be assimilated, had been implicit in the scheme to annex Scotland which the English House of Commons had considered in September 1651, and it remained an important element in the eventual plans for political incorporation, but progress towards this goal had been slow. Technical difficulties, stemming from the very disparity of the two systems, had proved considerable, although in some cases the English interpretation of Scots laws (for example, the laws of debt) had not proved unwelcome to the Scots. In the period of uncertainty of Glencairn's rising, however, the application of any law was to be preferred to no law at all, and there was little opportunity to implement an orderly integration of the two systems. But now, with the coming of more settled conditions, the new Council could hope to pursue Parliament's earlier aim and so further cement the political union of the two countries.

Several clauses of the Council's Instructions dealt with the collection, management and disbursement of the Scottish revenues. As a preliminary, the Council was ordered to 'certify the state of the whole revenue', where it came from, when it was paid, and how its yield might be improved. New emphasis was laid on two branches of the revenue, that formerly belonging to the Crown, the episcopate and deans and chapters, and that deriving from the customs and excise duties. The Council was specifically charged with seeing that all sums were paid into the Exchequer, and in the case of the excise, a new tax only recently imposed by an order of 16 May 1655,[8] they had special responsiblity for appointing commissioners to regulate its imposition and collection. The laying on of the excise and the erection of an Exchequer Court to adjudicate on matters concerning former Crown lands were, in fact, two of the most important issues with which Broghill had to deal in the coming months. Further evidence of Whitehall's current fiscal concern was given in the clauses which enjoined the Council to lessen the public expenses; to prepare a civil list which would allow the cost of the administration to be borne out of the customs revenue and one-third of the excise; and to cause the assessment to be levied on personal as well as real estates, as was the practice in England. These instructions reflected the spirit of administrative efficiency which the Council was to introduce into the sphere of civil government, as well as the growing realisation in Whitehall that to make budgetary ends meet, some retrenchment in government expenditure had to be effected along with an improved yield from all sources of income.

On religious matters, the Instructions of 24 June enjoined the Council to 'take care that the usual maintenance is received by pious and qualified ministers according to the Ordinance of 8 Aug. 1654' [*i.e.* 'Gillespie's Charter']; thus the Council was required to implement the system whereby boards of local ministers and elders, most of whom were Protesters or sectarians, were empowered to certify a candidate's fitness for the ministry before he should receive his stipend from the English Commissioners. This ordinance had hardly, if ever, been put into practical effect owing to the opposition of the Resolutioners and of Wariston's wing of the Protesting party, who saw in the decree not only the subordination of the church to the state but the victory of Gillespie's faction over the more orthodox and less self-seeking members of the party. The Instructions of 24 June indicated, however, that the English government was determined to persevere with its attempts to enforce the 'Charter', and so, by implication, with its policy of favouring the compliant minority of the Protesting party. But an altogether different emphasis was given to religious policy in another document, in whose drafting Broghill may have had a personal hand. This was a set of additional instructions for the Scottish Council, composed probably in August or early September 1655, which made specific recommendations on particular persons and policies.[9] Most of the issues touched upon were too trivial or too limited in their application to be included in the first set of Instructions, but the clauses on religion were sweeping enough to modify substantially the policies set forth in the latter. In the additional Instructions, the Council was ordered to ensure that the Commissioners for Visitation of Universities should go carefully about the planting of vacant churches with honest and faithful able ministers, without respect 'to any former order granted to Mr. Gillespie and others, that none shall be admitted without their recommendation, which was rather for their own eminency than the good of the work, as it now appears'. In another clause, the Council was empowered 'after conference with some of the most eminent of the ministers', presumably of both parties, to allow them fully to exercise their church discipline in synods, presbyteries and kirk sessions. These provisions did not mark any great shift in the régime's attitude towards presbyterianism as such, but they did portend a change in the Council's relations with the Scottish church parties; the policy of collaboration with Gillespie, divisive in its effects, was to give way to consultation with reasonable men of all parties. Quite why the two sets of instructions should conflict on these points is unclear, but interestingly enough the course of action which Broghill and the Council eventually followed contained elements from both sets of recommendations. Initially an attempt *was* made to revitalise 'Gillespie's Charter' and it was only when this failed that Broghill put forward proposals for a new approach to the problem, with the attempted formation of a third party in the church.[10]

Armed with both sets of instructions, however, the Council was well-equipped to address itself to Scottish affairs from 13 September onwards. In contrast to the glowing opinions which Broghill was later to win from some Scots — Nicoll described him in 1656 as 'weill beloved of all our Scottis natioun as knew him'[11] and Baillie as 'a man exceeding wise and moderat'[12] — little good was at first expected to come from a Council composed of 'six or seven English sojours, and two of our complying gentlemen'.[13] The latter were observed to revel in the outward splendour affected by the English, and while the English officers in Scotland eagerly anticipated the fruits of office from the administrative reorganisation embarked on by the Council, the Scottish people viewed with trepidation the possibility of new impositions being laid upon them.[14] English hopes and Scottish fears were both to some extent realised in the coming weeks, for Broghill and his colleagues quickly began to attack the problems mapped out for them by the Council in London with the vigour expected of new brooms. In their first few weeks of office, they touched on nearly all those areas of civil government most in need of reform: they began to reorganise the administrative and judicial machinery, supervise the imposition of the excise, tighten up measures for preserving law and order, and, not least of all, attempt a solution of the religious problem. Most of these problems proved more difficult to resolve than the Council had at first anticipated; some had to be juggled with for many months, while a few remained unsolved even when Broghill left Scotland in 1656. In addition to these concerns, the Council also had a permanent responsibility for maintaining internal security against the possibility of a royalist challenge, and so, as well as attending to matters related to finance, justice, law and order, and religion, Broghill and Monck supervised the construction of an intelligence network extending from Scotland to the continent of Europe.

ii. Finance

One of the first problems to which the Council addressed itself after assuming office was the imposition of an excise upon Scotland. As the Council's Instructions had indicated, this task was of major importance, since the anticipated yield from the excise had already been earmarked by the authorities to solve some of their most pressing financial problems. The suggestion that an excise should be levied in Scotland had been made by Monck in March 1655.[15] His idea had been to make Scotsmen responsible for the management of the tax, and to promise them that any amount levied over and above an agreed sum could be put towards easing the burden of the assessment. In this way the burden of the extra tax would appear to be mitigated, while the collectors would have an incentive to keep its yield as high as possible. Monck's underlying aim was, of course, to increase the state's revenue so that enough money could be allocated to pay his troops; the Scottish assessment, which had always been earmarked for this purpose, was continuing to prove woefully inadequate, while not enough money was being sent from England to make up the deficit. Some new expedient was clearly necessary. The Council responded by considering an appropriate order and declaration in May, approval being given by the Protector on the 16th.[16] The order began by recalling that the Ordinance of Union ordained that all taxes should be borne proportionably by the people of England and Scotland, and that the Instrument of Government had settled an excise to help maintain the army and navy in England and Ireland. Therefore, from 24 June 1655 the same rates which were levied in England and Wales were to be extended to Scotland. The Instructions for the Scottish Council, meanwhile, suggested some of the uses to which the new revenue could be put. One-third of the excise, together with the yield from the customs, was to pay the costs of the civil administration; while the rest of the excise, together with anything left over from the customs, plus all proceeds from assessments and sequestrations, was to go towards the pay of the forces and other contingencies.[17] Since regulating the excise was a highly technical business, the English Council decided to send a qualified person to Scotland to help get the scheme off the ground. Their choice eventually fell on Thomas Tucker, registrar to the (English) Commissioners for Appeals and regulating the Excise; the Scottish Council was ordered to appoint him one of its Commissioners for Excise during his stay in Scotland. The choice was a fortunate one, not least because on his return to London Tucker penned, in November 1656, a full report on his activities in Scotland[18] from which much of our knowledge of the imposition of this tax derives.

By 19 September, Broghill and his colleagues had chosen Richard Saltonstall, Edmund Syler and Sir James Macdowall of Garthland to serve with Tucker; their commission was not merely for the excise, but included customs and sequestrations as well.[19] Saltonstall and Syler had already served as revenue commissioners at Leith, and so, having had experience of both customs and sequestrations, they were obvious choices. Macdowall, who had been a commissioner for the Scottish excise in the 1640s, was picked because 'som of the councill . . . [were] of opinion, that it would be requisite to have one of the cuntry.' This policy, which echoed Monck's earlier suggestion that Scotsmen should be employed to manage the tax, no doubt also stemmed from a desire to profit from Macdowall's previous experience, for in one crucial respect the Council had decided to follow Scottish precedent and, as the covenanting government had done in 1650, to farm out, rather than to collect, the inland excise. In an attempt to preserve continuity with the Covenanters' efforts, Broghill 'caused a diligent search to be made in the excise bookes of thos times, the better to informe us, how we should proceed'.[20] In effect, the excise of all beer, ale and 'aqua-vitae' made and consumed in Scotland was to be farmed out, shire by shire, to the highest bidder, while the duty on imported or exported goods would be gathered by customs officers, who now acted as excise collectors in addition to their original duties. The duty on foreign and native salt was to be collected and accounted for separately.

The Commissioners decided that their first task should be to farm out the inland excise, and that initially the farms or leases should run for only four months, from 19 September 1655 to 19 January 1656. Despite the search in the record books, precedent was not very helpful, for circumstances had changed so much since 1650 that it was difficult to know what to accept as a realistic bid. The English, however, were not above giving market forces a helping hand. Tucker recalled that before the formal bidding took place, the Commissioners had private talks with each of the proposers to find out what would be his highest offer. On the basis of this information, the Commissioners then set the price at which to start the bidding, so that the farm could be let to whoever would push his bid furthest above this sum. Circumstances also forced the English to decide that, rather than let the farm of any shire go at a very low rate, they would instruct their own officials to collect the excise instead. This decision was arrived at after the magistrates of the Scottish burghs had tried to get the rules changed in their favour. The magistrates' complaint was that there was no provision for letting the farms of the principal burghs separately from those of the shires. Therefore, in order to preserve their corporate privileges, they attempted to exclude all other bidders so that the shire leases, and with them the burghs', would fall into their hands at a low rate. The magistrates believed that the Commissioners would have to give in to them if there were no other bidders, but when the Commissioners countered with the threat of collection, they in turn had to admit defeat. As a result, the Commissioners were able to attract higher bids from other people, and from those magistrates who were prepared to make a genuine offer to keep municipal affairs under their control.[21] Apart from Edinburgh, which had been given special permission to levy its own excise by a former grant of Council, Dundee was the only burgh to be farmed out separately.[22]

Tucker was strongly critical of the attitude of the burgh magistrates who, he maintained, 'doe usually exercise a kind of soveraignety over the people', and he extended this criticism to cover the activities of many of the Scots farmers. These he characterised as 'naturally rigid exactors, apt to avenge private quarrells or discontents, under colour and pretext of publique employment, and most of them generally strangers to the particular worke in which they engaged'. In this respect, English policy had backfired, for one of the reasons for entertaining Scots in the first place had been to make the new tax less obnoxious to the Scottish people.[23] The imposition of the tax was, in fact, expected to meet with considerable opposition. In September, Monck had suggested that, since 'people may be a little troublesome upon that occasion', another regiment of horse should be sent to Scotland before the laying on of the excise.[24] Tucker in due course reported plenty of trouble, although nothing on a scale which demanded vigorous military intervention. The blame for much of the unrest he put on people who had been disappointed in their efforts to bid for the farms; these men, he said, excited the populace against the excisemen, who were unable by themselves to impose sanctions on recalcitrant consumers. The Commissioners had earlier resolved to grant only the collective power to the farmers, reserving the 'Judiciall part' to themselves, so that the farmers could not personally threaten non-payers with legal penalties. In the next few months, the Commissioners were forced to reverse this decision and to allow the farmers greater control over those who refused to obey them.[25]

Many of these teething troubles had been overcome by the time the first leases fell in in January 1656. Thereafter the Commissioners decided to grant farms for a whole year and were gratified to find a greater number of proposers than before. (Tucker, however, could not resist attributing this to an 'innate propensity and inclination of being despoticall' on the part of many who wished to farm their own shires and burghs.)[26] A few intractable problems remained, such as the impossibility of finding farmers for the shires of Midlothian, Argyll and Bute,[27] but by the time of Tucker's departure from Scotland in the autumn of 1656, the imposition and collection of the excise was proceeding fairly smoothly.

Before his departure, Tucker also took the opportunity to reorganise the collection of the customs and the excise on foreign goods. This involved him in a journey to every port in Scotland and drew from him many pungent comments on the poor state of the country's trade and commerce. He noted contemptuously that although Scotland's geography would seem to favour commerce and traffic,

> yet the barrenesse of the countrey, poverty of the people, generally affected with slothe, and a lazy vagrancy of attending and followeing theyr heards up and down in theyr pastorage, rather than any dextrous improvement of theyr time, hath quite banished all trade from the inland parts, and drove her downe to the very sea-side, where that little which is still remayneing, (and was never greate in the most proude and flourishing times,) lives pent and shutt up in a very small compasse . . .[28]

As a result of his labours, Tucker was able to draw up an account of the receipts from customs and excise duties during his stay in Scotland. These showed that from October 1655 to October 1656 the yield from customs and foreign excise was around £12,800 stg., of which approximately £6000 came from the customs; this compares with a figure, estimated by a sub-committee of the House of Commons, of £9000 for customs alone in 1654.[29] The inland excise was farmed out from January 1656 to January 1657 for a total of £35,054; this was approximately 3½ times the sum raised in the first four months of the tax, which indicates that the Commissioners had made a fairly realistic initial estimate of how much the new farmers could and would bid. The excise on foreign salt accounted for another £550 *per annum*, and that on native salt for a few hundred pounds more.[30]

The imposition of the excise had in part been made necessary by the consistent failure of the assessment to yield anything like the nominal sum laid on the Scottish people. After a dramatic slump in the amount collected during the months when Glencairn's rising was at its peak, the yield had stabilised by the autumn of 1655 at a level of £7500 to £8000 per month.[31] This was still more than £2000 per month short of the desired maximum,[32] but Monck at least felt that the abatement was justified by the amount of land which had been burnt or wasted during the recent troubles. Nonetheless, in September 1655 the Council at Whitehall suggested to Monck, in answer to a plea for more money to carry on the work of building fortifications, that he should try to levy part of the £2000 allowed in abatements from those lands which had recovered from the holocaust.[33] Clearly, therefore, pressure was building up from Whitehall for another attempt to raise the full £10,000 per month from the Scottish people. During their first months in office, the Council in Scotland responded to this pressure with attempts to cut down the costs of collecting the tax, redistribute the burden so that it fell on personal as well as real estates, and enforce a proclamation calling for the full

£10,000 to be raised. Despite stringent efforts on all these counts, however, it is doubtful if the yield rose to more than £8000 or £8500 per month at any time in 1656.

By late October or early November 1655, Broghill and the Council had concocted a scheme for economising on the collectors' fees of nearly £5000 *per annum*, or just over £400 in any one month. Broghill's idea was to shift the burden of levying the cess on to the local gentry: each shire was to give the English Treasurer security for paying in the assessment, and then the gentry, taking it in turns quarter by quarter, were to 'take the paynes and care of levyinge it *gratis*'.[34] Broghill emphasised that not only would this be cheaper, but it would prevent inequalities in exaction, for if any gentleman tried to favour himself or his friends in one quarter, his neighbours would retaliate against him in the next. Although Broghill's motive for making this change was primarily fiscal rather than political, the new system carried one step further Lilburne and Monck's policy of involving the gentry in the tasks of local administration. Whether the local landowners regarded this onerous and painful duty as much of a concession is, however, a moot point.

Of more value to the gentry in their efforts to regain control of local affairs was, perhaps, the Council's subsequent decision to make all justices of the peace serve also as commissioners of the assessment. In effect, this united the old practice of appointing the shire gentry to sit on committees of revaluation with the recent scheme to make them responsible for collection. Broghill explained the advantages of the new measure in a letter to Thurloe of late December: by linking the assessment to the commission of the peace (plans for which had recently been completed), the Council would ensure that the gentry 'may by the benefit of the one commission be limited to acte upon the other; and wher we finde they will not acte upon both, they shall acte upon neither'. Broghill obviously believed that it was the commission of the assessment which the gentry would see as a benefit; and by using this as an incentive he attempted to get round the reluctance of some of the gentry to accept office as justices of the peace.[35]

The names of the commissioners of assessment for each shire were printed in a declaration of the Scottish Council, dated 21 December 1655; this also gave orders for raising a full £10,000 per month for the six months from 31 December 1655 until 1 July 1656. The text of the declaration,[36] which was proclaimed in Edinburgh at the beginning of January,[37] made no allowance whatsoever for abatements; indeed, it made the Council's intentions quite clear by listing exactly how much cess each shire and each burgh would be required to pay. Scots commentators took this document at its face value when they recorded their disgust at the increased exactions — Wariston, for one, called the imposition of £10,000 per month 'a crewel bondage and oppression to this poor land'.[38]

One of the specific grievances which the Scots had against the new order concerning the cess was that it attempted to levy tax on personal as well as real estates.[39] Due to the resultant howl of protest, this attempt did not in fact succeed, although the work of surveying and computing the amount of tax due from individual persons was certainly started in some, and probably in all, shires. Such a task could not be accomplished overnight. The declaration provided that the commissioners of assessment should hold a preliminary meeting before 10 January 1656, that a fortnight later they should meet again to receive the surveyors' returns, but that if the work were not completed in this time, then the cess was to be levied in the old manner for the months of January and February. Under no circumstances, however, was the work of surveying and valuation to be prolonged beyond 20 February. Linlithgowshire certainly needed the extra two months' grace, while in Perthshire also it was not anticipated that the full details would be ready before the end of February. Whether or not all the shires completed their returns, it was soon reported that '[t]here was such outcrying of the husbandmen that the gentry were glad to free them of their cess' on personal estates.[40]

As a result of this and other forms of protest, Scotland once more failed despite the Council's solemn pronouncements to produce £10,000 per month. In practice, the English did not really expect that it would, for the unbending attitude conveyed in the declaration notwithstanding, they were in fact prepared to allow abatements to the tune of £678 15s. 6d. per month.[41] These abatements were granted not merely to individuals, whose deficiencies might be made up by imposing an extra burden upon their neighbours, but also to whole shires, so that the total yield was affected. The amounts actually collected fell short of the target by much more than £678 — the Council of State in April 1656 was under the impression that only £8000 was being raised[42] — so that even the Council's revised estimate proved unrealistic. Nonetheless, the Council of State urged Broghill in April to consult with Monck on how the extra £2000 could be raised, and in June, with Broghill's full concurrence, the Council's formal order for the continuance of the assessment for six months longer again set the target at £10,000.[43]

Unfortunately, the allocation of abatements to specific individuals for these months is difficult to trace, for Monck's warrant-book, reflecting the fact that such matters were now being decided by the Council, is not as helpful for 1656 as for previous years. Nonetheless, during the year from September 1655 until August 1656, some familiar names do crop up: the laird of Glenorchy, Sir James Campbell of Lawers, Sir James Macdonald of Sleat, and the Earl of Perth's son, Lord Drummond, were all granted abatements, as was the royalist Earl of Atholl.[44] Concessions of various kinds were also given to Cameron of Lochiel, Lachlan Mackinnon of Strathordle, Dougal Macpherson of Badenoch, the Captain of Clanranald, the laird of Macleod and Lord Cranston.[45] Significantly, however, most of the abatements were made before January 1656 and many of the concessions, including grants for remission of arrears, which were made after December 1655 related to the period before the new order came into force. The Captain of Clanranald, for example, was in July 1656 given a remission of the arrears which he had accumulated before January of that year. It seems, therefore, that as far as he was able, Monck tried to continue that policy of favouring actual and potential supporters of the régime which he had forcefully pursued since 1654, but that the renewed pressure to raise £10,000 per month to some degree inhibited his efforts.

The laying on of the excise and the reorganisation of the assessment were two of the Council's most important attempts to improve the yield from the Scottish revenues, but this concern to increase income went hand in hand with a desire to cut down on public expenditure. On 22 September 1655, Broghill informed Thurloe that the civil list would be reduced, and that details would follow shortly. By early November, the Council had agreed on some retrenchment, but the full extent was not made known until February 1656, when the Council sent to London an estimate of 'The civil list of Scotland, with the respective salaries thereof'.[46] This showed that the Council had made a retrenchment of nearly £2800 *per annum* in the civil list, and that salaries would now put a charge of £20,134 10s. 10d. annually on the public receipts in Scotland. The reductions had not been effected merely by cutting down on lesser officials; such important figures as the Commissioners for Customs, Excise and Sequestrations, for example, had had their salaries reduced from £500 to £365 yearly.

Broghill's crowning achievement in the realm of financial administration would, he hoped, be the reorganisation of the Scottish Exchequer. This task fell into two parts: the remodelling of the Exchequer as an institution into which all the state's revenue would be paid and by which all accounts would be audited, and the erection of an Exchequer Court which would have cognisance of all 'concealed' revenue formerly belonging to the Crown. The restoration of the Exchequer's judicial function, therefore, represented an attempt to improve the revenue of the state by recovering rents and other dues formerly enjoyed by the Crown, while the other changes were an attempt to make the system of receiving, auditing and disbursing the revenue administratively more efficient and less costly. In both cases, the intention[47] was to bring Scottish and English practice into line so that the English Exchequer could keep a check on its Scottish subordinate.

Before leaving London, Broghill had busied himself 'in forminge a moddell, which might be cheape and cleer',[48] but his confidence that the Scottish Exchequer could swiftly and easily be set up in accordance with this plan was soon dispelled. The sticking-point turned out to be the 'judicial part', rather than the purely fiscal aspects, of the Exchequer's work, for difficulties soon arose over the limits of the Court's jurisdiction. Before the end of September, Broghill and the Council had decided that the Court should consist of two of the Judges and two councillors, along with the Auditor-General, and that it should sit only occasionally, and always in the afternoon, to transact business. Broghill anticipated that many of its cases would relate to the alienation of Crown lands by James I and Charles I, for the recovery of the rents due from these lands was to be one of the Court's prime tasks.[49] At this stage, the delay in setting the Court up was apparently due to the Council's ignorance of the exact powers of the Exchequer in England, for it was on this model that they desired to regulate the business in Scotland. When this information was forthcoming, however, it was discovered that if the Scottish Exchequer were given as wide powers as the English, then the 'Court of Session', or civil court, would lose most of its pleas, for Scottish land tenure was such that virtually all land was held directly or indirectly from the Crown; therefore all titles to land would automatically come within the purview of the new court. At the same time, the Council's desire to act in accordance with previous Scottish law and custom, as well as with current English practice, was creating another difficulty, for they could not see how to resolve the contradiction between the Scottish Act of Parliament of 1633, which had given wide powers, and the Act of 1640, which had given more limited powers, to the pre-war Exchequer Court. Despite their instructions to bring the laws and judicial systems of the two countries into line, the Council nonetheless emphasised that if grants of land made by the Stuart kings were to be resumed, it would have to be done by an authority holding powers under the laws of Scotland. These arguments Broghill carefully rehearsed in a letter to Cromwell of 23 October[50] in which he recommended to the Protector that the powers of the Scottish Exchequer be limited; and again in November, he affirmed the need to conduct the business of the Court in accordance with Scottish custom.[51] Little could be done, however, until the Council of State gave its decision on the extent of the new Court's jurisdiction, a decision for which Broghill waited impatiently, frequently complaining that his letters to the central government were not being answered.[52] At last, after Broghill had forcefully pointed out that until the Court was set up, the public revenue would suffer to the tune of £100 per week,[53] the Council delivered its decision. On 9 January, President Lawrence informed Broghill that it was thought fit to restrict the Court to settling matters which concerned either those parts of the revenue made away by King James or King Charles, contrary to the laws of Scotland, or else those lands and profits belonging to the bishops or any branch of the episcopal hierarchy, but now unduly alienated.[54]

The Scottish Council then lost little time in naming the new judges: they were to be George Smyth and William Lawrence, two of the English Commissioners for the Administration of Justice, and Samuel Disbrowe and William Lockhart, both councillors.[55] On 27 February, the Court of Exchequer issued a proclamation requiring owners of public lands (kirklands or lands of the king's patrimony) to produce their rights and infeoffments thereto, so that a complete rental might be drawn up. Those living south of the Forth were given until 1 April to produce the relevant documents, but more time was allowed for those in the north.[56] Evidently the response was disappointing, for on 29 July 1656 the Judges of the Exchequer issued another proclamation, threatening with loss of title any person who failed to produce the necessary proof by certain dates in September, October and November.[57] Despite the slow progress of this work, the Court was well established before Broghill left Scotland in August 1656. Its activities nonetheless continued to arouse a great deal of resentment among the Scots, with the result that in later years the authorities in Scotland saw fit to recommend that some of its powers be transferred to the central civil court, to avoid criticism that it was acting *ultra vires*.[58]

The four sets of measures described so far — those concerned with the laying on of the excise, the reorganisation of the assessment, the retrenchment in the civil list, and the remodelling of the Exchequer — constituted a serious attempt by Broghill and the Council to tackle the most pressing financial problems of the régime in Scotland. They had, in accordance with their Instructions, sought to increase revenue, limit expenditure and improve efficiency in the fiscal administration. But while the provision of an adequate revenue was in the long term vital for the continuation of both civil and military government in Scotland, the stability of the régime was in the short term much more bound up with the problems of maintaining public order and enforcing the law. Thus, at the same time as the Council was debating fiscal issues, it devoted considerable attention to other questions arising from the need to ensure domestic tranquillity. Here again the Council embarked upon some new expedients, notably the introduction of justices of the peace; but it also took care to refurbish old institutions and to carry on the measures of law enforcement which the army had pioneered in 1653-4 and for which it was still responsible.

iii. Justice, law and order

The administration of justice at the highest level had, since 1652, lain with seven Commissioners. Of the original members, four — Smyth, Moseley, Owen and Marsh — had been English and three — Lockhart, Swinton and Sir John Hope of Craighall — had been Scots. In 1653 Owen and Marsh were replaced by another two Englishmen, Henry Goodyear and William Lawrence, and in 1654 Hope was succeeded by the Scotsman Alexander Pearson of Southall.[59] Initially, none of the Scots judges was included on the commission to try criminal cases, but Hope and Pearson were subsequently added, perhaps because of their special knowledge of Scots criminal law.[60] The English judges had won no little favour among the common people by their firmness and impartiality, although, as the number of impoverished gentry who joined Glencairn to escape their creditors made clear, their strict interpretation of the law could have dangerous side-effects. On the whole, however, the English had good reason to be pleased with their successful take-over of the Scottish system, but this achievement, in itself, was not enough. Progress had still to be made towards a unification of Scottish and English law and legal practice, and it was to this end that Broghill, in accordance with clause five of the Council's Instructions, bent his energies.

Almost at once, however, Broghill had to contend with short-term practical difficulties in the administration of justice. In the summer of 1655, and indeed in the winter before that, the judges had failed to keep the sessions in the proper manner, not least because of the absence of Swinton, Lockhart and Smyth in England.[61] Now, when Swinton and Lockhart took up office as members of the Council, the court of justice was again effectively deprived of their services, so that only five judges remained for duty in the coming winter session. Of the five, only one, Alexander Pearson, was Scottish, and he was considered incompetent. This particular deficiency was made all the more serious by the Council's decision, in the first weeks of its life, to restore the outer house of the old Court of Session, for the outer house had to be staffed by an experienced man with knowledge of Scots law.[62] Its suppression by the English in 1652 had meant that all causes were heard by the whole bench sitting together (in the manner of the old inner house) instead of by a single judge who disposed of most actions at a 'first-round' hearing in the outer house and passed on only the most contentious cases to his colleagues in the inner house. The new system, as it operated from 1652 to 1655, was thus more expensive in manpower, and by the time Broghill had arrived in Scotland a considerable backlog of cases had built up. It was to help clear this backlog that the Council hearkened to a petition from the Faculty of Advocates and restored the outer house.[63]

Initially, Broghill had planned to fill up the vacancies on the bench, and indeed to increase the total number of judges, by appointing Englishmen, so that the long-term aim of assimilating the two systems would be brought one step nearer: unless at least four English judges were sent up, he informed Thurloe in September, 'we shall still continue Scotch'.[64] But the need to find a Scotsman to sit in the outer house temporarily overshadowed this aim. In November, the Council appointed two new Scottish judges, Sir James Learmonth of Balcomy and Mr. Andrew Kerr, who would take it in turns to perform the work of the outer house. Sir James Learmonth had been a Lord of Session in the 1620s and 1640s, and also a Commissioner of the Exchequer in the 1640s; his attraction for Broghill was that he had not subscribed to a private agreement made by those few members of the old Session who were willing to serve under the English, that they would accept office only on terms of life or good behaviour. The appointment of Kerr, hitherto merely an advocate, was also designed to show these Scottish judges that the Council was not dependent on them. If by making these appointments Broghill was forced to admit that no English judge could preside over the outer house, he nonetheless kept sight of his larger aim by recommending to Thurloe that, in addition to Kerr and Balcomy, at least one more eminent Englishman should be included in the commission.[65]

This last recommendation was given some urgency by the discovery, in late November or early December, that the status of the two Scots councillors, Lockhart and Swinton, was not as clear-cut as Broghill had at first thought. Initially, the problem seemed merely one of finance — were they to be included on the judicial payroll or not? — but soon Broghill realised that their actual presence on the bench might have profound implications for the government's policy of bringing the two legal systems into line. For if Lockhart and Swinton continued to act as judges, the Scots would outnumber the English on the bench, and so would be able successfully to resist all attempts at assimilation. As it was, the Scots were sticking hard to the letter of their statute law, in the face of English attempts to use the concepts of equity and good conscience to promote greater conformity between the two systems. As an example of the wrongs that might ensue if the existing state of affairs continued, Broghill cited the case of Lord Traquair, who had recently escaped conviction for perjury only because one of the Scots councillors had taken his place on the bench and swayed the decision in favour of the accused.[66] Broghill pressed Thurloe to seek a decision on Lockhart and Swinton's position from Cromwell. As a result, both were subsequently removed from the commission for the administration of justice for the year 1656,[67] so for the time being at least, Broghill got his way. Although the Council in Scotland continued to be troubled by the problem of Scottish versus English representation on the bench,[68] little else was done for the moment to promote that integration of the laws for which successive English governments had hoped.

The attention which Broghill paid to the commission for the administration of justice was also relevant to the enforcement of the criminal law in Scotland, not least because the English judges on the commission were responsible for holding periodic 'assizes' or circuit courts in the localities. Although the records for these criminal courts are scanty,[69] in 1656 hearings were certainly held, at any rate in the west, by Judges Smyth and Lawrence. In April and May 1656, they held courts at Glasgow, Ayr and Dumfries, and also at Jedburgh in Roxburghshire, where they dealt with a wide variety of cases adjudged to merit the death penalty, including sexual crimes (buggery, adultery and incest), murder, theft and blasphemy.[70]

By the time that Lawrence and Smyth heard these particular cases responsibility for committing such offenders to prison to await trial had devolved upon the newly created justices of the peace. The institution of justices and constables on the English model was seen by the English as a major contribution to the problems of maintaining peace and good government in the localities. As far back as April 1654, Monck had suggested that such a system 'would much conduce to the setling the Country' and had offered to submit a list of suitable appointees; but nothing was done until Broghill and the Council began to consider the matter in September 1655.[71] At the end of that month, letters were sent to all the garrison commanders in Scotland asking them to seek out likely candidates in the shires under their control. The officers were to ensure that the persons they nominated were able and faithful men, that their homes lay conveniently near the places where sessions would be held, and that they would be willing to accept a commission if offered it.[72] This last condition was doubtless seen as a precaution against the embarrassment of being turned down flat by those most hostile to the government, although in practice there was nothing to prevent such persons when approached, from returning an equivocal reply. In contrast to the diligence which the army showed in making these preliminary inquiries, Broghill himself refrained from meddling. He assured Thurloe that he had not named a single justice on his own initiative, and that his only intervention, undertaken on Thurloe's advice, had been to prevent the nomination of the Marquis of Argyle.[73]

By mid-November the Council had drawn up a list of instructions for the justices; this, along with a declaration enjoining all persons to give due obedience to the new officers, was formally proclaimed in Edinburgh on 19 December.[74] In the Instructions the justices were ordered to hold quarter-sessions in February May, August and October, beginning in February 1656. They were authorised not only to punish minor criminal offences but also to exercise the preventive power of binding suspected persons over to keep the peace; this, the Council hoped, would allow the justices to nip trouble in the bud before it assumed dangerous proportions. As custodians of the criminal !aw they were empowered to proceed against persons committing riot and to put into effect the laws against vagabonds trespassers and poachers, forestallers and regraters of markets, and profaners of the Sabbath. Their jurisdiction over the morals of the nation extended also to

'Mockers or Reproachers of piety', particularly persons found guilty of swearing and/or fornication, on whom they could impose severe fines, thus exercising a power formerly employed by the kirk sessions. Indeed the clergy complained so much at the loss of their 'pecuniary mulcts' that the Council was forced to decree that one half of the fines should be devoted to 'pious uses' in the parish in question, while the other half went to the informer and the arresting constable.[75]

Further clauses of the Instructions established the justices' importance as a link in the judicial hierarchy. They had responsibility for seeing that persons accused of serious crimes such as treason, murder, felony, incest and blasphemy were brought before the circuit judges, and were also required to superintend the work of the sheriffs. If they suspected any sheriff of inflicting inadequate punishments in cases of assault or of conniving at a prisoner's wrongful acquittal, they were to report him to the Council forthwith.[76] Finally, the justices of the peace were charged with a whole host of administrative duties which placed the social and economic welfare of the community very much in their hands: not only were they to make provision for the poor, the aged and the sick, but they were also to regulate wages and prices, reform gaols, see to the repair of roads and bridges and 'set down orders in the Countrey for governance in time of plague'.

Although Broghill recorded the Council's intention to establish justices and constables in Scotland 'with the power such ministers and officers have in England',[77] the Instructions of 1655 did not differ greatly from those which had been given to the Jacobean justices in Scotland in 1610 and 1617.[78] What had changed was the political climate in which they were expected to discharge their duties. As Broghill pointed out, it was the opposition of the magnates, and the competing claims of the heritable jurisdictions, that had prevented the Jacobean and Caroline system from taking root;[79] in the 1650s, however, the heritable jurisdictions of the nobility had been abolished and their political influence reduced, so that the commission of the peace now had a chance to operate effectively. Paradoxically, however, the success of the scheme after 1655 had quite a different significance from that which would have attended the success of James VI's venture. Under the Stuarts, it would have symbolised the victory of the central government over entrenched local interests, and of monarchical or state power over feudalism. Some of these elements were still present during the Interregnum: the scheme was, for example, a natural complement to the abolition by the Ordinance of Union of a feudal overlord's right to hold courts of justiciary, regality or barony. But in relation to the English Parliament's policy in 1651 of destroying the power of the nobility and gentry, the measure now put into force by Broghill and the Council marked a concession to the men of influence in the localities; and in comparison with the predominantly coercive, centralising and military tone of government over the last few years, it signified a move towards conciliation and co-operation with the local communities. In its attempts to enrol prominent Scottish civilians in the task of maintaining order and dispensing justice, therefore, the Council carried on and extended the efforts of Lilburne and Monck to suppress disorder by making the community responsible for the conduct of its members. In all, the measure marked the government's increasing willingness to effect a political compromise with at least some of the traditional holders of power in Scotland.

Notwithstanding the strong element of conciliation which the institution of justices of the peace embodied, the system was in practice firmly under the control of the army. An extant list of the justices for nineteen of the shires in Scotland[80] reveals that in every shire several army officers served on the commission of the peace; in all cases Monck's name appears, followed by those of the governors of the nearest garrisons and other high-ranking officers. The appointment of these men in itself seriously modified the extent to which the new scheme could be seen as a concession to civilian government, and to the Scottish community, for the job of the officers on the commission was to check the activities of the Scottish justices, and to see that the army's control over the maintenance of law and order was in no way diminished.

The names of the Scottish justices show, however, that in these nineteen counties the English asked for and received the support of a few peers, several of the greater gentry and a substantial number of lesser lairds and professional men. Conspicuously missing are the names of most of the leading nobility of Scotland; not only were they excluded by their royalist sympathies from being offered, far less accepting, such office, but it was not the purpose of the system to enrol these men specifically in the task of government. The intention was rather to use the influence of men of lesser rank, but of considerable standing nonetheless, to keep order in the localities and so to cut the ground from under the feet of any royalist nobleman who might attempt to foment rebellion. Some of the peerage had, of course, earned the commendation of the government before 1656 and their names do crop up as justices — thus the Earls of Tullibardine, Linlithgow and Wemyss and James, Lord Drummond were appointed in Perthshire; the Earl of Sutherland and George, Lord Strathnaver in Sutherland; Lord Cochrane in Ayrshire and the Earl of Hartfell in Dumfriesshire[81] along with, on average, one or two of the nobility in each county. The more substantial gentlemen accounted for a variable proportion of the justices in each shire. Their exact number, in relation to that of the lesser lairds, no doubt depended on the social structure of the several regions of Scotland as well as on the pattern of political allegiance; but rarely, it seems, did the greater gentry exceed the lesser lairds on the commission, and in many cases they were outnumbered by them. In both instances, however, the names of proven supporters of the régime crop up, as well as many less identifiable names: in Perthshire, for example, Sir Peter Hay of Meginch, Sir James Stuart of Grantully (son of Sir Thomas?), Sir James Campbell of Lawers, the fiar of Glenorchy[82] and the latter's factor, Henry Christie, appear alongside lesser known men of the name of Campbell, Menzies and Murray.

After the publication of the justices' Instructions in December 1655, it was some time before the English knew on whom they could depend for support, for despite the feelers which the army had been asked to put out in the autumn, some of those named on the first commissions refused to serve. The sticking-point was the oath which required them to accept office as 'one of the Commissioners and Justices of His Highness the Lord Protector's Peace'.[83] Alexander Brodie and his fellow-justices in Moray hesitated some months before complying,[84] while Col. Gilbert Ker, a prominent Protester who had been named in the commission for Roxburghshire, went further and adamantly refused to serve, on the grounds that to accept the employment would be sinful and unlawful, would contravene the word of the Lord and the Solemn League and Covenant, and would encroach upon the liberties of the kirk (this last being doubtless a reference to the justices' power over moral offences).[85] In April 1656, Broghill explained to Thurloe: 'Som ther are who scruple, others ther are, who deny; thes we strike out: those we give a monthe's time longer to advise; and then if they mend not, we shall serve them soe too.' Whatever Broghill meant by this last threat, in Brodie's case, at least, one suspects that his compliance followed the unsolicited visit of some English soldiers to his house.[86]

Apart from the unwillingness of individuals to accept the new employment, the English experienced some opposition as a result of the burghs' desire to resist any encroachment on their corporate privileges; in this case they resented the appointment of 'strangers' to serve on the commission of the peace within each town. In February 1656, Broghill and his colleagues were forced to grant a request from the town council of Edinburgh that only the local magistrates should be appointed as justices within the town, while orders were issued to Col. Ashfield in Glasgow to be careful of the sensitivities of that town.[87]

By April, however, Broghill was satisfied that '[o]ur busines of justices of the peace does begin to take som life, many considerable persons for interest and power haveing taken the oth'. In the same month, the governor of Ruthven Castle wrote in lyrical terms of the success of the system in the Highlands, which soon would be able to contend 'for civilitie' with the Lowlands.[88] But still more justices were needed, not only to fulfil the many judicial and administrative duties outlined in the Instructions, but also to serve *ex officio* as commissioners of the assessment. Thus when the orders for the laying on of the next six months' cess were issued in June, the senior officers in each shire were asked to send the names of men willing to take the oath and act as JPs to the Council with all convenient speed, so that the numbers on each commission might be made up.[89] Despite the apparent shortage of manpower, however, the system continued to operate efficiently during and after the summer of 1656 and to make a real contribution to the fight against disorder and unrest in Scotland.[90]

As a corollary to the appointment of justices of the peace, the Council drew up, in March 1656, a revised list of sheriffs for the several counties.[91] Whereas in previous years each shire had had two sheriffs-conjunct, one of whom was an English officer, most were now put under the jurisdiction of a single Scottish civilian. The new sheriffs, like the new justices, included several prominent supporters of the régime, such as Lord Strathnaver in Sutherland and Sir James Hamilton in Lanark;[92] others, like John Forbes in Banff or John Shaw in Ayr, are less well-known, but presumably their appointments were also made in recognition of services rendered to the English régime. In these, and most other, cases the men appointed were of much lower social status than their Jacobean or Caroline counterparts. In some shires it was not deemed proper, for security reasons, to put the office of sheriff entirely in civilian hands: this was so in Perthshire and Angus, both strategically placed on the Highland-Lowland line, where Cols. Daniel and Cobbett were appointed respectively, and in the Highland region itself. Here the issue was further complicated by the desire of the Scottish Council to divide the existing shires of Argyll and Inverness into five separate sheriffdoms. The proposal, which, it was feared, would excite the opposition of the Marquis of Argyle, was put forward by Broghill in a letter to the Council of State in February 1656, but action on it was delayed for some time.[93] Eventually only the area around Lochaber was erected into a shire by itself, thus, in effect, transforming the extraordinary judicial authority of the governor of Inverlochy into that of a normal sheriff.[94]

By breathing new life into the commission of the peace, and by refurbishing the commission for the administration of justice and the office of sheriff, Broghill and the Council had given fresh impetus to the work of maintaining law and order in a civilian context. This emphasis on the structure of the judicial machine did not, however, blind them to the fact that the content of English policy on matters not directly associated with the administration of justice could have an equally important bearing on the problem of maintaining law and order. In dealing with the problem of order, therefore, the Councils in Scotland and at Whitehall looked beyond the narrow limits of legal process and strict 'police-work' to wider considerations of the public good. Monck and Lilburne had faced the same issue when they maintained that leniency towards wrongdoers and a particular care for their material interests could contribute, along with coercion and punishment, to the pacification of the country. In the past, the belief that many of the nobility and gentry had joined the rebels because of material hardship had induced the government to give relief to debtors and to restrict the number of fines and forfeitures imposed by the Ordinance of Pardon and Grace; similar considerations, and the general desire for political conciliation, had inspired the lenient terms of the articles of capitulation. Now, in the aftermath of the rising, Broghill and the Council, and their colleagues in England, were faced with the consequences of this policy. Ironically, their task was in many cases the reverse of their predecessors': whereas Lilburne and Monck had pressed for the mitigation of a harsh policy in the interests of peace and equity, now the wheel had come full circle and the Council was called upon to help those whose just rights were being eroded by the results of such leniency. As before, these issues centred on the problems of debts, fines and forfeitures.

On 12 May 1655 the ordinance for relief of debtors, which had come into force a year previously, expired, leaving all debtors in Scotland exposed to the full rigour of the law. Shortly thereafter, Monck asked the Judges in Scotland to continue such measures of relief as had been permitted in the ordinance; otherwise, he warned, the excepted persons who were trying to pay off their fines as well as their debts might be driven to take up arms again to escape their creditors.[95] This argument was accepted by the Council of State when, in September 1655, it came to consider a petition from the Earls of Home and Hartfell and Sir Robert Douglas on behalf of many of the nobility and gentry in Scotland, which asked for the ordinance to be renewed. The Council recommended to their colleagues in Scotland that for the time being creditors should be pressed to accept satisfaction according to the old ordinance, and that justice should, as far as possible, be carried on according to the laws of England.[96] Laudable as these efforts were in their desire to prevent a recurrence of former troubles, they did not meet with the approval of the creditors, whose complaints were spearheaded by the burghs of Scotland in general, and the town council of Edinburgh in particular. The burghs contended that the order was greatly prejudicial to creditors' interests in that it allowed debts to be settled in land at a rate of twenty years' purchase; they, it seems, thought sixteen or fourteen years' purchase was a fairer price.[97] Nonetheless, in response to further pressure from Broghill, the Council of State went ahead with plans to provide a substitute for the ordinance which had expired in May 1655. An appropriate order was passed in its final form on 15 April, approved by the Protector on 12 May, and proclaimed in Edinburgh on 24 May.[98] The provision for twenty years' purchase still did not please the creditors, however, and for several months they kept up their refusal to make use of the order.[99]

In providing relief for debtors, the Council of State had especially borne in mind the fate of those persons who had been fined under the Act of Pardon and Grace. Not only did it wish to avoid driving them to desperate courses to escape their creditors, but it had a vested interest in smoothing their financial path so that they could pay their fines in full. Despite the substantial mitigation of these fines which the Council had granted in April 1655, a year later many offenders had still not paid up. On 16 April 1656, President Lawrence wrote to the Council in Scotland asking them to compute how much was in arrears, and how far the various charges which had been put on these fines were being met.[100] This last was a point of some importance, for the government was finding more and more that both the monetary fines and the forfeited lands of the persons named in the Act of Pardon and Grace were unable to satisfy the uses for which they had been earmarked.

The whole issue was exceedingly complicated, for it affected the rights not only of the excepted persons, but also of their creditors and of the people who had been promised donatives from the forfeited estates. It was, in fact, with the estates, rather than with the fines, that the Council at Whitehall was primarily to concern itself in the summer and autumn of 1656, but the two problems were in principle related. The connection arose from an ordinance passed on 31 July 1654 which allowed the holders of donatives to opt for payment in cash instead of in land if they so wished; the money, assessed at a rate of ten years' purchase, was to come out of the fines imposed on the excepted persons.[101] If all the grantees had been willing to accept money, and if the requisite sums had been forthcoming from the Exchequer, the problem of the donatives would have been solved. But since neither contingency had occurred, the problem of donatives remained to bedevil the fortunes of the forfeited persons and their creditors. It was not so much that the estates could not bear the charge of the donatives put upon them but that, if the donatives were satisfied, then there was little left over to satisfy the ordinary creditors. Originally, the government had provided that the debts of any one estate which was overburdened with donatives and other encumbrances could be met out of other forfeited lands,[102] but this policy had been vitiated by the release from sequestration of many estates after their owners had capitulated to Monck. This was true of the estates of the Earls of Seaforth, Loudon, Atholl and Glencairn, Lords Kenmure, Lorne and Mauchline and the laird of Womatt;[103] in addition, the Earl of Callander's estate was discharged late in 1655, and Lord Cranston's in the summer of 1656.[104] These lands 'would have yielded great relief to creditors';[105] but since they were not available, the situation as regards satisfying creditors was becoming critical.

These points were put forward to the central government by the trustees for the estates of excepted persons and by the creditors themselves. In December 1655, the trustees warned the Council that if any more grants were made on the forfeited estates, the creditors would suffer; they then followed this up in February 1656 with a complaint that the grant of lands made to Capt. Henry Ogle in November 1655 could not be fulfilled and a reminder that several previous grantees had likewise been disappointed.[106] Shortly thereafter, the trustees set out their case fully in a petition to the Protector which was presented by Col. David Barclay and considered by the Council in June. This recapitulated the points made in previous letters, emphasised particularly the difficulties caused by the discharge of so many estates by the terms of the articles of capitulation, and set forth an account of the remaining estates and the claims being made against them.[107]

The creditors, meanwhile, had registered their own protest in a petition which, interestingly enough, presaged the solution to the problem which the Council was eventually to adopt. Through the agency of Andrew Ramsay, the provost of Edinburgh, they asked that the forfeited estates might be freed from donatives and made liable to their just debts, and that to implement this 'the forfeit persons may be restored to their estates on paying as much as, with the rest [*i.e.* the fines] received, will answer the donatives at 10 years' purchase'. On 2 January 1656, this petition was referred to the Scotch committee.[108]

Despite the strength of these protests, it was some months before the Council at Whitehall took action. In part the delay was caused by the fact that many of the claims entered by creditors against the forfeited estates had not yet been approved by the commissioners appointed for that purpose; the work of processing such claims had come to a halt because so many of the commissioners were absent on business in London. Only after new commissioners had been appointed in April 1656 was it possible for the Council of State to get an accurate account of the debts lying on the forfeited estates.[109] By September 1656, however, the Council was able to consider a proposal to levy a fine of £40,000 on the forfeited persons so that the holders of donatives could be bought off and the original owners restored to their estates; they could then hold their estates free from any encumbrance provided they paid off all their debts within the next two years. It took another couple of months before the details were settled, but on 13 November the order was passed in its final form.[110] Thus, although the Council in Scotland had still to determine what proportion of the £40,000 fine each estate should bear, and to enforce payment of the money,[111] it was clear that by November 1656 the government in London had finally decided the fate of persons liable to sequestration and so had had the last word on an issue which had been central to English policy since 1651. In Scottish terms, it meant not only the return of several of the leading nobility to their family estates, but also the opportunity for their creditors to press home their claims against them. This, coupled with the straits to which many were reduced in order to raise their part of the £40,000,[112] meant that the new order was something of a mixed blessing for them; while, for the English, the whole issue illustrated the difficulties inherent in a policy which tried to satisfy key sections of the Scottish community and at the same time to reward faithful servants of the republican régime.

Despite the complexity of the problem, the English solution to it was in line with the general policy of enlisting the support of men of influence in the community in an attempt to maintain peace and stability in Scotland. Towards the end of the Council's first year in office an opportunity to test the success of this policy so far, and to extend its more conciliatory aspects, arose when elections were held for the second protectoral parliament. Just as in 1654 the parliamentary elections in Scotland had reflected the exigencies of English rule at a crucial point in Glencairn's rising, so now the elections of August 1656 were an important indicator of the developing nature of English administration in the north.

The elections of August 1656 produced the full complement of thirty members. Of these, 16 were English and 14 were Scots.[113] As in 1654, the English contingent included several army officers and executive officials. Numbered among the MPs were four serving army officers, Col. Thomas Fitch, the governor of Inverness, Col. William Mitchell, Col. Stephen Winthrop and Col. Edward Salmon. Two other Englishmen, Henry Whalley and George Downing, held important posts connected with the army, Whalley as Advocate-General and Downing as Scoutmaster-General.[114] Five of the remaining English members held high civil office and a further two (Robert Wolseley and Godfrey Rhodes) were commissaries.[115] The five high-ranking executive officials were Sir Edward Rhodes, Samuel Disbrowe, Nathaniel Whetham and Lord Broghill, all of whom were councillors, and George Smyth, one of the Commissioners for the Administration of Justice. Smyth and Disbrowe had also been appointed commissioners for claims on forfeited estates, an office not yet defunct, while Disbrowe had recently been awarded the office of Keeper of the Great Seal of Scotland and a Judgeship in the Exchequer.[116] The remaining three Englishmen were Robert Stewart, a London barrister, Dr. Thomas Clarges, Monck's brother-in-law, and Col. Henry Markham, one of the revenue commissioners in Ireland.[117]

Many of these men had, in addition to the 'pull' accruing to their own offices, ties of friendship or kinship with other men of influence in Scotland and England. Thus Clarges was related to Monck; Edward and Godfrey Rhodes were father and son; George Downing was the son of Emmanuel, clerk to the Scottish Council and was also related to Stephen Winthrop; and Markham was a friend of Broghill and Henry Cromwell. In addition, Whalley, Wolseley and Disbrowe had brothers of no mean importance in English politics.[118] This network of influence probably explains why, irrespective of Scottish opinion, these men were permitted by the authorities in Edinburgh and London to stand for Scottish constituencies; but it also meant that the Scots, however circumscribed their rights as electors might be, were represented by men who were, or who had access to, key figures in policy-making circles. In this way the Scots might hope that by gaining favour with influential Englishmen they could protect Scottish interests at Westminster.

On the other hand, the biographical details of the 14 Scots elected in 1656 suggest that a key English concern in these elections was to conciliate important sections of Scottish public opinion. The distinctive feature of the Scots MPs was that most were men of political and social standing in the localities. While few belonged to the higher echelons of the aristocracy, the majority were men of substance in the shires; in some cases their local influence had already been recognised and reinforced by their appointment as JPs earlier in the year. Into this category came the Earls of Moray and Tweeddale (members for the shires of Moray and Nairn, and East Lothian respectively); Lord Cochrane of Dundonald (Ayrshire and Renfrewshire); Sir John Wemyss of Bogie (Fife and Kinross); William Ker of Newton (Roxburghshire); Sir James Macdowall of Garthland (Wigtonshire); the three brothers William, George and John Lockhart (members for Lanarkshire, Lanark and adjacent burghs and Dunbartonshire, Argyll and Bute respectively); and John Swinton of Swinton (Berwickshire). The burghs also exhibited this pattern, for the provosts of Banff and Edinburgh and the town clerk of Dundee secured election. Dr. Alexander Douglas was chosen as member for Banffshire (of which county he had also been sheriff sometime before 1656); Andrew Ramsay for Edinburgh; and Sir Alexander Wedderburn of Blackness for Forfar and adjacent burghs.[119] Of these 13 men, at least eight had been appointed JPs in 1656,[120] as had the one other Scots MP, Col. David Barclay (member for the shires of Forfar and Kincardine), whose possession of the barony of Urie gave him an entrenched local interest as well.

As was the case with the elections of 1654, the relationship between favour with the English and influence with the Scots was essentially a reciprocal one. These men were allowed to prosecute their candidacy in 1656 not merely because the English sought to woo Scottish opinion through them, but because they had in many cases already shown their loyalty to, and willingness to work with, the English régime. This was especially true of those six men who held or had held some additional office of public trust, whether it be William Lockhart's recent appointment as ambassador in France, or his brother George's post as commissary of Lanarkshire.[121] George and John doubtless owed a lot to their elder brother's influence 'at court', but others could also call on friends to have a word in the right ear. William Ker of Newton was a friend not only of William Lockhart, but of the Earl of Tweeddale and of the local sheriff, Sir Andrew Kerr; Sir John Wemyss was a cousin of the Earl of Wemyss, lately appointed sheriff of Fife; Lord Cochrane's son was married to the daughter of the Earl of Cassillis, who was soon to be called to Cromwell's Other House; and Barclay's wife was related to the much-favoured Earl of Sutherland.[122] These family connections in many ways parallel the web of influence at work on the English side — the Disbrowes and the Lockharts, for example, exemplified the power of brotherhood in politics.

Taken together, the very factors which promoted the success of these men at the August poll meant that, after their election, they might be in a position to advance not only their own interests[123] and those of their friends and constituents, but those of the government as well. By implication, therefore, it is possible to see in the reasons for their success a mirror image of Monck and Broghill's conception of the developing nature of English administration in Scotland. In assessing why Monck and Broghill accepted the election of these particular fourteen Scots as 'fellow-guardians' of the English interest, one historian of the 1656 elections has expressed their underlying policy thus: to 'rely in the shires on the wealthiest and most traditional families who were willing to accept the protectorate; [to] encourage all the interests of the towns and wed them [to the government] by economic advantage'.[124] Such an attempt was entirely in line with the policy, adumbrated by Lilburne, developed by Monck and consolidated by Broghill in the years since 1653/4, of coming to terms with all but the most intransigently royalist of the nobility and gentry and admitting them to a share in the day-to-day work of government. The admission to Parliament of fourteen Scots, possessed almost to a man of wealth, status and power in their local communities, symbolised, as did so many English actions after the outbreak of Glencairn's rising, the fact that the radical policy of 1651/2 had been reversed. Ironically, however, the continuing dualism in English policy — the balance between coercion and conciliation, between oppression and co-operation — was even more neatly epitomised by the presence among the thirty MPs of many English officers and officials, not to mention those Scots who, like John Swinton and William Lockhart, had hitched their professional careers to the English interest. Overall, therefore, the results of these elections showed not only the increasingly conservative and civilian character of English rule in the mid-1650s, but also the continuing importance of the army's role in maintaining stability in the north.[125]

iv. The army and internal security

The importance of the army in enforcing law and order was manifest not only in the successful outcome of the 1656 elections. In many other ways the presence of the military in garrisons and camps throughout Scotland underpinned all the Council's 'civilian' efforts to promote domestic harmony, for it was the army's job not merely to assist the agents of the civil power in the execution of their duty, but to act as a police force in their own right and to enlist, under their aegis, the help of selected members of the community. In addition, the supervision of an intelligence network of spies and informers through which Monck and Broghill could trace the movements of royalist agents from abroad and track down their contacts in Scotland was a natural corollary of the army's other peacekeeping functions, for on this depended the régime's ability to isolate the spark of royalist conspiracy from the tinder of domestic unrest and so prevent a recurrence of those conditions which had created royalist rebellion in the years 1653/4.

After the suppression of Glencairn's rising, the army continued to allow certain Scotsmen to form guards or watches for the defence of the community against robbers and moss-troopers. Duncan Campbell of Auchline, with ten of his followers, was given a roving commission to apprehend robbers in the Highlands and Lowlands; while John Young, officially employed as assistant to the Deputy Scoutmaster-General of the army, was allotted the task of discovering any moss-troopers, thieves or idle persons lurking in the Borders.[126] The circumstances which had prompted Monck to permit certain groups of parishes or the gentlemen of certain shires to raise guards for the defence of their property against the common enemy had now largely passed; but well into 1656, and indeed for the rest of his time in Scotland, Monck continued to employ individual 'policemen' to catch 'desperate persons' and robbers.[127] These efforts, of course, merely supplemented the army's own work of finding out and arresting moss-troopers, murderers and robbers,[128] but neither the army nor the guards could operate efficiently without the help of the local community. For this reason, Monck took care to provide incentives for the Scots to hand over malefactors in their midst. In February 1656, in a gesture which he hoped would encourage others, he rewarded several persons in Fife for their help in apprehending robbers and other offenders; the reward money was raised from English officers who were enjoying the use of horses which they had seized from the country people in accordance with Col. Lilburne's proclamation of December 1653, but for which monetary compensation had not been given.[129] Such a move was doubly useful because it also enhanced the general reputation of the army for fair dealing among the local population. This in turn might help to persuade the Scots to co-operate with their beneficent governors — such, at any rate, had been the thinking behind the attempts of successive commanders to maintain a high standard of military discipline. In 1655-6 Monck carried on this tradition by ensuring that any soldier guilty of misconduct, such as the murder of a Scotsman[130] or the theft of a horse,[131] was severely punished, and that the provision of grass for the soldiers' horses[132] and the exaction of fire and candle money for the garrisons[133] were arranged equitably. Interestingly enough, at a time when some political accommodation was being sought with the gentry, the army was forbidden to quarter on gentlemen's houses, and any officer who disobeyed this order was severely reprimanded.[134] A similar ban was also put on quartering on the clergy.[135]

'Public relations' measures such as these might have some effect in the relatively settled areas of the Lowlands and northern coastal plains; but in the Highland zone, sterner means were required to boost the efforts of the army and its agents. Here Monck tried to ensure that the clan chiefs were held responsible for the wrongdoings of their clansmen; many had been bound to do so by the terms of their treaties of capitulation in 1655, but frequent reminders were necessary. In August 1656, for example, after several robberies had been committed in the Highlands, Monck ordered Lt. Col. Cotterell, Brayne's successor at Inverlochy, to make the clan chiefs produce the men responsible, or else give compensation to those who had been robbed; failing that, Cotterell was to confiscate the offending clan's cattle until some reparation was made, which course, Monck assured him, would 'make them leave of Thieving'.[136]

Closely allied to the army's work in suppressing theft was the control it exercised over the possession of arms. The two policies were obviously related, in that serious crimes, such as murder and robbery with violence, were encouraged, particularly in the Highlands, if would-be criminals had access to weapons; but of more fundamental importance was the link which the possession of firearms might provide between robbery and rebellion. Since the whole question of maintaining law and order in Scotland was bound up with the need to remove the conditions from which royalist revolt could spring, the restriction of firearms therefore had a crucial significance.

In the treaties of capitulation of 1655, some of the Highland chiefs had been allowed to retain their arms for defence against broken men and thieves within their bounds, but elsewhere permission had to be sought before arms could be carried. Although the licensing system, at least for small arms, became something of a formality,[137] permission was granted all the more readily if the applicant had done some service for the state; this was the case with Alexander Brodie the younger of Lethen, Sir Robert Innes, and Judge Swinton, whose followers were allowed to keep arms for the defence of his house while he was attending the Parliament in England.[138] Monck's generosity in issuing permits to friends of the state or to political neutrals did not preclude him from keeping a close watch on the movement of arms during times of particular crisis. Thus, in June 1656, when he suspected that messengers from the exiled court were especially active in Scotland, he ordered all warrants which had been granted to persons in Perthshire to be called in; a month later he extended this order to cover the whole of Scotland north of the Tay and coupled it with a warning to Major General Morgan to maintain strict control over the work of all gunsmiths in the region.[139] At the same time, it seems, Monck was not averse to arming the state's friends on a large scale; in April a pass was granted to a servant of Sir James Macdonald to transport 226 swords, 60 firelocks and 40 locks into Skye or elsewhere in Sir James's bounds.[140]

It is clear, therefore, that in the methods they employed for the punishment of crime and the control of firearms, the Council and the army showed themselves generally aware of the political overtones which apparently simple issues of domestic order might assume. Backing up these efforts to prevent political conspiracy from taking over and controlling the lawlessness of the outlying regions was the intelligence service which Monck operated from the autumn of 1655 on. The system over which he, and (for the period 1655-6) Broghill, presided depended for the gathering of information on agents' reports about the intentions of Charles and his supporters, and on the interception of letters to and from the friends of the king. The agents, spies and informers whom the English used were of three kinds: first, persons within Scotland, like David Drummond, a former minister in Perthshire, who were ostensibly ordinary citizens but whose loyalty to the English government (or desire for pecuniary gain)[141] led them to give occasional notice of suspicious happenings in their district or among their friends; secondly, 'professional' spies, recruited from within Scotland but sent abroad to discover the plans of the exiled court and of foreign governments friendly to Charles; and thirdly, agents like Major James Borthwick whose primary task it was to spy on *bona fide* royalist messengers who had entered the country to deliver letters and instructions from the king. The interception and deciphering of royalist letters, whether carried by hand or sent through the post, was essential to all forms of intelligence activity, for on this depended the identification of those Royalists within Scotland who were in touch with the exiles and who might provide the link between rebellion at home and invasion from abroad. Following methods pioneered by Thurloe in London, Monck confiscated letters from the king to his Scottish supporters, or alternatively merely intercepted and copied the most important of them so that he might allow the originals to reach their destination and so reveal the identity of the recipient. The information thus gleaned, together with news of the to-ings and fro-ings of suspected agents and reports of clandestine meetings among the clans, formed the stuff of which arrests were made, for it was Monck's repeated practice to round up leading Royalists (usually those who had taken a prominent part in Glencairn's rising) whenever he believed a fresh plot to be brewing. Many of the protagonists in the late rebellion spent several spells in prison after 1655, being released only on payment of heavy security when each scare had died down.

The first steps in the government's campaign to prevent a recurrence of unrest after the failure of Middleton and his allies began as early as September 1655, when Monck told Cromwell that 'Charles Stewart is indevouring to try what friends hee can make in this Countrey againe.'[142] In the following month the English gained possession of letters from Charles to Glencairn, Atholl and the Earl of Leven which contained thanks for past services and hopes for a speedy recovery of his fortunes in Scotland.[143] Monck also got wind of a mission to Scotland by Col. Borthwick, the brother of Major James, and one of Charles's most trusted agents. This led him to believe that Borthwick was preparing the ground for a new rising and that Charles might shortly send Middleton to stir up fresh trouble in Scotland.[144] His uneasiness grew even more when Robert Snype, a merchant burgess of Edinburgh, was arrested for smuggling in letters from the exiled king, and when Thurloe gave warning that conspirators in England were about to send emissaries north.[145]

By December 1655, therefore, Broghill and Monck had decided that not only must an agent be despatched to Cologne to get wind of Middleton's true intentions, but the known champions of the king's cause in Scotland must also be rounded up.[146] Suspicion fixed principally on Glencairn, but James Edmonston, laird of Womatt, was also held to be deeply involved. Shortly before Christmas Glencairn was imprisoned in Edinburgh Castle, and at the end of January 1656 orders were issued for the arrest of Womatt.[147] Meanwhile, information reached Broghill from several quarters which convinced him that fresh roguery was a-brewing and in the light of which he professed to discern a close connection between events in Ireland and in Scotland. The short sea passage between the two countries made traffic in men and ideas an easy matter, and so on 9 January the Council issued an order forbidding anyone to travel to Ireland without a licence.[148]

If, indeed, danger threatened from Ireland, it followed that security in the west and north-west of Scotland was of especial importance, and for this reason, perhaps, Broghill was peculiarly sensitive to news of Lorne's activities in Argyllshire. Reports that Lorne had declared for the king and had captured Mull with an armed band had ultimately to be discounted, but enough evidence remained to convince Broghill that Lorne was in close touch with the exiles. In the New Year it was discovered that the letters which Robert Snype had brought in were addressed to Lorne and McNaughton, while an informer wrote from Callander that Lorne had held a meeting of all his friends and that letters had come from the king to his (Lorne's) sister.[149] Not enough could be proved against him, however, to justify his arrest.

Despite this flurry of activity at the turn of the year, the fruits of the intelligence effort over the past few months had not, in fact, indicated that a royalist rising was at all likely, for the disaffection it had uncovered was localised and confined to words rather than deeds. Most significantly, despite the known presence of messengers from abroad (not to mention less tangible rumours that eight-score priests and Jesuits, dressed as beggars, were roaming the country as agents of the king),[150] Monck and Broghill had uncovered little hard evidence that Charles and his friends in Europe were seriously planning an invasion of Scotland. Nonetheless, Monck's efforts had been justified by the belief that, so far as royalist conspiracy went, prevention was better than cure and that the best way to deal with the threat of rebellion was to crush it before it got off the ground. After April 1656 he was even more convinced that vigilance should be continual and suspicion constant, for news reached Britain that Charles had concluded a treaty with Philip IV of Spain. This, for a brief spell, made the threat of invasion seem alarmingly real.

The treaty between Charles and Philip IV took the form of an offensive and defensive alliance in which the Spaniards, in return for the cession of Jamaica and relief for English Catholics, promised to provide Charles with 6000 troops for an invasion of England.[151] The treaty itself made no mention of Scotland but this did not rule out either the instigation of a rising *within* Scotland or the landing in the north of troops paid for out of other funds. The English authorities, moreover, although aware soon after the event that Charles and Philip had come to some agreement, probably did not know the exact terms of the treaty,[152] and so this, in conjunction with a lingering though unfounded suspicion that the Dutch might be willing to aid Charles, provided Broghill and Monck with good reason to be on guard against danger from abroad.

In the spring of 1656 Broghill enjoined his trusty informer David Drummond to be on the look-out for letters coming from Charles Stuart to some very eminent men in the country.[153] A close watch was also being kept on Glencairn, who had earlier been released from prison on payment of a heavy security; and Lorne was likewise under constant surveillance.[154] Broghill's suspicion that some conspiracy was afoot was strengthened in June when a ship carrying a cargo of arms and ammunition was apprehended off the coast of Aberdeen. The ship had been loaded at Middleburg in Zealand and so was confiscated under the Articles of

Peace, Union and Confederation lately concluded with the United Provinces. Although the master and mariners protested their innocence, the nature of the cargo and the fact that the ship was carrying more crew than seemed necessary suggested to the English that it was really a man-of-war which intended landing a party on the mainland.[155] An incident such as this highlighted a problem which was to become increasingly important in the coming months: the problem of securing the coasts of Scotland against a possible invader. In April Broghill had complained that all Scotland was without a man-of-war to guard the coast, and consequently Scots merchant vessels were an easy prey to pirates in the North Sea.[156] The commercial loss was bad enough, but when marauders could actually come ashore, as some Dunkirkers did in July at Elie in Fife,[157] the security of the state as well as of its merchant marine was obviously in jeopardy. In August 1656, these incidents took on added significance when information began to trickle in which suggested to Broghill and Monck that the alliance between Charles and Spain was about to bear fruit in a new attempt to topple the régime.

The relevant cluster of events, which together constituted the most serious threat to security Monck had to face after 1655, had two main elements, each of which might be linked with a possible invasion of Scotland. The first element indicated to Monck that a fresh insurrection was being planned in the Highlands, possibly with the help of Scots noblemen returned from exile; while the second, of which the main evidence was the presence of Spanish vessels in Hebridean waters, seemed to betoken more direct intervention by a foreign power in the affairs of the English Republic.

Early in August, news reached Edinburgh that Spanish ships had been spotted off the north-west coast of Scotland, that they had landed some men in the islands, and that they had taken in fresh supplies of provisions. Other reports seemed to indicate that the same fleet had lately sailed down the coast of Argyll, and Monck and Broghill, both of whom were already deeply suspicious of the motives of Lorne (and indeed of his father), were forced to conclude that the natives of Argyllshire had welcomed their coming.[158] Such news caused Broghill to reiterate the need for at least one man-of-war to patrol these waters, especially when, later in the month, further intelligence suggested the true reason for the Spanish presence. By mid-August, Broghill and Monck were convinced that the enemy's intention was to intercept Lt. General Brayne's party of men who were shortly to be shipped from Port Patrick to Jamaica.[159] By thus putting in jeopardy the success of the Western Design, Spain seemed poised to strike not only at the security of Scotland but at the integrity of Cromwellian policy as a whole. The burden of countering the threat fell upon Monck, who continued to receive in the next few weeks a series of reports about the Spanish naval presence off Islay. The largest estimate of Spanish strength put the number of vessels at 15 or 16 — quite enough for Monck to require the help of Henry Cromwell in Ireland (whence another party was to sail for Jamaica) in guarding the Scots forces if and when they should pass through St. George's Channel. In the event, Brayne's men did not sail until October, and by that time the enemy fleet had disappeared,[160] yet for those few weeks the west coast of Scotland had proved a vulnerable spot in the

Republic's defences.[161]

As the story of the Spanish ships unfolded, their relation to a possible invasion of Scotland or a rebellion therein had gradually dimmed, but this was not the case with other evidence of Spanish activities and intentions. Towards the end of August, Monck received a report that, far from concentrating the invasion effort on England, the King of Spain was planning to furnish Charles Stuart with money to raise 3 or 4000 men for a landing somewhere in the hills of Scotland.[162] Monck was sanguine of his chances of destroying such a force if ever it did appear in Scotland, but what made the report disturbing was its timing in relation to other signs of royalist conspiracy. In the course of August it became clear that messengers had arrived in Scotland from the exiled court: Thomas Straughan was arrested on suspicion of being a royalist intelligencer, and a close watch was ordered to be kept on Henry Knox, an associate of Balcarres, when he arrived from Holland in September.[163] In the hope of preventing an even greater traffic of royalist sympathisers between Scotland and the Continent, the Scottish Council re-enacted at the end of July an order prohibiting all skippers and seamen from transporting into or out of the country any person 'disaffected . . . to the peace and weilfair of this natioun' unless a licence had previously been granted in his behalf.[164]

In the next few weeks (by which time Broghill had departed for the Parliament in London), Monck's sifting of the intelligence reports produced the belief that the Royalists would attempt something in October. By early September he had taken care, in obedience to commands from London, to put the forces in Scotland in a ready posture and was confident of meeting any challenge that might arise either at home or from abroad.[165] It is clear that at this stage Monck firmly believed (or so, at any rate, he told Thurloe) that the invasion force which Charles was allegedly gathering in Flanders was aimed principally at Scotland. Monck's intelligencers assured him that the party was to be under the overall command of the Duke of York, who would be accompanied by Middleton and Balcarres.[166] Such rumours caused Monck to stress once again the need for an adequate patrol of the coasts, and even to request another regiment for service in Scotland. But whatever his desires for additional strength, he stood by his claim that no matter where they might land along the Scottish coast, royalist forces would either be challenged by the army at the point of their landing or else starved into submission in the hills.[167] Such confidence not unnaturally grew towards the beginning of October, when he heard that Charles was in financial difficulties in Europe and the Spanish West India fleet had been trounced by the English navy.[168]

Despite these signs that at the European end royalist plans were suffering a serious reverse, Monck did not relax his vigilance and control over likely supporters of the king's cause in Scotland. Indeed, the months of October and November 1656 saw the most concerted attempt so far to round up and imprison as many stalwarts of the cause as possible, without provoking too much resentment and disturbance among their friends and followers.[169] Lorne,[170] Seaforth,[171] Glengarry,[172] the Earls of Selkirk[173] and Buchan,[174] and Lord Forrester[175] were all apprehended, while lesser lights such as Roderick and

Norman Macleod,[176] Lt. Col. George Maxwell[177] and, later, the laird of Womatt[178] were forced to give fairly hefty sureties for their peaceable living. In addition, Monck daily secured 'divers common men' who might be likely to join Charles Stuart's party and foment a rebellion.[179] Some of the noblemen were released fairly speedily after giving in bonds for their future good behaviour — the Earl of Selkirk, for example, was set free less than six weeks after his arrest in mid-November — but others languished in prison until well into the New Year. At the same time, Monck kept up his search for agents in correspondence with the exiled court (Majors Strachan and Drummond were two of the men on the 'wanted' list in November), and was successful in intercepting further documents relating to royalist plans for Scotland.[180]

Although there were still fears that some men might land in the north of Scotland at the end of November, it became increasingly clear as Christmas approached that Charles's hopes of help from Spain were foundering and that, consequently, the threat of invasion had receded.[181] Moreover, although Strachan and his companion had eluded capture, Monck was confident that their mission in Scotland had accomplished little, and this, together with the preventive measures he himself had adopted against royalist noblemen, led him to believe that Charles's cause, and indeed the king himself, were much discouraged.[182] At the end of the year, therefore, the régime in Scotland was safe from external attack.

In retrospect it is clear that Monck and Broghill had attributed to Charles in his attempts to restore his fortunes in Scotland a diligence and determination which the king, in reality, sorely lacked. Whatever Monck and Broghill might think, after the failure of Middleton and Glencairn, Scotland occupied a very low place in Charles's priorities, for his energies, such as they were, were concentrated on planning an invasion of England (not of Scotland) with foreign help. Nor was there any party at the exiled court willing or able to reverse this scale of priorities, for by the mid-1650s the ascendancy of Hyde's 'Old Royalist' group in the counsels of the king was complete; there was thus little room for a revival of a 'presbyterian' pressure group which would focus attention on Scotland.[183] In one sense, therefore, Monck and Broghill had grossly overestimated the danger to Scotland from Charles's schemings abroad, and had been prone to take too seriously evidence of plans which had little hope of realisation. This did not mean, however, that the intelligence network was unjustified in practice. The whole point of having such a system was to anticipate trouble, not to wait until the trouble got out of hand, and so from this point of view the absence of serious royalist unrest was a testimony to the success of Monck's endeavours, not to their irrelevance. Many aspects of the Council's and the army's work in 1655-6 had in fact been devoted to ensuring that a phenomenon such as Glencairn's rising not only would not, but could not, occur again, and in this context the operation of an intelligence network and an internal security system was a useful and necessary adjunct to the army's other peacekeeping functions. It therefore contributed along with the Council's other policies on finance, justice, law and order to ensuring that by the end of 1656 the régime in Scotland was on a more sound and stable footing than at any time since 1651.

9

Broghill and the Church Parties, 1655 — 1657

IN settling the financial affairs of the northern kingdom and in attending to the administration of justice, Broghill and the Council had tackled two of the most important issues facing the republican government in Scotland. In addition to these concerns, however, the failure of the Scottish clergy to recognise the authority of the English government, the state of the Scottish church and, in particular, the split between Protesters and Resolutioners created problems which cried out for solution. Accordingly, during his year as President of the Council Broghill sought to enhance the stability of the régime by achieving some accommodation with the Scottish clergy. Here, in his dealings with the two major church parties, the President, acting in consultation with the Scottish Council, proved his ability to initiate as well as to implement government policy. For although he kept in close contact with the Protector and the Council of State in London through frequent correspondence with John Thurloe, the Council's Secretary, it was Broghill himself who suggested the major guidelines of English policy, and who, by his personal intervention at many crucial points in the negotiations with Resolutioners and Protesters, gave the execution of that policy its distinctive twist. In his letters to Thurloe on religious affairs, Broghill revealed much about himself, his attitude to politics, and his feelings towards the Scots. In particular, he showed that, although his methods were more subtle and devious than Monck's, in his handling of the religious issue he was no less ruthless and no less mindful of the fact that English interests were paramount than the commander-in-chief had been in his dealings with the Scottish community since 1654. For Broghill's conferences with the churchmen clearly reveal that behind the velvet glove of the negotiator there lay not only the cold calculation of an 'English' politician, but also the intellectual contempt of a man who cared little for the principles and interests of the parties he was manipulating. Perhaps because of these insights into the character of the man and the nature of English policy, the President's handling of religious matters has, more than any other aspect of his policy, caught the attention of later writers and has received substantial treatment in many works on the period.[1] Most probably, Broghill himself would have approved of such extensive coverage, for undoubtedly he regarded his dealings with the clergy to be of major importance for the settlement of Scotland and worthy of a large part of his time and energy. Nonetheless, the lasting success of his endeavours was not commensurate with the effort he put into the task, for he failed signally to resolve the disputes between the two church parties, or to win all-party agreement on the civil authority's role in the appointment of ministers. In the context of English policy towards Scotland, therefore, Broghill's dialogue with the ministry from 1655 to 1656, and the continuation of the debate in London in 1657, are not as significant as the sheer bulk of the evidence on the subject would seem to indicate. But still, the President deserves credit for two positive achievements: in his first few weeks of office he succeeded in persuading the Resolutioners to stop praying for the king, and towards the end of his time in Scotland he secured on an *ad hoc* basis the acquiescence of most of the clergy in a scheme for certifying the fitness of candidates for the ministry.

To a very large extent, Broghill's dealings with the clergy concerned the enforcement, or otherwise, of 'Gillespie's Charter', that ordinance passed by the Council of State on 8 August 1654 'for the better support of the universities in Scotland, and encouragement of publik preachers there'.[2] During Broghill's Presidency, the smouldering discontent of most Resolutioners and many Protesters with the terms of this ordinance came to a head, and the refusal of the clergy to abide by its provisions, when the Scottish Council made a strenuous effort to put it into effect, forced all parties to cast around for an acceptable substitute. At the outset, therefore, Broghill's religious policy was circumscribed by the treatment the ordinance had received since its inception in 1654.

Since 1651, the English government's relations with the clergy had been at best uneasy, and at worst bitterly hostile. During the period of royalist revolt, the Resolutioners' practice of praying for the king and so lending moral support to the rebels had incurred the wrath of Lilburne, who was inclined to blame the clergy for much of the political unrest in Scotland at that time. Only the Protesters escaped the commander-in-chief's blanket condemnation of the ministry, and in practice only Mr. Patrick Gillespie's faction could be represented as in any way willing to co-operate with the government.[3] The hint of Gillespie's compliance was enough, however, to encourage the English to build on his support. In March 1654 Cromwell, anxious 'to accommodate the Interest and to beget a good understanding between the People of God of different Judgements in this Nation', chose to summon him, along with Mr. John Livingstone and Mr. John Menzies, to London as a first step towards reconciling religious differences in Scotland.[4] That this overture to two Protesters and one Independent might be broadened into a genuine attempt to secure agreement among all parties was suggested two months later when, in May 1654, Messrs. Robert Blair and Robert Douglas, both Resolutioners, and Mr. James Guthry, a Protester of the Wariston faction, were issued with similar invitations. But since none of the last three consented to attend,[5] the field was left clear for Gillespie and his colleagues to press home their advantage at Whitehall, to the detriment of their opponents within and without the Protesting party.

When in London, however, Gillespie, Livingstone and Menzies (who arrived later than the other two) did not act as a united pressure group. Livingstone, the member who was most committed to maintaining presbyterian discipline, became increasingly disillusioned with life at the protectoral court and came home ahead of his colleagues; he had been unwilling to make the journey in the first place, and had agreed only after Lilburne had threatened to punish him for recalcitrance.[6] Gillespie and Menzies, on the other hand, continued to ingratiate themselves at court, not only as preachers sympathetic to the Independent cause but as hand-picked members of the Scottish universities; for both owed their academic office — Gillespie as Principal of Glasgow and Menzies as professor of divinity at Marischal College, Aberdeen — to English influence.[7] To their credit, they sought to further the interests of their colleges in London: in July 1654 it was clear that their presence at court was beginning to be felt when the Council voted £100 *per annum* out of the customs of Glasgow and Aberdeen to the universities there; this and a much larger grant of the revenues from the bishoprics of Galloway and Aberdeen was subsequently incorporated, after emendation, into the provisions of 'Gillespie's Charter'.[8]

Important as these concessions were for the universities concerned, it was the second part of the 'Charter', the section which dealt with admission to stipends, that really signified the triumph of Gillespie and Menzies in the counsels of the Protector. In this section the ordinance enjoined the Commissioners for Visiting the Universities to take care that, in the appointment of ministers to livings, 'respect be had to the choice of the more sober and godly part of the people, although the same should not prove to be the greater part', and that no person should be admitted who had not been certified to be 'a person of a holy and unblameable conversation, disposed to live peaceably under the present government', by a committee of 'triers', both clerical and lay, appointed for each of five districts in Scotland. The Commissioners for Visiting the Universities were further authorised to provide maintenance for ministers of gathered congregations in Scotland, and to eject scandalous or profane preachers.

In general outline, this scheme was obviously akin to the system of 'triers' which had been set up in England by the 'Ordinance appointing Commissioners for approbation of public Preachers' of 20 March 1654[9] — the month in which Cromwell had first decided to send for Gillespie and his colleagues. What made the ordinance of 8 August particularly significant in Scottish terms, and at the same time betrayed the influence of Patrick Gillespie in its drafting, was the names of the 57 Scottish 'triers'.[10] With few exceptions, the nominees were members of the Protesting party or else, in a handful of cases, outright Independents: this meant that in the planting of vacant churches any candidate put up by the Resolutioners would almost certainly be turned down, and that in the fullness of time the Protesters could hope to win a majority in the church. The Protesters would only achieve this goal, however, if they acted as a united party; if, in other words, Wariston and Guthry composed their differences with Gillespie. Ironically, the very feature of the ordinance which promised future supremacy to the Protesters — namely, the replacement of the authority of the established church courts, in which the Protesters were in an overall minority, by that of a commission where they were in the majority — augured ill for the prospects of unity within the party, for it served only to enhance the fears of Wariston and Guthry and their followers that Independency would creep in through the back door. Standing as they did for the maintenance of presbyterian church government in all its aspects, this section of the party could do nothing other than condemn the 'Charter'.[11] It is in fact hard to tell whether 'Gillespie's Charter' was more the cause, the effect or the accompaniment of the split within the ranks of the Protesters: had Patrick Gillespie not already broken with the orthodox members of the party and worked towards an accommodation with the English he would not have gone to London to seek Cromwell's favour in the first place, but had he not secured the passage of the ordinance, the breach between him and Wariston might not, thereafter, have been so wide. In the event, the refusal of many of the Protesters to act as 'triers' prevented the new scheme from getting off the ground.

But even if the 'triers' had consented to act, the Resolutioners would have refused to accept their decisions, for they were implacably opposed to the whole idea of the ordinance. They condemned it firstly on ideological grounds, because it circumvented the authority of the regular church courts, and secondly on party political grounds, because it spelled victory for their enemies, the Protesters. In October 1654, the synods of Lothian and Fife, both Resolutioner strongholds, issued declarations against it; and the ministers of Edinburgh, after denouncing it in their sermons, presented Monck with a written statement of their objections, which he then passed on to the Protector.[12] In all, the degree of opposition which the ordinance aroused amongst Protesters and Resolutioners prevented its being put into execution. Although Baillie affirmed that as soon as the details of the 'Charter' were known, Protesters in the synod of Glasgow and in the south 'begane to make use of it', Monck gave a more general view when in November he reported to the Protector that 'very few (if any) will act in it.'[13] Thus when Broghill arrived in Scotland in September 1655, he found that the ordinance of 8 August 1654 had remained a dead letter.

After the flurry of activity surrounding 'Gillespie's Charter', the year 1655 was, until Broghill's irruption on to the scene, relatively uneventful in religious affairs. The summer witnessed another abortive attempt by Mr. Robert Blair of Fife and Mr. James Durham of Glasgow to promote union between the two church parties. At their instigation, a conference was arranged for June 1655, but few from either party turned up. Of those who did, some, like Gillespie and Carstairs, were willing to consider a settlement on the lines of 'let bygones be bygones', but in the end the day was carried by Wariston's group of hardliners. They insisted that the Commission of 1650, on which the Protesters would have a majority, should be revived with authority to purge the ministry of all scandalous elements, and that before oblivion could be considered, their enemies would have to repent of their adherence to the Public Resolutions. Such terms were obviously unacceptable to the Resolutioners, and so the meeting broke up *re infecta.*[14] The Protesters, meanwhile, were unilaterally pursuing an idea of James Guthry's for reuniting the nation in a new Covenant; the details of this were a closely guarded secret, but its intention was almost certainly to stamp the Protesters' authority on the religious life of the nation.[15]

According to Wariston and to his colleague Mr. Robert Traill, Monck was fairly well disposed to the idea of the Covenant;[16] but it was otherwise with President Broghill. His distaste for the project was one of the first comments he made to

Thurloe on religious affairs in Scotland after taking up office in September.[17] In time Broghill was to veer away even more sharply from Monck's policy of favouring the Protesters, but in the autumn of 1655 he came north with few preconceptions or illusions about the attitude of either party in the church. Baillie believed that while still in England, Broghill had heard good reports of the Resolutioners' leaders from his sister-in-law Lady Clotworthy, and so was inclined from the start to heed their interests,[18] but the President himself expressed his views with greater impartiality and greater cynicism. Although he esteemed the Protesters the better sort of people, he told Thurloe, there was little to choose between the parties in their attitude to the English government; the Resolutioners 'love Charles Stuart and hate us', the Protesters 'love neither him nor us'. The only hope for the English, he averred, lay in exploiting the divisions between the two parties, although even the confident Broghill doubted that a 'real closure' could be effected: 'they are all,' he reported resignedly, 'a verry moovable people.'[19]

Yet, even as he wrote, events were pushing the President towards accommodation with the Resolutioners, and towards his first heady triumph in his dealings with the clergy. Within a fortnight of taking up office, Broghill had concluded an agreement with the Resolutioners on praying for the exiled king; the basis of the agreement was that the clergy promised to respect the ban on such prayers if the English relaxed the penalties previously imposed for disobedience. The clergy argued, somewhat tortuously, that they could not desist so long as the threat of losing their stipends remained, as to do so might suggest to the faithful that they had given in to the English through fear of financial loss; if, however, no such threat hung over their heads, their surrender would seem to stem purely from moral conviction and would be accepted as such by their congregations.[20]

The prospect of some concession by the Resolutioners on the matter of praying for Charles had been in the air for some time,[21] but the swift conclusion of the September discussions undoubtedly owed much to Broghill's firmness and diplomatic skill. Agreement was reached after Broghill had invited two leading Resolutioners, Messrs. David Dickson and Robert Douglas, to a private conference; in the course of the debate they were drawn to put forward the plan which Broghill ultimately followed, of lifting the penalties imposed on offenders. As this was a marked advance on previous discussions, when the Resolutioners had seemed in two minds as to whether they would surrender to the threat of greater, or to the promise of lesser, penalties, Broghill was quick to seize on the opportunity.[22] By 27 September the Council had drawn up and published a proclamation to take off and make null all former fines and penalties imposed on the ministry for praying for the king. By its terms, the English agreed to wait until 5 November following to see 'quhat good effectis this tendernes will produce'; after that date, the Council reserved the right to inflict whatever penalties it thought fit on wayward clergymen.[23]

The Resolutioners' response to this proclamation was encouraging. On 5 October, the ministers of Edinburgh and of surrounding presbyteries passed a resolution to stop praying publicly for the king, and sent word to their brethren throughout the land to do the same.[24] Although by the end of the year not every Resolutioner had seen fit to comply, the English felt justified in hailing the move as a great success — it was a great wonder and a great conquest, Thurloe told Henry Cromwell in Ireland.[25] The Resolutioners apparently found little difficulty in constructing an argument to justify their action to their adherents; in the statement they sent to the exiled king, they not only recited the arguments they had put forward to Broghill, but also explained that they had been afraid lest they be prevented from preaching altogether if they did not omit the forbidden prayers from their services (for such, they believed, was the import of the last part of the proclamation of 27 September).[26]

From his success in dealing with the Resolutioners, Broghill drew several morals. Earlier he had assured Thurloe that the only way to bring the clergy to heel was to adopt a firm stand, and to stick to it — too much harm had already been done by threatening measures which were never put into practice.[27] But firmness could be tempered by flexibility, especially when dealing informally with individuals: '[t]hey are a sorte of people,' he informed the Secretary, 'which if to be wrought upon, it must be by degrees, and pryvate conferences; for in all publike disputes men contend as much for creddit as for truth.'[28] Integral to this cool and realistic appraisal of the clergy's motives and aims was Broghill's belief that the internecine feuds of the Scottish churchmen could be manipulated in the English interest: if the Resolutioners drew closer to the government, he thought, not only would *their* support be gained, but the Protesters, too, would be forced to make approaches to the Council in order to keep abreast of their enemies in English favour.

In the following weeks, events seemed to justify Broghill's optimism in several ways. Sometime in October, just as he had predicted, the Protesters of the western presbyteries sent a deputation to Edinburgh to learn how an address from them to the Council would be received and to profess their willingness to 'owne the power now over them'.[29] From this tentative approach, Broghill managed to extract some measure of agreement from the Protesters that 'Gillespie's Charter' should be given a second chance. The Council had already, it seems, determined to put the ordinance into effect in accordance with their Instructions of 24 June; but when the delegation from the west, which included among its members Patrick Gillespie himself, asked of their own accord for a private meeting with Broghill, the President discerned a golden opportunity to promote the merits of the 'Charter'.

The meeting, which took place at Broghill's lodgings, was attended by Broghill, Monck and 'a faithfull minister of the gospell' named Collins on the English side, and two laymen and five ministers on the Protesting side.[30] The subject of 'Gillespie's Charter' was not at first broached, since discussion was for some time confined to the causes of the breach between the Protesters and their Resolutioner brethren. That this topic should take up so much of the conversation was hardly surprising, for the westerners' reason for sending delegates to Edinburgh in the first place had been a desire to clear themselves of the charge, put about by the Resolutioners, that they were less willing to explore the possibilities of union than their opponents.[31] At some stage in the discussion, Broghill saw a chance to kill two birds with one stone: he put it to the Protesters that the best way of ensuring union in the long term was to put the ordinance of 8 August 1654 into effect immediately. By admitting only worthy men into the ministry, Broghill reasoned, the ordinance would separate the wheat from the chaff, and when by such separation none but the good were left, agreement would be easy, and bad men would be kept out of the ministry as a matter of course. This neat solution appealed to some of the delegates (Gillespie among them, one imagines), but others voiced their fears that such a plan would entail the encroachment of the state upon the power of the church. This division of opinion remained even after the meeting had adjourned and the Protesters had retired to discuss the matter in private. Once again, therefore, the rift in the Protesters' ranks, which had been so obvious when the 'Charter' was first mooted in 1654, threatened to destroy its chances of success. But on this occasion Broghill was prepared to go ahead with the support of only one section of the Protesters, and accordingly, on 24 October 1655, the text of the ordinance was formally proclaimed to the Scottish people for the first time. In an accompanying declaration, the Scottish Council explained the previous history of the ordinance and announced that the persons named as 'triers' had until 1 December 1655 to declare their readiness to act; after this date the recalcitrant would be replaced by fresh nominees.[32] The search for substitutes had, in fact, already begun, for Broghill had asked those ministers who were willing to serve to propose others to fill the expected vacancies.[33]

This was, indeed, a necessary precaution, for the chances of enforcing the ordinance were slim. Broghill must surely have realised this, for not only had he failed to unite the Protesters on the issue, but he had also received from the Resolutioners a fresh statement of their reasons for refusing to acknowledge the validity of the ordinance.[34] In practice, he had made little advance on Monck's handling of the situation a year previously, for both then and now only Gillespie's wing of the Protester party was prepared to implement the ordinance. Moreover, at a general meeting of the Protesters in November, it became clear that Wariston and Guthry would continue to resist all Gillespie's efforts to win them over to his side. At this meeting, disputes between the two wings of the party were bitter, with Guthry pressing the advantages of his Covenant against Gillespie's attempts to promote his 'Charter'. Although neither project gained the approval of the party as a whole, the rejection of the Covenant was less important from the English point of view than the failure of the 'Charter' to win general acceptance.[35] What mattered most was that the disunity of the Protesters destroyed any slender hope the English might still have cherished that the ordinance could become a practical proposition.

The meeting at which these angry scenes took place had been ostensibly convened, not to discuss 'Gillespie's Charter', but to consider means for effecting a union with the Resolutioners. It arose, therefore, from the same circumstances which had prompted the western presbyteries to send Gillespie and his colleagues to Edinburgh in October and it was aimed as much at convincing the English of the Protesters' desire to unite with their brethren as at expressing that desire in terms of concrete proposals for union. In other words, the appearance of negotiation was more important to the Protesters than the reality. This was true, at any rate, of Guthry's faction; Gillespie seemed by all accounts to be more conciliatory towards the Resolutioners, but this was but another ploy to gain a majority within the church for the execution of his ordinance.

As a result of these discussions, a conference took place with the Resolutioners. It lasted for nearly three weeks, from 8 to 28 November, and during this time many papers were exchanged between the two sides. The Resolutioners, for their part, carried over to this meeting the set of overtures which they had put forward to the abortive meeting in June[36] and to which the Protesters had not yet submitted a reply. When it became clear that these were unacceptable to the other side,[37] the Resolutioners penned a fresh set of proposals which formed the basis for discussion in the last two weeks of the conference.[38] The Protesters, meanwhile, had drawn up their own conditions for union in a paper which predominantly reflected the uncompromising views of Wariston and Guthry, rather than those of Gillespie.[39] Each set of overtures was determined, above all else, by the numerical strength of the party concerned: thus, the Resolutioners' proposals reflected the interests of a party which, because it was in the majority, would benefit from the restoration of the old judicatories in which it could easily outnumber its opponents; while the Protesters, for their part, demanded either the purging of old institutions or the setting up of new ones where the disadvantages of being in the minority could be eliminated.

On the face of it, the Resolutioners' stance looked the more conciliatory. As in June, they were prepared to let bygones be bygones, on certain conditions. They offered to recommend the taking off of all censures which had been enacted against the Protesters for their refusal to accept the Acts of the General Assembly at St. Andrews and Dundee; they did not, however, propose to pronounce these Acts unlawful, as the Protesters would have wished, but they did concede that they would not force the Protesters to recognise their legality, if the Protesters in return ceased to press the validity of their declinatures. The Resolutioners promised to recommend to presbyteries and synods that all censures should be removed *de facto*, and whenever the next General Assembly should meet, they would press for an Act to be passed to ratify these procedures. The advantage to the Resolutioners lay in the fact that if normal relations were thus established in the working of the church courts, those who had all along adhered to the Public Resolutions would, by dint of being in the majority, retain the whip-hand.

What the Resolutioners absolutely refused to concede was the justice of the claims put forward by the Protesters in the fifth article of their Overtures of 9 November 1655. This article,[40] which was divided into two parts, embodied the very core of the Protesters' case, and to accept either of its clauses the Resolutioners would have had to concede all the points of their own argument. It was quite incompatible with anything the Resolutioners might themselves offer, and, not surprisingly, it proved the rock on which the conference foundered. In the first part of the article, the Protesters proposed that, to make the work of purging effectual, and to regulate all other public affairs of the church, including the settlement of party disputes within presbyteries or congregations, the

Commission and the Visitations appointed by the General Assembly of 1650 might be resurrected; if this did not please their opponents, then they suggested in the second clause that a special committee for the trial and censure of insufficient and scandalous ministers and elders should be appointed within the bounds of every synod, that this committee should consist of an equal number of persons from each party, and that it should also have authority to compose all divisions within the several presbyteries and congregations. By this means, the Protesters, who had the support of only one-sixth of the parish ministers in Scotland,[41] would achieve parity with their opponents when it came to planting and purging the church; and because these committees would be appointed by and would be answerable to the synods, just as the Commission had once been answerable to the General Assembly, their appointment would not contravene the principle of freedom from civil interference which Wariston held most dear[42] and which he had strenuously upheld in the face of Gillespie's attempts to implement his 'Charter'.

As a means of resolving the differences between the two parties, the Protesters' proposals were obviously useless, as far as the limits of the conference went, but this did not prevent the diehards of the party from exploring other means by which their demands could be met. After the conference had broken up, they determined, ironically, on an appeal to the civil power. With Monck's encouragement, the Wariston-Guthry faction submitted to the Scottish Council a petition in which they asked the English to recognise their sole right to exercise supreme jurisdiction over the church by authority of the Commission of 1650.[43] This, as Baillie rightly commented, was a more sweeping claim than ever Gillespie had made, for his 'Charter' had related only to the admission of ministers to their stipends; Guthry's wing of the party was now attempting 'ane usurpation of the whole immediat jurisdiction'.[44]

The petition was presented to the Council on 4 December 1655. Two months later the presbytery of Edinburgh submitted its reply. In a letter to Broghill of 30 January 1656, Messrs. Dickson, Douglas and Hutcheson informed the President that they and their colleagues utterly rejected the Protesters' claims and submitted for his consideration a paper entitled 'Some reasons why the Power of the Commission 1650 cannot now stand in force.'[45] In February the Resolutioners produced a petition of their own, in which they asked the Council to 'take off what restraints are putt upon the exercise of our kirk discipline and government, and permitt the ordinary judicatures to meet and act freely without interruption in matters ecclesiastick'.[46] Later in the month, at a meeting of the party in Edinburgh, they drew up further overtures requesting the Council to ensure that 'in contrarie plantations, the minister whose collation and ordination or admission are allowed by the ordinarie established judicatures of this Kirk, and he only, may be warranted to receive the established stipend and maintenance from the time of his admission'.[47] After the meeting broke up, four of the party's most prominent members, Dickson, Douglas, Sharp and Wood, reinforced these demands in a letter to Broghill wherein they affirmed their brethren's desire to see good order and government restored to the church and their belief that the President would be instrumental in promoting these ends.[48]

What, then, was the situation confronting Broghill after six months in office? The three main groups in the ministry — Gillespie's wing of the Protesting party, Wariston and Guthry's faction, and the main body of the Resolutioners — had each been brought in their separate ways to make some application to the English and to view the government as a court of appeal in their internal disputes. In theory, the clergy stood firm by their contention that the civil power had no right to interfere with or encroach upon the liberties of the kirk; but in practice each group was willing to seek the state's help in a bid to defeat its opponents. With the possible exception of Gillespie and his colleagues, the several contending parties did not so much require the state to negotiate, arbitrate or invent a solution to their problems as to recognise the justice of their case and to impose acceptance of it on their enemies. As Broghill had once explained to Thurloe,[49] any party might be won over to support the government if it were given power to suppress its rivals. But for Broghill, in February 1656, the favouring of one group to the exclusion of all others was no solution to the problem, for he was not convinced that any party could on its own provide a sufficient prop for the government. Although the one distinctive feature of his handling of religious policy so far had been his success in establishing closer contact with the Resolutioners, he was not yet prepared to embrace their demands wholesale. In a letter of 26 February to the Protector,[50] Broghill spelled out his view of the situation in his fullest statement on religious affairs since October 1655.

Broghill told Cromwell that both Resolutioners and Protesters had in their midst many honest and godly men, but neither party could be relied on, as it stood, to support the government. His plan, therefore, was to win over the best men from the existing parties and to form a new, third, party which would acknowledge the Cromwellian régime. This would probably consist of the bulk of the Resolutioners, the party having first been purged of its scandalous elements, and Gillespie's wing of the Protesters. The one group which did not figure in this plan, and to which Broghill was in fact bitterly opposed, was Wariston and his friends; these men he called 'Fifth-monarchy-presbyterians' and impugned as hostile to all authority, not merely to Oliver Cromwell's. To convince the Protector of the utility of this scheme, Broghill maintained that the formation of the new party would help to swing presbyterian opinion at home and abroad in favour of the government and so would destroy Charles II's standing with these groups. He then went on to reveal that he had already had talks with some of the leading men in the ministry and that their response to his overtures had been encouraging. Gillespie and Livingstone had concurred with his plans, and the Resolutioners had given assurances that they would live peaceably and inoffensively under the government and would purge all unfit ministers from their presbyteries and synods. The Resolutioners' meeting in Edinburgh earlier in the month had obviously given Broghill an opportunity to treat with their leaders, whom he identified as Douglas, Dickson, Wood, Hutcheson, Sharp and Smyth; but although their willingness to co-operate with the President was such that Broghill believed that by the summer the Resolutioners would all be praying for the government, it is clear that at this stage the party as a whole had not given its consent to — if indeed it knew of the existence of — Broghill's schemes for a 'third force'. Instead, the Resolutioners had put forward their pleas for the restoration of the powers of the church courts and so had, unwittingly or otherwise, provided Broghill with a bargaining-counter for use in future negotiations. Thus it was that he recommended to Cromwell that the ministry should be allowed 'to enjoy their discipline in things purely ecclesiastical and over such only as do freely submit unto it'; this proposed concession was clearly designed as the first stage in winning the Resolutioners over to wholehearted acceptance of his scheme. To reinforce his pressure on the party, Broghill further suggested that Cromwell write a letter of encouragement to the six leading Resolutioners; if these measures were followed, he assured the Protector, the enterprise had a good chance of success.

By the end of February 1656, therefore, the notion of compromise had entered into relations between Broghill and the churchmen. The likelihood that the Resolutioners would close with the government, and so fulfil the promise of their early dealings with Broghill, had substantially increased, but further progress depended on the result of deliberations in Whitehall. From March to August 1656 there were no new developments in religious affairs in Scotland, despite Broghill's repeated pleas[51] to Cromwell to tender some initiative to the Resolutioner leaders. 'Gillespie's Charter' still stood as the official means of certifying the fitness of entrants to stipends and of ejecting the unfit, but it could not be effectively enforced. To add to the government's difficulties, it was reported that the number of papists in the north had increased, and this called for action not only for religious reasons, but also because the activities of Jesuit missionaries were thought to be closely linked with plans for a royalist revival.[52] In March 1656, the Council accordingly announced that the death penalty would be imposed on any Catholic priest found in Scotland after the next Lord's day, and in June instructions were issued to the justices of the peace to take security from all papists for their peaceable living; papists were also to give up all arms and ammunition in their possession and to pledge themselves not to correspond with Charles Stuart or his agents.[53] The Scottish clergy heartily concurred with these measures, but felt that they had not gone far enough. In their view, the government's drive, being aimed at the political activities of Catholics rather than at Catholicism as such, did little to extirpate the papist menace at its roots; as they later complained, so long as papists gave bonds for their good behaviour, they would be free from further interference with their religion.[54] In order, therefore, to discuss more stringent measures against popery, and to make representations to Broghill on the subject, the Resolutioner-dominated synod of Lothian summoned two delegates from every presbytery to meet in Edinburgh in August. Very quickly, however, it became apparent that other forces were at work in this meeting, which was in effect a Resolutioner party conference. These forces were set in motion by the delegates' decision to ask the President what had become of their February petition concerning the admission of ministers to stipends.[55]

Up until then, during the spring and summer months of 1656, the ball had been very much in Whitehall's court. Broghill had provided the Protector and Council with the latest information on the state of the religious parties in Scotland, had sent on the petitions and protestations which the clergy had emitted on the issues arising from 'Gillespie's Charter', and had made recommendations for future action by the government. Responsibility for resolving the vexed question of 'the entry of ministers' thus fell on the committee for Scotch affairs of the Council of State, which in July 1656 delivered its report. On 31 July, the full Council accepted the committee's recommendation and accordingly instructed its colleagues in the north that henceforth they, the Council in Scotland, should order stipends to be paid to any minister or public preacher who they were satisfied was qualified according to the intention of the ordinance of 8 August 1654.[56] Thus, while retaining the spirit of the ordinance as to the fitness of ministers — that they should be persons of a holy and unblameable conversation etc. — this instruction did away with the functions of the provincial certifyers who, as the Council now admitted, had for the second time refused or neglected to act.

This instruction to the Council enabled Broghill to come closer to the Resolutioners who were, by a happy coincidence, gathered in Edinburgh when news of Whitehall's decision reached the northern capital. Broghill immediately communicated details of the new order to the party's leaders, thus providing a concrete answer to their query about their February petition. At this, the problem of popery was effectively eclipsed, as the Resolutioners' leaders began discussions with Broghill on the implications of the new measure. Broghill now saw his chance to meet some of the party's demands on the proper functioning of the church courts. By 12 August he had concluded an agreement with the Resolutioners to the effect that every presbytery in Scotland would undertake to certify to the Council the fitness of any minister whom they desired to be admitted to a stipend, and every minister so admitted would voluntarily engage to live peaceably and inoffensively under the government.[57] Thus the English received tacit recognition of their authority, even in church affairs, from the majority party in the church; while the Resolutioners were assured that an important aspect of church discipline would once again be handled by the regular judicatories. The extra-judicial and highly irregular provincial certifyers, whose existence would have threatened the orderly hierarchy of presbyterian church government, were pronounced dead.

The conclusion of this agreement marked the culmination of Broghill's dealings with the clergy in Scotland, for by the end of the month he had set out from Edinburgh to attend the Parliament at Westminster.[58] Although he remained in theory a member of the Scottish Council,[59] he never again visited the northern kingdom. As a result of his year's labours in church affairs, he had brought the Resolutioners closer to the government than ever before; even if they did not become the active supporters of the régime the President had hoped for, when he forecast that soon they would be praying for their conquerors, then at least they gave up the most violent expressions of their dislike for the English and loyalty to the king. To this extent, a truce had been called between the civil and religious authorities. More significantly, perhaps, for the quality of religious life in Scotland and for the performance of the church's pastoral duties, a *modus vivendi* had been found on the subject of the entry of ministers to their stipends. The system which in August 1656 had been agreed on between Broghill and the Resolutioners remained in operation until the Restoration.

Despite these achievements, however, it was not apparent at the time that Broghill's departure for London marked the end of a distinct phase in the government's religious policy towards Scotland, for hard on the heels of the Resolutioners' agreement with the government came another frenzied and acrimonious episode in the three-cornered dispute between the English and the church parties. In the course of the next year, both Resolutioners and Protesters, the latter being unwilling to accept the new order for the admission of ministers to stipends, made application to the authorities in Whitehall, the Protesters to have the new order overturned and a system of planting and purging committees of their own devising substituted, the Resolutioners to have the Council's order of 31 July 1656 upheld. The decision of both parties to plead their case before the Council of State seemed on the surface to fulfil Broghill's prediction that the Scottish clergy could be brought to vie with each other for English favour, but at a deeper level it reflected the implacability of the parties towards one another and the absolute failure of Broghill to do anything to heal the split within the church. However, absorbing as the debates were to the participants in London and to their colleagues back home, they produced no material alteration in the state of the church in Scotland or, despite many false alarms raised by the Protesters' ephemeral successes with the Council and with Parliament, in the nature of the government's religious policy in the north; at most they confirmed the trend towards accommodation with the Resolutioners which Broghill had done so much to promote. Their practical effect on the government of Scotland was therefore nil, but they are worth examining as the postscript to Broghill's intervention in religious affairs.

The chain of events which brought both parties to Whitehall began when Wariston and Guthry's wing of the Protesters received with horror the news of the Resolutioners' settlement with the government. Although one of their main objections was to the provision that every minister should, on his admission, engage to live peaceably under the government, they themselves were prepared to recognise the government to the extent of sending a delegate to Whitehall to ask that the new order be revoked.[60] Broghill at first thought that if their sense of outrage induced them in a roundabout way to court the English, it would be no bad thing, for he still had hopes of playing one party off against the other: but when he realised that the diehards in the party were bent on overturning the settlement completely, he begged Thurloe to intercede with Cromwell, and to impress upon him that those who wanted an alteration in the settlement were the bitterest enemies of the government in all Scotland.[61] The Resolutioners, meanwhile, had heard of the Protesters' design and, to forestall their efforts, commissioned James Sharp to go to Whitehall too; he in fact arrived in London well ahead of his adversaries, having travelled south with Broghill, now the avowed champion and patron of the Resolutioners. Early in November, Mr. James Simpson, minister at Airth in Stirlingshire, was sent up to London as the advance guard of the Protesters, but not until January 1657 was he joined by the full delegation, composed of Guthry, Gillespie, Wariston, and Sir Andrew Kerr of Greenhead.[62] Gillespie's presence in this commission is worthy of note, for in the summer of 1656 he had been willing to co-operate with Broghill and the Resolutioners in the working of the new order and had given the President hopes, however ill-founded, that he and his faction could be separated from their 'extremist' colleagues; now, however, he chose to stand alongside his Protesting brethren, even if he did not always play their game. These men went to London with the full approval of Monck who, in a letter to Cromwell of January 1657, averred that the Protesters 'are better to bee trusted then the other partie which are called the Generall Resolucion men',[63] an opinion which was clearly contrary to that of Broghill.

The Protesters came armed with four proposals to lay before the Protector. These were: (1) that in every synod a committee should be appointed of equal numbers of Resolutioners and Protesters, with power to plant and to purge the churches of all Malignants, (2) that a similarly composed committee should have power over all ecclesiastical matters, (3) that the Protector should appoint a committee to authorise ministerial stipends and (4) that the Protector should renew the Act of Classes of 1649 against Malignants.[64] These proposals were in many ways merely a repetition of the overtures which the Protesters had put before their opponents at the conference on union of November 1655, and which the Resolutioners had then found totally unacceptable. In London, the Protesters maintained that their scheme was the only way to rid the church of sinfulness and corruption but, as in 1655, the Resolutioners stood firm by the principle of restoration of the church courts, a principle which was not incompatible with their agreement with Broghill in August 1656.

An opportunity to plead these points came in February 1657, when Sharp and the five Protesters were called before the Protector. On two separate occasions, each side bombarded Cromwell with an account of the lamentable effects of the divisions within the church, but at this stage the Protesters did no more than hint at their proposed remedies. Gillespie made the interesting claim that the Protesters could call on the support of 200 ministers in Scotland (50 more than the Resolutioners would have had Broghill believe in 1655-6), and that in the province of Glasgow alone they had 25,000 adherents. Cromwell seemed rather sceptical of this claim, as indeed was Sharp, but on balance neither party really succeeded in winning the Protector's approval. Cromwell was, if anything, rather wearied by the whole tedious business, and ended the second conference with the wish that 'this bussiness were putt to some issue'.[65]

All parties doubtless shared the Protector's desire for action, but no further steps were taken to settle the affairs of the Scottish church until July. In the meantime, the Protesters brought off a successful *coup* with the help of their friends in Parliament. During the course of the debates on the Humble Petition and Advice, the Protesters agitated for a change in the clause relating to the eligibility of Scots to serve as, or vote for, MPs. As it stood, the Petition and Advice, although formally disfranchising Engagers, would have granted eligibility to all who had lived peaceably under the English government since

March 1652. The Protesters, however, were anxious to secure the exclusion of *all* Malignants not only from Parliament, but from other places of public trust as well. They therefore submitted a 'Proviso' which debarred from such office all those who had either invaded England in 1648, or had assisted, abetted or advised this invasion; the only exceptions were to be persons who had subsequently borne arms for the Protector or Parliament, and those who currently sat as MPs. The House passed this 'Proviso' on 15 June, and it received the Protector's consent on the 26th. The Protesters' triumph was to be short-lived, however, for when news of the Proviso reached Scotland, this threatened renewal of the Act of Classes of 1649 provoked an angry outcry. Monck warned Cromwell that it would be inexpedient to put the measure into effect, and by October 1657 the Council of State had decided to drop it. Its only practical effect was to create trouble and unrest during the Glasgow burgh elections of September 1657, when the Protester faction in the city tried to use it to defeat their opponents.[66]

The controversy surrounding the Petition and Advice had been one reason why the English authorities had delayed further action on the church issue; but on 14 July the Council of State at last decided to appoint a committee to hear both sides. At first, it looked as if the Protesters would repeat their transitory success as a political pressure group, for the committee apparently favoured their proposals. Sharp did little to help the Resolutioners' case by stating that he did not have a commission from any church court to deal with the question of union between the two parties; because of this his right to treat of the matters under review was not acknowledged by the committee. The Protesters therefore had a clear field for the presentation of their case. On 4 August, the committee accepted that case when it issued a report which substantially adopted the Protesters' proposals for planting and purging churches and for regulating most other ecclesiastical matters.

Sharp, who had a valuable ally in Thurloe, staved off disaster for his party by persuading the Council of State to hear his protests against the proposals at the same time as they considered the committee's report. As a result of these protests, and similar pleas from English presbyterian ministers, the Council decided not to implement the report but instead to write to the Scots ministers telling them to forget past differences and to concentrate their energies on 'the work of reformation'. The story was not yet over, for the Protesters made one last attempt to secure an alteration to the Council's order on disputed stipends, but again the influence of Sharp on Thurloe and of Thurloe on Cromwell ensured its defeat. In the event, the Council decided not to write to the Scots ministers after all, but merely to refer consideration of the dispute between Resolutioners and Protesters to the Scottish Council.[67] No progress was made by the Council in Scotland, however, and so, despite attempts by the churchmen themselves to effect a union in 1659-60, the split between Protesters and Resolutioners was still unhealed at the Restoration.[68]

The wearisome, and at times unedifying, spectacle of charge and counter-charge at Whitehall had thus resulted in the *status quo* of August 1656 being confirmed. The Resolutioners could claim to be the victors of the contest at London, if only because they had defeated the Protesters' attempts to disturb the compact which they had earlier made with Broghill and, through him, with the government. While Sharp was in London, Broghill had stood by the agreement for which he was responsible, and had proved a staunch ally of the Resolutioners. Thus he helped to ensure that his intervention in the affairs of the Scottish church had some lasting effect, and although he could not claim to have realised all his grandiose aims for promoting harmony between church and state, he could at least claim to have won valuable friends for the government. These friends were hardly the sort to support the régime through thick and thin — perhaps only by comparison with the strength of their former opposition can they be called friends at all — but the new understanding with them marked an advance on the hostility of previous years.

In this, and in other ways, Broghill's period as President of the Scottish Council had been a genuinely creative one, not only in the measures which he and his colleagues enacted and in the institutions they established, but also in the attitude of mind which Broghill himself brought to the task. Although his belief that he could manipulate any situation to English advantage (particularly where the Scottish clergy was concerned) bordered at times on arrogance and contempt for the people he was dealing with, he had a surer grasp of the long-term possibilities of a situation and a more sophisticated, 'political' outlook on affairs than anybody else holding high civil or military office in Scotland. Beside him, Monck was a plodder, but an indispensable plodder nonetheless. For on the army's ability to keep order in the provinces and supervise the day-to-day work of administration depended the practical success of many of the measures which the Council instituted. This was true not only of the year from September 1655 to August 1656, when Broghill was in Scotland, but even more so after his departure, when Monck was again the *de facto* ruler of the country. In the two years from September 1656 until the death of the Protector, it fell to Monck to consolidate the creative achievements of the Broghill era and to keep the government of Scotland ticking over efficiently. This was a period with few innovations in policy, when the political dynamism had clearly gone out of the régime, but one which saw much solid administrative endeavour; for the Scots people it was thus a period of orderly government, when life assumed something like a regular pattern and the sharpest edge had been taken off English domination.

10

The Consolidation of the Régime, August 1656 — September 1658

WHEN in late August 1656 Monck took over responsibility for civil and military affairs in the north, the executive in Scotland had been deprived of the services not only of Broghill but of several other able administrators as well. The Parliament at Westminster, to which Broghill had been elected as member for Edinburgh, claimed the attendance of thirty men, and at least half of these (Scots as well as English) held either an army commission or a civil office in the central administration. The exodus of these men to London was not without influence on the efficiency of the English administration and the calibre of its personnel. Most importantly, because so many councillors were elected as MPs, the business of the Council and of the Court of Exchequer was at a standstill for lack of a quorum from September 1656 until the end of March 1657,[1] and Monck had to plead with the Council at Whitehall to send some members north so that warrants for the collection of taxes could be legally issued. After many bitter complaints from Monck and some haphazard attempts by the Council of State to remedy the problem, the quorum was made up when Col. Scroope arrived at Dalkeith on the last Saturday in March 1657. Thereupon, after a gap of seven months, the Council reconvened and on 31 March issued an order for the levying of cess at £10,000 per month for six months, covering the three months just past and the months of April, May and June following.[2]

These seven months were the worst, but not the only, time when the demands of English politics and Whitehall's dilatoriness in attending to Scottish business prevented the administration in Scotland from running smoothly. In the summer of 1657 the supreme court of justice was severely undermanned, partly because two of the Scots judges had died, but also because several of the bench were attending the Parliament at Westminster.[3] Early in September the Council's work was again in jeopardy, this time because the Council at Whitehall had not sent down the commission for administering the new oath of office to their northern colleagues.[4] But in the following year Whitehall showed greater diligence in renewing the Instructions for the Scottish Council, which were due to expire on 24 June 1658. Fully a fortnight before the date of expiry, the Council of State had agreed on a new set and had sent them to Edinburgh, where they arrived on the 22nd. Since, however, the Protector did not sign the patent for putting them into effect until 3 July, it was mid-July before the 'new' Council could actually convene.[5]

The differences between these new Instructions and the previous ones of 1655[6] reflected some of the changes which had taken place in the government's attitude towards Scottish affairs during these years. Most noticeably, all mention of 'Gillespie's Charter' was dropped, thus confirming the results of Broghill's dealings with the clergy and of the debates between the two church parties before the Council of State in 1657. The Protesters' influence remained, however, in the clause which ordered that 'none [should] hold the office of magistrate who have been disabled' by the Humble Petition and Advice. The Council seemed thus to override the advice, and indeed the practice of General Monck, who had warned against the implementation of that clause in the constitution. The religious and political fears of the Protectorate were also displayed in the injunction 'to see that no Baptist holds any office of trust, nor practices at law, nor keeps a school', a warning which had not been deemed necessary in 1655.[7] Most prominent of all in the new document were a clutch of clauses dealing with financial and commercial matters. In 1655 it had been made clear that Whitehall expected its northern offshoot to make strenuous efforts to increase revenue and curtail expenditure in Scotland, and such matters had accordingly occupied a large part of Broghill's and the Council's time. By 1658, the need to make ends meet had become even more compelling, and recent efforts by the Scottish Exchequer to enforce the Protector's (formerly the Crown's) rights of property and casualty were given especial encouragement in the new Instructions. In 1658 the Council was empowered to 'reduce all Crown lands illegally alienated from the State', and to 'use effectual means to recover any part of the revenue concealed or detained'.

Despite the shortage of manpower and lack of co-operation from Whitehall with which Monck and the executive in Scotland were faced, the administrative machine stood up fairly well to the everyday tasks of government. Much of the credit, of course, was due to the army, which continued to guarantee security from foreign invasion and royalist unrest at home, and which generally ensured that the orders of the civil arm were enforced in the localities. Much was due also to the devolution of responsibility for maintaining law and order, and for performing sundry other administrative tasks, on to the shoulders of the local gentry, who now regularly acted as JPs, commissioners of assessment and spokesmen for their communities on *ad hoc* shire committees. Important also was the fact that between 1656 and 1658 no major new issues arose to trouble the uneasy peace between conquerors and conquered. The guidelines of English policy had long been set, and the Council and its agents concentrated now on implementing decisions already taken, and on refining the techniques of government. Overall, the conservative tendency of English rule made life easier, and more peaceful, for all concerned.

The problems to which the administration did address itself were primarily of two kinds: first, those dealing with matters of finance, ranging from the assessment, the excise, and the former Crown lands, to matters with more overtly political overtones, such as the £40,000 fine on forfeited estates and the interpretation of the laws of debt; and secondly, those pertaining to the administration of justice, the maintenance of law and order, and security against Royalists.

i. Finance

The Instructions with which the Council in Scotland had been issued on taking up office had charged them with the task of enquiring into the nature of the Scottish revenues, and of sending a particular account of these revenues, together with suggestions for their improvement, annually to the Council in Whitehall. Out of the former Crown revenue in Scotland, the expenses of the civil government were to be met, so that as the cost of that government grew in 1656 and 1657 the pressure on the executive in Scotland both to improve the revenue and cut down public expenses increased accordingly.

An important element in the total cost of carrying on all public affairs in Scotland was the payment of the civil list. This category of expenditure, which consisted largely of the salaries of the administrative officials but which, from 28 July 1657, included also the cost of 'fire and candle' for the garrisons,[8] was to be met out of the customs revenue and one-third of the excise. An account drawn up for the year January 1655 to January 1656 had shown that this source of revenue was inadequate to meet the charges made upon it, and indeed in June 1657 Monck had warned Thurloe that the cost of the civil government was already making inroads on the remaining two-thirds of the excise, which should have been set aside to pay the army's arrears.[9] This situation still obtained in August, after Monck had effected some retrenchment on the civil list, principally because the reduction of £3495, most of which was made on the cost of salaries, did not match the increase of over £5000 for 'fire and candle' money. The civil list now came to just under £26,000, so that only an increase in the relevant customs and excise duties, which in 1655-6 had provided nearly £23,000 towards the costs of civil government, or else a contribution from some other branch of the revenue, could make ends meet. To make matters worse, various other 'general and temporal contingencies', such as compensation to some who had suffered losses through their loyalty to the government during Glencairn's rising, had a claim also to be included on the civil list.[10]

The problem of finding that additional contribution from the revenue of Scotland brought the Council to investigate seriously the nature of the former Crown revenue; for although there were in theory other resources open to the government, such as the income from lands formerly under sequestration or the surplus proceeds of the £40,000 fine, these did not seem as elastic as the revenue from the old Crown lands. These had, of course, been appropriated at the conquest by the Commonwealth of England, and the dues from them now went to make up part of 'his highness's', instead of the king's, 'property and casualty'.[11] Investigation into the extent of these lands and into the alienation that had taken place under successive kings had been begun early in 1656, after Broghill and the Council had seen to the erection of an Exchequer Court. In February, and again in July 1656, proclamations had gone out requiring all holders of kirklands or lands of the king's patrimony to exhibit their titles before the Court at various specified dates. But the subsequent work of scrutiny was severely disrupted, for between

September 1656 and March 1657 the Exchequer Court was unable to sit for lack of a quorum. In April, however, the executive seems to have regained its interest in the subject,[12] for in that month a paper was prepared, probably with the help of William Purves, chief clerk in the Exchequer,[13] which outlined the relevant Scottish law and recommended that alienated lands should be recovered as soon as possible, lest men become more reluctant to surrender property the longer they were allowed to hold it.

Just how large a task the Exchequer would have if it sought to reduce all alienated lands, and so recover the lost rents, was revealed in July and August 1657, when Monck, the Judges of the Exchequer and the Auditor-General combined to prepare an account of the total revenue in response to an order from Whitehall. In its final form the account, which related to the year from January 1655 to January 1656, estimated that about half the 'property and casualty' revenue had been alienated by the Stuarts' land grants. The English reckoned that the full sum could amount to as much as £9622 17s. 0d. stg. *per annum,* if — but only if — the Exchequer could recover such alienated lands as the earldoms of Orkney, Huntingtore, Dunfermline, Islay, Bute, Stirling, Kelso, Arbroath and many others. In addition, although £4000-£5000 of 'property and casualty' revenue could presently be gathered in, various pensions were already charged on this sum; these, on an incomplete estimate, amounted to over £500.[14]

This was only the start of the Council's renewed investigation into the problem of the Crown lands. Around the turn of the year a revised statement of the revenue from this source was drawn up together with an account of the charges already made upon it. This document[15] showed that pensions or grants to the yearly value, not of £500, but of £2328 6s. 8d. had currently to be met by the Scottish Exchequer, while the rest of the proceeds was returned to the Exchequer in England for the Protector's own use and so could not be assigned towards public expenses in Scotland. In addition, it was pointed out, the fees from all the great offices of state had now been given away to their incumbents, so that Wariston, recently reinstated as Clerk Register, currently enjoyed the fees of the Court of Justice, William Lockhart the Signet, Disbrowe the Great Seal, Lord Strathnaver the Privy Seal, and Alexander Jaffray the profits of the Chancery. This, of course, relieved the government of direct responsibility for paying the lesser officials of these courts, but it nonetheless represented a loss to the public treasury. And besides, the Protector had given sundry grants of money to persons like the Marquis of Argyle, or to institutions such as the College of Glasgow, some of which were in payment for past public debts, but all of which increased the burden on the state's revenue.

The Council's activity in certifying the likely charges to be put upon the revenue of Scotland was not matched by equal success in reclaiming alienated Crown lands. The difficulties were formidable, and ranged from lack of the proper records, most of which were scattered around the Tower of London where they had been taken after Worcester,[16] to recurring uncertainty about the limits of the Exchequer Court's jurisdiction. In September 1657, Samuel Disbrowe conceded that to enlarge the Exchequer's powers further would be unwise, in view of popular feeling against the court, and that therefore the commissioners of the Scottish Exchequer should try to recover concealed or dilapidated estates by pleading their case before the Commissioners for the Administration of Justice in the ordinary civil courts. This procedure would depend for much of its success on the compliance of the Scots judges, but Disbrowe, alive to the fact that he and his Exchequer colleagues might otherwise be accused of lusting after power, was prepared to give it a trial.[17] Some measure of the horror with which many of the nobility viewed the government's move to reduce alienated estates was conveyed by a correspondent of the Earl of Morton. The Earl was defending his right and title to the earldom of Orkney, and his plight called forth the comment, 'I can not thinke they will proceid to such tyrannicall courses as to subwert the noblest families of our nation for your Lordp.'s is not the only case poynted at ther ar diwerse withe yow in the same conditione.' It also called forth the advice to use every means of pressure available, including attempting to win over Alexander Brodie, then a judge-designate, to promote his cause.[18] The prospect that Brodie and the other Scotsmen on the bench might succumb to the blandishments of the threatened nobility pointed to the drawbacks for the English of the whole procedure, but in April 1658 Disbrowe reiterated his belief that this was the surest, if not the quickest, way legally to repossess the state of the Crown's ancient patrimony.[19]

By the spring of 1658 the work of repossession seems to have made little progress, and even a year later 'his highness's property' still brought in only £5300 *per annum*.[20] In April 1658, however, the Council in Scotland had shown its determination to continue the task by drafting some proposals on the subject and by sending William Purves to London to explain them in person to the Council. Disbrowe highly recommended Purves's talents to Thurloe and said that some of the Exchequer's unpopularity had rubbed off on the clerk. Purves, he explained, had incurred the odium of his countrymen in no small degree by aiding the English in their work, and indeed the proceedings whereby all holders of 'public' lands were required to exhibit their titles to the Exchequer subsequently assumed the opprobrious epithet of 'Purves's Production'.[21] When in London, Purves attended meetings of the Council's committee for Scotch affairs, and succeeded in obtaining permission to have the registers relating to the Scottish revenue and the Exchequer sorted out from amongst the other records in the Tower and returned to Scotland. But more importantly, the committee advised the Council, after consulting Purves, that henceforth the recovery of that part of the revenue which had been alienated from the Crown by letters patent from the late king should be effected only with the consent of Parliament. In May 1658 the authorities in Scotland were notified accordingly, with the added injunction to be 'very vigorous' in the prosecution of the whole business. To this end, the Commissioners for the Administration of Justice were ordered to set aside every Friday to hear relevant pleas and, to strengthen the court, Samuel Disbrowe, Keeper of the Great Seal of Scotland since 1655 and now Chancellor, was ordered to sit with the judges. Two months later, in July 1658, he took his place as their President,[22] but since no Parliament was then sitting, the work of the judges could not bear full fruit.

Purves's mission to London had, in fact, been a tacit admission by the Scottish Council that the much-vaunted improvement of the former Crown revenue was making little headway. It was as well for the costs of civil government, therefore, that branches of the revenue other than the Crown's property-roll showed a much-increased yield, especially since the cost of salaries and related contingencies probably went up by nearly £2000 between 1656 and 1659.[23] The increase in revenue came mainly from the inland excise. In 1659 it was reckoned that the farm of the excise on beer, ale and 'aquavitae' brought in over £47,000 yearly; that the excise on salt brought in over £1600 and the export tax on coal another £2200; and that the customs and foreign excise yielded £12,500.[24] For 1656 the comparable figures (excluding the coal tax) had been over £35,000; approximately £1350; and nearly £16,000 respectively.[25] It was only the excise on liquor, therefore, that showed a significant increase — around £12,000, of which £4000 could in theory be used to pay for the civil government. The customs and foreign excise, by contrast, seems to have declined in yield by approximately £3500 between 1656 and 1659. What this represented in terms of net loss for the payment of the civil list is unclear, since two-thirds of the foreign excise, for which separate figures are not available, was assigned for payment of army arrears and not for the charges of civil government.[26] Although none of these figures is wholly reliable, it does seem that, with the increase in the charges on the civil list, there was still no substantial balance of income over expenditure in this particular sector of the state's finances by 1659. Moreover, the picture becomes even less favourable if the large number of pensions and 'temporary contingencies' charged on one branch or another of the revenue of Scotland is taken into account.[27]

In 1659, it was estimated that the charges on the civil list (including 'fire and candle' money for military guards) came to over £36,628 *per annum*. This, however, was only a small proportion of the total 'issues of Scotland', *i.e.* of the full cost of running the country, for over £270,000 was required annually to pay for the army. Of this sum a mere £72,000 was forthcoming from the yield of the monthly cess on Scotland, the remainder being, in theory, assigned from the English assessments.[28] The cess, therefore, met only one-quarter of the expense of maintaining the English army in Scotland, despite the fact that its imposition constituted a very real burden on the Scottish taxpayers. This burden was, however, made lighter after June 1657, for in that month Parliament reduced the rate from a nominal £10,000 to £6000 per month, thereby arriving at the sum of £72,000 on which the estimates of 1659 were based.

This reduction in the rate of the assessment was made with the full approval of Monck. When he heard that Parliament was debating the issue, he sent a special plea to Thurloe to consider the needs of Scotland, a poor country by English standards, whose resources had been much exhausted by the upheavals of war and the laying on of fines and forfeitures. The Scots clearly believed that they were paying a much higher proportion of their national income in this tax than were the English — even after the reduction, some calculated that Scotland was paying double or even treble the proportion demanded from England — and Monck stressed that only by the removal of this feeling of inequality could the Scots be reconciled to the present government. Monck's attitude, therefore, stemmed not from any humanitarian impulse but from clearsighted recognition of the needs, and the limitations, of the English régime in Scotland: so difficult was the task of collection, he averred, perhaps with some exaggeration, that the soldiers had almost as well go without their pay as gather it up.[29] The Bill setting the assessment on Scotland at the lower rate of £6000 per month passed the House on 22 June 1657. But what Parliament gave with one hand it took away, at least temporarily, with the other, for at the same time another Bill was passed which required an extra £15,000 to be levied on Scotland. This extraordinary assessment was to be spread over three months, and was designed to help meet the cost of the war with Spain.[30]

As Monck had intimated in his letters to Thurloe, the Scots' resentment of their tax burden, as well as their genuine impoverishment, was frequently reflected in difficulties over the collection of the cess. Some of the really hard cases, involving shires which were in arrears continuously for several years, were recorded in Monck's warrant-book, for the commander-in-chief usually found it necessary to issue special orders for dealing with such defaulters. In September 1656, for example, stern measures were adopted towards several persons in the Western Isles whose arrears since September 1654 totalled £1364 stg: if they refused to pay up, Monck told Lt. Col. Reade, their estates on the mainland were to be distrained upon until their debts to the state were paid.[31] Even without such special directives, the army had standing instructions to assist the civilian collectors if required, and so military intervention in this sphere was probably much more frequent and sustained than the number of orders which Monck issued on the subject would indicate. The responsibility for calling in military assistance fell, in the first instance, on the commissioners of assessment, so that often the matter would not go beyond the notice of the local gentry, the nearest army garrison and, of course, the defaulters themselves. What no doubt helped to make this system work smoothly was the fact that army officers stationed nearby were included on the commission of assessment for each shire. Thus, even if the Scots on the commission were reluctant to call in force against their neighbours, the officers were certain to protect English interests, and could take action without prior reference to Monck.[32]

The practice of having English officers on the commission proved its value when the number of Scotsmen who had taken the oath of office fell below the requirements for each shire. Such difficulties stemmed in part from the Council's decision to amalgamate the commission of the assessment with that for the peace, for the government was consequently deprived of the services of those who refused to take the oath as justices. But the commission for any shire might also be depleted by the death, departure to another district, or change in personal circumstances of any of its members, or again, the whole system might be jeopardised by the Exchequer's failure to issue the necessary commissions. Such was very nearly the case in October 1656, when the departure of Disbrowe for Westminster left the Exchequer without a quorum, but on that occasion Monck asked Judge Goodyear and his colleagues to assume responsibility for passing all new commissions under the seal.[33]

The changes which had taken place amongst the commissioners of assessment since 1656 were starkly revealed early in 1658, when the Scottish Council came to implement Parliament's orders for laying on the new cess of £6000 per month. This obviously required a complete revaluation and redistribution of the tax burden to take account of the reduction in the rate, and to this end Parliament had, in the enabling Act, named panels of commissioners for each shire. Since, however, the Act merely reiterated the Council's own nominations for the commission in December 1655, Monck had perforce to write to the Protector stating that such a list was hopelessly out of date. Parliament's list of June 1657, he said, took no account of those who had demitted office since 1656, or of those who had been appointed to fill the vacancies, and it was impossible to carry on the work with those few nominees who were willing and able to act; he therefore asked that the Scottish Council be given authority to add such new names as they thought fit.[34] It was also clear from this letter that the work of valuation lagged much behind the actual date on which the new rate came into force, although presumably collection of the tax had continued since June 1657, either at the old rate or at an estimated level for the new rate. The levying of the additional £15,000 to finance the war with Spain was likewise behindhand, and here, it seems, no money at all had been raised by February 1658.[35] Later in the year, further pressures were put on the system when the Council of State urged that the cess for the second half of the year be collected *ahead* of time; that due for the June quarter was to be paid in by 1 June, the instalment for the September quarter before 6 July, and the amount due in December by 6 October.[36] In view of the difficulties which the army and the collectors already had to cope with in gathering the cess, it seems highly unlikely that these demands were ever met.

The effect which the lowering of the assessment had on the policy of granting abatements is hard to determine. Such matters were now normally dealt with by the local commissioners or, at the highest level, by the Council. Only those cases which required special action by the army were recorded by Monck's secretary, and there seem to have been proportionately fewer of these in the period from September 1656 to September 1658 than before. Nonetheless, grants were recorded to such persons as the laird of Lenzie, James Cunningham, Hugh Campbell of Lix and Thomas Ker of Mersington,[37] but overall, it seems, the system of abatements continued to function in a routine way that demanded little attention from the commander-in-chief.

Any administrative problems relating to the cess that did arise could only make worse the already massive discrepancy between the nominal yield of the assessment and the cost of the army establishment for Scotland. From June 1657 the amount transferred from the English assessment to plug this gap was fixed at £11,400 per month.[38] By then, of course, the actual yield of the Scottish assessment had fallen by *at least* £2000 per month, but plans were also being made to effect an even greater reduction in the cost of the army. From December 1657 a new establishment took effect which amounted to £20,818 per month for pay and contingencies (fortifications being extra); this compared with a figure of £24,992 per month set in July 1655.[39] These economies elicited from Monck a storm of protest and criticism about the central government's handling of army affairs in the north.[40] He acidly pointed out that defects in the Council's methods of accounting meant that no money at all had been apportioned to pay the army in Scotland from 25 May to 25 June 1657. He further complained that their provision for the period from 23 June to 9 December 1657 was inadequate, that they had ignored the cost of disbanding those soldiers who were surplus to the requirements of the new establishment, and that, despite the allocation of two-thirds of the excise, the pay of the army in Scotland was still in arrears. Monck summed up his grievances by saying that the forces in Scotland were not being treated on an equal footing with those in England, and threatened to resign his command if the imbalance were not redressed.[41]

The establishment fixed in December 1657 was still in force when, in April 1659, the House of Commons called for an estimate of all public revenue and expenditure, both civil and military. The figures for Scotland showed that annual issues and expenses came to £307,271 12s. 8½d., of which the army establishment took up £270,643 4s. 2d. The income of Scotland from all sources came to £143,652 11s. 11d. The excess of expenditure over income was, therefore, £163,619 0s. 9½d., of which £148,200 was, in theory, met by the assignment from the English assessment. But this still left a small deficit, and in addition the state acknowledged debts of £93,827 13s. 0¾d. for the arrears of the army in Scotland and £1800 for the cost of building a citadel at Leith.[42] It is clear from these figures, therefore, that the maintenance of the army in Scotland constituted a serious drain on the resources of the state. The reality, moreover, was probably harsher still, for the neat figures of the accountants masked a generally hand-to-mouth approach towards financing the forces in Scotland, which resulted in confusion and delay in paying the soldiers actively responsible for peace and order in the north. But despite Monck's obvious disgruntlement and his hints that his officers were not at all happy with their conditions of service,[43] there is no evidence to suggest that these shortcomings affected the army's desire or ability to perform its peacekeeping duties.

Aside from such weighty matters as the assessment, the Crown lands, and the payment of the civil list, the government in Scotland had, finally, to deal with the aftermath of the Council's decision, in November 1656, to take off all sequestrations in Scotland in exchange for a composite £40,000 fine. In the past, this issue had always been treated not merely as a financial question but as one whose political and social overtones had profound implications for domestic peace. By 1657, however, the only matter still unsettled was the apportionment of the £40,000 fine amongst the thirteen persons whose estates were affected. In practice the money was in most cases put up not by the owners themselves, but by their creditors, since the whole idea behind the scheme was to discharge the donatives lying on these estates so that the creditors could themselves proceed to recover their just debts. This meant, of course, that the creditors and the owners had to engage in some hard bargaining before the terms on which the creditors put up the money could be agreed.[44] In the spring of 1657, the creditors were granted an extension of the time allowed for payment; the original order had set 25 March and 24 June 1657 as the dates on which the first and second moieties fell due, but these were now altered to 1 June and 1 October.[45] This extension was not, however, granted solely because of the creditors' difficulties in raising money; the Council in Scotland had also contributed to the delay by the length of time they took to apportion the total fine.[46] Not until 14 May 1657 did they publish a list of the first moieties which were due on 1 June, although the creditors may possibly have known of the details some time in advance of the official announcement. The individual fines ranged from £5275 upon the Earl Marischal to £195 on Major General Dalziel, and this, of course, was only the first instalment. On 19 August the Council set out the proportion of the second moiety, which in most, but not all, cases approximated to the first. Variations occurred where victims had in the course of the summer months successfully challenged the Council's first estimate and had been granted a rebate or, conversely, where the Council had seen fit to enlarge the fine.[47] Thus while Lord Bargany secured a reduction in his fine, from £1396 for the first instalment to £452 for the second, to rectify the overvaluation of his estate,[48] Lord Montgomery's actually went up from £379 to £1727. Montgomery's ill-fortune resulted from the Council's decision to dun him for £1400 assessed on the estate of his father, the Earl of Eglinton, but subsequently, on the advice of able lawyers, the Council admitted that this was a mistake and that Montgomery was not liable. Montgomery was therefore relieved of the additional burden, but only after his case had been laid before the Council in Whitehall.[49] The resolution of this and similar problems[50] meant that payment of the whole £40,000 was delayed long after October 1657, if indeed the full amount was ever paid at all. By February 1658, probably less than half lay in the hands of the Receiver-General, although over £38,000 had been paid out by the state to discharge donatives.[51]

As Monck, the Council and the revenue officials busied themselves with the imposition and collection of the £40,000 fine, little reference was made to the fears of political and social unrest which the régime in Scotland had previously voiced whenever the question of fines and forfeitures was raised.[52] In part, of course, this reflected the fact that what had started as a fundamental issue of English policy had now been whittled down to the mere details of the financial position of thirteen persons and their creditors. But it was also a sign that the political climate within which such administrative problems could be solved was now much calmer, and the country less prone to disturbance, than at any time since Worcester. The large measure of stability and security which the régime now enjoyed was in part a testimony to the success of Monck's intelligence system, through which he kept tabs on Charles Stuart's agents in Scotland and foiled their attempts to rekindle the royalist sympathies of the nobility and gentry. But it was even more a tribute to the success of the courts and other law enforcement agencies, both civil and military, in punishing crime, reconciling feuds and keeping under control the groundswell of unrest and disorder which the Royalists had used as a springboard for rebellion in 1653-4. In this as in earlier periods, therefore, the manner in which justice was dispensed and order preserved was crucial to the effective governance of Scotland.

ii. Justice, law and order

At the top of the judicial hierarchy, ultimate responsibility for determining civil actions lay, as before, with the Commissioners for the Administration of Justice. In the winter of 1656-7, the supreme court for civil causes[53] did not suffer the same interruption to its proceedings as did the Council or the Court of Exchequer, for although Smyth and Swinton were members of the Westminster Parliament,[54] there still remained in Edinburgh sufficient judges to carry on the winter session. By the opening of the summer session in June, however, death had depleted the ranks of the Commissioners, for on 12 May Alexander Pearson of Southall died in Edinburgh.[55] A few weeks later, Sir James Learmonth of Balcomy dropped dead while presiding over a hearing in court, thus bringing the number of judges present in Edinburgh down to four — one less than the quorum.[56] Balcomy's death was an especial blow because he had sat in the Outer House, a duty which could only be performed by someone versed in the intricacies of Scots law and legal practice. Even before Balcomy's demise on 26 June, Monck had urged the necessity of replacing Southall and of providing another judge for the Outer House. Feelers had been put out to Alexander Brodie of Brodie in the hope that he would fill the vacancy, but on 23 June Monck had to report to Cromwell that Brodie had peremptorily refused the appointment.[57] Monck recommended instead James Dalrymple, an honest man and a good lawyer, who was well known to his countrymen and to the English in Scotland, but who needed a good deal of coaxing before he would take on the job. Balcomy's sudden death provided the final push, and on 1 July 1657 Dalrymple hastily assumed his seat on the bench; a few weeks later, on 25 July, the Protector formally confirmed his appointment.[58]

Although Dalrymple's appointment enabled the court to go on to despatch a fair number of cases in July,[59] the judicial bench was still much under strength. But in November 1657, in time for the winter term, Sir Archibald Johnston of Wariston was added to the commission, having in the previous July been reappointed as Clerk Register,[60] and in January 1658 Alexander Brodie at last consented to accept a judgeship.[61] This brought the number on the bench up to nine and, significantly, Scotsmen were, for the first time, in a majority: four Englishmen — Smyth, Moseley, Goodyear and Lawrence — were outnumbered by five Scots — Kerr, Swinton, Dalrymple, Wariston and Brodie. By allowing this to come about, the government tacitly admitted two things: first, that the technicalities of Scots law were too complex for Englishmen to cope with alone, and second, that it was politically safe to give the Scots judges their head. This in turn implied that the ideal of assimilating the legal systems of England and Scotland had been quietly abandoned and that henceforth the more conservative, pragmatic aim of despatching as many legal actions in as short a time as possible would predominate. At the same time, however, the government made it clear that there were limits to its willingness to hand back to the Scots control over their own judicial system. In 1658, only the English Judges were included on the commission to hear criminal causes (although Swinton may have contrived to lend his opinion on occasion),[62] and from July of that year Samuel Disbrowe, the Chancellor, sat with the judges for civil causes as their permanent president.[63]

The new appointments to the bench allowed the court to deal with an increasing number of civil actions in the sessions of 1657-8.[64] Compared with the figures for previous years, the number of judicial decisions handed down from the bench showed a steep rise, a rise which probably reflected not only increased efficiency on the part of the judges but also the greater willingness of private persons to embark on litigation in the more settled atmosphere of the late 1650s.[65] The improvement in judicial administration proved to be short-lived, however, for by the end of 1658 Monck was again exercised over vacancies on the bench. On 26 September 1658 Judge Smyth died while on circuit at Inverness, and in the following month Judge Goodyear fell seriously ill. Monck asked for replacements, and although he expressed a strong preference for an Englishman, he acknowledged that the Council of State might well choose a Scot — surprisingly, perhaps, when both the recent casualties had themselves been English.[66] Despite the pressure from Monck, and other pleas from Judge Moseley[67] and from Wariston,[68] no new appointments were made before April 1659, when the downfall of the Protectorate put a stop to judicial proceedings in Scotland; as a result, in the winter session of 1658-9 only a few cases were dealt with.[69]

In pressing for the appointment of an Englishman, Monck stressed that the new recruit would be needed on the commission for criminal causes. As the time and place of Judge Smyth's death indicated, the practice of sending judges out on circuit to hear criminal cases had continued in the years since 1656, although little evidence remains as to the regularity of the sessions or the nature of the cases that came before the bench.[70] By this time, however, the activities of the circuit judges, while still an indispensable part of the government's machinery for administering justice and maintaining order, were reinforced and supplemented by other law-enforcement agencies. Giving judgment at an assize was only the final step in the long process of bringing an offender to book. Equally, if not more, important were the efforts of the justices of the peace, who had to present the offender for trial and take preliminary depositions from witnesses; the local community (including clan chieftains and men of influence in the shires) whose duty it was to hunt down, hand over to the authorities and give evidence against, suspected criminals; and last but by no means least, the army, whose responsibilities covered a wide range of peacekeeping duties, from the simple task of keeping prisoners in safe custody to actively seeking out and capturing the worst offenders. Paradoxically, although the army was the backbone of the whole process of law enforcement, that process was at its most effective when it functioned not as an offshoot of the military machine but as a co-operative venture between army and local community. Within the context of military occupation, the essence of the peacekeeping system built up by Monck after the suppression of Glencairn's rising was duality, not separation, of function. Thus local gentry and army officers were combined on the commission of the peace; clan chiefs and lesser lairds were required to exercise authority both as agents of the central government (whether as JPs or sheriffs) and as holders of quasi-feudal power (when they were held responsible for the wrongdoings of their tenants or clansmen); and private citizens took over some of the army's duties when they were given special powers to form guards or hunt down mosstroopers.

The Scottish JPs continued to play a key role in the government of the localities, but the number of occasions on which Monck had to intervene in the work of the justices suggests that the commission of the peace needed constant prodding from army headquarters to carry out its duties effectively. In April 1657, both Monck and Morgan found it necessary to ask the JPs of Banffshire and Aberdeenshire to keep an especial watch for robbers and loose men in their bounds, since some of the vagabonds roaming the area were suspected of having royalist connections, while in the previous month, Col. Fairfax, who was himself a JP in Fife, was told to rouse the rest of his colleagues to deal with some persons suspected of abetting thefts.[71] In June 1658 the governor of Dunstaffnage, Capt. Witter, was ordered to inquire into the misdemeanours of one Daniel Maclean of Brolos;[72] Witter was on the commission for Argyllshire and was told to choose any one of his fellow-justices to assist him in the inquiry. In this, as in other instances, it was not always made clear whether the army officer was being given orders in his purely military capacity, or whether he was being asked to take action as a JP; but since the object of the system was, in part, to blur the distinction, this may not have been unintentional. Not all the justices' work was, of course, concerned with crime. The justices of Midlothian (whose jurisdiction was still occasionally contested by the magistrates of Edinburgh) conscientiously laid down rates for wages and prices in 1656,[73] and in the same year James Fowler, who had discovered deposits of silver on the Earl of Sutherland's estate, asked that the JPs of Inverness, Ross and Sutherland be ordered to set all idle men to work on the project.[74]

Whilst the army could do much to ensure that the commission of the peace worked effectively, the system was not, in the short term, proof against the influence of a local magnate who wished to obstruct its authority. Such a one was the Marquis of Argyle, or so, at any rate, Monck was told in May 1657. The accusation came from a 'gentleman in Argyllshire' who fed information on the Marquis's conduct to David Drummond, one of Monck's paid intelligencers, and to Capt. Witter, the governor of Dunstaffnage. The informant maintained that ever since Argyle's return from London, where he had been soliciting the Council of State for financial aid, those of his friends who were on the commission of the peace had failed to perform their duties as justices and had acted as though they wished the authority of the commission to lapse completely.[75] Monck knew full well that the JPs of Argyllshire had been lax in their treatment of criminals long before Argyle returned to the shire,[76] but his increasing dislike of the Marquis caused him to give credence to Drummond's tale. The English had never in fact fully trusted Argyle, but during the years of royalist rebellion his assistance to them had been of such value that they had kept their hostility in check. For the moment, however, peace had been restored and so the régime was reluctant to go on buttressing his power — for this reason Broghill himself had taken steps to ensure that Argyle was chosen neither as a JP nor an MP for the shire,[77] and

Monck was now prepared to settle old scores.

What doubtless made the present incident so annoying to Monck was the fact that the commission of the peace had potentially a vital role to play in lessening the régime's dependence on the Marquis for control over Argyllshire. By enrolling the gentry in the service of the state, it bypassed, and so undermined, his semi-feudal authority. This, at any rate, was the theory; but Argyle's activities in the spring of 1657 showed that the reality was rather different. Through a series of meetings at Inveraray he was endeavouring to consolidate his influence with his friends and neighbours and to find out which of them, if any, held favour with the English, for he was apparently convinced that none could be loyal to him and to the English at the same time. Monck was assured[78] that these efforts by the Marquis to form a party of faithful supporters had a sinister purpose; that at the very least they were designed to impress on the English that Argyle was still a figure of considerable power and influence in Scotland, but that more likely they were a sign that he was preparing, if not to initiate, then certainly to facilitate, an attempt to restore the king. The Marquis's version of these events was, naturally, more straightforward: he stressed that his conferences with neighbouring clans (such as the Macgriggors, Clanranald and, above all, the Macleans) were designed simply to recover debts owing to him,[79] an explanation which accorded well with his known financial difficulties. One of these meetings at which the gentlemen of Argyllshire were present was almost certainly occasioned by Monck's sudden demand that reparation for the losses sustained by the army in Argyllshire in August 1652 should now be paid in full, in accordance with the articles concluded between Major General Deane and the Marquis in October of that year. While it was no doubt true that the Marquis and his followers had for over four years skilfully avoided payment of this sum (estimated by Monck at well over £700 stg.), Monck's decision to resurrect the issue in April 1657[80] was, above all, a symptom of his heightened suspicion of the Marquis's intentions. He might, therefore, have taken some comfort from a report that his peremptory demands had driven a wedge between Argyle and the lairds of Glenorchy and Cawdell who, supported by some other gentlemen, denied liability for an incident of which they had strongly disapproved at the time.[81] The full sum of £700 was probably paid in the course of the next twelve months, but memories of the incident still rankled when, in 1659, Monck bent all his energies to destroying Argyle's credit in London. In March 1659, he enjoined Disbrowe to stop the Marquis from taking his seat in Richard Cromwell's Parliament and from recovering the £12,000 which, he alleged, was owing to him by the state; depositions concerning the affair of 1652 were to be used as ammunition against the Marquis, of whom Monck now said, 'Truly I thinke in his Heart there is noe Man in the three Nations does more disaffect the English Interest than hee.'[82]

Whatever Argyle's true intentions in the spring of 1657, his uneasy relationship with Monck illustrated in acute form the dilemma facing the commander-in-chief in his efforts to preserve peace in the Highlands. As Monck had already recognised in many of his actions since 1654, law and order could not be maintained without the co-operation of the clan chiefs, but a problem arose over how to enrol these chieftains in the task of law enforcement without conceding to them a fair measure of independent power. In practice, Monck was insistent that clan chiefs should exercise control over their followers when the latter were suspected of robbery or other forms of violence. In October 1656, he warned the chief of the Macgriggors that he must stop his men marauding in Argyllshire, and issued strict instructions to Lt. Col. Reade to lay any disturbances caused by the men of Lochaber at the door of the laird of Lochiel. A letter was later sent direct to Lochiel warning him of the penalties for disobedience, and similar warnings were issued to the other chiefs in the region.[83] At the same time, Major John Hill was instructed to 'be very round' with the chieftains of Badenoch and to threaten them with the loss of their goods and livelihood if they did not stop their followers from thieving, while in November the lairds of Glencoe and Cawdell, the Stewart of Appin and several others (including the Earl of Atholl) received stiffly worded letters to the same effect.[84] The chieftains were faced with a simple choice: either they must capture the offenders, or they must suffer themselves. Monck, moreover, was able to name precisely the 'broken men' and robbers he wished to see arrested — one of the fruits, no doubt, of fostering contacts within the local community.

In the Lowlands, too, the army enlisted the help of particular noblemen in its fight against crime. Lord Blantire, for example, who had been named as a JP for Lanarkshire in 1656, was specifically mentioned in July 1658 and again in 1659 in connection with the arrest of thieves and mosstroopers.[85] In 1656, use was made of men with local influence who held office as JPs or sheriffs to control the passage of dangerous and suspected persons between Scotland and Ireland. Although a permit for the crossing could in theory be issued by any sheriff, commissary or two JPs, the opinion of some gentlemen as to the suitability of intending travellers was considered more valuable than others, and for the passage between Kintyre and Ireland the advice of Lord Neil Campbell was particularly requested.[86] Even within the commission of the peace, therefore, some were more useful than others, for the degree of assistance they could lend the army in its peacekeeping role depended on the extent of their local knowledge and power.

Underpinning all these efforts to employ members of the subject nation as policemen, gaolers, judges and spies in their own country was the overriding competence of the English army. At every point in the law enforcement process, the military was on hand to supervise and control the activities of its helpers and to undertake those tasks which armed might alone could perform. The most dangerous and elusive criminals had to be hunted down by armed parties; and the nearer their offence came to the type of unrest which had heralded royalist uprising in the early 1650s, the more likely the army was to intervene at first hand. There was, in fact, no clear distinction between the army's work as 'policemen' and as defenders of the security of the state, for as the English had already found to their cost, the worst forms of violent crime were closely akin to armed rebellion. Thus with or without the help of informers and specially commissioned *vigilantes*,[87] the army continued in the second half of the decade to take stern action against murderers, robbers and mosstroopers; to control the possession of arms and horses; to investigate all hints of mutterings against the régime; and to sift intelligence reports about the activities of Royalists.

Although mosstroopers were almost a dying breed in the more settled atmosphere of the later 1650s, a few continued to cause trouble, in the Borders as well as in Lanarkshire and other areas nearer the Highlands. Perhaps the most notorious case was that of Capt. Wishart, who had been shipped off to the Barbadoes during the late rebellion but had escaped and returned to Scotland in 1655. Reports that he had been seen came in from several quarters, but he eluded his captors until February 1657, when he was finally arrested in Stirlingshire through the offices of two informers whom the army paid handsomely for their pains.[88] Amongst the other criminals who passed through the army's hands — some to go for trial at the circuit courts, others, like the laird of Barfoot,[89] who was accused of hitting an English soldier, destined for a court-martial — were a few whose offences dated back several years. In August 1658, Monck ordered the arrest of John MacKenzie, who had murdered Capt. Powell, governor of Braemar, as long before as 1652, while in January 1658 five persons were arrested for murders committed in 1654.[90]

During these years, strict control continued to be exercised over the use of firearms and the possession of horses above the value of £5 stg. In October 1656 the governors of garrisons in strategic areas were reminded that they should issue permits for horses and for fowling pieces only to those gentlemen whose loyalty to the government was unquestioned, while in November 1656 and again in April 1658, orders were given that special care should be taken over the issuing of licences in the Border counties.[91] In September 1656 a consignment of imported weapons was seized at Fraserburgh; in March 1657 an illegal cargo of gunpowder was seized at Aberdeen, and an iron gun was discovered buried in the sands at Crail; while in November 1657 a cache of arms was uncovered in Elgin.[92] Although Monck's anxiety over these matters was greatest whenever he suspected that agents from the exiled court were present in Scotland, ready to exploit any signs of unrest, he was constantly aware that the unauthorised use of arms and ammunition posed a threat not only to the state but to private citizens as well, for their possession could be an incitement to, and a symptom of, strictly non-political crimes of robbery and violence.

Similarly, unguarded criticisms of the régime voiced in the taverns of the capital might simply betoken an excess of good cheer, or they might mask some underlying conspiracy — hence the close attention which Monck paid to all 'expressions' or 'utterances' against the government. In October 1656 the army took into custody a clergyman named Hamilton who became drunk and disorderly in an Edinburgh tavern one night and declared that he wished to see hanged any Scotsman who did not say he loved his king.[93] Other instances involved persons from various parts of the country: William Buchanan, laird of Drummakiell, was arrested by Col. Thomas Reade, the governor of Stirling, in September 1656;[94] Reade was later required to investigate the case of William Malloch, who had railed against the government while in Edinburgh, but whose companions seemed to come from Clackmannanshire;[95] while at other times suspicion alighted on Alexander Andrew, formerly sub-collector of the excise in Forfarshire, and several unidentified persons in the Borders.[96]

During these years the intelligence system which Monck and Broghill had built up in 1655-6 continued to function efficiently and to provide Monck with information in the light of which he could assess the seriousness of 'utterances' against the régime. From the beginning of 1657 it was clear that whatever interest Charles had once had in his northern kingdom had waned still further, and although rumours still trickled into army headquarters in the spring and summer of 1657 and again in the spring of 1658 that some invasion was being planned from abroad, Monck was confident that the army could deal with any domestic unrest that might ensue.[97] Nonetheless, consistent efforts were made to intercept letters from abroad and to keep tabs on both their carriers and their recipients. Royalist messengers were painstakingly tracked down. In February 1657 two men, one of whom was Alexander Bruce, brother to the Earl of Kincardine, were ordered to be questioned about their entertainment of messengers from abroad, and Bruce was required to lodge a surety of £6000 stg. for his peaceable living before being allowed to travel overseas.[98] Later in the year a search was made for one Dempster, a Jesuit, who was finally run to earth in June in the Canongate, where he was living under the name of Robert Logan.[99] Surveillance was also kept up over those noblemen, chieftains and gentlemen most fitted to head a king's party in Scotland.[100] Several times, moreover, Monck considered sending men of standing like Glencairn or Lorne into exile, most probably to England, to make sure that they were divorced from any likely conspiracy, but this idea was never followed up.[101] Indeed, in the course of 1657 and into 1658 Monck became more and more convinced, as was in fact the case, that such expressions of royalist activity as there were in Scotland, were happily isolated and in no way constituted a real challenge to the army's control over the country. Thus when news of Oliver Cromwell's last illness reached the north in September 1658, he could be sure that there was little chance of royalist sympathisers creating much stir on the death of the Protector.

By ceaseless vigilance and unremitting efforts, therefore, the English army sought to preserve law and order in Scotland. During the period from September 1656 to September 1658, no new methods were introduced, either by the army or by the Council, to help in the work of dispensing justice and preventing or punishing crime. The judicial institutions run by civilians, such as the circuit courts or the commission of the peace, had been set up either before or during Broghill's innovating period as President of the Council; while the techniques employed by the army to coerce and cajole the local community into good behaviour had all been pioneered during, or just after, Glencairn's rising. What Scotland required in these years was, from the English point of view, not a new initiative, but a policy of containment. Old methods, therefore, served very well if applied consistently and efficiently, for the problems they were devised to solve and the dangers they were designed to avert were no longer in a state of flux. The success of these measures is difficult to assess, but the overall impression to be gained from Monck's orders to his officers throughout Scotland and his reports to the government in London is that politically inspired unrest was certainly, and non-political crime was probably, very much on the decrease in these years. In

February 1657, Monck expressed his satisfaction with the way his policies were bearing fruit in the Highlands. He told Thurloe:

> I never had them in that order since I came into Scotland, that I have now and I thinke they will prove pretty firme to His Highnesse, for I finde them very punctuall in observing of any orders for apprehending any broken men or theeves in that country, which I could never bring them too (sic) till now of late.[102]

Several times during this period, Monck had little to tell Thurloe except that 'all things are quiett and well,' and although he occasionally referred to the malignant temper of the Scots,[103] he seemed convinced that the régime was, thanks to the good work of the army, on a sound and stable footing. The truth of his assertions was to be amply demonstrated in the last few months of 1658, when Scotland remained passive after the death of Oliver and calmly accepted the accession of his son Richard.

PART FOUR

THE ARMY IN SCOTLAND AND THE COLLAPSE OF THE REPUBLICAN REGIME, SEPTEMBER 1658 — MAY 1660

Introduction

THE period from the death of Oliver Cromwell on 3 September 1658 until the restoration of Charles II in May 1660 witnessed profound changes in the nature and composition of the government in England, changes which had a significant impact, legally and constitutionally, on the Anglo-Scottish union.

The political turmoils in England, as is well known, went through several phases. For the first few months after Oliver's demise there seemed every chance that the Protectorate would remain secure under his son, but after the summoning of Richard's first Parliament in January 1659 two sets of conflict, the first between the civilian and the army interests, the second between the 'New Cromwellians' and the adherents of the Good Old Cause, enmeshed to disrupt the political scene. By the spring of 1659 the army leaders under Fleetwood, who disliked Richard Cromwell's reliance on civilian 'courtiers', had deemed it politic to make common cause with the anti-Protectorate republicans who, as well as possessing civilian support, had considerable influence among the junior officers of the army. This uneasy alliance succeeded in bringing about the dissolution of Richard Cromwell's Parliament on 22 April, followed by Richard's resignation as Lord Protector, and the recall of the Rump on 7 May 1659. In the course of the summer, controversy grew between the civilian and the military supporters of the new Commonwealth; no agreement could be reached on the precise form the new government should take; and so by the autumn of 1659 the authority of the Rump had been thoroughly undermined. On 13 October the 'Wallingford House' clique of army officers, led by Fleetwood and Lambert, expelled the Rump, and with a few civilian supporters set up a Committee of Safety a fortnight later to cloak their military rule with some vestige of respectability. By December, however, it was clear that the Wallingford House men had failed to carry the whole army with them—the fleet in the Downs, the army in Ireland and the garrison of Portsmouth all sided with the Rump in the course of December. In the country as a whole the new régime was unpopular, its social basis was narrow, its enemies threatened a tax strike and, most significantly of all in the short term, order was visibly collapsing in London. As a result Fleetwood was unable to retain control either over the political situation or the army, and so he resigned his command of the forces to Speaker Lenthall on 24 December. Two days later the Rump resumed its sitting.

The second restoration of the Rump did not, however, mean a speedy return to stability or the quick enforcement of a political settlement, for like the previous régime the Rump was unpopular and lacked broadly based support. Many eyes therefore turned to General Monck, for he alone, with the army in Scotland at his back, seemed to have the power and the authority to produce order out of chaos.

Ever since the expulsion of the Rump in October, Monck had come out strongly in favour of the civilian, especially the parliamentary, interest against the machinations of Fleetwood and Lambert and had been taking steps to ensure that the army in Scotland would support him if he chose to intervene in English politics. By 8 December he had set up his army headquarters at Coldstream, and on 1 January 1660 he began his march on London, probably not at this stage with the intention of restoring the king but certainly with the desire to defend the authority of Parliament. When he arrived in London, however, he formed the opinion that the only way to restore stability was not simply to support the Rump against its detractors, as he had hitherto done, but to insist that those MPs who had been excluded from Parliament by Pride's Purge in 1648 should be readmitted. This having been done on 21 February, the Long Parliament was effectively restored and with it a majority of 'Presbyterians' who favoured a monarchy rather than a republic. In this way Monck made inevitable, even if he had not strategically planned for, the restoration of Charles II. On 16 March 1660 the Long Parliament dissolved itself to allow for the election of a Convention Parliament, which met in April. The strong monarchist majority therein ensured the return of the king, and on 8 May 1660 Charles was duly proclaimed.

The effect of all these tergiversations on the government of Scotland was greater in theory than in practice. Moreover, the impact of events in England takes on a different colour depending on whether one examines the constitutional union between the two countries, the functioning of the central executive in Scotland, or the day-to-day running of the country by the army and other local agencies.

After the death of Oliver Cromwell, the first challenge to the nature of the union between England and Scotland was made in Richard's Parliament by the anti-Protectorate republicans. In an attempt to deprive the 'court' of the support of the Scottish MPs, they argued that since the Humble Petition and Advice, under whose authority this Parliament met, had not spelled out the extent of Scotland's parliamentary representation at Westminster, Scottish MPs had no right to sit there. This attack was beaten off, but the reprieve for the Scottish MPs was short-lived. The restoration of the Rump in April 1659 had a drastic legal and constitutional effect, because it cancelled the Cromwellian Ordinance of Union and so removed the basis for Scottish representation in a combined Parliament. Although a new Bill of Union was considered throughout the summer, the project made no headway before the dissolution of the Rump; thereafter much uncertainty reigned—and was not dispelled by Monck's refusal to let Scots MPs sit in the Convention Parliament—over whether the union should be considered permanently dissolved. All these considerations were, however, somewhat abstract: more immediate in its impact on the administration of Scotland was the lack of a central executive in the north after April 1659. The downfall of the Protectorate deprived existing councillors, judges and revenue officials of authority to act, and despite efforts by the Rump to consider the problem of replacements, no new arrangements were made before October 1659. In that month, Monck spurned attempts by the Council of State to settle the administration of justice, if nothing else, and from then until the Long Parliament addressed itself to the problem in March 1660, no further progress was made. Even when commissioners and judges were appointed by the Long Parliament to take over the civil administration of Scotland, these moves had only a limited effect, for the officials had little time to take up their duties before the return of the king.

None of this meant, however, that while England was in political turmoil Scotland was either ungoverned or ungovernable. What is most striking about the period from September 1658 until May 1660, and what is most crucial for an understanding of the effectiveness of English rule in the north, is the fact that the day-to-day running of the country at the local level continued independently of, almost in isolation from, the political upheavals in England. It is true that at many crucial points the attention of Monck and his colonels, and indeed of the Scots people, was focused on events in the south, to the neglect, perhaps, of Scottish affairs; yet Scotland continued to be governed with relative efficiency, its unruly elements (of whatever political persuasion, or none) kept in check, and order consistently maintained, right up to the proclamation of the king. In large part this was due to the control of the army (even when it had been much depleted by Monck's withdrawal of the bulk of his forces south), and to the success of those peacekeeping measures which the English had gradually worked out in co-operation with the local community since the years of Glencairn's rising. From the standpoint of the Restoration, this stability was significant because it facilitated the return of the king. More importantly, however, in the context of the Interregnum, the state of Scotland in 1659-60 stands forth not as a pointer to the future but as a testimony to the past—as a tribute, that is, to the success, and not the failure, of English republican rule.

11

Continuity and Change under Richard Cromwell and the Rump, September 1658 — October 1659

i. The death of Oliver and stability in Scotland, September 1658 — May 1659

NEWS of Oliver's last illness produced varied reactions in the northern capital in the early days of September 1658. On the 2nd, the councillors and the Judges kept a private day of humiliation to ask the Lord to restore health to His Highness.[1] On the 4th, Scotland's few Anabaptists were reported to have sprung to life in anticipation of the Protector's demise.[2] On the 6th, Monck warned his chief subordinates to 'have a speciall eye over the Scotts' in the event of Cromwell's death and to be on the look-out, too, for 'discontented spiritts' amongst the soldiery; while on the 8th, he ordered several great guns which belonged to the state to be removed from their exposed positions in Leith into the safety of the citadel.[3] This order was issued as news arrived from the Council of State in Whitehall that Oliver's illness had proved fatal and that he had been succeeded by his eldest son, Richard.[4] Letters announcing this fact were accordingly sent off to the several regiments in Scotland, and the town council of Edinburgh was enjoined to attend the proclamation of Richard in the Scottish capital at 10 o'clock on the morning of 10 September.[5]

Richard was proclaimed at the Mercat Cross of Edinburgh, which was richly hung with tapestry for the occasion. The councillors, the Judges, the magistrates and town council of Edinburgh, some army officers and Monck himself were present, as were a few of the Scottish nobility. Soldiers lined the High Street with their colours flying and trumpets sounding, while guns went off from Edinburgh Castle, Leith citadel, and a frigate lying at anchor in Leith Road.[6] Thus speedily, but with some ceremony and no little solemnity, the succession was formally declared, and steps were then taken to ensure that Richard's accession was made known throughout the shires and burghs of Scotland.[7]

Once the formalities had been completed, Monck could turn to the vital task of ensuring that Richard's assumption of power was accepted both by the officers and men under his command, and by the Scots over whom they ruled. In his letter of 6 September and in his formal announcement of Oliver's death on the 8th, he had made it quite clear that he expected his colonels to clamp down on displays of dissent from either quarter, and in the month or so after Cromwell's demise he followed this up by taking further steps to ferret out and suppress any signs of unrest.

The army in Scotland (though not Monck himself) was at this time supposed by some to be faithful to the cause of the Fifth Monarchy men.[8] There had, indeed, been periods throughout the 1650s when radical principles had found favour with the Scottish forces and had momentarily threatened the cohesion of the army, its adherence to the Protectorate and its ability to ensure the stability of the régime. But the two most serious challenges — the 'Overton plot' of 1655[9] and the spread of Quakerism in 1657[10] — had been met by Monck with such firmness and determination that by January 1658 the army in Scotland had been thoroughly purged of all disaffected officers and soldiers.[11] The army's record of conformity with the prevailing mode of government was maintained when, after the dissolution of Parliament in February 1658, Major Packer voiced his opposition to the Protectorate and his adherence to the Good Old Cause. The regiments in Scotland once again toed the protectoral line by sending up addresses of loyalty to Oliver, some of them taking the opportunity explicitly to refute suggestions that the army in Scotland was sympathetic to His Highness's enemies.[12] Thus, up to the time of Oliver's death, Monck's army had ratified every retreat from republicanism and every 'swing to the right' made by the politicians in London. Nonetheless, the suspicion remained that despite their general's timely endeavours, radical dissidence had maintained a toehold amongst the Scottish forces.

Monck, too, may have scented danger beneath the surface calm, for in September or October 1658 he put a ban on all meetings of officers and soldiers designed 'to interpose in public affairs'.[13] Around the same time he and the other officers at headquarters organised the signing of two addresses of loyalty to the new Protector.[14] The first of these was a copy (sent north by Fleetwood) of an address from the 'Armies in England, Scotland, and Ireland' which had been signed on 20 September by 220 commissioned officers meeting at Whitehall.[15] The other, similar in tone to the first, had been drawn up independently by the officers in Edinburgh, and Monck sent it to Cromwell as evidence that the army in Scotland had not waited for promptings from the south before registering its loyalty to him. Copies of the address which had emanated from Whitehall were subsequently sent to and signed by the various regiments throughout Scotland.[16] Such was the apparent unanimity with which these northern forces welcomed the change in government that in late September a captain lately come from England averred: 'the truth is, general Mounck is of that prudence and discretion, that he doth ingage every man that knowes him, willingly and freely to doe that which is fitt.'[17] There were hints in the following month that some officers in Scotland would be glad to see a general besides Richard having the power to grant army commissions,[18] but despite this, at the end of the year Monck was confident of the morale of his army, and of their disinclination to join in the demand for higher pay which was agitating the forces elsewhere.[19]

Concurrent with, but ultimately dependent upon, Monck's efforts to maintain discipline and obedience in the army were his precautions against a renewal of unrest amongst the Scots. The death of Oliver had stimulated hopes, fostered by some of the clergy, that Scotland's fortunes would now improve; but such hopes stemmed more from a belief that the English would fall out amongst themselves than from any plan to foment native insurrection.[20] Monck was nonetheless zealous to prevent emissaries from the exiled court making contact with sympathisers at home, although, in truth, he had little cause for concern. On 21 September, and again on 12 October, he told Thurloe that no letters had reached Scotland from the exiled king. Rumours that some of Middleton's former officers had gathered in Holland to await Charles Stuart's commands likewise failed to perturb him, for he doubted their ability to gather men and money, to win help from a foreign power, or to link up with dissident elements in Scotland.[21] On 20 November, he assured Thurloe (who had been told a month earlier that the king was cultivating a cavalier faction in Scotland) that Charles Stuart had done nothing to promote evil designs in the country.[22] Nonetheless, he was quick to demand that known or suspected Royalists be arrested and questioned, lest they hold correspondence with the king,[23] and to order that a strict watch be kept on the sale of guns and gunpowder, especially in Edinburgh and the Borders.[24]

By December 1658 it was clear that the régime in Scotland was safe from a royalist challenge. Its radical opponents, too, had subsided, for although Quakers and Anabaptists were active in Edinburgh and Leith, their propaganda posed no real threat to the government.[25] For the time being, therefore, the régime seemed politically secure.

During these months problems nonetheless occurred at the administrative level which affected the day-to-day efficiency of government. Ironically, these difficulties were in the main unrelated to Oliver's death. It was indeed the case that many Scotsmen who held civil office seemed reluctant to subscribe an address of loyalty to the new Protector, and that delays were caused by the need to recast the public seals and renew the commissions of all office-holders on Richard's accession.[26] But these technicalities worried Monck and Disbrowe much less than unforeseen events such as the increase in the number of vacancies on the judges' bench. The death of Judge Smyth on 26 September and the sudden illness of Judge Goodyear put the winter sessions, especially the work of the Outer House, in jeopardy and occasioned frequent demands from Monck and Disbrowe that new appointments be made. Whitehall's failure to fill up the vacancies caused some interruption to the administration of justice, for in the winter sessions from November 1658 to February 1659 the remaining Commissioners could deal with only a few cases.

If Oliver's death had only a minimal impact on the efficiency of the civil administration, it did not seriously weaken the control of the army over Scottish affairs either. The evidence for the period between September 1658 and April 1659 is scanty, but what there is would seem to indicate that the army continued to tackle resolutely the type of problem with which it had successfully coped in the past. In addition to his earlier reports after Oliver's death, Monck assured Thurloe in February and March 1659 that the army had never been quieter or in a better condition than it was then, and that he was confident that it could be kept free from political agitation.[27] Its energies, therefore, could be turned to dealing with the

Scots. Its main concern continued to be the maintenance of law and order, and in particular the suppression of theft and unruly behaviour in the Highlands. The incidents it dealt with appear to have been minor, involving the actions of isolated criminals such as Hugh Fraser, a notorious robber, or Neil McLaughlan, a member of Maclean of Duart's household who had shot a public notary in Argyllshire.[28] A report in September 1658 that at least eighteen men were in arms in the hills was the only intimation of a major outbreak of robbery and violence. In this case, Monck took steps to remind local chieftains of their responsibility for maintaining order amongst their clansmen, and also to inform the local gentry and JPs of the need for care.[29] Conditions on the Highland line clearly required constant vigilance: in September 1658 permission was granted to the lairds of Lenzie and Buchanan to maintain armed retainers in Perthshire and Stirlingshire,[30] and passes were granted to individuals to carry arms in the Highlands on the assumption that travellers in that region were more likely to be attacked than in the Lowlands.[31]

At various times the army was called upon to assist the civil power in the execution of its duties, but in no way did these incidents denote widespread civil disobedience by the Scots. Difficulties were experienced in gathering the excise in Fife and Linlithgowshire which required the intervention of the army,[32] and in April 1659 the authority of the sheriff of Bute had to be upheld against the combined challenge of the lairds of Kaimes and Macnaughton.[33] In Orkney, however, the boot was on the other foot, for Sheriff Blair complained to Monck that Captain Watson, whose company was stationed at Kirkwall, was trying to usurp his judicial functions.[34] Such an incident must have displeased Monck greatly (if indeed Watson was to blame), for he was still anxious to maintain good relations and fair dealing between the army and the community.[35]

During the first quarter of 1659, little is known about civilian life in Scotland. The burghs held particular conventions in January and March;[36] circuit courts were held at Stirling, and probably elsewhere, in March;[37] and the supreme court sat, even if it did not transact much business, in January and February.[38] Such scattered references give little idea of how the civil government of Scotland was carried on. By the early spring of 1659, however, it is probable that, while the army continued to perform its peacekeeping functions efficiently, the civil administration was no longer working smoothly. In the higher echelons, there were already problems of manpower (*e.g.* the shortage of judges), and these were probably exacerbated by the election of several senior administrators, including five councillors, to the Parliament then sitting at Westminster. It is unlikely, therefore, that the Council or the Exchequer operated at full strength in these months, and in April Monck warned that unless some of the judges were sent home before 1 June, the summer sessions would be in jeopardy.[39] Paradoxically, few of the shortcomings in the civil administration can be traced *directly* to the build-up of political tension in England. Such difficulties had, to some degree, been experienced before, especially when the Parliament of 1656 had drawn so many officials away to London,[40] and it is only in retrospect that they assume the status of a major run-down in the administration.

The Parliament at Westminster, attendance at which had deprived Scotland of many of its top officials, was important for reasons other than its effect on the Scottish administration. Not only did its sitting bring disruption to the executive in Scotland, but the elections to it gave striking proof of Monck's control over Scottish affairs in the months after Oliver's death. It was quite clear that the government in Scotland had been little weakened by the Protector's death when in December 1658 and January 1659 the elections for representatives to sit in Richard Cromwell's Parliament produced a crop of members overwhelmingly amenable to the English and, more specifically, to the protectoral interest. At the same time, however, there were signs that, in contrast to the elections of 1654 and 1656, 'a number of native Scots were making concerted efforts to be elected',[41] so that Monck and Disbrowe had now to cope with, and eventually control, a greater display of Scottish initiative than ever before.

The Humble Petition and Advice of 1657 had provided that, before its dissolution, Oliver's second Parliament should decide on the proportion of representatives henceforth to be allotted to Scotland; but this had not been done before that body was dissolved on 4 February 1658. In the following December, therefore, the Council of State decided to retain the division of thirty seats (twenty for shires and ten for burghs) that had been set out in the ordinance of 27 June 1654, and on 14 December 1658 the writs, along with three for the Other House addressed to Monck, the Earl of Cassillis and Wariston, were accordingly sent north.[41] These were received in Edinburgh on 21 December[42] but, even before that, steps had been taken to ensure that the constituencies would elect members of whom the Secretary to the Council of State, John Thurloe, and other custodians of the protectoral interest would approve. On the 9th, Disbrowe asked for guidance on several points: should members of the Council in Scotland stand for election; if chosen, should they leave their posts to attend the Parliament; and did Thurloe have any candidates in mind for Scottish seats?[44] On the 17th, however, Monck told Thurloe that two of his most recent recommendations were unlikely to find places, for the question of candidates had already been settled. It had been necessary to make such arrangements at an early stage, for the Scots were intent upon getting members of their own nation elected.[45] Monck reiterated this point in letters of the 28th and 30th, and similar hints were dropped by Disbrowe.[46] Some of the trouble apparently stemmed from the Marquis of Argyle's determination to secure election, for try as they might, the English could not prevent his being chosen. In other cases Monck and Disbrowe were unable to meet Thurloe's demands not because of competition from independently minded Scotsmen, but because they themselves had already given pledges to other government nominees.[47] That some Scotsmen at least were content to make the best of this situation was suggested by Captain Langley, when he wrote: '. . . the Scots choose all For ends, (*i.e.* material advantage) None For love, those they love being the most Ridged and Contrary to the english interest.' It would have been pointless, he went on, to choose 'the most Ridged,' for quite apart from government disapproval, these men would have declined to serve, hating as they did anyone who had correspondence with the English. Disbrowe, too, suggested that self-interest would dictate the choice of members: Scotsmen, he reckoned, would be unwilling to bear the cost of sending a member to Westminster, and so would gladly accept a government nominee willing to pay his own expenses.[48]

It is clear, therefore, that Monck's confident assurances, before and after[49] the elections were held, that the MPs from Scotland would all prove faithful government supporters, masked a situation of some complexity. His assessment had, of course, a double implication, for it was as vital to know how the MPs stood in relation to the great issues agitating English politics as to gauge their commitment or otherwise to Scottish interests. Conversely, although the details of the 28 men who secured election[50] reveal that, as in 1654 and 1656, the English interest had emerged triumphant,[51] this was more a result of the efforts of the protectoral party in England to capture as many 'safe' seats as possible than a reflection of English policy towards Scotland as such.

Of the seventeen Englishmen, six were civilians who owed their nomination to connections with the protectoral party; some of them probably never even saw their Scottish constituencies. The six were Lawrence Oxborough (Forfar and adjacent burghs); Sir Peter Killegrew (Orkney and Shetland); Sir William Wheeler of Westminster (Banffshire); Dr. William Stanes (Dunbartonshire); Edward Sedgewick (Dornoch and adjacent burghs); and Thomas Waller (Linlithgow and adjacent burghs). None of these men had any discernible ties with Scotland and Scottish interests.[52] A seventh, Nathaniel Whetham Jr. (Nairnshire), was a political nonentity, but his father was a member of the Council in Scotland.[53] Dr. Thomas Clarges, who was elected for two groups of burghs, Peebles and Banff, was also in a class of his own, for as well as being approved by Thurloe, he was Monck's brother-in-law, was designated agent for Scottish affairs in London (in which capacity he acted as trusted messenger between Monck and the government in Whitehall), and had been an MP for Scotland in the Parliament of 1656.[54]

The remaining nine Englishmen fall into two categories. The first consisted of serving army officers: Major Ralph Knight (Sutherlandshire), who commanded a troop in Monck's own regiment of horse stationed at Linlithgow; Col. Thomas Fitch (Inverness-shire), governor of Inverness and member for the same constituency in 1656; Lt. Col. Roger Sawrey (Ayrshire), whose regiment was stationed at Ayr; and Major Jeremiah Tolhurst (Dumfries and adjacent burghs), governor of Carlisle and MP for the same seat in 1654.[55] In the second category there were five Englishmen, some of whom held army commissions but whose connections were primarily with the civil administration in Scotland. Four were councillors: Edward Rhodes (Perthshire); Col. Adrian Scroope (Clackmannanshire); Samuel Disbrowe (Midlothian); and Col. Nathaniel Whetham (St. Andrews *and* Edinburgh). Disbrowe, of course, held other offices, and all except Scroope had served in 1656 (Disbrowe also in 1654). A fifth man, John Thompson, who had been elected in 1654, was Auditor-General of the revenues in Scotland and sat for Edinburgh.[56]

The seventeen Englishmen, therefore, were either connected with the civil and military government of Scotland, or else they had friends at court. The eleven

Scotsmen likewise had some record of service to the Protectorate, with the possible exception of Archibald Murray of Blackbarony (Selkirkshire) who in any case declined, on the grounds of poverty, to take his seat.[57] Some were figures who ranked high in the administration: these included John Swinton (Berwickshire); Sir Andrew Kerr of Greenhead (Roxburghshire); George Lockhart (Lanarkshire), who was now Advocate General for Scotland;[58] Sir James Macdowall (Wigtonshire); and John Lockhart (Lanark and adjacent burghs), who had been appointed writer to the privy seal.[59] Swinton, Macdowall and the Lockhart brothers had all served in previous Parliaments, as had the Earl of Linlithgow (Kincardineshire)[60] and the Earl of Tweeddale (Haddingtonshire). The remaining three were Sir Alexander Gibson of Durie (Fife), who had been named as a JP in 1656;[61] Commissary William Ross (Dumfriesshire);[62] and the Marquis of Argyle (Aberdeenshire). Argyle's candidacy was, as we have seen, bitterly resented by Monck, who did all he could to thwart the Marquis's plans for self-advancement during his attendance at Westminster.

If, therefore, one regards Argyle as something of a maverick, one is left with the impression that what virtually all these MPs possessed was reliability. The vast majority had been tried and tested in protectoral politics and administration over the past few years. Despite the argument[63] that office-holders and men of influence might be capable, whatever their nationality, of advancing the interests of their constituents, it is difficult to regard these results as a victory for Scottish interests. Instead, they were at once a triumph for the court party, and evidence of Monck's continuing ability, with the help of a disciplined army, to bend Scottish fortunes to an English will. His achievement was all the greater for having overcome concerted Scottish opposition, of which traces survived in the election of the Marquis of Argyle. By January 1659, therefore, Monck had furnished ample proof of his control over Scottish affairs.

Notwithstanding the nature of the results, some Scots believed it worth while after the elections to furnish their MPs with a list of grievances to be raised in the House. Dr. Clarges, for example, was asked by his constituents to press for a reduction of the cess and the excise, and the easing of other financial burdens.[64] But when the debates in Parliament got under way, no attention was paid to such 'local' issues.[65] Instead, the whole question of Scotland's constitutional position was raised when the right of Scottish members to take their seats in the House came under fire. The ground for complaint was ostensibly that since Scotland's parliamentary representation had not been determined by the Humble Petition and Advice, she was not entitled to send members to Westminster; by implication, therefore, the nature of the union (but not its basic validity) was being called into question. In reality, the issue was one of republican versus protectoral interest, for the subservience of the Scottish members to the court party made their exclusion from the House a prime object of republican policy. The MPs for Scotland had thus become 'as much the object of a further exercise in fruitless factionalism as they were the subject of a determined constitutional challenge', for the issue of Scotland's relations with England had become submerged in the struggle to undermine the Protector's power.[66]

Although the question of the admission of the Scottish members had been broached several times during February,[67] it was not until 8 March that their exclusion was formally moved. Between 8 and 21 March many debates were held on the subject, until on the latter date a motion was carried by 211 to 120 votes that the question be put: thereupon the protectoral interest carried without a division the motion 'that the members returned for Scotland shall continue to sit this present Parliament'.[68] Although the legality of their presence under the Petition and Advice had still not been determined, the Scottish members had thus been given a reprieve. During the debates, several of them had spoken in support of their continuing presence in the House. Only Swinton had appeared to favour the republican suggestion that they withdraw until their constitutional position should be determined.[69] Whether or not such a united front can be construed as 'a substantial manifestation of genuine regard for the interests of Scotland and the future of the union',[70] it was certainly proof that the members for Scotland could be relied on to support the protectoral interest.

Such, then, was the nature of the Parliament which claimed the attendance of many senior members of the administration in Scotland. Administrative difficulties were to worsen when that Parliament ceased to sit. When Monck wrote to Thurloe on 14 April demanding the return of Wariston, Swinton and Lawrence to the judicial bench,[71] he was not to know that the dissolution of Richard Cromwell's Parliament on the 22nd, and the subsequent collapse of the Protectorate, would throw the English executive in Scotland into chaos. The civil administration was not to recover from its winter doldrums. Instead, as commissions granted to senior officials under the Protectorate lapsed, and the restoration of the Long Parliament cancelled the Cromwellian Ordinance of Union, Scotland's constitutional and administrative position was again thrown into the melting-pot. But if, in legal terms, chaos ensued, anarchy did not. Despite the absence of civil justice, the army maintained order and stability in Scotland, and thus provided the base from which Monck could march south to restore stable conditions in England.

ii. The restoration of the Rump and the collapse of the executive in Scotland, May 1659 — October 1659

For a fortnight after the dissolution of Parliament on 22 April, it was not clear what form the next government would take. As late as 3 May, Monck, who had been kept reasonably well informed by Fleetwood and the officers at Wallingford House, as well as by Thomas Clarges, of the army's recent proceedings, did not appear to realise that the collapse of the Protectorate was imminent.[72] When he did receive word that the army had effected the deposition of Richard and the restoration of the Rump,[73] he wrote to Fleetwood registering his and his officers' approval of the late transactions and echoing the sentiments expressed by the general council of officers in their Declaration of 6 May.[74] On the same day, 12 May, he also wrote to the Speaker signifying his army's allegiance to the Rump and expressing the hope that 'the measure of their Authority . . . (would) be adequate to the Nature and being of a Commonwealth'.[75] Monck's reasons for acting in this way were complex. His own opinion regarding the dissolution of Richard Cromwell's Parliament had not been entirely favourable, but at a specially convened meeting of officers at Edinburgh he appears to have learned that some of his subordinates had been 'wrought upon' by fellow-officers writing from London, in favour of restoring the Rump.[76] Perhaps to pacify them, or perhaps because of his own belief that the only thing to do with a *fait accompli* was to make the best of it, he decided, once the full story was known, to promise his adherence to the new régime and to send letters of support to Fleetwood and the Rump. Whatever Monck's own feelings, therefore, the fact remained that the army in Scotland had once more ratified a political *bouleversement* in England.

Monck's address to Parliament was well received when it was read in the House on 18 May.[77] On this day, the House also set about regulating Scotland's position vis-à-vis the commonwealth of England, for the restoration of the Rump meant that all proceedings regarding the Union which had taken place since April 1653 were legally cancelled. The ordinance of union of April 1654 was therefore null and void. On the 18th, the House referred the matter to a committee of the Council of State, who were to prepare a Bill for Union on the basis of Parliament's Declaration of 25 March 1652.[78] On 31 May this committee, which included Archibald Johnston of Wariston, duly took the matter into consideration and on 13 June recommended that an old Bill for Union, which had twice before been read in Parliament, should be taken up again.[79] But the House declined to take this advice, and on 25 June ordered a new Bill to be prepared.[80] This was read twice, after which it was referred to a committee of the whole House.[81] This committee sat eleven times in the course of August, September and the first week of October 1659, but it had not completed its deliberations when on 13 October the Rump was forcibly dissolved by the army.[82] The circumstances of 1653 were thus repeated, for once again failure to achieve a political settlement in England prevented the union of Scotland and England from receiving legislative sanction.

While the nature of the union was being debated by Parliament and the Council of State throughout the summer of 1659, it provoked little comment from the Scots themselves. On 24 May, Parliament was presented with an address from those deputies who had consented to the union in 1652, but its contents were vague, and demanded only that the union should be perfected in accordance with the parliamentary declarations of 1651 and 1652.[83] Only the leaders of the various religious groupings, including the Protesters and Resolutioners, made a determined effort to have their views represented in London. James Sharp, the Resolutioner spokesman, was present in the capital and anxiously watching the course of events, for he feared that Richard's downfall would cause the Protesters' star to rise in Whitehall. At the end of May he suffered the personal indignity of being hauled before the Council of State on suspicion of being implicated in a royalist plot.[84] Under interrogation, Sharp himself remained noncommittal about the religious aspects of the union, while the views of the other parties were, as he told Robert Douglas in Edinburgh, rather confused. Argyle and Wariston, for example, were in favour of 'the liberty of Presbyterian Government', with Argyle especially being vehemently opposed to the demand for religious toleration which he professed to discern in the petition from the deputies of 1652.[85] Sharp's main fear, however, seemed to be that these disputes would leave the way open for Patrick Gillespie to achieve a settlement in favour of his supporters, but by 7 June he was hopeful that Monck's intervention would check the Protesters' designs.[86] At the end of the month, Sharp was ordered to return to Edinburgh; early in July he made preparations for his journey in the belief that the current religious settlement would remain unchanged for some time.[87]

The controversy did not end there, however. Debates on the extent of the toleration to be granted in the new Bill held it up at the committee stage over the next few weeks. On 27 July a petition from the 'gathered churches' in Edinburgh and surrounding districts was presented to Parliament. It begged that the petitioners should be admitted to a share in 'those Gospel priviledges that the truly godly in England contend for' and that the new Bill of Union should safeguard them from interference by the presbyterian church in Scotland.[88] Apparently an attempt was made to insert a proviso to this effect into the Bill, for on 26 August the clause was attacked in committee by a staunch supporter of the presbyterian interest.[89] The issue remained unresolved, however, when Parliament was dissolved on 13 October.

Worrying as this aspect of the debate on the union was to the religious interests in Scotland, it was not a matter which profoundly affected the administration of the country. Much more serious in Monck's eyes, and more remarked on by Scots commentators, was the suspension of the Scottish Council and of judicial proceedings in Scotland. Although the commissions of the senior officials could have been renewed on an *ad hoc* basis and the structure of the central executive decided upon independently of the debate on the union, the two issues in fact went hand in hand, with the result that vital administrative details were not completed until the Bill for Union was in its final committee stages. Instructions for the commissioners of Parliament who were to replace the Council in Scotland had, in particular, to await settlement of the nature of the union. As a result, when the Bill for Union lapsed with the dissolution of Parliament, Scotland was still without a formally constituted central executive.

Discussion about the commissioners who were to be sent to Scotland had gone on in a general way ever since the Bill for Union had been taken into consideration by Parliament and the committee of Council. In July, Wariston reported much speculation amongst the English councillors and army officers on who should be sent north: Cols. Cooper and Kelsey, Sir James Harrington, Major Salwey, Alexander Brodie and Wariston himself were variously mentioned.[90] In August, Monck, who was becoming increasingly impatient at the delays in settling the government of Scotland, was assured that commissioners would be arriving soon, but not until 9 September did Parliament order the Council of State to peruse the instructions which had been drafted for the commissioners in 1651 and make some report.[91] By 15 September a new list of instructions had been drawn up which reflected the change in circumstances since 1651 but did not differ in essentials from the earlier draft.[92] The main differences lay in the clauses relating to finance — here the draft of 1659 accepted the reforms and innovations of the Council in Scotland over the past four years — but those clauses dealing with religion were very similar to the earlier model. As in 1651, a large degree of toleration was to be extended to the Scottish people, for the commissioners were instructed to pay stipends to such ministers or public preachers as were of pious life and conversation, well affected to the commonwealth, and suitably qualified to preach the Gospel. At Wariston's behest, one other change was made which confirmed the experiences of the last few years: a clause which sought to promote conformity between English and Scots law was omitted from the article dealing with courts of justice. On the whole, however, Wariston was scandalised at the speed with which these instructions passed the Council: it troubled him 'to see the poor nation so contemned and trampled upon, people not caring what they doe with it or to it . . .'[93] On 5 October the instructions were reported to and read in Parliament; whereupon the House referred it back to the Council to recommend persons fit to be commissioners.[94] There the matter lay when Parliament was dissolved on the 13th.

The failure to appoint parliamentary commissioners meant, in turn, that the settlement of justice in Scotland was delayed, for the two matters had come to be regarded as interdependent. On 19 May, the Committee of Safety had recommended to Parliament that an act be passed authorising the Commissioners for the Administration of Justice, the Commissioners of the Exchequer, and other judicial officers in Scotland who had been in office on 6 May last, to continue in their places until new commissions should be sent by authority of Parliament; but the House rejected this advice and referred the matter of judicial administration in Scotland to a committee of the Council.[95] For some time thereafter it was assumed that the granting of new commissions would be a matter for the parliamentary commissioners for Scotland, when and if they were ever appointed.[96] But in the course of the summer, and under promptings from Monck, Parliament and the Council occasionally considered the administration of justice in Scotland, in emergency fashion, as a subject in its own right.[97] On 9 September Parliament took this further and asked the committee which had been appointed to peruse the commissioners' instructions to consider also whether further instructions, or even a Bill, should be prepared to deal with judicial matters.[98] The Council debated this topic on 20 September and 4 October, by which date it had decided that a Bill should be prepared 'to settle Judges and other officers of justice in Scotland'.[99] On 5 October, when the commissioners' instructions were read in Parliament, the House ordered the Council to consider the names of persons fit to be Judges.[100] Thus far had the matter gone by 13 October.

It is clear, therefore, that since the restoration of the Rump there had been no sitting of the supreme judicatory in Scotland. This lack of justice was much lamented by Scots commentators, some of whom depicted the summer of 1659 as being 'without all law', a time when 'there were no judicatures in Scotland, no exercise of justice by any courts, supreme or inferior'.[101] Despite these sweeping statements, it does seem, however, that the burgh courts continued to function throughout the period and that sheriff courts remained in being until at least mid-July.[102] The position of the sheriffs had initially been regulated by an Act of Parliament of 11 May, which authorised justices of the peace and sheriffs in England, Scotland and Ireland to remain in and exercise the powers of their respective offices; but on 7 July a further declaration was issued which stated that this authority did not extend to the hearing of civil causes by sheriffs in Scotland. Until then, reported Nicoll, the sheriffs had held courts and given out decreets, but they ceased doing so when, around 15 July, they received word of the new declaration.[103]

Some sheriffs may nonetheless have continued to administer criminal justice of sorts after they had ceased to deal with civil actions: in September Lt. Col. Mann informed Monck that the sheriff of Inverness-shire had tried and sentenced a man to death for setting fire to a barn containing corn.[104] In the summer months local constables also were playing their part in thief-catching and peacekeeping,[105] and the justices of the peace existed in more than name only. Scattered references in Monck's warrant-book show that JPs were expected to exercise the duties of their office between May and September. In June the JPs of the shires of Stirling and Clackmannan were asked to assist in the arrest of some coalhewers who had run away from the mines in Linlithgowshire; in July two army majors were ordered, in their capacity as JPs, to examine someone suspected of spreading false and scandalous reports; while other entries showed that in August the JPs of Dumfriesshire were actively keeping the peace in their districts and that their colleagues in Galloway were being called to the assistance of the collectors of the excise.[106] It is unclear, however, whether regular quarter sessions were held during these months. The effectiveness of the JPs was further limited by the fact that the judges of the supreme court, who were currently without valid commissions, could not go on circuit that summer. This meant that JPs and other officers were unable to produce men accused of serious crimes before the circuit courts, and so dangerous criminals, while they could be caught, could not be tried.

In the short term, however, it was more vital for the peace of the country that malefactors should be sought out and apprehended than that they should be subjected to the full process of the law. The activities of the JPs and other civilian officials therefore played an important part in keeping Scotland free from any major outbreaks of disorder in the summer of 1659; but undoubtedly their efforts were secondary to those of the army. As the Council of State recognised in a placatory letter to Monck of 17 August, it was largely due to his faithfulness and diligence that Scotland had hitherto been kept quiet.[107] Had it not been for the army's continuing grip on the country and its suppression of disorder, Scotland might have produced symptoms of unrest similar to Booth's rising in England. As it was, Monck and the army performed their peacekeeping role successfully in two related spheres, in the detection of ordinary crimes of theft and violence and in the prevention of royalist unrest.

From May to October 1659, the army dealt with several cases of robbery. These included sheepstealing in Argyllshire in May;[108] the theft of cattle from the Earl of Airlie in June or July;[109] and large-scale outbreaks of thieving in Nithsdale,

Annandale and Perthshire during August and September.[110] Incidents such as these became more serious when the robbers were armed, as was the case in Perthshire,[111] and so Monck was swift to clamp down on the activities of mosstroopers — some of whom re-appeared in Lanarkshire and the Border counties in July[112] — lest their presence lead to fresh outbreaks of violence. In June he reported that about a dozen men had taken up arms around Glasgow and Stirling, but that he was confident of quashing them soon.[113] In August he told the Council of State that as many as 80 rogues had got together in the Highlands to steal cattle,[114] and in September Lt. Col. Mann warned him from Inverness that upwards of 20 men were roaming the district robbing at will. Mann's solution to the problem was to summon all the gentlemen of the name of Frazer and remind them of their collective responsibility for the behaviour of their clansmen; similar measures were to be taken with the Macintoshes, one of whom had joined with the marauding Frazers.[115]

The danger to the peace of the country which such incidents could pose was shown by other reports in the month of September. These emphasised the close connection between criminal behaviour and political unrest, of which Monck himself had been acutely aware when he shaped the army's peacekeeping policy after 1654. On 5 September Major Hill reported from Inverlochy that William Ferguson of Inveray and the laird of Scellitor had come out in arms for the cause of Charles Stuart. Although Hill was confident that other, more loyal, Highlanders could be induced to seek out and arrest the miscreants, he observed that they might nonetheless be joined in arms by a few thieves.[116] A week later Hill wrote to Monck about another instance of unrest, when Daniel Maclean of Brolos gathered together a party of twenty or so armed men in Mull. This attempt, which appeared to be politically motivated, had proved even less successful than the first, and again it was clear that other members of the clan were disposed to behave more peaceably.[117]

These incidents pointed several morals. First, they indicated that conditions in Scotland were not altogether tranquil: although there was no question of a serious challenge to the army's control of the country, there was nonetheless an increasing number of incidents towards the end of the summer involving fairly large groups of men and having a distinct political tinge, which threatened the peace of the commonwealth. Secondly, it was clear that these disturbances could derive strength from non-political criminal activity in the Highlands, as had been the case during Glencairn's rising. And thirdly, there were signs that some elements in Scotland were responsive to political developments in England. Hill reported that Ferguson of Inveray and Forbes of Scellitor had heard of the stirs in England and had aimed to be the first in Scotland to rise for the king, while in the aftermath of Brolos' attempt, steps were taken to inform the Highlanders of the failure of royalist designs in England, so that they might be discouraged from making similar plans in Scotland.

What mattered in the end, though, for the stability of the régime in Scotland was not that these symptoms of unrest had arisen, but that they were kept under control. In this respect, the various measures which Monck took in the course of the summer to forestall political, and more particularly royalist, unrest, had an important role to play, for together with the normal means of law enforcement employed by the army (such as the use of chieftains and loyal clansmen to keep watch on their fellows) they helped to prevent the disturbances of late August and September from assuming dangerous proportions.

In the measures which he took to counter the Royalists, Monck frequently acted on instructions from Whitehall. On this issue, the Council of State was anxious to secure Monck's co-operation, for indifferent as they were to Scotland's (and the general's) interest in the Bill for Union and the settlement of justice, the authorities in England were alive to Scotland's significance for the security of the commonwealth. On 17 May Monck had signified the dual role of his army and of the Scottish nation in this respect, when he assured the Committee of Safety that not only were the forces unanimous in support of the recent changes, but that the Scots too would be kept in good order and prevented from making contact with the king.[118] Shortly thereafter, the newly formed Council of State warned Monck of royalist designs in various parts of the country and asked him to be on his guard against Malignants in Scotland. This was followed at the end of May by a specific request to him to arrest and interrogate anyone suspected of contriving a royalist plot.[119] During June and early July, Monck was careful to search out any private stores of arms, particularly in Lanarkshire, and to examine persons accused of making speeches hostile to the commonwealth.[120] In mid-July these efforts were stepped up on orders from the Council. Monck was requested to take an engagement from all those in Scotland who had previously given bonds for their peaceable living, to the effect that they would not act against the commonwealth or do anything to aid Charles Stuart's cause; anyone refusing to give such parole was to be imprisoned forthwith. In addition, he was asked to implement a set of instructions which had been issued to the militia and army troops in England; these included orders to prevent or disperse sporting meetings, to seize arms and horses belonging to suspected individuals, and to keep a watch on strangers and suspicious meetings of all kinds.[121]

In the last week of July and the beginning of August, Monck set about putting these orders into effect. On 25 July he sent word to the governors of garrisons and the chief officers of the regiments in Scotland, informing them of the instructions which had been issued to their counterparts in England regarding meetings and the possession of arms and horses.[122] Then, on 28 July, he held a council of war at Dalkeith at which the issue of tendering the engagement to known Royalists was discussed. The form of the engagement was agreed upon and a circular letter despatched to the various commanding officers explaining the procedure to be followed.[123] The gentlemen under suspicion (a list of whose names was appended to the letter) were to be summoned to appear at the nearest garrison on 16 August; should they refuse to take the engagement, they were to be imprisoned, and even if they subsequently recanted they were not to be released until they had given in bonds of good security, the sums demanded ranging from £12,000 for Glencairn and Lorne to £500 for minor characters such as Col. George Keith and the future troublemaker in Mull, Daniel Maclean of Brolos. The engagement was obviously tendered ahead of time in some cases, for on 12 August Lt. General David Leslie, Sir James Lumsden and Col. James Hay were sent as prisoners to Edinburgh Castle for refusing it, while around the same date the Earls of Loudoun, Callander and Kelly, the Earl Marischal, Viscount Kenmore, the Marquis of Montrose and Lords Lorne, Napier and Dudhope were imprisoned in various garrisons throughout the country.[124] On 11 August the Earls of Glencairn and Rothes and Lord Montgomery subscribed to the engagement, possibly after a short period of imprisonment. By 7 September they had been joined in their assent by Dudhope and the Earl Marischal, both of whom were presumably released from prison thereafter, and by the Earl of Seaforth (who also had been in prison), the lairds of Glengarry and Lochiel, Col. George Keith and Lord Ogilvy.[125] Of the other names on the original list, only Maclean of Brolos is definitely known to have taken up arms against the commonwealth. The rest presumably took the engagement (as McNaughton intended) or else suffered imprisonment (as did Major James Livingstone and Major Charles Erskine), but the fate of Lord Reay, Col. Gilbert Stuart and Macleod of Dunvegan is uncertain.[126] On 20 September the Council of State wrote to Monck informing him that he could set free all those against whom no definite charge could be brought as long as they had given their parole, or some good security, or both.[127] As well as attending to these duties, in August Monck also implemented his instructions concerning the possession of arms and horses and kept tabs on persons accused of speaking 'divers words of dangerous consequence'.[128]

The authorities in England were well satisfied with the success of these measures and congratulated Monck on keeping Scotland quiet during the period of Booth's rising in England.[129] Gloomy observers in Scotland had believed that the Scots were only too anxious to join in the royalist or presbyterian plots of the English conspirators and had feared that 'we shall not only see their teeth, but feel them bite when they can'.[130] But pessimistic forecasts from Cornet Baynes that 'horrible outrages and inhuman cruelties would be acted in the midst of us' proved less accurate in the end than the Earl of Rothes' comment in September that there was 'no appearance but of the Injoyeinge of peace in this nation'.[131] Thus, by the early autumn of 1659 Monck and his officers had given proof of their ability to maintain law and order and to perform, in harness with the civilian population, the basic functions of government at a time when the machinery of civil administration had broken down. The absence of the top layer of the administration, in the form of the Council, the Judges and the Commissioners of the Exchequer, had not prevented the enforcement of law or, indeed, the raising of revenue, from taking place at grass-roots level. Parliament and the Council of State had contributed to this continuity by authorising local officials such as JPs, sheriffs and commissioners of assessment[132] to remain in office despite the delays in providing a central executive. But basically the credit for maintaining stability must go to the army, for it was the military who supervised the activities of local officials, who provided the ultimate bulwark against disorder and whose vigilance prevented royalist sympathisers from giving vent to their discontent. Yet the achievements of the summer of 1659 were not simply the product of Monck's diligence in these months; they were a tribute also to the success of those administrative and peacekeeping measures which the army and the Scottish Council had developed since 1655. The stability of Scotland in 1659 was thus the result of a cumulative effort by the English authorities to consolidate their hold on the country through measures of conciliation and co-operation with the local community as well as by military control. The importance of a powerful army in ensuring peace in Scotland was one lesson to be drawn from the summer of 1659; but the events of the following winter were to show that even when that military force was greatly reduced, the country could still remain free from major outbreaks of unrest.

12

The Army and the Downfall of the Republican Régime, October 1659 — May 1660

IN October 1659, the republican administration in Scotland entered upon its final phase, a phase during which the uncertainties of English politics were to dominate Scottish affairs. Although Monck's forces did not cross the Tweed until 1 January 1660, for the preceding three months the attention of the General and his officers was largely concentrated on events in England. Very soon after the expulsion of the Rump, it became clear that Monck would not only declare his allegiance to Parliament but would take positive steps to uphold its authority. Much of what he and his forces did between October and December 1659 was therefore designed to facilitate armed intervention in the south. What matters for the present study, however, is not the intricate details of the triangular relationship between Monck, the army in England and Parliament, nor Monck's part in restoring the king, but the effect of these actions on the government of Scotland. From this point of view the period from October 1659 to May 1660 falls naturally into two parts: the period from mid-October to December 1659 when Monck and his army were still in Scotland but intent on preparations for departure; and the period from January to May 1660 during which Major General Sir Thomas Morgan assumed command of the forces remaining in Scotland, and the country, though relieved of the bulk of its conquerors, waited quietly for the return of the king.

i. Preparations for the march into England, October — December 1659

From mid-October to December 1659 Monck pursued three related lines of action: he engaged in a pamphlet battle, and in negotiations, with the army in England; he took steps to ensure the support of his own army for the cause of Parliament; and he involved the Scots in measures to support his army's march into England and to ensure stability in Scotland during his absence.

In the war of words between the armies in England and Scotland which began after the expulsion of the Rump, Monck came out as a staunch defender of the civilian, and in particular the parliamentary, interest against what seemed to be a bid for power by an influential section of the army in England. Some inkling of Monck's views on the right relationship between the civil and the military power had already been given in September, for he had then refused to endorse the claims by Lambert and his colleagues, fresh from their success in quelling Booth's rising, to represent the Good Old Cause, and to conduct the affairs of the army free from civil interference.[1] After the interruption of the Rump it therefore came as no surprise when Monck declared himself ready to defend the liberty and authority of Parliament 'to the last drop my bloud' and made it clear, in letters to the Speaker, to Fleetwood and to Lambert, that he would if necessary employ the forces under his command to uphold the cause of Parliament.[2] In the last two weeks of October, messages flew thick and fast between Monck and his officers on the one hand, and Lambert, Fleetwood and the officers at Whitehall on the other, in which the latter sought repeatedly to justify their recent actions by claiming that the Rump had threatened the liberties of the people, while Monck stood equally firmly by his defence of Parliament.[3] Despite this seeming intransigence, Monck nonetheless responded favourably at the end of the month to a suggestion from Fleetwood that he should send representatives from the Scottish army to negotiate a settlement with the army in England.[4] Such a move was in fact welcome to both sides, because each needed time to consolidate its strength — Lambert's forces were reckoned less powerful than their putative strength of 12,000 might indicate, while Monck was inferior in numbers to Lambert and still unsure of the cohesion of his army.[5] At a Council of War in Edinburgh on 3 November, Fleetwood's offer was therefore taken up and three commissioners were appointed to treat with Lambert and Fleetwood.[6]

The results of the negotiations which then took place between the two parties were not at first sight favourable to Monck, for on 15 November his commissioners consented to an agreement which on several vital points went clearly contrary to his instructions, and to his views on the army's role in the state.[7] On the three important matters of the return of Parliament, the drafting of a new constitution, and the appointment of officers in the Scottish army, the commissioners agreed to formulae which gave much greater weight to the wishes of the English army leaders than Monck's defence of the civilian and parliamentary interest would allow. Monck and his trusted subordinates were despondent at news of this agreement, but it was not politic at that time for them summarily to repudiate it. Not only was there a desire to delay armed conflict with brother-officers as long as possible but, on a more practical level, more time was needed to organise the Scottish army for a march into England.[8] Therefore at the end of November and in the midst of further acrimonious exchanges between Monck and Fleetwood and Lambert, fresh instructions were issued to five commissioners — the three former plus two new ones — to resume negotiations. These were set to take place at Newcastle sometime after 7 December.[9] But although some talks took place at Alnwick between Monck's representatives and those of Lambert,[10] formal negotiations had not begun before the position of the army leaders in England had been so eroded that the need for an agreement was removed. December saw the downfall of the Wallingford House men. Pressure from those sections of the army which remained loyal to the Rump had gradually undermined their position, while in the last few weeks the country, and especially London, had been drifting towards anarchy.[11] Monck had been since mid-October in contact with the supporters of his cause in England and elsewhere, but in the event he did less to effect Fleetwood and Lambert's downfall than the innate unpopularity and tactical stupidity of the military clique.[12] Now, however, he was hailed by many (although not, ironically enough, by the restored Rumpers)[13] as the key to the restoration of stability, for he alone had the power and authority to impose order and enforce a political settlement. On 1 January 1660 he therefore began his march on London.[14]

If the circumstances which propelled Monck to the forefront of English politics were not entirely of his own making, the readiness of his army to march with their General did owe much to his efforts. For concurrently with the paper war against Fleetwood and Lambert, Monck had waged a vigorous campaign to root out all signs of disaffection amongst his soldiers. It was not the case that the officers and men of the Scottish army had from the first been unanimous in support of their General's stand for Parliament; cohesion and fidelity among the troops was won only at the cost of many dismissals and desertions. The initial unease felt by many officers thus gives the lie to the expressions of solidarity which Monck's early letters and declarations contained, but such propaganda was itself a powerful weapon in promoting the unanimity which Monck so desired.[15] By December 1659, by a mixture of coercion and persuasion, Monck had won the support of the Scottish forces for the cause of Parliament and his own designs, and so had achieved his second major objective of these months.

Between October and December 1659, Monck undertook an at times drastic remodelling of the army in Scotland, but the material on which he worked had already been affected by the Rump Parliament's attempted reorganisation of the forces between June and September. The Rump's instrument for this work had been the recently appointed committee for nomination of officers. This committee of seven, whose task it was to scrutinise the granting of all commissions, represented an attempt to subordinate the army to the Rump, but time was to show that its three civilian members, Vane, Hesilrige and Ludlow, were dominated by the four army representatives, Lambert, Disbrowe, Fleetwood and Berry.[16] Its attempts to tamper with the Scottish forces were bitterly resented by Monck, who even threatened to resign over the issue. Twice he wrote forceful letters to the Speaker asking that the officers of the Scottish army should remain unchanged, and although Parliament rebuked him for his interference, it nonetheless took steps to moderate the committee's zeal.[17] In the event, every regiment of horse and foot in Scotland suffered some change in its officers, but only five were drastically altered. In regard to his own regiments, Monck's pleas were particularly effective, for the committee resolved to make only minimum changes to their composition.[18]

It was of some significance for Monck's future plans that many of these changes were made too late to take practical effect before the breach came between the army in England and Parliament. One factor affecting the Scottish situation was that officers serving in Scotland were to receive their commissions from the commissioners whom Parliament was to appoint to replace the Scottish Council. Since these officials never took office during the lifetime of the Rump, many changes in the composition of Monck's forces were therefore delayed.[19] Nonetheless, the work of the committee for nomination of officers did pose problems for Monck when he came to review the political stance of his forces in October 1659. Many of the recent appointments proved to be of men who sided with the army leaders rather than with Parliament, for the Rump had been hoodwinked by the army representatives on the nominating commission into accepting men inimical to the civilian interest.[20] Even if such appointees had not received their commissions, and even if, like many officers in Monck's army, they were absent from their posts in Scotland, they had still to be dismissed from the army and replacements found for them before Monck could march a strong, united force south to the defence of Parliament. This task was therefore an important element in the remodelling of the army which Monck undertook on hearing of the expulsion of the Rump.

By October 1659, the army in Scotland consisted of three regiments of horse, one of dragoons, and ten regiments and a few companies of foot.[21] As soon as he received word of Parliament's interruption, Monck took steps to ensure the fidelity of the three regiments of foot, including his own, which were stationed in or near Edinburgh. The other foot regiments were remodelled in the course of October and November, as soon as emissaries from Monck could reach their far-flung quarters.[22] The regiments of horse were likewise remodelled in these months, but here the changes were necessitated by Monck's weakness in cavalry as well as by political dissidence. Out of the three regiments of horse and one of dragoons currently in Scotland, he contrived to mould four regiments of horse, all decently officered. This involved changing round several officers from one regiment to another to fill up vacancies and to compensate for desertions. It also required the transformation of Morgan's four troops of dragoons into six full troops of horse. The systematic remodelling of the horse began early in November, after Major General Morgan had arrived in Edinburgh.[23] Morgan had been absent from Scotland since 1657, having been appointed second-in-command of the expeditionary force in Flanders. Although he had returned to England in the autumn of 1658 after successfully acquitting himself at the battle of the Dunes, he had been unable to resume his command in Scotland because of illness. In October 1659 he was laid up in York with gout, and it was only by disguising his sympathies for Monck's cause that he was able to escape from the hostile Lilburne and make his way north. Once in Scotland he declared openly for Monck, and his adherence to their cause was much welcomed by the army there. Soon after his arrival he set about reorganising the horse with some vigour and was joined in this task by Adjutant General Smith.[24] Although there were only three regiments of horse to deal with, their task was not a simple one.[25] The general shortage of officers caused by dismissals, desertions and absenteeism necessitated a good deal of rearrangement among the remaining officers. In this respect Monck's own regiment of horse suffered most heavily, since many of its officers were transferred to other regiments to make up their strength.[26] Overall, of course, many vacancies were filled vertically, by promotion from within the regiment. Deficiencies in the ranks, which reflected a widespread shortage of manpower, were filled by divers means, including the mounting of foot soldiers. Undermanning in the foot regiments, in turn, was met in part by recruiting from amongst the Scots, although the extent to which this was done was much exaggerated by propagandists in England.[27]

Despite all these expedients, the four regiments of horse and ten regiments of foot available to Monck were almost certainly under strength. By the beginning of December, around one hundred and forty officers and non-commissioned officers had either deserted or been dismissed. Transfers and promotions could not make up for these losses — so much so, in fact, that Monck was induced to ask Clarges to find some officers in London and ship them to Scotland by sea — but at the same time Monck stalwartly refused to swell the ranks by arming more Scots.[28]

To offset these disadvantages, Monck could, however, count on several positive factors. Despite the arrears which were due to the army in Scotland,[29] his forces could expect to be paid for some months to come, for Monck had to hand various supplies of ready cash. In June Parliament had laid an assessment of £6000 per month on Scotland for the next twelve months and had ordered the total to be paid in two moieties, one on 1 August 1659, the other on 10 October. Monck had, however, put back the dates on which payment was due in order to ease the burden on the poverty-stricken Scots, so that as he prepared for his march into England he could rely on some of this money being gathered in. In August the Council of State had also granted a payment of £20,000 to Monck to tide him over until the cess for 1659-60 was collected, and so he could count on this sum too to bolster his finances.[30] In addition, customs and excise duties were still being gathered in and attempts were made to ensure the payment of other branches of the public revenue.[31] Baillie asserted that at the end of the year Monck had £50,000 stg. in his treasury;[32] even if this were an exaggeration, prompt payment of the forces looked like being one of Monck's major advantages over Lambert.

Apart from the £20,000 granted by Whitehall, the collection of these sums to pay the Scottish forces depended on the army's ability to retain control over the Scottish community. But for broader reasons than the supply of his army, such control was essential to Monck, for unless he could maintain order and stability in Scotland he could not withdraw the bulk of his forces into England. Nor indeed could he convince opinion in England that he was not selling the pass by surrendering Scotland to the Royalists.[33] Thus while he strove to wage a paper war against Lambert and Fleetwood and to effect the solidarity of his own army, Monck also took steps to ensure the tranquillity of Scotland. The measures he adopted were in many ways a logical extension of his peacekeeping policy since 1655, for they displayed a careful balance of consultation and co-operation on the one hand, with the assertion of continuing military control on the other.

Monck's plans for the government of Scotland during his absence belong more to the realms of police work than administration, for the collapse of the formal machinery of government continued in the winter of 1659/60 despite an attempt by the Council of State in its dying days to settle the administration of justice. At first the Council had been unwilling to contemplate such a step, but on 25 October, prompted by a petition from the city of Edinburgh, they ordered a letter to be sent to Monck authorising those Judges, Commissioners of the Exchequer, sheriffs and commissaries who had been in office at the last meeting of their courts to hold the next law term from 1 November. Monck refused, however, to recognise the Council's authority and complained that he had not received his orders from a lawfully constituted Parliament.[34] Thus, in his plans for the settlement of Scotland he chose to deny himself the support of the normal processes of law. Instead he relied heavily on the efficiency of that part of the army which was to remain in Scotland, and on help from the local community. In particular he tried to turn to his advantage the fear of disorder of the men of property, for just as this fear had led these men to co-operate with the régime as JPs and commissioners of assessment, so now, Monck hoped, it would persuade them to maintain stability in his absence.

Some confirmation that the landowners of Scotland were thinking along the same lines was provided by a set of proposals which a Perthshire gentleman, George Kinnaird of Drumrossie, submitted to Monck in October 1659.[35] Kinnaird was an arch-politician who came into his own after the Restoration, but nonetheless his views had something in common with the sentiments of men who valued order above all things. Although his motives for approaching Monck were undoubtedly selfish, they demonstrated how, by careful manipulation, Monck could keep the Scots in check. Kinnaird clearly held out the prospect of political unrest in Perthshire after the departure of the English forces. To counter this, he suggested that Monck allow the Scots noblemen and gentlemen north of the Tay to act with the remaining English officers for the maintenance of peace and that they be permitted to carry arms for this purpose. In a passage which brought out the political undertones in his message, he suggested that gentlemen of all persuasions be combined in the new peacekeeping force, so that whichever party should eventually triumph, Monck's friends could appear to be on the winning side. Shorn of its political subtleties, this document indicated the role which the gentry could play in preserving order in the localities, for Kinnaird's basic demands probably did not differ greatly from those of the gentry as a whole. Such at any rate was the impression Monck got in November when commissioners from the shires and burghs met in Edinburgh to put their points of view to him.

On 27 October, Monck took the decision to summon representatives of the shires and burghs to a meeting in the capital. Letters were despatched to the noblemen and gentlemen of the shires and to the magistrates of the burghs inviting them to select one of their number to convene in Edinburgh on 15 November, when they would hear what the General had to say 'about some affaires that concerne the countries att that time'.[36] The letter also included a request to the shires to furnish a certain number of baggage horses, each with a packman, for the use of the English army; these were to gather in Edinburgh by 20 November.[37]

On the appointed day the commissioners from the shires and burghs duly assembled in Edinburgh. The noblemen and gentlemen from the shires chose the Earl of Glencairn as their president, while the burghs chose Sir James Stewart, thus demonstrating the strange mixture of sympathies which had come to acknowledge Monck's authority, for Glencairn's royalist past consorted ill with Stewart's Remonstrant one.[38] The commissioners were treated to a brief speech from Monck in which he outlined his concern for the freedom of Parliament and the liberties of the people. 'Haveing a call from God and his people to march into England,' he said, he charged his hearers — 'you the nobility, gentlemen, sheriffe, and the rest of the justices of peace' — with preserving the peace of the commonwealth, suppressing all tumults and signs of correspondency with Charles Stuart, and countenancing the godly ministry and all who feared God in the land. He promised further to seek a reduction in the assessment from Parliament, but for the time being he demanded that the 'arrears' of the assessment for March, April, May and June 1660 should be speedily gathered in.[39]

On the following day the commissioners signified their compliance with Monck's desires, but asked the General for some concrete proposals on how they could prevent disorder or unrest in the shires, for they were, they said, unprepared for such a task. In addition they asked that watches be appointed on the Highland line and in the Borders to preserve the country from theft and robbery. Monck's response to this was the uncharacteristically feeble remark that he had not had time to consider specific measures, but that he would welcome suggestions from the shires when he next met their representatives on 12 December. On the need for watches at strategic points, he promised to appoint guards if the shires in question submitted further details and engaged for the peaceable conduct of the men so employed.[40]

Monck's dealings with the commissioners from 15 to 17 November were designed to be only the first round in his consultations with leaders of the Scottish community. His speech of 15 November was distributed in the form of a letter to the representatives, who were expected to carry it back to their constituents. Each shire was then required to elect a representative to attend Monck at Berwick on 12 December and there to discuss in more detail provisions for securing peace in Scotland. At the elections for the new commissioners, quite serious political controversy appears to have broken out in some shires. This was certainly true of Perthshire, where George Kinnaird became involved in a dispute which may have presaged the emergence of royalist versus republican conflict in the area. At the meeting of the shire, one faction expressed dissatisfaction with the man — probably Kinnaird — who had been chosen to represent them in Edinburgh and wanted to replace him with another nominee, but it seems that Kinnaird's candidature won through in the end. One local laird feared that a similar situation might arise in Forfar, for he wrote to Lord Ogilvy to inform him of the recent unrest in Perthshire. Fife, too, witnessed some controversy at the meeting of the shire.[41]

Owing to their poverty, different arrangements obtained for the burghs of Scotland. At the meeting at Edinburgh, Monck had initially decreed that the replies of the burghs to his letter of 15 November should be sent to the provost and bailies of Edinburgh and that they alone should be responsible for bringing the letters to Berwick. But at a meeting of the burgh commissioners on the 15th, it was decided that the representatives from Edinburgh should be joined by others from Linlithgow and Haddington. In the course of December the replies trickled in, making a total of forty-four messages to be presented to Monck.[42]

When the commissioners from the shires arrived at Berwick,[43] they elected five of their number to wait upon the General: these were the Earls of Glencairn, Rothes, Wemyss and Eglinton and Alexander Bruce,[44] brother to the Earl of Kincardine. In pursuance of their instructions to consider ways of preserving peace in Scotland, they submitted five proposals to Monck: (1) that he appoint a committee in each shire to regulate its affairs, (2) that each shire be allowed to raise a guard of horsemen for its defence, (3) that the shires be allowed to take up arms for Monck's assistance and their own defence if the projected negotiations between Monck's commissioners and Fleetwood's should fail, (4) that to achieve this aim arms might be made readily available and (5) that individual gentlemen and their servants might, if they were loyal to Monck, be allowed to carry arms.[45]

These proposals led to much heart-searching by Monck and his officers on whether the Scots should be allowed to arm to assist the English. In the end Monck decided that only under certain conditions and subject to strict controls would he permit them to do so, and then only for their own defence. This issue troubled Monck greatly and no doubt explains his earlier reluctance to commit himself to a specific policy for the security of Scotland. But his mind having been made up, Monck's reply to the commissioners at Berwick was precise and detailed. To their first proposal he replied in the affirmative, with the proviso that the committee should act with the consent of the nearest garrison commander and should engage to do nothing to the prejudice of the commonwealth, or in favour of Charles Stuart's interests. In reply to the second he allowed guards (the details of which he laid down) to be mounted in the shires adjacent to the Highlands, and promised to review the case of the other shires if and when he withdrew his army from Scotland. To the third he deferred an answer. To the fourth he promised 'to furnish them with fit means for their defence' whenever he judged it to be necessary, and in answer to the fifth he granted to such noblemen and gentlemen as should subscribe to live peaceably the right to wear their swords and to have armed attendants. In the face of protests from Glencairn that these provisions were inadequate, Monck remained adamant: only if the worst came — that is, only if he suffered military defeat at the hands of Lambert — would he allow the Scots to arm for his assistance.[46] After conveying these decisions to the commissioners personally, Monck subscribed letters to the shires intimating the substance of his resolves, and to the city of Edinburgh expressing thanks for the burghs' addresses of loyalty. Then in a letter to the governor of Stirling he again gave vent to his concern about arming the Scots and explained the recent proceedings as they related to Stirlingshire, a shire which occupied a key position on the Highland/Lowland line.[47]

The conferences at Edinburgh and Berwick revealed two things. First, they illustrated Monck's desire to involve the chief men of Scotland in his plans to march south. The growth in importance of the nobility as the discussions progressed is quite striking. Although it is impossible to say how many of the shire representatives were nobles at either meeting, it was clearly they, rather than the gentry or lairds, who played most part in dealing with Monck at first hand. Glencairn was their president in November, while in December four out of the five delegates who negotiated directly with Monck were noblemen, and here too

Glencairn played the leading role. This meant in effect that while Monck was absent in England, he was prepared to recognise the nobility, and of course the gentry, as custodians of the peace in Scotland. On the other hand, the limits to Monck's tolerance of these groups was made crystal clear by his refusal to let the Scottish community take up arms either for his assistance or their own defence. This again was a sign that in Monck's eyes the Scots were capable of taking an independent initiative which could give them control of Scotland and foreclose his options in England. Thus, so far as the Scots could not be relied on solely to observe the wishes and instructions of Monck's army, to that extent had they remained undaunted by the English conquest.

The state of Scotland on the eve of Monck's departure is hard to assess. Quaker observers — hardly the least prejudiced of sources — depicted Scotland as being in a mighty uproar, with the spirits of men set on fire, and the Scots ready to push the English out of their country.[48] Certainly there was an expectation of change. Small details like Glasgow's emergency resolution empowering the magistrates to take decisions in the name of the whole council; Edinburgh's policy of locking up its registers and mounting special guards at the gates; and Aberdeen's precautions against the incursion of robbers and broken men — all testify to the awareness of troubled times.[49] More seriously, news that some of the laird of Glengarry's men had taken up arms in November and were robbing innocent countrymen brought home to Monck only days before the Edinburgh conference the dangers of relaxing the army's control and of giving the Scots some freedom to act.[50] In December, the danger to the commonwealth was emphasised by news of a conspiracy being hatched at the Earl of Tweeddale's house in Edinburgh and of Viscount Kenmore's escape from imprisonment in Edinburgh castle.[51]

Yet these incidents were isolated and betokened the expectation of change rather than change itself. From October to December 1659, while Monck was treating with Fleetwood, remodelling his army and settling the Scots, there is no reason to believe that the country was more difficult to control than before. Of course, the knowledge that several regiments were about to march south and that English politics were in turmoil led to much muttering, and a little stirring, among the Scots, but two factors worked against this erupting into violence after Monck's departure. The first was the careful balance between co-operation and control which Monck had achieved in his settlement of the relations between the remaining English forces and the Scottish people. The second was the suspicion that Monck who, after all, had lately been seen to court the nobility, would in the end bring the Scots what they wanted and restore their king.

ii. Preparations for the king's return, January — May 1660

Although Monck had arrived in Berwick on 2 December and had set up his headquarters at Coldstream on the 8th, he did not cross the Tweed until 1 January 1660.[52] The crossing was effected in two stages: the infantry marched on 1 January, and the horse on the 2nd. Monck took with him six regiments of foot — his own, Fairfax's, Lytcott's, Reade's, Morgan's and Hubblethorne's — and four regiments of horse — his own, Knight's, Clobery's and Morgan's. In England, these regiments were formed into two divisions, the first under Monck's command and the second under Colonel Reade.[53] This left only four regiments in Scotland, all of foot: Mann's, Robson's, Overton's[54] and Hughes'. In the course of January, Monck sent Morgan's two regiments back to Scotland, and these were joined by another two, one of horse and one of foot, before the king's return.[55]

For some weeks after Monck's departure, the forces in Scotland, grouped in and around the four garrisons of Inverness, Perth, Leith and Stirling,[56] were without a resident commander-in-chief. Morgan, who was to fulfil that role, marched with Monck as far as York, which was reached on 11 January. From there his two regiments were ordered back to Scotland, but Morgan himself did not return to the north until late February.[57] His commission to command the forces in Scotland was issued by Monck from Northampton on 25 January,[58] a surprising delay on the General's part in completing the formalities for his successor.

Little evidence survives to show how the Scots reacted to Monck and Morgan's absence. Two observers, both of whom owed much to the English régime, reported that the Royalists were gaining ground. John Campbell, fiar of Glenorchy, informed his father that '[o]ur shyr hes gon to a great hight upon ye old Malignant accompt',[59] while John Baynes, Receiver-General of the revenues in Scotland, wrote from Leith that the malignant party had high hopes of Monck.[60] Such feelings put to the test the army's ability to stifle unrest. Captain Humphrey Mason, governor of Dunnottar Castle, found it difficult to make the gentlemen of the district observe Monck's restrictions on the bearing of arms. When the Earl of Atholl sent a party of 40 or 50 armed men into Forfarshire to apprehend one man, Mason was forced to ask Lord Ogilvy (commissioner for the shire) to clamp down on such broad interpretations of the right to mount guards.[61] Aberdeen's reaction to the escape of Viscount Frendraught from imprisonment in the Tolbooth was another sign of the times. Frendraught was a Royalist, and so to satisfy the neighbouring garrisons special efforts had to be made to effect his recapture.[62] But in the burghs as a whole, more settled conditions prevailed. The magistrates and councillors continued to transact business which, if not exactly routine, had a familiar ring: Glasgow was at odds with Patrick Gillespie over a vacant stipend, while Edinburgh appointed a master for the local grammar school.[63]

Some opportunity for the shires and burghs to express their opinions on recent events was given in February, when their commissioners gathered in Edinburgh at Monck's request. From Wooler in Northumberland on 2 January, Monck sent permits for one nobleman or gentleman from every shire, and one burgess from every burgh, to meet in Edinburgh to discuss the condition of Scotland.[64] Although he had by now crossed the Border, Monck was still mindful of Scottish interests. In January he sent his chaplain, Thomas Gumble, to London with instructions to secure fair treatment for Scotland from the English Parliament, and when he himself addressed the House on 6 February, he stressed Scotland's claim to be treated on an equal footing with England, particularly in matters of finance. His purpose in decreeing the meeting at Edinburgh was thus to enable the Scots to draw up a list of grievances which he would present to Parliament. But such a meeting had other uses. Monck used it as a platform from which to remind the shires that they still owed arrears of cess, and he made it clear that he would consider their grievances only if they showed their willingness in this and other respects to live peaceably and obey his instructions.[65]

In the event, only about half the shires and burghs in Scotland sent representatives to Edinburgh. For the shires, it was noticeable that the great majority of commissioners were members of the nobility, only four shires being represented by gentry or lairds.[66] It was also clear that the shires and burghs were not united in their view of what constituted Scottish interests, for they failed to reach agreement on the advice they wished to convey to Monck on the future conduct of Scottish affairs.[67] Although the shires and burghs met separately, they appointed a joint committee to consider a list of grievances and proposals. After two days' debate and a series of angry exchanges, no agreement could be reached on the final list, although at first some common ground had been revealed. Both sides were agreed that Monck should be asked to delay proceedings relating to Scotland until commissioners arrived from Edinburgh to advise him, and that these commissioners should represent the need to fix Scotland's tax burden at a level proportionate to that of England. Various measures were agreed concerning the encouragement of trade, the protection of shipping, and the establishment of a stable currency. Other provisions dealing with vacant stipends, the quartering of soldiers, and the release of prisoners of war likewise provoked little dissension, but the remaining issues caused such bitter disagreement that the whole purpose of the joint debates was destroyed. The burghs, on the one hand, disapproved of the shires' proposals for the revocation of gifts and annuities, while the shires disliked the burghs' intention to include in their list an article approving the union of England and Scotland. Somewhat surprisingly, the matter of the union, although a source of disagreement, did not figure as prominently in the debates of the conventions as other more 'domestic' issues. It was less contentious, for instance, than the burghs' desire for the speedy setting up of courts in Scotland and for the strict enforcement of the laws of debt. To this the nobility and gentry of the shires were vehemently opposed. They asked that the recommendation for a delay in proceedings relating to Scotland should be taken to include a deferment of judicial business, and they were more than anxious for an extension of the moratorium on debts. On this last point the discussions foundered, for here, more than on any larger issue of Anglo-Scottish relations, the two sides felt their interests at stake. Accordingly the burghs commissioned William Thomson to go to London to present their particular concerns, while the shires appointed Mungo Murray to convey their desires to the General. Murray, it was hoped, would be joined later by the Earls of Glencairn and Home and the lairds of Durie and Carden.

When these commissioners reached London in March, time was fast running out for the republican régime in Scotland. On 21 February Monck readmitted the secluded members to Parliament and so made the Restoration inevitable. Henceforth Scotsmen turned their attention to London and, eventually, to Breda — their intrigues there belong more properly to the reign of Charles II than to the Interregnum. Of events in Scotland between March and May 1660 little can be said, for almost nothing remains to show how the army coped with the problems of government as the régime in England crumbled. It seems safe to assume, however, that Scotland showed no signs of rising against its conquerors. Monck's precautions did much to keep the country passive, but many Scots were unwilling as well as unable to intervene in the settlement then unfolding in England. 'God forbid,' admonished Lauderdale, 'the stirring of Scotland at this time should be a pretence for hindering the peaceable doing of what Scotland is most concerned in.'[68]

Despite the politicians' preoccupation with the restoration of the monarchy, the last few months of the republican régime saw piecemeal attempts by Parliament and the Council of State to deal with the administration of Scotland. Measures relating to the raising of revenue for the commonwealth were passed in January and February, and applied to Scotland as well as England and Ireland. Acts for levying customs and excise duties were passed on 27 December and 25 January, and new commissioners for customs and excise at Leith were appointed on 15 February.[69] The assessment was regulated by an act of 26 January which set Scotland's share at the enormously high figure of £12,000 per month for six months, but by an order of 12 March the time allowed for payment was extended.[70] When, or even if, these sums were eventually gathered in is uncertain. Details of the new act were slow to reach Scotland, and the newsbooks were sometimes ahead of official channels in conveying word of recent transactions to Edinburgh. On 17 May Parliament found it necessary to pass an order enjoining prompt payment of the six months' assessment in England, and there is little reason to suppose that taxpayers in Scotland had discharged their obligations more swiftly. Some areas, like Fife, may have made their payments in a lump sum at the end of the six months' period, but even so it is extremely unlikely that much cess was gathered in before the recall of the king.[71]

Steps were also taken to provide a central executive for Scotland and to revive the administration of justice. In March the Council of State gave out the names of five persons to act as commissioners for managing the affairs of Scotland: Major General Morgan and Colonels Whetham, Twistleton, Daniel and Markham. Subsequently, Molyneux Disney was chosen to replace both Markham and Whetham. Although a quorum of the commissioners had arrived in Edinburgh by 2 May, they had not yet received their commissions, the delay apparently being caused by uncertainty over the style of their authority and by the opposition of James Sharp and others in London to the whole scheme.[72] On 5 May, however, Morgan, Twistleton and Disney wrote to the Council of State assuring them that as soon as the commissions arrived they would set up courts and enquire into the revenues. The insinuation of 'the Fanatick cavaleere' that the king would be back within days would not, they insisted, deflect them from the task.[73] But despite a possible attempt on their part to establish sheriff and commissary courts in Parliament's name (a device, said Nicoll, to ensure they were paid their salaries),[74] these commissioners did not act as servants of the English Republic. With the king's approval, however, they acted as a commission for the government of Scotland until August 1660.

In March, ten judges were also named. The bench was to consist of four Englishmen — Edward Moseley, Henry Goodyear, John Hewlie and a fourth man named Crook — and six Scotsmen — Sir John Wemyss, Sir James Hope, James Dalrymple, John Scougall, James Robertson and David Falconer. Provision was made for equal representation of English and Scots on the commission for criminal causes, but the differential in salary established in 1652 (£600 for English, £300 for Scots) was to be retained. Judges for the Court of Exchequer were appointed at the same time, they being the four Englishmen already named and John Thompson, the former Auditor-General. These nominations did not take effect before the proclamation of the king (the summer sessions would not in any case have met before June), and after the Restoration new appointments were made.[75]

These provisions for the government of Scotland were highly unpopular amongst many sections of the Scottish community and were attributed by Sharp and Lauderdale to Monck's insistence. Sharp was in London at this time at Monck's behest and with the concurrence of the ministry in Edinburgh. Although his instructions from his clerical brethren charged him with the oversight of church affairs,[76] he became heavily involved in London in secular politics, and so his letters to Robert Douglas and others in Edinburgh revealed much about the attitude of the English authorities to Scottish affairs. According to Sharp, Monck's desire to settle the government of Scotland was, despite his earlier pleas to Parliament to treat Scotland on an equal footing with England, strongly motivated by a wish to keep the country in subjection until the outcome of the Convention Parliament's debates should be known. Sharp and Lauderdale disliked the proposal to send commissioners and judges to Scotland and tried to represent the unwisdom of this course of action to Monck. They were supported by many members of the Council of State and attempts were made, apparently with success, to prevent the officials from leaving London. By the end of March, Monck's attitude seemed to have softened, for he assured Sharp that the despatch of judges to Scotland was only

> for the fashion, and in a month or two there would be a change; that it was necessity put him on it, and a little time would show it was not for Scotland's hurt.

Nonetheless, Sharp was convinced that English policy towards Scotland was dictated solely by self-interest. Englishmen, he wrote,

> incline to keep Scotland at under, and either incorporate, or make us distinct, as they shall find most serviceable to their interest.[77]

Sharp thus revealed that not only was there disagreement between Monck and his advisers on the administration of Scotland, but that the very fate of the union hung in the balance. Surprisingly, however, there seems to have been little direct discussion on the union as such. The most Monck did was to make it clear that he was unwilling to allow Scottish representatives to attend the Convention Parliament, although whether this reflected a personal desire to dissolve the union permanently, or merely to prevent the political activity surrounding elections, remained a mystery. Sharp and his brethren in Edinburgh were anxious that the

Scots should elect commissioners to attend the coming Parliament at Westminster, but Monck adamantly refused to allow the shires and burghs of Scotland (or even a select committee) to meet to elect MPs. He reiterated this decision at the end of March:

> as for sending commissioners from Scotland to the parliament [he told Sharp], it was neither for our [i.e. Scotland's] reputation or advantage; and that, if we be quiet, our business would be done to our mind.[78]

This meant that when the Convention Parliament met, there were for the first time since before Barebones' Parliament no Scottish representatives at Westminster. Thus the dissolution of the parliamentary union was confirmed, and was not to be revived after the king's return. Moreover, Monck's attitude to Scottish affairs in these months implied that in any future treaty with the exiled king Scotland would not be included. In these ways the indifference to Scotland which had so often been a feature of policy-making in Whitehall and Westminster over the preceding few years was again made apparent.

In Scotland, meanwhile, Sharp's correspondents were concerned not so much with the political aspects of the union as with the effect of the king's return on religion throughout the three kingdoms. In a letter to Sharp of 31 March, Robert Douglas reported that there were currently three shades of opinion in Scotland: the Protesters, who did not want the king at all; the Malignants, who wanted the king, but not 'upon covenant terms'; and those lovers of the 'religion and liberty of the nation' who wished the king to return 'upon the terms of the league and covenant'.[79] Douglas's sympathies obviously lay with the last group, but as time went on the reports from London showed that his hopes were to be disappointed. From March onwards, Sharp's letters had warned that 'to keep the covenant interest on foot' would be a difficult business. Even moderate presbyterianism of the English sort (Baillie's 'lame erastian presbytery') was unlikely to survive throughout the three nations, despite Parliament's votes in favour of the Westminster Confession of Faith and the Solemn League and Covenant on 2 and 5 March. As early as 10 March, he had written that moderate episcopacy was rearing its head, and by April he expressed grave doubts as to whether the king could be restored on Covenant terms.[80]

In Scotland, the strength of that Malignancy which Douglas so greatly feared was demonstrated at a meeting which the nobility and gentry convened on their own initiative in April 1660. In an attempt to secure some representation of the Scottish viewpoint in London, the idea had earlier been mooted, principally by Sharp and his friends, that the Scottish nobility should grant a commission to Lauderdale and Crawford-Lindsay to act on their behalf, since these two were already in London and had access to Monck. But Lauderdale, it seems, was too friendly with the Presbyterians to suit the nobility, who were increasingly reverting to old cavalier or 'malignant' principles.[81] On 5 April some noblemen and gentlemen therefore took matters into their own hands and, without a warrant from Monck, met in Edinburgh to elect commissioners to go to London.

The meeting, which was attended by thirteen noblemen and ten gentlemen, formally convened on 5 or 6 April under the presidency of the Earl of Rothes. In an effort to put their proceedings on a sound footing, they claimed the right to sit by virtue of the warrant which Monck had granted to the shire commissioners in February, and perhaps to emphasise this continuity they appointed as their commissioners to go to London the men who had been chosen for that task in February: the Earls of Glencairn and Home and the lairds of Carden and Durie. In order to strengthen their claim to represent Scottish opinion, they decided to confer with two representatives from the burghs. The two so chosen, most probably at the nobility's request, were Robert Murray and James Borthwick of Edinburgh, the men who had gone to treat with Monck at Berwick. In addition to appointing commissioners for London, the nobility and gentry made their political sympathies quite clear by drawing up a letter to the king in which they expressed their disappointment at having received no commands from him and their strong desire to serve him in any way he might now direct.[82]

Despite their representations abroad, the nobility and gentry obviously expected some good to come from the despatch of commissioners to London, for they appointed a committee to receive and disseminate any information they might send back from the capital.[83] But Glencairn and his colleagues achieved little. By the time they reached London, the elections to the Convention Parliament were in train and were producing results manifestly favourable to the return of the king. On 28 April, three days after the Convention Parliament met, Sharp signified to Douglas, who was still expressing horror at the prospect of a settlement not on Covenant terms, that 'the design of closing with the king now appeareth above board.' On 1 May, after Monck's dealings with Sir John Grenville and Charles Stuart had been revealed, it was clear that Parliament's invitation to the king to return would be on the basis of the Declaration of Breda.[84] Hence the question of a treaty, in which Scotland might or might not be included, did not arise.

Parliament's acceptance of the Declaration of Breda and the recall of the king on 1 May was the signal for Sharp and many other Scotsmen to go to Breda to pay court to His Majesty. Sharp went at Monck's suggestion, ostensibly to persuade the king to write to the presbyterian ministers in England and to inform him of matters in Scotland. Sharp asserted that he would not be 'accessory to any things prejudicial to the presbyterian government',[85] but this intention, if indeed it was sincere, could do nothing against the strong current running in favour of episcopacy. This, at least, was true for England — the cause of the Solemn League and Covenant was certainly dead — but for Scotland matters remained in doubt for some time longer. Douglas and the ministers of Edinburgh sent messages of encouragement and loyalty to Charles through Sharp and the Earl of Rothes, but these were not delivered until the king had landed in England. Nonetheless in Breda, according to Sharp, the king had displayed 'a great affection for our country and kirk' and was resolved 'not to wrong the settled government of our church'. Yet Charles was not inclined to be more specific on Scottish affairs — he told Sharp 'he would reserve a full communing about that till his coming to England'.[86] Thus when the king returned to English soil, little was known about his intentions towards Scotland, and it was only in the following year that his plans for the dismantling of presbyterian church government were revealed.

Meanwhile, various members of the laity had joined the brethren of Edinburgh in sending addresses to the king. When William Thomson, the town clerk of Edinburgh, signified his intention of going to Breda, the council drew up a letter of congratulation to be conveyed to His Majesty.[87] Sharp too was entrusted with several messages, including missives from Glencairn and the Earl of Crawford-Lindsay.[88] Members of the Scottish nobility currently in London (where they were to be joined by many others over the next few weeks) began to jostle for position around the king. Lord Paisley, the eldest son of the Earl of Abercorn and son-in-law of Speaker Lenthall, had already beseeched his uncle in Holland to find him a place in the king's household.[89] Opportunist gentlemen like George Kinnaird of Drumrossie contemplated the large number of offices that might now fall vacant. Kinnaird, in expectation of an administrative purge, asked a friend in Scotland for details of the Court of Session and other courts as they had been constituted in former times.[90] Noblemen who could not immediately make the journey to London, like the poverty-stricken Earl of Kelly, anxiously asked their friends in the capital to keep them apprised of events, and as May wore on more and more seemed determined to pay their respects to the king in person.[91] Those who, like the Marquis of Argyle, were afraid of reprisals for their collaboration with the Republic, waited longest before venturing to appear in court, while others, among them Cassillis, chose to stage their political comeback in Scotland rather than in the limelight of Whitehall.[92]

It is, then, not altogether correct to think that news of the king's return was received by every Scotsman with unalloyed joy. The recall of King Charles posed delicate problems requiring much tact for those who had lately held office or had in any way aided the republican régime. Others there were whose past was blameless, but who could not be sure of securing, amid the multitude of petitioners now importuning the king, that recognition and reward which they craved. A third group, comprising those who in the crucial years from 1648 to 1651 had expressed reservations about the wisdom of the Engagement or about the sincerity of the young king, were in an especially difficult position, for although their record against the English might be beyond reproach, they could not be sure that this would blot out the memory of their former crimes. The complexity of the Stuart kings' relations with the Scottish nobility and gentry and the many shifts in support for Covenanters and Royalists which had taken place over the past two decades meant, in effect, that the Restoration in Scotland had less obvious and clear-cut implications for the supporters of the monarchy than was the case in England.

Nonetheless, the celebrations which were held in Edinburgh to mark the proclamation of Charles II attested the people's relief at the return of the king. On 7 May, news of Parliament's resolution for his recall reached Scotland, 'to the comfort and joy of much pepill'. On 14 May the king was proclaimed in Edinburgh, after Morgan had reputedly done all he could to hinder the solemnities.[93] Nicoll graphically described the scene: the announcement at the Mercat Cross, followed by the ringing of bells, the sound of trumpets, cannons roaring and drums beating, with dancing in the streets and all other tokens of joy.[94] Or, as Wariston saw it:

> . . . great ryot, excesse, extravagancy, superfluity, vanity, naughtinesse, profanetye, drinking of healths; the Lord be merciful to us.[95]

EPILOGUE

The Restoration Settlement, 1660 — 1663

THE swiftness with which the Scots people reacted in celebrating the return of the king was not matched by Charles in the attention he gave to the affairs of his northern kingdom. For many months after his restoration, vestiges of the republican administration remained, and it was years rather than months before the true nature of the civil and religious settlement to be imposed on Scotland was fully revealed.

Until August 1660 the government of Scotland lay in the hands of the four commissioners — Morgan, Twistleton, Daniel and Disney — who had been appointed to that task by the republican régime. The arrival of these high-ranking officials in Edinburgh by the second week in May surprised the Scots, since by then all attention was focused on the king's recall, but the commissioners proceeded to assume executive authority in Scotland.[1] On 11 May they issued a proclamation announcing their appointment and continuing in office all those who had held positions of trust on 4 April 1659.[2] From then until 22 August they continued to exercise their authority, presumably with the king's approval, but in practice they took few positive measures to carry on the government of Scotland. They did, however, play a prominent part in the thanksgiving celebrations of 19 June, held to mark the king's return.[3]

The commissioners' authority ceased to exist when the government of Scotland was resumed by the Committee of Estates on 23 August 1660.[4] This change was the outcome of various discussions between Charles, his advisers and those members of the nobility and gentry of Scotland who were currently resident in London. Early in June some of the nobility had presented a petition to the king asking that Parliament be summoned, but discussion on this issue became clouded by debates over when and how the English forces in Scotland should be withdrawn. While refraining from giving a definite answer about the removal of the troops, Charles encouraged the Scots to draw up further proposals for the civil government of their country. This resulted in a petition from 'the Noblemen, Gentlemen and Burgess of your Majesties Antient kingdome of Scotland, mett at London' which asked that, until a meeting of Parliament could be held, Scotland might be governed by the king and the Committee of Estates appointed in 1651.[5] Not all the Scottish nobility were in favour of such a move, but the king brushed aside their objections and in a proclamation of 2 August ordered the Committee, or the remaining members of it, to convene in Edinburgh on 23 August.[6]

Meanwhile, in the course of July, the king made known his choice of ministers for Scotland. After some hesitation it was decided that Lauderdale should be

Secretary of State, and that Crawford-Lindsay should be Treasurer, Cassillis Justice-General, Sir John Fletcher King's Advocate, and Sir Archibald Primrose Clerk Register. The Earl of Middleton (the former Lieutenant General John Middleton) was to be the king's commissioner for Parliament, and the Earl of Glencairn was appointed Lord Chancellor.[7] The men thus chosen to occupy the highest offices of state in Scotland had had varied political careers. Although the five noblemen could all at some time have been classified as Covenanters, their support for the cause of the monarchy and their adherence to the religion of the Covenants had, since the 1640s, taken very different paths. Cassillis, a supporter of Argyle, had been an opponent of the Engagement and had been invited to attend the Cromwellian Other House in the 1650s;[8] Lauderdale and Crawford-Lindsay, hitherto strong supporters of presbyterianism, had both been Engagers but had suffered imprisonment after 1651;[9] while Middleton and Glencairn, the first an old ally of Leslie's, the other a 'royalist-covenanter' of Hamilton's party, had not only supported the Engagement but had actively promoted royalist rebellion in Scotland during the last decade.[10] The two gentlemen, Primrose and Fletcher, likewise had diverse political records: Fletcher had successfully practised as a criminal lawyer under the Republic, while Primrose, formerly a Montrosian and an Engager, had had his estates sequestered after Worcester. Both, however, were friends of Middleton, and this no doubt accounted for their rise to eminence in 1660.[11] After the Restoration, therefore, Charles chose to call into his service representatives of the various religious and political factions whose antagonisms had dominated Scottish politics, particularly in the late 1640s; but if he thereby hoped to achieve a broad consensus in favour of his policies in church and state, he was soon to be disappointed. In April 1661, Cassillis was deprived of his public office for refusing to take the oath of allegiance and supremacy before the king had made clear his intentions on church government;[12] in 1664, Crawford-Lindsay resigned his office rather than accept the introduction of episcopacy;[13] while the feud between Middleton and Lauderdale (who viewed with distaste and reluctance the king's support for the bishops) was a dominant feature of the early 1660s.[14]

Before these tensions reached their climax, however, it fell to Glencairn as Lord Chancellor to preside over the solemnities which accompanied the sitting of the Committee of Estates in the Parliament House in Edinburgh on 23 August 1660. At its first meeting nine nobles, ten barons or lairds and ten burgesses were present.[15] Much of the Committee's work over the next few weeks was concerned with the suppression of the Protester faction, for it was on them that odium chiefly fell for their compliance with the republican government. Accordingly, it was they who bore the brunt of royalist vengeance in 1660-1. The Committee of Estates' first act was to order the arrest of eleven Protesters who had assembled in Edinburgh on 23 August to draw up an address to the king. In their petition the Protesters congratulated the king on his restoration, but deplored the use of the Prayer Book in his household and made bold to remind him of his obligations to observe the Covenant throughout his dominions. Only one of the subscribers to this document escaped capture and imprisonment in Edinburgh castle.[16] The

Committee of Estates followed up this action with a ban on all unlawful meetings and conventicles, and on all seditious petitions and remonstrances.[17] The Royalists' dislike of the Protesters was further demonstrated by the king himself in a letter to the presbytery of Edinburgh, in which he stated his intention to uphold the Acts of the General Assembly of 1651, whose authority the Protesters did not recognise. The Committee of Estates, in turn, stepped up the campaign against the Protesters by forbidding the circulation of *Lex Rex* and *The Causes of God's Wrath*, two of their most cogent propaganda pieces, and by banning the adoption by any person of the Remonstrance of 1650. This enabled the Committee to arrest dissentient clergymen, including Patrick Gillespie and James Simpson, and to demand bonds from Protester laymen to the effect that they would disown the Western Remonstrance. Resolutioner synods, meanwhile, were encouraged to depose Protesting ministers.[18]

In the end all the Protester prisoners were released with the exception of James Guthry, who was tried before Parliament in 1661 and executed on 1 June.[19] Two prominent laymen who had been associated with the Protesters throughout their public careers, the Marquis of Argyle and Sir Archibald Johnston of Wariston, suffered the same fate. Argyle was imprisoned in England in the summer of 1660 after presenting himself at Charles's court, but was shipped home in December to be tried by the Scottish Parliament on charges of treason. These related not only to his conduct during the first and second civil wars, but also to the help he had given the English during Glencairn's rising. Argyle was found guilty and executed on 28 May 1661.[20] Two years later, in July 1663, Wariston, who had eluded arrest in 1660 despite a reward being offered for his capture, was tried before Parliament and executed. He faced charges concerning his participation in successive republican governments, for he had held the post of Clerk Register, had sat as a peer in the protectoral Parliaments and had been a leading member of the Council of State in the summer of 1659 and of the Committee of Safety set up by the army in October of that year.[21]

The Parliament which tried Guthry and Argyle had been summoned by Charles in a proclamation dated 10 October 1660. Two days later another proclamation remitted the trial of all persons concerned in the late troubles to that assembly.[22] Initially summoned for 12 December but postponed because of pressure of business in England, it eventually convened on 1 January 1661 with Middleton in attendance as king's commissioner.[23] According to Wodrow, the elections had been so carefully managed by the court party that only devotees of the royalist interest were returned.[24] The main work of the Parliament was embodied in the Act Rescissory of 28 March 1661. This Act, following upon others which affirmed the king's prerogative right to appoint officers of state, Privy Councillors and Lords of Session, to call Parliaments and to summon all subjects to take up arms, declared that the proceedings of all Parliaments since 1633, with the exception of that of 1650-1, were cancelled. Thus, in Mathieson's words, 'the whole political, and so far as recognised by statute, the whole religious revolution' of the past two decades was effaced. Many moderate Presbyterians were offended at this Act, for it annulled not only the work of the rigid Covenanters, but also the Parliament of

1641 which Charles himself had attended, and the Engagement of 1647 by which many Presbyterian-Royalists had upheld the king's interest.[25]

In the course of its sittings, Parliament had also attended to two more specific matters of concern for the carrying on of government in Scotland: the restoration of the courts of law and of judicial processes, and the supply of an adequate revenue for the king. Until the summer of 1661 the administration of justice was in abeyance, for in July 1660 the judges who had been appointed by the republican régime in the previous March were expressly forbidden to perform their judicial functions and were ordered to return to England.[26] At the beginning of 1661, Charles saw fit to exercise his prerogative right to appoint Lords of Session: fifteen ordinary lords and four extraordinary were duly named and their appointment confirmed by Parliament on 5 April 1661.[27] The names of the new judges revealed that, as with his officers of state, Charles was willing to entertain men with a covenanting past, but it was also clear that support for the Engagement, some sign of affection for the king's cause since 1650, or the patronage of Monck, Lauderdale or Middleton were equally important in procuring office in 1661.[28] The Court of Session, now reconstituted in the manner which had obtained before its sittings were interrupted on 28 July 1650, sat down in June 1661[29] and, so far as is known, proceeded to dispense justice in accordance with the laws and customs of Scotland in force before the English invasion. At this time sheriff and commissary courts were also ordered to reconvene,[30] and on 9 July Parliament passed a commission for, and instructions to, justices of the peace and constables.[31] In its instructions to the justices, Parliament evinced a desire to wipe out all trace of Cromwellian innovations and reforms, for the act of 9 July substantially re-enacted the Jacobean statute of 1617, with only minor amendments taken from Cromwellian practice. In particular, it was made clear that the nobility were not to be subjected to the power of the justices in the localities: no justice could proceed against a nobleman, prelate, privy councillor or lord of session for riot or breach of the peace, and any landed gentleman whose estate was worth ten chalders of victual or 1000 merks silver (Scots) was to have his case considered by the Privy Council if he refused to obey the justices. Thus, by employing the expedient of reporting high-born malefactors to the Privy Council, the régime made sure that the social and political pre-eminence of the nobility was asserted and the justices' importance was downgraded. Indeed, for the remainder of the century JPs were treated as mere agents of the Council whose prime duty it was to carry out the latter's orders.[32]

In the spring of 1661, Parliament also turned its attention to a settlement of the king's revenue. In October 1660, the Committee of Estates had authorised the levying of six months' cess at £6000 stg. per month, according to the proportions and valuations of 1653, and, mixing Cromwellian with covenanting practice, had also imposed an excise on goods which had been liable to such duty in 1647.[33] In 1661, however, the imposition of the cess was not renewed, for in March of that year Parliament voted the king an annuity of £40,000 stg. for life, to be raised solely from customs and excise duties.[34] Customs duties on inland salt and imported livestock, wines, salt, soap, tobacco, clothing and other goods were to provide one-fifth of this sum, while the remaining four-fifths was to come from an excise on home-brewed malt, whisky distilled at home, and imported whisky and beer. By imposing indirect taxes of this sort, Parliament was spreading 'the financial burden over the whole nation, to the proportional benefit of the landed class'.[35] Extraordinary revenue, in the form of a tax on landed wealth, was not raised until 1665. In that year a Convention of Estates voted a tax of fifty shillings upon every pound land of old extent to meet the exigencies of the Dutch War. In the imposition of this tax, payment of which was to be spread over five years, the Estates had clearly reverted to traditional (pre-1640) methods of apportionment and assessment; but on all subsequent occasions valued rent was, in accordance with Scottish covenanting and English republican practice, used as the basis for taxation. Indeed, after 1667 the sum of £72,000 Scots, or £6000 stg. per month, assessed on valued rent, became the standard unit of taxation upon land whenever extraordinary income was required, so that in this way the Cromwellian act of assessment of 1657 retained its influence on Scottish fiscal policy until the Union.[36]

After Charles's first Parliament rose on 12 July 1661, the government of Scotland passed into the hands of the Privy Council, the members of which had been nominated on Charles's authority alone. This body was, despite other parliamentary sessions, to be chiefly responsible for the government of the country throughout the rest of the reign. It met for the first time in Edinburgh on 13 July 1661. Although this and other sessions of the Council were held at Holyroodhouse, the real seat of power over Scottish affairs in fact remained in London. The Secretary was ordered to reside permanently in London, and four Englishmen — initially Clarendon, Monck (now Albemarle), Ormonde and Manchester — were added to the Council as special advisers. It was this section of the Council meeting in London, and not the larger body sitting in Edinburgh, which for the next few years laid down the main lines of policy towards Scotland. Thus, although a multitude of routine tasks continued to be transacted in Edinburgh, 'on all great questions of Church and State' the councillors 'received their instructions from the Secretary at Whitehall'.[37]

The work of the Council in its first few years was dominated by measures affecting the religious settlement of Scotland. In the summer of 1660, when the first discussions were taking place in London on the future settlement of the country, the king had appeared to favour the retention of the presbyterian system of church government. This at any rate was the impression conveyed by Sharp to his correspondents in Edinburgh, and it was also the construction which Douglas and his colleagues put on Charles's letter to them of 10 August.[38] In this letter, which the presbytery of Edinburgh received on 3 September and which they were asked to communicate to the other presbyteries within the nation, Charles promised to preserve the government of the church as settled by law. The Act Rescissory, however, removed the legal basis of the presbyterian system which had existed since 1638 and so deprived it of all civil sanction. Charles's true intentions were more clearly revealed in another Act of 28 March 1661, in which he declared his resolution to maintain the reformed religion as established by his father and grandfather, to settle the government of the Church in such a way as should be most agreeable to monarchical rule and the public peace, and meanwhile, notwithstanding the Act Rescissory, to allow the present administration by sessions, presbyteries and synods.[39]

Such a statement naturally aroused fears that episcopacy was about to be re-established. Several synods, including that of Fife, were resolved to protest against any interference with the presbyterian system, but they were dissolved on Middleton's orders before their petitions could reach either king or Parliament. The synod of Aberdeen, on the other hand, was positively encouraged to present its address, for it inclined towards episcopacy.[40] By the summer of 1661, it seems, Sharp had joined with Middleton, Clarendon and Ormonde in persuading the king and the Council at Whitehall that the restoration of the bishops was both right and timely.[41] On 5 September the Privy Council in Edinburgh considered a letter from Charles announcing his pleasure that episcopacy be established as the form of church government in Scotland, and on the following day an act of Council gave effect to this letter.[42] On 15 December 1661 four Scottish prelates — Sharp, Leighton, Hamilton and Fairfoul — were consecrated in London, and on 9 January 1662, after several presbyteries had begun to draw up protestations against this action, the Council in Edinburgh issued a proclamation prohibiting the meeting of presbyteries, synods or kirk sessions without the authority of the bishops.[43]

In the session of Parliament which began in April 1662, legislative sanction was given to the restoration of episcopacy. By an act of 27 May the 'ancient and sacred order' was fully restored. Burnet, relying heavily on the point that no synod or presbytery could now meet without authority from a bishop concluded that

[t]he whole government and jurisdiction of the church in the several dioceses was declared to be lodged in the bishops, which they were to exercise with the advice and assistance of such of their clergy as were of known loyalty and prudence: all men that held any benefice in the church were required to own and submit to the government of the church as now by law established.[44]

Clergymen were, indeed, required to take the oath of allegiance and supremacy which Parliament had contrived in April 1661 for all holders of public office, and to attend diocesan meetings held by the bishops. Attendance at any meeting not authorised by a bishop was declared unlawful. In addition 'it was made treason to preach or write against the king's prerogative and ecclesiastical supremacy or against episcopal government'. The campaign against presbytery was later in the year extended to the civil sphere, for those in public employment were forced to take an oath abjuring the Covenants and affirming that it was unlawful to take up arms against the king.[45]

Failure to take the oath of allegiance, to attend a diocesan meeting or to observe the anniversary of Charles' birth and restoration (29 May) all constituted grounds on which ministers could be deprived of their benefices. Similarly, ministers appointed under the statute for the abolition of lay patronage of 1649 (now of course rescinded) who failed to secure presentation by a lawful patron and collation by a bishop before 20 September 1662 were also to be deprived. To

Middleton fell the task of enforcing obedience to these commands. He began his work in the west, where the strong covenanting (and Protesting) tradition made it likely that most resistance to the new order would be met. Such, indeed, was the case. On 1 October the Privy Council, sitting at Glasgow, issued a proclamation requiring all ministers who had not secured presentation and collation by 20 September, or who had not observed the king's birthday, to cease preaching, to leave their parishes before 1 November (subsequently extended to 1 February 1663) and to move out of the bounds of their respective presbyteries. Over large areas of the west this proclamation was obeyed, so that many parishes, particularly in Clydesdale and Ayrshire, lost their ministers. In the synod of Galloway, where few nonconforming ministers obeyed the order to leave their parishes, wholesale deprivations took place. In the east, on the other hand, with the exception of the presbytery of Edinburgh, few ministers were deprived, although many of those who were allowed to remain in their parishes still refused to conform. In the north, however, nearly all the clergy conformed.[46] In all, 262 ministers in Scotland were deprived of their benefices as a result of these edicts,[47] a figure which represents between one-quarter and one-third of the total number of benefices in Scotland.

The reimposition of episcopacy was thus highly unpopular, certainly among the clergy and most probably among the laity, in those very areas which had shown themselves staunch in support of the Covenants and hostile to an uncovenanted king. These were the areas, moreover, which on account of their hostility towards the 'malignant party' had shown sympathy towards the English republicans both before and after 1651. Thus, by accident or design, the policy of deprivation allowed Charles to retaliate against many of those who over the past two decades had heaped indignities upon himself, his family and his kingly office. On the whole, however, Charles's religious settlement was far from being, in practice, the extremist measure of presbyterian legend. In so far as it effected a restoration, it was 'a restoration of the moderate episcopalian régime of James VI's middle years', whereby 'in the normal course of administration, the bishop exercised his authority within a framework in which the rights of both presbyteries and congregations were substantially safeguarded'. Contemporaries, therefore, might well have spoken 'of returning to the good old form of government by bishop and synod'.[48]

Once the religious settlement had been decided, Parliament was free to turn its attention to the question of indemnity for actions committed during the late troubles. This issue had in England been settled at the earliest possible opportunity after the king's return, but in Scotland it had been delayed until after the religious question was decided. Since those who, from a royalist point of view, might incur most guilt for their past actions were likely also to be opponents of episcopacy, the threat of exclusion from indemnity was kept hanging over their heads until after the religious alteration had been made. Delay in passing an Act of Indemnity was, in other words, a means of intimidating the Presbyterians.[49] In January 1662 Charles had given Middleton instructions concerning the projected act in which he itemised the categories of persons to be excluded from pardon. These were: all those found guilty of the murder of Charles I; those who had already been sentenced and declared fugitives by Parliament; and those who, being found guilty of opposing the Engagement of 1647, of supporting the Western Remonstrance or of complying with the usurper, should be made liable to fines by Parliament. Since the work of calculating these fines would be a heavy burden on Parliament's time, a small committee was to be set up to decide the details in advance and to submit recommendations to Parliament.[50] In the end, about 700 persons were excluded from the Act of Indemnity of 9 September 1662 and were subjected to heavy fines, the amounts collected being assigned to compensate Royalists who had suffered confiscation. The names of the excepted persons and the penalties imposed on them were detailed in a separate act.[51] The fines were, according to Charles's instructions, not to exceed one year's income from land, money or trade, but some latitude was allowed. Even more latitude was taken by Middleton, for prior to the exaction of the fines he had taken bribes from several parties who wished to avoid being named in the act. In all, the fines which, as Wodrow asserted, fell mainly on the western shires, amounted to over £1,000,000 Scots,[52] but the full amounts were never paid. The subsequent history of the act was complicated by the struggle for political power which developed between Middleton and Lauderdale, but in March 1663, at the time when Middleton was deprived of his office of king's commissioner, the operation of the act imposing the fines on the unlucky 700 was suspended. In 1664 the act was revived, but in the following year it was decided that only one half of the fines should be paid, the other half being waived on condition that the culprits signed the declaration renouncing the Covenants.[53]

Such are the outlines of the civil and religious settlement imposed on Scotland after the Restoration. There remains to be considered the fate of the main instrument of coercion and alien domination between 1651 and 1660: the English army in Scotland. At Charles' restoration, in accordance with an establishment prepared by Monck and approved by the Council of State in March 1660,[54] the forces in Scotland stood at six regiments of foot and two of horse. During the summer of 1660, members of the Scots nation resident in London pressed the king to withdraw these troops from Scotland, but it soon became clear that the king and the Earl of Clarendon were reluctant to do so until the new settlement was fully established. Although some assurances were given that the forces would be removed as soon as the money was raised to disband them, Sharp, for one, concluded in June that the garrisons would remain, at least until the following summer.[55] Nonetheless, on 30 August 1660 the English House of Commons was informed of a plan, devised by Monck, to reduce the forces to a mere three regiments of foot and one *troop* of horse. Accordingly, in November and December 1660 the regiments of foot of Robson, Hughes and Clarke, the regiment of horse of Lord Falkland (lately Saunders') and five of the six troops of Morgan's horse were disbanded. This left, in occupation of the four citadels of Leith, St. Johnstons, Ayr and Inverness and some minor garrisons in the Highlands, the three foot regiments of Morgan, Mann and Daniel (lately Overton's) and one troop of Morgan's regiment of horse.[56]

The forces remaining in Scotland had to contend with many incivilities from the native population. At times, anti-English feeling was given free rein.[57] A particularly vivid case was that of a riot in Stirling in November 1661 which took place when the magistrates and townspeople set upon a detachment of soldiers which had been sent from the castle to rescue some officers held prisoner in a local bailie's house. In the ensuing struggle cries of 'kill the rogues, kill the rogues' were flung at the soldiers and about eighteen or twenty of them were wounded. The sentiments expressed by the crowd were clearly anti-English, and the soldiers in turn expressed to Morgan their disgust at 'being trampled upon and made slaves' by such creatures.[58] Further difficulties were caused by the reluctance of some Scots to pay arrears of cess for the upkeep of the soldiers and by the unwillingness of the country people to provide straw and fodder for the horses in the garrisons.[59]

In June 1661, in a letter to Parliament Charles ordered the withdrawal of the remaining forces from Scotland. But before this could be effected, the citadels had to be dismantled so that no enemy of the state could make use of the fortifications which the English had built to subjugate Scotland. Work on the demolition of these fortresses proceeded tardily despite orders from the Privy Council in Edinburgh, but by the end of the year something had been done to render them useless.[60] It was, however, the need to provide troops for the service of Portugal that finally impelled the removal of the last remnants of the army from Scotland. In May 1662 'all the citidaillis quhairin the Englische sodgeris wer quarterit wer now emptyed' and their occupants shipped to Lisbon from Leith. With that, the military occupation of the country was ended 'and thair wes none in airmes in all Scotland, ather native or stranger, except the leiff gaird for his Majesteis use and weill of his subjectis.'[61]

NOTES

U

Notes

Introduction: Scotland's Relations with England, 1637 — 1651

1. The period covered by this introduction has recently been the subject of two studies by David Stevenson, *The Scottish Revolution 1637-1644: The Triumph of the Covenanters* (Newton Abbot, 1973) and *Revolution and Counter-Revolution in Scotland, 1644-1651* (London, 1977). Both have their origins in Dr. Stevenson's admirably detailed and convincing thesis, 'The Covenanters and the Government of Scotland 1637-1651' (Glasgow University, Ph.D. thesis, 1970). Many of the arguments in this introduction have been suggested by Dr. Stevenson's work, and the whole owes much to his pioneering scholarship.

2. Stevenson, *The Scottish Revolution 1637-1644* pp. 16-18. In the early years of his reign, James had retained his interest in Scottish affairs, but certainly after 1617 his commitment to and understanding of Scottish problems waned: Jennifer M. Brown, 'Scottish Politics 1567-1625', in Alan G. R. Smith (ed.), *The Reign of James VI and I* (London, 1973) esp. pp. 37-8.

3. Stevenson, *The Scottish Revolution 1637-1644* p. 313 (my emphasis).

4. Stevenson, *The Scottish Revolution 1637-1644* pp. 56-57; Stevenson, 'Thesis' p.72.

5. Stevenson, *The Scottish Revolution 1637-1644* p. 132.

6. For a full account of these proceedings see Stevenson, *The Scottish Revolution 1637-1644* pp. 116-126, 163-6, 192-6, 214-42. For a concise summary, see Gordon Donaldson, *Scotland: James V to James VII* (Edinburgh and London, 1965) pp. 322, 324, 327, 329.

7. Stevenson, *The Scottish Revolution 1637-1644* pp. 220-1.

8. Stevenson, *The Scottish Revolution 1637-1644* pp. 280-5; Donaldson, *Scotland: James V to James VII* p. 332.

9. Stevenson, *The Scottish Revolution 1637-1644* pp. 286-90; Donaldson, *Scotland: James V to James VII* p. 331. For the text of the Solemn League and Covenant, see S. R. Gardiner (ed.), *The Constitutional Documents of the Puritan Revolution 1625-1660* (3rd edn., Oxford, 1906) pp. 267-71.

10. C. V. Wedgwood, *The King's War 1641-1647* (London, 1958) pp. 294-6; Lawrence Kaplan, *Politics and Religion during the English Revolution: The Scots and the Long Parliament 1643-1645* (New York, 1976) pp. 18-26.

11. This argument is made explicit by Stevenson in 'Thesis' at pp. 383, 393, 419, 448, 453. See also Stevenson, *Revolution and Counter-Revolution* p. 56; Kaplan, *Politics and Religion* pp. 49, 60, 118.

12. For the negotiations, see Wedgwood, *The King's War 1641-1647* pp. 409-12, 418-9, and for the text of the proposals, Gardiner, *Constitutional Documents* pp. 275-86.

13. Wedgwood, *The King's War 1641-1647* pp. 526-7, 533-4, 545-6; Stevenson, *Revolution and Counter-Revolution* pp. 57-61, 64-6; S. R. Gardiner, *History of the Great Civil War 1642-1649* (4 vols., New York, 1965) iii, 3-4, 19-20, 22-5, 27-8, 71-6.

14. Gardiner, *Civil War* iii, 77; C. H. Firth and R. S. Rait (eds.), *Acts and Ordinances of the Interregnum* (3 vols., London, 1911) i, 833-8. This ordinance consolidated and made more explicit the provisions of two others passed in the previous year: see Firth and Rait, *A & O* i, 749-54 (ordinance of 19 August 1645 for regulating the election of elders); i, 789-97 (ordinance of 20 October 1645 concerning suspension from the Sacrament of the Lord's Supper). For a discussion of Erastianism and Parliament, see William M. Lamont, *Godly Rule* (London, 1969) chapter 5.

15. Stevenson, *Revolution and Counter-Revolution* p. 63.

16. For the Newcastle Propositions, and the king's first answer to them, see Gardiner, *Constitutional Documents* pp. 290-306, 306-8. For the progress of the negotiations, Wedgwood, *The King's War 1641-1647* pp. 565-9, 573-5; Gardiner, *Civil War* iii, 127-8, 131-7.

17. Wedgwood, *The King's War 1641-1647* pp. 601-12; Stevenson, *Revolution and Counter-Revolution* pp. 85-8.

18. Stevenson, *Revolution and Counter-Revolution* pp. 91, 93.

19. Gardiner, *Constitutional Documents* pp. 347-53; Gardiner, *Civil War* iv, 39-41; Donaldson, *Scotland: James V to James VII* p. 337; W. L. Mathieson, *Politics and Religion* (2 vols., Glasgow, 1902) ii, 81-2.

20. Gardiner, *Civil War* iv, 51-2.

21. Donaldson, *Scotland: James V to James VII* p. 337; Mathieson, *Politics and Religion* ii, 82-7; Gardiner, *Civil War* iv, 87-90. For Hamilton's dissembling tactics, see Stevenson, *Revolution and Counter-Revolution* pp. 121-2.

22. On 1 March 1648, the commission of the kirk had issued a declaration against the Engagement: A. F. Mitchell and J. Christie (eds.), *The Records of the Commissions of the General Assemblies of the Church of Scotland* (3 vols., Scottish History Society, 1892-1909) i, 373-82. As preparations were made for war against England, the Commission's opposition continued to be forcibly expressed in a Humble Representation of 28 April 1648: Mitchell and Christie, *Records* i, 489-512. The General Assembly declared the Engagement unlawful in July: Mathieson, *Politics and Religion* ii, 93-4.

23. See Stevenson, *Revolution and Counter-Revolution* p. 118.

24. Mathieson, *Politics and Religion* ii, 89-90; Gardiner, *Civil War* iv, 132, 155-6.

25. Mathieson, *Politics and Religion* ii, 99-103; Donaldson, *Scotland: James V to James VII* pp. 338-9; Stevenson, *Revolution and Counter-Revolution* p. 124.

26. Stevenson, *Revolution and Counter-Revolution* pp. 125-6.

27. Donaldson, *Scotland: James V to James VII* p. 339; Mathieson, *Politics and Religion* ii, 106-7; S. R. Gardiner, *History of the Commonwealth and Protectorate* (3 vols., London, 1897-1901) i, 16. For the text of the Act, see *The Acts of the*

Parliaments of Scotland eds. T. Thomson and C. Innes (12 vols., London, 1814-75) vi (2), 143-7.

28. Donaldson, *Scotland: James V to James VII* p. 213; Rosalind Mitchison, *A History of Scotland* (London, 1970) p. 229. For the Scots' attachment to the Stuart line, see Jennifer M. Brown, 'Scottish Politics 1567-1625' p. 23.

29. *APS* vi (2), 157; Gardiner, *C and P* i, 20.

30. Gardiner, *C and P* i, 22-3, 71, 74-5.

31. Stevenson, *Revolution and Counter-Revolution* p. 154.

32. Gardiner, *C and P* i, 204-8.

33. Gardiner, *C and P* i, 214-5, 219-27. For accounts of the negotiations which especially highlight the role of the Prince of Orange, see S. R. Gardiner (ed.), *Letters and Papers illustrating the relations between Charles II and Scotland in 1650* (Scottish History Society, 1894) pp. 39-41, 41-2, 43-7, 51-4, 55-9, 59-60, 61-2, 64-7, 70, 73-6, 84-6.

34. Gardiner (ed.), *Charles II and Scotland* pp. 105-6; Stevenson, *Revolution and Counter-Revolution* pp. 160-1, 168.

35. Gardiner (ed.), *Charles II and Scotland* pp. 88-9.

36. Gardiner, *C and P* i, 256, 263-5.

37. Gardiner, *C and P* i, 266-7, 311. This pressure culminated in Charles being forced to sign a declaration on 16 August 1650 in which he swore to uphold the Covenants and abhor Malignancy, for the text of which see Mitchell and Christie, *Records* iii, 33-40.

38. Gardiner, *C and P* i, 301-2, 303, 307, 316.

39. Stevenson, *Revolution and Counter-Revolution* pp. 174-5; Mathieson, *Politics and Religion* ii, 121-2.

40. Quoted in Gardiner, *C and P* i, 368.

41. This move had a corresponding effect on English politics, for 'the Rump was now able to portray the war as a national rather than as a religious one, as a struggle against royalism rather than against presbyterianism.': Blair Worden, *The Rump Parliament 1648-1653* (Cambridge, 1974) p. 240.

42. Gardiner, *C and P* i, 372-6.

43. Stevenson, *Revolution and Counter-Revolution* p. 175.

44. Mathieson, *Politics and Religion* ii, 128-9; Gardiner, *C and P* i, 369-71.

45. Gardiner, *C and P* i, 370-1; Stevenson, *Revolution and Counter-Revolution* pp. 187, 188; Stevenson, 'Thesis' pp. 708-9.

46. Gardiner, *C and P* i, 378.

47. Stevenson, *Revolution and Counter-Revolution* p. 188.

48. Mathieson, *Politics and Religion* ii, 131; Gardiner, *C and P* i, 381; Mitchell and Christie, *Records* iii, 130, 132; Stevenson, *Revolution and Counter-Revolution* pp. 190-1; Thomas McCrie (ed.), *The Life of Mr. Robert Blair . . . with Supplement . . . by . . . Mr. William Row* (Wodrow Society, 1848) pp. 247-8.

49. Gardiner, *C and P* i, 381; Mathieson, *Politics and Religion* ii, 132.

50. Row, *Life of Blair* pp. 250-1. For the text of the Public Resolutions, Mitchell and Christie, *Records* iii, 159-60.

51. For the texts of the protests *against* the Resolutions, see Mitchell and

Christie, *Records* iii, 173-82 (presbytery of Stirling), 196-9 (presbytery of Glasgow), 243-51 (presbytery of Aberdeen), 255-8 (presbytery of Paisley), 274-6 (presbytery of Deer), 276-9 (presbytery of Irvine), 298-303 (presbytery of Ayr), 362-3 (presbytery of Hamilton), 390-2 (presbytery of Lanark), 392-3 (synod of Glasgow and Ayr).

52. For texts of declarations *in support of* the Resolutions, see Mitchell and Christie, *Records* iii, 379-81 (synod of Fife), 386-7 (synod of Angus), 418-9 (synod of Moray), 421-2 (synod of Perth), 429-31 (presbytery of Chanonry).

53. Mitchell and Christie, *Records* iii, 356-8; *APS* vi (2), 654-5; Row, *Life of Blair* pp. 268-9.

54. Mitchell and Christie, *Records* iii, 367-70, 388, 404, 432, 439-44; Row, *Life of Blair* pp. 269-72.

55. *APS* vi (2), 676-7, 683-4.

56. Stevenson, *Revolution and Counter-Revolution* pp. 197-202.

57. Gardiner, *C and P* i, 381, 387-9, 391-3; John Willcock, *The Great Marquess* (Edinburgh and London, 1903) pp. 257, 273-4.

58. Mathieson, *Politics and Religion* ii, 136-8; Row, *Life of Blair* pp. 273-8 (for a full and reliable account of the proceedings).

59. The movements of the English army from Dunbar to Lambert's victory at Hamilton may be traced in W. S. Douglas, *Cromwell's Scotch Campaigns 1650-1651* (London, 1898) pp. 117-187.

60. Sir John Hope was an ordinary lord of session, as was his brother Sir James Hope of Hopetoun. The story has it that the third brother, Sir Alexander Hope, was first accused of putting forward the proposal to abandon southern Scotland, but when arrested, he said that Sir John Hope was to blame: Gardiner, *C and P* i, 387; George Brunton and David Haig, *An Historical Account of the Senators of the College of Justice* (Edinburgh and London, 1832) p. 290. Sir James is included in the story by Stevenson, *Revolution and Counter-Revolution* p. 196.

61. Gardiner, *C and P* i, 422-4; Douglas, *Cromwell's Scotch Campaigns* pp. 271-88; Stevenson, *Revolution and Counter-Revolution* pp. 205-6.

62. Gardiner, *C and P* i, 431.

63. Thus in Stevenson, *Revolution and Counter-Revolution* p. 207, following the estimate of Charles's strength on leaving Scotland put forward by Sir James Turner, *Memoirs of his Own Life and Times* (Bannatyne Club, 1829) p. 94. Note, however, that Gardiner put the number of the Scots leaving Stirling at 20,000 (*C and P* i, 431) and that Cromwell estimated the strength of Charles's army at Worcester to be 16,000 (Gardiner, *C and P* i, 442n).

64. Gardiner, *C and P* i, 467; C. H. Firth (ed.), *Scotland and the Commonwealth* (Scottish History Society, 1895) pp. i, 1-5.

65. Firth, *S and C* pp. xviii, 8-9, 23, 320; John Nicoll, *A Diary of Public Transactions* (Bannatyne Club, 1836) pp. 56-7.

Chapter 1: The Subjugation of Scotland, September 1651 — January 1652

1. Firth, *S and C* pp. 6, 7, 10; HMC *Portland* i, 615; Henry Cary, *Memorials of the Great Civil War in England from 1646 to 1652* (2 vols., London, 1842) ii, 352; Maurice Ashley, *General Monck* (London, 1977) p. 88.

2. Firth, *S and C* p. 10 and n; H. G. Tibbutt, *Colonel John Okey 1606-1662* (Bedfordshire Historical Record Society, 1955) pp. 43, 45.

3. There had been some disagreement over the best means of defending the town and the English incursion evidently took the Scots by surprise: Firth, *S and C* pp. 11-12; Nicoll, *Diary* p. 58; G. R. Kinloch (ed.), *The Diary of Mr. John Lamont of Newton 1649-1671* (Maitland Club, 1830) p. 34; Tibbutt, *Colonel John Okey 1606-1662* p. 45.

4. Firth, *S and C* pp. 12-13; Gardiner, *C and P* i, 468. As Gardiner notes, accounts of the numbers killed vary between 5 and 800. In his letter to the Speaker of 1 September (Cary, *Memorials of the Great Civil War* ii, 351) Monck mentions 500, but Clarke in a letter of 5 September mentions nearly 800 (*ibid.* ii, 366). Lamont (*Diary* p. 34) says 5-600. In his letter to the Speaker Monck reported 200 taken prisoner, whereas the account printed in Firth, *S and C* at p. 12 estimates 500; Nicoll, (*Diary* p. 58) estimates 4-500. Likewise there is a variation in the number of ships reported to have been captured: the account in Firth, *S and C* p. 12 states 'about 190', Monck's letter to the Speaker states 60, and Lamont's estimate is nearly 200 (*Diary* p. 34).

5. Firth, *S and C* pp. 13, 15, 324-5; Nicoll, *Diary* p. 58; Gardiner, *C and P* i, 468-70; Robert Steele (ed.), *Tudor and Stuart Proclamations* (2 vols., Oxford, 1910) 3rd part (Scotland) Nos. 2075, 2076.

6. For the records of these courts-martial, see Worcester MS. xxi, and the selections therefrom in Godfrey Davies (ed.), 'Dundee Court-Martial Records 1651' *Miscellany III* (Scottish History Society, 1919) pp. 3-67.

7. Firth, *S and C* pp. 14, 323.

8. Firth, *S and C* p. 14; John Stuart (ed.), *Extracts from the Council Register of the Burgh of Aberdeen 1643-1747* (Scottish Burgh Records Society, 1872) p. 122; John Barclay (ed.), *Diary of Alexander Jaffray* (Aberdeen, 1856) pp. 58-9; Peter Toon, *God's Statesman: The Life and Work of John Owen* (Exeter, 1971) pp. 46-7.

9. Firth, *S and C* p. 15; *Aberdeen Council Register* pp. 123-4; Tibbutt, *Colonel John Okey 1606-1662* p. 46.

10. Firth, *S and C* pp. 17, 320-2; Bulstrode Whitelocke, *Memorials of the English Affairs* (4 vols., Oxford, 1853) iii, 349.

11. For the events leading up to the surrender, see *Calendar of State Papers, Domestic Series 1651-2* pp. 6, 82, 86; Worcester MS. xx f77v; Nicoll, *Diary* pp. 71, 73, 75; *Journals of the House of Commons* vii, 64, and for the date of the articles of rendition, see Worcester MS. xlv 19 January 1654. A fuller account of the castle's significance is given in F. D. Dow, 'The English Army and the

Government of Scotland 1651-1660' (York University, D.Phil. thesis, 1976) pp. 31-3.

12. Worcester MS. xxf14; Cary, *Memorials of the Great Civil War* ii, 352, 365-6.

13. Worcester MS. xix f131; *CJ* vii, 23; Ashley, *General Monck* p. 91. The additional cost was to be £17,218 12s. 0d. per month.

14. Worcester MS. xx ff37, 63.

15. Firth, *S and C* p. 326; Stevenson, *Revolution and Counter-Revolution* p. 209. The Earl of Seaforth and the Mackenzies had undertaken to provide 740 armed men: NLS MS. Adv. 29.2.9, Balcarres Papers f216.

16. Worcester MS. xx f14; Firth, *S and C* p. 335.

17. Worcester MS. xx ff30v, 34; Bodl. Lib. Tanner MS. lv f90.

18. Firth, *S and C* p. 337 (extract from *Mercurius Scoticus*—this is cited by the *Oxford English Dictionary* as the earliest use of the word 'Tories' in a Scottish context, meaning 'robbers, bandits or outlaws').

19. Worcester MS. xx f34.

20. Firth, *S and C* pp. 20-1, 339, 340-1; Worcester MS. xx f37.

21. It is unclear when each arrived in Scotland, but by December both were active in the civil and military administration. On 23 October, Parliament had named them (and six others, including Monck) as commissioners for settling the civil affairs of Scotland: *CJ* vii, 30 and see *infra* p.

22. Firth, *S and C* p. 343.

23. Worcester MS. xx f63; J. Y. Akerman (ed.), *Letters from Roundhead Officers written from Scotland and chiefly addressed to Captain Adam Baynes. July MDCL—June MDCLX* (Bannatyne Club, 1856) pp. 38, 39; David Laing (ed.), *The Diary of Alexander Brodie of Brodie* (Spalding Club, 1863) p. 16; Ian Grimble, *Chief of Mackay* (London, 1965) p. 166.

24. Firth, *S and C* p. 34 and n; *LRO* p. 45.

25. Worcester MS. xx f77; Firth, *S and C* p. 343.

26. Douglas, *Cromwell's Scotch Campaigns* pp. 167n, 204n, 256, 276n; Firth, *S and C* pp. 8 and n, 28, 340, 341; Worcester MS. xx f66.

27. Worcester MS xx ff66, 70; Firth, *S and C* p. 28.

28. Worcester MS. xx f63; Worcester MS. xxii f20.

29. Bodl. Lib. Tanner MS. lv f90; Worcester MS. xx f63; Worcester MS. xxi f55 (cf. Davies, 'Dundee Court-Martial Records 1651' pp. 39-42).

30. Firth, *S and C* p. 29.

31. Worcester MS. xx f63. It is not clear from the report whether the sums were in £ Scots or £ sterling.

32. Firth, *S and C* pp. 22-3; Stevenson, *Revolution and Counter-Revolution* p. 209. For the summonses to Balcarres to appear at Dunkeld and Dumbarton, see NLS MS. Adv. 29.2.9, Balcarres Papers ff213, 215 both dated 11 September from Finlarig (near Killin).

33. D. Hay Fleming (ed.), *Diary of Sir Archibald Johnston of Wariston* Vol. II 1650-1654 (Scottish History Society, 1919), 143.

34. Firth, *S and C* pp. 16-17.

35. Firth, *S and C* p. 26n; Stevenson, *Revolution and Counter-Revolution* p. 209.

36. Worcester MS. xx ff23, 31v; Firth, *S and C* pp. 333, 335; *CJ* vii, 33; Gardiner, *C and P* ii, 72.

37. Firth, *S and C* p. 335; Stevenson, *Revolution and Counter-Revolution* p. 210; Worcester MS. xx ff23, 29 (later reports tended to confirm the English belief that Argyle had been instrumental in summoning the Parliament, although it was by then clear that others had also been implicated in the project: *ibid.* ff34, 40v; Firth, *S and C* p. 19).

38. Firth, *S and C* pp. 19-20; 338-9; Whitelocke, *Memorials* iii, 370; Bodl. Lib. Tanner MS. lv f90; Worcester MS. xx f29.

39. Firth, *S and C* pp. 20, 27; Worcester MS. xx ff63, 77.

40. Firth, *S and C* pp. 29, 344; Worcester MS. xx f77v; C. S. Terry (ed.), *The Cromwellian Union* (Scottish History Society, 1902) pp. 2, 4, 5.

41. For debates and decisions in Whitehall and Westminster leading up to the despatch of these commissioners, see *infra* pp.

42. Firth, *S and C* pp. xxxiv.

43. *LRO* pp. 38, 39, 40, 42, 45.

44. Davies, 'Dundee Court-Martial Records 1651' pp. 45, 47, 59-60, 61, 64; *LRO* p. 38.

45. Lamont, *Diary* pp. 34, 35; *Aberdeen Council Register* p. 125; Marguerite Wood (ed.), *Extracts from the Records of the Burgh of Edinburgh 1642 to 1655* (Edinburgh, 1938) p. 263.

46. Firth, *S and C* p. 31. This is also borne out by the calculations entered by Clarke in Worcester MS. xxiii ff71-75v (MS. xxiii is a notebook dealing with the imposition of the cess for 1651-2, but its entries are, for the early months of the conquest, fragmentary and difficult to interpret).

47. David Stevenson, 'The financing of the cause of the Covenants, 1638-51', *Scottish Historical Review* li (1972) pp. 106-7, 113-23.

48. Firth, *S and C* pp. 328-30, 331-2; Worcester MS. xx f14.

49. J. D. Marwick (ed.), *Extracts from the Records of the Burgh of Glasgow 1630-1662* (Scottish Burgh Records Society, 1881) pp. 213, 214; *Aberdeen Council Register* pp. 125, 126, 127.

50. Terry, *CU* pp. 1-2; Firth, *S and C* p. 30; *LRO* p. 42; W. H. Dawson, *Cromwell's Understudy: The Life and Times of General John Lambert* (London, 1938) pp. 144-5.

51. Worcester MS. xxiii ff4-29v; SRO E/901/1 Valuation Rolls of 1649. These figures did not necessarily give the English a true picture of the rental of each shire, since the figures for 1649 had in some cases been artificially heightened to meet the requirements of the covenanting government. Nor did it help them to understand how the Scots had determined the contribution of each shire to the monthly maintenance of 1649-51, for the valuation rolls of 1649 had never in fact been used for that purpose: see Dow, 'Thesis' pp. 50n, 51n.

52. Firth, *S and C* p. 31.

53. Nicoll, *Diary* p. 69; Worcester MS. xxiii ff82-84v.

54. Worcester MS. xxii f29; Firth, *S and C* p. xxx, and see *infra* p. 58.
55. Brunton and Haig, *Senators of the College of Justice* p. 345.
56. Firth, *S and C* p. xxviii; Nicoll, *Diary* pp. 65, 66, 69, 75.
57. Steele 3rd pt. No. 2084.
58. Firth, *S and C* pp. 334, 344, 346-8, xxxiv; Steele 3rd pt. Nos. 2081, 2083.
59. Terry, *CU* pp. 2, 3; Firth, *S and C* p. xxxiv; Nicoll, *Diary* pp. 64, 65, 66, 69.
60. Mitchell and Christie, *Records* iii, 513; Row, *Life of Blair* p. 285; D. G. Barron (ed.), *In Defence of the Regalia, 1651-2* (London, 1910) p. 95; Stevenson, *Revolution and Counter-Revolution* pp. 208-9.
61. Row, *Life of Blair* p. 285; Wariston, *Diary* ii, 140-4.
62. Row, *Life of Blair* pp. 286-7; Wariston, *Diary* ii, 144-50; Firth, *S and C* p. 336; Worcester MS. xx ff6v, 14, 23.
63. Wariston, *Diary* ii, 147; Jaffray, *Diary* pp. 59-60, 166-8.
64. Nicoll, *Diary* pp. 61-2.
65. Firth, *S and C* pp. 31, 339-40; Worcester MS. xx f29v.
66. Worcester MS. xx f44.
67. Row, *Life of Blair* pp. 287-8; cf. Firth, *S and C* p. 19.
68. Worcester MS. xx ff29, 49.
69. Gardiner, *Constitutional Documents* p. 269; David Laing (ed.), *The Letters and Journals of Robert Baillie* (3 vols., Edinburgh, 1842) iii, 175-6.
70. Firth, *S and C* p. 328; *Aberdeen Council Register* p. 124; Worcester MS. xx f7.
71. Worcester MS. xx ff34, 66; D. C. Mactavish (ed.), *Minutes of the Synod of Argyll 1652-1661* (Scottish History Society, 1944) p. 223.
72. Firth, *S and C* pp. 19-20; Worcester MS. xx ff29, 42.
73. Firth, *S and C* pp. 30, 343; Lamont, *Diary* p. 36; HMC *Various Collections* v, 152.
74. Nicoll, *Diary* pp. 63, 72; Row, *Life of Blair* p. 289.
75. Nicoll, *Diary* pp. 71-2; Row, *Life of Blair* pp. 289-90.
76. Row, *Life of Blair* pp. 290-1; Firth, *S and C* pp. 32-3; Nicoll, *Diary* pp. 72-3; Terry, *CU* pp. 7-10; Whitelocke, *Memorials* iii, 386-7, 389-90; W. Stephen (ed.), *Register of the Consultations of the Ministers of Edinburgh and some other Brethren of the Ministry* (2 vols., Scottish History Society, 1921-30) i, 1-12.
77. Terry, *CU* p. 3.
78. Terry, *CU* pp. 2, 4; Firth, *S and C* pp. 29-30.
79. Terry, *CU* pp. 6-10.
80. Terry, *CU* pp. 5-6.
81. *CJ* vii, 12-13; Whitelocke, *Memorials* iii, 349.
82. *CJ* vii, 14. On 6 September Major John Cobbett had been granted lands of £100 stg. *per annum* but this was not confirmed until 15 October 1652: *CJ* vii, 191. For grants to other army officers, see *CJ* vii, 132, 147; Firth, *S and C* p. xxxii.
83. *CJ* vii, 14, 19-20, 22; Terry, *CU* p. xvii; Firth, *S and C* p. xxiii. Proposals to subjugate Scotland to the Commonwealth of England had first been aired, in the pages of *Mercurius Politicus,* in January 1651, when the war against Scotland began to be seen in national rather than religious terms: Worden, *The Rump Parliament* pp. 240, 254.

84. Wariston, *Diary* ii, 143; A. C. Swinton, *The Swintons of that Ilk and their Cadets* (Edinburgh, 1883) p. 65.

85. *CSPD 1651* p. 474; *CSPD 1651-2* p. 65; *CJ* vii, 30, 31, 47, 56; Terry, *CU* pp. xx-xxi and n, xxiii and n.

86. For the text of the Declaration, see Terry, *CU* pp. xxi-xxiii (and for other locations, see *ibid.* p. xxi n).

87. *CJ* vii, 21, 30; *CSPD 1651* pp. 455, 489; Terry, *CU* p. xvii and n.

88. *CJ* vii, 21, 47, 49, 53; *CSPD 1651* p. 492; *CSPD 1651-2* p. 48; Nicoll, *Diary* p. 79; Terry, *CU* pp. xvii, xviii-xx and notes, xxiv.

89. For the text of the Instructions, see C. H. Firth (ed.), *Scotland and the Protectorate* (Scottish History Society, 1899) pp. 393-8.

90. *LRO* p. 43 (the writer was Cornet John Baynes).

Chapter 2: The Political Settlement of Scotland and Union with England, January 1652 — April 1653

1. There they took up residence in the 'great hous and castle' belonging to the Earls of Buccleuch and were guarded by four companies of Col. Alured's regiment: Nicoll, *Diary* p. 79; Terry, *CU* p. xxiv note 7; Firth, *S and C* p. 31; Worcester MS. xxii f13.

2. This newspaper had been printed at Leith from July to December 1651: Firth, *S and C* p. 315n.

3. *LRO* p. 43; Worcester MS. xxii f13.

4. Worcester MS. xxii f14 (dated 24 January) states that the Commissioners had issued the summonses for the counties by that date. The printed summons cited in Steele 3rd pt. No. 2085 is also dated 24 January but refers specifically to burghs summoned for 13 February, as does the summons (itself undated) printed in Terry, *CU* pp. 11-12. Evidence from Wood, *Extracts Edin. Recs. 1642 to 1655* p. 266 suggests that Edinburgh's printed summons was dated 21 January.

5. Terry, *CU* p. xxv note 4. The franchise in the shires was held, in accordance with an Act of Parliament of 1587, by 'all the barons and freeholders (tenants in chief) who possessed land worth more than 40 s[hillings] of old extent per annum and were not nobles'. (Note, however, that the Earl of Annandale was elected to serve as a deputy for Perthshire in March 1652: Terry, *CU* p. 128.) The burgh commissioners to a Parliament were elected by the councils of the burghs. Stevenson, *The Scottish Revolution 1637-1644* p. 167.

6. By 24 January the dates for attendance had been fixed: Terry, *CU* p. 10. A list of these is printed *ibid.* pp. 12-4; there 12 February is given as the second date, although it seems from other evidence (cited in note 4 *supra*) that this was subsequently changed to 13 February.

7. B.L.Add.MS. 38091 f98.

8. Nicoll, *Diary* p. 80; Steele 3rd pt. No. 2086; Gardiner, *C and P* ii, 67 dates this declaration inaccurately as 21 January, because of confusion between the Old and New Styles of dating. See also *CJ* vii, 37; *CSPD 1651-2* p. 26.

9. For a brief account of the competence of sheriff, commissary, regality and baron courts in the mid-seventeenth century, see Dow, 'Thesis' p. 82 notes 1-3.

10. See *infra* pp.

11. Nicoll, *Diary* p. 80; Worcester MS. xxii f22.

12. Nicoll, *Diary* p. 81; Terry, *CU* pp. xxv, 18 (the latter establishes that some deputies had in fact arrived by 12 February); Gardiner, *C and P* ii, 67. According to Lamont (*Diary* p. 37), the Declaration was also proclaimed at other mercat crosses throughout the kingdom: if the usual procedure were followed, the proclamations outside the capital would be *after* 12 February. Terry is clearly wrong in assuming (*CU* p. xxv) that only when the Declaration had been proclaimed were the summonses sent to the shires and burghs.

13. Terry, *CU* p. 23.

14. For the text of the Explanation, see *APS* vi (2), 809; Nicoll, *Diary* pp. 83-4 (for the version pertaining to East Lothian; the date of proclamation is erroneously given as 11 February, *i.e.* the day before the proclamation of the Declaration of 28 October); Worcester MS. xxii f27; Steele 3rd pt. No. 2088. Protection was not to extend to mosstroopers or to the murderers of English soldiers.

15. Terry, *CU* p. 14-5.

16. Terry, *CU* p. xxviii and Document CLIX (facing p. 84—the original of this *schema* is to be found in PRO SP 25/138 [Minute Book of the Committee of Parliament appointed to confer with the Deputies sent from Scotland] pp. 22-5).

17. Terry, *CU* pp. 177, 178.

18. See *supra* pp.

19. Terry, *CU* pp. 26-7.

20. Row, *Life of Blair* pp. 292-4; Baillie, *Letters and Journals* iii, 173.

21. Terry, *CU* pp. 11, 16; Baillie, *Letters and Journals* iii, 174; Bodl. Lib. Carte MS. 103 f163 cf. Wariston, *Diary* ii, 153, 154.

22. Firth, *S and C* p. 211.

23. Terry, *CU* pp. xxvii, 15-6.

24. Terry, *CU* p. 26; Lamont, *Diary* pp. 36, 38.

25. Wood, *Extracts Edin. Recs. 1642 to 1655* pp. 266, 268, 269, 270; Terry, *CU* p. 23.

26. *Aberdeen Council Register* pp. 128-9; Terry, *CU* pp. 46 and n, 55.

27. Terry, *CU* p. 39.

28. Terry, *CU* pp. 34-5; *Glasgow Burgh Recs.* pp. 218-9; Stevenson, 'Thesis' p. 738.

29. Terry, *CU* pp. 118-20.

30. Terry, *CU* pp. 112-5.

31. Terry, *CU* p. 35n; Nicoll, *Diary* p. 89.

32. Terry, *CU* Document CLIX (PRO SP 25/138 pp. 22-5), 74-5, 153; PRO SP 25/138 pp. 18, 19.

33. After Glasgow, Kirkcudbrightshire, and Morayshire had converted their dissents to assents, the number of acceptances totalled 73.

34. Baillie, *Letters and Journals* iii, 175; Terry, *CU* p. 109.

35. Terry, *CU* pp. 37-8, 56-7, 51-3, 36-7, 58-9, 50, 49, 50-1.

36. Terry, *CU* pp. 76-7.

37. Terry, *CU* p. 38.

38. These were Sir James Macdowall of Garthland and Sir Andrew Agnew of Lochnaw (Wigtonshire) and Sir James Hamilton of Orbiston and (probably) John Douglas of Kayston (Dunbartonshire): Terry, *CU* pp. 38, 53. Agnew was appointed a sheriff in 1656; Douglas was a JP in 1656; Hamilton was an MP in 1654 and a JP in 1656; and Macdowall was an MP in 1654, 1656 and 1659, a commissioner for claims on forfeited estates in 1654, and a commissioner for customs and excise in 1655. For these, see Terry, *CU* pp. lvi, lxiii, lxxix; Firth, *S and P* pp. 311, 316; Firth and Rait, *A* & *O* ii, 878.

39. See *e.g.* Terry, *CU* pp. 42, 44, 78, 81, 128, 158, 162.

40. See *e.g.* Terry, *CU* pp. 60, 77, 101, 107, 148, 160.

41. See *e.g.* Terry, *CU* p. 53 (Desires of Edinburgh and eleven other burghs) cf. *ibid.* p. 171 (Argyllshire's reference to Solemn League and Covenant.)

42. For a typical example reflected in most of the Desires, see Terry, *CU* pp. 39-41.

43. Terry, *CU* p. 82 cf. p. 91 (Fife).

44. Terry, *CU* pp. 41, 156-7.

45. See *e.g.* Terry, *CU* pp. 43, 44, 54, 129, 158, 163. For the difficulties encountered by the Earl of Airlie when trying to raise ready cash in February 1652, see SRO Airlie MSS. GD 16/34/25, the Earl of Airlie to Lady Ogilvy (his daughter-in-law) 19 February 1652.

46. Terry, *CU* p. 54.

47. Terry, *CU* p. 80.

48. Terry, *CU* p. 61.

49. Terry, *CU* p. 125.

50. Terry, *CU* pp. 61, 108, 155-6, 160.

51. Terry, *CU* pp. 123-6. There is, however, little evidence in the text of the Desires themselves to justify Hugh Trevor-Roper's statement that '[f]rom the outer fringes of the country, where the kirk was not yet firmly planted, a faint voice might seem to welcome the union for the social change it might chance to bring': H. R. Trevor-Roper, 'Scotland and the Puritan Revolution' in *Religion, the Reformation and Social Change* (London, 1967) p. 439.

52. Terry, *CU* pp. 68-9, 84, 85, 98-9; Bodl. Lib. Tanner MS. lv f158.

53. For the text of the Tender, see Terry, *CU* pp. 98-9. Whitelocke (*Memorials* iii, 406) gave the number of shires reported to Parliament as 20 and the number of burghs as 35, figures which correspond to the number of decipherable entries in *CJ* vii, 105-6. Further assents were reported to the House on 23, 26 March, 2 April and 14 May 1652: see Terry, *CU* p. xxx note; *CJ* vii, 107, 111, 113, 132.

54. Terry, *CU* p. xxxi; *CJ* vii, 107, 110-1; *CSPD 1651-2* p. 185.

55. The text of the Declaration is printed in Terry, *CU* pp. 140-4. The names of those shires and burghs whose assents were reported on 26 March were inserted into the Declaration by order of the House: *CJ* vii, 111.

56. *CJ* vii, 111-2; *CSPD 1651-2* p. 199; Terry, *CU* pp. 149-50.

57. *CJ* vii, 107, 118. Also on 23 March, the House referred the Commissioners'

fourth and fifth proposals to the Council of State and charged them with bringing in an act for preventing robberies upon the Borders and for settling disputes over fishing rights in the Tweed: *CJ* vii, 107. This last answered some of the Desires of Roxburghshire: see Terry, *CU* p. 61.

58. Steele 3rd pt. No. 2092; Terry, *CU* pp. xxxii and n, xxxiii and n; Firth, *S and C* p. 41; *CJ* vii, 132 (for the report of 14 May).

59. Terry, *CU* p. 179; *Glasgow Burgh Recs.* pp. 234, 235; Wood, *Extracts Edin. Recs. 1642 to 1655* p. 287; SRO Stair MSS. GD 135/136 (for Fife).

60. Cf. the names of the deputies appended to the text of the assents throughout Terry, *CU,* and the list of the August deputies printed *ibid.* Document CLIX (PRO SP 25/138 pp. 22-5).

61. Terry, *CU* pp. xxxiii note, 181-3; Worcester MS. xxiv f10; J. D. Marwick (ed.), *Extracts from the Records of the Convention of the Royal Burghs of Scotland 1615-1676* (Edinburgh, 1878) pp. 358-65. The meeting of the burghs took the form of a General Convention. It was intended that the meeting at Edinburgh should attend to business which had been postponed when the last General Convention, held at Cupar in July 1650, had been abandoned due to the troubled times. But in the event, these matters were again held over, until November 1652: *ibid.* pp. 358, 365; Louise B. Taylor, *Aberdeen Council Letters* (6 vols., London, 1942-61) iii, 209.

62. This list follows Terry, *CU* Document CLIX (and hence PRO SP 25/138 pp. 22-5).

63. The report forms PRO SP 25/138 pp. 15-25; the 'matter of fact' is expressed diagrammatically in Terry, *CU* Document CLIX.

64. PRO SP 25/138 pp. 15-17, 20; cf. Terry, *CU* p. xxxiv.

65. PRO SP 25/138 pp. 18-19, 21; cf. Terry, *CU* pp. xxxiv-xxxv.

66. Terry, *CU* p. xxxvi; *CSPD 1651-2* p. 441 (PRO SP 25/138 p. 4).

67. Terry, *CU* p. xxxvii and n2; *CJ* vii, 189, 190, 229.

68. See the minute-book of the Committee, PRO SP 25/138.

69. Row, *Life of Blair* p. 300.

70. *CSPD 1651-2* p. 439 (PRO SP 25/138 pp. 3-4) cf. Terry, *CU* p. xxxviii and n 1.

71. *CSPD 1651-2* pp. 441-2 (PRO SP 25/138 pp. 4-6) cf. Terry, *CU* p. xxxviii.

72. *CSPD 1651-2* p. 448 (PRO SP 25/138 pp. 7-8).

73. *CSPD 1651-2* p. 456 (PRO SP25/138 pp. 9-12) cf. Terry, *CU* pp. xxxviii-xxxix. The judicatories in Scotland were continued by an order of Parliament of 26 October: *CJ* vii, 195.

74. *CSPD 1651-2* pp. 458, 459-60 (PRO SP 25/138 pp. 12-13, 13-25); *CJ* vii, 203 cf. Terry, *CU* p. xxxix.

75. *CSPD 1651-2* p. 467 (PRO SP 25/138 p. 26) cf. Terry, *CU* pp. xxxix-xl.

76. *CSPD 1651-2* p. 475 (PRO SP 25/138 pp. 27-8) cf. Terry, *CU* p. xl. It should be noted that there is no official record of the deputies being informed of the House's decision of 29 October; their queries concerning their status could, therefore, conceivably have arisen out of simple ignorance.

77. *CSPD 1651-2* pp. 484-5, 488, 491, 495 (PRO SP 25/138 pp. 29-30, 30-3); Terry, *CU* pp. xl-xli; *CJ* vii, 227, 229.
78. *CSPD 1652-3* pp. 38-9 (PRO SP 25/138 pp. 36-8) cf. Terry, *CU* p. xli.
79. *CSPD 1652-3* pp. 51-2 (PRO SP 25/138 pp. 40-2) cf. Terry, *CU* p. xlii.
80. *CSPD 1652-3* p. 60 (PRO SP 25/138 pp. 43-5) cf. Terry, *CU* p. xlii.
81. *CSPD 1652-3* pp. 215-6 (PRO SP 25/138 pp. 58-9); *CJ* vii, 263, 265 cf. Terry, *CU* pp. xlii-xliii.
82. *CSPD 1652-3* p. 97 (PRO SP 25/138 p. 46).
83. PRO SP 25/138 p. 48; *CSPD 1652-3* pp. 131-2.
84. *CSPD 1652-3* pp. 156-7 (PRO SP 25/138 pp. 52-4); *CJ* vii, 253.
85. *CSPD 1652-3* pp. 210, 215 (PRO SP 25/138 pp. 57-8, 58-9).
86. *CSPD 1652-3* pp. 269-70 (PRO SP 25/138 pp. 64-5).
87. Terry, *CU* p. xliv; *CSPD 1652-3* pp. 303-4.
88. Terry, *CU* pp. xliv-xlv and notes; *CSPD 1652-3* p. 310.
89. Terry, *CU* pp. xlviii-xlix and notes; Firth and Rait, *A & O* ii, 813-22, 871-5, 875-83, 930-2.
90. Lamont, *Diary* p. 46.

Chapter 3: Attempts at Pacification and the Birth of Revolt, March — December 1652

1. For the form of the officers' oaths, see Terry, *CU* pp. 178-9.
2. The Charter to the Assenting Burghs, which also describes the form of oaths to be taken by municipal officers, is printed in Terry, *CU* pp. 63-5.
3. Wood, *Extracts Edin. Recs. 1642 to 1655* pp. xxvi, 261, 310-2.
4. *Aberdeen Council Register* p. 125; *Glasgow Burgh Recs.* p. 213.
5. The Desires of some of the burghs implied that the administration of justice had lapsed, certainly after 31 January 1652: see *e.g.* Terry, *CU* p. 108 and cf. Wood, *Extracts Edin. Recs. 1642 to 1655* p. xxvi.
6. Terry, *CU* p. 65.
7. Terry, *CU* pp. 154-5, 165; Firth, *S and C* pp. 39-40; Worcester MS. xxii f60.
8. Terry, *CU* pp. 16, 85, 97, 101-4; Wood, *Extracts Edin. Recs. 1642 to 1655* pp. 270, 271, 272; *The Lord Provosts of Edinburgh 1296 to 1932* (Edinburgh, 1932) p. 43. For Stewart, see Stevenson, *Revolution and Counter-Revolution* pp. 188, 203.
9. Terry, *CU* pp. 65-6, 67, 164; *CJ* vii, 132.
10. Terry, *CU* pp. 174-5 and n; *CJ* vii, 132; *CSPD 1651-2* p. 210. Two Scottish judges were probably added later to the commission for criminal causes: G. W. T. Omond, *The Lord Advocates of Scotland* (2 vols., Edinburgh, 1883) i, 160.
11. The English had great difficulty in persuading some Scots to accept the post of Clerk. Some scrupled to accept office under the English régime; one man was interviewed four times by the Judges, but still refused, as a matter of conscience, to serve: Wariston, *Diary* ii, 161, 164, 165; SRO Breadalbane MSS. GD 112/39/891 A. Henderson to the laird of Glenorchy the younger 10 May 1652.

12. Nicoll, *Diary* p. 95; the Keeper of the Signet is described by Nicoll as 'Mr. Clerk, Inglischeman.'

13. Among other honours, Lockhart and Swinton were appointed members of the Council for Scotland in 1655, and Lockhart was appointed ambassador to France. Each is discussed at many points in the following chapters, but see also H. R. Trevor-Roper, 'Scotland and the Puritan Revolution' pp. 415-6, 433, 442-3.

14. Brunton and Haig, *Senators of the College of Justice* pp. 289-90 and *supra* p.   Trevor-Roper confuses Sir John Hope with his brother Sir James Hope of Hopetoun in 'Scotland and the Puritan Revolution' p. 415.

15. *DNB* s.v. Lockhart, Sir William, of Lee (1621-1676).

16. *DNB* s.v. Swinton, John (1621?-1679); Swinton, *The Swintons of that Ilk* pp. 64-77. Swinton is said to have become a Quaker in 1657, after the visit of George Fox to Scotland: *ibid.* p. 69; Sir James Balfour Paul, 'The Diary of Sir James Hope 1646-1654', *Miscellany III* (Scottish History Society, 1919) p. 159n.

17. Firth, *S and C* p. 43; Nicoll, *Diary* p. 96; Lamont, *Diary* p. 42.

18. Worcester MS. xxii ff77, 96.

19. This argument is developed fully in Parts Two and Three.

20. Worcester MS. xxiv ff25, 29; xxviii ff25-28; Nicoll, *Diary* pp. 102, 219.

21. Worcester MS. xxiv, f25.

22. Worcester MS. xxiv, f29; Omond, *The Lord Advocates of Scotland* i, 161; Lamont, *Diary* p. 47. For some reported cases of witchcraft in Scotland between 1651 and 1660, see G. F. Black, *A Calendar of Cases of Witchcraft in Scotland, 1510-1727* (New York, 1938) pp. 63-5.

23. Nicoll, *Diary* p. 104.

24. Terry, *CU* pp. 1, 17.

25. Firth, *S and C* p. xxxi; Wariston, *Diary* ii, 158, 159-60.

26. Lamont, *Diary* p. 37. SRO Leven and Melville MSS. GD 26/7/176 (petition of Alexander Earl of Leven to Parliament in 1659, after the recall of the Rump). For the sequestration of another prisoner captured at Alyth, John Lord Bargany, see SRO Bargany MSS. RH 4/57/33 (orders by the subcommissioners for sequestration 'for the counties of Dumfries, Wigton, Carrick, part of Ayr') and Sir Hew Hamilton Dalrymple, *A Short Account of the Hamiltons of Bargany* (Edinburgh, 1897) pp. 10-2.

27. Lamont, *Diary* pp. 39, 40.

28. For the names of some of those whose estates had been sequestered by 1653, see 'An Abstract of the Sequestrations of Scotland drawn from the Accompts of the sub-Commissioners delivered in upon oath for the Crops or years 1651 and 1652', Bodl. Lib. Carte MS. 74 f460. It also appears that the estates of some people in the shires of Ayr, Renfrew and Kirkcudbright who had not accepted the union had been sequestered by 1653: *CSPD 1652-3* p. 416 (dated 16 June 1653).

29. See Part Two.

30. Worcester MS. xxii f29; Firth, *S and C* p. xxx.

31. Worcester MS. xxiii ff85v-89.

32. Worcester MS. xxiii ff89v-92v. Further abatements were allowed to certain

shires for the keeping of armed guards; by the end of the year, this applied to some parishes in Stirlingshire, Perthshire and Caithness: *ibid.* ff92v-93v.

33. See *infra* pp.

34. Firth, *S and C* pp. 44-5 and n; Worcester MS. xxii f101.

35. Baillie, *Letters and Journals* iii, 187, 193, 202, 203, 216, 217, 219; Hew Scott (ed.), *Fasti Ecclesiae Scoticanae* (7 vols., Edinburgh, 1915-28) iii, 267, 482.

36. For evidence of Lilburne's favour towards Protesters, see Worcester MS. xlv 12 May 1653; Scott, *Fasti* ii, 33 and *infra* pp. . But in at least three other cases concerning admission to benefices, Lilburne favoured a candidate who had been deposed in 1649 for *not* preaching against the Engagement: Worcester MS. xlv 14 May, 12 August, 10 December 1653; Scott, *Fasti* i, 215, 233, 363.

37. Baillie, *Letters and Journals* iii, 206-8, 237-59; J. D. Mackie, *The University of Glasgow 1451-1951* (Glasgow, 1954) pp. 108, 109.

38. Wood, *Extracts Edin. Recs. 1642 to 1655* pp. 277-9, 304; Sir Alexander Grant, *The Story of the University of Edinburgh during its first three hundred years* (2 vols., London, 1884) ii, 247.

39. Row, *Life of Blair* pp. 297, 301; Jaffray, *Diary* pp. 65, 166-8; Wariston, *Diary* ii, 173; Lamont, *Diary* p. 47.

40. Row, *Life of Blair* p. 300; Lamont, *Diary* pp. 44-5, 47.

41. Worcester MS. xxiv f1v; Lamont, *Diary* p. 39.

42. Row, *Life of Blair* pp. 295-6; Mitchell and Christie, *Records* iii, 513, 514; Wariston, *Diary* ii, 165-7.

43. See *e.g.* Baillie, *Letters and Journals* iii, 178, 179, 182-3.

44. Row, *Life of Blair* pp. 296-7; Wariston, *Diary* ii, 179-83; Worcester MS. xxiv f7.

45. Lamont, *Diary* p. 44; Baillie, *Letters and Journals* iii, 174; for the harassment of Protesters, see Wariston, *Diary* ii, 171, 175, 176, 187.

46. Lamont, *Diary* p. 44.

47. Lamont, *Diary* p. 48; Firth, *S and C* pp. 53-4; R. B. Hannen, 'Cupar, Fife, 1652-1659', *Baptist Quarterly* N. S. vol. x (1940-1), 46-7.

48. Firth, *S and C* p. 370; Baillie, *Letters and Journals* iii, 178; Nicoll, *Diary* p. 91.

49. E. B. Underhill (ed.), *Records of the Church of Christ gathered at Fenstanton, Warboys and Hexham 1644-1720* (Hanserd Knollys Society, 1854) p. 301.

50. Firth, *S and C* pp. 38-9; *CJ* vii, 123; Worcester MS. xxii f71v.

51. SRO Hepburne Papers RH9/18/29 Items 34, 35, 36, 37 and 41; David Stevenson, 'The English and the Public Records of Scotland, 1650-1660' *Miscellany One* (Stair Society, 1971) pp. 159, 160-1; Firth, *S and C* p. 334; *CJ* vii, 127.

52. Barron, *In Defence of the Regalia, 1651-2* pp. 28-9, 121, 122; *CSPD 1651-2* pp. 230, 231.

53. Barron, *In Defence of the Regalia, 1651-2* pp. 17-9, 110-2, 124-8, 132-3; O. Ogle, W. H. Bliss, W. D. Macray and F. J. Routledge (eds.), *Calendar of the Clarendon State Papers* (5 vols., Oxford, 1872-1970) ii, 118, 129, 136.

54. Barron, *In Defence of the Regalia, 1651-2* pp. 30, 33, 122-3, 134-5; Worcester

MS. xxii ff86, 96. The articles of capitulation are dated 24 May, and not 26 May as is stated by Gardiner, *C and P* ii, 70.

55. On the later fate of the regalia, see Gardiner, *C and P* ii, 70-1.

56. See *supra* pp.

57. Terry, *CU* p. 17.

58. Firth, *S and C* p. 34; Terry, *CU* pp. 131-3; Worcester MS xxii f49.

59. Firth, *S and C* pp. 37-8, 40-1, 42.

60. Terry, *CU* pp. 170-3

61. Terry, *CU* p. 180.

62. The fortifications at Inverlochy and Leith were not begun until 1654 and 1656 respectively, but those at Ayr and Inverness, like that at St. Johnstons, were started in the spring of 1652. As well as being designed for defensive purposes, the citadels served also as barracks: Firth, *S and P* pp. xxxix-li (for a valuable account of the construction of these citadels); C. H. Firth, *Cromwell's Army* (4th edn., London, 1962) p. 294n. In addition to these major fortresses, smaller garrisons were established at many points throughout Scotland. By the beginning of 1653, these included Edinburgh, Dundee, Aberdeen, Inchgarvie, Linlithgow, Dumbarton, Stirling, Burntisland, Tantallon Castle, Bass Island, Inchkeith, Ruthven Castle, Braemar, Blair Atholl, Dunkeld, Brodick and Dunnottar Castles, Dunstaffnage, Dunnolly and Orkney: Firth, *S and C* pp. 116-8.

63. *CSPD 1651-2* pp. 199, 200; Worcester MS. xxii f72.

64. At the end of 1651 the army in Scotland had numbered about 12,000 men; at the end of 1652 it was to number around 18,000, divided almost equally between field forces and those accommodated in settled garrisons: see Worcester MS. xxiv f81v. In January 1653, reductions were made in the numbers within the various regiments as well as in the number of regiments *per se;* this meant that the foot were reduced to just over 12,000 and the horse to around 2200: Firth, *S and C* pp. xxxii-xxxiii and 114n.

65. Worcester MS. xxii f104; Gardiner, *C and P* ii, 73.

66. Firth, *S and C* pp. 45-6.

67. Worcester MS. xxii f110; Firth, *S and C* p. 361; Willcock, *The Great Marquess* p. 280.

68. Firth, *S and C* pp. 361, 362, 363, 364, 365; Willcock, *The Great Marquess* pp. 281-2.

69. Firth, *S and C* p. 365.

70. Firth, *S and C* p. 50n; Willcock, *The Great Marquess* p. 283.

71. For the text of the agreement, see Firth, *S and C* pp. 48-50; Willcock, *The Great Marquess* pp. 282-3. The Marquis's houses of Inveraray and Carrick could be garrisoned 'uppon extraordinary necessity'.

72. Worcester MS. xxiv f20; Firth, *S and C* p. 366.

73. Firth, *S and C* pp. 368-9, 55-7; Willcock, *The Great Marquess* pp. 284-5; Worcester MS. xxiv f46. The harsh reprisals inflicted on the Highlanders, as well as Argyle's influence, no doubt also conduced to an agreement, for which see Firth, *S and C* p. 53. Argyle communicated the results of his negotiations with Deane to a meeting of the gentlemen of the shire in late November: SRO

Breadalbane MSS. GD 112/39/892. The money due to be paid by the shire to the English was still owing in 1657: see *infra* p. 224.

74. Firth, *S and C* pp. 57-8.

75. Willcock, *The Great Marquess* p. 285.

76. Firth, *S and C* p. 367; cf. *ibid.* pp. 360, 363, 364-5 for other references to the mountainous territory.

77. Firth, *S and C* pp. 361, 362, 365; cf. Row, *Life of Blair* p. 298; and Worcester MS. xxiv ff3, 4.

78. Bodl. Lib. Tanner MS. liii f92.

79. Sir Walter Scott (ed.), *Military memoirs of the Great Civil War, being the military memoirs of John Gwynne; and an account of the Earl of Glencairn's expedition* . . . (Edinburgh, 1822) p. 191 (reprinted from *Mercurius Politicus* No. 117) cf. Firth, *S and C* pp. 363, 366.

80. *CSPD 1651-2* p. 2; *Cal.Cl.S.P.* ii, 110.

81. Barron, *In Defence of the Regalia, 1651-2* pp. 17, 110-2; *Cal.Cl.S.P.* ii, 118, 124, 127.

82. Gardiner, *C and P* ii, 389; Firth, *S and C* p. 137.

83. Gardiner, *C and P* ii, 389-90; Firth, *S and C* pp. 46-7, 50-3; *Cal.Cl.S.P.* ii, 138. For Middleton, see Stevenson, *Revolution and Counter-Revolution* pp. 102, 105, 110, 114; Firth, *S and C* p. xlii; *CSPD 1651-2* pp. 101-2, 108, 231.

84. Firth, *S and C* pp. 47-8, 65-70; *Cal.Cl.S.P.* ii, 158, 166; Gardiner, *C and P* ii, 390; George F. Warner (ed.), *The Nicholas Papers* (3 vols., Camden Society, 1886-97) i, 313. But in December, Hyde expressed doubts about Glengarry's fitness to Nicholas: Firth, *S and C* p. 53n.

85. Gardiner, *C and P* ii, 390.

86. Worcester MS. xxiv ff46, 72, 76; Daniel Mackinnon, *Origin and Services of the Coldstream Guards* (2 vols., London, 1833) i, 55-6.

87. Worcester MS. xxiv f76; Lamont, *Diary* p. 50.

Introduction to Part Two

1. Stevenson, *The Scottish Revolution 1637-1644* pp. 263-4; Sir James Balfour Paul (ed.), *The Scots Peerage* (9 vols., Edinburgh, 1904-14) iv, 247-8.

2. *Scots Peerage* i, 519.

3. *Scots Peerage* iv, 548, vii, 508-9.

4. *Scots Peerage* i, 361; Firth, *S and C* p. xlvii.

Chapter 4: Lilburne and the Growth of Revolt, January 1653 — April 1654

1. Firth, *S and C* pp. 62, 72n; *CSPD 1652-3* pp. 8, 37. Commissions were also issued to Col. Robert Overton to command the forces in the west of Scotland and

to Col. Thomas Morgan for the forces on the north side of the Tay, in each case under Lilburne's overall authority. Lilburne was given separate commissions to command all ships in the Firth of Forth and to hold courts-martial: Firth, *S and C* pp. 62-5; Worcester MS. xxiv f87v.

2. Sir Charles Firth and Godfrey Davies, *The Regimental History of Cromwell's Army* (2 vols., Oxford, 1940) i, 264-9; *DNB* s. v. Lilburne, Robert (1613-1665).

3. Firth, *S and P* p. 82.

4. Worcester MS. xxiv f90; *CSPD 1652-3* p. 114.

5. Firth, *S and C* p. 79n.

6. Worcester MS. xxiv f107v. The same report also stated that the collector of the assessment for Ayrshire, Mr. Boyd, had helped to raise horses and arms for the late king, and would therefore now be apprehended.

7. Worcester MS. xxiv f109.

8. Worcester MS. xxiv f111.

9. Firth, *S and C* p. 79.

10. Firth, *S and C* pp. 85, 88-9.

11. Firth, *S and C* pp. 84, 87; *CSPD 1652-3* pp. 190, 194.

12. Firth, *S and C* pp. 96, 122; Worcester MS. lxxxvi f30.

13. Firth, *S and C* pp. 122, 126.

14. The unwillingness of some chieftains and nobles to join the Royalists openly and the disputes within the leadership are discussed more fully in section ii, *infra*.

15. Firth, *S and C* p. 185.

16. Firth, *S and C* pp. 127-8, 140 and n, 148, 149, 151, 153, 221.

17. Firth, *S and C* p. 144n.

18. Firth, *S and C* pp. 146, 147; Gardiner, *C and P* ii, 391-2.

19. Firth, *S and C* pp. 143-4.

20. Gardiner, *C and P* ii, 396.

21. After being ejected in 1649 from his office as Lord Justice-General for having supported the Engagement, Glencairn made a comeback to political life, along with many other Royalists and Engagers, in 1651. In March 1651, he was appointed to the committee for managing the affairs of the army, although his repentance for supporting the Engagement was not accepted by the commission of the kirk until May. When Charles marched into England, Glencairn was one of those left behind to raise new levies in Scotland, and in October 1651 he was associated with Loudoun's plan to summon Parliament to Killin. From then until his assumption of the royalist command in June/July 1653 he appears to have lain low: Stevenson, *Revolution and Counter-Revolution* pp. 194, 200, 206; Firth, *S and C* p. 19.

22. Firth, *S and C* pp. 90-2, 99-102, 103; *Cal.Cl.S.P.* ii, 188; Gardiner, *C. and P* ii, 396-7.

23. *Nicholas Papers* ii, 15; *Cal.Cl.S.P.* ii, 250.

24. Firth, *S and C* pp. 194, 196; Worcester MS. xxv f114Av.

25. Baillie, *Letters and Journals* iii, 250; cf. Firth, *S and C* p. 185.

26. Firth, *S and C* p. 228.

27. Worcester MS. lxxxvi ff 100, 105v; Worcester MS. xlv 10, 27, 28 June,

22 July, 2 September, 7, 13 October 1653; 13 January, 19, 20 March 1654.

28. Firth, *S and C* p. 307.

29. SRO Murthly Castle MSS. Grandtully Correspondence GD 121 Box 88 Bundle 1 Alexander Macdonnell to the laird of Grandtully 10 July 1653; Worcester MS. xxvi f9v; Firth, *S and P* p. 34.

30. Firth, *S and C* pp. 186n, 190-1, 193; Worcester MS. lxxxvi f75.

31. Firth, *S and C* pp. 203, 221-2, 227, 231; Nicoll, *Diary* p. 116; Lamont, *Diary* p. 61.

32. Firth, *S and C* pp. 265, 276, 286.

33. For a fuller discussion of the Royalists' expedition to Argyllshire and Kintyre and of the Marquis's relations with Lilburne, see *infra* pp.

34. Worcester MS. xxv f125v; cf. Firth, *S and C* pp. 199, 204-5.

35. Firth, *S and C* p. 240; cf. *ibid.* pp. 242, 243.

36. Firth, *S and C* pp. 265, 270-1, 272-3, 282-3; Worcester MS. lxxxvi f150v.

37. Firth, *S and C* p. 282; Worcester MS. xxv f162.

38. Firth, *S and C* pp. 286, 304, 305 and n; Worcester MS. lxxxvi f139v.

39. Firth, *S and C* p. 302n; Firth, *S and P* p. 9; Worcester MS xxvi f1v. In November, Kinoule had been arrested by Col. Daniel, and in a letter to Lilburne had not only protested his loyalty but had warned the commander that arresting persons merely on suspicion was 'the high way to make all this contrey doubtfull of their oune condition and shal possiblie make burst forth humours, which ane even and gentle hand in the government of affaires might have stopt or smothered.' B.L.Add.MS. 6399 f60.

40. *A Collection of the State Papers of John Thurloe* . . . ed. T. Birch (7 vols., London, 1742) i, 3 and see *infra*

41. Worcester MS. 1 f6v (reprinted in *TSP* ii, 27); Worcester MS. lxxxvi f139v; *TSP* ii, 18.

42. *TSP* ii, 4, 5.

43. Firth, *S and P* pp. 36, 41; Wariston, *Diary* ii, 207; Brodie, *Diary* pp. 107, 109, 110; SRO Brodie Papers GD 247 Box 64 Bundle 10 Item 1 (Account of the losses sustained by Alexander Brodie . . .).

44. Firth, *S and P* pp. xvii, 19, 36, 41; *TSP* ii, 18.

45. Firth, *S and P* pp. 43, 46-7; *TSP* ii, 95.

46. Firth, *S and P* p. 47.

47. Firth, *S and P* p. 46.

48. *TSP* ii, 95; Firth, *S and P* pp. 42, 52, 54.

49. Firth, *S and P* pp. 25-30, 52, 56; *Cal.Cl.S.P.* ii, 310-2; Gardiner, *C and P* ii, 407.

50. *Nicholas Papers* ii, 70; Wariston, *Diary* ii, 220.

51. Firth, *S and P* pp. 52, 56, 58-9, 67.

52. Firth, *S and P* pp. 62, 65, 74, 81; *Gwynne's Memoirs* pp. 172-4.

53. Firth, *S and P* pp. xxv-vi, 88-9, 91, 95; *LRO* p. 66.

54. Firth, *S and P* p. 90; Gardiner, *C and P* ii, 410.

55. Worcester MS. xxiv f109; Worcester MS. xxv f39.

56. SRO Glencairn MSS. GD 39/2/51.

57. SRO Glencairn MSS. GD 39/2/53.
58. SRO Glencairn MSS. GD 39/2/49.
59. SRO Glencairn MSS. GD 39/2/52; *ibid.* GD 39/2/61.
60. SRO Glencairn MSS. GD 39/2/50; cf. Firth, *S and C* pp. 122, 151.
61. Firth, *S and C* p. 142 and n; Worcester MS. xxv f66v; *LRO* p. 57.
62. Firth, *S and C* pp. 141, 183-4.
63. Firth, *S and C* pp. 193, 262; Worcester MS. xxv f162.
64. *Gwynne's Memoirs* pp. 215-6.
65. Firth, *S and C* p. 145.
66. Terry, *CU* p. 156; Worcester MS. xxiii f93; Firth, *S and C* p. 175.
67. Firth, *S and C* pp. 82-3.
68. Worcester MS. xxv f39.
69. See Firth, *S and C* pp. 88-9.
70. Firth, *S and C* p. 95 (for Badenoch); for the use of the assessment to compensate allies and win friends, see *infra* pp.
71. Terry, *CU* p. 172; Firth, *S and C* pp. 49, 56, 169, 197n, 204. In January 1652 the English had believed that Argyle was levying the assessment but putting it into his own pocket: Terry, *CU* p. 10.
72. Willcock, *The Great Marquess* pp. 280-1, 295-6; Firth, *S and C* p.166. A letter probably written to Argyle by Lilburne in mid-September contains allusions to the Marquis's financial affairs: Worcester MS. lxxxvi f97.
73. David Masson, *The Life of John Milton and History of his Time* (7 vols., London, 1859-94) iv, 487-94; Firth, *S and C* p. 73 and n; Worcester MS. lxxxvi f56v; Gardiner, *C and P* ii, 155.
74. Firth, *S and C* p. 134. Although an adherent of the king, Sir Robert's relations with the leaders of the king's cause in Scotland in 1653 were somewhat equivocal. His connections with his brother-in-law Balcarres, and with the latter's messenger to the court abroad, Col. Bampfield, worked to his disadvantage when sometime around August, these men were implicated in a design to undermine Glencairn's authority. Moray thus suffered guilt by association and so incurred the displeasure of Hyde and his faction abroad: Alexander Robertson, *The Life of Sir Robert Moray* (London, 1922) pp. 78-97.
75. SRO Glencairn MSS. GD 39/2/49.
76. Firth, *S and C* p. 161.
77. Firth, *S and C* pp. 165-7; Willcock, *The Great Marquess* p. 289.
78. Firth, *S and C* pp. 167-9.
79. SRO Breadalbane MSS. GD 112/39/894.
80. See Willcock, *The Great Marquess* pp. 25-6.
81. This concern extended to the sea round Orkney and Shetland and to the Irish Channel, as well as to Hebridean waters: *CSPD 1651-2* p. 255; *CSPD 1652-3* pp. 36, 45, 138, 143, 190, 194, 263; *CSPD 1653-4* pp. 140, 189, 200, 212.
82. Firth, *S and C* p. 221 and n, 226, 275; *TSP* i, 478; cf. Willcock, *The Great Marquess* p. 292.
83. Willcock, *The Great Marquess* p. 292; Firth, *S and C* p. 275 and n; SRO

Glencairn MSS. GD 39/2/65, Lord Kenmore to the Earl of Glencairn 22 September 1653.

84. Willcock, *The Great Marquess* pp. 291, 383; Firth, *S and C* pp. 241-3, 257 and n; SRO Glencairn MSS. GD 39/2/64, Lord Lorne to the Earl of Glencairn 3 September 1653.

85. SRO Glencairn MSS. GD 39/2/59.

86. SRO Glencairn MSS. GD 39/2/69.

87. Firth, *S and C* pp. 308-10.

88. Glencairn's aunt, Lady Anna Cunningham, was the grandmother of the Duchess of Hamilton; hence the late Dukes of Hamilton had been Glencairn's cousins: *Scots Peerage* iv, 245, 375.

89. Towards the end of 1653, Glencairn told Charles that 'Argyle only has hindred all this summer's service': Firth, *S and P* p. 309.

90. Baillie, *Letters and Journals* iii, 250.

91. Firth, *S and C* p. 185.

92. *Nicholas Papers* ii, 6, 20; *Cal.Cl.S.P.* ii, 229, 233, 238. Bampfield, one of Thurloe's most valuable agents, continued to be 'deeply integrated into Royalist conspiratorial circles in Paris until at least 1655': Antonia Fraser, *Cromwell: Our Chief of Men* (London, 1973) p. 518; David Underdown, *Royalist Conspiracy in England 1649-1660* (New Haven, 1960) p. 63.

93. SRO Glencairn MSS. GD 39/2/60; *ibid.* GD 39/2/62.

94. Baillie, *Letters and Journals* iii, 250-1; cf. Worcester MS. 1 f17v 'Advice concerning Glencairne's waiving his Commission & managing affairs by a Council', written by Bampfield in late 1653.

95. *TSP* i, 495 (this letter from Charles to Balcarres was intercepted); Firth, *S and C* p. 247; *Cal.Cl.S.P.* ii, 333; *Nicholas Papers* ii, 71 (but cf. *ibid.* p. 65, where Nicholas was told by Hyde that Balcarres was 'wholly governed by his Majesty.'). For Balcarres' attempts to oust Glencairn, see also Robertson, *The Life of Sir Robert Moray* pp. 85-92, 95-7.

96. Baillie, *Letters and Journals* iii, 251; Firth, *S and C* p. 222; John Willcock, *A Scots Earl in Covenanting Times* (Edinburgh, 1907) p. 49.

97. Willcock, *The Great Marquess* pp. 291-2; Willcock, *A Scots Earl* pp. 51-3; Baillie, *Letters and Journals* iii, 250; Firth, *S and C* p. 257.

98. *TSP* ii, 3-4; Alexander Mackenzie, *The Macdonalds of Glengarry* (Inverness, 1881) p. 50; Willcock, *A Scots Earl* pp. 56-61; cf. *Cal.Cl.S.P.* ii, 325.

99. Firth, *S and P* pp. xxv-vi; Gardiner, *C and P* ii, 407-8.

100. Firth, *S and P* pp. 20-1; Gardiner, *C and P* ii, 406.

101. Nonetheless, Lilburne did not leave Scotland until 31 May, or after: *LRO* p. 71.

Chapter 5: Lilburne and the Scottish People, January 1653 — April 1654

1. Gardiner, *C and P* ii, 404.
2. Firth, *S and C* pp. 126-7.
3. Firth, *S and C* p. 242; Firth, *S and P* p. 65.
4. Firth, *S and C* pp. 231, 241, 244, 265-6, 274, 276, 286; Worcester MS. lxxxvi f153v; Nicoll, *Diary* p. 112. Lilburne also wanted Major Tolhurst's force at Carlisle to be strengthened to deal with trouble in Galloway: Worcester MS. lxxxvi f139v.
5. See *supra* pp. 42-3.
6. Firth, *S and C* p. 266; Firth, *S and P* p. 62.
7. See *supra* pp. .
8. For a full discussion of 'Gillespie's Charter', see *infra* pp. 196-8. For the text of the ordinance, see Nicoll, *Diary* pp. 166-7; Firth and Rait, *A & O* iii, cxiv-cxv; *APS* vi (2), 832.
9. Firth, *S and C* p. 242; Firth *S and P* p. 41.
10. Firth *S and C* pp. 108-9; Row, *Life of Blair* p. 305.
11. In May 1653 Nicholas reported to Hyde that, according to one of the royalist spies who had lately come down from Scotland, the Protesters were in favour of having an elective king, and that this might possibly be Argyle. Nicholas suspected that Cromwell hoped in time to introduce the notion of an elective kingship into England, and that the experiment in Scotland was planned as a trial-run: *Nicholas Papers* ii, 9.
12. Firth, *S and C* pp. 192n, 242, 266, 271.
13. Firth, *S and C* pp. 127, 162, 193, 222, 241, 271.
14. See *e.g.* Firth, *S and C* pp. 369-70.
15. Firth, *S and C* p. 161.
16. Firth, *S and C* pp. 162-3 and n; Baillie, *Letters and Journals* iii, 225, 244; Nicoll, *Diary* p. 110; Row, *Life of Blair* p. 307; Gardiner, *C and P* ii, 394-5.
17. Firth, *S and C* p. 163; Baillie, *Letters and Journals* iii, 244; Row, *Life of Blair* p. 308. cf. Gardiner, *C and P* ii, 395 and n.
18. Worcester MS. xxv f90v, for a copy of the paper.
19. Firth, *S and C* p. 163n; Worcester MS. xxv f93v; Row, *Life of Blair* p. 308; Steele 3rd pt. No. 2102.
20. Worcester MS. xxv f93v, for a copy of this paper.
21. Firth, *S and C* p. 192n, 222; Nicoll, *Diary* pp. 111-2; Steele 3rd pt. No. 2104; cf. Baillie, *Letters and Journals* iii, 228.
22. Lamont, *Diary* p. 59.
23. Lamont, *Diary* p. 60.
24. Nicoll, *Diary* p. 121.
25. Firth, *S and C* p. 192.
26. Firth, *S and C* p. 193; Lamont, *Diary* p. 59; Worcester MS. xxv f114. For the interruption of the presbytery of Cupar, see Row, *Life of Blair* pp. 308-9. Lilburne had previously given Col. Fairfax blanket permission to disperse unauthorised

meetings in Fife, or to send 'some discreet officer' to observe those which did have a warrant: Worcester MS. xlv 6 August 1653.

27. Baillie, *Letters and Journals* iii, 252.

28. Worcester MS. xlv 17, 18 July 1653, 13 March 1654; Worcester MS. xlvi 21 October 1654; Worcester MS. xlvii 7 August 1655, 21 February 1656; Worcester MS. xlviii 12 December 1657.

29. Wood, *Extracts Edin. Recs. 1642 to 1655* pp. 317, 323, 325; Nicoll, *Diary* p. 115; *Recs.Conv.RBS* pp. 368-70; Worcester MS. xlv 27 September 1653.

30. Worcester MS. lxxxvi f100; Wood, *Extracts Edin. Recs. 1642 to 1655* pp. 322-3; Nicoll, *Diary* p. 114; *CSPD 1653-4* p. 138; Firth, *S and C* p. 228.

31. Firth, *S and C* pp. 148-9 (cf. *ibid.* p. 83, where in a letter of 14 February 1653 Lilburne stated that he was considering measures to control the clan chiefs).

32. Worcester MS. lxxxvi f87; Steele 3rd pt. No. 2103; Lamont, *Diary* p. 58; Firth, *S and C* p. 156n; SRO Airlie MSS. GD 16/50/71, James Law to the Earl of Airlie 28 July 165[3]. Sorners were masterful beggars, or begging vagrants.

33. Firth, *S and C* pp. 145, 196-7.

34. Worcester MS. lxxxvi ff 111, 117-117v, 118; Firth, *S and C* p. 282; SRO Duntreath MSS. GD 97/3/132, Substance of the Engagement to the Commonwealth by the Gentlemen of Stirlingshire 29 November 1653.

35. Firth, *S and C* pp. 174-9, 258; Worcester MS. lxxxvi f153v. Caithness was also allowed to keep a guard (see Worcester MS. xlv 5 November 1653) and permission was specifically granted to the fiar of Glenorchy, Sir Thomas Stuart of Grantully, and the Earls of Airth and Perth to do likewise (see Worcester MS. xlv 20 and 28 July 1653).

36. See *e.g.* Worcester MS. xlv 2 August (Earl of Moray), 3 August (Sir James Macdowall), 17 August (Alexander Straughan, servant to Viscount Arbuthnott), 22 November (George Dundas of Dundas), 15 December 1653 (William Lowrie, laird of Blackwood).

37. Firth, *S and C* pp. 155-6; Steele 3rd pt. No. 2101.

38. Firth, *S and C* pp. 229-30; Steele 3rd pt. No. 2105.

39. Firth, *S and C* p. 259. The request was repeated a month later: Worcester MS. xlv 30 November 1653.

40. Wood, *Extracts Edin. Recs. 1642 to 1655* pp. 326, 331.

41. *TSP* ii, 221; Nicoll, *Diary* p. 124; Steele 3rd pt. No. 2110.

42. See *e.g.* Worcester MS. xlv 20 March 1654, where the fine on the burgh of Selkirk was reduced to £30 stg. on account of its poverty. Other burghs, mostly in the Lowlands, were similarly fined around this time.

43. Worcester MS. lxxxvi f117.

44. Firth, *S and C* pp. 298-300.

45. Nicoll, *Diary* p. 131; cf. Worcester MS. xlv 6 January 1654.

46. From the date of the proclamation, Lilburne's order-book (Worcester MS. xlv) records a large number of such concessions. Noblemen were usually asked for written engagements that they would not use their horses against the Commonwealth; gentlemen or lairds frequently escaped having to sign such a bond. For some examples, see Worcester MS. xlv 27 December 1653 (Lord

Blantire and the laird of Tarbert), 5 January (Earl of Linlithgow), 6 January (Sir Alexander Gibson of Durie), 14 January (the people of Ayrshire), 19 January 1654 (the gentlemen of Berwick). In keeping with his faith in the people of the west, Lilburne specifically stated that he believed many in Ayrshire were peaceably inclined towards the government when he granted them permission to keep their horses.

47. Firth, *S and C* pp. 139, 141-2, 154-5. For protection for the orchards etc. of various nobles and lairds, see, *e.g.*, Worcester MS. xlv 4 May (the Earl of Winton and Lord Kingston), 6 May (Duchess of Hamilton), 6 July (Sir Walter Murray), 28 July 1653 (Earl of Panmure).

48. Worcester MS. lxxxvi f57; Worcester MS. xlv 14 May, 18 June 1653.

49. Firth, *S and C* p. 162; Worcester MS. lxxxvi f115.

50. Firth, *S and C* p. 149.

51. Worcester MS. lxxxvi f89; Worcester MS. xlv 11 July 1653; Firth, *S and C* pp. 159, 170-9.

52. Worcester MS. xlv 23 July 1653. For references to the committees for valuation during Lilburne's term of office, see Worcester MS. xlv 31 May (Fife), 24 June (Nithsdale), 1 July (Wigtonshire), 15 July (Stirlingshire), 25 July (Renfrewshire), 26 July (Inverness and Ross), 3 August (Aberdeenshire), 23 August, 12 September (Dunbartonshire), 7 October, 11 February 1654 (Peeblesshire), 10 October (Linlithgowshire), 13 October 1653 (Galloway). Disputes over valuations were settled by the army: Worcester MS. xlv 16 February, 1 March 1654.

53. Worcester MS. xxii f29; *CJ* vii, 195; *CSPD 1652-3* p. 303.

54. These conclusions result from adding up the columns of figures in the tables of valuation and assessment printed in Firth, *S and C* pp. 174-9.

55. Worcester MS. xxv f155; Worcester MS. lxxxvi f120v (Lilburne to Rowe, cf. *ibid.* f121, Lilburne to Capt. Richard Deane); Firth, *S and C* pp. 287-8.

56. Firth, *S and P* p. 22.

57. Worcester MS. xlv 7 September 1653 and 5 March 1654 (laird of Lethen), 7 February 1654 (Earl of Linlithgow and laird of Meginch). 24 February 1654 (laird of Grantully), and see *infra* p. 154. For other abatements on wasted lands see Worcester MS. xlv 28 July 1653 (Earls of Airth and Perth), 9 February 1654 (laird of Edzell).

58. Worcester MS. xlv 19 August, 14 September 1653 (laird of Glenorchy), 19 September 1653, 16 February 1654 (Macdonald of Sleat), 4 January 1654 (Marquis of Argyle). For Glenorchy, see also Firth, *S and C* pp. 222-3; and for Sir James Macdonald, Firth *S and C* pp. 188, 199-200 and Worcester MS. xlv 2 September 1653, 20 January, 30 January 1654 (concerning protection for North Uist and other islands belonging to him).

59. Worcester MS. lxxxvi f76v; Firth, *S and C* p. 191.

60. Firth, *S and P* p. 36.

61. Firth, *S and P* p. 44; cf. *ibid.* pp. 19, 21.

62. Diarists of the period such as Nicoll and Lamont and leading figures such as Baillie make frequent reference to the impoverishment of the nobility and gentry.

Baillie's oft-quoted lamentations express the Scottish point of view succinctly: 'Our Nobilitie, weell near all are wracked . . . ' and 'Our Noble families are almost gone . . . ' (*Letters and Journals* iii, 249, 387).

63. Firth, *S and C* p. 185.

64. For Thomas Ker, laird of Mersington, see Firth, *S and C* p. 77; for Viscount Frendraught, Worcester MS. xlv 7 February 1654; for Lothian, Worcester MS. lxxxvi f69, Worcester MS. xlv 6 July 1653, 30 January, 22 February 1654; for Mar, Firth, *S and C* p. 239; for Huntly, Firth, *S and C* p. 289, Worcester MS. lxxxvi f126. For other recommendations to the Judges, see Worcester MS. xlv 8 October (laird of Glenorchy), 23 November (lairds of Ralston and Halibaith), 10 December 1653 (Lord Ramsay) and 30 January 1654 (laird of Assynt).

65. Firth, *S and C* pp. 266-7, 289.

66. Firth, *S and C* pp. 295-6, for the full text of the proposals.

67. Firth, *S and P* pp. 15, 19, 21.

68. See *infra* p. 120.

69. See *infra* pp. 121-2.

Chapter 6: Monck and the Suppression of Revolt, April 1654—September 1655

1. Firth, *S and P* pp. xix, 90-1.

2. See Gardiner, *C and P* ii, 410.

3. Firth, *S and P* p. 20; Worcester MS. xxiv ff 107v, 127; Worcester MS. xxv f 8v; C. H. Firth (ed.), *The Clarke Papers* (4 vols., Camden Society, 1891-1901) iii, 3; *LRO* p. 52.

4. Firth, *S and P* pp. 76-80.

5. *CSPD 1654* p. 76.

6. Firth, *S and P* p. xviii; see also Gardiner, *C and P* ii, 398-9, 401, 405.

7. *CSPD 1653-4* pp. 212, 279, 349, 351; Firth, *S and P* pp. 40, 42 and n, 49.

8. *CSPD 1654* pp. 57, 70, 86; Firth, *S and P* pp. 90-1, 147.

9. *CSPD 1654* p. 76; Firth; *S and P* pp. 94, 98, 106, 108, 144.

10. Firth, *S and P* pp. 93, 94, 99.

11. *CSPD 1654* p. 219; Firth, *S and P* p. 192.

12. Firth, *S and P* p. xix; Firth and Davies, *Regimental History* i, 228, 233, 256, 368; ii, 401.

13. Firth, *S and P* pp. 108, 111 and n; *LRO* p. 73; B.L.Add. MS. 25347 ff 11-12.

14. Lilburne had mentioned this problem in a letter to Cromwell of 28 March 1654: Firth, *S and P* pp. 62-3.

15. Firth, *S and P* pp. 63, 77, 78, 79.

16. Firth, *S and P* p. 90; *CSPD 1654* p. 147; *TSP* ii, 261-2 (for the text of the proclamation); Steele 3rd pt. No. 2116.

17. For a warning to the Earl of Airth, see Worcester MS. xlv 17 May 1654 cf. Worcester MS. xlv 8 June 1654 (Sir John Auchmootie); Worcester MS. xlvii 29 May 1655 (John Watson).

18. But see Worcester MS. xlvi 22 February 1655 (Kippen); Worcester MS. xlvii 28 May (Ayrshire), 30 June 1655 (Forres).

19. *CSPD 1654* p. 77.

20. *CSPD 1654* pp. 100, 165; Firth, *S and P* p. 98; Firth and Rait, *A & O* ii, 898-9 (cf. Worcester MS. xxvi f71v, where the text of the ordinance has been transcribed); Steele 3rd pt. No. 2118.

21. Even when the texts of former Bills of Union and Oblivion had been incorporated into *ordinances,* these were frequently referred to as *Acts* by contemporaries.

22. Terry, *CU* pp. xlviii-l; *CSPD 1653-4* pp. 297-8, 364, 365, 382; *CSPD 1654* pp. 90, 113. For the Instrument of Government, see Firth and Rait, *A & O* ii, 813-22 esp. pp. 813, 814.

23. For the text of the Ordinance of Union, see Firth and Rait, *A & O* ii, 871-5. A summary is given in *CSPD 1654* pp. 90-1.

24. *CSPD 1653-4* pp. 369, 392; *CSPD 1654* p. 90; Firth and Rait, *A & O* ii, 883-4; SRO Dalhousie MSS. GD 45/1/124 (for another copy of the ordinance).

25. Firth and Rait, *A & O* ii, 875-83.

26. Firth, *S and P* p. 77; *TSP* ii, 261.

27. Gardiner, *C and P* ii, 412; Nicoll, *Diary* p. 125.

28. See *infra* pp.

29. For the text of the ordinance, see Firth and Rait, *A & O* ii, 884-8.

30. *CSPD 1653-4* pp. 377, 381, 404, 425; *CSPD 1654* pp. 32, 90.

31. Terry, *CU* pp. li-lii and note 1; Nicoll, *Diary* pp. 124-5; Firth, *S and P* pp. 99, 100; Worcester MS. xlvii 6 June 1655. The delay in proclaiming the Protectorate was probably caused by slowness in passing the Acts of Union and of Pardon and Grace, which were to be presented to the Scottish people at the same time. In January 1654 Lilburne had several times in letters to Lambert expressed his surprise that he had not been ordered to make the necessary arrangements for proclaiming the Protectorate, and on 25 April 1654 Monck mentioned to Lambert that the delay was 'a cause of some unsetlednesse in the people': Firth, *S and P* pp. 16, 17-8, 23, 95; cf. *TSP* ii, 18 and Terry, *CU* pp. l-li and n.

32. Wariston, *Diary* ii, 251; Lamont, *Diary* p. 70; Nicoll, *Diary* pp. 125-6; Baillie, *Letters and Journals* iii, 251.

33. Wariston, *Diary* ii, 251.

34. Firth, *S and P* pp. 90, 93, 95.

35. Firth, *S and P* pp. 95, 96, 97, 101-2, 103; *CSPD 1654* pp. 102, 135.

36. Firth, *S and P* pp. 97, 103; Gardiner, *C and P* ii, 414-5.

37. Firth, *S and P* p. 104.

38. Firth, *S and P* pp. 57, 104, 108, 110; Willcock, *The Great Marquess,* p. 384.

39. Worcester MS. xlv 23 June 1654; Firth, *S and P* p. 145; *LRO* p. 75.

40. Firth, *S and P* pp. 104-111 (where the place-name on each letter indicates Monck's whereabouts on a particular day); Gardiner, *C and P* ii, 415.

41. Firth, *S and P* pp. 111, 113, 133; *LRO* pp. 71, 72, 73.

42. *LRO* pp. 71, 72, 73; Firth, *S and P* p. 105.

43. The following paragraphs tracing Monck's marches through the Highlands in June and July are based largely on the 'Narrative of Proceedings in the Hills from June 9 to July 1654' written by Monck after Morgan's defeat of Middleton on 19 July. This is printed in Firth, *S and P* pp. 149-53. Other sources are indicated where necessary.

44. *LRO* pp. 73, 74; Firth, *S and P* pp. 133-6, 137-8.

45. Firth, *S and P* p. 138; *LRO* p. 75.

46. *LRO* p. 75; *TSP* ii, 388-9.

47. *TSP* ii, 389; Firth, *S and P* p. 138; *LRO* pp. 75, 78; Worcester MS. xlv 1 July 1654; cf. Gardiner, *C and P* ii, 416-7.

48. *LRO* p. 78.

49. *LRO* pp. 78, 79; Firth, *S and P* pp. 138, 139 n; Gardiner, *C and P* ii, 416.

50. *LRO* p. 78.

51. *LRO* pp. 79, 80; *TSP* ii, 465; Gardiner, *C and P* ii, 417.

52. Firth, *S and P* pp. 143-4; *LRO* pp. 81-2.

53. Cf. *TSP* ii, 465.

54. *TSP* ii, 465; *LRO* pp. 82-3.

55. Firth, *S and P* pp. 145-6; *TSP* ii, 475.

56. *TSP* ii, 465; *LRO* pp. 82-3.

57. *TSP* ii, 475; cf. Gardiner, *C and P* ii, 417.

58. *TSP* ii, 483.

59. *TSP* ii, 483; *LRO* pp. 83, 87; Gardiner, *C and P* ii, 418-9.

60. On 26 July he signed a proclamation making the lands of the Earl of Sutherland over to Lord Reay, at Creith in Sutherland: SRO Reay MSS. GD 84/2/211.

61. *LRO* p. 84.

62. *LRO* p. 84; Turner, *Memoirs* pp. 109-11.

63. *LRO* p. 84; Firth, *S and P* p. 152.

64. Firth, *S and P* pp. 152, 153; *LRO* p. 87.

65. *LRO* pp. 87, 90, 91; *TSP* ii, 526, 533.

66. *LRO* pp. 90, 92, 93; *TSP* ii, 526, 555; Firth, *S and P* p. 154.

67. *LRO* p. 92; *TSP* ii, 533, 555.

68. The texts of the treaties are printed in Firth, *S and P* pp. 158-61 (Atholl), 165-8 (Glencairn), 177-9 (Kenmore), 187-9 (Montrose); and Worcester MS. 1 f65v (Forrester). Sir Arthur Forbes was also captured at the end of August: Firth, *S and P* pp. 173-4.

69. Forrester seems to have been an exception to this rule: Firth, *S and P* pp. 167, 175; Worcester MS. 1 f65v.

70. Firth, *S and C* p. 295; Firth, *S and P* pp. 47, 65, 99-100 and, especially, p. xxxii; *TSP* ii, 555 (where Monck advocates the levying of regiments for foreign service in a letter of 21 August 1654). The same motive lay behind plans to transport prisoners to the plantations (see *e.g. LRO* p. 87); for many prisoners, such plans were cancelled by the treaties of capitulation, so that an attempt to enrol

these men in military service abroad may have seemed a suitable alternative to the English.

71. *TSP* ii, 527.

72. Firth, *S and P* pp. 175-7; *LRO* pp. 92, 97.

73. The name is used by Cornet John Baynes, *LRO* p. 97.

74. *LRO* pp. 97-8; Firth, *S and P* pp. 176-7; Willcock, *The Great Marquess* p. 386; B.L.Add.MS. 15858 f168; Worcester MS. xlvi 19 September 1654. See also Baillie, *Letters and Journals* iii, 288 for the suggestion that the incident was staged by Argyle because he no longer wanted a garrison in his territory.

75. Firth, *S and P* p. 194.

76. Firth, *S and P* pp. 157, 162, 190, 212, 216, 259.

77. See *e.g.* Firth, *S and P.* p. 190; Worcester MS. 1 f67v.

78. Firth, *S and P* pp. 156, 157, 162, 190, 195, 202, 212, 216. On 5 December 1654, the House of Commons resolved, after some debate, to levy only £8000 on Scotland for the next three months, thus implicitly accepting some of Monck's objections to the higher figure, but in 1655 attempts were again made to raise the full £10,000: *CJ* vii, 395; Worcester MS. xxvi f171.

79. Firth, *S and P* pp. 186, 192-3, 216. It was calculated that by 24 December 1654 arrears of pay amounted to £60,415 12s. 7½d: *TSP* iii, 43, but cf. the higher figure of £77,215 10s. 11½d. given in Firth, *S and P* p. 218.

80. Firth, *S and P* p. 187; *TSP* ii, 619.

81. Firth, *S and P* pp. 200, 204-5; Nicoll, *Diary* p. 149; Worcester MS. xlvi 14 December 1654.

82. Firth, *S and P* p. 244.

83. Firth, *S and P* pp. 199-200, 201.

84. Firth, *S and P* p. 201n; *LRO* p. 105; Worcester MS. xlvi 31 October 1654.

85. Firth, *S and P* pp. 200, 201 and n, 203-4.

86. Worcester MS. xlvi 23 October, 16 November 1654; Nicoll, *Diary* pp. 140, 143.

87. Worcester MS. xlvi 9 December 1654, 19 January 1655; *TSP* iii, 28; Willcock, *The Great Marquess* p. 385; Willcock, *A Scots Earl* p. 70.

88. Worcester MS. xxvi f173v; Firth, *S and P* pp. 223 n1, 225 n1; *TSP* iii, 28, 42.

89. *TSP* iii, 3, 28. At the end of October, and again at the end of December, Charles sent several messages to his supporters in Scotland: Firth, *S and P* pp. 205-11, 226-30. The period from the autumn of 1654 to the spring of 1655 saw many attempts to enlist the services of William Davidson, a merchant in Amsterdam: Firth, *S and P* p. 196 and n; *TSP* ii, 260, 319, 374; *Nicholas Papers* ii, 106, 115, 117, 128, 283; *Cal.Cl.S.P.* iii, 4, 36.

90. *TSP* iii, 99; Firth, *S and P* pp. 223 n1, 225 n1, 234-7 (for Seaforth's treaty of capitulation). Monck gave as a reason for his speed in concluding the treaty with Seaforth the fact that his estate was burdened with debt, so that the agreement involved no loss to the commonwealth: *ibid.* p. 234.

91. Worcester MS. xlvi 18, 24 April 1655.

92. Worcester MS. xlvi 29 March 1655.

93. Firth, *S and P* pp. 224-5, 233, 246-7, 247-8 and nl, 249-50; Worcester MS. xxvii f43Av.

94. SRO Reay MSS. GD 84/2/212.

95. For a summary of this affair, see Gardiner, *C and P* iii, 70-6. Letters and papers relevant to it are printed in Firth, *S and P* pp. 234, 238-9, 240-3, 244, 250, 251-3.

96. Firth, *S and P* pp. 223-4, 225-6.

97. Firth, *S and P* pp. 257, 258; Worcester MS. xxvii f64; Worcester MS. xlvi 19, 24, 27 March 1655.

98. Firth, *S and P* p. 259.

99. SRO Reay MSS. GD 84/2/213, copy of a letter signed by Middleton, Dalziel and Drummond to Lord Reay 30 March 1655.

100. Firth, *S and P* pp. 285-8; Worcester MS. xlvii 12 May 1655.

101. SRO Reay MSS. GD 84/2/213; *ibid.* GD 84/2/214, General Monck to Lord Reay 5 May 1655 (Grimble, *Chief of Mackay* p. 169 wrongly states that Reay *received* a letter from Monck on 5 May); Firth, *S and P* pp. 280-2; Worcester MS. xlvii 5 May 1655.

102. Firth, *S and P* pp. 269-72 (Lorne), 273-6 (McNaughton), 276-80 (Lochiel), 282-4 (Selkirk).

103. Firth, *S and P* pp. 291-3; Worcester MS. xlvii 10 May, 22 June, 17 July 1655.

104. Worcester MS. 1 f123v; Worcester MS. xlvii 5 May, 7 June 1655. Firth, *S and P* p. xxviii states that Glengarry signed on 8 June. Loudoun's capitulation predated all those mentioned above, being signed on 12 March 1655: *ibid.* pp. 254-6.

105. SRO Reay MSS. GD 84/2/213; Firth, *S and P* p. 272n.

106. Worcester MS. xlvii 7 June, 2 August 1655.

107. Firth, *S and P* p. 279. After the arbitrators had delivered their verdict, this concession was retracted by the English: Worcester MS. xlvii 2 January, 11, 12 February, 30 April, 22 May 1656.

108. Firth, *S and P* p. 287.

109. Firth, *S and P* pp. 266, 268.

110. Worcester MS. xlvii 17 July 1655.

111. Firth, *S and P* p. 268.

112. See *e.g.* Firth, *S and P* pp. 266, 267, 289, 290, 293.

113. *CSPD 1655* pp. 251-2, 260-3, 310; Firth, *S and P* pp. lii-liii, 296 and n. In October 1655 the regiments of foot were reduced to eleven.

114. Firth, *S and P* pp. 305-6; cf. *ibid.* pp. 289-90.

115. Firth, *S and P* pp. 298-300, 302-6. Monck's estimate of £1000 was considerably less than the figure of £5000 per month which he had put forward in July 1654: *ibid.* p. 147.

116. Firth, *S and P* pp. 302-3.

Chapter 7: Monck and the Scottish People, April 1654 — September 1655

1. For Perth, see Worcester MS. xlvi 11 November 1654, 16 January 1655; for Stirling, *ibid.* 26 October 1654.

2. For Roxburgh and adjacent counties, see Worcester MS. xlv 9 May 1654, Worcester MS. xlvi 9 January 1655; for Caithness, *ibid.* 15 November 1654.

3. Worcester MS. xlvi 11 September 1654 (fiar of Glenorchy), 23 February 1655 (Stuart of Grantully). For other lairds to whom this privilege was granted, see Worcester MS. xlvi 24 November (laird of Graden), 9 December (laird of Buchanan), 12 December 1654 (laird of Gartmore); Worcester MS. xlvii 2 July (laird of Duffra), 4 July 1655 (laird of Luss). On 21 November 1654, the lairds of Glenorchy and Lawers and other heritors in the area had, in addition, been requested to assist the army with what forces they could muster: Worcester MS. xlvi 21 November 1654.

4. Worcester MS. xlvi 2 November 1654.

5. For these commissions, see Worcester MS. xlv 24 July (James Futhy), 25 July 1654 (John Dempster); Worcester MS. xlvi 4 September (William Stanfield), 21 September and 21 December (James Wemyss and Henry Mair or Mace), 8 December 1654 (Archibald Moore); Worcester MS. xlvii 21 June 1655 (Henry Farr and John Richardson).

6. Worcester MS. xlvii 7 May 1655.

7. Worcester MS. xlvi 12 February 1655.

8. Worcester MS. xlv 7 August 1654; Worcester MS. xlvi 4 September 1654.

9. Worcester MS. xlvii 21 June 1655.

10. Worcester MS. xlvii 21 June 1655.

11. Worcester MS. xlvii 6 June 1655 (cf. *TSP* iii, 520).

12. Possibly, however, before Brayne's departure, the area around Lochaber had been formed into a separate shire and the governor of Inverlochy's extraordinary judicial authority had been transformed into that of a normal sheriff: see *infra* p.

13. Firth, *S and P* p. xliii; Worcester MS. xlvii 30 May 1656. Cotterell's appointment was short-lived; by September 1656, he had been replaced by Lt. Col. Robert Reade, who in turn was superseded by Major John Hill in May 1657: Worcester MS. xlviii 30 September 1656, 28 May 1657.

14. Worcester MS. xlvii 22 June 1655.

15. Firth, *S and P* p. 98.

16. See *infra* pp.

17. See *infra* pp.

18. Worcester MS. xlv 5 May (Resolutioners), 19 August 1654 (Protesters); Worcester MS. xlvi 17 October 1654 (Protesters).

19. Nicoll, *Diary* p. 135; Wariston, *Diary* ii, 305-6; Firth, *S and P* p. lviii.

20. Worcester MS. xlvi 10 March 1655.

21. Lamont, *Diary* p. 86; Steele 3rd pt. No. 2120.

22. Worcester MS. xlvi 4 and 5 April (Dumfries), 7 April 1655 (Galloway).

23. Worcester MS. xlvi 11 April (presbyteries in Berwickshire), 12 April (synod of Merse), 16 April (synod of Lothian), 20 April 1655 (presbyteries in Perthshire); Worcester MS. xlvii 7 and 25 June (synod of Aberdeen), 8 June (synod of Fife), 18 June (synod of Perthshire), 14 July (presbyteries and synod of Caithness), 17 July 1655 (presbyteries and synod of Angus and Mearns).

24. Worcester MS. xlvii 7 and 25 June 1655.

25. Worcester MS. xlvii 11 May, 12 June 1655. Craw had initially been recommended to the Commissioners by Lilburne: Worcester MS. xlv 12 May 1653. Cf. Scott, *Fasti* ii, 33.

26. Worcester MS. xlvi 19 April 1655; Worcester MS. xlvii 9 July 1655; *Recs. Conv. RBS* pp. 371-87, 398-413.

27. *Recs. Conv. RBS* pp. 387-90, 391-6, 396-8; Wood, *Extracts Edin. Recs. 1642 to 1655* p. 363.

28. Firth, *S and P* p. 195. Monck repeated this sentiment in 1657: *TSP* vi, 529.

29. *CSPD 1654* p. 296.

30. Wood, *Extracts Edin. Recs. 1642 to 1655* pp. 346, 350, 386; *Aberdeen Council Register* p. 144; Taylor, *Aberdeen Council Letters* iii, 241; Nicoll, *Diary* p. 138.

31. For a discussion of these MPs, see Hugh Trevor-Roper, 'Scotland and the Puritan Revolution' pp. 415-7, and for their role in the religious issue which caused the dissolution of Barebones' Parliament, *ibid.* p. 433. Sir James Hope had been appointed a Commissioner for the Administration of Justice in May 1653, one year later than his brother, Sir John Hope of Craighall: *CSPD 1652-3* p. 311.

32. Terry, *CU* pp. lii-liv; *CSPD 1654* pp. 197-9, 220, 223; Firth and Rait, *A & O* ii, 930-2.

33. *CSPD 1654* p. 228.

34. Paul J. Pinckney, 'The Scottish representation in the Cromwellian parliament of 1656', *Scottish Historical Review* xlvi (1967) p. 96. For the relevant clauses of the Instrument of Government, see Firth and Rait, *A & O* ii, 817.

35. Whitelocke, *Memorials* iv, 132 (quoted in Pinckney p. 96); *LRO* p. 89 (cited in Pinckney p. 96).

36. For twenty-one of the twenty-two, see Terry, *CU* pp. lv-lvii; Pinckney p. 96ff. The twenty-second member, James Stuart of Maynes, MP for Orkney and Shetland, is referred to in Worcester MS. xlvi 19 October 1654. See also Dow, 'Thesis' p. 352.

37. Worcester MS. xlvi 2 October 1654.

38. Terry, *CU* p. lvi note 8; Firth, *S and C* pp. 140n, 148, 157; Firth, *S and P* p. 154. Bressie's fortunes continued to be mixed; by November 1655 he had gone bankrupt but from May 1657 he was acting as a subcommissioner for the excise on native salt: *ibid.* p. 320 and n3; Worcester MS. xlviii 27 May 1657.

39. Firth and Rait, *A & O* ii, 878; Terry, *CU* p. lvi and notes; Firth, *S and C* p. 44.

40. Wilkie apparently had an unhappy time in London, for he was in prison in 1655: *TSP* iii, 554.

41. These were Swinton, Lockhart, Macdowall, Wedderburn, Sword and Hamilton. According to Terry (*CU* p. xxxvi and notes), Hamilton probably did

not make the journey to London, since there is no record of his being paid for his attendance there.

42. See Terry, *CU* pp. 32 and 46 (Thomson), 38 (Macdowall), 53 (Hamilton), 55 (Sword), 57 (Lockhart).

43. Swinton and Lockhart: see *supra* p. 148.

44. Terry, *CU* p. lvi note 4; Firth and Rait, *A* & *O* ii, 878, 885. For Lockhart's marriage to Robina Sewster, see *DNB* (Lockhart, Sir William, of Lee).

45. Firth and Rait, *A* & *O* ii, 878, 885.

46. Firth, *S and C* p. 175.

47. Swinton and Lockhart were to be members of the Scottish Council in 1655: Firth, *S and P* p. 306 note 3. Macdowall was appointed a commissioner for excise and customs in 1655 and acted as a judge in Admiralty matters in 1659: *TSP* iv, 48, vi, 517, vii, 199; Worcester MS. li f82. The future JPs were Swinton, Lockhart, Barclay, Hamilton, George Earl of Linlithgow and James Earl of Hartfell: Firth, *S and P* pp. 308-16; for Hamilton as sheriff, see *ibid.* p. 316.

48. Baillie, *Letters and Journals* iii, 289.

49. Pinckney, pp. 105, 113.

50. *CSPD 1654* p. 312. The four members of the committee who were also MPs were George Smyth, John Swinton, William Lockhart and Samuel Disbrowe: SRO Hay of Haystoun Papers GD 34/811, Copy of the ordinance of 19 August 1654.

51. Pinckney p. 100; Firth, *S and P* p. 311; Nicoll, *Diary* p. 59.

52. *CSPD 1655-6* p. 8.

53. Terry, *CU* p. lvi n2; Firth and Rait, *A* & *O* ii, 882; Lamont, *Diary* p. 77.

54. Pinckney p. 111; *CSPD 1654* p. 283. For papers relating to the Keith family's attempts to obtain relief from sequestration, see SRO Murray of Ochtertyre MSS. GD 54/1/354-6 and GD 54/1/534. In a letter to her lawyer of 13 August 1654, the Countess Marischal acknowledged Barclay's help in this matter: *ibid.* GD 54/1/354.

55. Firth, *S and P* pp. 36, 41; Worcester MS. xlvi 19 September 1654.

56. Firth, *S and C* p. 265.

57. For Sir James Macdonald of Sleat, see Worcester MS. xlvi 13 January 1655 (cf. 25 April 1655); for the fiar of Glenorchy, *ibid.* 11 September, 27 October 1654; for Sir Thomas Stuart of Grantully, *ibid.* 18 December 1654, Worcester MS. xlvii 23 July 1655; for the Earl of Sutherland, Worcester MS. xlvi 25 January, 8 March 1655, Worcester MS. xlvii 19 June, 22, 25 August 1655; for the laird of Lawers, Worcester MS. xlvi 4 October 1654, Worcester MS. xlvii 28 August 1655.

58. For the laird of Foulis, see Worcester MS. xlvii 7 May 1655; for the laird of Lethen, Worcester MS. xlv 29 April 1654, Worcester MS. xlvi 14 October 1654; for the laird of Luss, *ibid.* 23 September, 17 November 1654; for Viscount Arbuthnott, *ibid.* 8 March 1655, Worcester MS. xlvii 23 June, 14 July 1655; for Baron Comrie, Worcester MS. xlvi 4 October 1654. Another such supporter was the laird of Meginch: *ibid.* 21 September 1654. For other references to abatements for 'losses', which do not state by whom the latter were perpetrated, see *ibid.* 2 October (laird of Assynt), 26 October 1654 (Lord Duffus), 17 August 1655 (Earl of Southesk and Sir Alexander Carnegie).

59. For Atholl, see Worcester MS. xlvi 23 September 1654, Worcester MS. xlvii 15 June 1655; for Glengarry, *ibid.* 7 June 1655.

60. Worcester MS. xlvii 27 June (Earl of Perth and Sir Thomas Drummond, and laird of Edinample), 30 June 1655 (Mr. David Drummond).

61. Worcester MS. xlvii 25 May 1655.

62. Worcester MS. xlvi 25 October 1654 (Glenorchy), 31 March 1655 (Macdonald); Worcester MS. xlvii 2 August (Menzies), 23 August 1655 (Stirling).

63. Worcester MS. xlvi 2, 16 November 1654, 6 March 1655.

64. For Glenorchy, see Worcester MS. xlvi 21 November, 18 December 1654, 16 January, 6 April 1655; for Assynt, *ibid.* 27 March, 18 April 1655.

65. Worcester MS. xlv 16 May 1654.

66. Worcester MS. xlvi 16 December 1654, 20 March 1655; B. L. Add. MS. 38848 f27.

67. Worcester MS. xlvii 22 May 1655.

68. Worcester MS. xlv 15 August 1654 (Macdonald); Worcester MS. xlvi 19 September and 1 November 1654 (Bruce). Monck also asked that Bruce be considered for a Judgeship, should a vacancy occur: Firth, *S and P* p. 214.

69. For the JPs who assumed office in 19 of the shires of Scotland in 1656, see Firth, *S and P* pp. 308-16. For the appointment of sheriffs and commissaries, which also show that loyal supporters of the régime had been awarded, *ibid.* pp. 316-8. See also *infra* pp.

70. Worcester MS. xlvi 9 January 1655 and Worcester MS. xlvii 4 May 1655 (Roxburgh); *ibid.* 13 June (Midlothian), 18 June (Sutherland), 21 June (Inverness), 27 June (Clackmannan), 2 July (Ayr), 28 July and 25 August (Berwick), 4 August (Kirkcudbright), 13 August 1655 (Perth).

71. For the setting up of shire committees, see Worcester MS. xlvi 27 April 1655 and Worcester MS. xlvii 8 June 1655 (Peebles); *ibid.* 19 May (Perth), 4 July (Fife), 25 August 1655 (Forfar). The English were anxious to prevent these shire committees from meddling in the work of valuations for, or other matters pertaining to, the assessment: Worcester MS. xlvi 27 April 1655; Worcester MS. xlvii 19 May 1655.

72. Firth and Rait, *A & O* ii, 881.

73. *CSPD 1654* pp. 158, 163, 223, 249, 251, 265.

74. *CSPD 1654* pp. 246, 263, 285, 307, 312. James Beattie, *History of the Church of Scotland during the Commonwealth* (Edinburgh, 1842) at p. 253 attributed the Council's decision to mitigate the fines to Patrick Gillespie's influence at the protectoral court.

75. See SRO Hay of Haystoun Papers GD 34/811. This ordinance is not printed by Firth and Rait.

76. In the course of this study, the following collections have come to light: SRO Airlie MSS. GD 16/50/55 and GD 16/50/69 (petitions relating to James, Earl of Findlater, Alexander, Lord Duffus, Patrick, Earl of Panmure, John, Earl of Dalhousie and several papers relating to George, Lord Banff); SRO Hay of Haystoun Papers GD 34/811 (papers relating to Gilbert, Earl of Erroll); SRO Dalhousie MSS. GD 45/1/126-8 (papers relating to the Earl of Panmure); SRO

Duntreath MSS. GD 97/3/136-43 (papers relating to Sir James Livingstone of Kilsyth); B. L. Add. MS. 23113 f36 (testimony on behalf of Sir John Scott of Scotstarvet); B. L. Add. MS. 34195 f53 (testimony on behalf of Sir John Wauchope of Niddrie).

77. Worcester MS. xlvi 14 October 1654.

78. Worcester MS. xlvi 2 October (laird of Balhousie, Earl of Perth and Lord Drummond), 7 October (Earl of Ethie), 13 October (Earl of Tullibardine and the laird of Craigmillar), 14 October (Earl of Perth and Lord Drummond), 16 October 1654 (Sir John Scott).

79. *CSPD 1655* pp. 70-2, 86, 103, 116, 117-8. The results of the Council's deliberations are also recorded in Worcester MS. xxvii f74 and SRO Dalhousie MSS. GD 45/1/126.

80. *CSPD 1655* pp. 129-30.

81. See *e.g.* SRO Dalhousie MSS. GD 45/1/128 (Earl of Panmure); SRO Duntreath MSS. GD 97/3/143 (Sir James Livingstone of Kilsyth); B. L. Add. MS. 35125 f55 (Lord Duffus); Bodl. Lib. Rawlinson MS. A 34 p. 45 (Earl of Perth and Lord Drummond).

82. See *e.g.* *CSPD 1655* pp. 278, 319 and *CSPD 1655-6* p. 8 (petition of James, Earl of Hartfell); *ibid.* pp. 24 (petition of James, Lord Coupar) and 150 (petition of the Earl of Moray). A letter of complaint from the Council of State in Whitehall to the Council in Scotland in April 1656 indicated that some of the fined persons had failed to make the required payments: *ibid.* p. 279.

83. See *infra* pp. 183-5.

Chapter 8: Monck, Broghill and the Council, September 1655 — August 1656

1. *CSPD 1655* pp. 58-9, 90, 103.

2. Firth (ed.), *Clarke Papers* iii, 31, 32. At first the rumours had been based on the assumption that a Lord Deputy and Council, rather than a President and Council, would be appointed: *ibid.* iii, 25.

3. *CSPD 1655* p. 152; *TSP* iii, 423, 711; *LRO* p. 118; Firth, *S and P* p. 306 and n 3; C. H. Firth, *The Last Years of the Protectorate 1656-1658* (2 vols., New York, 1964) ii, 91 note 1. Each member of the Council received a salary of £600 *per annum,* with the exception of President Broghill, who got £1000.

4. *DNB* s.v. Boyle, Roger, Baron Broghill, and first Earl of Orrery (1621-1679).

5. Firth (ed.), *Clarke Papers* iii, 42; Firth, *S and P* p. 306. In Edinburgh, on 18 June, a special committee was set up by the town council to prepare lodgings for them: Wood, *Extracts Edin. Recs. 1642 to 1655* p. 379.

6. *CSPD 1655* pp. 108-110 and 255-6 (for the full text of the Instructions, including amendments).

7. For Monck's Instructions, see Firth, *S and P* pp. 76-80.

8. For a full discussion of the imposition of the excise, see *infra* pp. 168-71.

9. *TSP* iii, 496-8 (for the full text of the additional instructions). The date of this document is suggested by internal evidence. Cf. Firth, *S and P* p. 307n.

10. For a full discussion of the early history of 'Gillespie's Charter' and of Broghill's dealings with the church parties, see Chapter Nine.

11. Nicoll, *Diary* p. 183.

12. Baillie, *Letters and Journals* iii, 315.

13. Baillie, *Letters and Journals* iii, 288.

14. Brodie, *Diary* p. 154; Baillie, *Letters and Journals* iii, 290; *LRO* pp. 118-20.

15. Firth, *S and P* pp. 260-1.

16. *CSPD 1655* pp. 160, 164, 171; *APS* vi (2), 827-9 (for the text of the order).

17. *CSPD 1655* p. 109. By September, it had been estimated that the arrears of the army up until 23 July 1655 amounted to £96,576 16s. 11d., and this was to be the first charge on two-thirds of the excise, but, as Monck pointed out, this sum was not likely to be realised for another two or three years: Worcester MS. 1 f138; Firth, *S and P* p. 307. Cf. *CSPD 1655* pp. 322, 343; *CSPD 1655-6* p. 20.

18. 'Report by Thomas Tucker upon the settlement of the revenues of excise and customs in Scotland, A.D. MDCLVI' in *Miscellany* (Scottish Burgh Records Society, 1881). Information on Tucker's appointment, after the Council of State had first chosen, on 12 July 1655, George Foxcroft as their commissioner, is to be found *ibid.* p. xvi. Cf. *CSPD 1655* pp. 241, 291, 304-5.

19. Tucker, *Report* p. 2; *TSP* iv, 48 (printed in Tucker, *Report* pp. xvi-xviii). Saltonstall demitted office in December 1655 and was succeeded by Col. Leonard Lytcott: Tucker, *Report* pp. xxi note 4, 15; *TSP* iv, 222, 559.

20 *TSP* iv, 48 (cf. Tucker, *Report* pp. xvi-xviii). For the Covenanters and the excise, see Stevenson, 'The financing of the cause of the Covenants, 1638-51', esp. pp. 103-5, 106, 115.

21. Tucker, *Report* pp. 2-4.

22. Tucker, *Report* pp. 11, 31-2, 33. After January 1656, the tack of Dundee was given to Sir Alexander Wedderburn, collector of the assessment and friend of the English: *ibid.* p. 34. For the grant to Edinburgh of a tax of 4d. Scotch on all ale and beer brewed and sold in Edinburgh from 1 April 1654 to 10 November 1657, see *CSPD 1654* pp. 50, 69; *CSPD 1655* p. 109; Nicoll, *Diary* pp. 172-3.

23. Tucker, *Report* pp. 3, 8, 9.

24. Firth, *S and P* p. 305.

25. Tucker, *Report* pp. 7, 9.

26. Tucker, *Report* pp. 9, 11.

27. See Dow, 'Thesis' p. 401 notes 3 and 4.

28. Tucker, *Report* p. 16.

29. Tucker, *Report* pp. 35-46; *The Antiquarian Repertory* [chiefly compiled by Francis Grose; Thomas Astle] (4 vols., London, 1807-9), ii 3 (this estimate is accepted by Firth, *LYP* ii, 115 note 1). The Commons committee, reporting in October 1654, incidentally recommended that an excise be laid upon Scotland, and thought that it would yield £9000 *per annum*.

30. Tucker, *Report* pp. 33, 34, 35. All Tucker's figures are slightly higher than the Council's estimates prepared in February 1656 and printed in *TSP* iv, 526-30.

Ashley quotes the figure of £48,820 for a year's farm (of the excise) and allegedly bases this on Tucker's tables, but clearly this sum relates to *all* customs and excise duties, both farmed and collected: Maurice Ashley, *Financial and Commercial Policy under the Cromwellian Protectorate* (2nd edn., London, 1962) p. 91.

31. Firth, *S and P* p. 295. During the rising, Monck's estimates of the yield from the assessment had fallen as low as £7300, and even at one point to £6000, per month: *ibid.* pp. 157, 212.

32. In December 1654, acting perhaps on the recommendation of the sub-committee set up to examine the state's revenue, Parliament had temporarily accepted the figure of £8000 per month as a realistic estimate of the potential yield from the Scottish cess, but it never quite lost sight of the higher target of £10,000: *The Antiquarian Repertory* ii, 8; *CJ* vii, 395.

33. Firth, *S and P* pp. 298-9, 302-4, 304-5; *CSPD 1655* p. 356.

34. *TSP* iv, 127.

35. *TSP* iv, 342-3. For the appointment of JPs, see *infra* pp. . Broghill's plans to merge the two commissions met with an initial difficulty, for in the early months of 1656 some men who had been nominated to both offices attempted to act as commissioners for the assessment, but not as justices. The Council had therefore to ordain that no one should act as an assessment commissioner unless he had first taken the oath as a justice. The disinclination of some nominees to take this oath meant that they were struck off both commissions: this, in turn, created shortages of manpower on the commissions but preserved the principle that the two bodies should be staffed by the same men: B.L.Add.MS. 38848 f63.

36. *APS* vi (2), 837-45; cf. Steele 3rd pt. No. 2131.

37. Nicoll, *Diary* p. 173.

38. James D. Ogilvie (ed.), *Diary of Sir Archibald Johnston of Wariston* Vol. III 1655-1660 (Scottish History Society, 1940), 21; Brodie, *Diary* p. 172; Nicoll, *Diary* p. 168; Baillie, *Letters and Journals* iii, 318.

39. Prior to 1656, tenants, particularly those who held their lands by leases, could in theory be charged cess on their personal estates, but details of this and of exactions on other types of personal estates remain obscure. For the case of tenants, see Worcester MS. xxiii f92 (1652), and Worcester MS. xliii (unfoliated volume containing references to such levies in 1653 and 1654). When committees for valuation were appointed in the summer of 1653, their terms of reference were apparently limited to the rents in each shire: Firth, *S and C* p. 180; Worcester MS. xlv 23 July 1653.

40. *APS* vi (2), 842, 844; Row, *Life of Blair* p. 324; SRO Dundas of Dundas MSS. GD 75/619, Instructions by the commissioners of Linlithgowshire to the surveyors for levying the cess 24 January 1656; SRO Murthly Castle MSS. GD 121 Grandtully Correspondence Box 88 Bundle 1 Declaration of the commissioners for Perthshire 7 January 1656; *ibid.* Robert Andrew to [Sir Thomas Stuart?] 21 January 1656.

41. Worcester MS. xliii (unfoliated volume): entry entitled 'Abatement given to the severall Shires & Burghes in Scotland for the Six Monthes Assessment.'

42. *CSPD 1655-6* p. 249.

43. *CSPD 1655-6* pp. 249, 364; *TSP* v, 86.

44. For Glenorchy, see Worcester MS. xlvii 11 September 1655, 29 April 1656; for Lawers, *ibid.* 22 October 1655, 30 June 1656; for Drummond, *ibid.* 15 September 1655; for Atholl, *ibid.* 3 October 1655; for Macdonald of Sleat, *ibid.* 24 March 1656.

45. For Lochiel, see Worcester MS. xlvii 10 September 1655, 30 April 1656; for Cranston, *ibid.* 21 September 1655; for Mackinnon of Strathordle, *ibid.* 5 March 1656; for Macpherson of Badenoch, Worcester MS. xlviii 9, 16 July, 25 August 1656; for the Captain of Clanranald, *ibid.* 18 July 1656; for Macleod, *ibid.* 21 August 1656.

46. *TSP* iv, 49, 127, 526-30 (for the statement of February 1656).

47. See *CSPD 1655* p. 322.

48. *TSP* iv, 49.

49. *TSP* iv, 57. For a full list of the officers of the Court after it was finally established, see *ibid.* iv, 528.

50. *TSP* iv, 105-6. The difference between the Acts of 1633 and of 1640 was that whereas the former granted the Exchequer power to try all causes relating to the king's property, the latter (passed by the Covenanters) limited it to trying matters concerning the managing of the king's rents and casualties. Thus the Court was denied the right to decide the validity of infeoffments, since this was reserved to the Court of Session: *APS* v, 35, 285.

51. *TSP* iv, 129.

52. *TSP* iv, 184, 250, 324, 342.

53. *TSP* iv, 329.

54. *CSPD 1655-6* pp. 106, 107; *TSP* iv, 407.

55. Nicoll, *Diary* p. 173.

56. Nicoll, *Diary* pp. 174, 175-7; Steele 3rd pt. No. 2134.

57. Steele 3rd pt. No. 2143.

58. See *infra* pp.

59. Firth, *LYP* ii, 90 note 3 (and authorities there cited); Brunton and Haig, *Senators of the College of Justice* pp. 346-7; Omond, *The Lord Advocates of Scotland* i, 158. For the Council of State's deliberations on the recall of, and the choice of replacements for, Marsh and Owen, see *CSPD 1653-4* pp. 139, 143, 202, 273. Sir James Hope of Hopetoun had also been appointed a Commissioner for the Administration of Justice in May 1653 but was dismissed in July of the following year, probably because of his support for the religious radicals in Barebones' Parliament: *CSPD 1652-3* p. 311; Nicoll, *Diary* p. 132; *TSP* iv, 269; Trevor-Roper, 'Scotland and the Puritan Revolution' p. 433.

60. Omond, *The Lord Advocates of Scotland* i, 160. Swinton may also have participated in criminal proceedings on occasion: *TSP* iv, 323.

61. Firth, *S and P* p. 214 and note 1 (citing Nicoll, *Diary* p. 155); Baillie, *Letters and Journals* iii, 288; SRO Mey MSS. GD 96 Jo. Nisbet to the laird of Mey 25 June 1655.

62. *TSP* iv, 268-9; Firth, *LYP* ii, 106.

63. *TSP* iv, 268 (in which Broghill explained to Thurloe the workings of the

inner and outer houses); William Forbes, *A Journal of the Session* (Edinburgh, 1714) p. xvi; Aeneas Mackay, *Memoir of Sir James Dalrymple, 1st Viscount Stair* (Edinburgh, 1873), p. 59. For the working of the Court of Session, see also The Rt. Hon. Lord Cooper of Culross, 'The Central Courts after 1532', in *An Introduction to Scottish Legal History* (Stair Society, 1958) pp. 341, 343.

64. *TSP* iv, 57.

65. *TSP* iv, 268-9; Brunton and Haig, *Senators of the College of Justice* p. 277; Lamont, *Diary* p. 95; Nicoll, *Diary* p. 168.

66. *TSP* iv, 269, 324; Firth, *LYP* ii, 107-8.

67. See *TSP* iv, 528.

68. See *infra* pp.

69. See Omond, *The Lord Advocates of Scotland* i, 160-1.

70. Worcester MS. xxviii ff25-8. Winter sessions were also held in the north in October 1655: Brodie, *Diary* p. 161.

71. Firth, *S and P* pp. 98, 106; *TSP* iv, 57.

72. Worcester MS. xlvii 28 September 1655.

73. *TSP* iv, 250.

74. *TSP* iv, 250; Nicoll, *Diary* p. 172; Steele 3rd pt. Nos. 2126, 2130; Firth, *S and P* pp. 403-5 (for an abstract of the Instructions, from which quotations are here taken); *APS* vi (2), 832-6 (for the full text of the Instructions). Cf. Donaldson, *Scotland: James V to James VII* p. 348.

75. Row, *Life of Blair* p. 327.

76. See Omond, *The Lord Advocates of Scotland* i, 162-3.

77. *TSP* iv, 57.

78. C. A. Malcolm (ed.), *The Minutes of the Justices of the Peace for Lanarkshire 1707-1723* (Scottish History Society, 1929) pp. xxi-xxii. Cf. Donaldson, *Scotland: James V to James VII* pp. 224-6; J. Irvine Smith, 'The Transition to the Modern Law 1532-1660', in *An Introduction to Scottish Legal History* p. 40.

79. *TSP* iv, 57 cf. Smith, 'The Transition to the Modern Law 1532-1660' p. 40. Malcolm, however, stressed that in the early seventeenth century 'the chief disputes . . . were not between the Justices and the owners of private heritable jurisdictions but between the Justices of shires and the Justices of burghs': *The Minutes of the Justices of the Peace for Lanarkshire 1707-1723* p. xvii.

80. Firth, *S and P* pp. 308-16. Clarke's list probably gives the names of those who *accepted* office as justices, rather than those who were offered it.

81. For the granting of favour to these men, or to their families, in the period between April 1654 and September 1655, see *supra* Chapter Seven *passim.* For Sutherland and Hartfell, see *supra* pp. 152-4, 159, and *infra* pp. 182, 186. George Lord Strathnaver, son of the Earl of Sutherland, was appointed a sheriff in 1656 and later succeeded his father as Keeper of the Privy Seal: Firth, *S and P* p. 390 and see *infra* p.

82. For grants of favour to these men and to their families between April 1654 and September 1655, see *supra* Chapter Seven *passim.*

83. Row, *Life of Blair* p. 327; cf. Wariston, *Diary* iii, 25. For the oath, see Firth, *S and P* p. 403.

84. Brodie, *Diary* pp. 176, 178, 182, 183.

85. *TSP* iv, 479-80.

86. *TSP* iv, 741; Brodie, *Diary* p. 182.

87. Marguerite Wood (ed.), *Extracts from the Records of the Burgh of Edinburgh 1655 to 1665* (Edinburgh, 1940), p. 10; Worcester MS. xlvii 21 February 1656.

88. *TSP* iv, 741; Firth, *S and P* p. 321.

89. Worcester MS. xlvii 20 June 1656.

90. See Donaldson, *Scotland: James V to James VII* pp. 348-9; Firth, *LYP* ii, 108.

91. Firth, *S and P* pp. 316-7 (for the names of the sheriffs); Brodie, *Diary* p. 174.

92. For Sir James Hamilton, see *supra* pp. 47, 150-3.

93. *TSP* iv, 500; *CSPD 1655-6* p. 224; Worcester MS. xxviii f11v.

94. Bodl. Lib. Rawlinson MS. A34 p. 73 cf. *TSP* iv, 129. However, Capt. John Hill, Governor of Ruthven Castle, was referred to as sheriff of Badenoch in a letter of 30 October 1655: Worcester MS. xlvii 30 October 1655.

95. Worcester MS. xlvii 22 May 1655.

96. *CSPD 1655* pp. 284, 319. Such a recommendation, of course, also served the purpose of bringing the two legal systems into line, in addition to giving Scots creditors the benefit of a more lenient law. For the law relating to debt in England at this time, see Ivan Roots, 'Cromwell's Ordinances: The Early Legislation of the Protectorate', in G. E. Aylmer (ed.), *The Interregnum: The Quest for Settlement 1646-1660* (London, 1972) p. 148.

97. Wood, *Extracts Edin. Recs. 1642 to 1655* pp. 390, 393, 396, 397; *Recs. Conv. RBS* pp. 433-5.

98. *CSPD 1655-6* pp. 203, 224, 274-5; Nicoll, *Diary* pp. 178-9, 180; Steele 3rd pt. Nos. 2138, 2139.

99. Baillie, *Letters and Journals* iii, 317.

100. *CSPD 1655-6* p. 279.

101. *CSPD 1654* pp. 186, 195, 220, 260, 276.

102. This was provided for in the ordinance for settling the estates of several excepted persons of 12 April 1654: Firth and Rait, *A & O* ii, 886-7.

103. See *CSPD 1655-6* p. 362.

104. *CSPD 1655-6* pp. 53-4, 363, 375; *CSPD 1656-7* p. 14 cf. Worcester MS. xxviii ff32, 47.

105. *CSPD 1655-6* p. 362 cf. B.L.Add.MS. 23113 f40.

106. B.L.Add.MS. 23112 f40; *TSP* iv, 548-9 (cf. *CSPD 1655-6* p. 30).

107. *CSPD 1655-6* pp. 361-3.

108. *CSPD 1655-6* p. 94.

109. *CSPD 1655-6* p. 279; Nicoll, *Diary* p. 180. The original commissioners for claims on forfeited estates had been named in the Act of Pardon and Grace of 12 April 1654: Firth and Rait, *A & O* ii, 878.

110. *CSPD 1656-7* pp. 108, 129, 134-5, 151, 158.

111. See *infra* pp.

112. The young Duchess of Hamilton, for example, had to sell personal belongings, including beds, a set of embroidered chairs and a furred mantle to

raise the necessary money. Her fine was £7000 stg: Rosalind K. Marshall, *The Days of Duchess Anne* (London, 1973) p. 30.

113. A full list of members, accepted by Pinckney as accurate, is given in Terry, *CU* pp. lxii-lxiii. Three of the members on this list, Col. Edward Salmon, George Downing and the Earl of Moray, did not in fact take their seats as MPs for Scottish constituencies: see Dow, 'Thesis' p. 479 note 1.

114. Pinckney pp. 101, 104.

115. For the commissaries, see Firth, *S and P* p. 317. Some doubt remains about the identification of Wolseley (cf. Terry, *CU* p. lxiii n9).

116. Pinckney pp. 104-5; Firth and Rait, *A & O* ii, 878; Nicoll, *Diary* pp. 173, 183-4.

117. Pinckney p. 105. Stewart, despite his Scottish name, is identified by Pinckney as 'the London barrister and later master in chancery for whom Secretary Thurloe wrote a letter in the next election': *ibid.* p. 105 and n. cf. *TSP* vii, 572.

118. Pinckney pp. 104-5, 102n.

119. For Douglas, Ramsay and Wedderburn see Terry, *CU* pp. lxii n5, lxiii n8, lvi; Pinckney p. 109.

120. The eight were Douglas, Wemyss, Tweeddale, Swinton, Ker, William and George Lockhart, Cochrane: see Firth, *S and P* pp. 308-16.

121. The other four were Barclay (a trustee for the estates of excepted persons), Swinton (judge and councillor), Sir James Macdowall (Commissioner for the Excise), and Sir Alexander Wedderburn (collector of the assessment; he was also a tacksman of the excise).

122. Pinckney, pp. 109 and n2, 108, 107, 111. The Earl of Sutherland had won the favour of the English principally because of his family's inclination towards congregationalism and because of his hostility towards Lord Reay, one of the Royalists who had participated in Glencairn's rising. In 1655 the Earl had been granted abatements of cess because of the devastation his lands had suffered at the hands of the Royalists; in 1656 he was appointed a JP, and in 1657 he was to be appointed Keeper of the Privy Seal: Firth, *S and P* pp. 83, 316; Nicoll, *Diary* pp. 207, 208; Worcester MS. xlvi 21 January, 8 March 1655; Worcester MS. xlvii 19 June, 22 August, 25 August 1655.

123. Several of the Scots MPs had personal reasons for seeking election and gaining access to government circles. The Earl of Moray was being pressed for payment of his fine (Pinckney, p. 106); Barclay wished his title to the barony of Urie confirmed (p. 111); Tweeddale wanted to gain control over the young Countess of Buccleuch (p. 107); Swinton hoped that the forfeiture imposed on his lands by the Scottish Parliament in 1651 would be revoked by the Council of State (pp. 108-9); and Wemyss wanted to protect his own and his family's interest in the salt-pans of Leith and the coal-mines of Fife (p. 108).

124. Pinckney p. 113.

125. During the life of the 1656 Parliament, Scotland's constitutional position came under debate twice at Westminster—once when a Bill of Union (designed to replace the Ordinance of Union of April 1654) was debated in the House between

October 1656 and February 1657 but failed to become law, and again when Parliament considered the Humble Petition and Advice in the spring and summer of 1657. See Dow, 'Thesis' pp. 484-8 and *infra* pp.

126. Worcester MS. xlvii 10 September (Young), 30 October 1655 (Campbell).

127. For permission to John Miller to act in this capacity, see Worcester MS. xlvii 23 January 1656 and Worcester MS. xlviii 1 July 1656; and for Alexander Hendry, Worcester MS. xlvii 21 February 1656.

128. For arrests for murder, see Worcester MS. xlvii 31 October, 5, 13, 19 November 1655, 25 February, 19 April 1656; for arrests for robbery, see *ibid.* 14, 17 December 1655, 31 January, 29 February 1656.

129. See Worcester MS. xlvii 27 February 1656.

130. See Worcester MS. xlvii 4 October, 3 December 1655.

131. See Worcester MS. xlviii 4 August 1656.

132. See Worcester MS. xlvii 20 December 1655, 27 March, 16 April, 21 June 1656; Worcester MS. xlviii 18 July, 1 August 1656.

133. For fire and candle money and other matters relating to the army's quarters, see Worcester MS. xlvii 11 September, 1 November, 14 December 1655, 22, 30 January, 21 February, 5 March, 26 April, 21 June 1656; Worcester MS. xlviii 18 July 1656.

134. See Worcester MS. xlvii 28 February, 22 May 1656 (*bis*); Worcester MS. xlviii 3, 14 July 1656.

135. See Worcester MS. xlvii 10, 29 November 1655, 18 June 1656.

136. See Worcester MS. xlviii 12 August 1656.

137. But cf. Firth, *LYP* ii, 109: 'Ex-royalists, who had not proved their intention to live peaceably, found it difficult to obtain such privileges . . .'

138. For Brodie, see Worcester MS. xlvii 18 February 1656 and Worcester MS. xlviii 7 August 1656; for Innes, *ibid.* 4, 7 August 1656; for Swinton, *ibid.* 5 September 1656.

139. Worcester MS. xlvii 20 June 1656; Worcester MS. xlviii 4 July 1656.

140. Worcester MS. xlvii 25 April 1656.

141. Monck's order-books contain several references to the fees paid to Drummond: Worcester MS. xlviii 1 April 1657 (£21); 14 July 1657 (£25 for expenses incurred by another on Drummond's behalf, for which Drummond had already paid); 27 October 1657 (£21). In 1657 he therefore received a regular fee of five shillings per day; at this time he was officially styled deputy to the Scoutmaster-General. He had earlier received other tokens of Cromwellian favour: see *e.g.* Worcester MS. xlvii 30 June 1655 (abatement of cess), 5 July 1655 (recommendation to enjoy the church living attached to the chapel of Holyroodhouse).

142. Firth, *S and P* p. 307.

143. *TSP* iv, 162-3; Firth, *S and P* pp. 297-8.

144. *TSP* iv, 104-5, 187, 222, 223; iii, 732, 733; Worcester MS. xlvii 23 November 1655.

145. Worcester MS. xlvii 23 November, 4 December 1655, 9 January 1656; *TSP* iv, 223.

146. *TSP* iv, 187, 221, 250, 271.

147. Nicoll, *Diary* p. 172; Worcester MS. xlvii 31 January 1656 (for suspicions of Womatt, see also *TSP* iv, 291).

148. *TSP* iv, 372, 400; Nicoll, *Diary* p. 173.

149. *TSP* iv, 372, 401; Bodl. Lib. Rawlinson MS. A27 p. 687; Willcock, *A Scots Earl* pp. 77-8.

150. *TSP* iv, 400.

151. *Cal. Cl. S. P.* iii, 109-110; Underdown, *Royalist Conspiracy* p. 178.

152. D. L. Hobman, *Cromwell's Master Spy* (London, 1961) pp. 101-2; *TSP* v, 301; Worcester MS. xxviii f21.

153. *TSP* iv, 726.

154. *TSP* v, 17-8. Cf. Worcester MS. xlvii 6 March 1656.

155. *TSP* v, 86; Worcester MS. xxviii f38v. (A Dutch ship had earlier been cast aground near Tain: *TSP* v, 25; Worcester MS. xxviii f16v).

156. *TSP* iv, 741.

157. Worcester MS. xlviii 30 July 1656.

158. *TSP* v, 301-2.

159. *TSP* v, 322-3. For Brayne's orders, see Bodl. Lib. Rawlinson MS. A56 f27.

160. *TSP* v, 323, 348, 375-6, 396; S. A. G. Taylor, *The Western Design* (2nd edn., London, 1969) p. 125.

161. Although Monck and Broghill accepted the reality of the Spanish threat off the north and west coasts of Scotland, it must be noted that other English sources maintain silence on the subject (but see *CSPD 1656-7* pp. 398, 408 for two reports of Spanish ships being sighted off the coasts of Scotland in August 1656). It is unlikely, however, that the reports which reached Edinburgh were complete fabrications, but Monck's informants may well have spun out or embroidered some scanty items of information to suit the ears of their paymasters. In particular, the number of reported sightings, and the length of time over which they took place, may reflect the informant's basic inclination to feed news to his masters 'by instalments' and so to inflate artificially the importance of his information.

162. *TSP* v, 348 (cf. *ibid.* v, 315).

163. Worcester MS. xlviii 13, 20, 30 August 1656. Monck was not to know that Balcarres was out of favour with the king: see Dow, 'Thesis' pp. 562-3.

164. Nicoll, *Diary* pp. 182-3; Steele 3rd pt. Nos. 2129, 2144.

165. *TSP* v, 396; Firth (ed.), *Clarke Papers* iii, 71; Worcester MS. xlviii 19 August 1656. Around this time, Robert Baillie alleged to a correspondent in Middleburg that '[t]he King is so farr forgot here, that not one man, so farr as I know, keeps any correspondence with him; nor doe we hear at all what he does or intends': *Letters and Journals* iii, 321.

166. *TSP* v, 422; Worcester MS. xxviii f75; Nicoll, *Diary* pp. 186-7.

167. *TSP* v, 396, 479-80, 505. His demand for another regiment was to replace that of Col. Salmon, which had been ordered to England.

168. *TSP* v, 479, 500; Nicoll, *Diary* p. 186.

169. *TSP* v, 500.

170. Worcester MS. xlviii 14 November 1656, 3 January 1657; SRO Rollo of Duncrub MSS. GD 56/143(6); Nicoll, *Diary* p. 187.

171. *TSP* v, 500; Nicoll, *Diary* p. 187; Brodie, *Diary* p. 190; Worcester MS. xlviii 17 October 1656.

172. *TSP* v, 500; Brodie, *Diary* p. 190; Worcester MS. xlviii 17 October, 29 December 1656, 8 January 1657.

173. Nicoll, *Diary* p. 187; *TSP* v, 602; Worcester MS. xlviii 14 November, 27 December 1656; SRO Ogilvy of Inverquharity MSS. GD 205 Portfolio 10, the Duchess of Hamilton to Lady Belhaven, 18 November 1656.

174. Worcester MS. xlviii 5 December 1656.

175. Nicoll, *Diary* p. 187; Worcester MS. xlviii 14 November 1656.

176. Worcester MS. xlviii 11 October 1656, 15 January 1657. Roderick's bond was set at £600 stg., Norman's at £400, but this was later raised to £600.

177. Worcester MS. xlviii 27 October 1656 (bond of £1000 stg.).

178. Worcester MS. xlviii 15 January 1657. The laird of Womatt's security had earlier been set at £1000 stg: Worcester MS. xlvii 6 May 1656; Worcester MS. xlviii 19 September 1656. For other sureties during the period 1657-8, see *ibid.* 3 January 1657 (Lorne — £5000 stg.); 18 September 1657 (Lord Forrester — £3000 stg.); 29 October 1657 (Seaforth — £6000 stg.); 25 November 1657 (Glengarry — £3000 stg.); 11 May 1658 (Glencairn — £10,000 stg.); 4 August 1658 (Sir Mungo Murray — £2000 stg.).

179. *TSP* v, 500.

180. *TSP* v, 602-3. John Monroe and Henry Mackay were arrested in December for attempting to take letters overseas: Worcester MS. xlviii 6, 20 December 1656.

181. *LRO* p. 131; *TSP* v, 707.

182. *TSP* v, 726-7.

183. For a fuller discussion of the court in exile and Charles's attitude towards Scotland, see Dow, 'Thesis' pp. 557-63.

Chapter 9: Broghill and the Church Parties, 1655-7

1. The most helpful accounts are to be found in F. N. McCoy, *Robert Baillie and the Second Scots Reformation* (Berkeley, California, 1974), pp. 180-4; Mathieson, *Politics and Religion* ii, 172-5; Trevor-Roper, 'Scotland and the Puritan Revolution' pp. 433-6.

2. For the text of the 'Charter', see Nicoll, *Diary* pp. 164-7; Firth and Rait, *A & O* iii, cxii-cxv; *APS* vi (2), 831-2.

3. For Lilburne's policy towards the church and the church parties, see *supra* pp.

4. B. L. Egerton MS. 2620 f11. Cf. Baillie, *Letters and Journals* iii, 243; Nicoll, *Diary* p. 127; Row, *Life of Blair* p. 313.

5. *Consultations* i, 70-1; Row, *Life of Blair* pp. 315-6; Firth, *S and P* p. 102; Nicoll, *Diary* p. 127.

6. Row, *Life of Blair* pp. 313, 317; Wariston, *Diary* ii, 273, 274; Baillie, *Letters and Journals* iii, 282.

7. For Gillespie, see *supra* pp. 59, 101-2, and for Menzies, Trevor-Roper, 'Scotland and the Puritan Revolution' p. 425.

8. *CSPD 1654* pp. 249, 264; Nicoll, *Diary* pp. 165-6; Baillie, *Letters and Journals* iii, 282. The grant to the universities did not form a separate charter, as stated in McCoy, *Robert Baillie* pp. 170, 174.

9. Cf. Firth, *LYP* ii, 94 and note.

10. These are named in the ordinance: see Nicoll, *Diary* pp. 166-7; Firth and Rait, *A & O* iii, cxiv-cxv; *APS* vi (2), 832.

11. Wariston, *Diary* ii, 308-9; *Consultations* i, 57-69; McCoy, *Robert Baillie* pp. 173-4.

12. Row, *Life of Blair* p. 319; Baillie, *Letters and Journals* iii, 283; Firth, *S and P* p. 211; *Consultations* i, 71-80; McCoy, *Robert Baillie* p. 173.

13. Baillie, *Letters and Journals* iii, 282; Firth, *S and P* p. 211. When the 'Charter' was proclaimed in October 1655, the accompanying declaration stated that it had not previously been implemented owing to the refusal of the 'triers' to act: Nicoll, *Diary* p. 163; *APS* vi (2), 831.

14. Wariston, *Diary* iii, ix, 2, 3, 4; *Consultations* i, 90; Baillie, *Letters and Journals* iii, 279-80.

15. Wariston, *Diary* iii, xi-xiii, 1, 7, 8, 11; Baillie, *Letters and Journals* iii, 297.

16. Wariston, *Diary* iii, 10.

17. *TSP* iv, 37-8.

18. Baillie, *Letters and Journals* iii, 295.

19. *TSP* iv, 49 (quoted in part in Firth, *LYP* ii, 95).

20. The clergy's argument turned on a literal interpretation of the wording of the ban of March 1655. This prohibited anyone from paying a stipend to any minister 'as hath alreddie, or sall heireftir, by praying for the pretendit king, contravene . . .' the ban. The Resolutioners argued that this wording meant that 'the penalty should continue, tho' the fault did not.' Nicoll, *Diary* p. 152; *TSP* iv, 56.

21. Baillie, *Letters and Journals* iii, 281; Wariston, *Diary* iii, 6.

22. *TSP* iv, 49.

23. Nicoll, *Diary* pp. 160-1; *TSP* iv, 58; Steele 3rd pt. No. 2122.

24. Nicoll, *Diary* p. 162; *Consultations* i, 89-90.

25. Baillie, *Letters and Journals* iii, 296; *TSP* iv, 88.

26. Firth, *S and P* pp. 321-3.

27. *TSP* iv, 49.

28. *TSP* iv, 73.

29. *TSP* iv, 127-9, for Broghill's exhaustive account of the subsequent negotiations.

30. 'Collins' was probably John Collins, who had been sent to Scotland by the Council of State in 1654 to dispense the Gospel: *CSPD 1654* p. 195. The Protester delegation included Sir Andrew Kerr, Sir George Maxwell, Mr. Patrick Gillespie and Mr. John Livingstone.

31. See Wariston, *Diary* iii, xvi; Baillie, *Letters and Journals* iii, 296.
32. Nicoll, *Diary* pp. 163-4; *APS* vi (2), 830-1 (for the text of the declaration); Steele 3rd pt. No. 2124.
33. *TSP* iv, 129.
34. *TSP* iv, 129.
35. Baillie, *Letters and Journals* iii, 297; cf. Wariston, *Diary* iii, xviii, 12-13; McCoy, *Robert Baillie* p. 181.
36. *Consultations* i, 90-1.
37. *Consultations* i, 104-7.
38. *Consultations* i, 111-9 (for the Resolutioners' proposals); *ibid.* i, 119-26, 126-34, 134-42, 142-6, 146-60, 161-84 (for the subsequent debates on these proposals).
39. *Consultations* i, 92-4 cf. Wariston, *Diary* iii, 11-15; Row, *Life of Blair* p. 326.
40. *Consultations* i, 93.
41. Cf. *TSP* iv, 558. This figure is accepted by Firth, *LYP* ii, 96; Mitchison, *A History of Scotland* p. 235; Donaldson, *Scotland: James V to James VII* p. 353; McCoy, *Robert Baillie* p. 186 note, and most other authorities.
42. Wariston, *Diary* iii, 15.
43. Wariston, *Diary* iii, xvii, 18-19; *TSP* iv, 255-7; Baillie, *Letters and Journals* iii, 300, 305.
44. Baillie, *Letters and Journals* iii, 300.
45. *Consultations* i, 184-90; Baillie, *Letters and Journals* iii, 305.
46. *Consultations* i, 191-3.
47. *Consultations* i, 194-7.
48. *Consultations* i, 198-201.
49. *TSP* iv, 49.
50. *TSP* iv, 557-9.
51. See *TSP* iv, 597, 700-1.
52. *TSP* v, 86; Row, *Life of Blair* p. 324; *Minutes of the Synod of Argyll* pp. 82, 109, 121-2; *CSPD 1655-6* pp. 234, 324, 365.
53. *TSP* iv, 700; Firth, *S and P* pp. 329-30.
54. *Consultations* i, 201-2.
55. Row, *Life of Blair* pp. 327-8; *Consultations* i, 201-2.
56. *CSPD 1656-7* pp. 45, 48; *APS* vi (2), 761.
57. *Consultations* i, 202-3; *TSP* v, 301.
58. Before his departure, the town council of Edinburgh gave a banquet in his honour: Nicoll, *Diary* p. 183.
59. Broghill seems to have been renominated when the Council's instructions were renewed in June 1658: Nicoll, *Diary* p. 221.
60. McCoy, *Robert Baillie* p. 184.
61. *TSP* v, 322, 336.
62. McCoy, *Robert Baillie* p. 189; cf. Row, *Life of Blair* pp. 329, 330.
63. Firth, *S and P* p. 345.
64. McCoy, *Robert Baillie* pp. 189-90.
65. McCoy, *Robert Baillie* pp. 190-1 (and authorities there cited); *Consultations* i, 355; *Consultations* ii, x; Row, *Life of Blair* pp. 330-2.

66. McCoy, *Robert Baillie* pp. 191-2, 195-6 (and authorities there cited); *Consultations* ii, xi-xii cf. Firth and Rait, *A & O* ii, 1049-50. And for a full discussion, see Ellen D. Goldwater, 'The Scottish Franchise: Lobbying during the Cromwellian Protectorate', *The Historical Journal* xxi (1978), 27-42.

67. McCoy, *Robert Baillie* pp. 193-5 (and authorities there cited); *Consultations* ii, xvii.

68. *Minutes of the Synod of Argyll* pp. xxvii-xxxii.

Chapter 10: The Consolidation of the Régime, August 1656 — September 1658

1. Nicoll, *Diary* p. 194.

2. *TSP* v, 396, 707, 726; vi, 92, 156; Firth, *S and P* p. 349; *CSPD 1656-7* pp. 209, 214, 240; Nicoll, *Diary* p. 194.

3. *TSP* vi, 329, 339, 372; Nicoll, *Diary* p. 198.

4. *TSP* vi, 498, 516, 517, 520.

5. *CSPD 1658-9* pp. 52, 57, 60-1; *TSP* vii, 203, 268; Worcester MS. li f52.

6. For the text of the Instructions of 1658, see *CSPD 1658-9* pp. 60-1; for those of 1655, see *CSPD 1655* pp. 108-10, 255.

7. Shortly after these Instructions came into force, Capt. Timothy Langley, deputy governor of Leith, began to send to Thurloe regular reports on the activities of the Scottish Anabaptists (and Quakers), particularly those in Edinburgh and Leith: *TSP* vii, 371, 403, 527, 554.

8. *TSP* vi, 470 (cf. Firth, *S and P* p. 360).

9. *TSP* vi, 366.

10. These figures may be deduced from *TSP* vi, 445, 470-2. Excise duties did later increase: see Firth, *LYP* ii, 118 and *infra* p. 216.

11. The term 'property and casualty' is fully discussed in David Stevenson, 'The King's Scottish Revenues and the Covenanters, 1625-1651', *The Historical Journal* xvii (1974) p. 17. Briefly, 'property' had heretofore consisted of fixed revenues and rents from Crown lands, payments from royal burghs, customs duties, and the impost on wines. 'Casualties' had included feudal casualties, escheats, compositions and other profits of justice.

12. In December 1656 the Council of State had given the Scottish authorities an additional prod by demanding that £10,000 should be paid from property and casualty revenues into the *English* Exchequer: *CSPD 1656-7* p. 191.

13. The paper is at Worcester MS. xxix ff 48-49v. Despite ill-feeling aroused by his services to the Republic, Purves attained high office after the Restoration. He was appointed King's Solicitor for life in September 1662, and also became Procurator of the Church of Scotland: see Sir William Purves, *Revenue of the Scottish Crown, 1681* ed. D. Murray Rose (Edinburgh and London, 1897) pp. xvii-xviii.

14. *TSP* vi, 424, 444-5, 469-72. Monck first sent an account of the revenue on 6 August, but a fortnight later an amended and expanded version was despatched,

which also concerned itself with retrenchments in the civil-list.

15. Worcester MS. li f30.

16. *TSP* vi, 445. For the sad condition of the registers pertaining to private rights, see Stevenson, 'The English and the Public Records of Scotland, 1650-1660' p. 163.

17. *TSP* vi, 516.

18. SRO Morton MSS. GD150 Box 97, J. Douglas to the Earl of Morton 5 December 1657. For the history of the Earldom of Orkney and its relation to the Crown in the 17th century, see Sir William Purves, *Revenue of the Scottish Crown, 1681* pp. 122-4.

19. *TSP* vii, 59.

20. *CJ* vii, 628.

21. *TSP* vii, 59; Sir William Purves, *Revenue of the Scottish Crown, 1681* p. xvi.

22. *CSPD 1657-8* p. 373; *CSPD 1658-9* pp. 18, 20; Worcester MS. xxx f84; Nicoll, *Diary* pp. 215, 216.

23. Cf. *TSP* vi, 472 and *CJ* vii, 629.

24. *CJ* vii, 628.

25. For 1656, see *TSP* vi, 445 and Tucker, *Report* pp. 33-46. The figure for the salt tax is based solely on Tucker, *Report* pp. 34-5. The figure of £16,000 for customs and foreign excise is that assumed by Monck etc. at *TSP* vi, 445; the figure given by Tucker for October 1655 to October 1656 is £12,800 (pp. 35-46).

26. This is clear from *TSP* vi, 445.

27. One of the largest of these grants was embodied in an order of the Lord Protector and Council of 11 September 1656 in favour of the Marquis of Argyle. Argyle was granted part of the excise on wines and strong waters to repay a debt, owing to him by the old Committee of Estates but now assumed by the English government, of £12,116 13s 4d. stg. From 10 November 1657, he was to get half the said excise, providing that he did not exceed £3000 in any one year, until the debt was paid in full, but by April 1659 he had received only £1000. *CSPD 1656-7* p. 107; *CJ* vii, 640; Willcock, *The Great Marquess* p. 296.

28. *CJ* vii, 628-30. An estimate, dated 30 December 1658, of the civil-list in Scotland which appears in Monck's letter-book gives a figure of £28,166 11s. 8d. 'besides Temporary Contingencies': Worcester MS. li f62.

29. *TSP* vi, 330, 351; Firth, *LYP* ii, 116-7.

30. Worcester MS. xxix ff 84v, 90; *CJ* vii, 567-8, 577; Firth and Rait, *A & O* ii, 1142-1162, 1234-1249.

31. Worcester MS. xlviii 30 September 1656.

32. For an example of how this worked in practice, see Worcester MS. xlviii 2 November 1657.

33. Worcester MS. xlviii 20 October 1656.

34. B.L.Add.MS. 38848 f63; *CSPD 1657-8* p. 344.

35. SRO Breadalbane MSS. GD 112/39/911.

36. *CSPD 1657-8* p. 382.

37. Worcester MS. xlviii 19 September 1656 (Lenzie); 26 September (Cunningham); 30 September (Campbell); 1 October (Ker).

38. *CSPD 1657-8* p. 316; Worcester MS. li f24v; Worcester MS. xxx f122.

39. Firth, *S and P* pp. 373-81 (for the new establishment); cf. Firth, *LYP* ii, 115 n2.

40. *TSP* vi, 552, 557; Firth, *S and P* pp. 366-71; *CSPD 1657-8* pp. 161, 281; Worcester MS. li ff 14v, 26v, 36, 40.

41. Firth, *S and P* pp. 371-2; Worcester MS. li f24v.

42. For the full estimates presented to the House, see *CJ* vii, 628-30, 640.

43. Firth, *S and P* p. 373.

44. For an example, see B.L.Add.MS. 23113 f57; cf. *TSP* vi, 366.

45. *CSPD 1656-7* pp. 134, 361.

46. Monck later complained that the Council had not been given enough time to apportion the fine equitably: *CSPD 1657-8* p. 284.

47. SRO Dalhousie MSS. GD 45/1/129 (for the text of the declaration); Worcester MS. xxx ff 26v-28v (for both moieties: another copy is at SRO Bargany MSS. RH 4/57/85).

48. SRO Bargany MSS. RH 4/57/37: Petition of John Lord Bargany to the Council in Scotland.

49. *TSP* vi, 537; *CSPD 1657-8* pp. 128, 284; *CSPD 1658-9* p. 41.

50. See *e.g.* *CSPD 1657-8* p. 65 (Sir Thomas Thompson); *CSPD 1657-8* p. 301 (Earl Marischal).

51. Worcester MS. xxx f27 (this document should be dated c. February 1658); *TSP* vi, 859.

52. The subject of the laws of debt (which had previously always been related to that of fines) raised little stir during this period, except that in January 1657 debtors expressed concern lest Parliament overturn the Council of State's order of 15 April 1656 and complained that because of the uncertainty, the judges were procrastinating. The Council agreed to tell the judges to get on with the business before them, but the letter was not sent until March: *CSPD 1656-7* p. 246; cf. Nicoll, *Diary* p. 184.

53. Englishmen as well as Scots now came increasingly to refer to this court by its old name of 'the court of session' and to its judges as 'lords of session', in a way which paralleled the reintroduction in England and Scotland of titles, offices etc. reminiscent of the former monarchy.

54. For Swinton's uncertain status as a judge, see *supra* p. But from January 1657, he was certainly paid as a judge, a decision reached by the Council while Swinton was conveniently in London: *CSPD 1656-7* p. 239. The arguments which applied to Swinton ought also to have held good for William Lockhart, but there is no notice of his receiving a salary; in any case his diplomatic appointment would have precluded him from actively fulfilling the judgeship, if in fact he still held it (cf. Firth, *S and P* p. 385, where he is counted as a judge in 1659, but not so for 1658 by Nicoll, *Diary* p. 222).

55. Lamont, *Diary* p. 98.

56. Nicoll, *Diary* p. 198; Lamont, *Diary* p. 99; *TSP* vi, 372.

57. *TSP* vi, 329, 339, 367; Wariston, *Diary* iii, 97.

58. *TSP* vi, 367 (partly quoted in Brunton and Haig, *Senators of the College of Justice* p. 362); *ibid.* p. 364.

59. See *The Decisions of the English Judges during the Usurpation* (Edinburgh, 1762): unpaginated volume.

60. Firth, *LYP* ii, 107; Brunton and Haig, *Senators of the College of Justice* p. 308; Wariston received his commission in September: *Diary* iii, 100. According to Nicoll, his appointment led to a great increase in legal fees etc: *Diary* p. 213.

61. Firth, *LYP* ii, 107; Nicoll, *Diary* p. 210.

62. Nicoll, *Diary* p. 222; Firth, *S and P* p. 386.

63. Nicoll, *Diary* p. 215; Firth, *S and P* p. 385; *CSPD 1658-9* p. 18.

64. *The Decisions of the English Judges during the Usurpation* (1762).

65. This willingness is reflected in some family papers of the period: see *e.g.* Stirling of Ardoch Papers (SRO GD24 Section 2 Vol. 5) where the emphasis is very marked; and the Breadalbane MSS. (SRO GD 112) for the concerns of the Campbells of Glenorchy.

66. Nicoll, *Diary* p. 219; *TSP* vii, 445, 450.

67. Bodl. Lib. Rawlinson MS. A43 f159.

68. Bodl. Lib. Rawlinson MS. A61 f271; cf. Wariston, *Diary* iii, 92, 93.

69. *The Decisions of the English Judges during the Usurpation* (1762).

70. But see Dow, 'Thesis' p. 520 for some evidence relating to 1659.

71. *TSP* vi, 162, 208; Worcester MS. xlviii 26 March 1657.

72. Worcester MS. xlviii 10 June 1658. Maclean was suspected of plotting against the government; for his royalist sympathies in September 1659, see *infra* p.

73. Firth, *S and P* pp. 405-11; for the hostility of the magistrates of Edinburgh, see Wood, *Extracts Edin. Recs. 1655 to 1665* p. 50.

74. *TSP* v, 702 (for Fowler, see also *TSP* v, 723; Worcester MS. xlviii 15 October 1656).

75. *TSP* vi, 295.

76. Worcester MS. xlviii 24 October 1656.

77. *TSP* iv, 250; v, 295.

78. In a letter from 'an honest gentleman in Argyllshire to Mr. David Drummond' of 31 May 1657: Bodl. Lib. Rawlinson MS. A51 f70. This was then transmitted to Monck, and by him to Thurloe: *TSP* vi, 341.

79. *TSP* vi, 295; Bodl, Lib. Rawlinson MS. A51 f70 (cf. *TSP* vi, 306).

80. Worcester MS. xlviii 9 April, 10 April 1657 (cf. Worcester MS. xlviii 3 July, 30 December 1657).

81. *TSP* vi, 295.

82. Firth, *S and P* pp. 411, 412-15.

83. Worcester MS. xlviii 4 and 29 October 1656 (Lochiel); 24 October 1656 (Macgriggor).

84. Worcester MS. xlviii 4 October 1656 (to Hill); 18 November 1656 (to Glencoe and others).

85. Worcester MS. xlviii 2 July, 12 July 1658; Firth, *S and P* p. xxv.

86. Worcester MS. xlviii 14, 24 October 1656; and see additional entry on flyleaf.

87. For persons granted special permission to hunt down robbers, mosstroopers etc., see Worcester MS. xlviii 20 October 1656 (John Richardson and John Farr), 10 November 1656 (Capt. William Ross), 21 January 1657 (Duncan Campbell of Auchline), 15 April 1657 (James Miles), 24 June 1658 (name in shorthand).

88. Firth, *S and P* p. 247; Worcester MS. xlviii 9 September, 11 October, 14 October 1656, 25 February, 2 March, 5 March 1657.

89. Worcester MS. xlviii 6 December 1656.

90. Worcester MS. xlviii 3 August 1658; 20 and 22 January 1658.

91. Worcester MS. xlviii 10 October 1656, 24 November 1656, 7 April 1658.

92. Worcester MS. xlviii 25 September 1656, 3 March 1657, 13 March 1657, 20 November 1657.

93. *TSP* v, 499; Worcester MS. xlviii 14 October 1656.

94. For Buchanan's arrest and his subsequent fate, see Worcester MS. xlviii 16 September, 4 November, 5 December 1656, 9 January, 29 January 1657.

95. Worcester MS. xlviii 15 June 1657.

96. Worcester MS. xlviii 20 August 1658 (Andrew), 23 April 1658 (the Borders: for control of arms there, see entry dated 7 April). Another case was reported involving James Tate, whose provenance is unknown: Worçester MS. xlviii 27 January, 10 February 1658.

97. See Dow, 'Thesis' pp. 552-3, 555-6.

98. Worcester MS. xlviii 6 February, 14, 16, 18 March 1657.

99. Worcester MS. xxix f87; *TSP* vi, 366-7.

100. *TSP* vi, 184, 208, 292.

101. *TSP* v, 17; vi, 81, 436.

102. *TSP* vi, 52.

103. See *e.g.* Firth, *S and P* pp. 347-8; *TSP* vi, 81, 664.

Chapter 11: Continuity and Change under Richard Cromwell and the Rump, September 1658 — October 1659

1. Worcester MS. xxx f153; *TSP* vii, 374.

2. *TSP* vii, 371.

3. Worcester MS. xlix 7 and 8 September 1658; Firth, *S and P* p. 383.

4. Worcester MS. xxx f155v.

5. Firth, *S and P* p. 384; Wood, *Extracts Edin. Recs. 1655 to 1665* p. 116.

6. Worcester MS. xxx f158; Nicoll, *Diary* p. 216.

7. Richard was proclaimed at Kirkcaldy on 13 September, at Cupar on the 15th and at Inverlochy on 5 October. News of Oliver's death first reached Aberdeen on 14 September: Lamont, *Diary* p. 107; Firth, *S and P* p. 384; Jaffray, *Diary* p. 119. For Monck's letter to the High Sheriff of Sutherland announcing Oliver's death and Richard's succession, see B. L. Stowe MS. 185 f131.

8. Godfrey Davies, *The Restoration of Charles II, 1658-1660* (San Marino, 1955) p. 18; *TSP* vii, 415.

9. See *supra* pp. 138-9.

10. Firth, *S and P* pp. 350-2, 362-3; Firth, *LYP* ii, 103. Some idea of the number of Quakers dismissed from the army in 1657 may be gleaned from Monck's warrant-book. According to the entries there, the dismissals occurred in two phases, the first from March to May 1657 and the other from October to December. In the first over 20 soldiers were dismissed, in the second somewhat under 20: Worcester MS. xlviii 2, 13, 27 March; 16, 22 April; 9, 15, 20, 25, 29 May; 16, 26, 27 October; 20, 21 November; 22 December 1657.

11. Firth, *LYP* ii, 122.

12. Firth, *LYP* ii, 45-7; Firth (ed.), *Clarke Papers* iii, 140. For the addresses of loyalty from the regiments in Scotland, see Worcester MS. xxx ff 25v, 32, 33v, 34v, 36, 37v, 43, 46, 48v, 52, 54, 57, 60v, 66, 70v, 71v, 75v, 80.

13. *TSP* vii, 452.

14. *TSP* vii, 404, 411, 414, 435.

15. Davies, *Restoration* p. 8; Worcester MS. xxx ff 164-8.

16. *TSP* vii, 416, 446.

17. *TSP* vii, 411.

18. *TSP* vii, 436. Cf. Davies, *Restoration* p. 34.

19. *TSP* vii, 545. Cf. Davies, *Restoration* p. 40.

20. *TSP* vii, 403, 411, 416.

21. *TSP* vii, 404, 435, 411.

22. *TSP* vii, 521; *Cal. Cl. S. P.* iv, 102.

23. *TSP* vii, 445, 509, 545; Worcester MS. xlix 4 October 1658. Nonetheless the Earls of Rothesay and Glencairn were both released from prison in December on payment of heavy security, £6000 in Rothesay's case and £12,000 in Glencairn's: Worcester MS. xlix 1, 6 December 1658.

24. Worcester MS. xlix 15 October, 17 December 1658. The Council issued a proclamation in October banning the import of arms and ammunition without special licence after 1 December: Nicoll, *Diary* pp. 219-20; Steele 3rd pt. No. 2163.

25. *TSP* vii, 403, 527, 554.

26. *TSP* vii, 422, 435; Worcester MS. xxx f170; SRO Breadalbane MSS. GD 112/39/923; Nicoll, *Diary* p. 218.

27. *TSP* vii, 616, 623. But some members of the army in Scotland (notably Col. Ashfield) were causing Thurloe alarm because of their anti-protectoral stance in the debates of the Parliament then sitting at Westminster: *TSP* vii, 638. For a discussion of the Scottish representatives in Richard Cromwell's Parliament, see *infra* pp. 237-40.

28. Worcester MS. xlix 28 October, 3 November 1658; Worcester MS. cclvii George Campbell to General Monck 21 April 1659; SRO Airlie MSS. GD 16/34/33 Earl of Airlie to Lord Ogilvy 23 February 1659 (concerning the theft of the Earl's property).

29. Worcester MS. xlix 18 September 1658.

30. Worcester MS. xlix 17 September 1658.

31. See *e.g.* Worcester MS. xlix 16 February 1659.

32. Worcester MS. xlix 27 September, 19 October 1658, 22 January 1659.

33. Worcester MS. cclvii. The true information of Corporal Vavasour . . . 14 April 1659; the laird of Kelburne to Major Crispe 11 April 1659; same to General Monck 14 April 1659.

34. Worcester MS. cclvii Sheriff Blair to General Monck 29 April 1659.

35. See *e.g.* Worcester MS. xlix 4 February 1659 (payment for grass for horses), 23 March 1659 (ban on soldiers shooting pigeons etc.).

36. *Recs. Conv. RBS* pp. 474-84.

37. Worcester MS. xxxi f63.

38. *The Decisions of the English Judges during the Usurpation* (1762).

39. *TSP* vii, 656.

40. See *supra* pp.

41. James A. Casada, 'The Scottish representatives in Richard Cromwell's parliament', *Scottish Historical Review* li (1972), 130.

42. Terry, *CU* p. lxxvii; Casada, 'The Scottish representatives . . .' p. 129. For the relevant clause of the Humble Petition and Advice, see Firth and Rait, *A & O* ii, 1051. After asking the Protector's advice Monck declined to attend owing to pressure of business in Scotland: *TSP* vii, 579, 583. Wariston did attend, setting out for London on 11 January: Wariston, *Diary* iii, 105. When the Other House was first created, Scotland had been given four seats; Monck, Wariston, William Lockhart of Lee, and the Earl of Cassillis were then invited to attend, but none took their seats: Terry, *CU* pp. lxxv-lxxvi; Firth, *LYP* ii, 86.

43. *TSP* vii, 574, 575 (not 22 December as stated by Casada, 'The Scottish representatives . . .' p. 129).

44. *TSP* vii, 555 (cf. Casada, 'The Scottish representatives . . .' p. 130).

45. *TSP* vii, 572.

46. *TSP* vii, 583, 584; Wariston, *Diary* iii, 105 (cf. Casada, 'The Scottish representatives . . .' p. 130).

47. *TSP* vii, 584.

48. Bodl. Lib. Rawlinson MS. A63 f56; *TSP* vii, 555.

49. *TSP* vii, 613.

50. All thirty constituencies returned a member, but two candidates, Dr. Thomas Clarges and Col. Nathaniel Whetham were elected twice, for separate Scottish districts; hence only 28 individuals were chosen. For the complete list, see Worcester MS. xxxi ff1-3; see also H. N. Mukerjee, 'Scottish Members of Richard Cromwell's Parliament' *Notes and Queries* clxvi (1934), 65. Since another two candidates, Dr. William Stanes and Lawrence Oxborough, were elected by English constituencies and chose to sit for them, only 26 members formed the Scottish contingent in Parliament: James A. Casada, 'Scottish Members of Parliament: 1659', *Notes and Queries* N. S. xviii (1971), 295.

51. More so, in one way, than in previous years, for the proportion of 17 Englishmen to 11 Scots (raised to 18 to 10 when Henry Whalley was elected in place of Archibald Murray of Blackbarony, who declined to serve) was higher than in 1654 or 1656. For Whalley, see Casada, 'The Scottish representatives . . .' p. 131.

52. Casada, 'The Scottish representatives . . .' pp. 141-2. I reject Casada's

identification of Waller (p. 138) in favour of that given by Terry, *CU* p. lxxix: in Worcester MS. xxxi f2 he is described as 'Thomas Waller of Grayes Inn Esq.'—for his election on 6 January 1659, see Worcester MS. li f61v.

53. Casada, 'The Scottish representatives . . .' p. 140.

54. Casada, 'The Scottish representatives . . .' p. 141; *TSP* vii, 492.

55. Casada, 'The Scottish representatives . . .' pp. 138-40. To this group may also be added Henry Whalley, Judge Advocate of the army in Scotland. Fitch was not an adherent of the protectoral party, and hence his election deviated from the norm: *ibid.* p. 139.

56. Casada, 'The Scottish representatives . . .' pp. 137-8, 139, 140. For Thompson and Whetham see Wood, *Extracts Edin. Recs. 1655 to 1665* p. 129.

57. Casada, 'The Scottish representatives . . .' p. 131.

58. Worcester MS. xxxi f1; Nicoll, *Diary* p. 215.

59. Worcester MS. xxxi f2; cf. Nicoll, *Diary* p. 239.

60. Monck especially recommended him to Thurloe in a letter dated 25 January: Bodl. Lib. Rawlinson MS. A63 f54 (cf. H. N. Mukerjee, 'Scottish Members . . .' p. 65).

61. Casada, 'The Scottish representatives . . .' pp. 135-6. Lamont, *Diary* p. 110.

62. Casada, 'The Scottish representatives ...' p. 136; Ross was also recommended by Monck, *TSP* vii, 633 (cf. H. N. Mukerjee, 'Scottish Members . . .' p. 65).

63. As advanced by Professor Pinckney in his analysis of the 1656 elections.

64. Worcester MS. li ff60v-61.

65. Cf. Casada, 'The Scottish representatives . . .' pp. 143-4.

66. Casada, 'The Scottish representatives . . .'p. 145; Terry, *CU* p. lxxxvii. Cf. Firth (ed.), *Clarke Papers* iii, 176.

67. Terry, *CU* pp. lxxxi-lxxxii. For references to the problem of the Scottish members in parliamentary debates between 31 January and 7 March, see J. T. Rutt (ed.), *Diary of Thomas Burton Esq.* (4 vols., London, 1828) iii, 17, 28, 29, 31, 71, 75, 76, 119, 225, 269, 345, 346, 407, 561; iv, 57.

68. Terry, *CU* pp. lxxxii-lxxxviii; Casada, 'The Scottish representatives . . .' pp. 144-5; Worcester MS. xxxi ff 48, 50v, 56, 59v; Firth (ed.), *Clarke Papers* iii, 183-4. For the debates, see Burton, *Diary* iv, 87-223. For Monck's reaction to them, see *TSP* vii, 638.

69. Casada, 'The Scottish representatives . . .' p. 145.

70. Casada, 'The Scottish representatives . . .' p. 146.

71. *TSP* vii, 656.

72. Firth (ed.), *Clarke Papers* iii, 188, 194, 195; iv, 3 note 4; Davies, *Restoration* p. 86; Sir Richard Baker, *Chronicle of the kings of England from the time of the Romans government unto the death of King James . . . whereunto is added the reign of King Charles I, and the first thirteen years of . . . King Charles II . . . 7th impr.* (London, 1679) p. 644.

73. Exactly when and how Monck heard this news is not clear. A letter from the officers in England to Monck of 3 May, enclosing the resolutions of the General

Council of 28 April, made no mention of a recall of the Rump, and such a step may not have been decided upon until 5 May: Firth (ed.), *Clarke Papers* iv, 1-2, 4-6; Davies, *Restoration* pp. 87, 89. For the resignation of Richard on 25 May, see *ibid.* p. 100.

74. *TSP* vii, 669-70 (cf. Worcester MS. xxxi f111). For the pleasure of some officers in Scotland at Lambert's return, see *LRO* p. 140. On 17 May Monck told the Committee of Safety that the army in Scotland was 'very unanimous' in favour of the recent transactions: Firth (ed.), *Clarke Papers* iv, 10.

75. Worcester MS. xxxi f114v (for other locations, see Firth (ed.), *Clarke Papers* iv, 10 note 2); *CSPD 1658-9* p. 347.

76. Baker, *Chronicle* p. 644; Ashley, *General Monck* p. 152; and cf. note 74 *supra.*

77. Worcester MS. xxxi f124.

78. *CJ* vii, 658.

79. Davies, *Restoration* p. 103; Bodl. Lib. Rawlinson MS. C. 179 [Minute book of the proceedings of the Council of State from 19 May to 10 August 1659] p. 34; *CJ* vii, 681-2.

80. *CJ* vii, 693.

81. *CJ* vii, 736, 740.

82. *CJ* vii, 745, 749, 754, 757, 763, 768, 773, 775, 779, 789, 792.

83. *CJ* vii, 664; Nicoll, *Diary* pp. 242-3.

84. Davies, *Restoration* p. 127; *Consultations* ii, 179, 180, 181; Bodl. Lib. Rawlinson MS. C. 179 p. 24. For the decision to send Sharp to London in January 1659 and his instructions, see *Consultations* ii, 147-50.

85. *Consultations* ii, 184, 185.

86. *Consultations* ii, 187, 188. Sharp's fear of the Protesters was shared by Baillie: *Letters and Journals* iii, 396.

87. *Consultations* ii, 189, 191, 192; Bodl. Lib. Rawlinson MS. C. 179 p. 115.

88. *CJ* vii, 736; Nicoll, *Diary* p. 245 cf. Firth (ed.), *Clarke Papers* iv, 51. The Quakers also seem to have contemplated a petition: Wariston, *Diary* iii, 131.

89. Terry, *CU* p. xcii cf. Wariston, *Diary* iii, 133.

90. Wariston, *Diary* iii, 126, 127.

91. Worcester MS. li f90v; *CSPD 1659-60* pp. 119, 183; Wariston, *Diary* iii, 134; *CJ* vii, 775.

92. *CSPD 1659-60* p. 200; for the instructions, B. L. Egerton MS. 1048 f176 (for the older instructions, see Firth, *S and P* pp. 393-8).

93. Wariston, *Diary* iii, 136.

94. *CSPD 1659-60* p. 240; *CJ* vii, 792.

95. *CJ* vii, 659.

96. *Consultations* ii, 189.

97. Bodl. Lib. Rawlinson MS. C. 179 p. 74; *CSPD 1659-60* p. 78; *CJ* vii, 749; Firth (ed.), *Clarke Papers* iv, 37.

98. *CJ* vii, 775-6; *CSPD 1659-60* pp. 183, 190.

99. *CSPD 1659-60* pp. 214, 237.

100. *CJ* vii, 792.

101. Firth, *S and P* pp. 385, 391; Baillie, *Letters and Journals* iii, 430; Row, *Life of Blair* p. 338.

102. Nicoll, *Diary* pp. 265, 266, 244-5. Burgh elections were held in October 1659 (see *e.g.* Wood, *Extracts Edin. Recs. 1655 to 1665* p. 165; *Glasgow Burgh Recs.* p. 428) but there was no general convention of burghs in July; instead a particular convention met: *Recs. Conv. RBS* pp. 486-90.

103. *CJ* vii, 648, 707; Firth and Rait, *A & O* ii, 1270-1; Steele 3rd pt. No. 2164; Nicoll, *Diary* p. 244.

104. Worcester MS. cclvii Lt. Col. Mann to General Monck 17 September 1659. On 19 July 1659 the deputy sheriff of Roxburgh wrote to Monck about a dispute over church seats: HMC *Leyborne-Popham* p. 119.

105. Worcester MS. cclvii Major Crispe to General Monck 6 June 1659; Lt. Col. Mann to General Monck 17 September 1659.

106. Worcester MS. xlix 6 June, 29 July, 15, 25 August 1659.

107. Worcester MS. li f90v (cf. *CSPD 1659-60* p. 119).

108. Worcester MS. xlix 27 May 1659; Worcester MS. cclvii George Campbell to Wm. Clarke 24 May 1659.

109. Worcester MS. xlix 7 July, 15 August 1659. Cf. SRO Airlie MSS. GD 16/50/73(C) General Monck to the Earl of Airlie 30 September 1659.

110. Worcester MS. xlix 22 August, 9 September 1659.

111. Guards were ordered to be mounted in Perthshire in September as a defence against the incursions of 'broken men': Worcester MS. xlix 9, 30 September 1659.

112. Worcester MS. xlix 12, 29 July 1659.

113. Firth, *S and P* p. 416.

114. Bodl. Lib. Tanner MS. li f113.

115. Worcester MS. cclvii Lt. Col. Mann to General Monck 17 September 1659.

116. HMC *Leyborne-Popham* p. 120. A commission was issued on 12 September for the raising of an armed band of 30 men to pursue the lairds of Jura and Scellitor: Worcester MS. xlix 12 September 1659.

117. HMC *Leyborne-Popham* pp. 121-2.

118. Firth (ed.), *Clarke Papers* iv, 10.

119. *CSPD 1658-9* p. 358; Firth (ed.), *Clarke Papers* iv, 15-6; Worcester MS. li f69v.

120. Worcester MS. xlix 25 June, 1, 5 July 1659; HMC *Leyborne-Popham* p. 117.

121. Worcester MS. li ff 78, 78v, 79v; *CSPD 1659-60* pp. 27, 53. Monck had allowed a race meeting to be held at Jedburgh in May: Worcester MS. xlix 20 May 1659.

122. HMC *Leyborne-Popham* p. 120.

123. Firth (ed.), *Clarke Papers* iv, 25-6, 26-8.

124. Worcester MS. xlix 12, 16 August 1659; Firth (ed.), *Clarke Papers* iv, 41.

125. Firth (ed.), *Clarke Papers* iv, 41; Nicoll, *Diary* p. 247; Baillie, *Letters and Journals* iii, 430.

126. Worcester MS. xlix 16 August 1659 (for Livingstone and Erskine: the latter was not on the original list); HMC *Leyborne-Popham* p. 121.

127. *CSPD 1659-60* p. 210; Firth (ed.), *Clarke Papers* iv, 56.

128. Worcester MS. xlix August 1659 *passim* (horses); 8, 9 August 1659 (dangerous words).

129. *CSPD 1659-60* p. 119 (cf. Worcester MS. li f90v).

130. *LRO* p. 146.

131. SRO Seafield MSS. GD 248/556/1 Earl of Rothes to [Earl of Findlater?] 7 September 1659. Cf. Baillie, *Letters and Journals* iii, 430.

132. The Council of State asked Monck on 16 July to issue orders to the commissioners for gathering in the cess: Worcester MS. li f84. Commissioners of assessment were, of course, also JPs; for an order to them to meet to provide straw for the army, see Worcester MS. xlix 17 August 1659. For delays in collecting the assessment, Davies, *Restoration* p. 176 and Wood, *Extracts Edin. Recs. 1655 to 1665* p. 163 and for evidence that the excise was being collected, Worcester MS. xlix 25 August 1659.

Chapter 12: The Army and the Downfall of the Republican Régime, October 1659 — May 1660

1. Davies, *Restoration* pp. 147-8; Firth (ed.), *Clarke Papers* iv, 57-9 and authorities there cited.

2. Worcester MS. xxxii f23; Worcester Coll. pamphlet AA. e. 5[23]; Nicoll, *Diary* pp. 252-4 cf. Firth (ed.), *Clarke Papers* iv, 67n.

3. For a fuller account of these exchanges, see Dow, 'Thesis' pp. 610-2 and authorities there cited.

4. Firth (ed.), *Clarke Papers* iv, 70-4, 77-8.

5. Davies, *Restoration* p. 172.

6. Firth (ed.), *Clarke Papers* iv, 85-8, 96-7; Worcester MS. lii f8v.

7. Davies, *Restoration* pp. 172-3; Worcester MS. xxxii f123. For the instructions see Firth (ed.), *Clarke Papers* iv, 97-9.

8. Davies, *Restoration* pp. 173-4; Wariston, *Diary* iii, 152, 153, 154.

9. Davies, *Restoration* p. 174; Firth (ed.), *Clarke Papers* iv, 126-9, 129-31, 131-2, 143-51, 162-3, 163-4.

10. Firth and Davies, *Regimental History* i, 140; HMC *Leyborne-Popham* p. 133.

11. Davies, *Restoration* pp. 180-5; Austin Woolrych, 'Last Quests for a Settlement 1657-1660', in Aylmer (ed.), *The Interregnum: The Quest for Settlement 1646-1660* pp. 200-1. News of the army in Ireland's decision caused celebrations by the English garrisons in Edinburgh and Leith: Nicoll, *Diary* p. 261.

12. At times, indeed, his 'prospects did not seem very bright' as his feelers at first found little response: Davies, *Restoration* p. 167. For Monck's communications with the gathered churches and with congregational ministers, see Worcester MS. xxxii f24; Firth (ed.), *Clarke Papers* iv, 70, 81 and notes, 89-91, 118, 121, 151, 184, 212; Davies, *Restoration* pp. 174-6. For relations with the Irish army, see Worcester MS. xxxii ff 44v, 119, 130-2; Firth (ed.), *Clarke Papers* iv, 95-6 (notes). For a letter to the garrison at Hull, see Worcester MS. xxxii f44v and

for one to Vice Admiral Goodson, Worcester MS. xxxii f133. For relations with London, Worcester MS. lii f16v; Firth (ed.), *Clarke Papers* iv, 134-7 and notes. An account of dealings with Fairfax is given in Davies, *Restoration* pp. 177-80.

13. The Rump had reassembled on the night of 26 December. The letters which the Speaker subsequently sent to Monck, although acknowledging the General's influence on recent events, contained no mention of his projected march south and were thought by Monck's chaplain to be 'as cold as the night' in their attitude to the General: Woolrych, 'Last Quests for a Settlement 1657-1660' pp. 201-2; Davies, *Restoration* pp. 187-9, 259, 266 and note 49.

14. Mackinnon, *Origin and Services of the Coldstream Guards* i, 85.

15. Davies, *Restoration* p. 176.

16. Davies, *Restoration* pp. 105-6.

17. Firth (ed.), *Clarke Papers* iv, 16-7, 22-3; Davies, *Restoration* p. 110; Ashley, *General Monck* pp. 155-6.

18. For fuller details, see Dow, 'Thesis' pp. 616-7. There were no changes made in Morgan's regiment of dragoons: Firth and Davies, *Regimental History* i, 312.

19. Baker, *Chronicle* pp. 648-9.

20. Davies, *Restoration* p. 111.

21. Firth and Davies, *Regimental History* i, xxix-xxx; *CSPD 1658-9* p. 358.

22. See Dow, 'Thesis' pp. 618-20.

23. Firth and Davies, *Regimental History* i, 139, 312.

24. Davies, *Restoration* p. 178; *DNB* s.v. Morgan, Sir Thomas (d. 1679?).

25. See Dow, 'Thesis' pp. 621-2.

26. Firth and Davies, *Regimental History* i, 139-40, 289.

27. Davies, *Restoration* p. 177. In August Monck had been ordered to recruit each troop to 80 and each foot regiment to 800, but it is not clear how far this process had gone before the breach between the English army and Parliament: *CSPD 1659-60* p. 84; Worcester MS. li f89. For the relevant order from Monck to the recruiting sergeants, see Worcester MS. xlix 2 September 1659; cf HMC *Fitzherbert* p. 3.

28. Davies, *Restoration* pp. 163, 177. For a Quaker comment on desertions, see Swarthmore MSS. Vol. IV f268.

29. These had been assessed at over £148,000 by March 1659: Worcester MS. li f65v.

30. Firth and Rait, *A & O* ii, 1284-6; Davies, *Restoration* p. 176. Baker, *Chronicle* p. 667 gives 10 October and 10 December as the dates fixed by Monck for payment of the cess, but Edinburgh was preparing to pay the first four months' in September and the rest by 20 November: Wood, *Extracts Edin. Recs. 1655 to 1665* pp. 163, 170.

31. Firth and Rait, *A & O* ii, 1349-51; Worcester MS. xlix 25 October, 9, 14, 18 November 1659.

32. *Letters and Journals* iii, 438.

33. Cf. comments reported in Firth (ed.), *Clarke Papers* iv, 140, 143.

34. Worcester MS. lii f1; *CSPD 1659-60* p. 256; Wariston, *Diary* iii, 147-8; Wood, *Extracts Edin. Recs. 1655 to 1665* p. 167; Nicoll, *Diary* p. 256. (Despite the

creation of the Committee of Safety, the Council of State had continued to sit until 25 October: Davies, *Restoration* p. 154).

35. SRO Rossie Priory MSS. GD 48/1101, letter dated 26 October 1659 and 'Queries for my lord general Monck.' For Kinnaird's career after 1660, see *DNB*, Kinnaird, George Patrick, first Baron Kinnaird (d. 1689).

36. Firth (ed.), *Clarke Papers* iv, 78-9. Although the summons stipulated one representative, Perthshire nominated two; SRO Rossie Priory MSS. GD 48/1141 (cf. *infra* p.). For some burgh selections see *Glasgow Burgh Recs.* p. 431; *Aberdeen Council Register* p. 183; Wood, *Extracts Edin. Recs. 1655 to 1665* pp. 172-3.

37. Firth (ed.), *Clarke Papers* iv, 79; *Glasgow Burgh Recs.* p. 430; Swarthmore MSS. Vol IV f279v.

38. For Stewart's support of the Western Remonstrance in 1650 and his subsequent recantation in 1651, see Stevenson, *Revolution and Counter-Revolution* pp. 188, 203, and for his hostile attitude to the English in 1652, see *supra* p. 54. Shortly after his appearance at the Edinburgh convention in November 1659, he was suspected of dealing with Lambert, but he denied this: Firth (ed.), *Clarke Papers* iv, 211.

39. Firth (ed.), *Clarke Papers* iv, 113-5; Davies, *Restoration* p. 226; Nicoll, *Diary* p. 257.

40. Firth (ed.), *Clarke Papers* iv, 115-6, 120-1.

41. SRO Airlie MSS. GD 16/50/75 (Ogilvy was later elected commissioner for Forfar: *ibid.* GD 16/50/76); Firth (ed.), *Clarke Papers* iv, 205. Baillie wrote that 'after Monck's march, some stickling there was in the west to have had meetings in shyres for new Commissioners': *Letters and Journals* iii, 446. For instructions to Kinnaird as to how he should behave at Berwick, see SRO Rossie Priory MSS. GD 48/1142.

42. Wood, *Extracts Edin. Recs. 1655 to 1665* pp. 177-9; *Aberdeen Council Register* p. 184.

43. Some, including Argyllshire, were almost certainly late and probably did not arrive at all; for Argyllshire's apologies, see Worcester MS. cccxliv.

44. Bruce, a known Royalist, was shortly to go on a mission to the king in exile: Turner, *Memoirs* pp. 131-2.

45. Firth (ed.), *Clarke Papers* iv, 190; Baker, *Chronicle* p. 674.

46. Firth (ed.), *Clarke Papers* iv, 190-1; Baker, *Chronicle* pp. 674-5; Davies, *Restoration* pp. 226-7; Nicoll, *Diary* p. 260.

47. Worcester MS. xxxii f158v; Firth (ed.), *Clarke Papers* iv, 192, 194-5.

48. Swarthmore MSS. Vol. IV ff 279, 279v, 268.

49. *Glasgow Burgh Recs.* p. 430; Wood, *Extracts Edin. Recs. 1655 to 1665* pp. 174, 179; *Aberdeen Council Register* p. 185.

50. Worcester MS. xlix 12 November 1659.

51. Firth (ed.), *Clarke Papers* iv, 200-1; Worcester MS. xxxii f166v; Nicoll, *Diary* p. 259.

52. Nicoll, *Diary* p. 258; Davies, *Restoration* p. 176; Mackinnon, *Origin and Services of the Coldstream Guards* i, 85.

53. Firth (ed.), *Clarke Papers* iv, 238, 248n; Firth and Davies, *Regimental History* ii, 568 (Reade commanded the second division because Morgan was ill). Two companies of Morgan's regiment of foot were left in Scotland: *ibid.* ii, 496.

54. But three companies were in England: Firth and Davies, *Regimental History* ii, 559.

55. Firth (ed.), *Clarke Papers* iv, 248n; Firth and Davies, *Regimental History* ii, 497; Bodl. Lib. Carte MS. 103 f652.

56. Row, *Life of Blair* p. 340.

57. Mackinnon, *Origin and Services of the Coldstream Guards* i, 86; Firth and Davies, *Regimental History* i, 313-4; HMC *Leyborne-Popham* p. 147; Nicoll, *Diary* pp. 274, 276.

58. Worcester MS. xlix 25 January 1660.

59. SRO Breadalbane MSS. GD 112/39/928.

60. *LRO* p. 154.

61. SRO Airlie MSS. GD 16/50/78.

62. *Aberdeen Council Register* p. 185.

63. *Glasgow Burgh Recs.* p. 434; Wood, *Extracts Edin. Recs. 1655 to 1665* p. 184.

64. SRO Duntreath MSS. GD 97/3/150.

65. Davies, *Restoration* p. 268; Nicoll, *Diary* pp. 272-3; B. L. Egerton MS. 2618 f57.

66. B.L.Add.MS. 23113 f80.

67. For the proceedings see B.L.Add.MS. 23113 ff 80 *et seq.; Recs.Conv.RBS* pp. 490-503; Davies, *Restoration* pp. 230-1; Nicoll, *Diary* p. 272.

68. Osmund Airy (ed.), *The Lauderdale Papers* (2 vols. Camden Society, 1884-5) i, 8.

69. Firth and Rait, *A & O* ii, 1353-5, 1416-7; *CJ* vii, 844.

70. Firth and Rait, *A & O* ii, 1355-1403; *CJ* vii, 872.

71. Davies, *Restoration* p. 347; *LRO* p. 156; Lamont, *Diary* p. 120.

72. Worcester MS. xxxiii f1; SRO Rossie Priory MSS. GD 48/1102b; *Mercurius Politicus* 15-21 March 1660; *Mercurius Publicus* 16-23 May 1660; Nicoll, *Diary* p. 278; Robert Wodrow, *The History of the Sufferings of the Church of Scotland* ed. R. Burns (4 vols., Glasgow, 1828-30) i, 14, 18.

73. B. L. Sloane MS. 1519 No. 108.

74. Nicoll, *Diary* pp. 282-3. For further discussion of these officials, see *infra* p. .

75. Worcester MS. xxxiii f1; Nicoll, *Diary* p. 278; Brunton and Haig, *Senators of the College of Justice* pp. 346-7.

76. Wodrow i, 5 (around the beginning of March, Lauderdale and Crawford-Lindsay were released from prison, and hence Lauderdale was able to join Sharp in making representations to Monck and the Council: *ibid.* i, 8, 9); Davies, *Restoration* p. 227.

77. Wodrow i, 13-4, 18.

78. Wodrow i, 14, 15, 17, 18; Davies, *Restoration* p. 228.

79. Wodrow i, 16-7.

80. Wodrow i, 8, 9, 18; Davies *Restoration* pp. 229, 297-8.

81. Wodrow i, 10, 11, 16.

82. B.L.Add.MS. 23113 f83; *Consultations* ii, 204; Wood, *Extracts Edin. Recs. 1655 to 1665* p. 193; *Cal.Cl.S.P.* iv, 620. The four commissioners from the shires had probably never fulfilled their mission to go to London in February.

83. B.L.Add.MS. 23113 f83.

84. Wodrow i, 21; Davies, *Restoration* pp. 320-32, 338-42.

85. Wodrow i, 21-2.

86. Wodrow i, 22-5, 29-30.

87. Wood, *Extracts Edin. Recs. 1655 to 1665* pp. 195, 197-8.

88. *Consultations* ii, xxxix; Wodrow i, 28; Bodl. Lib. Carte MS. 30 f598.

89. Bodl. Lib. Carte MS. 30 ff 609, 621.

90. SRO Rossie Priory MSS. GD 48/1102; GD 48/1102b. Cf. Burnet's comment: 'The disposal of Scotch places in the Government was being privately and provisionally considered by Lauderdale's friends in January.' Gilbert Burnet, *History of My Own Time* ed. Osmund Airy (2 vols., Oxford, 1897) i, 152n.

91. B.L.Add.MS. 23113 ff 105, 111; Lamont, *Diary* p. 128; Nicoll, *Diary* p. 295; Baillie, *Letters and Journals* iii, 443.

92. B.L.Add.M.S. 23113 f111; *CSPD 1659-60* p. 441; Willcock, *A Scots Earl* pp. 84-5.

93. Row, *Life of Blair* p. 350.

94. Nicoll, *Diary* pp. 283-4; one cannoneer was blown up when the guns were fired: *ibid.* p. 284.

95. Wariston, *Diary* iii, 183.

Epilogue: The Restoration Settlement, 1660-1663

1. *Mercurius Publicus* 18-25 April, 16-23 May 1660; B. L. Sloane MS. 1519 No. 108.

2. Steele 3rd pt. No. 2172.

3. Nicoll, *Diary* pp. 292-4; *Mercurius Publicus* 27 June-4 July, 4-11 July 1660.

4. See *CSPD 1660-1* p. 205 (I reject Firth and Davies's assumption that the commissioners' authority lasted until 28 August: *Regimental History* ii, 497).

5. Wodrow i, 38, 44; *Lauderdale Papers* i, 32-3.

6. Wodrow i, 51; Nicoll, *Diary* p. 297.

7. *Mercurius Publicus* 29 August-5 September 1660; Wodrow i, 49, 51, 52; Burnet, *History* i, 199.

8. *Scots Peerage* ii, 480 cf. *supra* p. 329.

9. *Scots Peerage* iii, 36; v, 303-4 cf. *supra* pp.

10. See Part Two *passim.*

11. For Fletcher, see Omond, *The Lord Advocates of Scotland* i, 171-2; Burnet, *History* i, 191 and note 2. For Primrose, see Omond, *The Lord Advocates of Scotland* i, 171; Burnet, *History* i, 190-1; Brunton and Haig, *Senators of the College of Justice* pp. 352-5.

12. *Scots Peerage* ii, 480; *APS* vii, 162.

13. *Scots Peerage* iii, 36; Mathieson, *Politics and Religion* ii, 197.

14. For an extensive account of the feud between Lauderdale and Middleton, see Burnet, *History* i, chapters 2, 3, 4 and 8; cf. Mathieson, *Politics and Religion* ii, 197-200.

15. Nicoll, *Diary* p. 298.

16. Nicoll, *Diary* p. 298; Mathieson, *Politics and Religion* ii, 176-7; Donaldson, *Scotland: James V to James VII* p. 361.

17. Steele 3rd pt. No. 2186.

18. Mathieson, *Politics and Religion* ii, 177-8; Steele 3rd pt. Nos. 2188, 2189.

19. Mathieson, *Politics and Religion* ii, 178; Nicoll, *Diary,* p. 335.

20. Nicoll, *Diary* pp. 334-5; Willcock, *The Great Marquess* pp. 302-31; Mathieson, *Politics and Religion* ii, 178-9.

21. Mathieson, *Politics and Religion* ii, 178-80; Steele 3rd pt. No. 2180; Burnet, *History* i, 364-5.

22. Steele 3rd pt. Nos. 2191, 2191a.

23. Steele 3rd pt. No. 2195; Nicoll, *Diary* p. 308.

24. Wodrow i, 90.

25. Mathieson, *Politics and Religion* ii, 181.

26. *Mercurius Publicus* 11-18 July 1660.

27. *APS* vii, 123-4.

28. Bibliographical details of the new Lords of Session may be found in Brunton and Haig, *Senators of the College of Justice* pp. 283, 299-300, 312-3, 319-20, 342-3, 350-80. Two ordinary lords, James Robertson and John Scougall, had been named in the abortive commission of March 1660. The only man to have served previously as a judge under the English Republic was Sir James Dalrymple, afterwards Viscount Stair; for his skilful cultivation of Monck's friendship and that of the king, see Mackay, *Memoir of Sir James Dalrymple* pp. 67-71. Mackay also noted (*ibid.* p. 70) Sir George Mackenzie's opinion that 'in the nomination of the College of Justice, each great man was allowed a friend or two, till the list was compleat.'

29. *APS* vii, 189, 193; Nicoll, *Diary* pp. 329, 335-6.

30. *APS* vii, 189; Nicoll, *Diary* p. 329.

31. *APS* vii, 306-13.

32. Malcolm (ed.), *The Minutes of the Justices of the Peace for Lanarkshire 1707-1723* p. xxiii.

33. Steele 3rd pt. Nos. 2192, 2193. For the imposition of the excise by the Covenanters, see Stevenson, 'The financing of the Cause of the Covenants, 1638-51' pp. 103-5, 106, 109, 111-3, 115, 120.

34. *APS* vii, 78, 88-95.

35. Donaldson, *Scotland: James V to James VII* p. 360.

36. Robert S. Rait, *The Parliaments of Scotland* (Glasgow, 1924), pp. 499-500.

37. *The Register of the Privy Council of Scotland* ed. P. Hume Brown. 3rd series. Vol. I 1661-1664 (Edinburgh, 1908) pp. v-vi. Cf. Burnet, *History* i, 202-3.

38. Steele 3rd pt. No. 2181; Wodrow i, 40, 51, 52-3; Donaldson, *Scotland: James V to James VII* pp. 361-2; Mathieson, *Politics and Religion* ii, 177.

39. Mathieson, *Politics and Religion* ii, 184.
40. Burnet, *History* i, 218; Mathieson, *Politics and Religion* ii, 184.
41. Mathieson, *Politics and Religion* ii, 184-8; Burnet, *History* i, 234-5.
42. *Reg. P.C. Scot. 1661-1664* pp. xix, 28-9, 30-2; Steele 3rd pt. No. 2210.
43. *Reg. P.C. Scot. 1661-1664* pp. 125-6, 130-1; Burnet, *History* i, 238-49, 250; Mathieson, *Politics and Religion* ii, 188; Steele 3rd pt. No. 2221. In addition, Bishop Sydserf (formerly of Galloway) was still alive; he was now appointed to the bishopric of Orkney. Hamilton was given the diocese of Galloway, Fairfoul Glasgow, Sharp St. Andrews, and Leighton Dunblane.
44. Mathieson, *Politics and Religion* ii, 188; Burnet, *History* i, 253.
45. Mathieson, *Politics and Religion* ii, 181, 188, 189; Burnet, *History* i, 257; *Reg. P.C. Scot. 1661-1664* pp. 260-1.
46. Steele 3rd pt. Nos. 2232, 2238, 2241; Mathieson, *Politics and Religion* ii, 189-93; Donaldson, *Scotland: James V to James VII* p. 365.
47. Mitchison, *A History of Scotland* p. 251.
48. Donaldson, *Scotland: James V to James VII* pp. 362-3. In general, for religious policy after the Restoration see Julia M. Buckroyd, 'The evolution of ecclesiastical policy in Scotland 1660-81' (Cambridge Ph.D. thesis, 1976).
49. Wodrow i, 271; Burnet, *History* i, 229-30; Mathieson, *Politics and Religion* ii, 197.
50. *Lauderdale Papers* i, 103-5.
51. *APS* vii, 415, 520.
52. Burnet, *History* i, 258; Wodrow i, 271, 275-6.
53. Steele 3rd pt. Nos. 2272, 2274, 2286; Burnet, *History* i, 383; Willcock, *A Scots Earl* pp. 126-7; Mathieson, *Politics and Religion* ii, 199; Mitchison, *A History of Scotland* p. 250.
54. Bodl. Lib. Carte MS. 103 f652.
55. Wodrow i, 38, 40, 44, 45; Burnet, *History* i, 194-5.
56. Firth and Davies, *Regimental History* i, 230; ii, 497; *Mercurius Publicus* 29 August-5 September 1660.
57. On 24 August 1660, the Committee of Estates had deemed it necessary to issue a proclamation commanding that no disorders or insolencies be committed by anyone in Scotland against any member of the English nation: Steele 3rd pt. No. 2187.
58. HMC *Leyborne-Popham* pp. 190-2; Worcester MS. cclvii Capt. John Bardsley to Major General Morgan 28 November 1661.
59. Steele 3rd pt. No. 2192; Wodrow i, 84; Wood, *Extracts Edin. Recs. 1655 to 1665* pp. 240, 277; HMC *Leyborne-Popham* p. 192; Firth and Davies, *Regimental History* ii, 497-8.
60. *Reg. P.C. Scot. 1661-1664* pp. ix, x, 6-7, 97.
61. Firth and Davies, *Regimental History* ii, 498-9; Nicoll, *Diary* p. 367.

BIBLIOGRAPHY
of works cited in the Notes

Y

I. MANUSCRIPT SOURCES.

Bodleian Library, Oxford.

Carte MSS. 30, 74, 103.

Rawlinson MSS. A27, A34, A43, A51, A56, A61, A63 (unpublished Thurloe material). C179 (Minute book of the proceedings of the Council of State from 19 May to 10 August 1659).

Tanner MSS. li, liii, lv.

British Library, London.

Add. MSS. 6399; 15858 (correspondence of Sir Richard Browne); 23113 (Lauderdale correspondence); 25347 (papers relating to Matthew Alured); 34195; 35125 (Lauderdale papers); 38091; 38848 (Hodgkin Papers).

Egerton MSS. 1048; 2618; 2620 (letters of Oliver Cromwell).

Sloane MS. 1519.

Stowe MSS. 185.

Friends' House, London (Society of Religious Friends).

Swarthmore MSS. Vol. IV.

National Library of Scotland, Edinburgh.

MS. Adv. 29.2.9 Balcarres Papers.

Public Record Office, London.

SP 25/138 (Minute Book of the Committee of Parliament appointed to confer with the Deputies sent from Scotland).

Scottish Record Office, Edinburgh.

E. Exchequer Papers:—

E/901/1 Valuation Rolls of 1649.

GD. Gifts and Deposits:—

GD 16 Airlie MSS.
GD 24 Stirling of Ardoch Papers.
GD 26 Leven and Melville MSS.
GD 34 Hay of Haystoun Papers.
GD 39 Glencairn MSS.
GD 45 Dalhousie MSS.
GD 48 Rossie Priory MSS.
GD 54 Murray of Ochtertyre MSS.
GD 56 Rollo of Duncrub MSS.
GD 75 Dundas of Dundas MSS.

GD 84 Reay MSS.
GD 96 Mey MSS.
GD 97 Duntreath MSS.
GD 112 Breadalbane MSS.
GD 121 Murthly Castle MSS., Grandtully Correspondence.
GD 135 Stair MSS.
GD 150 Morton MSS.
GD 205 Ogilvy of Inverquharity MSS.
GD 247 Brodie Papers.
GD 248 Seafield MSS.
RH. Register House microfilm:—
RH4 Bargany MSS.
RH9 Hepburne Papers.
Worcester College, Oxford.
MSS. xix-xxxiii: note-books.
MS. xliii: warrants concerned with the raising of the cess and (from the other end) documents relating to the size and cost of the army.
MSS. xlv-xlix: warrant-books.
MSS. l, li, lii, lxxxvi: letter-books.
MS. cclvii: Clarke MSS. from Littlecote 1615-1720.
MS. cccxliv: copy of Argyllshire's letter to Monck December 1659.

II. PRINTED PRIMARY SOURCES.

i. General printed.

The Acts of the Parliaments of Scotland eds. T. Thomson and C. Innes (12 vols., London, 1814-75).
Osmund Airy (ed.), *The Lauderdale Papers* (2 vols., Camden Society, 1884-5).
J. Y. Akerman (ed.), *Letters from Roundhead Officers written from Scotland and chiefly addressed to Captain Adam Baynes. July MDCL-June MDCLX.* (Bannatyne Club, 1856).
The Antiquarian Repertory [chiefly compiled by Francis Grose; Thomas Astle] (4 vols., London, 1807-9).
Sir Richard Baker, *Chronicle of the kings of England from the time of the Romans government unto the death of King James . . . whereunto is added the reign of King Charles I, and the first thirteen years of . . . King Charles II . . . 7th impr.* (London, 1679).
John Barclay (ed.), *Diary of Alexander Jaffray* (Aberdeen, 1856).
D. G. Barron (ed.), *In Defence of the Regalia, 1651-2* (London, 1910).
G. F. Black, *A Calendar of Cases of Witchcraft in Scotland, 1510-1727* (New York, 1938).

Calendar of State Papers, Domestic Series 1651-1660 ed. M. A. E. Green (11 vols., London, 1877-86).
Henry Cary, *Memorials of the Great Civil War in England from 1646 to 1652* (2 vols., London, 1842).
Godfrey Davies (ed.), 'Dundee Court-Martial Records 1651', *Miscellany III* (Scottish History Society, 1919).
The Decisions of the English Judges during the Usurpation (Edinburgh, 1762).
C. H. Firth (ed.), *The Clarke Papers* (4 vols., Camden Society, 1891-1901).
C. H. Firth (ed.), *Scotland and the Commonwealth* (Scottish History Society, 1895).
C. H. Firth (ed.), *Scotland and the Protectorate* (Scottish History Society, 1899).
C. H. Firth and R. S. Rait (eds.), *Acts and Ordinances of the Interregnum* (3 vols., London, 1911).
D. Hay Fleming (ed.), *Diary of Sir Archibald Johnston of Wariston* Vol. II 1650-1654 (Scottish History Society, 1919).
William Forbes, *A Journal of the Session* (Edinburgh, 1714).
S. R. Gardiner (ed.), *The Constitutional Documents of the Puritan Revolution 1625-1660* (3rd edn. Oxford, 1906).
S. R. Gardiner (ed.), *Letters and Papers illustrating the relations between Charles II and Scotland in 1650* (Scottish History Society, 1894).
HMC *Fitzherbert.*
HMC *Leyborne-Popham.*
HMC *Portland,* i.
HMC *Various Collections,* v.
Journals of the House of Commons, vii.
G. R. Kinloch (ed.), *The Diary of Mr. John Lamont of Newton 1649-1671* (Maitland Club, 1830).
David Laing (ed.), *The Diary of Alexander Brodie of Brodie* (Spalding Club, 1863).
David Laing (ed), *The Letters and Journals of Robert Baillie* (3 vols., Edinburgh, 1842).
Thomas McCrie (ed.), *The Life of Mr. Robert Blair . . . with Supplement . . . by . . . Mr. William Row* (Wodrow Society, 1848).
D. C. Mactavish (ed.), *Minutes of the Synod of Argyll 1652-1661* (Scottish History Society, 1944).
C. A. Malcolm (ed.), *The Minutes of the Justices of the Peace for Lanarkshire 1707-1723* (Scottish History Society, 1929).
J. D. Marwick (ed.), *Extracts from the Records of the Burgh of Glasgow 1630-1662* (Scottish Burgh Records Society, 1881).
J. D. Marwick (ed.), *Extracts from the Records of the Convention of the Royal Burghs of Scotland 1615-1676* (Edinburgh, 1878).
A. F. Mitchell and J. Christie (eds.), *The Records of the Commissions of the General Assemblies of the Church of Scotland* (3 vols., Scottish History Society, 1892-1909).
John Nicoll, *A Diary of Public Transactions* (Bannatyne Club, 1836).
James D. Ogilvie (ed.), *Diary of Sir Archibald Johnston of Wariston* Vol. III 1655-1660 (Scottish History Society, 1940).

O. Ogle, W. H. Bliss, W. D. Macray and F. J. Routledge (eds.), *Calendar of the Clarendon State Papers* (5 vols., Oxford, 1872-1970).
Sir James Balfour Paul (ed.), 'The Diary of Sir James Hope 1646-1654'. *Miscellany III* (Scottish History Society, 1919).
Sir William Purves, *Revenue of the Scottish Crown, 1681* ed. D. Murray Rose (Edinburgh and London, 1897).
The Register of the Privy Council of Scotland ed. P. Hume Brown 3rd series Vol. I 1661-1664 (Edinburgh, 1908).
J. T. Rutt (ed.), *Diary of Thomas Burton Esq.* (4 vols., London, 1828).
Sir Walter Scott (ed.), *Military memoirs of the Great Civil War, being the military memoirs of John Gwynne; and an account of the Earl of Glencairn's expedition . . .* (Edinburgh, 1822).
Robert Steele (ed.), *Tudor and Stuart Proclamations* (2 vols., Oxford, 1910) 3rd part (Scotland).
W. Stephen (ed.), *Register of the Consultations of the Ministers of Edinburgh and some other Brethren of the Ministry* (2 vols., Scottish History Society, 1921-30).
John Stuart (ed.), *Extracts from the Council Register of the Burgh of Aberdeen 1643-1747* (Scottish Burgh Records Society, 1872).
Louise B. Taylor, *Aberdeen Council Letters* (6 vols., London, 1942-61).
C. S. Terry (ed.), *The Cromwellian Union* (Scottish History Society, 1902).
A Collection of the State Papers of John Thurloe . . . ed. T. Birch (7 vols., London, 1742).
H. G. Tibbutt, *Colonel John Okey 1606-1662* (Bedfordshire Historical Record Society vol. 35, 1955).
'Report by Thomas Tucker upon the settlement of the revenues of excise and customs in Scotland A.D. MDCLVI', *Miscellany* (Scottish Burgh Records Society, 1881).
Sir James Turner, *Memoirs of his own Life and Times* (Bannatyne Club, 1829).
E. B. Underhill (ed.), *Records of the Church of Christ gathered at Fenstanton, Warboys and Hexham 1644-1720* (Hanserd Knollys Society, 1854).
George F. Warner (ed.), *The Nicholas Papers* (3 vols., Camden Society, 1886-97).
Bulstrode Whitelocke, *Memorials of the English Affairs* (4 vols., Oxford, 1853).
Marguerite Wood (ed.), *Extracts from the Records of the Burgh of Edinburgh 1642 to 1655* (Edinburgh, 1938).
Marguerite Wood (ed.), *Extracts from the Records of the Burgh of Edinburgh 1655 to 1665* (Edinburgh, 1940).

ii. Pamphlets.

Three Letters from the Lord General Monck, Commander in Chief of the Forces in Scotland, and one of the Commissioners by Act of Parliament for the Government of the Army of this Commonwealth, viz. To Mr. Speaker, to the Lord Fleetwood, to the Lord Lambert. 20 October 1659.

iii. Newspapers.

Mercurius Politicus 15-21 March 1660.

Mercurius Publicus 18-25 April, 16-23 May, 27 June-4 July, 4-11 July, 11-18 July, 29 August-5 September 1660.

III. SECONDARY SOURCES.

i. Books and essays.

Maurice Ashley, *Financial and Commercial Policy under the Cromwellian Protectorate* (2nd edn., London, 1962).
Maurice Ashley, *General Monck* (London, 1977).
James Beattie, *History of the Church of Scotland during the Commonwealth* (Edinburgh, 1842).
Jennifer M. Brown, 'Scottish Politics 1567-1625', in Alan G. R. Smith (ed.), *The Reign of James VI and I* (London, 1973).
George Brunton and David Haig, *An Historical Account of the Senators of the College of Justice* (Edinburgh and London, 1832).
Gilbert Burnet, *History of my Own Time* ed. Osmund Airy (2 vols., Oxford, 1897).
The Rt. Hon. Lord Cooper of Culross, 'The Central Courts after 1532', in *An Introduction to Scottish Legal History* (Stair Society, 1958).
Sir Hew Hamilton Dalrymple, *A Short Account of the Hamiltons of Bargany* (Edinburgh, 1897)
Godfrey Davies, *The Restoration of Charles II 1658-1660* (San Marino, 1955).
W. H. Dawson, *Cromwell's Understudy: The Life and Times of General John Lambert* (London, 1938).
Dictionary of National Biography.
Gordon Donaldson, *Scotland: James V to James VII* (Edinburgh and London, 1965).
W. S. Douglas, *Cromwell's Scotch Campaigns 1650-51* (London, 1898).
C. H. Firth, *Cromwell's Army* (4th edn., London, 1962).
C. H. Firth, *The Last Years of the Protectorate 1656-1658* (2 vols., New York, 1964).
Sir Charles Firth and Godfrey Davies, *The Regimental History of Cromwell's Army* (2 vols., Oxford, 1940).
Antonia Fraser, *Cromwell: Our Chief of Men* (London, 1973).
S. R. Gardiner, *History of the Commonwealth and Protectorate* (3 vols., London, 1897-1901).
S. R. Gardiner, *History of the Great Civil War 1642-1649* (4 vols., New York, 1965).
Sir Alexander Grant, *The Story of the University of Edinburgh during its first three hundred years* (2 vols., London, 1884).
Ian Grimble, *Chief of Mackay* (London, 1965).
D. L. Hobman, *Cromwell's Master Spy* (London, 1961).
Lawrence Kaplan, *Politics and Religion during the English Revolution: The Scots*

and the Long Parliament 1643-1645 (New York, 1976).
William M. Lamont, *Godly Rule* (London, 1969).
The Lord Provosts of Edinburgh 1296 to 1932 (Edinburgh, 1932).
F. N. McCoy, *Robert Baillie and the Second Scots Reformation* (Berkeley, California, 1974).
Aeneas Mackay, *Memoir of Sir James Dalrymple, 1st. Viscount Stair* (Edinburgh, 1873).
Alexander Mackenzie, *The Macdonalds of Glengarry* (Inverness, 1881).
J. D. Mackie, *The University of Glasgow 1451-1951* (Glasgow, 1954).
Daniel Mackinnon, *Origin and Services of the Coldstream Guards* (2 vols., London, 1833).
Rosalind K. Marshall, *The Days of Duchess Anne* (London, 1973).
David Masson, *The Life of John Milton and History of his Time* (7 vols., London, 1859-94).
W. L. Mathieson, *Politics and Religion* (2 vols., Glasgow, 1902).
Rosalind Mitchison, *A History of Scotland* (London, 1970).
G. W. T. Omond, *The Lord Advocates of Scotland* (2 vols., Edinburgh, 1883).
Sir James Balfour Paul (ed.), *The Scots Peerage* (9 vols., Edinburgh, 1904-14).
Robert S. Rait, *The Parliaments of Scotland* (Glasgow, 1924).
Alexander Robertson, *The Life of Sir Robert Moray* (London, 1922).
Ivan Roots, 'Cromwell's Ordinances: The Early Legislation of the Protectorate', in G. E. Aylmer (ed.), *The Interregnum: The Quest for Settlement 1646-1660* (London, 1972).
Hew Scott (ed.), *Fasti Ecclesiae Scoticanae* (7 vols., Edinburgh, 1915-28).
J. Irvine Smith, 'The Transition to the Modern Law 1532-1660', in *An Introduction to Scottish Legal History* (Stair Society, 1958).
David Stevenson, 'The English and the Public Records of Scotland, 1650-1660', in *Miscellany One* (Stair Society, 1971).
David Stevenson, *Revolution and Counter-Revolution in Scotland, 1644-1651* (London, 1977).
David Stevenson, *The Scottish Revolution 1637-1644: The Triumph of the Covenanters* (Newton Abbot, 1973).
A. C. Swinton, *The Swintons of that Ilk and their Cadets* (Edinburgh, 1883).
S. A. G. Taylor, *The Western Design* (2nd edn., London, 1969).
Peter Toon, *God's Statesman: The Life and Work of John Owen* (Exeter, 1971).
H. R. Trevor-Roper, 'Scotland and the Puritan Revolution', in *Religion, the Reformation and Social Change* (London, 1967).
David Underdown, *Royalist Conspiracy in England 1649-1660* (New Haven, 1960).
C. V. Wedgwood, *The King's War 1641-1647* (London, 1958).
John Willcock, *The Great Marquess* (Edinburgh and London, 1903).
John Willcock, *A Scots Earl in Covenanting Times* (Edinburgh, 1907).
Robert Wodrow, *The History of the Sufferings of the Church of Scotland* ed. R. Burns (4 vols., Glasgow, 1828-30).
Austin Woolrych, 'Last Quests for a Settlement 1657-1660', in G. E. Aylmer

(ed.), *The Interregnum: the Quest for Settlement 1646-1660* (London, 1972).
Blair Worden, *The Rump Parliament 1648-1653* (Cambridge, 1974).

ii. Theses.

Julia M. Buckroyd, 'The evolution of ecclesiastical policy in Scotland 1660-1681' (Cambridge University, Ph.D. thesis, 1976).
F. D. Dow, 'The English Army and the Government of Scotland 1651-1660' (York University, D.Phil. thesis, 1976).
David Stevenson, 'The Covenanters and the Government of Scotland 1637-1651' (Glasgow University, Ph.D. thesis, 1970).

iii. Articles.

James A. Casada, 'Scottish Members of Parliament: 1659', *Notes and Queries* N. S. xviii (1971), 295.
James A. Casada, 'The Scottish representatives in Richard Cromwell's parliament', *Scottish Historical Review* li (1972), 124-47.
Ellen D. Goldwater, 'The Scottish Franchise: Lobbying during the Cromwellian Protectorate', *The Historical Journal* xxi (1978), 27-42.
R. B. Hannen, 'Cupar, Fife, 1652-1659', *Baptist Quarterly* N.S. vol. x (1940-1), 45-9.
H. N. Mukerjee, 'Scottish Members of Richard Cromwell's Parliament', *Notes and Queries* clxvi (1934), 65.
Paul J. Pinckney, 'The Scottish representation in the Cromwellian parliament of 1656', *Scottish Historical Review* xlvi (1967), 95-114.
David Stevenson, 'The financing of the cause of the Covenants, 1638-51', *Scottish Historical Review* li (1972), 89-123.
David Stevenson, 'The King's Scottish Revenues and the Covenanters, 1625-1651', *The Historical Journal* xvii (1974), 17-41.

Index